Brian Komar

SAMS
Teach Yourself

TCP/IP Networking

in 21 Days

SAMS

201 West 103rd St., Indianapolis, Indiana, 46290 USA

Sams Teach Yourself TCP/IP Networking in 21 Days

Copyright © 2002 by Sams Publishing

International Standard Book Number: 0-672-32353-2

Library of Congress Catalog Card Number: 2001096704

Printed in the United States of America

First Printing: March 2002

05   04   03   02   4   3   2

Trademarks

Warning and Disclaimer

DEVELOPMENT EDITOR
Maryann Steinhart

MANAGING EDITOR
Charlotte Clapp

ACQUISITIONS EDITOR
Dayna Isley

PROJECT EDITOR
Elizabeth Finney

COPY EDITOR
Linda Seifert

INDEXER
Sandra Henselmeier

PROOFREADERS
Bob LaRoche
Juli Cook

TECHNICAL EDITORS
Ronald Beekelaar
Marc Charney

TEAM COORDINATOR
Lynne Williams

INTERIOR DESIGNER
Gary Adair

COVER DESIGNER
Aren Howell

PAGE LAYOUT
Susan Geiselman

Contents at a Glance

Contents

About the Author

Brian Komar is the president of Komar Consulting, Inc., in Winnipeg, Manitoba. Brian has worked in partnership with Microsoft Corporation over the past three years as a subject matter expert on network security and Windows 2000 Active Directory design. Over the past year, Brian has spent the majority of his time researching the deployment of Public Key Infrastructure (PKI) and the various technologies that depend on a PKI to provide authentication and encryption services.

Between writing assignments, Brian speaks at industry conferences around the world, such as WinConnections, MCP TechMentor, Microsoft Tech Ed, and the Microsoft Enterprise Conference (MEC). Brian is known for delivering the "under the hood" sessions that look at the details of technology and reveal how systems really work in a network.

In his spare time, Brian enjoys relaxing with his wife Krista and planning for his next travel adventure. Brian can be reached at bkomar@komarconsulting.com.

Dedication

This book is dedicated to Johnston Smith, David Chaze, and David Beeston, my high school English teachers. I still use today the basics that you taught me in organizing my thoughts, and transforming them into a written document. I thank you for the foundation that you provided me.

Acknowledgments

There are several people that I would like to thank who were directly or indirectly involved with the creation of this book.

First, I would like to thank Dayna Isley, Maryann Steinhart, Ronald Beekelaar, and Marc Charney for all their help in developing *Sams Teach Yourself TCP/IP Networking in 21 Days*. My gratitude to them cannot be expressed in words, but know that I am in your debt for the assistance provided. And Dayna, a special thanks to you for convincing me to proceed with the project.

I would also like to acknowledge the great people at Pearson Technology Group. My first writing opportunities were at New Riders, a division of Pearson, and the people involved with Pearson have always been the best. I have worked with several publishers over the years, but nowhere else have I made as many friends as with Pearson.

Special thanks goes out to Peter Sellers of EDS. Your immediate response when asked to help with the deployment chapter was most appreciated, and the work you did was top notch as usual. Peter and I have known each other for about two years through some trainer preparation courses that I delivered for EDS. The effort he puts into a class as both a trainer and as a student carries into his writing and I am glad that he contributed to this book.

Lastly, I would like to thank my wife Krista who puts up with my endless travel, late hours, and continued chatter about computers. I know that you put up with a lot, but without you, there would be no balance in my life.

Tell Us What You Think!

As the reader of this book, *you* are our most important critic and commentator. We value your opinion and want to know what we're doing right, what we could do better, what areas you'd like to see us publish in, and any other words of wisdom you're willing to pass our way.

You can email or write me directly to let me know what you did or didn't like about this book—as well as what we can do to make our books stronger.

Please note that I cannot help you with technical problems related to the topic of this book, and that due to the high volume of mail I receive, I might not be able to reply to every message.

When you write, please be sure to include this book's title and author as well as your name and phone or fax number. I will carefully review your comments and share them with the author and editors who worked on the book.

Email: networking@samspublishing.com

Mail: Mark Taber
           Associate Publisher
           Sams Publishing
           201 West 103rd Street
           Indianapolis, IN 46290 USA

Introduction

Welcome to *Sams Teach Yourself TCP/IP Networking in 21 Days*. This book introduces you to many of the tasks and concepts required to administer a TCP/IP network. Much of the material in this book is based on material that I have used in classroom training and presented at technical conferences and consulting engagements, and research that I have performed over the last few years.

This book is intended for a extensive audience. The material ranges from introductory topics, covering the history of the Internet and basic network concepts, and then progresses into advanced topics such as DNS configuration and SNMP management. Each chapter includes information on the functionality of a protocol and how to implement the protocol in a networking environment.

This book is structured to teach you the basics of TCP/IP. The content includes new technologies that have evolved in recent years including Internet Protocol Security (IPSec), wireless LANs, RADIUS authentication, and Public Key Infrastructures (PKI).

I have organized the book into loose "sections." Each section covers one aspect of TCP/IP implementation and design. Within a section, you'll find related topics that build on each other in each day of material. Do not consider this a race to the finish, though. Read the material at your own pace. There is a lot of material included in each "day" of the book. If you feel overwhelmed, take a break, and then come back to the material a few days later. I remember when I first started learning about TCP/IP. I would read and reread material trying to figure out the protocols. After a few days off to recuperate, I found that suddenly the information made sense! There was no turning back.

In the first section of the book (Days 1 and 2), the topics are of an introductory nature. They help build a solid foundation of how the TCP/IP protocol suite has evolved. Included in this material is an introduction to networks, network layered models, and how standards are developed on the Internet. These first chapters can be skipped by a more experienced reader.

The second section (Days 3–5) takes a more in-depth look at how IP addresses are assigned in a network, overviews the more commonly implemented protocols in the TCP/IP suite, and then digs in on the topic of subnet masking. The subnet shortcut table that I use in Day 5's material is an excellent tool to use when determining the IP address ranges to implement for your network.

The third section (Days 6–8) looks at the topic of name resolution in a TCP/IP network. When you connect to resources on a network, you do not enter the IP address for every host to which you want to connect. Instead, you use logical names to represent the network servers. This section looks at DNS and NetBIOS name resolution in a TCP/IP network and includes both theory and practical deployment information.

Days 9–11 round out the basics of TCP/IP. Topics included in this section are routing of IP packets on the network and the protocols used to build the routing tables, methods of auto-assigning IP address information to network hosts, and authentication in a TCP/IP network. I have separated authentication as a separate day because authentication is the key to network security. Unless you can identify who is connecting to a resource, there is no way to restrict access to that resource.

Days 12 and 13 introduce the topic of security in a TCP/IP network. With the recent attacks on network security ranging from distributed denial of service (DDoS) attacks to the Code Red and Nimda trojans, our society is becoming more cognizant of network security issues. This section looks at methods of encrypting transmitted data, both at the application and IP layers, and overviews how firewalls can be used to protect network resources exposed to the Internet.

After you complete the material up to and including Day 13, the book moves into the application layer of the TCP/IP stack. Days 14–18 look at different types of applications that run on TCP/IP networks. These applications include remote command applications, file transfer protocols, e-mail protocols, SNMP management, and remote access to networks. Each day's material has been updated to reflect advances and changes in how these applications are used in today's networks.

In Day 19, I look at some of the newer uses of TCP/IP in networking. I look at how TCP/IP networks are implemented in both ATM and wireless environments. In addition, the day's material looks at how voice-over-IP can be used to reduce long-distance phone charges. (Trust me, I use this technology when speaking to Asia and contacting my wife at home.)

I see Day 20 as one of the more popular chapters in the book. The material looks at configuring TCP/IP on the operating systems used in today's home and corporate networks. With the ever-growing popularity of Linux, the chapter includes TCP/IP configuration tips for Linux clients, and configuration information for the latest versions of software from Microsoft and Novell.

The final day's material looks at the potential future of the Internet Protocol, IPv6. I am not sure when we will deploy IPv6, but I do know that the day will come when we move to this expanded IP addressing method. The material covers the basics of how IPv6 works and offers solutions on how IPv4 and IPv6 networks can interoperate with each other.

Questions at the end of each chapter will help you review the material covered that day. Detailed answers to these questions can be found in Appendix B at the back of the book. I provide several pen-and-paper exercises that require you to create configuration files or solve subnet masking problems.

The examples in this book come primarily from the Microsoft networking environments. I have included information on configuration in other network operating systems, such as Linux and Unix where appropriate, and generally discuss protocols based on their RFC definitions. In the past year I have learned through research projects at Microsoft that following the RFCs helps greatly when you want to interoperate between operating systems.

The following conventions are used throughout the book:

- Commands that you type in at a command prompt or in a dialog box are displayed in a bold, monospaced font, such as

  `netstat -a`

- TCP/IP configuration files and their paths are printed in a monospaced typeface, such as `/etc/services`.

- **RFC 1878** · If there is a specific RFC related to the topic being discussed, an RFC icon, such as the one shown here, appears beside the text referring to the specific RFC number.

- Most keywords in the text are *italicized* to draw attention to them. Definitions for keywords can be found in Appendix D, "Glossary."

- A code continuation character (➡) is used before a line of code that is really a continuation of the preceding line. Sometimes a line of code is too long to fit as a single line on the page. If you see ➡ before a line of code, remember that it's part of the line immediately above it.

- Throughout the book, you will find several sidebars, such as this one:

Contacting the Author

If you have any questions regarding the material discussed in this book, please drop me a line at my e-mail address, bkomar@komarconsulting.com.

The book also contains Notes, Tips, Cautions, and Warnings to help you spot important or useful information more quickly. Some of these are helpful shortcuts, and some alert you to pitfalls you can avoid.

DAY 1

The History of the Internet

This first day of your 21-day exploration of TCP/IP discusses where it all started. It discusses the evolution of the Internet and the driving force behind the TCP/IP protocol suite. The first section provides an overview of the Internet's development and its growth over the years.

The second section examines the governing bodies of the Internet and the roles they play in its continued growth in size and technology.

Finally, you learn about the defining documents of the TCP/IP protocol suite: Requests for Comment (RFCs). This section discusses the process of creating RFCs and the maturity cycle of a Request for Comment.

This day can be skimmed or skipped by more experienced readers. It is provided to help inexperienced users learn about the development of the Internet, the makeup of its governing bodies, and the role of TCP/IP in its growth.

How Did the Internet Begin?

Understanding the evolution of the Internet you know today helps to explain how the TCP/IP protocol has evolved. The evolution has been driven by different forces through the years, beginning with the 1957 launching of Sputnik by the USSR. The United States formed the Advanced Research Projects Agency (ARPA), within the Department of Defense, to lead the U.S. in science and technology applicable to the military.

In 1962, Paul Baran was commissioned by the U.S. Air Force to develop a method that would enable the U.S. to maintain control over its military even after a nuclear attack. Baran had to develop a decentralized solution so that if a major U.S. city were to be destroyed, the military could still counterattack. The final proposal was to implement a packet-switched network.

Packet switching breaks down data that travels over the network into datagrams (or packets) that are labeled to include source and destination addresses. These packets are forwarded from computer to computer until they reach the intended destination computer. If an initial connection is unavailable, the packets should be able to find an alternate route to the destination. The destination also can request that packets lost during transmission be re-sent by the source computer when the data is reassembled at the destination (see Figure 1.1).

FIGURE 1.1

Requesting that a lost packet be re-sent.

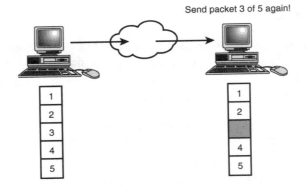

Send packet 3 of 5 again!

Stage I: The ARPAnet

In 1968, Bolt, Beranak, and Newman (BBN) was contracted by ARPA to build this packet-switching network known as the ARPAnet. The following were the initial four sites connected:

- University of California at Los Angeles—Network Measurements Center using a Xerox DSS 7:SEX

- Stanford Research Institute—Network Information Center using an SDS940/Genie
- University of California at Santa Barbara—Culler-Fried Interactive Mathematics using an IBM 360/75:OS/MVT
- University of Utah—Graphics using a DEC DPD-10/Tenex

The network was wired together using 50Kbps circuits and was managed by information message processors (IMP) that ran on Honeywell 516 minicomputers. The protocol used to communicate between hosts was the network control protocol (NCP), which enabled hosts running on the same network to transfer data.

Protocols in a Network

A *protocol* is an agreement used for communication between two networked hosts. The protocol defines how data should be packaged for transmission on the network so the receiving host can unpackage it on reception. For two hosts to communicate on a network, they must be using the same protocol.

By 1972, the ARPAnet had increased to 32 nodes. Ray Tomlinson created an e-mail program that enabled a user to send personal messages across the network. This application started moving the network away from its military roots. Academics using the ARPAnet began to use it to communicate with remote colleagues. Mailing lists also started evolving at this time. The Advanced Research Projects Agency was renamed the Defense Advanced Research Projects Agency (DARPA).

In 1973, development began on the protocol suite now known as the Transmission Control Protocol/Internet Protocol (TCP/IP) protocol suite. Vinton Cerf headed this development from Stanford along with Bob Kahn from the DARPA. The major goal of this protocol was to enable separate computer networks to interconnect and communicate with one another.

In 1976, two major networking developments occurred. Bob Metcalfe of Xerox developed Ethernet, which allowed for the development of local area networks (LANs). The other major development was the implementation of SATNET, the Atlantic packet satellite network that linked the United States with Europe.

"Internet" Versus "internet"

In 1982, the term internet was defined as a connected set of separate networks using the TCP/IP protocol suite. The Internet was defined as connected TCP/IP internets. This book continues this distinction, using the term Internet to refer to the global network.

By 1983, the ARPAnet had been split into the ARPAnet and the MILNET (Military Network). This separated the public portion of the ARPAnet from the military component. The year 1983 also was the cutoff for use of NCP on the ARPAnet. All participating networks had to switch to TCP/IP. With the splitting of the ARPAnet, the Internet Activities Board (IAB) was established to promote continued use of the ARPAnet.

As a result of the increase in participants on the ARPAnet and the MILNET, the University of Wisconsin introduced a better name-resolution method. The domain name space (DNS) provided a distributed database of hostname-to-IP-address resolution. This database replaced the static host files that had to be maintained at each host on the ARPAnet. Domain name servers maintain the domain name space. These DNS servers each contain a portion of the entire domain name space.

Stage II: NSFNET

In 1985, the National Science Foundation began deploying new T1 lines at 1.544Mbps for the next generation of the ARPAnet, known as the NSFNET.

With the movement toward the NSFNET, the National Science Foundation introduced two enhancements to the TCP/IP protocol. The Network News Transfer Protocol (NNTP) was introduced to increase Usenet News performance, and Mail Exchanger (MX) records were developed for use with DNS servers.

By the time the NSFNET T1 backbone was completed, traffic had increased greatly, revealing the need for more bandwidth. Advanced Network Systems (ANS) was assigned the task of researching a high-speed networking solution. This started the migration to a T3, 45Mbps, backbone on NFSNET. While the migration was still taking place, the Department of Defense officially took the ARPAnet out of service.

The Internet continued to grow. The National Science Foundation created InterNIC to monitor the following Internet services:

- Directory and database services provided by AT&T.
- Registration services provided by Network Solutions, Inc.
- Information services provided by General Atomics.

Internet traffic continued to increase, resulting in a movement to an Asynchronous Transmission Mode (ATM) network backbone running at 145Mbps.

The Internet Today

Today, the backbone networks of independent Internet service providers carry most Internet traffic. Providers include MCI, AT&T, Sprint, UUnet, ANS, and many others.

In addition, domain name registration services are outsourced to external vendors such as register.com and country-based registration sites, such as the Canadian Internet Registration Authority, located at http://www.cira.ca.

Who Is in Charge of the TCP/IP Protocol?

The Internet Society was established in 1992 to oversee the internetworking technologies and applications of the Internet. Its primary function is to promote and encourage the growth and availability of the Internet. This includes the development of future protocols for use on the Internet.

Within the Internet Society, additional advisory groups are responsible for the development of the Internet. These groups include the Internet Architecture Board, the Internet Engineering Task Force, and the Internet Research Task Force.

The Internet Architecture Board (IAB)

The Internet Architecture Board (IAB) is the technical advisory group within the Internet Society. Its jurisdiction includes the following:

- Setting Internet standards
- Managing the Requests for Comment publication process
- Reviewing the operation of the Internet Engineering Task Force (IETF) and the Internet Research Task Force (IRTF)
- Performing strategic planning for the Internet to identify long-range problems and opportunities
- Acting as an international technical-policy representative for the Internet
- Resolving technical issues outside the mandates of the IETF and the IRTF

When first established, the IAB was known as the Internet Activities Board. Every member of the IAB was responsible for investigating an area of concern. Each member chaired a task force that investigated a pressing issue facing the Internet.

In the summer of 1989, the continuing growth of the Internet led to the restructuring of the IAB. The existing structure was too flat and needed to be organized into separate task forces—the Internet Research Task Force (IRTF) and the Internet Engineering Task Force (IETF) (see Figure 1.2).

FIGURE 1.2

The Internet Architecture Board architecture.

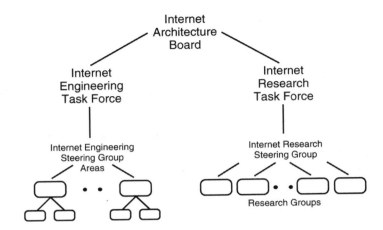

The Internet Engineering Task Force (IETF)

The Internet Engineering Task Force primarily is concerned with short- to medium-length projects. Any technical problems and needs that arise as the Internet develops also fall within the mandate of the IETF. The IETF existed even before the Internet Architecture Board reorganization. Before the reorganization, the IETF included more than 20 working groups, each of which investigated a specific problem. The entire IETF met regularly to hear from the working groups and to discuss the proposed standards of the TCP/IP protocol suite.

Due to its growth, IETF meetings became too large for a single person to chair. With the reorganization of the Internet Architecture Board, the IETF split into separate areas. Each area was assigned to research specific issues, and each was assigned a manager. These managers and the chairman of the IETF make up the Internet Engineering Steering Group (IESG).

Technical areas investigated by the IETF include

Applications	Internet services
Operations	Network management
Host and user services	Routing
Security	OSI integration

During the course of an investigation, the IESG publishes an Internet draft. The Internet draft is the first stage in developing a new RFC. The draft has the format of an RFC, but undergoes revision during this process.

Note The current listing of Internet drafts on which the IETF is working can be found at http://www.ietf.org/ID.html.

1

The Internet Research Task Force (IRTF)

The Internet Research Task Force heads all research activities related to TCP/IP protocols, including any proposed changes to the Internet architecture in general. Many projects, after being researched by the IRTF, are passed on to the IETF for further development.

Within the IRTF, the Internet Research Steering Group (IRSG) functions as an advisory board. The IRSG sets priorities and coordinates all research projects.

Requests for Comment (RFCs)

All the standards of the TCP/IP protocol are published by the Internet Architecture Board in the form of Requests for Comment, better known as RFCs. The problem with RFCs is that, although all TCP/IP standards are published as RFCs, not all RFCs specify standards.

When looking through the list of RFCs at sites such as www.ietf.org, you might notice that some numbers are missing. These RFC numbers were assigned for proposed RFCs that never made it to print. There are some published RFCs that definitely do not describe Internet standards; you can examine RFC 968 titled "Twas the night before start-up" by V.G. Cerf. This RFC is a comical look at the problems a network administrator can face when installing a network. Another humorous RFC is RFC 0527 titled "ARPAWOCKY" by D.L. Covill. This RFC brings home the point that network administrators have their own language when discussing technology.

The Hitchhiker's Guide to the Internet

RFC 1118 is titled "The Hitchhiker's Guide to the Internet." It is an excellent document that provides help to new Internet users. It supplies information about how the direction of the Internet is determined. It also defines many common terms used when discussing the Internet and discusses how to acquire information from the Internet.

Requests for Comment do not use a prescribed format. Anyone can submit a proposal for publication as an RFC. Incoming documents are reviewed by a technical expert, the

IETF or IRTF, or the RFC editor and then are assigned a classification. This classification determines whether the contents of the RFC are considered a standard of the TCP/IP protocol suite.

The following are standard classifications of RFCs:

Required. All required RFCs must be implemented on all TCP/IP hosts and gateways.

Recommended. Although they are not required, recommended RFCs generally are implemented by all TCP/IP hosts and gateways.

Elective. An elective RFC does not have to be implemented. If it is implemented, however, its configuration has been defined fully in an elective RFC.

Limited use. A limited-use RFC is not intended for general use.

Not recommended. These RFCs are not recommended for implementation.

The Maturation Process of an RFC

Requests for Comment go through a maturation process before they are accepted as an Internet Standard. The six maturity levels of an Internet standard are shown in Table 1.1.

TABLE 1.1   Internet Standard Maturity Levels

Maturity Level	Description
Internet Standard	This specification is granted after the RFC has reached a high degree of technical maturity. The IESG has established this RFC as an official standard protocol and has assigned the protocol an STD number. It sometimes is easier to find the Internet Standard for a protocol by viewing the STD documents rather than RFCs. When an RFC has been deemed to be an Internet Standard, it also is assigned a standard number (as well as its original RFC number).
Draft Standard	This specification is well understood and is known to be stable. It can be used as a basis for developing the final implementation. At this stage, substantial testing and comment on the RFC are desired. There is still a possibility that the protocol might change before it becomes a standard protocol.
Proposed Standard	This specification has gone through an intensive review process. Implementing and testing by several groups is desired. You should expect changes to be published before it becomes an Internet Standard.
Experimental Protocol	This designation generally is applied to protocols that are not recommended for implementation unless your network is participating in the experimentation process. It is not intended for operational use.

TABLE 1.1 continued

Maturity Level	Description
Informational Protocol	These are protocols developed by vendors or other standards organizations outside the scope of the IESG. They are published to provide information about their specifications to the Internet community.
Historic Protocol	These protocols are unlikely to become standards. They have been phased out, replaced by newer protocols, or dropped due to a lack of interest.

Keep in mind that, when a document is published, it is assigned an RFC number. If in time the RFC needs to be updated, a new RFC is published with a new RFC number, rendering the previous RFC obsolete. Reference the RFC index (`http://www.ietf.org/iesg/1rfc_index.txt`) to ensure you have the most recent RFC for a specific topic.

Finding the Current RFC for a Specific Protocol

Two common methods are used to find the most current RFC that relates to a specific protocol. The Internet Architecture Board publishes a quarterly memo called the IAB Official Protocol Standard; it contains a list of the most recent RFCs related to each protocol. You also have the option to view the Standard One (STD0001) document. This first standards document contains up-to-date lists of all Internet standard protocols. The document also contains lists of RFCs that have attained the following maturity levels: Draft Standard protocols, Proposed Standard protocols, Experimental protocols, Informational protocols, and Historical protocols.

The maturity process of a protocol becoming an Internet standard is shown in Figure 1.3.

The following is the maturity process of an RFC:

1. A protocol is brought forward as a standard to the IESG. Only the IESG can recommend that a protocol enter the standards track. Likewise, a protocol moves from one state to another along the standards track based only on the recommendations of the IESG.

2. The transition from a proposed standard to a draft standard can take place only after the protocol has been a proposed standard for at least six months.

3. The transition from a draft standard to an Internet standard can take place only after the protocol has been a draft standard for at least four months.

Figure 1.3

*The maturity process
of an Internet
Standard.*

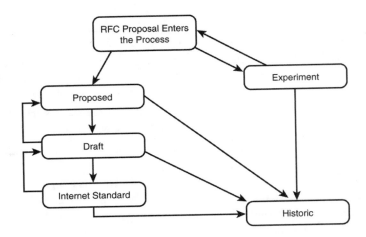

4. Occasionally, it might be determined that a protocol is not ready for standardization. It then is assigned to an experimental state. To be placed back in the standards track, the protocol must be resubmitted by the IESG after being reworked.

5. Sometimes a protocol is replaced by another protocol. It then is moved to the historic state. This can occur at any part of the process.

Obtaining RFCs

Requests for Comment can be obtained from the Internet using FTP or Web methods. The following sections show you how to retrieve RFCs using different techniques. No matter which method you use, one of the first documents you retrieve should be rfc-index.txt. This document contains an up-to-date list of all RFCs released until that point in time. This list includes descriptions of each RFC and is stored in reverse chronological order. It also states whether an RFC has become obsolete and been replaced by a new RFC.

Retrieving RFCs Using FTP

RFCs can be retrieved from ftp://ftp.ietf.org/rfc. Anonymous users can access this site using the account anonymous or ftp and their e-mail account as the password.

Use this command to retrieve a specific RFC: **Get rfc####.txt**, where #### is the RFC number.

The following example shows a connection to the FTP site at ftp.ietf.org using a text-based FTP client:

```
C:\RFCs>ftp ftp.ietf.org
Connected to www2.ietf.org.
```

```
220 www2.ietf.org NcFTPd Server (licensed copy) ready.
User (www2.ietf.org:(none)): ftp
331 Guest login ok, send your complete e-mail address as password.
Password:bkomar@komarconsulting.com
230-You are user #4 of 50 simultaneous users allowed.
230-
230 Logged in anonymously.
ftp> cd /rfc
250 "/rfc" is new cwd.
ftp> get rfc1918.txt
200 PORT command successful.
150 Opening ASCII mode data connection for rfc1918.txt (22270 bytes).
226 Transfer completed.
ftp: 22777 bytes received in 0.53Seconds 42.98Kbytes/sec.
ftp> bye
221 Goodbye.
```

Remember to set the default directory to the location where you want to store the
RFC document. In this example, the RFC1918.txt file will be stored in the c:\RFCs
directory. You can change the local directory during an FTP session using the
lcd *directoryname* command.

Obtaining RFCs Through the World Wide Web

Requests for Comment also can be retrieved using the World Wide Web. The IETF provides a search engine for finding RFCs at: http://www.ietf.org/rfc.html.

At this Uniform Resource Locator (URL), you can retrieve an RFC by RFC number. You
can also retrieve a specific RFC by connecting to
http://www.ietf.org/rfc/rfcNNNN.txt.

Tip

There are several Web sites that store RFCs. One of the easiest ways to
find an RFC in Microsoft Internet Explorer is to type **find RFC ####** in the
address bar. This takes you directly to a Web page containing the
indicated RFC.

Note

Appendix A, "RFC Reference," includes a list of all released RFCs to date of
publication of this book. These RFCs are listed by category.

Applying What You Have Learned

Today's material helps you understand how the Internet has evolved since its inception in
the late 1960s. The Internet has been the primary driving force in the evolution of the

TCP/IP protocol suite. Knowing how the TCP/IP suite has evolved over the years can help you appreciate the development of the protocol.

Spend some time reviewing Appendix A and the list of RFCs. You don't need to read every single RFC. Instead, pick an area of technology that interests you and read its definition in the appropriate RFC. The following questions test your ability to find the appropriate RFC based on Appendix A.

Test Your Knowledge

Here are questions to check what you've learned today. The answers can be found in Appendix B, "Test Your Knowledge: Answers."

1. What type of network is the Internet based on?
2. Which RFCs are related to the Telnet protocol?
3. What group within the Internet Society is in charge of researching short- to medium-term projects?
4. When an RFC is categorized as obsolete, is it removed from the list of RFCs?
5. Can an RFC be updated after it has been released?
6. What methods can be used to retrieve the text of a specific RFC?
7. Why are some RFC numbers missing? Why would they not exist?
8. At what stage of the RFC development process can modifications be made to an RFC?

Preview of Day 2

Next you'll learn about types of networks. The discussion includes local area networks (LANs) and wide-area networks (WANs). If you know how networks are installed and how communication occurs in each class of network, you will better understand how TCP/IP transmits information between hosts on remote networks.

After discussing types of networks, Day 2 then compares the OSI Reference model and the TCP/IP layered model. The OSI model provides a design standard for network systems, while the TCP/IP layered model is an actual network system that is implemented today. If you know how a network model can be implemented in a layered format, you will better understand what happens to data when one application connects to another.

DAY 2

Network Types and Open Systems Architecture

The goal for today's material is to gain a better understanding of some of the common local area network (LAN) and wide area network (WAN) topologies. You also will learn about the Open System Interconnect (OSI) reference model and its implications for network design and compare it to the Transmission Control Protocol/Internet Protocol (TCP/IP) layered model.

This section covers the following topics:

- Local area networks
- Wide area networks
- The need for open systems
- The OSI reference model
- The TCP/IP layered model

If you are already familiar with the topics of local and wide area networks, you might want to skip ahead today to the section, "What Are Open Systems?"

Defining Network Types

Before you learn how to implement TCP/IP in your network, you first need to understand the common types of network topologies that exist. Understanding how information travels in specific LAN and WAN environments can help you determine which topology to implement in your organization.

Local Area Networks (LANs)

Local area networks (LANs) are the most common networks. A LAN has the following characteristics:

- The network operates in a contained area. This could be a single floor in a building or simply within a single building.
- The hosts within the LAN are interconnected with high-bandwidth network connections such as Ethernet or token ring, or use newer technology such as wireless networks.
- All facets of the LAN often are privately managed. No third parties are required for connectivity solutions.
- LAN services are available on a 7-day, 24-hour basis.

Among network operating systems, there are two basic types of local area networks: peer-to-peer and server-based.

Peer-to-peer networks operate with no dedicated servers on the network. Each host functions as both a client and a server. The user at each host determines what information or peripherals he is willing to share with the other members of the network. Peer-to-peer networks generally are relegated to smaller organizations; they do not scale well to larger ones. They have several security issues as a result of each host's capability to control its own security, which decentralizes security control.

In *server-based networks*, at least one host is dedicated to server functionality. Client computers do not share any information with other computers. All data is stored on the central server. Most corporate networks are based on this methodology. Within a server-based network, servers can play several roles. These roles include the following:

- **Directory servers**. These provide a central directory service for management of users, groups, and host objects to allow for centralized authentication and authorization using the central directory.
- **File and print servers**. These provide a secure repository for all data. They also can manage print queues that provide access to network-sharable print resources.

- **Application servers**. These provide the server side of client/server applications. In a client/server environment, the client runs a small version of the program that allows connectivity to the server. The server side of the application is used to perform processor-intensive queries on behalf of the client. Examples of application servers include Web servers and database servers.

- **Mail servers**. These provide electronic-message capabilities for the clients of the network. With the use of gateways, mail transport can take place between heterogeneous mail systems.

- **Security servers**. These provide security to the local area network if it is connected to any larger networks such as the Internet. Security servers include firewalls and proxy servers. Security servers are discussed on Day 13, "Protecting Your Network."

- **Remote access servers**. These enable external data flow to occur between the network and remote clients. A remote client can use a modem to dial in to the local area network, or alternatively, use a technology known as tunneling or Virtual Private Networks (VPNs) to connect to the remote network over a public network such as the Internet. The system that allows the remote client to connect to the corporate network is the remote access server. A remote access server can be configured with one or more modems to allow external access to the network, or one or more virtual ports to allow tunnel connections. After the client has connected to the remote network, the user can function as if he or she were directly connected to the network using a network card.

When implementing a local area network, several facets of the network must be considered. These include the location of the computers, the location of the cables, and the connectivity hardware required. The term used to define these network design issues is *network topology*. The following four LAN topologies are commonly in use today:

- Bus networks
- Star networks
- Ring networks
- Dual-ring networks

Bus Networks

A bus network is the simplest method used to network computers. A bus network consists of a single cable that connects all computers, servers, and network peripherals in a single network segment (see Figure 2.1).

FIGURE 2.1

A bus topology network.

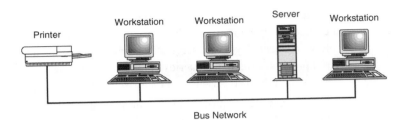

Bus Network

Hosts on a bus network communicate with each other by putting information on the cable addressed to the physical address of the network card used to connect the destination computer to the segment. This physical address is called the Media Access Control (MAC) address.

Network Cards and MAC Addresses

Each networkcard is assigned a unique MAC address. MAC addresses are 12-digit hexadecimal addresses such as 00-01-0E-6F-6D-62. Each network card manufacturer is assigned a prefix to be used for its network cards. It is the responsibility of the network card manufacturer to be sure no two of its cards have the same MAC address.

When data is put on the network, it actually travels to all computers in the local network. Each computer examines the destination MAC address to see whether it matches the computer's MAC address. If it matches, the computer reads the information. If it doesn't match, the computer discards the information.

Ethernet networks are the most common implementations of bus networks. Ethernet networks use a method called Carrier Sense Multiple Access with Collision Detection (CSMA/CD). This means only one computer at a time can send data on the bus network. If a host wants to transmit data and detects there is already data on the network, it waits for the network to clear before transmitting its information. If two hosts simultaneously start to transmit data on the network, a collision occurs. The hosts can detect that a collision has occurred. One of the transmitting hosts transmits a jam signal. This causes the collision to last long enough for all other hosts to recognize it. Each transmitting host waits a random amount of time before trying to retransmit the data. This time interval is randomized to prevent two hosts from repeatedly sending collision packets on the network.

Wiring Standards in a Bus Network

Networked computers commonly are linked using network cabling. The following are two wiring standards for communications on a bus network:

- **10BASE-2.** Also known as thin ethernet, it allows network segments up to 185 meters on coaxial cable.

- **10BASE-5.** Also known as thick ethernet, it allows network segments up to 500 meters on coaxial cable.

Another common wiring standard implemented in local area networks is the 10Base-T standard. This standard is discussed in the section about star networks.

Hardware Utilized in a Bus Topology Network

Both thin ethernet and thick ethernet require the following additional network hardware to link the hosts:

- BNC connectors
- Terminators
- AUI connectors

British Naval Connector (BNC) connectors enable the various thinnet coaxial cable segments to interconnect. Each host has a T-connector that is used to link the cable segment to a host computer (see Figure 2.2).

FIGURE 2.2

BNC connector types.

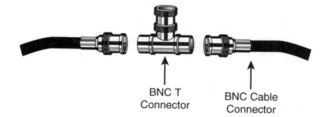

BNC T
Connector

BNC Cable
Connector

A terminator is placed at each end of the coaxial cable to absorb any free signals. Because data travels the entire cable to every host on the network segment, it is possible for data to continue to travel on the network even after it has reached the destination host. Terminators absorb these free signals to prevent the electronic signal from bouncing back on the segment, which prevents other hosts from transmitting data. In a bus network, all open cable ends must be terminated. If they are not, it can lead to the network being down.

Troubles with Terminators

I have faced troubles with terminators on a few occasions. I was teaching at a remote site, for example, and a technician was reinstalling systems in the room next to me.

During the reinstall, he unplugged the coaxial cable from a T-connector. My classroom was connected to the same network segment. None of my students were able to connect to my computer. To solve the problem, we terminated our network segment before it reached the other classroom, and all network communication resumed normally

Attachment Unit Interface (AUI) connectors commonly are used with thick ethernet cabling. These devices use a DB15 connector to link to the network card (see Figure 2.3).

FIGURE 2.3

An AUI connector.

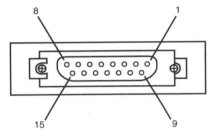

The AUI connector plugs its male-pronged DB15 connector into the female-pronged DB15 connector on the network card.

Mixing Media

At times, you might encounter a situation in which the computers in your office are networked using one type of cable medium, but the network cards do not support that cable medium. In this situation, it sometimes is easier to purchase transceivers to convert the network cards instead of purchasing new network cards.

Transceivers have two interfaces. One interface is a BNC connector and the other is an AUI connector. This enables a network card with an AUI interface to be used on a bus network utilizing BNC connectors. The transceiver passes information between the two connectors so the AUI-type network card can still participate in the network.

Star Networks

In a star network, cable segments to a central connection unit, or hub, connect all computers (see Figure 2.4).

The star topology is the most prevalent network topology implemented in networks today. The chief advantage of the star topology over the bus topology is that, if a cable segment is broken, only the host connected to the hub on that cable segment is affected. The following are other benefits of using a star topology:

FIGURE 2.4

A star topology network.

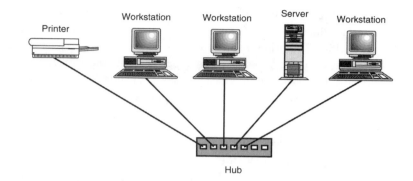

- It is easy to stack hubs to increase the number of ports that a host can link into the hub stack. This helps star-based networks to grow in size.
- Different cable types can be used to connect to the hubs.

When implementing a star network, you use different cabling types than in a bus network. The most common wiring standard used with star-based networks is 10BASE-T wiring, which carries Ethernet signals on inexpensive twisted-pair wiring. The following five categories of unshielded twisted pair (UTP) cables can be used:

- **Category 1 (Cat1).** Used in traditional UTP telephone cable. It can carry only voice traffic, not data.
- **Category 2 (Cat2).** Certified for data transmissions of up to 4 Megabits per second (Mbps)(early token ring).
- **Category 3 (Cat3).** Certified for data transmissions of up to 10Mbps (ethernet).
- **Category 4 (Cat4).** Certified for data transmissions of up to 16Mbps (token ring).
- **Category 5 (Cat5).** Certified for data transmissions of up to 100Mbps (fast ethernet).

New Categories for Twisted-Pair Wiring

Three new categories are referred to when talking about twisted pair wiring categories: Cat5e, Cat6, and Cat7. Cat5e uses more stringent specifications than Cat5 and offers better performance. The Cat5E standard is approved by the Electronic Industries Association/Telecommunications Industry Association (EIA/TIA) and the Institute of Electrical and Electronics Engineers (IEEE). Cat6, not an official standard, supports frequencies up to 350MHz, about two and a half times the specification for Cat5. The Telecommunications Industry Association is currently working on Draft 6 for Cat6. Finally Cat7 uses a copper core wiring that supports frequencies up to 600MHz. Because of its use of copper, Cat7 will require shielded wiring rather than unshielded wiring. At this time, Cat7 is a working item and even earlier in the standardization process.

Depending on the type of wiring you implement, different cable connectors are used to interface the wiring segments with the network cards. RJ45 connectors commonly are used with UTP wiring. RJ45 connectors look much like phone connectors, but they are about twice as big. In some cases, especially with older token-ring network cards, DB9 connectors are used to interface the network cabling with the network cards. DB9 connectors look like AUI connectors, except there are 9 pins rather than 15 pins on the connector.

Wireless Star Topologies

Wireless networks using the 802.11 standard use a Wireless Access Point (WAP) as the central connection unit. Devices connect to the WAP using wireless network cards and the 802.11 standard. 802.11 communications can reach speeds of 11Mbps. For more information on Wireless networking, please see Day 19 "IP over New Technologies."

Ring Network

In a ring network, all the computers are joined in a logical circle. Data travels around the circle and passes through each computer. In a physical layout, a ring network appears to be the same layout as a star network. The key difference is the connection unit known as a Multi-Station Access Unit (MAU). Within the MAU, data signals are passed in a ring from one host to the next (see Figure 2.5).

FIGURE 2.5

A ring topology network.

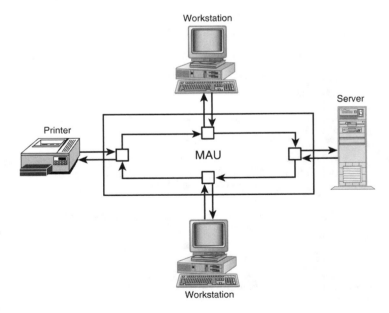

Data is transmitted around the ring using a method called *token passing*. When a host needs to transmit data, it modifies the token with the data it wants to send and configures the token with the MAC address of the destination host. The data passes by each computer until it reaches the destination host. The destination host modifies the token to indicate that the data was received successfully. After the sending host verifies that the data was received, the frame is removed from the network. The token is released so that another host on the network can transmit data.

Only a single token exists in a ring topology network. If a client wants to transmit data and the token is in use, he must wait. Although this sounds inefficient, the token travels at a very fast rate. If the total cable length for a network is 400 meters, a token can circle this ring around 5,000 times per second.

> The best analogy for a token-ring network is a campfire stick. Anyone sitting around a campfire can speak only when holding the campfire stick. After a person has spoken, she passes the campfire stick to the person sitting at her left. If someone forgets to say something when holding the stick, he must wait until everyone else has had a turn using the campfire stick.

Dual-Ring Networks

Dual-ring networks commonly run the Fiber Distributed Data Interface (FDDI). FDDI is limited to a maximum ring length of 62 miles and operates at 100Mbps.

There are differences between token ring and FDDI when it comes to token passing. A computer on an FDDI network can transmit as many frames as it can produce in a preset time interval before letting the token go. In addition, several frames can circulate the ring at once. This gives an overall edge in speed to FDDI over token ring.

Traffic in a dual-ring network consists of two similar streams flowing in opposite directions (see Figure 2.6).

FIGURE 2.6

A dual-ring topology network.

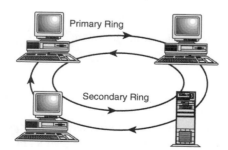

One ring is called the primary ring; the other ring is the secondary ring. Under normal operation, all data flows on the primary ring, and the secondary ring remains idle. The secondary ring is used only if a break occurs in the primary ring. The ring automatically reconfigures itself to use the secondary ring when necessary and continues to transmit.

Workstations generally are connected only to the primary ring. These single-attachment hosts connect to the ring using a dual-attached concentrator (DAC). These clients only have a connection to the primary ring. The DAC and dual-homed stations have connections to both the primary and secondary rings. When the primary ring is broken, only stations with dual connections are involved in calculating an alternative route.

The primary medium for an FDDI network is fiber-optic cable. This means

- An FDDI network is more secure because it does not emit electromagnetic-field signals that can be tapped.
- An FDDI network can transmit over longer distances without the use of repeaters to strengthen the signal.
- An FDDI network is immune to electromagnetic noise.

Wide Area Networks (WANs)

LAN implementations have physical and geographic limitations. Wide area networks (WANs) meet a need for networking that requires connectivity over larger distances.

Most WANs are simply combinations of local area networks and additional communications links between the LANs. The following terms are used to describe the scope or size of a WAN:

- **Metropolitan area networks (MANs).** MANs are WANs in a small geographic area. Generally, they are localized to a single city or region.
- **Campus area networks (CANs).** CANs is a common designation for WANs that link regions of a university campus.

For practical implementation, these are no different from a wide area network except for the area they physically cover.

Communications over a WAN use one of the following transmission technologies:

- Analog
- Digital
- Packet switching

Analog and digital technologies commonly are implemented as point-to-point technologies. In other words, they are configured between two distinct hosts. Packet switching, on the other hand, links several hosts using a mesh or cloud technology. Any host participating in the cloud can establish a session to another host in the cloud.

The following sections discuss these technologies in more detail.

Analog WAN Connectivity

Analog phone lines can be used to connect networks despite the poor line quality and slower speeds. The public-switched telephone network (PSTN) was primarily designed for voice traffic; it also can be used for data traffic. Remote users connecting to the home network from the road often use PSTN access. Although it is possible to purchase a dedicated analog line to connect networks, the cost of a conditioned line generally is prohibitive, and other networking solutions are investigated.

Digital Wide Area Network Connectivity

A more common method of linking a WAN is to use digital data service (DDS) lines. DDS provides a point-to-point synchronous connection. A company can lease dedicated circuits that provide full-duplex bandwidth by setting up a permanent link from each endpoint of the network.

Digital lines are preferable to analog lines due to increased speed and lack of transmission errors. Digital traffic does not require a modem. Instead, data is sent from a router on a network to a channel service unit/data service unit (CSU/DSU) (see Figure 2.7).

FIGURE 2.7

Communications over a digital network.

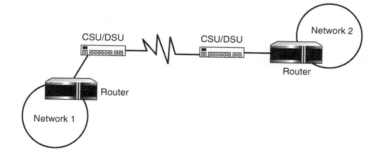

The CSU/DSU converts network data into digital bipolar signals that can traverse the synchronous communications environment.

The following are common digital connectivity methods:

- T1/E1
- T3/E3
- ISDN
- Switched 56

T1/E1

T1 service (known as E1 in Europe) is the most widely used digital service at higher data speeds. T1 can transmit a full-duplex signal at a rate of 1.544Mbps. It can be used to transmit voice, data, and video signals.

Because of the high cost of a T1 line, many subscribers opt for fractional-T1 service. Instead of using a T1's full bandwidth, the subscriber uses one or more T1 channels. Each T1 channel is a 64Kbps increment.

T3/E3

T3 service (known as E3 in Europe) can provide voice and data-grade service at speeds up to 45Mbps. This is the highest-capacity service available to the consumer today. As with T1 service, fractional-T3 service is available as an alternative to multiple T1 lines.

Integrated Services Digital Network (ISDN)

ISDN is an interLAN connectivity method that can carry data, voice, and imaging signals. Two flavors of ISDN are available: basic rate and primary rate.

Basic rate ISDN provides two bearer channels (known as B channels) that communicate at 56Kbps; an 8Kbps link-management channel; and one data channel (known as a D channel) that carry signal and link management data at a rate of 16Kbps. A network using both B channels can provide a 128Kbps data stream.

Primary rate ISDN can provide the entire bandwidth of a T1 link by providing 23 B channels and one D channel. In Europe, 30 B channels are used. The D channel under primary rate ISDN communicates at 64Kbps and still is used only for signal and link-management data.

ISDN is a demand-dial interface. Instead of remaining active at all hours, it demand-dials whenever a connection is required.

Switched 56

Many telephone companies offer LAN-to-LAN digital dial-up services. Switched 56 is a circuit-switched version of a 56Kbps DDS line. The key advantage of a switched 56 line over a dedicated line is that it can be enabled on demand. This eliminates the cost of a dedicated WAN connection.

Asymmetric Digital Subscriber Line (ADSL)

A technology that enables digital data transmission over existing copper phone lines. Both normal phone signals and the digital data transmission share the same infrastructure, with the DSL connections transmitting data at rates of 1.5 Mbps to 9 Mbps to the subscriber and from 16 kilobits per second (kbps) to 800 kbps to the service provider.

Although some organizations might find the upload bandwidth too small, home users generally are a good fit for the increased download bandwidth. To use ADSL, a digital modem must be installed.

Packet-Switching Networks

Packet-switching networks enable you to transmit data over an any-to-any connection. Sometimes a packet-switched network is described as a mesh network. When information is transmitted over the network, it is not known what path the information will take between the sender and the recipient of the data (see Figure 2.8).

FIGURE 2.8

A packet-switching network.

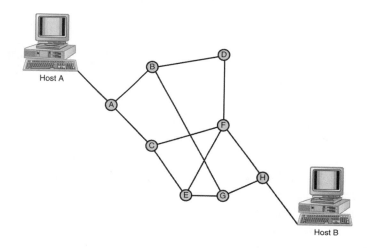

The original data is broken into smaller packets. Each packet is tagged with the destination address and a sequence number. As the packet traverses the network between the source and destination hosts, it travels on the best current path. Each packet travels along its own unique best current path. This way, if a network link goes down during the transmission of a stream of packets, not all the packets have to be re-sent. Some of the packets will have found an alternate route when the link went down.

Figure 2.8 shows one path that can be taken from Host A to Host B. In the diagram, a packet has been routed from Host A to Host B by crossing the networks located at A, C, F, and H. If the network located at F goes down, packets that have arrived at network C need to find an alternate route to network H. One possible alternative is to traverse networks E and G to arrive at network H.

At the destination host, the packets might arrive at different times or out of sequence. Because each packet has a sequence number, however, the original message can be rebuilt. The destination host also can request that missing packets be re-sent based on the missing sequence numbers.

Packet-switching networks are fast and efficient. They have their own method of managing routing traffic. For customers, they offer high-speed network links that are affordable. Charges are implemented on a per-transaction basis rather than a flat-rate fee.

The following are three common implementations of packet-switching networks:

- X.25
- Frame relay
- Asynchronous transfer mode (ATM)

X.25 Networks

X.25 was developed in the 1970s to provide users with WAN capabilities over public data networks. Phone companies developed it, and its attributes are international in nature. It is administered by an agency of the United Nations called the International Telecommunications Union (ITU).

In an X.25 network, a host calls another host to request a communications session. If the call is accepted, the two systems can begin a full-duplex information transfer. Either host can terminate the session.

A point-to-point connection takes place between data terminal equipment (DTE) at the client site and data circuit-terminating equipment (DCE) at the carrier's facilities. The DTE is connected to the DCE through a translation device known as a packet assembler/disassembler (PAD). The DCE connects to packet switching exchanges (PSEs), more commonly known as switches. The switches interconnect with each other until they reach the DCE of the destination host. This DCE connects to the DTE of the host to complete the communications session (see Figure 2.9).

FIGURE 2.9

An X.25 network.

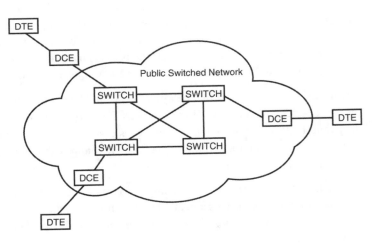

An association known as a virtual circuit accomplishes the end-to-end communication between the two DTEs. Virtual circuits enable communication between two defined endpoints to take place through any number of intermediate nodes. These nodes do not have to be a dedicated portion of the network. The circuit is not a physical data link; it is bandwidth that can be allocated on demand. The following are the two types of virtual circuits:

- **Permanent virtual circuits (PVCs).** PVCs are used for common data transfers known to occur on a regular basis. Although the route is permanent, the client pays only for the time the line is in use.

- **Switched virtual circuits (SVCs).** SVCs are used for data transfers that are sporadic in nature. The connection uses a specified route across the network. The route is maintained until the connection ceases.

The X.25 protocol contains many error-correcting algorithms. They exist because X.25 first was implemented across PSTNs that required this feature.

Frame Relay

Network communications have moved toward digital and fiber-optic environments. There is less need for the error checking found in the X.25 protocol. As a result, many large corporations use Frame Relay to connect their remote offices to the corporate headquarters. Frame Relay provides fast, variable-length packet-switching over digital networks. Frame Relay includes a cyclic redundancy check (CRC) algorithm that can detect whether a packet is corrupted and can discard it. It does not, however, ask for retransmission of the data. It leaves that up to the higher levels of the protocol.

Frame Relay uses permanent virtual circuits (PVCs) so the entire path between two hosts is known from end to end. This creates an optimal network environment in which the path between two hosts is predetermined. Instead of always having to calculate the best path to a remote host, the PVC has predetermined that route. In addition, because the hosts are connected using a common frame relay network, packets do not have to be fragmented due to differing Maximum Transmission Units (MTUs). The MTU is the largest packet size that can be used on a network segment. Frame relay networks all have the same MTU, removing the issues with differing MTUs.

Frame Relay also includes the following local management interface (LMI) extensions:

- Virtual circuit status messages provide information about PVC integrity. They report the addition of any new PVCs and the deletion of existing PVCs. These status messages prevent hosts from sending messages to a PVC that has ceased to exist.

- Multicasting is an optional LMI extension that enables a host to send a single frame destined for multiple recipients. This reduces overall network traffic because a single frame can be sent to multiple hosts instead of one message per host.

- Global addressing provides globally significant connection identifiers. Frame Relay uses data link connection identifiers (DLCIs) to identify a circuit ID. When global addressing is implemented, each connection has a globally unique ID. This ID is known to all other connections (see Figure 2.10).

FIGURE 2.10

Global addressing under Frame Relay.

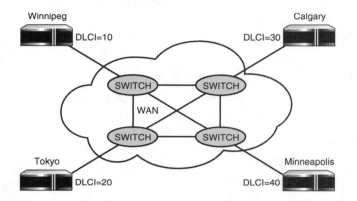

If Winnipeg must send a frame to Minneapolis, Winnipeg places a value of 40 in the DLCI field and sends the frame into the Frame Relay network. When the frame arrives in Minneapolis, the network changes the DLCI field contents to 10. This shows that the frame came from the Winnipeg network. This addressing scheme enables the WAN to function using the same methods as a LAN.

- Simple flow control provides an XON/XOFF flow-control mechanism. Frame Relay includes simple congestion-notification messages that enable the network to inform user devices when network resources are approaching a congested state. The simple flow control LMI extension is provided for devices that cannot use these notification messages and that need some level of flow control.

Asynchronous Transfer Mode (ATM)

Asynchronous transfer mode (ATM) uses advanced technology to segment data into cells at high speeds. Each cell is a fixed length, consisting of 5 bytes of header information and 48 bytes of payload data. The use of a fixed-length packet results in higher transfer speeds because the network spends less time processing incoming data. It also helps in planning application bandwidth. Cells cross the ATM network by passing through devices known as ATM switches. These switches analyze header information to switch the cell to the next ATM switch that ultimately leads to the destination network. ATM enables more than one computer to transmit at the same time through the use of multi-plexers. The topic of TCP/IP over ATM is discussed more fully on Day 18 "Dial-Up Networking Using TCP/IP."

When an ATM device wants to establish a connection with another ATM device, it sends a signaling request packet to the ATM switch on its network (see Figure 2.11).

FIGURE 2.11

A signaling request transits the network.

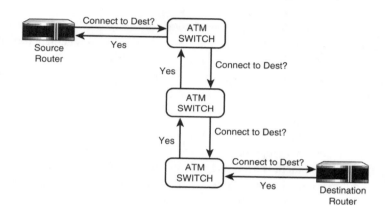

2

The request includes the ATM address of the target ATM device as well as quality of service (QoS) parameters. The QOS parameters essentially set minimum guidelines that must be met for transmission. They include values for peak bandwidth, average sustained bandwidth, and burst size. If the actual traffic flow does not meet the QOS specifications, the cell can be marked as discard-eligible. This means any ATM switch that handles the cell can drop the cell in periods of congestion. At each switch, the signaling request is reassembled and examined. If the switch table has an entry of the destination ATM device and the ATM switch can accommodate the QOS requested for the connection, it forwards the cell to the next ATM switch. When the cell signaling request reaches the destination endpoint, it responds with an accept message.

That wraps up the basics of the various network types that can be implemented for your network. The next section looks at a concept, Open Systems, that allows standard-ized protocols to be developed that provide network connectivity over the networks we deploy.

What Are Open Systems?

The concept of open systems is derived from a need for standardization. Many people have encountered a situation in which they must choose between competing products. The major problem is that if you buy BigCorp's XYZ product, you are tied to that prod-uct as your networking solution.

The goal of open systems is to reduce vendor-specific solutions. You should be able to choose among vendors to provide the actual products used when you implement your solution. You should be able to change your mind down the road and switch to a different vendor's solution without having to redesign your entire network. The solution should be able to plug in to the place held by the former product.

TCP/IP is a good example of an open system for a protocol suite. Through the use of RFCs, all TCP/IP standards are fully documented. They have been designated as required or elective components to be included in a vendor's implementation of TCP/IP. The goal of TCP/IP is to provide connectivity between heterogeneous systems. You might have to make some choices about how you implement the connectivity. By using TCP/IP, however, you know you have an underlying framework that is available on most platforms.

Be careful with the term *open systems*. Many times it is bandied about as the end-all and be-all, almost a religion. Competing products drive the market to come up with better solutions. If there is absolutely no difference between Product A and Product B, why would you not always choose the cheaper of the two products? People need a reason to buy a product. What differentiates one product from the next?

Use of Layered Models

In networking, layered models often are used to represent the various networking functions that must be performed. The following are reasons for using layered models:

- They divide all the functions of a network's operation into less-complex elements.
- They enable vendors to focus design and development on specific areas.
- They enable buyers to replace all components at a specific layer with components produced by a different vendor.
- They make it possible for layers to remain unaffected by changes in other layers of the network—as long as each layer presents an interface with which the layers above and below it can communicate.
- They provide a framework for network development.
- They divide the complexity of networking into easy-to-learn subsets of network operations.

When working in a layered model, each layer should be concerned only with the layers immediately above and below it. Many times, the adjacent layers are referred to as the n+1 and the n−1 layers, in reference to the currently observed layer (see Figure 2.12).

FIGURE 2.12

The interaction between network layers.

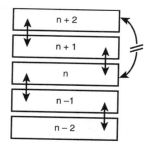

The n layer of the network only can communicate with the n+1 and n−1 layers. It is not possible for the n layer to communicate with other layers without transferring information through the n+1 or n−1 layers.

The Open System Interconnection (OSI) Reference Model

In the early 1980s, the International Standards Organization (ISO) saw the need to develop a network model to help vendors create interoperable network solutions. It developed what is now known as the Open System Interconnection (OSI) reference model. Even though other networking models have been created, they often are related back to the OSI reference model when vendors want to provide education about their products.

The OSI reference model is made up of the following seven distinct layers:

- Physical
- Data link
- Network
- Transport
- Session
- Presentation
- Application

The OSI reference model describes how information makes its way from an application on one host system to an application on another host system. As information descends through the network layers on the sending host, it changes its format through each layer. The data from higher layers is prepended with header information from the layer directly below it (see Figure 2.13).

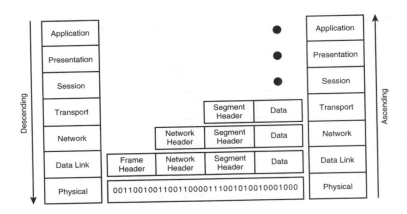

FIGURE 2.13

Data encapsulation in the OSI reference model.

The diagram in Figure 2.13 shows that, as data descends through the left-side host, the previous layer's header and data combination is encapsulated within the next layer's header layer; for example, the original data of an e-mail message is encapsulated within a segment header. The segment header ensures that the message hosts are able to reliably communicate with each other.

At the network layer, the data (which now comprises the segment header and the original data passed from the higher layers) is placed within a packet that contains a network header. This network header includes the source and destination logical addresses. In a TCP/IP internetwork, these are the IP addresses of the source and destination hosts. These addresses assist in packet routing between the two hosts over the internetwork.

At the data link layer, the network header and its data are encapsulated within a frame header. The frame header defines how the information will be transported through the network interface onto the physical network. Each device on the network requires framing to connect to the next device in the network. The frame header also includes the physical addresses of the source and destination hosts.

Finally, at the physical layer, the frame header and its data are converted into a format that enables the information to be transmitted on a network medium such as network cabling.

When the data is received at the destination host, the bits are converted back to a frame header and its data. As the information moves up through the network layers, each header is used to determine how to move the data up through the layers. At each layer, the previous layer's header information is stripped off so that the data is back in the same format it was in when transmitted by the matching layer on the source host.

Now that the basic features of the OSI reference model have been reviewed, the following sections briefly examine each specific layer of the model. Each layer has a preset function it must perform. As data descends through the layers, the upper layer's header and data become the data section of the next lower layer. Data cannot skip a layer as it descends through the OSI model. This simplifies the process of data transmission. It also enables new protocols to be developed because they must simply interact with the layers above and below the layer in which they are implemented.

The Physical Layer

The physical layer defines the electrical currents, physical pulses, or optical pulses that are involved in transporting data from the Network Interface Card (NIC) of a host to the communications system. This layer includes the connection to the communications system. The requirements and characteristics for transmission generally are documented in standards such as the V.35 or RS-232 standards. The physical layer is responsible for transmitting bits from one computer to another using media such as Cat5 cabling.

The Data Link Layer

The data link layer sends data frames from the network layer to the physical layer. When the data link layer receives bits from the physical layer, it translates these bits into data frames. A data frame commonly includes the following components:

- **Destination ID.** This ID usually is the MAC address of the destination host or the default gateway.
- **Sender ID.** This ID usually is the MAC address of the source host.
- **Control information.** This includes information such as the actual frame type, routing, and segmentation information.
- **Cyclic redundancy check (CRC).** CRC provides error correction and verifies that the destination reference host receives the data frame intact.

The data link layer is divided into two sublayers—the logical link control (LLC) and media access control (MAC). The LLC sublayer provides error control and works primarily with the network layer to support connectionless or connection-oriented services. The MAC sublayer provides access to the actual LAN medium. It primarily functions with the physical layer.

The Network Layer

The network layer determines the best way to move data from one host to another. It manages the addressing of messages and the translation of logical addresses (such as IP addresses) to physical addresses (MAC addresses).

The network layer also determines the route data traverses between source and destination hosts. If the packets being transmitted are too large for a destination host's topology, the network layer compensates by breaking the data into smaller packets. These packets are then reassembled at the destination.

2

The Transport Layer

The transport layer segments and reassembles data into a data stream. It provides an end-to-end connection between source and destination hosts. When data is transmitted from a source to a destination host, the data is segmented into smaller collections of information. The segments are numbered sequentially and are sent to the destination host. When the destination host receives the segments, it sends an acknowledgment of their receipt. If a segment is not received, the destination host can request that a specific segment be re-sent. This provides error control for data transport.

The Session Layer

The session layer enables two applications on separate hosts to establish a communication connection called a session. These sessions ensure that messages are sent and received with a high degree of reliability.

The session layer performs security functions to make sure two hosts are allowed to communicate across a network. The session layer coordinates the service requests and responses that occur when applications communicate between hosts.

The following are common protocols and interfaces that function at the session layer:

- **Winsock.** Many protocols use the Winsock programming interface. This interface defines the ports, protocols, and addresses of two hosts that are going to communicate on a network.
- **Remote Procedure Calls (RPCs).** An RPC is a redirection mechanism that enables a request to be built on a client and then executed on a server at the security level of the client.
- **X Window systems.** These permit intelligent terminals to communicate with Unix computers as if they were directly attached.

The Presentation Layer

The presentation layer determines how data is formatted when exchanged between network computers. The data received from the application layer is translated into a commonly recognized, intermediary format.

The presentation layer also is responsible for all translation of data, encryption of data, character set conversions, and protocol conversions. The presentation layer is responsible for syntax conversion between two communicating hosts, for example, if one of the hosts used the ASCII standard for its text and data representation and the other host used EBCDIC.

The following are common presentation formats handled by the presentation layer:

- **ASCII.** The American Standard Code for Information Interchange is an 8-bit character set used to define all alphanumeric characters. It is the most common implementation of text transmissions on computers.
- **EBCDIC.** The Extended Binary Coded Decimal Interchange Code is a text representation method used extensively on IBM mainframe and minicomputers.
- **External data representation (XDR).** XDR is used by applications such as NFS and NIS to provide a universal format for text transmission between two hosts. It facilitates text transmissions between two hosts using different text representations (such as EBCDIC and ASCII).

The Application Layer

The application layer enables programs to access network services. It does not deal with programs that require only local resources. To use the application layer, a program must have a communications component that requires network resources.

The following are types of programs currently in use that use the application layer:

- **Electronic mail.** The application layer provides network communication services. Common implementations include products such as Microsoft Exchange Server and Lotus Notes.
- **Electronic Data Interchange (EDI).** The application layer provides improved business flow for ordering, shipments, inventory, and accounting between associated businesses.
- **Conferencing applications.** The application layer enables users in remote locations to use conferencing applications such as video, voice data, and fax exchange. A common program that uses this technology is Microsoft NetMeeting.
- **World Wide Web.** Through the use of browsers, such as Internet Explorer or Netscape Navigator, users can view information in formats such as text, graphics, sound, and video from remote network locations. The most common Web servers in use today include Apache Web Server, iPlanet Web Server, and Microsoft Internet Information Server (IIS).

The TCP/IP Layer Model

The TCP/IP layer model is based on a four-layered network (see Figure 2.14).

Within the four layers, specific boundaries are observed. In the Network layer, only physical MAC addresses are used for address resolution. Even when an interface does not have a physical address—as is the case with a modem—an auto-generated physical address is used. Modems are commonly used to connect to networks, yet they do not have a physical MAC address. When a modem connects to the network, an auto-generated physical address is assigned to the modem so communication can take place.

FIGURE 2.14

The TCP/IP four-layer model.

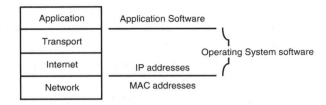

In the Internet layer, logical IP addresses are mapped to the physical MAC addresses. Each host in a TCP/IP internetwork is assigned a unique IP address. This address identifies hosts and identifies the subnetwork on which a host resides.

All protocols used in the Transport and Internet layers are provided by the operating system. Applications do not have to provide their own transport or internetworking protocols. This makes it easier for applications to be deployed on different operating systems. The application only has to interface with either Transmission Control Protocol (TCP) or User Datagram Protocol (UDP) as a transport protocol.

All protocols and software used in the Application layer are application-dependent. You can switch the underlying protocols, and many of the applications will continue to operate. You can, for example, use a Java-based FTP client on both a LINUX client or on a Windows 2000 client. The Java-based FTP client will still operate in this environment because the FTP software functions beyond the operating system. It interfaces with whatever TCP/IP protocol stack is used. This concept is known as boundary layers. A new protocol at any of the four layers of the TCP/IP model only needs to interact with the layer immediately above or below the level in which it functions.

The following sections go into more detail about the processes completed in each layer of the TCP/IP layer model.

The Network Layer

The network layer merges outgoing frames on the wire and pulls incoming frames off the wire. The format used by these frames depends on the network topology implemented.

The network layer adds a preamble at the beginning of the frame and adds a cyclical redundancy check (CRC) to ensure that the data is not corrupted in transit. When the frame arrives at the destination, the CRC value is recalculated to determine whether the data has been corrupted in transit. If the frame arrives intact, it is passed up to the Internet layer. If the frame is corrupted, it is discarded at this point.

Issues with Frame Types

On a single network segment, all hosts must use the same frame type for communication to occur. Multiple frame types can be run on a single network segment, but only hosts with same frame types can actually communicate.

The Internet Layer

The Internet layer provides three primary functions: addressing, routing, and packaging. The Internet Protocol (IP) resides in this layer of the TCP/IP protocol layer suite. IP provides connectionless, nonguaranteed delivery of information. This means the IP protocol does not perform any checks or measures to make sure the destination host has received the information successfully. Packets could be lost or could arrive out of order.

When information arrives from the transport layer, the IP protocol adds a header to the information. The header includes the following information:

- **Source IP address.** This is the IP address assigned to the sending host.
- **Destination IP address.** This is the IP address assigned to the target host.
- **Transport protocol.** The protocol used by the transport layer is stored within the IP header. This way, when the datagram arrives at the destination system, the Internet layer knows whether to transfer the datagram using the TCP or UDP protocols.
- **Checksum.** This ensures that the data arriving at this layer has not been corrupted in transit.
- **Time-to-Live (TTL).** Each time the datagram crosses a router, the TTL is decreased by a value of at least one. When the TTL reaches a value of zero, the datagram is dropped from the network.

The Internet layer also determines how to route a datagram to a destination host. If it is determined that the destination IP host is on the same network segment, the datagram is sent directly to the destination host. If IP determines that the destination host is located on a remote network segment, IP uses the source host's routing table to determine the best route to reach the network on which the remote host is located. If there is not an explicit route in the routing table, the source host uses its default gateway to send the datagram to the remote host. (The default gateway is the preferred router a host uses to route traffic to remote network segments.)

Other processes that occur in the Internet layer are fragmentation and reassembly. Sometimes, when information is transferred between network segments, the network segments might not use the same network topology. The recipient's network topology cannot work with the same datagram size as the sending host's network. In this case, IP breaks data into smaller pieces. When the data is received at the destination host, the smaller pieces are reassembled into the original data packet. When the data is broken up, the following information is appended in each separate packet:

- **Flag.** The fragment flag bit in the IP header of each packet fragment is set to designate that the data has been fragmented. On the last packet fragment, the flag bit is not set because no more fragments follow.

- **Fragment ID.** When a datagram is broken into smaller pieces, the fragment ID identifies all the pieces of the original datagram. This information is used by the client to reassemble the datagram.

- **Fragment offset.** When the smaller pieces are reassembled into a single datagram, the fragment offset determines the order in which the fragments should be reassembled.

The Transport Layer

The transport layer provides end-to-end communication between hosts using ports. The following two protocols are provided in the TCP/IP layer model to transport data:

- Transmission control protocol (TCP)
- Universal datagram protocol (UDP)

TCP provides connection-oriented communication on a TCP/IP network. When two hosts communicate using the TCP protocol, a session must be established between the two hosts. This is so each host can determine the next sequence number the other host will be using. A TCP connection provides a level of reliability. Transmissions use sequence numbers and acknowledgments to make sure the destination host successfully receives the data. If a destination host does not receive a specific packet, it can request that the source host resend the packet (see Figure 2.15).

FIGURE 2.15

TCP uses sequence numbers to ensure delivery.

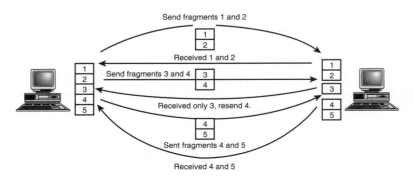

In Figure 2.15, the host on the left has segmented a data package into five segments. It sends segments 1 and 2 to the host on the right. When the host on the right receives the fragments, it acknowledges their receipt. The host on the left then sends the next two fragments (fragments 3 and 4). For whatever reason, the host on the right receives only the third fragment. When it sends the acknowledgment, it only acknowledges the receipt of fragment 3. The host on the left resends fragment 4 and also sends fragment 5. On receipt, the receiving host acknowledges both fragments. Now it can reassemble the data into its original format. The TCP protocol is covered in depth on Day 4 "Core Protocol of the TCP/IP Suite." Topics discussed include the TCP three-way handshake and the use of sliding windows in TCP data transmissions.

A UDP protocol provides connection-less service. It is not guaranteed that the destination host will receive the information. Applications that use UDP are on their own to be sure data is successfully delivered to the recipient host. The only provision you have in a UDP packet is that there is a checksum value within its header. The checksum makes it possible to determine if the data was corrupted in transit.

A common analogy used when comparing the TCP and UDP protocols is the post office versus a courier service. The post office is much like the UDP protocol. When you place a letter to your friend in the mailbox, it is not guaranteed that the mail will get to him. Most of the time it reaches him successfully. When you must be sure that a business associate receives a package, however, you are not going to use a typical mail service. Instead, you use a courier service to be sure the business associate receives the package in a predetermined amount of time. Along the way, you can check the progress of the package by either phoning, or checking the status on the courier's Web site. When the business associate receives the package, she acknowledges its receipt by signing for the package.

Just as it costs more to use a courier service rather than the post office, there is additional cost on the network when using the TCP protocol. Periodically, the recipient host must send an acknowledgment that it has received the last transmissions successfully. The sending host often waits for an acknowledgment before it continues to send data.

You, as a network administrator, do not have a choice which transport protocol to implement. This is determined by the higher-level application using the transport protocol. Many applications use TCP so they do not have to provide reliable data transport. The TCP protocol can handle reliable transmission of data using sequence numbers and acknowledgments. An application that uses UDP has to ensure reliability on its own.

Note

Some protocols and their associated applications, such as the Domain Name Server (DNS), can use both UDP and TCP for data transmissions. In the case of DNS, UDP is used when the DNS client sends DNS requests to a DNS

server. TCP is used when a master DNS server sends a zone transfer to a
secondary DNS server. DNS is discussed in detail on Day 6, "Resolution of IP
Addresses and Logical Names," and Day 7, "Configuring Domain Name
Servers."

The Application Layer

Network-based applications function on the application layer in the TCP/IP layer model.
Network-based applications refers to applications that connect to or communicate with
remote network hosts. Network applications that run on a TCP/IP network generally fit
into one of two categories:

- Winsock applications
- NetBIOS applications

Winsock applications use the Windows Sockets service application-programming interface (API). These include utilities such as FTP, Telnet, SNMP, and IRC.

NetBIOS applications use NetBIOS names and messaging services over a TCP/IP network. The Windows NT 4.0 network operating system still uses NetBIOS names for its
networking name resolution, while newer versions of the Microsoft network operating
system such as Windows 2000 and Windows .NET Server, are less dependent on
NetBIOS name resolution.

Comparing the OSI Model to the TCP/IP Model

The following comparisons can be made between the seven-layer OSI reference model
and the four-layer TCP/IP model (see Figure 2.16):

- The TCP/IP layer model combines both the physical and data link layers of the
  OSI model into the TCP/IP model's network layer. The TCP/IP model does not dif-
  ferentiate between the physical network cards and their drivers. This enables
  TCP/IP to be implemented in any network topology.
- The Internet layer of the TCP/IP model corresponds to the network layer of the
  OSI reference model. Both layers provide addressing and routing services.
- The transport layer in each model enables end-to-end communication sessions to
  occur between two hosts.
- The application layer in the TCP/IP model combines the session, presentation, and
  application layers of the OSI model. The TCP/IP model includes all issues of how
  data is represented and how sessions are maintained within the definitions of an
  application.

FIGURE 2.16

Comparing the OSI and TCP/IP layer model.

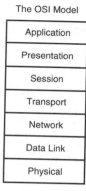

The OSI Model

| Application |
| Presentation |
| Session |
| Transport |
| Network |
| Data Link |
| Physical |

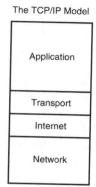

The TCP/IP Model

| Application |
| Transport |
| Internet |
| Network |

2

Applying What You Have Learned

Here are questions to check what you've learned today. The answers can be found in Appendix B, "Test Your Knowledge: Answers."

Test Your Knowledge

1. What are the primary differences between a Frame Relay network and an X.25 network?

2. What is the primary difference between ATM and Frame Relay networks?

3. What advantages does an FDDI network have over a token-ring network?

4. Describe the major differences between a peer-to-peer network and a server-based network.

5. What element does Quality of Service (QoS) add to ATM transmissions?

Match the OSI reference model layers to their functionality.

6. Application   a. Determines the best route from source to destination

7. Presentation   b. Enables programs to access network resources

8. Session   c. Performs a binary transmission

9. Transport   d. Provides an end-to-end connection between a source and destination hosts

10. Network   e. Responsible for translation of all data

11. Data link   f. Divided into two sublayers

12. Physical   g. Coordinates service requests and responses between two hosts

13. What are the four layers of the TCP/IP layer model?

14. What is meant by the term boundary layer?

15. What layers of the OSI model can be matched to the Network Interface layer of the TCP/IP layer model?

16. What functionality is provided by the Transport layer in the TCP/IP layer model?

Preview of Day 3

Tomorrow's material digs into the Internet protocol. Topics include the basic formatting of an IP address, the various classes of IP addresses, and general information about the use of subnet masks.

The end of the day overviews some features of IPv6. If you are interested in a more detailed description of IPv6, see Day 21, "IPv6, the Future of TCP/IP?"

DAY 3

Internet Protocol (IP) Addresses

Today you will learn about the assignment of IP addresses to hosts. This chapter discusses the rules for assigning IP addresses. Also, we'll look into how subnet masks are used to determine what portion of a 32-bit address is used to represent the network and what portion is used to identify a host on that network. The following topics are covered today:

- The assignment of IP addresses
- A comparison of dotted-decimal notation versus binary representation
- The classes of IP addresses
- The role of a subnet mask in routing decisions
- How a sending host determines if routing is required to reach the destination host
- The role of Private Address Ranges
- The future of IP addressing

Internet Protocol Address Basics

IP addresses uniquely identify each host on a TCP/IP internetwork. A host can be a computer, a terminal, a router, a printer, or even a hub. You can think of it like this: A host is any physical device on your network that fits one of the following properties:

- You use this device to access other devices on the network or to the Internet.
- You connect to this device as a shared network component.
- You need to manage this device to be sure it is functioning correctly.

Every host in a TCP/IP internetwork requires a unique IP address. This IP address must be unique across the entire internetwork. With a large worldwide network such as the Internet, a number-assigning authority is required. For the Internet, the Internet Assigned Number Authority (IANA) sets policies regarding how IP addresses are assigned and has delegated the responsibility of managing Internet IP addressing to regional authorities:

- Asia Pacific Network Information Centre (APNIC) http://www.apnic.net/
- American Registry for Internet Numbers (ARIN) http://www.arin.net/
- Réseaux IP Européens (RIPE Network Coordination Centre) http://www.ripe.net/

When you attach your network to the Internet, you most likely will contact a local Internet Service Provider (ISP) to provide your office (or home) with connectivity to the Internet. You will obtain your network's pool of IP addresses from your ISP. If your ISP needs additional IP addresses for assignment to clients, it will either contact its ISP, or if it is a member of one of the regional authorities, it will request IP address pools from its regional authority.

What happens if a host uses the same IP address as another host on the network? The answer depends on your implementation of TCP/IP. It is guaranteed that one of the hosts will not be able to communicate with other hosts on the network. In fact, if the TCP/IP stack is well coded and the two hosts are on the same subnet, a warning message may be issued to both hosts, making them aware that a duplicate IP address has been found on the network.

How Do You Write an Address?

Each IP address is a binary stream of 32 1s and 0s. This is why the current version of IP addressing is known as 32-bit addressing. It would be confusing if addresses were written in this manner. Therefore, dotted-decimal representation is used for IP addresses. Before dotted-decimal representation is discussed, however, you should briefly review the binary number system.

Binary Representation

The binary numbering system consists of only two digits: 0 and 1. All numbers are represented as streams of 0s and 1s. Figure 3.1 shows the representation of numbers 0 through 15 in the binary system.

FIGURE 3.1

Binary representation of numbers 0 through 15.

	128's	64's	32's	16's	8's	4's	2's	1's	
0	0	0	0	0	0	0	0	0	=0
1	0	0	0	0	0	0	0	1	=1
2	0	0	0	0	0	0	1	0	=2
3	0	0	0	0	0	0	1	1	=2+1
4	0	0	0	0	0	1	0	0	=4
5	0	0	0	0	0	1	0	1	=4+1
6	0	0	0	0	0	1	1	0	=4+2
7	0	0	0	0	0	1	1	1	=4+2+1
8	0	0	0	0	1	0	0	0	=8
9	0	0	0	0	1	0	0	1	=8+1
10	0	0	0	0	1	0	1	0	=8+2
11	0	0	0	0	1	0	1	1	=8+2+1
12	0	0	0	0	1	1	0	0	=8+4
13	0	0	0	0	1	1	0	1	=8+4+1
14	0	0	0	0	1	1	1	0	=8+4+2
15	0	0	0	0	1	1	1	1	=8+4+2+1

The column values of 128, 64, 32, 16, 6, 4, 2, and 1 are all powers of 2. In other words, the 1s column actually is the value 2^0. The 2s column is the value 2^1. Figure 3.2 shows the translations for the eight columns. This collection of 8 bits is referred to as an octet of information. Remember that 8 bits also is referred to as a byte of information.

FIGURE 3.2

Calculating each of the binary columns for an octet.

2^n		Dec	Actual
2^0	=	1	1
2^1	=	2	2
2^2	=	4	2 x 2
2^3	=	8	2 x 2 x 2
2^4	=	16	2 x 2 x 2 x 2
2^5	=	32	2 x 2 x 2 x 2 x 2
2^6	=	64	2 x 2 x 2 x 2 x 2 x 2
2^7	=	128	2 x 2 x 2 x 2 x 2 x 2 x 2

As you can see, each column is a power of 2. As you move left through the columns, each column is 2 times the number in the previous column.

 Note   Although it might seem trivial to review the binary numbering system, it is a good idea to practice translating numbers between 0 and 255 to binary numbers. When working with advanced IP addressing issues, such as calculating pools of IP addresses for use in subnet masking, this knowledge can greatly reduce the amount of time spent at this task.

The number 131, for example, would be represented as 128 + 2 + 1. In binary, this is 10000011. The number 63 would be represented as 32 + 16 + 8 + 4 + 2 + 1, which is 00111111 in binary.

The good news is you only work with up to eight digits, or an octet, when working with binary and IP addresses. The 32-bit address is represented in dotted-decimal format using four octets of information. These four 8-bit collections form the 32-bit IP address for a host.

What is the highest decimal digit allowed for an octet? If you convert 11111111 to decimal, you have 128 + 64 + 32 + 16 + 8 + 4+ 2 + 1 = 255. Therefore, the largest value allowed for any of the decimals in dotted-decimal format is 255. The lowest is 00000000, or simply 0.

Dotted-Decimal Notation

It is difficult and tiresome to write addresses in binary. Instead of using binary, therefore, dotted-decimal notation is more commonly used for addresses.

An IP address (as previously mentioned) comprises four octets of information to make up the 32-bit address. Each octet is more commonly written in decimal notation.

For example, the IP address

`01111111 00000000 00000000 00000001`

is more commonly written as 127.0.0.1, and is referred to as the *loopback address*. The loopback address represents the local host where you are sitting. It is a reserved address that ensures that data sent to the loopback address is never transmitted on the network.

Each octet of information is translated into its decimal equivalent. The octets are then separated using a period between each octet.

IP Address Classes

On a single network segment, all IP hosts share the same network address. Each host on that segment must have a unique host portion of the address. Five pools of IP addresses have been designated as classes of IP addresses. Only the first three can be assigned to hosts on a network.

Each of the first three classes of IP addresses is composed of a network and host portion of those IDs. Figure 3.3 shows the details of the address classes.

FIGURE 3.3

The five classes of IP addresses.

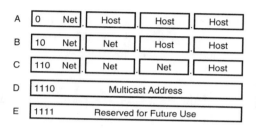

Class A Addresses

A Class A address allocates 8 bits to the network portion of the address and 24 bits to the host portion of the address. A Class A address has a first octet value between 1 and 126. These numbers are represented in binary by patterns that resemble 0#######. This allows for 126 distinct networks of 16,777,214 hosts per network. These numbers are determined using the following calculations:

- The first digit of the first octet in a Class A address is 0; this leaves 7 bits to create each unique network ID. The value of 2^7 is 128. Two addresses cannot be used, however. The value 0 cannot be used as a network ID. The value 127 also cannot be used because it is reserved for loopback functions. This leaves 126 unique network IDs.

- There are 24 bits left for the host ID. The value of 2^{24} is 16,777,216. A host ID cannot be all 0s or all 1s. This eliminates two host IDs from the pool, resulting in 16,777,214 unique hosts per network.

For example, if your IP address is 10.237.16.88 network, the 10 (being the first 8 bits of the IP address) represents the network portion of the IP address. The host portion would be 237.16.88, but you could be assigned any value between 0.0.1 and 255.255.254.

Class B Addresses

A Class B address allocates 16 bits to the network portion of the address and 16 bits to the host portion of the address. A Class B address has a first octet value between 128 and 191. These numbers are represented in binary by patterns that resemble 10######. This allows for 16,384 unique networks with 65,534 hosts per network. These numbers are determined using the following calculations:

- The first two digits of the first octet of a Class B address are 1 and 0; this leaves 14 bits to represent each unique network ID. If you calculate 2^{14}, you determine the total number of Class B network IDs to be 16,384.
- There are 16 bits left for the host ID. The value of 2^{16} is 65,536. A host ID cannot be all 0s or all 1s. This removes two host IDs from the pool, resulting in 65,534 unique hosts per network.

For example, if your IP address is 172.18.16.88 network, the 172.18 (being the first 16 bits of the IP address) represents the network portion of the IP address. The host portion would be 16.88, but you could be assigned any value between 0.1 and 255.254.

Class C Addresses

A Class C address allocates 24 bits to the network portion of the address and 8 bits to the host portion of the address. A Class C address has a first octet value between 192 and 223. These numbers are represented in binary by patterns that resemble 110#####. This allows for 2,097,152 unique networks with 254 hosts per network. These numbers are determined using the following calculations:

- The first three digits of a Class C address are 1, 1, and 0; this leaves 21 bits to represent each unique network ID. If you calculate 2^{21}, you determine the total number of Class C network IDs to be 2,097,152.
- There are 8 bits left for the host ID. The value of 2^8 is 256. A host ID cannot be all 0s or all 1s. This removes two host IDs from the pool, resulting in 254 unique hosts per network.

For example, if your IP address is 192.168.222.88 network, the 192.168.222 (being the first 24 bits of the IP address) would represent the network portion of the IP address. The host portion would be 222, but you could be assigned any value between 1 and 254.

Class D Addresses

Class D addresses are reserved for multicast group usage and cannot be assigned to individual hosts on a network. For example, a video media server can send a video signal to all hosts on the network that register a specific multicast address. The data is transmitted to the multicast address as the destination, and all members of the multicast group receive the data.

A Class D address has a first octet value between 224 and 239 and is represented in binary with a pattern matching 1110####. The remaining 28 bits represent the multicast group to which the host belongs.

Class E Addresses

Class E addresses are experimental addresses that are not available to the public. They have been reserved for future use. A Class E address has a first octet value between 240 and 255. This is represented in binary with values that match the pattern 1111####.

General Guidelines for IP Addressing

The following are general guidelines for assigning network and host IDs:

- All hosts on the same physical network segment should have the same network ID.
- Each host on a network segment must have a unique host portion of the IP address.
- A network ID can never be 127. This value has been reserved for loopback functions.
- A host ID cannot be all 1s. This also represents a broadcast address for the local network.
- A network ID cannot be all 0s. This represents the local network.
- A host ID cannot be all 0s. It is customary to represent a network using the network portion of the ID with a host ID set to all 0s. This cannot be allocated to an individual host.

Special IP Addresses

Some IP addresses have been reserved and cannot be assigned to individual hosts or be used as network IDs. These reserved addresses include the following:

- Each network address is represented by the network ID with the host ID set to all 0s. Table 3.1 shows the format for each IP address class's network address.

TABLE 3.1 Network Addresses by Class

Class	Network ID
A	w.0.0.0
B	w.x.0.0
C	w.x.y.0

- A network ID with the host ID set to all 1s represents a network's broadcast address. Table 3.2 shows the format for each IP address class's broadcast address.

TABLE 3.2   Broadcast Addresses by Class

Class	Network ID
A	w.255.255.255
B	w.x.255.255
C	w.x.y.255

- The IP address 255.255.255.255 is reserved as the limited broadcast address. This address can be used at any time when the network ID is not yet known by a host. Routers generally are configured not to forward this broadcast beyond the local network segment.

- The network address 127 is reserved for loopback functions. It cannot be assigned to a network segment.

- The IP address 0.0.0.0 is reserved to mean this host. This is an option only when a host such as a DHCP client is starting up and has not yet received an IP address. This topic is discussed on Day 9 "Gateway and Routing Protocols."

The Role of Subnet Masks

Subnet masks designate which bits of an IP address represent the network portion and which bits represent the host portion. Default subnet masks are used with Class A, Class B, and Class C IP addresses, as follows:

Class A: 255.0.0.0

Class B: 255.255.0.0

Class C: 255.255.255.0

The Class A subnet mask tells you the first 8 bits of the IP address represent the network portion of the address. The remaining 24 bits represent the host portion of the address. Let's say a host has the IP address 10.25.65.32. Using the default subnet mask, the network address would be 10.0.0.0. The host component of the address would be 25.65.32.

The Class B subnet mask tells you the first 16 bits of the IP address represent the network portion of the address. The remaining 16 bits represent the host address within the network. If a host has the IP address 172.20.33.33, the network portion of the address would be 172.20.0.0. The host component would be 33.33.

The Class C subnet mask tells you the first 24 bits of the IP address represent the network portion of the address. The remaining 8 bits represent the host address within the network. If a host has the IP address 192.168.2.3, the network portion of the address would be 192.168.2.0. The host component would be 3.

The ANDing Process

When a source host attempts to communicate with a destination host, the source host uses its subnet mask to determine whether the destination host is on the local network or a remote network. This is known as the *ANDing process.*

The AND function has the following properties:

- If the two compared values are both 1, the result is 1.
- If one of the values is 0 and the other is 1, the result is 0.
- If both of the compared values are 0, the result is 0.

The source and destination IP addresses are compared to the source's subnet mask using the ANDing process. An AND result is created for each of the addresses. If the result is the same, the hosts are on the same network. If the result is different, the destination host is on a remote network. All traffic destined for that remote host should be directed to the router indicated in the source host's routing table. If no explicit route is defined in the routing table, the traffic is directed to the source host's default gateway.

Figure 3.4 shows two hosts that want to communicate. Host A (with IP address 172.16.2.4) wants to communicate with Host B (with IP address 172.16.3.5). If the subnet mask for Host A is 255.255.0.0, will the hosts communicate using local transmissions or will they send information to the default gateway?

FIGURE 3.4

Using the ANDing process.

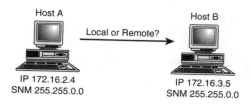

When converted to binary, the address 172.16.2.4 is as follows:

`10101100 00010000 00000010 00000100`

When converted to binary, the address 172.16.3.5 is as follows:

`10101100 00010000 00000011 00000101`

If the ANDing process is performed, the result for Host A using its subnet mask of 255.255.0.0 is

```
HOST A's IP Address    10101100 00010000 00000010 00000100
Host A's Subnet Mask   11111111 11111111 00000000 00000000
ANDING Result          10101100 00010000 00000000 00000000
```

The result for Host B is

```
HOST B's IP Address    10101100 00010000 00000011 00000101
Host A's Subnet Mask   11111111 11111111 00000000 00000000
ANDing Result          10101100 00010000 00000000 00000000
```

As you can see, the two results match. This indicates that, as far as Host A is concerned, the two hosts are on the same physical network. Communication can occur directly between the two hosts. In fact, the same holds true because host B would have the same subnet mask since the hosts are on the same network.

Day 5, "The Art of Subnet Masking," further examines the art of subnet masking. It also examines the use of nonstandard subnet masking to further segment a group of IP addresses into smaller segments. This process, which ignores the default subnet masks used by address classes, is commonly referred to as Classless Internet Domain Routing (CIDR).

Common Subnet Mask Problems

As previously discussed, the subnet mask determines whether a destination host is on the local network or a remote network. Most troubleshooting of subnet masking is performed using the WINIPCFG, IPCONFIG, and PING utilities.

The IPCONFIG Utility

In some TCP/IP implementations, the IPCONFIG utility is called IFCONFIG. Whatever the name, this utility reveals the current TCP/IP configuration for the host on which the command is run. This includes the configuration of the IP address, subnet mask, default gateway and DNS server, and other TCP/IP configuration settings.

The following are symptoms that incorrect subnet masks have been implemented on your network:

- You can communicate with hosts on the local network, but you can't communicate with remote hosts.
- You can communicate with all hosts on the remote network except one specific host. When you try to communicate with that host, you receive messages such as Timed out warnings.
- You can't communicate with a host on the local network because your host believes it is located on a remote network and incorrectly forwards the packet to the default gateway.

Local Network Addresses

Three pools of IP addresses have been reserved for use on local networks that are either behind firewalls and proxy servers or not connected to the Internet in any manner. The reserved address pools, known as private network addressing, are

- 10.0.0.0 through 10.255.255.255
- 172.16.0.0 through 172.31.255.255
- 192.168.0.0 through 192.168.255.255

These addresses were created to provide networks not attached to the Internet with a pool of IP addresses that do not conflict with any addresses currently in use on the Internet. If networks using these reserved addresses link to the Internet in the future, they do not have to worry about an address conflict with any other network on the Internet.

The network in Figure 3.5 uses the network address 192.168.3.0 for the private network. In this example, the firewall has a component known as the Local Address Table (LAT). The Local Address Table designates that the internal interface of the firewall is on the 192.168.3.0 network. Any hosts using an IP address that belongs on the 192.168.3.0 network must be located on the internal side of the firewall. A host trying to connect from the Internet side of the firewall will be stopped by the firewall for security reasons.

FIGURE 3.5

Use of private addresses.

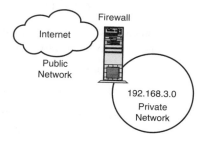

Why Private Addresses Were Created

When I first started to set up firewalls, I was not aware of the reserved local address tables. I used the network address 131.107.0.0 with the subnet mask 255.255.0.0 for my internal network.

I thought I correctly configured this network range into the firewall's LAT and communications function—until someone attempted to send e-mail to a recipient at microsoft.com. The mail server for the domain microsoft.com was located at 131.107.3.42. When the e-mail was forwarded to our firewall, it resolved the Mail Exchanger (MX) record for microsoft.com and determined that it needed to forward the mail to 131.107.3.42. Using its LAT table, the firewall determined that this server must be located somewhere on our local network. The mail was not successfully delivered—ever!

Besides preventing address conflicts with the Internet, private network addressing also reduces the demand for public network IP addresses. When data is sent from the private network to public network, the original source address information is translated to an ISP-obtained outbound address. This process is known as network address translation (NAT).

 Note

NAT is discussed in Day 13, "Protecting Your Network."

The NAT process helps prevent external attackers from determining the IP addresses in use on your private network, as well as reduce the demands for public network addresses. For example, if you had thousands of hosts behind your firewall, you would only require a single public network IP address for outbound traffic, rather than one per host on the private network.

The Future of IP Addressing (IPv6)

Even with the use of private network addressing, the growth of the Internet will eventually result in the current IP addressing scheme running out of addresses. The IETF, recognizing this, has been commissioned to create the next generation of the IP address.

Several published RFCs lay out the needs for the new protocol. This new release of the IP protocol, now known as IPv6, should begin to replace the current IPv4 as the pool of available IPv4 addresses dries up.

The following are major changes in the next release of IPv6:

- **Expanded addressing capabilities.** The address size for IPv6 will be 128 bits, which will provide a larger pool of IP addresses for the Internet. This pool will provide each Internet user with a pool of IP addresses equal to the total number of IP addresses available on the Internet today.

- **Simplification of the IP header.** Much of the IPv4 header information has been made optional or has been dropped entirely. This will speed up processing of the IP header information by receiving hosts.

- **Improved extensibility of the IP header.** The IP header has been formatted to provide more efficient forwarding, more flexibility on the length of option fields, and easier inclusion of new options in the future. This will enable the IP header to change as the protocol evolves over the next few years, without having to redesign the entire header format.

- **Improved flow control.** IP datagrams will be able to request better quality of service. This will include time-specific delivery of information and the capability to request a minimum bandwidth availability or real-time service.

- **Increase security.** The IP header will include extensions to support authentication of source and destination hosts, and better assurance of noncorruption of data. This also will provide the option of encrypting data as it is transported over the network within the IP header construct.

These IP protocol enhancements should help the Internet continue to grow. They also should help continue the increase in functionality provided to applications using TCP/IP as their base protocol suite. Specific information about IPv6 is discussed on Day 21, "IPv6, the Future of TCP/IP?"

Applying What You Have Learned

The material covered today is the starting point for understanding how to configure TCP/IP on a network. Today you learned about the notation used to represent IP addresses, the five classes of IP addresses, and the function of the subnet mask. This chapter also provided a brief overview of what IPv6 will provide for future use of the TCP/IP protocol suite.

Test Your Knowledge

Here are questions to check what you've learned today. The answers can be found in Appendix B, "Test Your Knowledge: Answers."

1. Convert the decimal numbers in Table 3.3 to binary representation.

TABLE 3.3 Converting from Decimal to Binary

Decimal	Binary
127	
0	
76	
248	
224	
57	
135.56.204.253	

2. Convert the binary numbers in Table 3.4 to decimal format.

TABLE 3.4 Converting from Binary to Decimal

Binary	Decimal
11100110	
00011100	
01010101	
11001100	
11001010 00001100 10100011 11110010	
00011011 10001001 01111111 10000101	

3. Identify the address class of the IP addresses in Table 3.5.

TABLE 3.5 Identifying Address Classes

IP Address	IP Address Class
131.107.2.8	
127.0.0.1	
225.34.56.7	
129.33.55.6	
10.2.4.5	
223.223.223.223	

4. What is the broadcast address for a host with IP address 172.30.45.67, assuming the default subnet mask is implemented on the network?

5. What is the network address for a host with IP address 201.200.200.15, assuming the default subnet mask is implemented on the network?

6. Assume that you are an ISP in Malaysia. If you have run out of IP addresses for assigning to your clients, where would you go to obtain new pools of IP addresses?

7. Based on the network in Figure 3.6, can the host named SUSAN communicate with the host named KELLY?

FIGURE 3.6

A sample network.

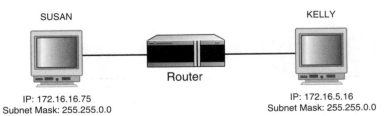

SUSAN
IP: 172.16.16.75
Subnet Mask: 255.255.0.0

Router

KELLY
IP: 172.16.5.16
Subnet Mask: 255.255.0.0

8. What subnet mask could be used to enable SUSAN and KELLY to communicate correctly?

9. What pools of IP addresses have been reserved for use on local area networks by the Internet Assigned Number Authority?

10. How does NAT reduce the demand for public network addresses?

11. What advantages does IPv6 have over IPv4?

Preview of Day 4

Tomorrow, you begin to look specifically at the core protocols within the TCP/IP protocol suite and the role that they play within the TCP/IP layered model. After you complete this lesson, you will be ready to attack more advanced topics such as subnet masking.

3

DAY 4

Core Protocols of the TCP/IP Suite

Today we look at the protocols in the TCP/IP suite that exist at the Internet and Transport layers of the TCP/IP layer model.

In the Internet layer of the TCP/IP layer model, four protocols exist for determining addressing and connectivity in an IP-based network, and we'll examine them all:

- Address Resolution Protocol (ARP)
- Internet Protocol (IP)
- Internet Control Message Protocol (ICMP)
- Internet Group Management Protocol (IGMP)

In the transport layer of the TCP/IP layered model two protocols are used for the transmission of data over the network. Transmission Control Protocol (TCP) provides guaranteed delivery of data, while User Datagram Protocol (UDP) provides nonguaranteed delivery.

Specifically, the following topics will be discussed:

- How the decision is made to use guaranteed delivery or nonguaranteed delivery of data
- Which applications are designed for use with TCP and UDP
- The fields of TCP and UDP headers
- How TCP establishes and terminates a session
- How sliding windows improve transmission performance when using TCP
- The well-known TCP and UDP ports

Defining the Core Protocols in the IP Layer Model

In Day 2, "Network Types and Open systems Architecture," we looked at the details of the TCP/IP layer model. Within the Internet and transport layers of the model, there exist several core protocols that provide common functionality to TCP/IP-based application protocols. The following sections discuss how these core protocols work and how they interact with each other as data is transmitted between the layers in the TCP/IP layer model.

Protocols in the Internet Layer

In the TCP/IP layer mode, the Internet layer provides all addressing, packaging, and routing functions. The protocols in this layer either interact with the physical network components in the network interface layer or provide logical addressing information to the transport layer. The following protocols are considered to be Internet layer protocols:

- Address Resolution Protocol (ARP)
- Internet Control Message Protocol (ICMP)
- Internet Protocol (IP)
- Internet Group Management Protocol (IGMP)

Address Resolution Protocol (ARP)

RFC 826 For two hosts to communicate successfully on a network segment, they must resolve each other's hardware addresses. This is accomplished in the TCP/IP protocol suite using Address Resolution Protocol (ARP). ARP resolves a destination host's IP address to a MAC address. It also makes sure the destination host is able to resolve the sender's IP address to a MAC address.

Frequently on a network, a client computer communicates with a central server. Instead of querying each time for the server's MAC address, the ARP protocol caches resolved MAC addresses for future use in what is known as the *ARP cache*. If a target IP address' MAC address is found in the ARP cache, this MAC address is used as the target address for communication.

Note

> For multihomed (multiple interfaced) hosts, a separate ARP cache is maintained for each interface in the computer.

The following rules must be followed when maintaining the ARP cache:

- Each new entry is configured with a Time-To-Live (TTL) value. The actual value depends on the operating system in use. When the Time-To-Live value decrements to a value of 0, the entry is removed from the ARP cache.

- If a new entry is not reused within an OS-defined period of time, it is removed from the ARP cache.

- In some TCP/IP implementations, the Time-To-Live value is reset to its initial value every time an entry is reused in the ARP cache.

- Each implementation of TCP/IP sets a maximum number of entries in the ARP cache. If the ARP cache fills up and a new entry must be added, the oldest entry in the ARP cache is removed to make room for the new entry.

The ARP Process

When a host needs to communicate with another host on a local network segment, the following process is used (see Figure 4.1):

1. The calling host checks its ARP cache to determine whether there is an entry for the IP address of the destination host.

2. If an entry cannot be found, the calling host creates an ARP packet that asks the destination host to reply with its MAC address. Included in the ARP packet are the IP address and MAC address of the calling host so the destination host can add this information to its ARP cache. This ARP packet is sent to the Ethernet broadcast address FF-FF-FF-FF-FF-FF. This means every host on the segment investigates the packet.

3. Each host investigates the ARP packet to see whether the destination host IP address in the ARP packet matches its IP address. If it does not, the packet is

ignored. If it matches, the destination host adds the IP address and MAC address information of the sending host to its ARP cache.

FIGURE **4.1**

The ARP process when communicating with a local host.

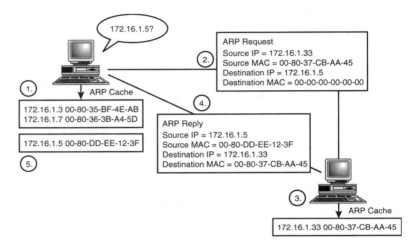

4. The destination host creates an ARP reply containing its IP address and MAC address information. This reply is returned to the calling host.

5. The calling host adds the IP address and MAC address information to its ARP cache. Communication now can begin between the two hosts.

The process differs when the target host is located on a remote network (see Figure 4.2). This can be determined by comparing the target host's IP address to the sending host's IP address/subnet mask combination as discussed in Day 3's lesson in the section "The ANDing Process."

FIGURE **4.2**

The ARP process when communicating with a remote host.

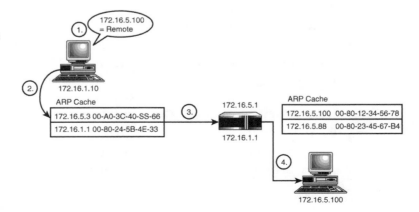

The following process is used to communicate with a host on a remote network:

1. The sending host determines whether the destination host is located on a remote network. The sending host inspects its TCP/IP configuration and finds the address for its default gateway. The *default gateway* is the router on the host's network segment where all outbound network traffic is directed.

The Implementation of Default Gateways

Not all TCP/IP implementations use default gateways. If they are not used, explicit routes, also known as static routes, are configured for each remote network. If the remote network is not defined in the routing table, traffic cannot be sent to that remote network. In these implementations, the sending host determines which router the data must be sent to so that the data reaches the remote network. ARP is used to find the selected router's MAC address.

---

2. The sending host inspects its ARP cache to see whether it has recently resolved the MAC address of the default gateway. If it hasn't, the host sends an ARP packet to determine the MAC address using the same local ARP resolution method previously discussed.

3. The data is transferred to the default gateway.

4. The default gateway now inspects the destination host's IP address. If the default gateway has an interface on the network segment on which the host is located, it inspects its ARP cache for an entry for the destination host. If the default gateway does not have an interface on the network segment on which the destination host is located, it uses its routing table to determine to which router to pass the information. It inspects its ARP cache for the MAC address of the target router's interface. If it does not have an entry in the ARP cache, it uses ARP to determine the MAC address.

4

ARP in Real Life (We Wish)

An analogy that I have used in the classroom is that ARP is much like asking someone of the opposite sex for his or her phone number at a night club and always being successful. You start the conversation with, "Hi, my name is Brian (your IP address) and my phone number (MAC address) is 555-1111." The only difference with ARP and reality, is that the person you approach is obligated to answer truthfully and respond with something like "Hello, Brian. My name is Krista, and my phone number is 555-2222." You never have to worry about receiving a false phone number when using ARP.

The ARP Packet

The ARP packet structure is shown in Figure 4.3. This packet format is used for both the ARP protocol and the Reverse Address Resolution Protocol (RARP). The RARP protocol is discussed in Day 9, "Gateway and Routing Protocols," with the topic of automatic configuration.

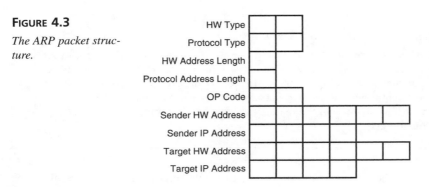

FIGURE 4.3

The ARP packet structure.

Table 4.1 describes each field in an ARP packet.

TABLE 4.1   The ARP Packet Fields

Field	Definition
Hardware Type	Designates the type of hardware used in the network layer.
Protocol Type	The field indicates the protocol address type in the protocol address fields. For an IP address, this value is set to 08-00.
Hardware Address Length	The length in bytes of the hardware address. For Ethernet and token ring networks, this is 6 bytes.
Protocol Address Length	The length of the protocol address. For IPv4, this is 4 bytes (or 32 bits).
Op Code	Determines whether the packet is a request or a reply. Possible values include: (1) ARP request, (2) ARP reply, (3) RARP request, or (4) RARP reply.
Sender's hardware address	The hardware address of the sending host.
Sender's protocol address	The IP address of the sending host.
Target's hardware address	The hardware address of the target host. This is set to `00-00-00-00-00-00` in an ARP request.
Target's protocol address	The IP address of the target host.

Using the ARP Command

Each TCP/IP protocol suite provides an ARP command for viewing and modifying the ARP cache. In Windows XP, the ARP command can be used for three purposes: viewing the ARP cache, adding a static entry to the ARP cache, and removing an ARP cache entry.

The following command is used to view the ARP cache:

```
ARP -a [IP address]
```

This command displays all the current ARP cache entries. You can use [IP address] to optionally provide the parameters. This parameter filters the ARP command so only the physical addresses for the specified IP address are displayed. Use this when you are trying to determine the MAC address for a single IP address, and there are several entries in the ARP cache. In Windows 2000, you also can use the ARP -g command with the same results.

When Should I Use the ARP Command?

Typically, a user does not use the ARP command unless he is troubleshooting network connectivity problems. ARP is best left to the TCP/IP protocol stack when it resolves IP addresses to MAC addresses.

4

To add a static entry to the ARP cache that will not expire according to normal ARP cache rules, use the following command:

```
ARP -s "IP Address" "Physical Address"
```

If you want to add a static entry for the host 172.16.2.16 with MAC address 0080D7225FBF, for example, type the following command:

```
ARP -s 172.16.2.16 00-80-D7-22-5F-BF
```

Note that the MAC address uses a hyphen to separate each pair of hexadecimal characters. It generally is not recommended that you add static entries to the ARP cache. If a network card failed or was replaced on host 172.16.2.16, you would not be able to communicate with this host because you would have the incorrect MAC address.

Static ARP Entries Really Are Not That Static

Static ARP entries remain in the ARP cache until the host is restarted. When this occurs, the ARP cache is flushed and static entries are not re-created. If an IP address has been assigned a static entry in the ARP cache, and if an ARP broadcast sent on the network suggests a different physical address, the new address replaces the old address in the ARP cache.

A common scenario where this might occur is with a two-node cluster. When failover occurs, the cluster server will send out ARP broadcasts indicating the new MAC address for the shared IP address used by the cluster. All clients will update their ARP cache with the new MAC address information for the shared IP address used by the cluster.

If you want to remove an incorrect entry from the ARP cache (such as an incorrectly entered static entry), use the following command:

```
ARP -d "IP address"
```

If you want to remove your previous entry for the host at 172.16.2.16, type the following:

```
ARP -d 172.16.2.16
```

Hosts Can Update ARP Packets

Although the ARP packet is sent with a specific host's IP address, other hosts still inspect the ARP packet to see whether it is intended for them. If a host notices that the ARP packet contains an IP address/MAC address combination that does not match an entry in its ARP cache, it updates its cache with the information in the ARP packet. This information is more timely and should be trusted over an entry in the ARP cache.

Internet Control Message Protocol (ICMP)

RFC 792   RFC 1276   The Internet Control Message Protocol provides an error-reporting mechanism and controls messages to the TCP/IP protocol suite. This protocol was created primarily to report routing failures to the sending host.

The following functions can be performed by the ICMP protocol:

- Provide echo and reply messages to test the reliability of a connection between two hosts. This usually is accomplished with the PING (Packet Internet Groper) command.

- Redirect traffic to provide more efficient routing when a router becomes congested due to excess traffic.

- Send out a time-exceeded message when a source datagram has exceeded its allocated Time-To-Live and has been discarded.

- Send out router advertisements to determine the address of all routers on a network segment.

- Provide a source-quench message to tell a host to slow down its communications when the communications are saturating a router or a network WAN link.

- Determine what subnet mask is in use on a network segment.

> **Routing Protocols**
>
> Routing is discussed on Day 9, "Gateway and Routing Protocols." See Day 9's material when reviewing the concept of routing and the functionality provided by routing protocols.

The ICMP Packet Format

The ICMP packet format is shown in Figure 4.4, and its fields are described in Table 4.2.

FIGURE 4.4

The ICMP packet structure.

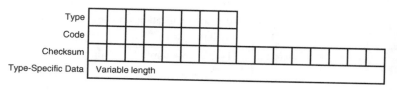

4

TABLE 4.2   The ICMP Packet Fields

Field	Definition
Type	This 8-bit field indicates the type of ICMP packet being transmitted. The following are possible types:
	0: Echo Reply
	3: Destination Unreachable
	4: Source Quench
	5: Redirect Message
	8: Echo
	11: Time Exceeded
	12: Parameter Problem
	13: Time Stamp
	14: Time Stamp Reply
	15: Information Request
	16: Information Reply

TABLE 4.2   Continued

Field	Definition
Code	This field provides additional information not provided in the Type field for the destination host. For example, for a Destination Unreachable message (type=3), the following error codes are available: 0—Network unreachable 1—Host unreachable 2—Protocol unreachable 3—Port unreachable 4—Fragmentation needed 5—Source route failed 6—Destination network unknown 7—Destination host unknown 8—Source host isolated 9—Communication with destination network administratively prohibited 10—Communication with destination host administratively prohibited 11—Network unreachable for type of service 12—Host unreachable for type of service
Checksum	This field provides error detection for the ICMP portion of the packet.
Type Specific Data	This data depends on the type of functionality ICMP is providing. If it's Echo Request/Echo Reply (the most common), this information includes an identifier and a sequence number that are used to identify each echo request sent and each reply.

Using the ICMP Protocol to Troubleshoot Connectivity

One of the most common problems a network administrator faces is determining why a specific computer cannot communicate with the rest of the network. Many times, it is the result of an incorrect TCP/IP protocol configuration. The ICMP protocol can help determine which configuration parameter potentially is incorrect.

Figure 4.5 shows a test network on which you could test the TCP/IP configuration for a host with IP address 172.16.2.200.

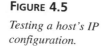

FIGURE 4.5

Testing a host's IP configuration.

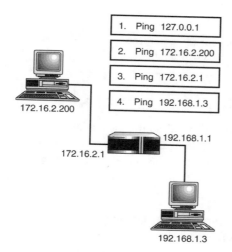

| 1. Ping 127.0.0.1 |
| 2. Ping 172.16.2.200 |
| 3. Ping 172.16.2.1 |
| 4. Ping 192.168.1.3 |

172.16.2.200

192.168.1.1

172.16.2.1

192.168.1.3

4

Use the following procedure to test your computer's IP configuration:

1. Start by pinging a reserved IP address. This address (known as the loopback address) is 127.0.0.1. If you ping this successfully, the TCP/IP protocol suite has been installed correctly.

2. Ping the IP address assigned to your host (in this example, 172.16.2.200). If you can ping this IP address, the IP address has been configured correctly on your host. This also indicates that TCP/IP has been bound to a network interface card (NIC).

3. Ping the IP address of the configured default gateway. Pinging this address proves you can communicate with another host on the same network segment. If you cannot do this, try pinging a different host on the same network segment. If neither ping works, you probably have an incorrect subnet mask configured. If you can ping one host but not the other, be sure you have the correct addresses and that both hosts are running. In this example, you would ping 172.16.2.1.

4. Finally, ping an IP address for a host on a remote network segment. This proves all routing functions are working correctly. If this does not work, double-check your subnet mask. If it is incorrect, TCP/IP might assume the remote host actually is a local host and won't be able to communicate properly with it. All packets destined for the remote host won't be properly directed to the default gateway on the network segment. In this example, 192.168.1.3 could be pinged to test this step.

A Shortcut for Host Testing

When testing a host's configuration, you actually could just perform Step 4. Here's why: If you can ping the host at 192.168.1.3, you successfully used your default gateway. Because the response returned to your computer, you have configured your IP address correctly. For all this to occur, you must be running the TCP/IP protocol.

Internet Protocol (IP)

RFC 791 The Internet Protocol provides all logical addressing of hosts. Each host is assigned a unique IP address for the network on which it is running. The IP protocol is connectionless. For two hosts to communicate using the IP protocol, they do not have to establish a session first. Data is exchanged between the systems using a best-effort delivery system.

As with any protocol that provides network addressing, the Internet Protocol comprises both network and host components as discussed in yesterday's material. By comparing a destination computer's IP address with its own source IP address and subnet mask, IP can determine whether the packet must be routed to the destination host or can be sent directly to it by using the ANDing process.

The format of an IP packet is shown in Figure 4.6.

FIGURE 4.6

The IP packet format.

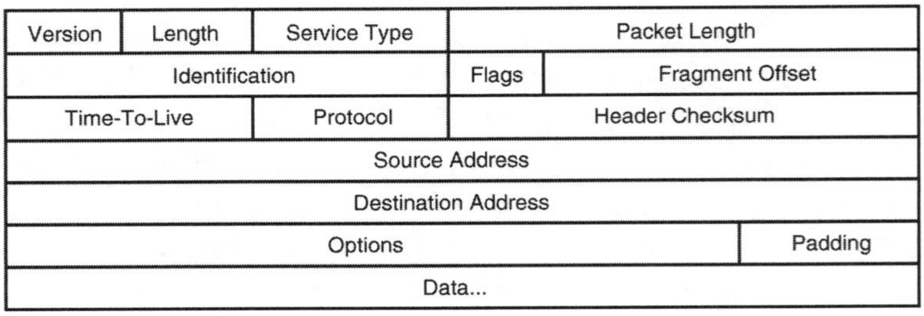

Version	Length	Service Type		Packet Length	
Identification			Flags	Fragment Offset	
Time-To-Live		Protocol	Header Checksum		
Source Address					
Destination Address					
Options					Padding
Data...					

The following fields exist in an IP packet:

- **Version.** This field indicates which version of the IP protocol is used for formatting the IP datagram. The current version of the IP protocol is version 4, but work is continuing on the IPv6 protocol. If the receiving computer cannot handle the IP protocol version, it simply drops the packet. The length of the Version field is 4 bits.

- **Length.** This field indicates the IP header's length. All fields in an IP packet are of fixed length except the IP Options and Padding fields. This field determines the dividing line between the header and data portions of the packet. The Length field is subtracted from the Packet Length field to determine where the data starts.

- **Service Type.** This field informs IP how to handle the IP packet. It includes the five subfields shown in Figure 4.7.

Precedence	Delay	Thru-put	Reliability	Unused

- **Precedence.** This subfield sets the importance of a datagram. This 3-bit subfield can range from a value of 0 (normal) to a value of 7 (network control). The higher the number, the more important the packet. Theoretically, higher precedence packets should be routed to the destination address faster than lower precedence packets.

- **Delay, Throughput,** and **Reliability.** These subfields all specify the desired transport of the packet. These three subfields usually are all set to 0. If they are set to 1, they indicate that low delay, high throughput, and high reliability are desired. When multiple routes are available to a remote network, these subfields can be used to determine which route to take.

- The last two bits of the Server Type field currently are unused in IP version 4.

- **Packet Length.** This field contains the total length of the IP packet. This includes all data and the IP header.

- The next three fields—**Identification, Flags,** and **Fragment Offset**—are known as packet fragmentation fields. They play a part in the fragmentation and reassembly processes. In an IP internetwork, information can travel between different network topologies including Ethernet, token ring, and FDDI networks. Each network topology is constrained by the amount of data that can fit into a single frame on the network. When data is transferred between differing topologies, it sometimes must be broken into smaller fragments that can be transported across the other network topology.

The size of these fragments is based on the maximum size that can be handled by the network topology across which the datagram is traveling. When a packet is fragmented, a mechanism also must be provided that enables the original packet to be reassembled at the destination host.

- **Identification.** This field contains a unique identifier that marks the original datagram. If an original packet is broken into three fragments, each of the three fragments has the same Identification field.

- **Flags.** This 3-bit field controls fragmentation. The first bit currently is unused. The second bit is the Don't Fragment (DF) bit, and the third bit is

4

the More Fragments (MF) bit. If the DF bit is set to 1, the datagram cannot be fragmented. If the data is transferred to a network that cannot handle frames of this size, the datagram is dropped (because it cannot be fragmented). This often is used for circumstances in which packet size is being tested and the packet should not be fragmented into smaller fragments. The MF bit is set to 1 when an original packet has been fragmented. The MF bit indicates that more packets follow the current packet. In the last packet of a fragment, the MF bit is set to 0. This indicates that no more packets follow.

- **Fragment Offset.** This field is used in conjunction with the MF bit when reassembling the fragmented packet. Many times, the destination host receives the fragmented packets out of order. The MF bit, Identification field, and Fragment Offset field help determine how to rebuild these fragmented packets into the original packet. The offset value always is based on the beginning of the message.

Walking Through a Fragmentation Example

If a 1500-byte packet must be broken into fragments not larger than 700 bytes, the following would occur: The first fragment would be assigned the same ID as the original 1500-byte packet. The MF bit would be set to 1, and the Fragment Offset would be set to 0. The second fragment would have the same ID as the original packet and also would have the MF bit set to 1. The Fragment Offset for the second fragment would be set to 700. The final fragment would have the same ID as the original packet. This would be the final packet, so the MF bit would be set to 0 because no more fragments follow. The fragment offset would be set to 1400 for this packet.

- **Time-to-Live** (TTL). This field indicates how long a datagram can exist on a network. Each time the packet crosses a router, its value decreases by at least one second. When the TTL field reaches a value of 0, the datagram is discarded at the current router. A message is sent to the source host stating that the packet was dropped using the ICMP protocol so the source host could resend the packet.

- **Protocol.** This field indicates which high-level protocol was used to create the information stored in the data portion of the packet. This field assists in moving the packet up to the correct protocol in the TCP/IP layer model. It also defines the format of the data portion of the packet. A protocol identification number (PIN) assigned by the Network Information Center (NIC) represents each protocol. ICMP, for example, is protocol number 1; TCP is protocol number 6.

- **Header Checksum.** This field makes sure the header information has not been corrupted in transit. This checksum is only for the header portion of the packet. It results in reduced processing at each router because the checksum is not calculated on the entire packet. The Header Checksum must be recalculated at every router the packet traverses. This is because the TTL field decrements at each router, necessitating that a new checksum be calculated.

- **Source Address** and **Destination Address.** These fields contain the 32-bit IP addresses of the source and destination hosts. These values are not changed in transit, unless the address information is translated by Network Address Translation (NAT) devices.

- **Options.** This field can be composed of several codes of variable length. More than one option can be used in an IP packet. If more than one is used, the fields appear consecutively in the IP header. Each option is eight bits long and consists of three subfields.

  - The first bit represents the *copy flag*. It determines how this option should be treated when an original packet is fragmented. If the copy flag is set to 0, the option only should be copied to the first fragment. If the copy flag is set to 1, the option should be copied to all fragments of the original packet.

  - The *option class* is represented by two bits. The option class can have one of four values assigned to it. A value of 0 means the option has to do with a datagram or a network control. A value of 2 means the option is used for debugging or measurement purposes. Values of 1 and 3 are reserved for future use and have not been defined yet.

  - The *option number* represents the final five bits.

    Each allowable combination of option class and option number is shown in Table 4.3.

TABLE 4.3   Valid IP Option Classes and Option Numbers

Option Class	Option Number	Description
0	0	End of option list.
0	1	Used for padding. Indicates that no option has been set.
0	2	Security options for military applications.
0	3	Loose source routing. This option indicates a sequence of IP addresses that should be used as the route to a destination host. Loose source routing enables multiple network hops to exist between designated source addresses.
0	7	Used to trace routes to a destination. Useful for determining which exact route was traversed between a source and destination host. Each router that handles the IP packet adds its IP address to the options list.

TABLE 4.3   continued

Option Class	Option Number	Description
0	9	Strict source routing. As with loose source routing, strict source routing specifies a routing path to a destination host. The difference is that, if the designated route cannot be followed, the packet is discarded.
2	4	Internet time stamp that enables time stamps to be recorded along a route. Each router records its IP address and a time stamp, indicating the time the router handled the packet. This time is based on milliseconds since midnight Greenwich Mean Time (or Universal Time). Due to nonsynchronization of clocks, these times only should be considered estimates of the exact time.

Caution

Source routing is a common method used by hackers to redirect and hijack an application session. By using source routing in an ICMP packet, hackers can ensure that packets are returned through their hosts for inspection. Typically, firewalls are configured to automatically drop ICMP packets if the source routing or loose source routing option is enabled to prevent hijacking or observation of sessions.

- **Padding.** This field's contents are based on the options selected for an IP packet. The padding ensures that the datagram's header is rounded to an even number of bytes.

Internet Group Management Protocol (IGMP)

At times, instead of sending information from a source host to a single destination host, you will need to send information to multiple destination hosts. One method is to use *broadcasting*. There are two major issues with broadcasting. First, all hosts on the network segment must examine the packet to determine whether it is intended for them. Second, many routers are configured not to forward broadcasts to other network segments. Both these issues can cause congestion on the network.

An alternative to broadcasting is *multicasting*. Instead of an IP packet's destination being all machines on the network, the destination can be a specific group of computers. Multicast packets are delivered using User Datagram Protocol (UDP).

The following are some facts about IP multicast groups:

- All multicast addressing is based on Class D IP addresses, which range from 224.0.0.1 through 239.255.255.255.

- Many address are reserved for specific usages. For example, the address 224.0.0.1 represents the *all hosts* group. This group includes all IP hosts and routers participating in IP multicasting on a network segment.

- An IP host can dynamically join or exit an IP multicast group at any time.

- IP multicast addresses should appear only as destination addresses. They rarely appear as source addresses because multicast addresses are not usually bound to network interface cards. Some forms of Unix do allow this capability. In these cases, a multicast address can appear as the source address.

The fields in an IGMP version 2 packet (shown in Figure 4.8) are as follows.

FIGURE 4.8

The IGMP packet structure.

Type	Max Response Time	Checksum
Group Address		

- **Type.** This field indicates the type of message included in the IGMP packet. Acceptable values include:

  - 0x11—An **IGMP membership query** used to either determine which multicast groups have members on an attached network or a group-specific query that determines whether a specific multicast group has members on an attached network.

  - 0x12—An **IGMP version 1 membership report** included for backward compatibility with IGMPv1.

  - 0x16—An **IGMP version 2 membership report** used to report that a host is a member of a specific IGMP multicast group.

  - 0x17— An **IGMP version 2** *Leave group* **message** used to report that a host has removed itself from a specific IGMP multicast group.

- **Max** (Maximum) **Response Time.** This field is only used by IGMP Membership Query messages to specify the maximum allowed time before sending a responding membership report. The value is reported in 1/10 second units. For other IGMP messages, this value is left at 0 and ignored by both sender and receiver of the message.

4

> **IGMP Improvements in Performance**
>
> IGMPv1 did not use this portion of the IGMP packet. By implementing a maximum response time, latency can be decreased for scenarios such as the time between the last host leaving a multicast group, and the routing protocol being notified that no more members exist for the group.
>
> - **Checksum.** This field is a checksum for the entire IGMP message. It makes sure the information has not been corrupted in transit. The same algorithm used for calculating IP header checksums also is used for IGMP checksums.
>
> - **Group Address.** This field contains the IP multicast of the group in which a host is reporting membership. In the case of a multicast general query, this field is set to all zeroes.

Connection Versus Connectionless Traffic

The two protocols in the transport layer of the TCP/IP layered model provide transport mechanisms for applications over a TCP/IP network. The TCP protocol delivers guaranteed or reliable delivery of information. UDP delivers information using a nonguaranteed or best effort method.

At first glance, you might write off the UDP protocol. If delivery is not guaranteed, why would you use this transport protocol? The answer is in the overhead involved with a guaranteed protocol such as TCP. Two hosts exchanging data using TCP must exchange status information in addition to the actual exchange of data. This status includes acknowledgment messages that indicate whether previous segments were received successfully, whereas, UDP-based application protocols can transmit data much more efficiently and potentially faster with less overhead.

Transmission Control Protocol (TCP)

RFC 793 In its simplest implementation, a guaranteed protocol waits to be sure the recipient host receives a segment of information before it transmits the next available segment (see Figure 4.9).

When the recipient machine receives data from the sending machine, the recipient machine sends an acknowledgment packet that indicates the next segment it expects to receive. If the recipient host acknowledges every segment, the traffic involved with the file transfer doubles.

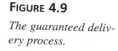

FIGURE 4.9

The guaranteed delivery process.

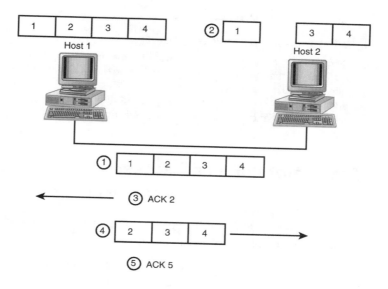

User Datagram Protocol (UDP)

In some circumstances, guaranteed delivery is not required. UDP delivers a best-effort attempt to transfer data between two hosts. Error detection can be performed when using the UDP protocol, but it is the responsibility of the higher-level application using UDP as its transport protocol. UDP can send information to a destination host without first establishing a session with that host. When timely delivery is important, UDP delivers information to a host faster than TCP. An example of this is Simple Network Management Protocol (SNMP).

SNMP monitors a network and is alerted to problems in the physical topology of the network. This is accomplished using traps. A *trap* is a triggered event based on a rule. Let's say, for example, a host is configured to issue a trap when its hard disk space is less than 100MB. The trap is sent immediately after the condition exists. If TCP were used instead, the host first would have to establish a session with the SNMP management system before it could send the SNMP trap. UDP enables the SNMP trap to be sent as soon as the trap event occurs.

Another common example is a radio station transmitting over the Internet using RealAudio. A host sending a RealAudio feed does not want every packet of data to be acknowledged by the recipient host. The playback quality would be greatly reduced if each packet were acknowledged.

> **What Transport Do Multicasts Use?**
>
> By definition, multicasts are transmitted from a single host to multiple hosts that are members of the target multicast group. The goal of a multicast is to send a single transmission of data that multiple hosts can read. The sending host cannot wait for acknowledgments from every recipient before it sends the next packet of data. As a result, all multicast applications use UDP as the underlying transport protocol.

The Use of Ports and Sockets

Both TCP and UDP act as an intermediary between applications and the Internet Protocol (IP) to provide transport over an internetwork. So far, you have learned that individual hosts are assigned IP addresses (made up of the network and host IDs) to uniquely identify themselves on an internetwork.

An issue that needs to be resolved—besides which host information must be sent to—is which application running on the host should receive the information. This can be resolved using ports.

Ports provide an application endpoint on a host and can be any number between 0 and 65,535. Ports numbered between 0 and 1,023 are defined as *well-known ports* that have been pre-assigned an associated application by the Internet Assigned Number Authority (IANA). Lists of specific TCP and UDP ports can be found later in this chapter.

Port numbers on the client side are generated dynamically by the operating system when the client attempts to connect to the remote host. The random port numbers are generated with a minimum value of 1,024 (because the ports between 0 and 1,023 are reserved for the well-known ports).

When a source host wants to communicate with a Winsock-based application running on another host, it connects to the server's application port number. The actual address connected to is the server's IP address and port number. The combination of IP address, transport protocol, and port number is called the *socket address*.

When a TCP session is established, both hosts participating in the session must agree to participate. The following two distinct functions take place:

- The host functioning as the server performs a passive open. The *passive open* indicates to the operating system on which port the application is willing to accept connections. This port is said to be in a *listening state*.
- The host functioning as the client contacts its operating system for a port assignment when it requests to connect to the server's application. This is an *active open*

because the session actually is established at this point between the client and server hosts.

It is possible for a single port on a host to have multiple sessions connected to it. Let's say, for example, two clients are connecting to a mail server using SMTP to send mail (see Figure 4.10).

FIGURE 4.10

Multiplexing a TCP port.

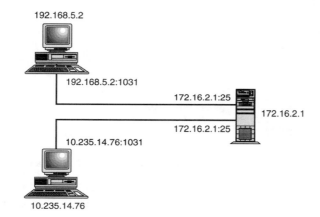

The client with IP address 192.168.5.2 is using TCP to send mail to the mail server at IP address 172.16.2.1. At the same time, the client with IP address 10.235.14.76 also is connected to the mail server for the purpose of sending mail. Both clients dynamically use port 1031 at the client side. How does the server know which client sent which message? This is handled using the full-socket information. The client at the top socket address is 192.168.5.2:1031. This is one endpoint for communication and 172.16.2.1:25 is the other. The bottom host's socket address is 10.235.14.76:1031. This is one endpoint and the other is 172.16.2.1:25. End-to-end communication sessions often are referred to as *virtual circuits*.

Messages are not intermixed because TCP uses both endpoints when identifying a communication stream. Even though both communication streams use port 1031 on the client side and communicate with 172.16.2.1:25, they also have unique socket addresses at the client side. This distinguishes the two mail sessions.

Note

Figure 4.10 displays an unlikely scenario. Because client hosts are randomly assigned a port over 1,024 when they connect to a server, the chance of two client systems connecting to a server using the same client port is highly unlikely.

Transmission Control Protocol

RFC 793   As previously mentioned, the TCP protocol affords reliable, connection-oriented
delivery in the TCP/IP protocol suite. The TCP protocol provides the following
features to the TCP/IP protocol suite:

- A mechanism for reliable communication between two hosts using an unreliable
  base protocol (IP).
- A start-up sequence to establish an end-to-end communication session.
- A mechanism to reassemble data that arrives out of order (based on its sequence
  numbers).
- The capability for a source host to distinguish between different applications running on a destination host (based on their port numbers).
- Timers that enable retransmission of lost packets to occur in a timely manner.
- Simplified application development. Because TCP handles acknowledgments and
  retransmission of lost or corrupted data, the applications do not have to provide
  this service.

The following are some well-known Winsock applications that use TCP as their transport
protocol:

- FTP
- Telnet
- SMTP mail servers
- Web servers

As discussed in Day 2, "Network Types and Open Systems Architecture," a good analogy for the TCP protocol is a guaranteed courier service such as DHL or UPS. When you
send a package using DHL or UPS, you can track its delivery. You also can be sure your
desired recipient receives the package because he must sign to acknowledge receipt.

The TCP Header Format

TCP segments are sent within an Internet datagram. The format of a TCP header is
shown in Figure 4.11. Its fields are as follows:

- **Source Port.** This 16-bit field contains the TCP port used by the local host for the
  TCP connection.
- **Destination Port.** This 16-bit field contains the TCP port used by the remote host
  for the TCP connection.

FIGURE 4.11

The TCP header format.

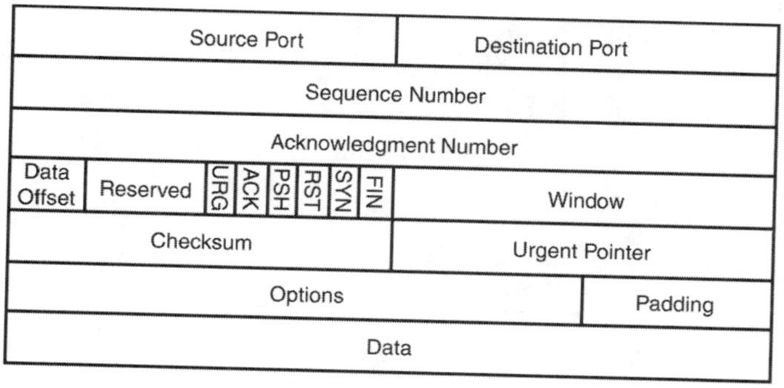

- **Sequence Number.** This 32-bit field indicates the order in which segments should be reassembled at the destination host. This field also is used during the TCP/IP three-way handshake to synchronize sequence numbers.
- **Acknowledgment Number.** This 32-bit field indicates which sequence number the sending host expects to receive next from the destination host.
- **Data Offset.** This 4-bit field indicates the size of the TCP header in 32-bit words. Using the Data Offset field, you can determine where the data begins in the TCP segment.
- **Reserved.** This 6-bit field is reserved for future use. It should be set to all zeros.
- **Urgent Control Bit** (URG). If this 1-bit field is set to 1, the Urgent Pointer field is significant and should be read.
- **Acknowledgment Control Bit** (ACK). If this 1-bit field is set to 1, the Acknowledgment Number field is significant and should be read.
- **Push Control Bit** (PSH). If this 1-bit field is set to 1, the segment is requesting that a push function take place. This occurs when an application wants to send its data stream immediately instead of waiting for the transmission buffer to be full before delivery takes place.
- **Reset Control Bit** (RST). If this 1-bit field is set to 1, this TCP packet is requesting that the connection be reset.
- **Synchronize Control Bit** (SYN). This 1-bit field indicates that sequence numbers should be synchronized. This occurs during the establishment of a TCP session.
- **Finish Control Bit** (FIN). If this 1-bit field is set to 1, the sending host has no more data to send.
- **Window.** This 16-bit field indicates how many octets of data the sending host is willing to accept at a time. This establishes the sending and receiving window sizes in TCP Sliding Windows.

4

- **Checksum.** The checksum makes sure the TCP header and payload have not been corrupted in transit. It also covers some of the fields found in the IP header. These fields (shown in Figure 4.12) are known as the *pseudo-header*.

  The checksum is calculated using a mathematical technique called the *one's complement*.

Source IP Address		
Destination IP Address		
Zeros	Protocol	TCP Length

Explanation of One's Complement

The one's complement is a common checksum technique. Let's say, for example, you want to calculate the one's complement of the following value:

    0000100010101111

If the number has a 0 as a placeholder, the one's complement of a 0 is a 1. Similarly, the one's complement of a 1 is a 0. Therefore, the following is the one's complement of the preceding number:

    1111011101010000

In binary arithmetic, the one's complement is one way to represent a negative number. The only problem with using the one's complement for negative numbers is that it results in two values for zero.

Take, for example, the number 1 (or 00000001 in binary). If you calculate the one's complement of this number, you get 11111110. Adding these two numbers should produce a value of 0. Instead, it adds up to 11111111 in binary, as follows:

    00000001
    11111110

    11111111

Therefore, when using the one's complement, both 00000000 and 11111111 can represent zero. UDP itself uses 11111111 when a checksum is calculated to have a value of 0.

- **Urgent Pointer.** If the Urgent Control Bit field is set to 1, this field is then interpreted. It designates which portion of the data is urgent by giving an offset from the sequence number in this segment. It points to the sequence number that follows the urgent data.

- **Options.** This variable-length field can contain one or more of three possible options: (0) End of Option List, (1) No-Operation, or (2) Maximum Segment Size.

The End of Option List option is used at the end of all options in the TCP segment, not after each individual option. The No-Operation option is used between options to align subsequent options on a word boundary. The Maximum Segment Size option is used during the synchronization sequence to set the maximum size segment a host can receive.

- **Padding.** This field makes sure the TCP header ends on a 32-bit boundary. The padding is done with all zeros.

- **Data.** The actual data included in the TCP segment.

The Establishment of a TCP Session (TCP Three-Way Handshake)

When a host wants to communicate with a destination host using TCP, the destination host must agree to communicate. If the destination host does not agree to communicate, a TCP session cannot be established. This session establishment is called the *TCP three-way handshake* (see Figure 4.13). Here's how it works:

FIGURE 4.13

The TCP three-way handshake.

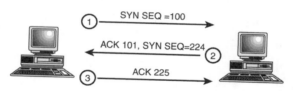

1. The computer that wants to establish a session sends a TCP packet with the SYN (synchronize) flag set to 1. This indicates that the sending host wants to synchronize sequence numbers with the destination host. It also sends its current sequence number to the destination host. For example, in Figure 4.13, the computer on the left sends sequence number 100 as its initial sequence number.

2. The destination host, if it wants to establish the communication session, responds with an acknowledgment. (Setting the ACK flag to 1 indicates that the response is an acknowledgment.) The acknowledgment references the next sequence number it expects to receive. This establishes the TCP connection in one direction. To establish the connection in the return direction, the destination host also sets the SYN flag to 1 and sends its current sequence number. In Figure 4.13, the computer on the right acknowledges the first computer's sequence number by responding that it expects to receive sequence number 101 next. The computer on the right also establishes that its initial sequence number is 224.

3. The original source host responds to the destination host's TCP packet with an acknowledgment that includes the sequence number it expects to receive next. This

establishes a full-duplex connection. In Figure 4.13, the first computer verifies the second computer's sequence number by responding that it expects the next TCP packet to be sequence number 225.

The actual sequence numbers are chosen randomly at the sending host. After a sequence number has been established, it continues to increment by one for each segment of data transmitted. By attaching a sequence number to every segment of data transmitted, the TCP protocol can keep track of all transmitted information, even though the underlying protocol might be unreliable in nature (such as IP). The sending host keeps a copy of the data it has transmitted in a send buffer until it receives an acknowledgment that the data has been received successfully at the destination. This way, if an acknowledgment is not received, it can resend the same segment.

Closing a TCP Session

A modified three-way handshake is used to close a TCP session. The closing must occur in both directions for the TCP session to cease to exist. It is possible, however, for one direction to terminate before the other direction has completed transmitting.

The following are the steps involved in closing a TCP session, as shown in Figure 4.14.

FIGURE 4.14

Closing a TCP session.

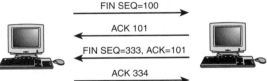

1. After communicating over a TCP session for a while, an application determines that it no longer needs the session. It indicates that it wants to end the session by sending a TCP segment with the FIN flag turned on.

2. TCP sends an acknowledgment segment containing the next expected sequence number. This is sent independently because the application software at the receiving end must be informed that the connection has been closed. This can take some time, and the sending host should be informed that the segment with the FIN flag set has been received.

3. After the application completes its shutdown, it uses TCP to send a segment with the FIN flag set to indicate that it also has completed the session. It still contains an acknowledgment for the original FIN segment.

4. The original host sends an acknowledgment containing the sequence number expected next by the other host.

Message Flow Using TCP

After the full-duplex connection has been established, communication can begin between the two hosts.

An application in the upper layers of the TCP/IP layer model passes a stream of data to TCP. TCP receives the stream of bytes and assembles them into segments. If the stream of data does not fit into a single segment, each separate segment is given a sequence number. This sequence reorders the segments into the original data stream at the recipient host.

During the TCP/IP three-way handshake, the hosts have the option to exchange their maximum segment size during the synchronization process. This is the maximum size used for each TCP data segment to be transmitted. The window size is exchanged in every TCP segment. This enables the window size to be adjusted during a transmission if necessary.

Figure 4.15 shows how a transmission between two hosts can occur.

FIGURE 4.15

Communication using TCP.

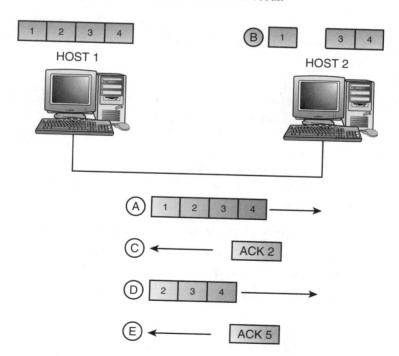

In the figure, Host 1's TCP protocol has a data stream that needs to be transmitted to Host 2. Based on the segment size negotiated during the TCP three-way handshake, the data stream must be broken into four segments.

Host 1 sends all four segments to Host 2 using a sliding window (discussed in the next section). This is shown in step A of Figure 4.15. Unfortunately, only segments 1, 3, and 4 arrive successfully at Host 2 (step B).

When Host 1 sent the four segments, it also set retransmission timers for each segment. *Retransmission timers* indicate when a segment should be re-sent if no acknowledgment is received. There is no nack (negative Acknowledge) feature in TCP. If the retransmission time reaches zero, Host 1 resends that segment.

Note   When the sending host's retransmission timer reaches zero and the segments in the send window are re-sent, the retransmission timer is reset to double the previous amount of time. This acknowledges that the previous segments were not received successfully and provides a longer time frame for the delivery of the next attempt.

Assume that Host 2 only received segments 1, 3, and 4 successfully. Host 2 returns an acknowledgment to Host 1 indicating it received only the first segment successfully (step C). As with all acknowledgments, Host 2 acknowledges using the next segment number it expects to receive.

Host 1 sends segments 2, 3, and 4 again (step D). Even though Host 2 already received segments 3 and 4, it is not a problem to send these segments again. When Host 2 receives these segments successfully, it can reassemble the original stream of data and pass it up to the upper-layer application for which it was destined. Host 2 simply discards the extra copies of segments 3 and 4. An error does not need to be sent to Host 1 stating that two copies of segments 3 and 4 were received. To show that it has now received segments 2, 3, and 4 successfully, Host 2 sends an acknowledgment indicating that it expects to receive segment 5 next (step E).

TCP Sliding Windows in Transmission

The example in the preceding section described a typical TCP transmission. TCP uses a method known as *sliding windows* to get better performance out of a TCP transmission.

During the TCP three-way handshake, the two hosts exchange transmit window sizes. The receiving host sets its receive window size to equal the sending host's transmit window size. The window size indicates the maximum number of segments that can be sent at any one time. This window size is included in every segment transmitted to the other host.

The sending host creates a send window set to its maximum transmission size. The example in Figure 4.16 shows a window size of six segments.

FIGURE 4.16

The sending host uses a sliding window size of six segments.

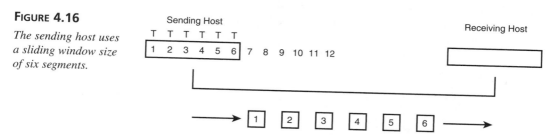

The sending host can send segments 1 through 6 to the receiving host. When the sending host sends the six segments, an individual retransmission timer is set on each individual segment. If only segments 1, 2, and 5 are received, the receiving host sends back an acknowledgment containing the segment number 3. This indicates that it received segments 1 and 2. Even though it also received segment 5, it only can indicate that it received the first two contiguous segments.

The sliding window at the sending host slides to the right past the two acknowledged segments. Segments 7 and 8 now can be transmitted to the receiving host (see Figure 4.17) in addition to the retransmission of segments 3, 4, 5, and 6.

FIGURE 4.17

The sliding window now enables segments 7 and 8 to be sent.

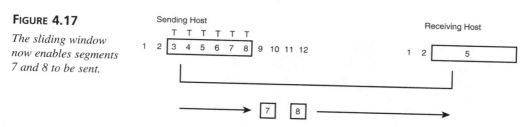

If no acknowledgment is received for segments 3 through 6 sent in the original window, their retransmission timers eventually reach zero. When this occurs, the segments are re-sent and the retransmission timer is reset to twice the initial value (see Figure 4.18).

FIGURE 4.18

Segments 3 through 6 are re-sent when the retransmission timers reach zero.

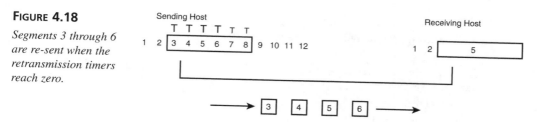

When the receiving host has received all segments up to and including segment 7, it sends an acknowledgment indicating that the next segment it expects is segment 8. The send window slides past segments 3 through 7 now that they have been acknowledged. Segments 8 through 12 are now sent to the receiving host. Retransmission timers are set on each of the segments, and the process begins again (see Figure 4.19).

FIGURE 4.19

The final segments are delivered.

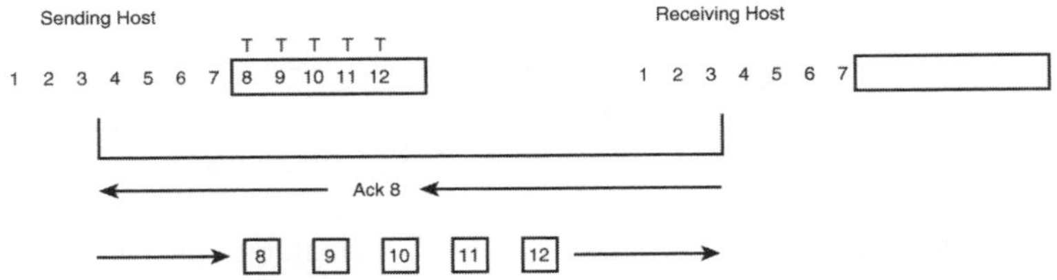

As you can see, using a sliding window can increase the performance of a TCP data transfer. In addition to acknowledging what segments it wants to receive next, it also indicates how many segments it can accept in its receiving window. It is this current window size information that leads to an increase in performance.

A TCP window can be too big, however. If you manually configured the window size too large, too many segments could be lost during transmission. This causes more data resends due to the retransmission timers expiring.

Delayed Acknowledgment Timers on the Recipient

The receiving host does not have to wait for the entire receive window to fill before it sends an acknowledgment to the sending host. An acknowledgment also can be sent whenever two contiguous segments are received. This is why an acknowledgment was sent to acknowledge segments 1 and 2. In some implementations of TCP, the recipient host starts a timer known as the *delayed acknowledgment timer* when it receives a segment. When the delayed acknowledgment time reaches zero, it also sends an acknowledgment to the sending host. This enables an acknowledgment to be sent even if two contiguous segments were not received.

Configuring Sliding Window Size in Windows NT, Windows 2000, and Windows XP

You can define a custom sliding window size by modifying the Windows NT, Windows 2000, or Windows XP Registry. In Windows NT, you set the value TCPWindowSize in the following Registry location:

        HKEY_LOCAL_MACHINE\System\CurrentControlSet\Services\Tcpip\Parameters

In Windows 2000, Windows XP, and Windows .NET Server, the value is defined in a slightly different Registry location:

```
HKEY_LOCAL_MACHINE\System\CurrentControlSet\Services\Tcpip\
    Parameters\Interfaces\<interface>
```

The datatype for the TCPWindowSize value is REG_DWORD. This entry does not exist by default. Its default value is the smaller of the following:

- Four times the maximum TCP data size on the network
- 8,192 rounded up to an even multiple of the network TCP data size

For an Ethernet segment, the default is tuned to 8,760 bytes for Windows NT and 17,520 bytes for Windows 2000, Windows XP, and Windows .NET Server. To keep the defaults, be sure the TCPWindowSize value does not exist. It already is tuned for best performance on an Ethernet network.

The States of a TCP Connection

During its lifetime, a TCP connection goes through a series of state changes as the client and server transmit data. A TCP connection moves from one state to the next due to various events, including user calls such as OPEN, SEND, RECEIVE, CLOSE, ABORT, and STATUS. The following states can exist for a TCP connection:

- LISTEN. In this state, a host is waiting for a connection request from any remote host.

- SYN-SENT. A host has sent a connection request and is waiting for a return request to complete the full-duplex connection.

- SYN-RECEIVED. The host is waiting for an acknowledgment of its connection request. It already has received and sent a confirmation request.

- ESTABLISHED. The normal state used for data transfer between two hosts. It represents an open connection between the two hosts.

- FIN-WAIT1. The host is waiting for either a connection termination request from the remote host or an acknowledgment of the connection termination request it sent earlier.

- FIN-WAIT2. The host is waiting for a connection termination request from the remote host.

- CLOSE-WAIT. This state represents the time when the TCP connection waits for the connection termination request from the upper-level application.

- CLOSING. The host is waiting for a connection termination request acknowledgment from the remote host.

- LAST-ACK. The host is waiting for acknowledgment of the connection termination request it already sent to the remote host.
- TIME-WAIT. The host is waiting a sufficient amount of time to be sure the remote host has received the acknowledgment of its connection termination request.
- CLOSED. This is not a state at all. It refers to the fact that no connection exists between the two hosts.

Viewing TCP Connection States

When you have established a session to another host using TCP, you can examine the connection states for your session using the command NETSTAT with the following parameters:

```
NETSTAT -A -P TCP
```

The -A ensures that all ports are displayed, no matter what their state, and the -P TCP ensures that only TCP-based ports are shown.

Common TCP Ports

The IANA has designated several default port numbers for use with the TCP protocol. If these ports also can be accessed by the UDP protocol, the UDP protocol typically uses the same port numbers.

Some of the more common TCP ports are shown in Table 4.4. They are stored in the Services file located in the /etc directory on Unix-based systems and in the <systemroot>\System32\Drivers\Etc folder on Microsoft operating systems.

TABLE 4.4   TCP Port Number Examples

Port	Service Name	Aliases	Description
0			Reserved
1	TCPMUX		TCP port service multiplexer
5	RJE		Remote job entry
7	ECHO		Echo service
9	DISCARD	SINK NULL	Discard service
11	SYSTAT	USERS	Active users
13	DAYTIME		Returns date and time
17	QOTD	QUOTE	Quote of the day
19	CHARGEN	TTYTST SOURCE	Character generator

TABLE 4.4   continued

Port	Service Name	Aliases	Description
20	FTP-DATA		File Transfer Protocol—data
21	FTP		File Transfer Protocol—control
23	TELNET		Telnet
25	SMTP	MAIL	Simple Mail Transfer Protocol
37	TIME	TIMESERVER	Time
42	NAME	NAMESERVER	Host name server
43	WHOIS	NICNAME	Who is service
53	DOMAIN	NAMESERVER	Domain name server
67	BOOTPS		Bootstrap protocol server
68	BOOTPC		Bootstrap protocol client
77	RJE	NETRJS	Any private RJE service
79	FINGER		Finger
80	HTTP	WWW	WWW's Hypertext Transmission Protocol
88	KERBEROS	KRB-5	Kerberos authentication
101	HOSTNAMES	HOSTNAME	NIC hostname server
102	ISO-TSAP		ISO TSAP
103	X400		X.400
104	X400-SND		X.400 SND
105	CSNET-NS		CSNET mailbox name server
110	POP3	POSTOFFICE	Post Office Protocol 3
111	SUNRPC		Sun RPC Portmap
113	AUTH	AUTHENTICATION	Authentication service
117	UUCP-PATH		UUCP path service
119	NNTP	USENET	Network News Transfer Protocol
139	NBSESSION	NETBIOS-SSN	NetBIOS Session Service
143	IMAP		Internet Mail Access Protocol
389	LDAP		Lightweight Directory Access Protocol
443	HTTPS		HTTP using SSL Security
445	MICROSOFT-DS		Microsoft Directory Services
464	KPASSWD		Kerberos Password
540	UUCP	UUCPD	uucp daemon
543	KLOGIN		Kerberos authenticated rlogin

4

TABLE 4.4   continued

Port	Service Name	Aliases	Description
544	KSHELL	CMD	Kerberos remote shell
636	LDAP/S		LDAP using SSL Security
666	DOOM		Doom from ID software
993	IMAP/S		IMAP4 using SSL Security
995	POP3/S		POP3 using SSL Security
1433	MS-SQL-S		Microsoft SQL Server
1723	PPTP		Point-to-Point Tunneling Protocol
3389	WinTerm		Windows Terminal Services

> **Note**
>
> The IANA maintains the most comprehensive list of transport layer protocols and their associated ports at http://www.iana.org/assignments/protocol-numbers.

User Datagram Protocol

 The User Datagram Protocol (UDP) provides nonguaranteed delivery of information at the transport layer. UDP delivers information to a remote host with little overhead. No mechanisms exist to make sure the destination host successfully receives the package. Any application using UDP for its transport mechanism needs to include the following services:

- Retransmission of lost data
- Fragmentation and reassembly of large data streams
- Flow control
- Congestion avoidance

UDP only provides a basic checksum to make sure the UDP datagram has not been corrupted during transport. In spite of its shortcomings, UDP does have some benefits. It provides services such as multicasts and broadcasts that are not available using TCP.

In local area networks, which generally do not have delivery problems, data transfer over UDP generates less network traffic than TCP. This is because acknowledgment packets are not sent whenever data is received.

The User Datagram Protocol Header Format

The User Datagram Protocol header uses the following format (see Figure 4.20):

FIGURE 4.20

The UDP header format.

Source Port	Destination Port
Length	Checksum
Data...	

- **Source Port.** This 16-bit field is optional for UDP. It contains the port used if a reply needs to be sent to the sending system. If not used, this field is filled with zeros.

- **Destination Port.** This 16-bit field contains the destination port address on the recipient host. This provides an endpoint for communication.

- **Length.** This 16-bit field contains the length in octets of the UDP header and its data payload.

- **Checksum.** This 16-bit field makes sure the UDP packet has not been corrupted in transit. It is calculated much like the TCP header's checksum. The calculation of the checksum requires some information from the IP header. This information, known as the *pseudo-header*, contains the fields shown in Figure 4.21.

FIGURE 4.21

The UDP pseudo-header.

Source IP Address		
Destination IP Address		
Zeros	Protocol	UDP Length

- **Data.** This variable-length field contains the upper-level application data to be transported using UDP.

The following are some well-known applications that use UDP:

- Trivial File Transfer Protocol (TFTP)
- Simple Network Management Protocol (SNMP)
- Domain name server (DNS)

Communication Using UDP

When a source host wants to communicate with a destination host using UDP, a session does not need to be established (unlike with TCP). The source host's application knows which port it needs to communicate with on the destination host. If the source application needs replies, it also includes its port address in the UDP header.

The UDP datagram is encapsulated as data in an IP datagram (see Figure 4.22).

4

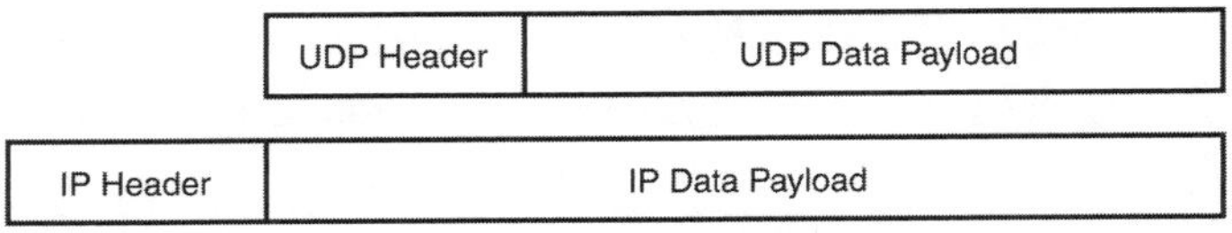

FIGURE 4.22

A UDP header and data is encapsulated in the IP data payload.

UDP Header	UDP Data Payload

IP Header	IP Data Payload

When the IP datagram arrives at the destination host, the IP header is stripped away revealing the original UDP header and data payload. The destination port number is determined from the UDP header, and UDP transfers the data to that designated port number.

If the designated port number is not available on the destination host, an ICMP error message is sent back to the host. The error message states that the port was unreachable, and the datagram is discarded.

Common UDP Ports

The Internet Assigned Number Authority also has designated several default port numbers for use with UDP. Some of the more common UDP port numbers are shown in Table 4.5. If you compare Table 4.4 with Table 4.5, you can see that several ports are available in both TCP and UDP. The two protocols always strive to use the same port number.

TABLE 4.5   UDP Port Number Examples

Port	Service Name	Aliases	Description
0			Reserved
7	ECHO		Echo service
9	DISCARD	SINK NULL	Discard service
11	SYSTAT	USERS	Active users
13	DAYTIME		Returns date and time
17	QOTD	QUOTE	Quote of the day
19	CHARGEN	TTYTST SOURCE	Character generator
37	TIME	TIMSERVER	Time
39	RLP	RESOURCE	Resource location
42	NAME	NAMESERVER	Host name server
43	WHOIS	NICNAME	Who is service
53	NAMESERVER	DOMAIN	Domain name server
67	BOOTPS		Bootstrap protocol server

TABLE 4.5 continued

Port	Service Name	Aliases	Description
68	BOOTPC		Bootstrap protocol client
69	TFTP		Trivial FTP
88	KERBEROS		Kerberos authentication
111	SUNRPC		Sun Microsystems RPC
123	NTP	NTPD NTP	Network time protocol
137	NBNAME		NetBIOS name service
138	NBDATAGRAM		NetBIOS datagram service
161	SNMP	SNMP	Simple Network Management Protocol network monitor
162	SNMP-TRAP	SNMP	Simple Network Management Protocol traps
445	MICROSOFT-DS		Microsoft Directory Services
464	KPASSWD		Kerberos Password
500	ISAKMP	IKE	Internet Key Exchange
512	BIFF	COMSAT	Unix Comsat
513	WHO	WHOD	UNIX Remote Who daemon
514	SYSLOG		System log
525	TIMED	TIMESERVER	Time daemon
666	DOOM		Doom ID Software
1701	12TP		Layer Two Tunneling Protocol
1812	RADIUS		Radius Authentication
1813	RADACCT		Radius Accounting
2049	NFS		Sun nfs

Determining What Ports Are in Use

Users learning TCP/IP often want to determine what ports actually are in use. Day 13, "Protecting Your Network," shows how knowledge of the ports associated with applications are used to configure a security device known as a *firewall*. A firewall protects your network by only allowing desired protocols to enter your network, by defining the protocols based on port information and protocol identifiers.

Depending on your skill level, or desire to type, you can use both text-based and graphical utilities to determine port status.

Using Text-Based Tools

In Windows 2000 and Windows XP, you can use the NETSTAT command to reveal which ports are in use. A similar command can be found in all implementations of TCP/IP.

The following is the syntax of the NETSTAT command:

```
NETSTAT [-a] [-e] [-n] [-s] [-p protocol] [-r] [interval]
```

Descriptions of the options are as follows:

Option	Description
-a	Shows all current connections and all ports currently in a listening state.
-e	Shows Ethernet statistics.
-n	Shows all addresses and ports in numerical format. The NETSTAT command usually resolves IP addresses to hostnames using host-name resolution and resolves port numbers to service names using the Services file.
-s	Shows the statistics by protocol. It can be combined with the -p protocol option to show statistics only for a specific protocol.
-p protocol	Shows only the connections for the specified protocol. Possible protocols include TCP, UDP, IP TCPv6, UDPv6, and IPv6.
-r	Displays the current routing table.
interval	Sets the update interval for showing active connections.

The following code shows a portion of the results displayed when the computer named BKCLIENT connects to a computer named SIDESHOWBRI. Currently connected applications include FTP and WWW.

```
C:\> netstat

Active Connections

  Proto  Local Address        Foreign Address          State
  TCP    BKClient:1168    SIDESHOWBRI.komarconsulting.com:ftp ESTABLISHED
  TCP    BKClient:1249    SIDESHOWBRI.komarconsulting.com:HTTP  ESTABLISHED
  TCP    BKClient:1250    SIDESHOWBRI.komarconsulting.com:HTTP  ESTABLISHED
  TCP    BKClient:1251    SIDESHOWBRI.komarconsulting.com:HTTP  ESTABLISHED
  TCP    BKClient:1252    SIDESHOWBRI.komarconsulting.com:HTTP  ESTABLISHED
  TCP    BKClient:1253    SIDESHOWBRI.komarconsulting.com:HTTP  ESTABLISHED
  TCP    BKClient:1254    SIDESHOWBRI.komarconsulting.com:HTTP  ESTABLISHED
  TCP    BKClient:1255    SIDESHOWBRI.komarconsulting.com:HTTP  ESTABLISHED
  TCP    BKClient:1256    SIDESHOWBRI.komarconsulting.com:HTTP  ESTABLISHED
```

From this listing, you can see that the BKCLIENT computer is using port 1168 when communicating with the FTP server on SIDESHOWBRI. The port used on SIDESHOWBRI is port 21, the ftp port, used by the FTP server for receiving FTP commands from an FTP client.

You also can see that the BKCLIENT computer has eight separate TCP sessions connected to port 80 on SIDESHOWBRI. When a Web page is downloaded, each individual graphic or object on the page is transferred with a unique TCP session. On BKCLIENT, the port numbers were assigned in ascending numeric order as they were established.

The following code shows the results of issuing the NETSTAT command on SIDESHOWBRI during these sessions.

```
Proto   Local Address          Foreign Address           State
TCP     sideshowbri:ftp       BKCLIENT.komarconsulting.com:1168  ESTABLISHED
TCP     sideshowbri:ftp-data  BKCLIENT.komarconsulting.com:1169  TIME_WAIT
TCP     sideshowbri:HTTP      BKCLIENT.komarconsulting.com:1249  ESTABLISHED
TCP     sideshowbri:HTTP      BKCLIENT.komarconsulting.com:1250  ESTABLISHED
TCP     sideshowbri:HTTP      BKCLIENT.komarconsulting.com:1251  ESTABLISHED
TCP     sideshowbri:HTTP      BKCLIENT.komarconsulting.com:1252  ESTABLISHED
TCP     sideshowbri:HTTP      BKCLIENT.komarconsulting.com:1253  ESTABLISHED
TCP     sideshowbri:HTTP      BKCLIENT.komarconsulting.com:1254  ESTABLISHED
TCP     sideshowbri:HTTP      BKCLIENT.komarconsulting.com:1255  ESTABLISHED
TCP     sideshowbri:HTTP      BKCLIENT.komarconsulting.com:1256  ESTABLISHED
```

Note that all the entries in the NETSTAT results are now reversed. This is because you are now viewing the TCP end-to-end communication session from the point of view of SIDESHOWBRI.

4

Don't Know the Port Numbers for a Protocol?

If you had run NETSTAT withthe -n parameter, the output only shows the numeric values for ports, not the logical names read from the Services file.

The NETSTAT command also can determine which UDP services are in a listening state on a computer. The following code shows the results of a NETSTAT -a -p UDP command:

```
U:\>netstat -a -p UDP

Active Connections

  Proto  Local Address        Foreign Address        State
```

```
UDP    sideshowbri:echo       *:*
UDP    sideshowbri:discard    *:*
UDP    sideshowbri:daytime    *:*
UDP    sideshowbri:qotd       *:*
UDP    sideshowbri:chargen    *:*
UDP    sideshowbri:name       *:*
UDP    sideshowbri:tftp       *:*
UDP    sideshowbri:135        *:*
UDP    sideshowbri:snmp       *:*
UDP    sideshowbri:1027       *:*
UDP    sideshowbri:1038       *:*
UDP    sideshowbri:1046       *:*
UDP    sideshowbri:1073       *:*
UDP    sideshowbri:1074       *:*
UDP    sideshowbri:1083       *:*
UDP    sideshowbri:1084       *:*
UDP    sideshowbri:1268       *:*
UDP    sideshowbri:domain     *:*
UDP    sideshowbri:bootp      *:*
```

In this list of UDP services, you can see the following UDP-transport–based applications running on SIDESHOWBRI:

- A DHCP server (sideshowbri:bootp)
- A trivial FTP server (sideshowbri:tftp)
- A domain name server (sideshowbri:domain)
- An SNMP agent (sideshowbri:snmp)

The NETSTAT command can help troubleshoot the ports in use between a client host and a server host.

Using Graphical Tools

Many graphical user interface (GUI) tools are available that allow easier determination of open ports on local and remote computers. In comparison to the NETSTAT tool, the GUI tools are generally used to probe remote computers, rather than the local computer for port information. Two commonly used GUI port scanners are provided by WinScan (www.prosolve.com) and NetScan Tools (www.netscantools.com).

Using WinScan

WinScan, a port scanner from Prosolve Network and Security Consulting, is a dedicated freeware port scanner that allows you to scan either a single host or a complete network for open ports.

Like the NETSTAT command, the WinScan tool uses the Services file to resolve port numbers to service names. Figure 4.23 shows the WinScan dialog box where all options are easy to configure.

FIGURE 4.23

The WinScan port scanner.

As shown in Figure 4.23, the WinScan port scanner can be configured to scan both TCP and UDP ports and displays all results within the single dialog box.

4

Scanning the Local Computer

By configuring the WinScan port scanner to scan the localhost IP address of 127.0.0.1, the WinScan port scanner will show all open ports on the local computer, rather than just those on remote computers.

Using NetScanTools

NetScanTools is a comprehensive suite of TCP/IP utilities from Northwest Performance Software, Inc. Rather than just providing port scanning capabilities, NetScan tools offers utilities ranging from Ping options to name server lookups.

In NetScanTools 4.22, the option to perform a Port Probe (see Figure 4.24) allows you to probe either single hosts or an IP subnet range.

As with WinScan, you can also define the port range and timeout options for a port scan. You can also scan the local host by scanning the 127.0.0.1 IP address.

FIGURE **4.24**

The NetScanTools Port Probe.

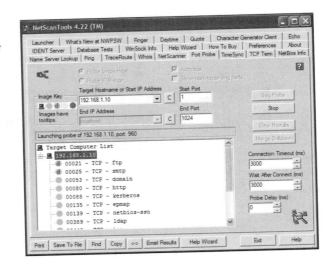

Applying What You Have Learned

Today's material covered a lot of information. You have researched the protocols that exist in both the Internet and Transport layers of the TCP/IP layer model.

In addition, the final section looked at how port scanners can be used to determine what services are running, or what connections exist, at a local or remote computer. Both text and graphical utilities can be used to perform port scanning functions.

Here are questions to check what you've learned today. The answers can be found in Appendix B, "Test Your Knowledge: Answers."

Test Your Knowledge

1. What physical address is obtained by the ARP protocol when the destination host is located on the same network segment?

2. What physical address is obtained by the ARP protocol when the destination host is located on a remote network segment?

3. What services are provided by the ICMP protocol?

4. Does the IP protocol provide connection-oriented or connectionless service?

5. Why is multicasting preferred over broadcasting when sending data to multiple hosts?

6. What is the difference between the TCP and UDP protocols?

7. How does TCP provide reliable transport?

8. What is a delayed acknowledgment timer?

9. Describe the TCP three-way handshake process.

10. Can a sliding window be configured too large?

11. If the TCP window size of the sending host is smaller than the receive window of the destination host, which computer adjusts its TCP window size?

12. What fault tolerance is provided in a UDP header?

13. What is a TCP pseudo-header?

14. Connect to a Web site using a Web browser. After you have connected, start a command prompt and type the following command:

```
netstat -a -n
```

What port are you connected to on the Web server? What port(s) are you using on your host system?

Preview of Day 5

Subnet masking is one of the most difficult tasks that a TCP/IP expert faces in TCP/IP networking. Tomorrow's material provides detailed steps that can be used to define non-default subnet masks. The following topics are covered:

- Determining which subnet mask is required based on the number of subnets required on the network

- Determining the maximum number of hosts that can exist on a network segment given a specific subnet mask

- Determining the pools of IP addresses used for each network segment based on the network IP address and the selected subnet mask

The method described revolves around using a subnet shortcut table that makes the calculations easier to perform.

4

DAY 5

The Art of Subnet Masking

Today you will learn what a subnet is, how to modify it, and why you might want to modify it. Today's material covers the following aspects of modified subnet masking:

- Determining when a customized subnet mask is required
- Deciding how many unique subnets are required
- Deciding whether the subnet mask chosen provides enough host IP addresses for each subnet
- Determining the network address, broadcast address, and pool of IP addresses for a specific network address/subnet mask combination
- Determining the need for variable-length subnet masking
- Understanding the concept of Classless Internet Domain Routing (CIDR)

The Need for Customized Subnets

Many times, when working with an assigned network address from your Internet Service Provider (ISP), situations arise that require you to segment the network using a subnet mask that is not the default subnet mask for the network address. An IP address, as discussed on Day 3, "Internet Protocol (IP) Addresses," is logically broken into network and host portions. In a subnetting scenario, the host portion of the address is further broken into a subnet portion and a host portion. Figure 5.1 shows the default subnet mask assigned to Class A addresses. If eight more bits are taken from the host portion of the address, these additional bits represent the subnetwork that this network address represents. The combined network and subnet portions of the subnet mask are known as the *extended network prefix*.

FIGURE 5.1

Extending the network prefix for a Class A address.

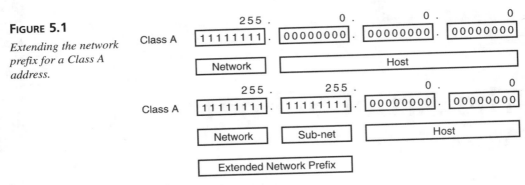

The most commonly asked question is, "Why would I want or have to do this?" The following circumstances require you to consider subnetting a network:

- If your network uses mixed topologies, such as ethernet and token ring, you need to segment the network based on topology. Each of these segments requires a unique network address.
- You need to redirect network traffic to isolate bandwidth-intensive applications or hosts to their own segment of the network or to reduce the effect of broadcast packets by segmenting the network.
- You want to reduce the number of addresses you might need from your ISP for your network.
- You want to distribute IP addresses more efficiently on your network. If you have two network segments joined by a serial connection, you only need two addresses for that segment. It is wasteful to allocate an entire Class C address range (254 addresses) to this segment.

- You want to divide a range of IP addresses between network segments. Each network segment requires a contiguous pool of IP addresses. Rather than acquire a separate pool for each network segment, a pool can be subnetted so that each network segment is assigned an IP subnet of addresses.

The process of subnetting an assigned network address is based on the following questions that must be answered:

- How many network segments does the network need addresses for today? A *network segment* is a physical section of the network separated from all other areas by a routing device.
- How many network segments will the network need in the future?
- How many hosts will be needed on the largest segment of the network today?
- What will the future needs be for hosts on any one segment of the network?

The right subnet masking decision is the one that correctly answers all these questions.

Determining a Subnetting Solution

The next three subsections guide you through a step-by-step solution for determining which subnet mask meets a network's subnetting needs. This solution helps you determine the number of subnets required, the number of hosts provided for each subnet, and the pool of IP addresses for each subnet.

The goal of this section is to determine a new separation point between the network and host portions of the IP address instead of using the default subnet mask based on the IP address class. Remember that when a host attempts to communicate with a second host, it performs the ANDing process. It uses the ANDing function against both its own IP address and the target host's IP address. If the ANDing function's results are the same, the hosts are on the same network segment. If the results are different, the destination host is on a remote network, and the data is sent to the default gateway.

 Note

If you need to refresh your memory, the ANDing process was discussed in detail on Day 3 in the section "The ANDing Process."

As a result of this process, the subnet mask takes a specific amount of host bits from the address and makes them part of the network portion of the address. The ANDing process then is performed on the modified subnet mask.

Determining the Number of Subnets

The first step in choosing a modified subnet mask is to determine how many subnets a network requires. Each network segment requires a unique network ID. The network in Figure 5.2, for example, requires eight unique network IDs.

FIGURE 5.2

A sample network.

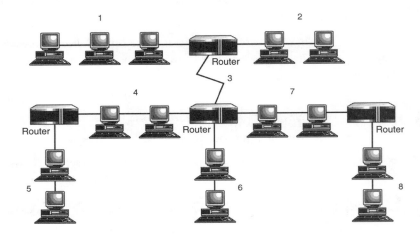

Some people might initially question why network 3 requires network IDs because there are no hosts on this segment. You must keep in mind, however, that each router on these segments has a network interface that requires an IP address.

Assume this network can use the Class B address 126.32.0.0. Using the default Class B subnet mask 255.255.0.0, this allocates the first 16 bits, or 126.32, to represent the network address. The remaining 16 bits represent the host component of the address.

You need to use some of the 16 host bits to segment this network address into the required 8 segments. A process is used to determine how many bits are needed from the host portion of the address to accomplish this. Because you require eight networks, the bits taken from the host portion of the address need to provide at least eight different combinations.

The first step is to convert the number 8 into its binary representation, which is 1000.

What If the Bits Are All Ones?

A special case exists in which this method does not work. If the number of networks required converts to all ones in binary, you must take an additional bit to represent the number of networks required. If the number of networks is seven, for example, this converts to 111 in binary. In this case, 4 bits are required to make up seven subnetworks. This is because subnetwork addresses of all zeros or all ones are not allowed in many network implementations.

The number 8 is represented using 4 bits. These 4 bits must be taken from the host portion of the address to represent the network portion of the address (see Figure 5.3).

FIGURE 5.3

Taking 4 bits from the host portion of the IP address.

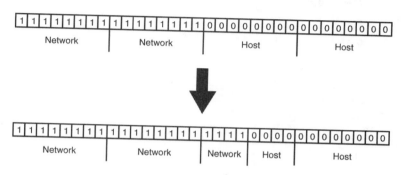

In this case, because the IP address is a Class B address, the host portion of the address includes the third and fourth octets of the 32-bit address. The 4 bits are taken from the leftmost bits. This results in the new subnet mask represented in Figure 5.3.

The third octet is now represented as 11110000, which translates to 240 in the decimal system. This means you can use the subnet mask 255.255.240.0 to segment this network into at least eight subnetworks.

Alternate Notation

It often is difficult to work with decimal-represented subnet masks. Another common method represents the number of bits required for the network portion of the address as a decimal number following the network address in dotted decimal format. The network ID 126.32.0.0 with the subnet mask 255.255.240.0, for example, is represented as 126.32.0.0/20 in this notation. This shows that the first 20 bits of this network address represent the network. This shorthand method can be less clumsy to use than the standard representation of a subnet mask.

How many unique network addresses can be allocated using this subnet mask? Table 5.1 shows all the possible combinations that can be created using these four bits.

5

TABLE 5.1   Determining All Possible Network Combinations for a 240-Subnet Mask

Binary	Decimal
00000000	0
00010000	16
00100000	32
00110000	48
01000000	64
01010000	80
01100000	96
01110000	112
10000000	128
10010000	144
10100000	160
10110000	176
11000000	192
11010000	208
11100000	224
11110000	240

Sixteen possible combinations can be created using unique patterns for the first 4 bits of an octet. This does not always provide 16 separate subnets for addressing. Some routing protocols do not advertise both the network address and the subnet mask. In these cases, you cannot use a subnet ID that is all zeros. This is because the network ID for the network 126.32.0.0/16 is equivalent to the subnetwork address 126.32.0.0/20. Unless the routing protocol advertises the subnetwork mask, both network addresses simply appear as 126.32.0.0, and you cannot tell the difference between them. The broadcast address for the network ID 126.32.240.0/20 is 126.32.255.255. This is the same as the broadcast address for the network ID 126.32.0.0/16. Again, without the subnet mask included, you do not know which network's broadcast address is represented by 126.32.255.255. This leaves you with 14 valid subnetwork addresses.

Zero Subnetting

Routers that support advanced routing protocols that transmit the subnet mask when they propagate routing information often have an option that enables use of the 0 subnet. This is called *zero subnetting*. Many Internet service providers implement this form of subnetting because it does not waste any IP addresses when they segment their address pool.

The following equation can be used as a shortcut for determining the number of networks:

$2^n - 2$

In this equation, n represents the number of bits required for the subnet mask. Table 5.2 shows how many subnets are available if you use up to one octet of bits from the host portion of an address.

TABLE 5.2   Number of Subnets Provided by n Bits of the Host Address

n Bits	Formula	# of Subnets
1	$2^1 - 2$	0
2	$2^2 - 2$	2
3	$2^3 - 2$	6
4	$2^4 - 2$	14
5	$2^5 - 2$	30
6	$2^6 - 2$	62
7	$2^7 - 2$	126
8	$2^8 - 2$	254*

*If you use additional bits from the host portion of the address, the number of subnetworks provided continues to grow using this formula.

5

Does this handle your future network growth needs? It depends. You have to look at expected expansion within the organization. If you require 14 subnets today, this number is probably insufficient for future growth.

Determining the Number of Available Hosts

The next step in subnet masking is to determine the number of hosts available on each segment of the network. This is calculated by first determining the number of bits left to represent the host portion of the address. In the example, this is 12 bits.

The number of hosts provided by each segment of this network addressing scheme is calculated using the same formula:

$2^n - 2$

In this equation, n is the number of bits left to represent the host portion of the address. The number 2 is subtracted from this number because a host address typically cannot be all zeros or all ones. Remember that a host address of all zeros represents this network, and a host address of all ones is the broadcast address for that host.

The subnet mask 255.255.240.0 against the Class B address 126.32.0.0 gives you $2^{12} - 2 = 4{,}094$ hosts per segment.

This should be a sufficient number of hosts for future growth on each network segment.

Establishing the Available Pools of IP Addresses for a Subnet Mask

The final step in determining a subnetting solution is to identify the actual addresses that would be used for the network segments.

The first addresses to be determined are the actual network addresses that would represent each of the individual subnetworks. Table 5.1 showed the actual decimal representations of the 16 different network addresses for a 240 subnetwork mask. Using these values, you would come up with the network addresses in Table 5.3.

TABLE 5.3   Network Addresses for a 255.255.240.0 Subnet Mask

Binary Network Address	Dotted Decimal Notation
~~10011100 00100000 00000000 00000000~~	~~126.32.0.0~~
10011100 00100000 00010000 00000000	126.32.16.0
10011100 00100000 00100000 00000000	126.32.32.0
10011100 00100000 00110000 00000000	126.32.48.0
10011100 00100000 01000000 00000000	126.32.64.0
10011100 00100000 01010000 00000000	126.32.80.0
10011100 00100000 01100000 00000000	126.32.96.0
10011100 00100000 01110000 00000000	126.32.112.0
10011100 00100000 10000000 00000000	126.32.128.0
10011100 00100000 10010000 00000000	126.32.144.0
10011100 00100000 10100000 00000000	126.32.160.0
10011100 00100000 10110000 00000000	126.32.176.0
10011100 00100000 11000000 00000000	126.32.192.0
10011100 00100000 11010000 00000000	126.32.208.0
10011100 00100000 11100000 00000000	126.32.224.0
~~10011100 00100000 11110000 00000000~~	~~126.32.240.0~~

As previously discussed, the network addresses 126.32.0.0 and 126.32.240.0 often are not used if routing protocols that do not transmit subnet masks are used.

The second addresses to be determined are the broadcast addresses for each network. The broadcast address is represented by a host address of all ones. Table 5.4 shows the broadcast addresses for each of these segments.

TABLE 5.4   Broadcast Addresses Using a 255.255.240.0 Subnet Mask

Binary Network Address	Dotted Decimal Notation
10011100 00100000 00011111 11111111	126.32.31.255
10011100 00100000 00101111 11111111	126.32.47.255
10011100 00100000 00111111 11111111	126.32.63.255
10011100 00100000 01001111 11111111	126.32.79.255
10011100 00100000 01011111 11111111	126.32.95.255
10011100 00100000 01101111 11111111	126.32.111.255
10011100 00100000 01111111 11111111	126.32.127.255
10011100 00100000 10001111 11111111	126.32.143.255
10011100 00100000 10011111 11111111	126.32.159.255
10011100 00100000 10101111 11111111	126.32.175.255
10011100 00100000 10111111 11111111	126.32.191.255
10011100 00100000 11001111 11111111	126.32.207.255
10011100 00100000 11011111 11111111	126.32.223.255
10011100 00100000 11101111 11111111	126.32.239.255

5

The final step is to create a pool of addresses for each of the networks. The pool begins with the address immediately following the network address and ends with the address before the broadcast address. Table 5.5 summarizes all the information for each network address.

TABLE 5.5   Address Pools for the 126.32.0.0/20 Network

Network Address	Beginning Address	Ending Address	Broadcast Address
126.32.16.0	126.32.16.1	126.32.31.254	126.32.31.255
126.32.32.0	126.32.32.1	126.32.47.254	126.32.47.255
126.32.48.0	126.32.48.1	126.32.63.254	126.32.63.255
126.32.64.0	126.32.64.1	126.32.79.254	126.32.79.255

TABLE 5.5   Continued

Network Address	Beginning Address	Ending Address	Broadcast Address
126.32.80.0	126.32.80.1	126.32.95.254	126.32.95.255
126.32.96.0	126.32.96.1	126.32.111.254	126.32.111.255
126.32.112.0	126.32.112.1	126.32.127.254	126.32.127.255
126.32.128.0	126.32.128.1	126.32.143.254	126.32.143.255
126.32.144.0	126.32.144.1	126.32.159.254	126.32.159.255
126.32.160.0	126.32.160.1	126.32.175.254	126.32.175.255
126.32.176.0	126.32.176.1	126.32.191.254	126.32.191.255
126.32.192.0	126.32.192.1	126.32.207.254	126.32.207.255
126.32.208.0	126.32.208.1	126.32.223.254	126.32.223.255
126.32.224.0	126.32.224.1	126.32.239.254	126.32.239.255

Building a Subnet Shortcut Table

The steps to determine the correct subnet mask and the associated pools of addresses can take several calculations. This section shows you some shortcuts that can be taken to determine the network addresses, the pools of IP addresses, and broadcast addresses for each subnet.

To determine subnet calculations, you can use a table consisting of three rows of information (see Figure 5.4).

FIGURE 5.4

Building a subnet shortcut table.

# of Bits	1	2	3	4	5	6	7	8
Incrementing Value								
Subnet Mask								
# of Networks								

In this table, you must calculate the increment value for each column, the subnet mask values to be used, and the number of subnetworks each subnet mask provides.

The first row to be calculated is the increment value row. This is based on the actual binary value each column represents. In the "Binary Representation" section of Day 3, you learned that octet values can be represented as a string of eight binary bits. These bits have the values shown in Figure 5.5.

FIGURE 5.5

Calculating the incrementing value row.

# of Bits		1	2	3	4	5	6	7	8
Incrementing Value		128	64	32	16	8	4	2	1
Subnet Mask									
# of Networks									

A Trick for Calculating Incrementing Values

If you cannot remember each binary bit place value, you can calculate them by entering a value of 1 in the rightmost column. As you move left, each column is double the value of the previous column. The second column from the right, for example, has a value of 2. This continues until you reach the final column, which has a value of 128.

These increment values determine the starting addresses of each pool of addresses provided by a specific subnet mask.

The second row of the table determines the subnet mask value based on the number of bits taken from the host portion of the address. These values are calculated by totaling the binary bit place values up to that column. The first column has a bit value of 128, so the subnet mask for that column also is 128. If you use two bits to represent the subnet mask, the subnet mask value is 128 + 64 = 192. If you use three bits to represent the subnet mask, the subnet mask value is 128 + 64 + 32 = 224. When you calculate the subnet mask value for all eight columns, the results look like Figure 5.6.

5

FIGURE 5.6

Determining the subnet mask values.

# of Bits		1	2	3	4	5	6	7	8
Incrementing Value		128	64	32	16	8	4	2	1
Subnet Mask		128	192	224	240	248	252	254	255
# of Networks									

An Alternative Calculation to Find Subnet Mask Values

Because you already have calculated the binary bit place value for each column, you also can use the following formula to calculate each column's subnet mask:

```
256 - Incrementing Value
```

This results in the same values for the subnet mask. The first method, however, does provide a better rationale of how the subnet values actually are determined.

The final step in building the table is to calculate the number of subnets provided by each subnet mask. The following is the formula for calculating the number of subnets provided:

$2^n - 2$

In this formula, n is the number of bits used to represent the subnet mask. If three bits are used to represent the subnet mask, for example, this provides $2^3 - 2 = 6$ pools of IP addresses. Figure 5.7 shows the table after all # of Networks values have been calculated.

FIGURE 5.7

The completed subnet shortcut table.

# of Bits	1	2	3	4	5	6	7	8
Incrementing Value	128	64	32	16	8	4	2	1
Subnet Mask	128	192	224	240	248	252	254	255
# of Networks	0	2	6	14	30	62	126	254

What If I Need More than 8 Bits?

There are a few catches when you need to grab more than 8 bits to represent the subnet mask. For the incrementing value, just continue from the leftmost column. If you require 9 bits, for example, this is represented using an increment value of 128. The subnet mask is made up of 9 bits. The first 8 bits are represented by 255, and the last bit is represented by 128. Finally, the number of networks provided by 9 bits is $2^9 - 2 = 510$ networks.

The following examples use the completed subnet shortcut table shown in Figure 5.7.

Using the Subnet Shortcut Table for a Class A Address

This section walks you through an example of using the subnet shortcut table to determine an optimal subnet mask for a scenario.

A network has been assigned the 65.0.0.0 network address by your ISP. You want to segment the network into four subnetworks. The largest segment of this network requires addressing for 8,000 hosts, but this number could grow to 10,000 hosts in the next two years. What subnet mask can be used uniformly across the network to provide the required results?

Using Figure 5.7, you can see that if you want to provide at least four subnetworks, you need to look at the third column, which provides six subnetworks. This provides growth for two additional networks in the future.

The associated subnet mask in this column is 224. For a Class A address, this is a subnet mask of 255.224.0.0. This also can be represented in shorthand notation as 65.0.0.0/11, representing the 11 bits that now represent the network portion of the address. The 11 bits are made up of the default 8 bits assigned to a Class A address and the 3 additional bits used by the subnet mask.

This leaves you with 21 bits to represent the host portion of the address. If you calculate $2^{21} - 2$, the number of hosts per subnetwork is 2,097,150. This is much more than the requirement of supporting 10,000 hosts per segment.

Finally, using the table, you can see that the incrementing value for a 224 subnet mask is 32. Table 5.6 shows how all network addresses can be determined using this incrementing value. The left column is created by continually adding the incrementing value to itself until the actual subnet mask value is reached.

TABLE 5.6 Using the Increment Value of 32

Increment Value	Network Address	Beginning Address	Ending Address	Broadcast Address
n	65.n.0.0	65.n.0.1	$65.n_{next}-1.255.254$	$65.n_{next}-1.255.255$
~~0~~	n/a	n/a	n/a	n/a
32	65.32.0.0	65.32.0.1	65.63.255.254	65.63.255.255
64	65.64.0.0	65.64.0.1	65.95.255.254	65.95.255.255
96	65.96.0.0	65.96.0.1	65.127.255.254	65.127.255.255
128	65.128.0.0	65.128.0.1	65.159.255.254	65.159.255.255
160	65.160.0.0	65.160.0.1	65.191.255.254	65.191.255.255
192	65.192.0.0	65.192.0.1	65.223.255.254	65.223.255.255
~~224~~	n/a	n/a	n/a	n/a

5

Note that the values of 0 and 224 are not used in this example. They can be used if the network uses a routing protocol that advertises the subnet mask in addition to the network address.

The broadcast addresses and pools of IP addresses can easily be calculated by completing Table 5.6 using the calculations in each row header.

Using the Subnet Shortcut Table for a Class B Address

This next example uses the subnet shortcut table to calculate subnets for a Class B address.

In this example, assume that on your private network, you have decided to implement the RFC 1918 Class B address of 172.28.0.0. You want to segment the network into 18 different subnets. The largest network segment requires 1,800 host addresses.

Using the subnet shortcut table in Figure 5.7, you can see that providing 18 subnetworks requires 5 bits of the host address. This provides a maximum of 30 subnets. A total of 21 bits is used to represent the network ID. This leaves a total of 11 bits to represent the host address. Eleven host bits provide $2^{11} - 2 = 2,046$ hosts per network segment.

This appears to meet the requirement of 18 subnetworks of 1,800 hosts. This solution provides for up to 30 networks of growth and enables each subnet to have up to 2,046 hosts. Therefore, the network ID 172.28.0.0 with subnet mask 255.255.248.0 can be used for this subnetworking example.

The actual calculation of network address, beginning addresses, ending address, and broadcast address is performed as shown in Table 5.7. The increment value used for the calculation of all addresses is 8 (as indicated in Figure 5.7) when you use 5 bits for the network mask.

TABLE 5.7 Subnetwork Addresses for 172.28.0.0/21

Increment Value	Network Address	Beginning Address	Ending Address	Broadcast Address
n	172.28.n.0	172.28.n.1	$172.28.n_{next} -1.254$	$172.28.n_{next} -1.255$
8	172.28.8.0	172.28.8.1	172.28.15.254	172.28.15.255
16	172.28.16.0	172.28.16.1	172.28.23.254	172.28.23.255
24	172.28.24.0	172.28.24.1	172.28.31.254	172.28.31.255
32	172.28.32.0	172.28.32.1	172.28.39.254	172.28.39.255
40	172.28.40.0	172.28.40.1	172.28.47.254	172.28.47.255
48	172.28.48.0	172.28.48.1	172.28.63.254	172.28.63.255
64	172.28.64.0	172.28.64.1	172.28.71.254	172.28.71.255
72	172.28.72.0	172.28.72.1	172.28.79.254	172.28.79.255
80	172.28.80.0	172.28.80.1	172.28.87.254	172.28.87.255

TABLE 5.7   continued

Increment Value	Network Address	Beginning Address	Ending Address	Broadcast Address
88	172.28.88.0	172.28.88.1	172.28.95.254	172.28.95.255
96	172.28.96.0	172.28.96.1	172.28.103.254	172.28.103.255
104	172.28.104.0	172.28.104.1	172.28.111.254	172.28.111.255
112	172.28.112.0	172.28.112.1	172.28.119.254	172.28.119.255
120	172.28.120.0	172.28.120.1	172.28.127.254	172.28.127.255
128	172.28.128.0	172.28.128.1	172.28.135.254	172.28.135.255
136	172.28.136.0	172.28.136.1	172.28.143.254	172.28.143.255
144	172.28.144.0	172.28.144.1	172.28.151.254	172.28.151.255
152	172.28.152.0	172.28.152.1	172.28.159.254	172.28.159.255
160	172.28.160.0	172.28.160.1	172.28.167.254	172.28.167.255
168	172.28.168.0	172.28.168.1	172.28.175.254	172.28.175.255
176	172.28.176.0	172.28.176.1	172.28.183.254	172.28.183.255
184	172.28.184.0	172.28.184.1	172.28.191.254	172.28.191.255
192	172.28.192.0	172.28.192.1	172.28.199.254	172.28.199.255
200	172.28.200.0	172.28.200.1	172.28.207.254	172.28.207.255
208	172.28.208.0	172.28.208.1	172.28.215.254	172.28.215.255
216	172.28.216.0	172.28.216.1	172.28.223.254	172.28.223.255
224	172.28.224.0	172.28.224.1	172.28.231.254	172.28.231.255
232	172.28.232.0	172.28.232.1	172.28.239.254	172.28.239.255
240	172.28.240.0	172.28.240.1	172.28.247.254	172.28.247.255

5

Using the Subnet Shortcut Table for a Class C Address

This final example works through Class C subnetting. Class C subnetting sometimes is more confusing, but the same methodology can be used to calculate the correct subnet mask for a given subnetting situation.

In this example, a network has acquired the address 197.5.6.0 from its local ISP. You need to segment the network into seven different subnets, with each subnet providing a maximum of nine hosts.

Using the subnet shortcut table, you see that four bits must be used to provide seven sub-networks. Using four bits means using a 240 subnet mask. For a Class C address, this is represented as 255.255.255.240 (or in shorthand notation, 197.5.6.0/28).

This leaves four bits to represent the host address. The calculation of $2^4 - 2$ shows that you have provided for 14 hosts per segment.

This solution meets all your business needs. All that is left is to create a table of network addresses (see Table 5.8). As with Class A and Class B addresses, start with the first column containing your increment values. For a 240 subnet mask, these values are incremented by 16s. Note that for a Class C address, the actual calculations for the columns change a bit.

TABLE 5.8   Network Addressing for 197.5.6.0/28

Increment Value	Network Address	Beginning Address	Ending Address	Broadcast Address
n	197.5.6.n	197.5.6.n+1	$197.5.6.n_{next} - 2$	$197.5.6.n_{next} - 1$
~~0~~	n/a	n/a	n/a	n/a
16	197.5.6.16	197.5.6.17	197.5.6.30	197.5.6.31
32	197.5.6.32	197.5.6.33	197.5.6.46	197.5.6.47
48	197.5.6.48	197.5.6.49	197.5.6.62	197.5.6.63
64	197.5.6.64	197.5.6.65	197.5.6.78	197.5.6.79
80	197.5.6.80	197.5.6.81	197.5.6.94	197.5.6.95
96	197.5.6.96	197.5.6.97	197.5.6.110	197.5.6.111
112	197.5.6.112	197.5.6.113	197.5.6.126	197.5.6.127
128	197.5.6.128	197.5.6.129	197.5.6.142	197.5.6.143
144	197.5.6.144	197.5.6.145	197.5.6.158	197.5.6.159
160	197.5.6.160	197.5.6.161	197.5.6.174	197.5.6.175
176	197.5.6.176	197.5.6.177	197.5.6.190	197.5.6.191
192	197.5.6.192	197.5.6.193	197.5.6.206	197.5.6.207
208	197.5.6.208	197.5.6.209	197.5.6.222	197.5.6.223
224	197.5.6.224	197.5.6.225	197.5.6.238	197.5.6.239
~~240~~	n/a	n/a	n/a	n/a

Variable-Length Subnet Masking

RFC 1878   Even using the subnetting methods already discussed, the potential to waste IP addresses still exists. If you review the solution in the first example, you'll notice several thousand IP addresses are wasted. Because the solution had to use the same subnet mask for all segments, you were bottlenecked into an inefficient solution.

Variable-length subnet masking (VLSM) enables each subnet to have its own unique subnet mask. This means a network is not locked into a fixed maximum number of networks with a fixed maximum number of hosts. This leads to more efficient use of an organization's IP address space.

The use of VLSM depends on a routing protocol that contains information about the subnet mask for each route. If the subnet mask is not included in the routing protocol, as is the case with RIP version 1, then you must use the same subnet mask for each network segment.

A VLSM Routing Example

VLSM is a better method of subnetting for most networking solutions. Let's say, for example, that a company with offices in Toronto, Minneapolis, and Seattle wants to implement the private network address 172.30.0.0, a Class B address. In each city, there are four offices. The largest office on each segment will have no more than 1,500 hosts. Within each office, several departments need to maintain separate pools of IP addresses (see Figure 5.8).

FIGURE 5.8

Another sample network.

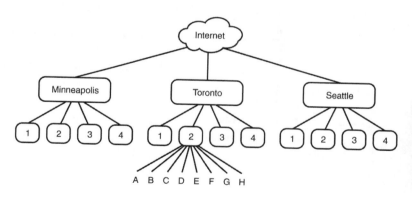

With VLSM, the initial four questions for determining which subnet mask to use become the following:

- How many total subnets does this level need today?
- How many total subnets will this level need in the future?
- How many hosts are on this level's largest subnet today?
- How many hosts will there be on this level's largest subnet in the future?

These questions must be answered at each level of the network design. Using Figure 5.8, you can see that the top hierarchy level currently requires three subnetworks, one for each of the three cities. If you use a 255.255.224.0 subnet mask at this level, it provides six networks of 8,190 hosts. This initial network mask leaves some room for growth. You have three additional networks available, and even if all four offices in a city grew to the maximum of 1,500 hosts, you still have around 2,190 host IP addresses available.

The pools of IP addresses for this solution are shown in Table 5.9.

TABLE 5.9 Network Addressing for 172.30.0.0/19

Increment Value	Network Address	Beginning Address	Ending Address	Broadcast Address
n	172.30.n.0	172.30.n.1	172.30.n_{next}–1.254	172.30.n_{next}–1.255
0	n/a	n/a	n/a	n/a
32	172.30.32.0	172.30.32.1	172.30.63.254	172.30.63.255
64	172.30.64.0	172.30.64.1	172.30.95.254	172.30.95.255
96	172.30.96.0	172.30.96.1	172.30.127.254	172.30.127.255
128	172.30.128.0	172.30.128.1	172.30.159.254	172.30.159.255
160	172.30.160.0	172.30.160.1	172.30.191.254	172.30.191.255
192	172.30.192.0	172.30.192.1	172.30.223.254	172.30.223.255
224	n/a	n/a	n/a	n/a

Figure 5.9 shows how these pools of IP addresses could be deployed to each of the three networks.

FIGURE 5.9

Assigning network addresses to the three cities.

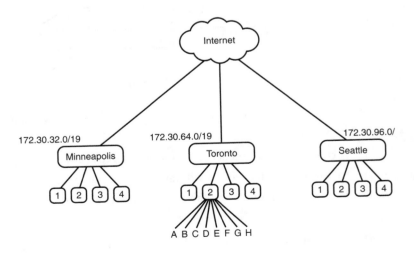

Looking specifically at Toronto, you know you need to provide four network segments within this city. Again, you can use two bits for the subnet mask. The issue now, however, is that this is an additional two bits from the host portion of the address. This leads to using a subnet mask of 255.255.248.0 for each of these four network segments.

Note

Some of you may notice that we are using two bits to create four network segments. This is because VLSM requires zero subnetting. This means that the subnets of 00 and 11 are allowed.

The pools of IP addresses for each of these segments are shown in Table 5.10.

TABLE 5.10   Network Addressing for 172.30.64.0/21

Increment Value	Network Address	Beginning Address	Ending Address	Broadcast Address
n	172.30.n.0	172.30.n.1	$172.30.n_{next}-1.254$	$172.30.n_{next}-1.255$
64	172.30.64.0	172.30.64.1	172.30.71.254	172.30.71.255
72	172.30.72.0	172.30.72.1	172.30.79.254	172.30.79.255
80	172.30.80.0	172.30.80.1	172.30.87.254	172.30.87.255
88	172.30.88.0	172.30.88.1	172.30.95.254	172.30.95.255
~~96~~	n/a	n/a	n/a	n/a

If the pool of IP addresses assigned to the downtown office is 172.30.64.0/21, the final step is to determine how to allocate a pool of addresses to each department. If you have eight separate departments that require a separate pool of IP addresses, you need to use another 3 bits of the host portion of the address. Table 5.11 shows the pools of IP addresses you can create using an additional three bits.

5

TABLE 5.11   Network Addressing for 172.30.64.0/24

Increment Value	Network Address	Beginning Address	Ending Address	Broadcast Address
n	172.30.n.0	172.30.n.1	172.30.n.254	172.30.n.255
64	172.30.64.0	172.30.64.1	172.30.64.254	172.30.64.255
65	172.30.65.0	172.30.65.1	172.30.65.254	172.30.65.255
66	172.30.66.0	172.30.66.1	172.30.66.254	172.30.66.255

TABLE 5.11   continued

Increment Value	Network Address	Beginning Address	Ending Address	Broadcast Address
67	172.30.67.0	172.30.67.1	172.30.67.254	172.30.67.255
68	172.30.68.0	172.30.68.1	172.30.68.254	172.30.68.255
69	172.30.69.0	172.30.69.1	172.30.69.254	172.30.69.255
70	172.30.70.0	172.30.70.1	172.30.70.254	172.30.70.255
71	172.30.71.0	172.30.71.1	172.30.71.254	172.30.71.255

This provides eight pools of 254 addresses. As long as each subnet requires no more than 254 host addresses, this is a potential network solution at each office.

Conditions That Must Exist for VLSM to Occur

If you are considering implementing VLSM for your network, the following conditions must exist for a successful implementation:

- The routing protocol must support advertising of a route's subnet mask. (Routing protocols are discussed in Day 8, "Configuring NetBIOS Name Servers.")

- The routing algorithm must be based on the longest match route. In the preceding example, the following routes could have been used to describe a department in the Toronto downtown office (see Figure 5.10).

FIGURE 5.10

Choosing the longest match route to 172.30.65.17.

```
172.30.0.0/16   = 10101100 00011110 01000000 00000000
172.30.64.0/19  = 10101100 00011110 01000000 00000000
172.30.64.0/21  = 10101100 00011110 01000000 00000000
172.30.65.0/24  = 10101100 00011110 01000001 00000000
```

If you are looking for the host 172.30.65.17, all four routes can be used to refer to the host. The final route, however, is the longest match for this address. The *longest match route* is much more specific and should be selected over all other routes when a routing algorithm is determining the path to that network.

- For efficient routing tables, address pools must be assigned to match the physical topology. The preceding example illustrated that if someone at a partner office wants to reach the Toronto downtown office, the initial route for the 172.30.0.0

network reaches the boundary router for the organization. The routing table on this router recognizes that the route is for a client in the Toronto office and routes it to the 172.30.64.0/19 network. From there, it further distinguishes that it is from the downtown office and routes it to the 172.30.64.0/21 network. Finally, it is distributed to the third-floor network at 172.30.66.0/24.

Note

> The 172.30.0.0/16 network is a private network address, and is not accessible from the Internet. This example assumes that the partner organization is also connected to the company's private network. For example, the partner may be connected to the corporation's private network using a leased line.

Each of the preceding prerequisites must be met for VLSM to be implemented on the network. Of these prerequisites, the last one requires the most thought and planning when you design your network.

Classless Inter-Domain Routing

RFC 1517-1520 The exponential growth of the Internet has raised concerns about the availability of IP addresses and the capability of the Internet to handle the associated routing tables. In response to these concerns, the concept of Classless Inter-Domain Routing (CIDR) was developed. The following are features of CIDR:

- CIDR removes the concept of Class A, Class B, and Class C addresses. Every address is simply an address that contains network and host portions. There is not a predefined subnet mask based on the first bits of the address.

- CIDR supports *route aggregation*. A single route can represent the address space of thousands of actual routes. Using a single routing entry to represent several networks can help keep the Internet backbone routing tables smaller and more efficient.

By removing the limitations of Class A, B, and C addresses, a pool of addresses can be formed using any contiguous pool of IP addresses. Any arbitrary-sized network can be created to fit an organization's networking needs.

For CIDR to be implemented, all routers must be able to advertise both the network address and the subnet mask for the network. This network mask determines what bits represent the network.

5

> **What About Supernetting?**
> Sometimes, CIDR is referred to as *supernetting*. The basic concept is still that you can create collections of addresses that usually are separate networks.

Table 5.12 shows some common CIDR address blocks that can be created.

TABLE 5.12   Common CIDR Block Ranges

Network Prefix Length	Dotted Decimal Representation	Hosts per Segment	Class B Network Complement	Class C Network Complement
/13	255.248.0.0	524,286	8 Bs	2048 Cs
/14	255.252.0.0	262,142	4 Bs	1024 Cs
/15	255.254.0.0	131,070	2 Bs	512 Cs
/16	255.255.0.0	65,534	n/a	256 Cs
/17	255.255.128.0	32,766	n/a	128 Cs
/18	255.255.192.0	16,382	n/a	64 Cs
/19	255.255.224.0	8,190	n/a	32 Cs
/20	255.255.240.0	4,094	n/a	16 Cs
/21	255.255.248.0	2,046	n/a	8 Cs
/22	255.255.252.0	1,022	n/a	4 Cs
/23	255.255.254.0	510	n/a	2 Cs

The biggest concern a network administrator should have with CIDR addressing is that several TCP/IP implementations do not allow a subnet mask to be assigned if it is shorter than the default subnet mask. If *every* host in the network does not support this, you cannot deploy a CIDR-based network.

The same methods are used to calculate CIDR addressing as to calculate VLSM addressing. The most important attribute used when choosing a CIDR addressing pool, however, is the number of hosts required per segment. If the number of hosts required per segment is greater than 254, a network can be assigned a supernet of Class C addresses rather than a Class B address. This generally results in a more efficient deployment of IP addresses.

Applying What You Have Learned

The best way to master subnet masking is to work through several subnetting examples. The questions for this chapter review subnetting examples for Class A, Class B, and Class C addresses. The answers can be found in Appendix B, "Test Your Knowledge: Answers."

Test Your Knowledge

1. Assuming you use the 10.0.0.0/8 network, how many bits do you need to use from the host portion of the address to create 115 subnets?

2. What extended network prefix must be used for the subnetwork example?

3. What are the network address, broadcast address, and pool of IP addresses for the third subnet?

   Network address =

   Broadcast address =

   Beginning address =

   Ending address =

4. Assuming you use the 172.30.0.0/16 network address, how many bits do you need to use from the host portion of the address to create 14 subnets?

5. What extended network prefix must be used for the subnetwork example?

6. What are the network address, broadcast address, and pool of IP addresses for the third subnet?

   Network address =

   Broadcast address =

   Beginning address =

   Ending address =

7. Assuming you use the 192.168.23.0/24 network address, how many bits do you need to use from the host portion of the address to provide for 10 subnets?

8. How many hosts does this provide for each subnet?

9. Assuming you use the 192.168.23.0/24 network address, complete the following table of addresses for all available network addresses:

5

Network Address	Beginning Address	Ending Address	Broadcast Address

10. For the following host IP addresses, determine the network address and broadcast address for the network in which they participate:

- 172.16.67.16 with subnet mask 255.255.240.0
- 192.168.54.76 with subnet mask 255.255.255.224
- 157.76.2.198 with subnet mask 255.255.255.128

Figure 5.11 shows a network that requires a variable-length subnet mask solution. You want to create a solution that does not waste IP addresses and that provides a routing solution that matches the topology.

FIGURE 5.11

Design a VLSM solution for this network.

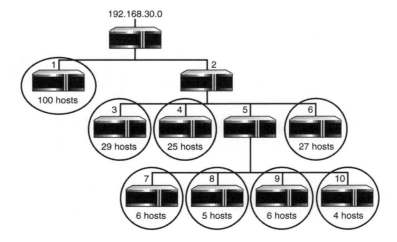

Answer the following questions about this network:

11. What network address can be used for the subnetwork #1?

    ____.____.____.____/____

12. Identify the network addresses that can be used for subnetwork #3, subnetwork #4, and subnetwork #6.

13. What are the broadcast addresses for subnetworks 7, 8, 9, and 10?

The following questions review Classless Inter-Domain Routing. Remember that the key to performing CIDR is to not apply the default subnet mask to the IP address. You are now taking bits from the network address rather than from the host portion of the address.

14. What network address can be used to aggregate the following pool of network addresses?

    198.163.32.0/24198.163.33.0/24

    198.163.34.0/24198.163.35.0/24

    198.163.36.0/24198.163.37.0/24

    198.163.38.0/24198.163.39.0/24

15. For the following CIDR networks, complete the missing information for each network address.

    Beginning Address: 200.200.64.1
    Ending Address: ____.____.____.____
    Subnet Mask: 255.255.252.0

    Beginning Address: ____.____.____.____
    Ending Address: 172.39.255.254
    Subnet Mask: 255.248.0.0

    Beginning Address: 198.16.0.1
    Ending Address: 198.31.255.254
    Subnet Mask: ____.____.____.____

Preview of Day 6

Tomorrow, you learn how TCP/IP allows logical names to represent IP addresses on a network. Specifically, tomorrow's material looks at the two most common naming services used in TCP/IP networks: host names using the Domain Name System (DNS) and NetBIOS naming.

We look at how name resolution is performed so that ultimately, a logical name such as www.komarconsulting.com is resolved to an IP address, and then resolved to a MAC address on the subnet where the www.komarconsulting.com host resides.

DAY 6

Resolution of IP Addresses and Logical Names

In the preceding days, you examined the actual addressing scheme used in a TCP/IP network. Today's material reviews two of the primary methods used to apply logical names to these IP addresses: hostnames and NetBIOS names.

These two methods make it easier for users to access resources, such as servers, workstations, and other devices, on a TCP/IP network. In your network system, you can apply one or both of these resolution methods.

In the last few years, dynamic updates have been introduced to domain name servers to allow DNS clients to automatically send updates of their DNS information to the DNS server, rather than requiring the DNS administrator to manually configure updates.

Today's material also looks at some of the key text files that can be configured in a TCP/IP environment. You will learn the specific parameters that can be set and the syntax within each file.

Resolving IP Addresses to MAC Addresses

For communication to take place between two computers, the computers' network cards must be able to locate each other. In a TCP/IP network, each host is assigned an IP address to represent that host on the network. As you saw in Day 4, "Core Protocols of the TCP/IP Suite," Address Resolution Protocol (ARP) is used to resolve an IP address to the MAC address of the network card. Remember, even though you are now considering assigning logical names to a host, this step *must* occur for actual communications to take place.

Resolving Logical Names to IP Addresses

Instead of working with IP addresses to locate hostnames, it is preferable to use logical names. The following name-resolution methods can be performed on a TCP/IP network:

- Hostname resolution
- NetBIOS name resolution

> **Pick a Name, Any Name**
>
> There are no specific rules for naming schemes when naming the devices on your network. For example, one of my clients used *The Simpsons* cartoon as the basis for his naming scheme. Every computer or network device was named after a character in *The Simpsons*. Other clients named their computers after Greek mythological characters.

Actual use of these logical names takes place in the application level of the TCP/IP layer model (see Figure 6.1).

FIGURE 6.1

Resolving logical namesto MAC addresses.

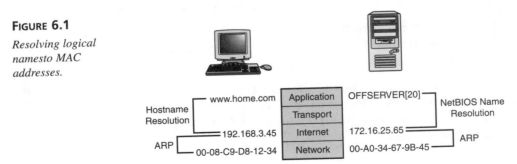

As you can see, either hostname resolution or NetBIOS name resolution is used to resolve the logical name to an IP address. The resolution method used depends entirely on the application that needs to resolve the name. NetBIOS applications use NetBIOS name resolution; Winsock applications use hostname resolution.

After the IP address has been determined for the logical name, ARP is used to determine the actual MAC address. Remember from Day 4, "Core Protocols of the TCP/IP Suite," that the MAC address resolved by ARP depends on whether the destination host is on a local or remote network. If the destination is on the same network as the source, ARP resolves the actual MAC address of the destination host. If the destination host is on a remote network, ARP finds the MAC address of the router used to send the data to the remote network. The frame is transmitted to the selected router, which forwards it to the destination host's network.

The following sections examine the specific actions taken in both hostname resolution and in NetBIOS name resolution.

Hostname Resolution

Hostname resolution has been used since the beginning of the Internet. Originally, all information was stored in a centralized HOSTS.TXT file. Any new hosts on the Internet registered their hostnames and IP addresses into this central file maintained by the Network Information Center.

All participating hosts on the Internet downloaded this centralized file to their own systems. As the Internet grew, the need to move away from this centralized file became evident. The following problems were noticed:

- Updates occurred on a daily basis because of the increased size of the Internet.
- The Stanford Research Institute's network—where the HOSTS.TXT file existed—became a bottleneck for the Internet.
- A hostname could not be duplicated *anywhere* on the Internet because of the flat nature of the name space.
- Name updates took a few days to become visible to the Internet as a whole.

The suggested solutions all advised that the new name-resolution method be hierarchical in design. The other key suggestion was that the database be distributed in nature rather than centralized. This way, each organization could maintain its own hostnames.

The Domain Name Space

The *domain name space* is a tree-like structure representing all the domains that make up the name space for the Internet. The *root domain* is at the top of the tree (see Figure 6.2).

6

FIGURE **6.2**

*The domain name
space.*

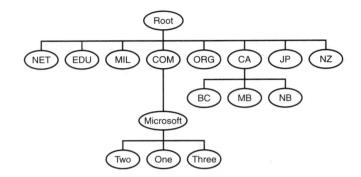

The root domain does not have an actual text label; it is expressed using a period (.).

Below the root domain are the top-level domains. There are two variations of top-level domains. In the first variation, the top-level domains represent types of organizations. The second variation uses a two-digit code to represent the country in which an organization is located. Table 6.1 shows the current top-level domains.

TABLE 6.1   Top-Level Domain Names

Name	Description
com	Commercial organizations
edu	Educational institutions and universities
org	Not-for-profit organizations
net	Network facilities
gov	U.S. non-military government organizations
mil	U.S. Military government organizations
num	Phone numbers
arpa	Reverse lookup domains
xx	Two-digit country codes (such as CA for Canada, NZ for New Zealand, and TW for Taiwan)
biz*	Businesses
info*	General information
aero*	Aviation related businesses
pro*	Professionals
coop*	Cooperatives

TABLE 6.1 continued

Name	Description
name*	Individuals
museum*	Museums

* These generic top-level domains have been added because of the need to expand the domain name space. Most organizations desire a COM top-level domain name and find that their first few choices are already taken. This should provide additional expansion starting in late 2001.

Second-level domains, which contain hosts and other subdomains, exist below the top-level domains. Figure 6.2 shows four second-level domains. Microsoft is an example of an organization that has registered a second-level domain in the COM top-level domain. MB, BC, and AB represent a separation technique used by the US and CA country domains; in this case, they represent individual provinces within Canada. MB stands for Manitoba, BC stands for British Columbia, and AB stands for Alberta. This provides a complete geographic breakdown within a country's top-level domain.

One represents a subdomain below the Microsoft.com second-level domain. If you want to view the Web pages of a Web server in the One domain, type `www.one.microsoft.com`—the uniform resource locator (URL) for the site—in a browser. A hostname that includes its full domain name path is called a fully qualified domain name (FQDN). If you are sitting at another host in the `one.microsoft.com` domain, you can refer to the server using just its hostname, www. The FQDN makes sure the application knows that the full path to the host is specified in the URL.

The `one.microsoft.com` Site

The `one.microsoft.com` domain is used for hosting certified professional information. For example, if you are a Microsoft Certified Professional (MCP), you can review program information by browsing `https://partnering.one.microsoft.com/mcp` where the name of the Web server is `partnering` and it is in the domain `one.microsoft.com`.

Acquiring a Second-Level Domain

You cannot use just any second-level domain name on the Internet. You must register your domain name with InterNIC. One site you can visit to search for available domain names and register a domain name is `http://www.register.com/`. Be prepared to perform some searches to determine whether the name you want is already taken.

6

Hostname Resolution Process

The process used when a computer needs to resolve a hostname to an IP address is shown in Figure 6.3.

FIGURE 6.3

The hostname resolution process.

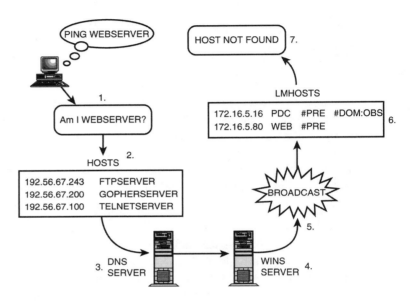

1. Is the name you are trying to resolve the name of the host you are working on?

2. Is the name you are trying to query located in the HOSTS file? (The HOSTS file is discussed in detail later today.)

3. Does the DNS server have an entry for this host?

Resolving Hostnames for Microsoft Clients

Microsoft clients have access to additional methods for resolving hostnames because of their dependence on NetBIOS names. Some NetBIOS name-resolution methods also can be used to resolve a hostname. These additional resolution steps start at Step 4. Non-Microsoft clients deliver a host-not-found message if the name is not resolved in the first three steps.

4. Is the hostname registered with the Windows Internet Name Service (WINS) server?

Note A WINS server is Microsoft's implementation of a NetBIOS name server, which maintains a database that stores NetBIOS name to IP address mappings.

5. Can the hostname be resolved using a local network broadcast?

6. Is the hostname included in the LMHOSTS file? (The LMHOSTS file is discussed in detail later today.)

If none of these resolution methods finds an IP address for the target hostname, the application returns an error message stating that the hostname could not be found. This is Step 7 in Figure 6.3.

Roles in the Domain Name Space (DNS) System

Within the domain name space system, the following key components are involved in the name-resolution process:

- The domain name space
- Resolvers
- Name servers

The domain name space (as previously discussed) is the distributed, hierarchical database that contains all hostnames to IP addresses on the Internet. This database resolves the requested hostname to an IP address (or vice versa).

Resolvers are the actual clients attempting to resolve a hostname to an IP address. The resolver functionality either is built in to the calling application or is running on the host computer as part of the TCP/IP protocol stack.

Name servers are the physical hosts that accept the requests from the DNS resolvers and that return the IP address for the requested hostname, or the answer to the query posed by a DNS resolver. Depending on the resolution method configured, the name server returns the IP address corresponding to a hostname, the hostname corresponding to an IP address, a response stating that the hostname is unknown, or a referral to another name server that can resolve the request.

The following roles can be played by each name server:

- Primary name server
- Secondary name server
- Master name server
- Caching-only name server

6

Primary Name Server

A *primary name server* manages a zone of information. A zone encompasses the part of the domain name space for which the particular name server is responsible. The zone files are stored locally on the primary name server, and all modifications to these zone files should be performed only at this server. A primary name server's zone of authority can encompass more than one domain. It can manage subdomains below a specific domain, or it can host the zone files for several different second-level domains (see Figure 6.4).

FIGURE 6.4

Name server's zones of authority.

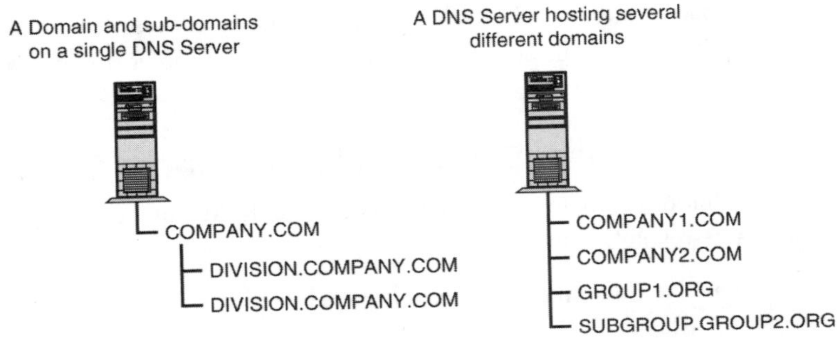

A Domain and sub-domains on a single DNS Server

- COMPANY.COM
  - DIVISION.COMPANY.COM
  - DIVISION.COMPANY.COM

A DNS Server hosting several different domains

- COMPANY1.COM
- COMPANY2.COM
- GROUP1.ORG
- SUBGROUP.GROUP2.ORG

Zone files do not necessarily map on a one-to-one basis to domain names. For example, Figure 6.5 shows a possible zone distribution for the company `xyz.com` with subdomains `research`, `marketing`, and `sales`. Although it is possible to create a single zone to hold all four domains (`xyz.com`, `research.xyz.com`, `marketing.xyz.com`, and `sales.xyz.com`), administration may require the distribution shown in Figure 6.5.

Secondary Name Server

A *secondary name server* obtains its zone information from another name server that has a copy of the zone file. The other name server could be another secondary name server, or it could be a primary name server. The actual transmission of the zone information is called a *zone transfer*.

The following are some reasons that secondary name servers are implemented:

- An additional name server with the same zone data can help balance traffic between the two servers.
- An additional name server can be located at a remote site to increase the speed of hostname resolution for the resolvers at that remote site.

- An additional name server for a zone can provide fault tolerance in case one of the name servers is down.

- A secondary name server is required if you are registering your domain with InterNIC.

FIGURE 6.5

Distributing zone files for the xyz.com *domain.*

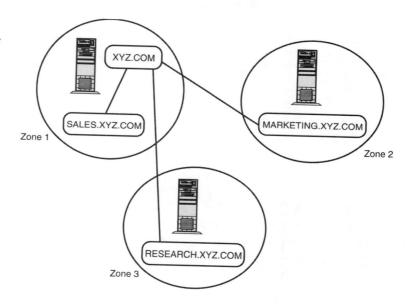

Zone 1
XYZ.COM
SALES.XYZ.COM
MARKETING.XYZ.COM
Zone 2
RESEARCH.XYZ.COM
Zone 3

Secondary name servers are sometimes referred to as Slave name servers because they only store copies of the original zone data files. No updates are performed on the zone files stored on a secondary name server.

Master Name Server

A *Master name server* is a name server that transfers its zone files to a secondary name server. Although you might assume that only primary name servers function as Master servers, it also is possible for a secondary name server to function as a Master server. This generally occurs when network links dictate the flow of traffic. Figure 6.6 shows a network in which it might be better for a secondary name server to function as a Master name server.

A secondary name server must be configured with the IP address of its Master name server. When the secondary name server boots, it communicates with its configured Master name server and initiates a zone transfer of the DNS data.

In addition, the primary name server can be secured by configuring what IP addresses can request zone transfers. This prevents an attacker from determining your network

6

topology by requesting a zone transfer from an unauthorized DNS secondary name server.

FIGURE 6.6

A scenario in which a secondary name server functions as a Master name server.

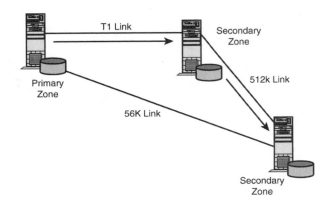

Caching-Only Name Server

A *caching-only name server* does not store any zone data file information locally. Whenever a host queries a caching-only server, it makes the request on behalf of the resolver, caches the result, and returns the IP address for the requested host to the resolver. If another host makes the same request, the caching-only server uses its cached information to fulfill the request.

This implementation of DNS is useful for a slow WAN link. Instead of having a secondary name server that requires that an entire zone transfer be sent to it regularly, a caching-only server can be located at the remote location. Only actual requests and responses are sent to the caching-only server. Frequently visited locations are stored in cache and do not require WAN traffic for resolution.

All in One

A DNS Server can actually play all roles in your DNS environment. For one zone, say example.com, your DNS server may be the primary name server and all updates to the zone are recorded at that DNS Server.

In addition, the DNS server may function as a secondary DNS server for the komarconsulting.com zone.

Finally, through the use of forwarders, where your DNS server forwards unresolved DNS queries to another DNS server, your DNS server may cache results for other domains, such as Microsoft.com to increase performance for DNS resolvers.

Microsoft's Active Directory Integrated Zones

In Windows 2000 and Windows .NET Server, a Microsoft DNS server can store its zone data in Active Directory, rather than in text files as shown in Figure 6.7.

FIGURE 6.7

Active Directory-integrated zones store data in the domain naming context.

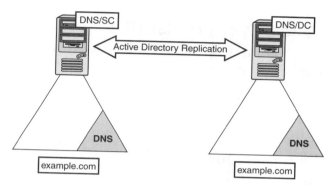

The following advantages are gained by using this method:

- DNS updates can be written at any of the DNS servers hosting the Active Directory-integrated zone. All DNS servers are write-enabled, and the updates are replicated using Active Directory replication.

- A separate DNS zone transfer topology does not have to be developed. All DNS information is replicated to domain controllers in the domain using Active Directory replication.

- DNS updates can be secured using Active Directory permissions. If DNS dynamic updates, discussed later in the chapter, are enabled, Active Directory-integrated zones can prevent the "hijacking" of a DNS resource record by defining permissions that only the computer that initially registered the DNS resource record can modify the resource record.

The Active Directory-integrated zone is fully interoperable with DNS servers that implement secondary zones, and can act as a Master zone for a secondary name server.

In fact, because the Active Directory-integrated zone is stored within the domain partition, secondary name servers must be used to make the information in the zone available at other DNS servers located in different domains in the forest.

6

Note

Windows .NET Server introduces a new partition, known as an application partition, that works around this issue. A writable copy of an application partition can be hosted at any designated domain controller in the forest. A DNS administrator can designate which domain controllers in the forest will host the application partition.

Query Types Under DNS

The following types of queries can be requested by a resolver when it queries a name server:

- Recursive
- Iterative
- Reverse

Recursive Queries

In a *recursive query*, the designated name server must either respond with the requested hostname's IP address or return an error. Many times, the name server changes its role to be a resolver and asks its configured name server to find the hostname's IP address (see Figure 6.8).

Figure 6.8

Performing a recursive DNS query through a firewall.

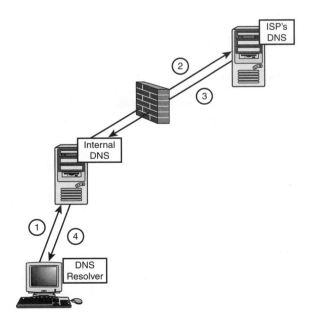

For example, the following process can take place as the DNS resolver attempts to resolve the IP address of the host named www.microsoft.com.

1. The DNS resolver makes a recursive query to the internal DNS server, requesting the IP address for www.microsoft.com.

2. The internal DNS server, being unable to resolve the query, performs a recursive query to the ISP's DNS server. The ISP's DNS server is selected because it is configured as a forwarder for the internal DNS server.

3. The ISP's DNS server returns the IP address for www.microsoft.com to the internal DNS server. The internal DNS server adds the www.microsoft.com hostname and the corresponding IP address to its cache.

Note

> There may be additional name resolution processes that take place at the ISP's DNS server in its attempt to resolve the IP address for www.microsoft.com.

4. The internal DNS server returns the IP address to the calling DNS resolver.

This configuration is useful for a local network located behind a firewall on the Internet. In this case, it is necessary to configure the firewall to allow the internal DNS server to forward DNS queries to the company's Internet Service Provider's DNS Server. The internal DNS resolvers cannot make queries to any DNS Servers located beyond the firewall. The only computer that can *forward* queries to the exterior network is the internal DNS Server. Using a recursive query, the internal DNS Server can pass the resolver's request to the ISP's DNS server and can provide a response to the IP address of the desired host.

Firewall Configuration

The firewall must be configured to only allow the internal DNS server to forward DNS queries to the ISP's DNS server. All other clients on the internal network must be blocked to prevent queries being sent to other DNS servers on the Internet.

6

Iterative Queries

In an iterative query, the queried name server only has to provide its best answer to the DNS resolver. The response could be the actual IP address of the requested host, a name-could-not-be-resolved error, or a referral to a different DNS server that might provide the IP address for the requested hostname (see Figure 6.9).

Figure 6.9

An iterative DNS query.

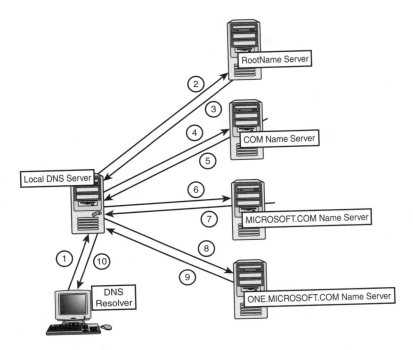

Figure 6.9 actually shows a combination of recursive and iterative queries. Follow these steps to resolve the name `partnering.one.microsoft.com`:

1. The DNS resolver makes a recursive query to its DNS server, requesting the IP address for `partnering.one.microsoft.com`.

2. The DNS server, not having the result in its DNS cache, does not have a forwarder configured to perform another recursive query. Instead, it sends an iterative name query to a root name server for `partnering.one.microsoft.com`.

Internet Root Name Servers

ICANN maintains 13 root servers that are spread around the world. The 13 servers are mirrors that contain the same information. This information is the IP addresses of all top-level domain registries. When a request is sent to a root DNS server, the response will direct the querying DNS server to contact the required top-level domain DNS server.

---

3. The root name server returns to the local name server the IP address of a COM top-level domain server to try next.

4. The local name server sends another iterative request to the COM name server, asking it to resolve `partnering.one.microsoft.com`.

5. The COM name server responds with the IP address of the `microsoft.com` authoritative name server.

6. The local name server sends another iterative query to the `microsoft.com` name server, asking it for the IP address of `partnering.one.microsoft.com`.

7. Assuming that the `one.microsoft.com` subdomain is stored in a separate zone file on another name server, the `microsoft.com` name server responds with the IP address of the `one.microsoft.com` authoritative name server.

8. The local name server sends another iterative query to the `one.microsoft.com` name server, requesting the IP address of `partnering.one.microsoft.com`.

9. The `one.microsoft.com` name server responds with the IP address `partnering.one.microsoft.com`. If the name does not exist in this domain, it returns an invalid hostname response at this point.

10. The local name server first caches the IP address for `partnering.one.microsoft.com` and the IP addresses of any intermediate name servers used in the resolution process. After it has added the hostname and corresponding IP address to cache, it returns the IP address to the calling DNS resolver.

Reverse Queries

A Reverse query occurs when you attempt to find the associated fully qualified domain name for an IP address. Rather than trying to determine the IP address for a given hostname, you are trying to find the hostname for a specific IP address.

This common task is performed by network security analysts when they try to resolve the IP address of a host in a security log to a hostname on the Internet.

This also is commonly used when setting rules on a firewall to restrict access to specific sites. If a rule has been established that network users should not be granted access to `www.badstuff.com`, the firewall also can be configured to perform reverse lookups. This prevents users from typing in the address `192.168.5.67` and circumventing the rule to block access.

Performance Tuning for DNS

A key performance factor for a DNS server is the capability to cache recently resolved hostnames. When a DNS server resolves a hostname for a resolver, it places the resolved hostname into its cache. The next time that hostname is queried, instead of going through the process of resolving that same name, the IP address can be returned from the cache.

6

This capability is based on the Time-To-Live (TTL) field in a DNS reply message. The TTL field designates when the DNS record should be removed from the cache of a DNS name server.

The TTL field is honored when a record is resolved from another name server's cache. Figure 6.10 shows how the TTL field is honored during a DNS resolution process.

FIGURE 6.10

DNS servers honor the TTL field when resolving a hostname.

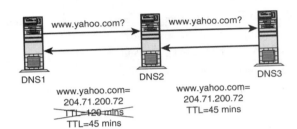

DNS1 has forwarded a DNS query to DNS2. DNS2 has forwarded the DNS query to DNS3. DNS3 was able to resolve www.yahoo.com to the address 204.71.200.74. It also returns that the TTL for this address is 45 minutes. When DNS2 adds the hostname/IP address combination to its cache, it also sets the TTL to 45 minutes, even though its default TTL for all records is 120 minutes. It does so because DNS3 can only guarantee this result for another 45 minutes. The same holds true when DNS1 adds the hostname/IP address combination to its cache. Configuring the TTL for a zone is covered tomorrow (Day 7, "Configuring Domain Name Servers").

Improving DNS with Dynamic Updates

RFC 2136 The biggest issue faced by DNS administrators is the fact that DNS until recently only supported manual updates to the DNS zone files. Although manual updates ensure security, by requiring appropriate rights to modify the zone file, with ever changing networks the updates rarely were modified in a timely fashion.

DNS Dynamic updates allow a host to register DNS resource records dynamically with their configured DNS server. When a change is made to IP address information, the host can update its host (A), Pointer (PTR), or related service locator (SRV) resource records dynamically with the DNS server.

DNS UPDATE Message Header Format

A DNS UPDATE message uses the message header format shown in Figure 6.11.

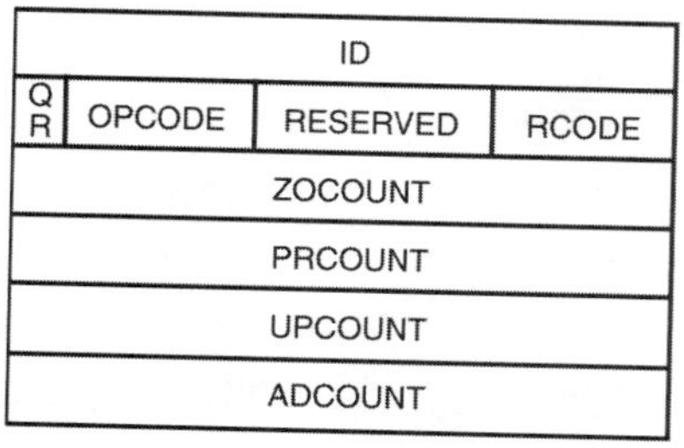

FIGURE 6.11

DNS UPDATE *message format.*

ID			
Q R	OPCODE	RESERVED	RCODE
ZOCOUNT			
PRCOUNT			
UPCOUNT			
ADCOUNT			

The following fields are included in the DNS UPDATE message header:

- **ID.** This field is a 16-bit identifier generated by the entity that generates the DNS UPDATE message. An example of this might be a DHCP server or the host that supports dynamic update. This identifier is used by the requestor to match a reply from the DNS server to an outstanding request.

- **QR.** This is a 1-bit field that specifies whether the message is a query (0) or a response (1).

- **OPCODE.** This is a 4-bit field that specifies the operation to be performed by the DNS message. For an UPDATE message, this value is set to 5.

- **RESERVED.** This 7-bit field is reserved for future use and should be set to a value of all zeros.

- **RCODE.** This field is used in DNS UPDATE response messages. Acceptable values are listed in Table 6.2.

TABLE 6.2   Response Code Options

Code	Value	Description
NOERROR	0	No error condition exists.
FORMERR	1	The name server was unable to parse the requested data because of a format error.
SERVFAIL	2	The name server encountered an internal error during the processing of the request.
NXDOMAIN	3	The name being updated does not exist.
NOTIMP	4	The name server does not support the UPDATE feature.
REFUSED	5	The name server refused to perform the requested operation for a policy or security reason.
YXDOMAIN	6	A resource record already exists for the name being added.
YXRRSET	7	A resource record set that should not exist does exist.

6

TABLE 6.2 continued

Code	Value	Description
NXRRSET	8	A resource record set that should exist does not exist.
NOTAUTH	9	The server is nonauthoritative for the zone named in the Zone section.
NOTZONE	10	A name used in the Prerequisite or Update section is not within the zone denoted in the Zone section.

- **ZOCOUNT.** This field contains the number of resource records in the Zone section.
- **PRCOUNT.** This field contains the number of resource records in the Prerequisites section.
- **UPCOUNT.** This field contains the number of resource records in the Update section.
- **ADCOUNT.** This field contains the number of resource records in the Additional Data section.

The Zone Section Format

Within each DNS message, a Zone section contains the DNS resource records to be updated. The format of the Zone section is shown in Figure 6.12.

FIGURE 6.12

The Zone section format.

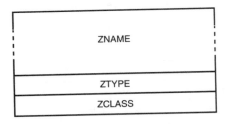

The following fields are included in the zone section of a DNS message:

- **ZNAME.** This field contains the zone name to be updated. All records must be in the same zone; therefore, there is only one zone record per DNS update message.
- **ZTYPE.** This field must contain the SOA record type. The SOA record is required, because updates can only be written at the primary name server referenced in the SOA record.
- **ZCLASS.** This field contains the zone's class. This field most likely contains IN to indicate that it is an Internet class resource record.

New Functionality Provided by Dynamic Updates

The following are two new features DDNS adds to the existing DNS service:

- Propagation of updates to the primary DNS server for a zone
- Notification of updates

Propagation of DNS Updates

DNS UPDATE messages provide a mechanism for the automatic addition, deletion, or modification of DNS resource records. With the implementation of IP addressing services such as DHCP, the possibility of new hosts requiring entries in DNS has grown dramatically. Previously, a manual update method could be used to maintain the DNS zone's Master file. The possibility of rapidly changing IP address assignments, however, increases the need for this automated process.

When a DNS UPDATE message is received by a DNS sever, a set of predefined prerequisites determines whether the UPDATE is processed. These prerequisites can include the following:

- **Resource record set exists (value independent).** At least one resource record with the specified NAME and TYPE must exist.

- **Resource record set exists (value dependent).** A set of resource records with the specified name and type must exist. In addition, this set of resource records must have the same members with the same resource data as the record set specified in the UPDATE message.

- **Resource record set does not exist.** No resource records with the specified NAME and TYPE can exist in the zone specified.

- **Name is in use.** At least one resource record with the specified NAME must exist in the specified zone.

- **Name is not in use.** No resource record of any type can exist in the zone.

Which prerequisite is used depends on the type of update performed on the resource records. An actual modification UPDATE, for example, cannot use the prerequisite "Name is not in use" because it depends on changing existing data. If the prerequisite is met, the processing of the UPDATE message can occur.

Updates are processed as follows:

1. If a system failure occurs during the processing of the Update section, the DNS server sends an RCODE message of SERVFAIL to the requestor. All updates applied to the zone so far are rolled back to their previous state.

6

2. Any Update resource records whose CLASS matches the ZCLASS are added to the zone. If a duplicate record exists, it is replaced with the updated data.

3. If the Update resource record's CLASS and TYPE are both set to ANY, all zone resource records with the same name are deleted. The only exception is when NAME is the same as ZNAME. These deletion requests are ignored.

4. If the Update resource record's CLASS is NONE, all zone resource records that match the Update resource record for the fields NAME, TYPE, RDATA, and RDLENGTH are deleted. Again, the only exception is when NAME is equal to ZNAME. This represents an SOA or name server (NS) record.

After the updates are complete, the zone's serial number in the SOA record should be incremented. Remember, the secondary zones use this value to determine whether updates have been performed on the Zone database.

Notification of Updates

RFC 1996   RFC 1996 addresses the issue of slow propagation of new and changed data in a DNS zone. It introduces a new transaction known as a DNS NOTIFY. This transaction enables Master servers to inform their Slave servers that a change has occurred in the zone.

This changes the typical zone update mechanism from a polling model to an interrupt model. This implementation only allows for changes to the zone's Start of Authority (SOA) record to be announced. This should meet the needs of DNS because any changes to resource records should be accompanied by a change to the zone's serial number stored in the SOA record. The serial number tracks when changes occur to any resource records. By changing the zone's serial number, you can indicate that resource records have been added, deleted, or modified.

NOTIFY messages can use either UDP or TCP for transport. (UDP is the preferred method.) TCP must be implemented when a firewall prevents UDP datagrams from being transmitted or when a resource record's modified size is too large for a UDP datagram.

When the DNS NOTIFY datagram is received, the Slave DNS server should behave as if it has reached its REFRESH interval. In other words, it immediately should query its Master DNS to determine whether the serial number stored in the SOA record is greater than the one currently stored in its zone files. If it is greater, a zone transfer should be initiated to update all the resource records for the zone.

If a DNS server functions as both a Slave and a Master DNS server, the NOTIFY protocol should be implemented so it only informs Slave servers after the SOA record has been updated. In other words, the Slave server should only function as a Master server using the DNS NOTIFY protocol after it has successfully completed its own zone transfer from its Master server.

Securing Dynamic Updates

The use of dynamic updates in your DNS environment can leave you with the possibility of rogue clients "hijacking" a DNS resource record from a server on your network.

There are two ways that DNS updates can be secured. The method you use depends on the DNS solution you implement at your organization:

- **BIND DNS Servers.** Berkeley Internet Daemon (BIND) DNS server, running version 8.0 or higher allows dynamic updates. At a BIND DNS server, you can restrict dynamic updates to only specific hosts, by using the {Allow-update <IP ADDRESS>;} option in the named.conf file for a specific zone. This entry only allows hosts from the specific IP address to perform dynamic updates.

Caution

Restricting updates to only specific IP addresses does not necessarily prevent the hijacking of IP addresses. For example, if you restrict dynamic updates to a DHCP server's IP address, it is still possible for two hosts to register with the DHCP server using the same hostname.

In this case, the first host's DNS resource record will be overwritten by the second host's, even though you restricted updates to the DHCP server. This is because both updates were performed by the DHCP server when the clients were assigned IP addresses at startup.

- **Windows 2000 and Windows .NET DNS Servers.** Microsoft implements secure dynamic updates when using Active Directory-integrated zones. Secure dynamic updates use the Microsoft security model to apply permissions to all DNS resource records. When a host adds a resource record to DNS using DNS dynamic update, the permissions for the resource record are set so that only that host can modify the contents of the resource record. If another host attempts to "hijack" the resource record, the attempt fails due to the permissions set on the resource record.

The alternative to hostname resolution is NetBIOS name resolution. NetBIOS name resolution is typically associated with Microsoft networks.

6

NetBIOS Name Resolution

The NetBIOS names method also is used on networks to apply logical names to computers and their services. The NetBIOS interface is an Application Programming

Interface that enables communications to take place between a client and a server computer using human names to represent each other. The following are services provided within NetBIOS:

- Name registration and release by clients
- Name resolution
- Session establishment and termination
- Support for reliable connection-oriented data transfer
- Support for connectionless datagram transfer

The NetBIOS names are restricted to 16 bytes in length. The first 15 bytes uniquely represent the NetBIOS resource on the network. The last byte represents the actual NetBIOS service that the NetBIOS resource is hosting. Each NetBIOS service has its own unique identifier that is used when registering the NetBIOS name.

Comparing NetBIOS Names to Socket Numbers

Both NetBIOS and Winsock have methods for identifying the applications and services running on a server or client. In NetBIOS, each service is assigned a NetBIOS name that includes a unique 16th character to represent that service. These service numbers are well known, and a client connects to the service using this NetBIOS name.

In Winsock, each service or application has a preconfigured port on which it listens for connections from clients. The clients know the port to which they should be connecting.

With both systems, the client also has a unique NetBIOS name or port that is used as its side of the communication system.

NetBIOS resources can include both unique names that can be registered only by a single computer and group names that can be registered by multiple computers. Table 6.3 lists some of the more common NetBIOS names.

TABLE 6.3   Common NetBIOS Names

Name	NetBIOS Suffix	Type	Description
Computername	00	Unique	Workstation service.
msbrowse	01	Unique	The Master browser for the segment uses this NetBIOS name to broadcast and receive domain announcements on a segment.

TABLE 6.3 continued

Name	NetBIOS Suffix	Type	Description
Computername	03	Unique	Messenger service requests for a specific computer name.
Username	03	Unique	Messenger service requests for a specific user name.
Computername	06	Unique	RAS server service.
Domainname	1B	Unique	Domain Master browser.
Domainname	1D	Unique	Master browser on a segment.
Computername	1F	Unique	NetDDE service.
Computername	20	Unique	Server service.
Computername	21	Unique	RAS client service.
Computername	BE	Unique	Network monitor agent.
Computername	BF	Unique	Network monitor application.
Domainname	00	Group	Domain or group membership.
Domainname	1C	Group	All domain controllers for a domain up to a maximum of 25 entries. The first entry always is the primary domain controller (PDC).
Domainname	1E	Group	Registered by all computers that participate in browser service elections.

For example, if my computer is named HELIX, is a member of the BKTRADERS domain, and I am logged on as BKOMAR, the NetBIOS names registered by my computer could include the following:

```
    Name                Type       Status
    - - - - - - - - - - - - - - - - - - - - - - - - - - - - - - -
    HELIX         <00>  UNIQUE     Registered
    BKTRADERS     <00>  GROUP      Registered
    HELIX         <20>  UNIQUE     Registered
    BKTRADERS     <1E>  GROUP      Registered
    BKTRADERS     <1D>  UNIQUE     Registered
    ..__MSBROWSE__.<01> GROUP      Registered
    HELIX         <03>  UNIQUE     Registered
    BKOMAR        <03>  UNIQUE     Registered
```

A NetBIOS client must be configured to determine how it resolves NetBIOS names on the network. The NetBIOS node type is the property that determines this. The following different configurations can be set:

6

- A B-node client (broadcast) is configured to use only broadcasts for NetBIOS transactions. If the target NetBIOS computer is not on the same network segment, communication probably will not take place.

- A P-node client (peer) is configured to only perform NetBIOS transactions with an NetBIOS name server (NBNS). The NBNS accepts the NetBIOS name registrations of all hosts configured to use the NBNS and stores them in an accessible database. If the NBNS does not have a record of the desired NetBIOS name, the client cannot connect to the desired host.

- An M-node client (mixed) first attempts to find the NetBIOS name on the network using a broadcast. If this fails, it then queries the configured NBNS to see whether it has a record of the NetBIOS name.

- An H-node client (hybrid) first attempts to resolve a NetBIOS name using a NBNS. If a record does not exist for the NetBIOS name on the NBNS, the client then resorts to a broadcast on the local network segment. This generally is the preferred configuration on a NetBIOS network because it reduces broadcast traffic yet enables a broadcast to take place if a NetBIOS name has not been registered on the NBNS.

Note

> Microsoft clients can use another NetBIOS name-resolution method known as enhanced B-node. A NetBIOS name is first resolved using a broadcast message. If this does not work, the Microsoft client checks a locally configured file named LMHOSTS to see whether an IP address is stored in the file for the desired NetBIOS name. The LMHOSTS file is discussed in the "TCP/IP Configuration Files" section later today.

NetBIOS Name-Resolution Process

NetBIOS name resolution is the process of resolving a NetBIOS name to an IP address. After the NetBIOS name has been resolved to an IP address, ARP enables the IP address to be translated to a MAC address.

The NetBIOS name-resolution process is shown in Figure 6.13. This process assumes the client is configured as an H-node client.

1. The first resolution attempt determines whether the NetBIOS name is a locally registered name. If it is, communication takes place using the localhost IP address (127.0.0.1) so that no network traffic is generated by the request.

2. The NetBIOS name cache is checked to see whether the NetBIOS name has been resolved recently. If found, the IP address related to the NetBIOS name is used.

FIGURE 6.13

The NetBIOS name-resolution process for an H-node client.

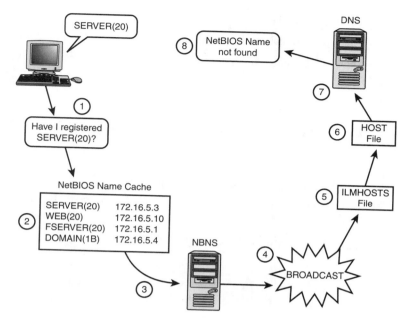

3. A request is sent to the client's configured NetBIOS name server (NBNS). This server accepts automatic registration of NetBIOS name/IP address combinations from its configured clients. If the name is found in the NBNS database, the IP address is returned to the calling client.

4. A local broadcast is issued, asking the client that has registered the desired NetBIOS name to respond with its IP address.

Non-Microsoft clients that use NetBIOS services cease their attempts to resolve a NetBIOS name at this point. Microsoft clients have access to additional methods for resolving NetBIOS names. These additional resolution steps start at Step 5.

5. The NetBIOS name could exist in the computer's LMHOSTS file. If found, the configured IP address is used.

6. The NetBIOS name could exist in the computer's local HOSTS file. If found, the configured IP address is used.

7. The client's configured DNS server is queried to determine whether a host record exists for the desired NetBIOS name. If it does, the IP address is returned to the calling client.

8. If all these methods fail to resolve the NetBIOS name to an IP address, an error message informs the calling client that the NetBIOS name could not be found.

6

Transactions in NetBIOS Networks

The following basic transactions take place with NetBIOS names:

- Name registrations
- Name discoveries
- Name releases

NetBIOS Name Registrations

NetBIOS name registration occurs whenever a NetBIOS host is started. Each NetBIOS name a host wants to register is either broadcast on the network or sent directly to the NBNS. (This depends on the NetBIOS node-type configuration.) If the name registration is for a unique NetBIOS name, the name cannot already be registered on the network. If it is, the registering host receives a not-acknowledged message.

The following four types of NetBIOS names can be registered with a NetBIOS name server:

- **Unique.** This name type can only be registered to a single IP address. If another host attempts to register this NetBIOS name, the registration is rejected with a not-acknowledged message.
- **Normal group.** This name type is not registered to a specific host or hosts. It simply states that the normal group exists on the network and is assigned the limited broadcast address of 255.255.255.255.
- **MultiHomed.** This single, unique name type stores multiple addresses. It indicates a host with multiple network cards bound to NetBIOS over TCP/IP. Each multihomed group name can contain a maximum of 25 IP addresses.
- **Domain name.** This NetBIOS name type includes as many as 25 IP addresses for a single NetBIOS name. It is used for hosts that all can deliver an identical service, such as logon authentication in a Windows NT domain.

NetBIOS Name Discoveries

NetBIOS name discoveries occur any time a NetBIOS client needs to resolve another NetBIOS name to an IP address. Depending on the NetBIOS node-type configuration, this name discovery either is sent to an NBNS or is issued as a local network broadcast. Either the NBNS or the host that owns the NetBIOS name responds.

NetBIOS Name Releases

NetBIOS name releases occur whenever a NetBIOS application or service for which a NetBIOS name has been registered is stopped. This occurs, for example, when a user logs off the network. When a user performs the logoff sequence, the NetBIOS name USERNAME[03] is released because the user no longer is logged on to the network. When the user logs on again, the NetBIOS name is registered at the IP address of the host on which he is working. The messenger service can continue to reach him, even if he logs on to a different computer.

NetBIOS Name Servers

NetBIOS name servers provide a registration location for NetBIOS clients. A NetBIOS client sends its configured NetBIOS names and IP address to its configured NetBIOS name server. The NetBIOS name server either enters the NetBIOS name/IP address combination into its database or returns a Negative Acknowledge message for the registration. When a Negative Acknowledge message is received, the client must evaluate the severity of this error. If the error is for a computer-name registration, the host halts all TCP/IP services because a duplicate computer name has been found on the network. If it is simply a username registration, the Negative Acknowledge message can be ignored. This is the case when a user is logged on to two or more hosts.

The advantage of a NetBIOS name server is that it can handle clients with dynamically assigned IP addresses. If a client receives a new IP address, the client sends a new NetBIOS name registration to register the new IP address. Alternatively, if dynamic DNS is implemented, the client can also update his host name registration with his configured DNS server.

Another advantage is the reduction in network traffic related to NetBIOS name services. Clients can send a directed packet to a NetBIOS name server when trying to resolve a NetBIOS name. This is much more efficient than using a local network broadcast that must be examined by all hosts on the network segment.

The most widely known implementation of a NetBIOS name server is Microsoft's Windows Internet Name Service (WINS). Configuration and troubleshooting of the WINS server are covered in Day 8's material, "Configuring NetBIOS Name Servers."

6

Comparing NetBIOS Name Servers with DNS Servers

Although both NetBIOS name and hostname resolution ultimately provide logical name-to-IP address resolution, some key differences do exist, as follows:

- NetBIOS names must be registered on the network. If the name being registered is a unique NetBIOS name, then the name must not already be registered on the network. If the NetBIOS name is registered, the registration will fail.

- DNS servers can use aliases to assign multiple logical names to a single IP address for the same service.

- NetBIOS names can automatically be registered with a NetBIOS name server. Only if a DNS server supports DNS dynamic updates can automatic registrations take place. Currently, only BIND versions greater than version 8.0 and Microsoft DNS Servers in Windows 2000 and Windows .NET Server support DNS dynamic updates.

- NetBIOS names exist for each service a computer is hosting. A single computer can register numerous NetBIOS names. DNS only requires a single host record for a resource. Some additional records (such as Mail Exchanger records and Service Locator records) indicate special services provided by a host.

- After NBNS replication is configured, NetBIOS name servers can exchange only changed records. The name servers perform an initial full replication to synchronize their databases. From that point on, they only send new and updated records. DNS servers must support incremental zone transfers (IXFR) to enable only changed resource records. Until recently, most DNS servers only supported full zone transfers (AXFR), where all zone information is sent from the Master name server to its Slave name server when updates are requested.

Despite these differences, additional overhead is involved when both name resolution services are implemented in the same network.

Moving Away from NetBIOS

With the advances in DNS to support dynamic updates, there is a movement away from the use of NetBIOS. Microsoft provided the capability to unbind NetBIOS from TCP/IP in Windows 2000.

This does not mean that you can immediately remove NetBIOS from the network. If you have legacy clients (Windows 9x or Windows NT) or applications that require NetBIOS, such as Windows 2000 clustering services, you will need to support NetBIOS on the network.

TCP/IP Configuration Files

As you have seen in the discussion of logical name resolution, several text files play a major part in the configuration of the TCP/IP protocol. These files are located in the Unix /etc directory; on Windows NT and higher clients, they are located in the %systemroot%\system32\drivers\etc directory.

The actual configuration files include

- HOSTS
- NETWORKS
- SERVICES
- PROTOCOL
- LMHOSTS (Microsoft clients only)
- RESOLV.CONF

HOSTS

The HOSTS file is used by TCP/IP to resolve hostnames to IP addresses. The following shows the syntax of the HOSTS file. This example shows a HOSTS file with multiple entries:

```
127.0.0.1               localhost
126.54.94.97            rhino.acme.com
39.25.63.10             x.acme.com
172.16.2.16             sideshowbri    brian    instructor
```

As you can see, the host named sideshowbri can be reached at IP address 172.16.2.16. The additional names on this configuration line are aliases. They also can be used instead of sideshowbri to refer to the host.

> **Caution**
>
> As previously discussed, the HOSTS file is one of the first files referenced during the hostname resolution process. An IP address configured incorrectly in this file can result in a host never being reached, even if entered correctly at a DNS server.
>
> Another issue with the HOSTS file is that, in some implementations of TCP/IP, hostnames are case sensitive. The most common way to represent a hostname is in lowercase.

6

If you are considering implementing HOSTS files on your clients, a major issue to consider is that the files must be updated manually at each host on the network. For this reason, it is common to implement DNS instead. Remember that modification of the HOSTS file does not require a reboot. The HOSTs file is read any time that hostname resolution takes place.

NETWORKS

The NETWORKS file is used to create logical names for network IP addresses. The following is an example of a NETWORKS file:

```
loopback        127

winnipeg        172.16

calgary         172.17

minneapolis     192.168.5
```

By creating entries in the NETWORKS file, you can refer to these networks using their logical names in TCP/IP configuration commands, such as the creation of static route entries in a routing table.

SERVICES

The SERVICES file contains the text names for well-known port addresses used by both TCP and UDP. The following is a partial listing of a SERVICES file:

```
echo            7/tcp
echo            7/udp
discard         9/tcp       sink null
discard         9/udp       sink null
systat          11/tcp
systat          11/tcp      users
daytime         13/tcp
daytime         13/udp
netstat         15/tcp
qotd            17/tcp      quote
qotd            17/udp      quote
chargen         19/tcp      ttytst source
chargen         19/udp      ttytst source
ftp-data        20/tcp
ftp             21/tcp
telnet          23/tcp
smtp            25/tcp      mail
.
.
.
rscsa           10010/udp
rscsb           10011/udp
qmaster         10012/tcp
qmaster         10012/udp
```

Many port scanners and utilities use the SERVICES file to translate port numbers to logical names. For example, if a port scanner determines that TCP port 21 is open, it reports that FTP is open.

> One of the big misconceptions about the SERVICES file is that the file is used to define the ports used by applications. In other words, it is believed that an application reads the SERVICES file to determine what port to use. This is incorrect. The SERVICES file is used by diagnostic tools to report what port it has discovered.

PROTOCOL

The PROTOCOL file contains the protocol ID numbers for the standard TCP/IP protocols. These protocol ID numbers are referred to in the IP header to designate which protocol is piggybacked on the IP protocol. The following is an example of the PROTOCOL file:

```
ip        0    IP       # Internet protocol
icmp      1    ICMP     # Internet control message protocol
ggp       3    GGP      # Gateway-gateway protocol
tcp       6    TCP      # Transmission control protocol
egp       8    EGP      # Exterior gateway protocol
pup       12   PUP      # PARC universal packet protocol
udp       17   UDP      # User datagram protocol
hmp       20   HMP      # Host monitoring protocol
xns-idp   22   XNS-IDP  # Xerox NS IDP
rdp       27   RDP      # "reliable datagram" protocol
rvd       66   RVD      # MIT remote virtual disk
```

This file is not changed very often. It can be edited, however, to add a new protocol that you want to refer to by a mnemonic.

LMHOSTS

The LMHOSTS (Lan Manager HOSTS) file is used only in Microsoft networks that require NetBIOS name resolution. This file provides the following capabilities:

- The capability to autoload NetBIOS names into the NetBIOS name cache
- The capability to refer to a centralized LMHOSTS file
- The capability to provide resolution to a login server located across a WAN boundary

6

> If a NetBIOS name server is included in a network using NetBIOS name resolution, it is not necessary to implement LMHOSTS files. This is because the NetBIOS name-resolution method first attempts to resolve the NetBIOS name using a NetBIOS name lookup to the NetBIOS name server. You can,

however, still include LMHOSTS files on key servers in case the NBNS fails. This ensures that remote NetBIOS hosts still can communicate if the NBNS fails.

The following is an example of an LMHOSTS file:

```
102.54.94.100        ntw
102.54.94.105        win95
102.54.94.97         rhino        #PRE      #DOM:networking
102.54.94.123        popular      #PRE
102.54.94.117        localsrv     #PRE

#BEGIN_ALTERNATE
#INCLUDE \\localsrv\public\lmhosts
#END_ALTERNATE
```

Placing the #PRE parameter in a line of the LMHOSTS file means that this name should be preloaded into the NetBIOS name cache. This results in faster NetBIOS name resolution.

The #DOM:Domain entry signifies that the entry can function as an authenticating server for the Domain domain.

The #INCLUDE line specifies the location of the centralized LMHOSTS file. The file always is noted using a universal naming convention (UNC)-styled network reference. The UNC name is based on the following syntax:

```
\\SERVER\SHARED RESOURCE\FILE
```

where SERVER is the NetBIOS name of the server on which the resource is located. SHARED RESOURCE refers to the logical name designated as an entry point to the server's files resources, and FILE represents the centralized LMHOSTS file.

When you use the #INCLUDE line, it is important that the server name be referenced earlier in the LMHOSTS file. This is because the file is parsed sequentially. If the SERVER name is not previously referred to, the shared LMHOSTS file's location cannot be resolved. The server's entry must include a #PRE entry in its definition so that its IP address is loaded into the NetBIOS name cache.

The #BEGIN ALTERNATE and #END ALTERNATE tag lines indicate that a redirection is to occur. The redirection generally is to a centralized LMHOSTS file on a central file server. These lines provide multiple locations for storing a centralized LMHOSTS file.

Tip

> The LMHOSTS file should only contain name-resolution entries for NetBIOS computers not located on the same network segment. Local segment hosts are resolved using an NBNS lookup or broadcast before the LMHOSTS file even is consulted.

RESOLV.CONF

The RESOLV.CONF file is used on Unix hosts to store their DNS configuration information. It generally is located in the /etc directory. The following is the format of the RESOLV.CONF file:

```
;

; Data file for a client

;

domain        online-can.com

nameserver    172.16.2.3

nameserver    172.16.3.3
```

where domain represents the domain portion of a fully qualified domain name, and nameserver represents the IP addresses of your configured DNS servers. The order in which they occur in the file is the order in which connection is attempted.

If the RESOLV.CONF file does not exist on a Unix host, it is assumed that the DNS service is running on the local host.

Applying What You Have Learned

Here are questions to check what you've learned today. The answers can be found in Appendix B, "Test Your Knowledge: Answers."

Test Your Knowledge

1. What are some of the key differences between hostname resolution and NetBIOS name resolution?

2. What top-level domains exist on the Internet today? Why has there been a need to add additional generic top-level domains?

3. If a target host's IP address is configured incorrectly in a computer's HOSTS file but correctly in DNS, will communication occur successfully? Why or why not?

6

4. If a target host's IP address is configured correctly in a computer's HOSTS file but incorrectly in DNS, will communication occur successfully? Why or why not?

5. Compare and contrast a recursive DNS query with an iterative DNS query.

6. What can be done to increase performance on a DNS server?

7. What four NetBIOS node-type configurations can be set for a client? Which node types help reduce network traffic?

8. What three basic NetBIOS name transactions occur on a NetBIOS network?

9. What advantages does dynamic DNS provide over DNS?

10. If you want to use a centralized LMHOSTS file located on a server named PRIMARY in a share named NETLOGON, what lines need to be added to the LMHOSTS file? PRIMARY's IP address is 172.18.56.35.

11. What versions of BIND DNS and Microsoft DNS support dynamic DNS updates?

12. What security risks can exist when dynamic updates are implemented in DNS?

Preview of Day 7

Tomorrow you will examine domain name server configuration in more detail.

You will approach DNS Server configuration from the point of view of both a BIND-compliant DNS server and a Microsoft Windows DNS server. This includes all configuration files and the various types of resource records that can be created.

DAY 7

Configuring Domain Name Servers

Today's material starts with an overview of the process that takes place when an organization registers a domain name on the Internet.

We'll also inspect the DNS message format, including the message header, the Question section, and the format of a returned resource record. Then we'll examine the actual configuration of a DNS server.

Two commonly used DNS servers in networks today include: Berkeley Internet Name Daemon (BIND)-compatible DNS servers and Microsoft DNS servers. We'll examine the configuration of both DNS server types.

Note

There are other DNS solutions available but most of the market uses BIND DNS or Microsoft DNS, so today focuses on these two implementations.

Finally, we'll take a look at common configuration problems with these DNS implementations, and you will learn how the NSLOOKUP command can help you troubleshoot configuration problems.

Registering a DNS Domain Name

Before you start configuring DNS servers, you must register a DNS domain name on the Internet. In recent years, the process of registering domain names for the Internet has moved from InterNIC to regional registration authorities. For example, in North America, you can register new domain names at www.register.com by following these steps:

1. The person applying for the domain name first must determine whether the desired name already is in use. Register.com provides a utility at its home page that allows you to check for a domain name using several of the common extensions (see Figure 7.1).

FIGURE 7.1

Searching for a specific domain name.

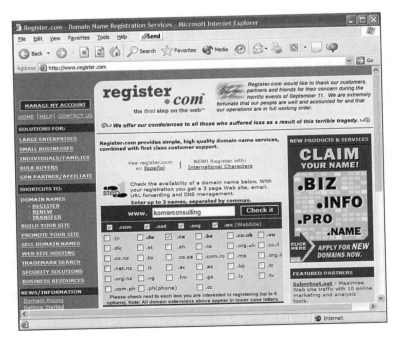

The home page runs a Whois search to determine if the domain name you want to use is already registered on the Internet. The Whois search also provides the administrative, accounting, and technical contacts if the domain name is already registered.

2. The search indicates what domain names are available based on your search criteria (see Figure 7.2).

FIGURE 7.2

Identifying available domain names.

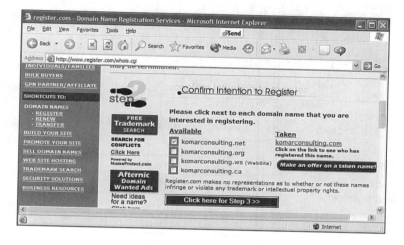

In this case, the names komarconsulting.net, komarconsulting.org, komarconsulting.ws, and komarconsulting.ca are all available, but, komarconsulting.com is not available (I registered it a few years ago).

3. Assuming that you want to register komarconsulting.net, you would select the check box next to komarconsulting.net, and then click the Click Here for Step 3 button.

4. To register a domain with register.com, you now must either create an account with register.com, or authenticate using an existing account. Both methods provide register.com with both an organization and administrative contact for the domain name you are registering.

Note

The organization and administrative information is used to create a record for your new DNS domain in InterNIC's Whois database. Your DNS domain information also is placed in the zone files for your authoritative DNS domain so that DNS domain name requests can be processed against your DNS domain.

5. The final step is to determine how long you want to register the domain for and how you want to pay for the domain name registration. After this information is provided, the transaction is completed and you now own an Internet domain name.

7

DNS Message Formats

RFC 1034   **RFC 1035**   **RFC 2136**   As with other protocols, DNS uses specific message formats for the querying and transfer of DNS data.

Within a DNS message, the following major sections need to be detailed:

- The DNS message header
- The DNS Question section
- Resource record format

The DNS message header format, shown in Figure 7.3, contains the following fields:

FIGURE 7.3

The DNS message header format.

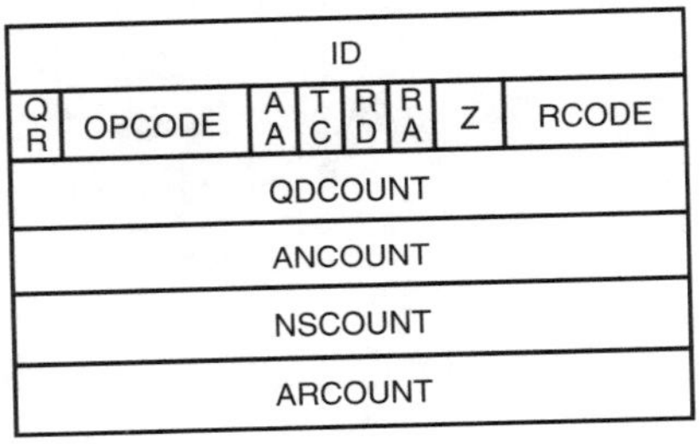

- **ID.** This 16-bit identifier is assigned by the program that generates a DNS query. This identifier also is used in the subsequent reply so the requestor can match the reply to the originating request.
- **QR.** This 1-bit field indicates whether the DNS message is a request (0) or a response (1).
- **OPCODE.** This 4-bit field specifies the type of query being formulated. A standard query has a value of 0, an inverse query has a value of 1, a server status request has a value of 2, and an update message has a value of 5. All other values up to 15 are reserved for future use.
- **AA.** This 1-bit field is only set in responses. When set, it indicates that the responding name server is an authority for the domain name in the DNS request message.
- **TC.** This 1-bit field stands for Truncation. It is set to 1 if the message was truncated because the length was longer than permitted on the transmission channel.
- **RD.** This 1-bit field stands for Recursion Desired. If set to 1, it indicates that the DNS resolver wants the DNS name server to use a recursive query.

- **RA.** This 1-bit field indicates that the responding name server can perform a recursive query. RA stands for Recursion Available.
- **Z.** This 3-bit field is reserved for future use and should be set to all zeros.
- **RCODE.** The 4-bit Response Code field is only set in a DNS response message. It indicates whether an error has occurred. Allowed values include the following:

Value	Error	Description
0	NOERROR	The DNS response was formulated with no errors.
1	FORMERR	The DNS name server could not interpret the format of the DNS request.
2	SERVFAIL	The DNS name server was unable to process the query because of an error that occurred at the name server.
3	NXDOMAIN	If the DNS response is from an authoritative name server, the name referenced in the DNS request does not exist.
4	NOTIMP	The DNS name server does not support this DNS request message.
5	REFUSED	The DNS name server has refused to process the DNS request because of a policy or security setting.
6	YXDOMAIN	If the DNS response is from an authoritative name server, a name that should not exist in the DNS zone, does exist.
7	YXRRSET	If the DNS response is from an authoritative name server, a resource record set that should not exist in the DNS zone, does exist.
8	NXRRSET	If the DNS response is from an authoritative name server, a resource record set that should exist in the DNS zone, does not exist.
9	NOTAUTH	The name server that the DNS query is sent to is not authoritative for the zone named in the Zone Section.
10	NOTZONE	A name used in the Prerequisite or Update Section of a DNS request, is not within the zone denoted by the Zone Section.
11–15		Reserved for future use.

- **QDCOUNT.** This 16-bit field specifies the number of entries in the DNS Question section.
- **ANCOUNT.** This 16-bit field specifies the number of resource records returned in the Answer section.

7

- **NSCOUNT.** This 16-bit field specifies the number of name server resource records in the Authority Records section.
- **ARCOUNT.** This 16-bit field specifies the number of resource records in the Additional Records section.

The Question section contains data when a DNS resolver sends a DNS request message. The Question section follows the DNS message header when a DNS resolver sends a DNS request message. Figure 7.4 shows the format of the Question section.

FIGURE 7.4

The Question section format for a DNS message.

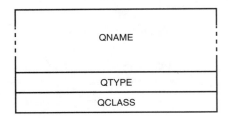

The Question section contains the following fields:

- **QNAME.** This variable-length field contains a requested domain name. It is represented as a sequence of labels, in which each label consists of a `length` octet followed by that number of octets.
- **QTYPE.** This 16-bit field specifies the type of the query. This field matches a type value for a specific resource record. Some general `QTYPE` values match more than one type of resource record.
- **QCLASS.** This 16-bit field specifies the class of the query. Typically, this is set to `IN` for Internet.

The Answer, Authority, and Additional sections all use the same format (see Figure 7.5). The Additional section contains resource records required in addition to the resource records returned in the Answer or Authority section. If a Start of Authority record is returned in the Authority section, for example, the related Answer (A) record for the authoritative name server also should be returned.

FIGURE 7.5

The resource record format.

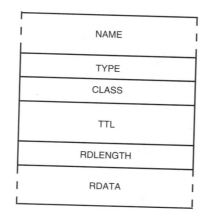

| NAME |
| TYPE |
| CLASS |
| TTL |
| RDLENGTH |
| RDATA |

The format includes the following fields:

- **NAME.** This variable-length field contains the domain name to which the resource record information pertains.
- **TYPE.** This 16-bit field contains the type of resource record being returned in the information.
- **CLASS.** This 16-bit field contains the class of the data being returned in the RDATA field. The most common class returned is IN for Internet.
- **TTL.** This 32-bit field specifies the time (in seconds) that the resource record can be stored in cache before it must expire. If the value is set to zero, it may not be cached after being returned to the DNS resolver.
- **RDLENGTH.** This 16-bit field indicates the length in octets of the RDATA field.
- **RDATA.** This variable-length field describes the resource. The format of this field is based on the entries in the TYPE and CLASS fields.

Resource Records

A domain name server contains several resource records in its configuration files. These resource records help a DNS resolver find specific hosts on the network to which they need to connect. Although, most often, a host uses DNS to resolve a hostname to an IP address, DNS also is used to find a host that provides a specific service on the network (such as mail processing or name server service). Table 7.1 lists the resource records that can be included in the configuration files of a DNS server.

7

TABLE 7.1   DNS Resource Record Definitions

Record Alias	Numeric	Record Type	Description
A	1	Address	Maps a hostname to an IP address.
NS	2	Name server	Identifies a DNS authoritative name server for the DNS domain.
CNAME	5	Canonical name	Creates an alias for a specified hostname. The CNAME record cannot match any other existing DNS name. Common usage includes providing aliases such as WWW or FTP.
SOA	6	Start of Authority	Indicates that the named DNS server is the best source of information for the data within the named DNS domain.
MB	7	Mailbox	An experimental record that indicates a DNS host with the specified mailbox.
MG	8	Mail group	An experimental record specifying that a mailbox is a member of a mailing group or list.
MR	9	Mailbox rename	An experimental record that specifies a mailbox is a proper rename of the other specified mailbox.
NULL	10		Null resource record.
WKS	11	Well-known service	Describes the services provided by a particular protocol on a particular interface.
PTR	12	Pointer	Maps an IP address to a hostname. It is used in reverse lookup zones to refer back to hostnames.
HINFO	13	Host information	Provides information about the specified hostname, including CPU Type and Operating System.
MINFO	14	Mailbox information	An experimental record that specifies a mailbox that is responsible for a mailing list or mailbox.
MX*	15	Mail exchanger	Indicates the mail server for a DNS domain name. This named host either processes or forwards mail for the DNS domain name.
TXT	16	Text	Associates general text information with an item in the DNS database. This is commonly used to indicate a host's location.
RP	17	Responsible person	Indicates the person responsible for the specified DNS domain or host.

TABLE 7.1 continued

Record Alias	Numeric	Record Type	Description
AFSDB	18	AFS database	Provides the location of an Andrew File System (AFS) cell database server or a Distributed Computing Environment (DCE) cell's authenticated name server. AFS is a network file system similar to NFS, but it is meant to be deployed in a wide area network environment.
X.25	19	X.25	A variation of the address record that maps the hostname to an X.121 address used in an X.25 network. This resource record is used in conjunction with an RT record.
ISDN	20	Integrated Services Digital Network	A variation of the address record. Instead of mapping a hostname to an IP address, however, it is mapped to an ISDN address. This resource record is used in conjunction with the RT record.
RT	21	Route through	Indicates an intermediate host used to route packets to a destination host. The RT resource record is used in conjunction with ISDN or X.25 resource records.
AAAA	28	IPv6 address	Maps a hostname to an IPv6 address.
SRV	33	Service locator	Provides the location of services on a network including the server hosting the service and the TCP or UDP port address of the service.
A6	38		Updated resource record for mapping hostnames to IPv6 addresses.

* *The mail exchanger (MX) records replaced the extinct mail destination (MD) and mail forwarder (MF) resource records.*

Configuring a BIND DNS Server

The configuration of a Berkeley Internet Name Daemon (BIND) DNS server depends on the configuration of several text-based files and databases. They have to be either created from scratch or modified from a base template. The following files must be defined:

- The DNS named configuration file
- The DNS cache file

7

- The DNS forward-lookup files
- The DNS reverse-lookup files

The `named.conf` File

A BIND-compatible DNS server uses the named daemon for its DNS service. At startup of the named daemon, the boot file `named.conf` is read to configure the following information:

- The directory in which the remaining DNS configuration files are located.
- The options used by the named daemon.
- The name of the named cache file that contains mappings to the Internet DNS root servers.
- The name of any primary domains for which the DNS server is authoritative and the database file that contains the resource records for that domain.
- The name of any secondary domains for which the DNS server is authoritative and the name of the local file that contains the resource records. There can be more than one secondary entry in the `named.conf` file. These entries also indicate the IP address of the master DNS server for this zone file.
- The name of an alternative DNS name server that can be queried if this domain is not authoritative for the queried domain resource record.

This information is used by the named DNS daemon (or service) when it starts. The named daemon processes all DNS requests based on the configuration information in the configuration files.

 Note

In earlier versions of BIND DNS servers, the `named.conf` file was called `named.boot`. In BIND 8.x, you can run `/usr/sbin/named-bootconf /etc/named.boot >> /etc/named.conf` to convert the `named.boot` file to the proper `named.conf` syntax.

The Options Section

Global options can be defined that affect all zones defined for the DNS server. These options can greatly affect the zone definitions that follow, so the options sections should be placed near the top of the `named.conf` file.

Here's how the global options section is formatted:

```
Options {
    Option1;
    Option2;
};
```

The following options can be defined in the Options section:

- `directory "path"`. The directory where all zone files are stored. The path must be enclosed with quote characters. For example, `"/usr/local/named"`.

- `notify yes|no`. Indicates whether the DNS server will notify configured secondary name servers when changes are detected in zone files.

- `forwarders ip addresses`. Configures to what IP addresses unresolved DNS queries are forwarded. Multiple IP addresses can be provided.

- `check-names option`. Controls how the DNS server will handle non-RFC compliant hostnames in DNS queries. The following keywords can be used with this option:

  - `Master [option]`. Defines how non-RFC compliant hostnames are handled in the master zone file.

    The `[option]` can be defined as `ignore`, where the non-RFC record is ignored and processing continues normally; `warn`, where the error is logged and processing continues normally; and `fail`, where the name is rejected.

  - `Slave [option]`. Defines how non-RFC compliant hostnames are handled when received in a zone transfer from a master server. The same options are available for the Slave as for the Master.

  - `Response [option]`. Defines how to handle non-RFC compliant hostnames received in response to a DNS query. The same options are available for the Response as for the Master.

You'll see examples of these options in the A Sample `named.conf` File section and Listing 7.1 a little later in the chapter.

> **Note**
>
> Additional options can be defined for the Options section. You can view the complete list of options at
> `http://nim.cit.cornell.edu/usr/share/man/info/en_US/a_doc_lib/files/aixfiles/named.conf.htm`.

7

Zone Definitions

The primary purpose of the `named.conf` file is to define the zones that are hosted by the DNS server. The zone definitions include the names of the zones hosted by the DNS server, the type of zones, and specific configuration settings for each zone file.

When you define a zone in the `named.conf` file, the following syntax is used:

```
Zone "domain name" IN {
    Option1;
    Option2;
};
```

where the `"domain name"` is the name of the zone. For a forward-lookup zone such as abc.com, this would be formatted as `"abc.com"`. For a reverse-lookup zone for the `192.168.24.0/24` network, the reverse-lookup zone would be represented as `"24.168.192.in-addr.arpa"`. Within the zone definition, the following options are commonly specified:

- `type` *type*. The type of zone hosted by the DNS server. A `master` zone hosts the writable copy of the zone file on the local disk system, a `slave` zone receives its zone data from an indicated master server, a `stub` zone only replicates the `NS` resource records from its master server, and a `hint` zone describes a source for information not contained in local zone files.

- `file` *path*. Indicates the file used to store zone data for master zone and is optional for `slave` and `stub` zones. The file is typically named `db.zonename`.

- `masters {hostlist;}`. For `slave` and `stub` zones, the master server for zone transfers is indicated.

- `check-names` *option*. The same syntax is used within a zone definition as that used for global options. The `check-names` *option* defined for a zone takes precedence over the global option setting.

- `allow-update {hostlist;}`. Enables dynamic updates for the zone and indicates which hosts, or subnets are allowed to perform dynamic updates. A specific IP address can be indicated, a subnet address, or the keyword any can be included.

- `allow-transfer {hostlist;}`. Defines what hosts can receive zone transfers of this zone. This option restricts zone transfers and prevents an attacker from dumping all zone records. If you define the *hostlist* to be **none**, this prevents all attempts to transfer the contents of the zone using a zone transfer mechanism.

A Sample `named.conf` File

When you put all the options together, you can configure a DNS server to host specific zones, and control how zones are maintained by the DNS server. Listing 7.1 is an example of a named.conf file hosting the example.com, 0.168.192.in-addr.arpa, and 0.0.127.in-addr.arpa zones, and acting as the secondary for the subsidiary. example.com zone.

LISTING 7.1   Sample named.conf File

```
options {
    directory "/usr/local/named";
    notify yes;
    check-names master warn;
};
zone "example.com" in {
    type master;
    file "db.example";
    check-names master ignore;
    allow-transfer { 192.168.0.7; };
    allow-update {192.168.0.5; 192.168.0.6;  192.168.0.100;};
};
zone "subsidiary.example.com" in {
    type slave;
    masters {10.10.10.10;};
    allow-transfer { 192.168.0.9; };
};


zone "0.168.192.in-addr.arpa" in {
    type master;
    file "db. 0.168.192.in-addr.arpa";
    allow-transfer { 192.168.0.7; };
    allow-update {192.168.0.5; 192.168.0.6; 192.168.0.100;};
};
zone "0.0.127.in-addr.arpa" in {
    type master;
    file "db.127.0.0";
};
zone "." in {
    type hint;
    file "db.cache";
};
```

Cache File

The DNS cache file contains a list of the root domain name servers. This file can use any name as long as the name implemented matches the name referenced in the named.conf file.

7

Configuration Update

The DNS cache file's contents should be verified periodically. The root domain name servers change from time to time, and this file should be updated to include any new root servers that have been implemented. An updated version of the DNS cache file can be retrieved from the following location:

```
ftp://rs.internic.net/domain/named.cache
```

The contents of this file can be pasted into the existing DNS cache file, replacing its current contents.

Listing 7.2 shows the latest version of the DNS cache file.

LISTING 7.2   DNS Cache File

```
;
;           last update:    Aug 22, 1997
;           related version of root zone:   1997082200
;
;
;
; formerly NS.INTERNIC.NET
;
.                           3600000   IN  NS   A.ROOT-SERVERS.NET.
A.ROOT-SERVERS.NET.         3600000       A    198.41.0.4
;
; formerly NS1.ISI.EDU
;
.                           3600000       NS   B.ROOT-SERVERS.NET.
B.ROOT-SERVERS.NET.         3600000       A    128.9.0.107
;
; formerly C.PSI.NET
;
.                           3600000       NS   C.ROOT-SERVERS.NET.
C.ROOT-SERVERS.NET.         3600000       A    192.33.4.12
;
; formerly TERP.UMD.EDU
;
.                           3600000       NS   D.ROOT-SERVERS.NET.
D.ROOT-SERVERS.NET.         3600000       A    128.8.10.90
;
; formerly NS.NASA.GOV
;
.                           3600000       NS   E.ROOT-SERVERS.NET.
E.ROOT-SERVERS.NET.         3600000       A    192.203.230.10
;
; formerly NS.ISC.ORG
;
```

LISTING 7.2   continued

```
.
F.ROOT-SERVERS.NET.          3600000     NS     F.ROOT-SERVERS.NET.
                             3600000     A      192.5.5.241
;
; formerly NS.NIC.DDN.MIL
;
.
G.ROOT-SERVERS.NET.          3600000     NS     G.ROOT-SERVERS.NET.
                             3600000     A      192.112.36.4
;
; formerly AOS.ARL.ARMY.MIL
;
.
H.ROOT-SERVERS.NET.          3600000     NS     H.ROOT-SERVERS.NET.
                             3600000     A      128.63.2.53
;
; formerly NIC.NORDU.NET
;
.
I.ROOT-SERVERS.NET.          3600000     NS     I.ROOT-SERVERS.NET.
                             3600000     A      192.36.148.17
;
; temporarily housed at NSI (InterNIC)
;
.
J.ROOT-SERVERS.NET.          3600000     NS     J.ROOT-SERVERS.NET.
                             3600000     A      198.41.0.10
;
; housed in LINX, operated by RIPE NCC
;
.
K.ROOT-SERVERS.NET.          3600000     NS     K.ROOT-SERVERS.NET.
                             3600000     A      193.0.14.129
;
; temporarily housed at ISI (IANA)
;
.
L.ROOT-SERVERS.NET.          3600000     NS     L.ROOT-SERVERS.NET.
                             3600000     A      198.32.64.12
;
; housed in Japan, operated by WIDE
;
.
M.ROOT-SERVERS.NET.          3600000     NS     M.ROOT-SERVERS.NET.
                             3600000     A      202.12.27.33
; End of File
```

DNS Forward-Lookup Files

Your DNS server hosts the zone configuration files for your domain. These configuration files are called forward-lookup zone files. Each DNS server contains entries for these forward-lookup configuration files in the named.conf file. Remember, primary zones have the actual configuration changes performed on the locally stored files. Secondary zones receive a copy of the configured zone files from their master server, as indicated in the secondary configuration lines of the named.conf file.

7

Listing 7.3 is an example of a typical forward-lookup zone configuration file.

LISTING 7.3   Forward-Lookup Zone Configuration File Example

```
@                 IN        SOA     example.com. _administrator.example.com (
                            200109250001    ; serial
                            10800           ;refresh
                            3600            ;retry
                            604800          ;expire
                            86400           ;TTL
                            )
                  IN        NS      ns1.southpark.com.
                  IN        NS      ns2.southpark.com.
ns1.example.com.  IN        A       192.168.0.3
ns2.example.com.  IN        A       192.168.0.4
zephyr            IN        A       192.168.0.5
lynx              IN        A       192.168.0.6
www               IN        CNAME   zephyr.example.com.
ftp               IN        CNAME   zephyr.example.com.
proxy             IN        CNAME   lynx.southpark.com.
mail              IN        CNAME   ns2.southpark.com.
southpark.com.    IN        MX      10      ns2.southpark.com.
southpark.com.    IN        MX      20      lynx.southpark.com.
_ldap._tcp   600  IN        SRV     0 100 389   lynx.southpark.com
_kerberos._udp 600 IN       SRV     0 100 88    lynx.southpark.com
```

The following sections discuss the formatting of common resource records found in a forward-lookup configuration file.

Start of Authority (SOA) Resource Record

The key resource record in a forward-lookup configuration file is the Start of Authority (SOA) resource record. It defines which name server functions as the primary name server and how it treats the data configured for the domain.

The SOA resource record uses the following syntax:

```
@       IN    SOA     <Source Host>  <Contact Email>      (
                      <Serial Number>
                      <Refresh Time>
                      <Retry Time>
                      <Expiration Time>
                      <Time to Live>
                      )
```

- @. This is used like a variable. It refers to the named.conf file. In that file, it recorded that the db.example file contained the resource records for the example.

com domain. If this file was saved as db.example, the @ character references the domain example.com.

- <Source Host>. This is the fully qualified domain name (FQDN) of the host that stores the master copy of the domain configuration file. Be sure you don't forget the period after the FQDN.

Caution

The period indicates that this is the absolute path to the hostname. If you do not add a suffix period, DNS appends the domain name to the path. A missing period, for example, would cause cartman.southpark.com to be parsed to cartman.southpark.com.southpark.com. This is one of the most common DNS configuration file errors. Always double-check all your entries because it is easy to miss typing a period.

- <Contact Email>. This is the e-mail address of the contact for this domain configuration file. Note that the @ character is replaced with a period in this resource record. This is because the @ symbol represents the domain name for the zone.

Caution

A problem can arise if the contact's e-mail address contains a period. If the contact's e-mail address is brian.komar@komarconsulting.com, for example, the contact e-mail name is formatted as brian\.komar.komarcon-sulting.com. The backslash (\) indicates that the first period actually is part of the contact's mailbox name and allows the use of a period in a contact's e-mail address.

- <Serial Number>. The value in this field is used by a secondary name server to determine whether a zone transfer must take place to update the configuration files on the secondary name server. If the serial number on the master name server is higher than the serial number on the secondary name server, the secondary name server initiates a zone transfer.

Tip

You can use the date you make the configuration change as the serial number for the zone. The serial number in Listing 7.3 represents that this change was written September 25, 2001. The trailing 0001 indicates that this was the first update performed on that date. This format ensures that the new serial number always is higher than any previous serial numbers.

7

- `<Refresh Time>`. This field configures how frequently a secondary name server checks to see whether its zone information is up-to-date. This value is stored in seconds. In Listing 7.3, `10800` represents that the secondary server checks to see whether an update has taken place every three hours. If your DNS changes infrequently, a higher value can be configured.

- `<Retry Time>`. This field configures how the secondary server reacts if it fails to contact its master server at the refresh time interval. This usually is set to be a shorter value than the refresh time. In Listing 7.3, the retry time is configured to `3600` seconds, or one hour.

- `<Expire Time>`. This field configures how long a secondary server can continue to provide DNS replies from out-of-date configuration files. In Listing 7.3, the expire time is set to `604800` seconds, or seven days. This means that, if a secondary server is unable to contact its master server for more than one week, it ceases to respond to DNS resolver requests for that domain.

- `<Time to Live>`. The Time to Live (`TTL`) field indicates how long another DNS name server can cache responses from this DNS server. This value can be set to a higher value if your resource record IP addresses do not change frequently. In Listing 7.3, the TTL was set to `86400` seconds, or 24 hours.

Name Server (NS) Resource Records

Name server (`NS`) resource records indicate which DNS servers are authoritative for a domain. Be sure to include NS resource records for the primary name server and all secondary name servers.

The following is the syntax of an NS record:

```
<domain name>  IN    NS      <name server>
```

- `<domain name>`. The domain for which the indicated name server contains a zone configuration file and related resource records.

- `<name server>`. The FQDN for the name server that is authoritative for the indicated domain name.

In Listing 7.3, you might notice that the `<domain name>` field is missing. This is because of the `NS` resource records' location in the configuration file. If the first field is left blank in a resource record, it is assumed to have the same value as the previous resource record that does have a value in its first field. In Listing 7.3, the `SOA` record has a value @ (the name of the domain) in its first field. Therefore, these `NS` resource records are both for the `example.com` domain.

> **Note**
>
> For an NS record, always refer to an address (A) record and not a canonical name (CNAME) record. An NS record must refer to a valid address record in the DNS resource records for a domain.

Address (A) Resource Record

The address (A), or host, resource record resolves an IP address to a given hostname. The following is the format of an address record:

```
<host name>    IN      A       <IP Address>
```

- `<host name>`. This field contains the logical name assigned to a host.
- `<IP Address>`. This field contains the IPv4 address assigned to the indicated host. If the address is an IPv6 address, an AAAA or A6 resource record is used.

In the sample configuration file in Listing 7.3, four address records have been configured. You might notice that ns1 and ns2 are represented by FQDNs. Because zephyr and lynx are represented by their hostnames, when they are resolved, the domain name example.com is appended to the hostnames.

> **Caution**
>
> Be sure to include address resource records for all hosts that are commonly accessed on the network or that provide network services. Also be sure an address record exists for any hostnames referenced in Start of Authority (SOA), name server (NS), or mail exchanger (MX) resource records. These records must reference hosts with an existing address record.

Canonical Name (CNAME) Resource Records

Canonical name (CNAME) resource records provide the capability to create aliases for hosts. By using aliases, you can change which computer might host an Internet service (such as Web services) without having to modify an actual address (A) record. You are not restricted to naming your Web servers with the hostname WWW. The following is the syntax of a CNAME resource record:

```
<alias>        IN      CNAME       <hostname>
```

- `<alias>`. This field indicates the alias that also can be used to refer to the hostname.
- `<hostname>`. This field contains the actual hostname configured for the host using an address (A) record. Be sure to end the hostname with a period if you use an FQDN.

7

> **Tip**
>
> It is not recommended to create a CNAME record that references another CNAME record. Although this actually works, it sometimes can become quite difficult to troubleshoot a DNS configuration error. You might have to refer to several CNAME records before you find the actual address record to which they all refer.

Mail Exchange (MX) Resource Records

A mail exchange (MX) resource record indicates where mail destined for the domain should be sent and processed. Multiple MX records can exist for a domain so load-balancing or fault tolerance can be provided for a domain's e-mail services.

The following is the format of a mail exchange resource record:

```
<domain name>    IN    MX      <cost>    <mail server>
```

- `<domain name>`. The domain name for which the mail exchanger processes mail.
- `<cost>`. This field enables a preference to be set for specific mail exchangers. The routing decision is based on a least-cost method. The lower the configured cost, the higher the preference for delivery. If you configure two MX records to have the same cost, load-balancing takes place between the two mail exchangers. Mail usually is routed to a higher-cost mail exchanger only if a lower-cost mail exchanger cannot be reached.
- `<mail server>`. This field represents the hostname of the mail exchanger that processes the mail. The hostname set in this field should be resolved by an address record rather than by a CNAME record. Some mailer software cannot resolve the MX record if it points to a CNAME record.

In the configuration file shown in Listing 7.3, two MX records are configured: one for ns2.example.com and one for lynx.example.com. Because the cost for ns2 is set to 10 and the cost for lynx is set to 20, mail most often is directed to ns2.example.com for any mail addressed to name@example.com. If the ns2 host is down for any period of time, mail is directed to lynx.example.com.

Service Locator (SRV) Resource Records

RFC 2782 A Service Locator (SRV) resource record is widely used in Windows 2000 Server and Windows .NET Server Active Directory environments. The SRV resource record is used to advertise services available on the network, including Lightweight Directory Access Protocol (LDAP), Kerberos Distribution Centers, and Global Catalog servers.

The following is the format of a service record:

```
<_Service>.<_Protool>.<Domain> <TTL> IN SRV <Priority> <Weight> <Port> <Target>
```

- <_service>. The name of the service that the service locator record is describing. The service is prefixed with the "_" character to prevent collision with an existing A or CNAME resource record.
- <_protocol>. The transport protocol used to connect to the advertised service. Typically, the protocol is set to either transport control protocol (TCP) or User Datagram Protocol (UDP).
- <Domain>. The DNS domain name that is hosting the advertised service.
- <TTL>. The Time-to-Live for the resource record. A DNS client that receives the resource record will cache the resource record only for the time indicated by the TTL field.
- <Priority>. Used to describe preference when multiple servers host the same service. A value from 0 to 65535 can be assigned with a preference to lower-numbered priorities.
- <Weight>. If two SRV resource records exist for a service with the same priority, weight will be used to determine which service to attempt connections with. As with priority, a value from 0 to 65535 can be assigned, but the preference is to higher-weighted SRV resource records if multiple SRV resource records exist with the same priority.
- <Port>. The port on which the target server hosts the service. The port can be a value between 0 and 65535 and is typically assigned to the standard port used by the advertised service.
- <Target>. The DNS name of the server that is hosting the advertised service.

In the example zone file shown in Listing 7.3, two SRV resource records exist for the example.com domain. The lynx server hosts two services: The _ldap service is available by connecting to lynx.example.com:tcp 389 and the _kerberos service is available by connecting to lynx.example.com:udp 88.

Reverse-Lookup Files

In some cases, a DNS resolver needs to resolve a given IP address to a hostname or an FQDN. A reverse-lookup file provides this functionality under DNS.

The zone files for the reverse-lookup zones are based on the network addresses for an IP network. The IP addresses are in reverse order in the reverse-lookup zone files. Table 7.2 shows the naming schemes required for Class A, Class B, and Class C networks.

7

TABLE 7.2   DNS Resource Record Definitions

IP Network Class	IP Address Format	Reverse-Lookup Zone Name
Class A	w.x.y.z	`w.in-addr.arpa`
Class B	w.x.y.z	`x.w.in-addr.arpa`
Class C	w.x.y.z	`y.x.w.in-addr.arpa`

If the network address for your network is `10.0.0.0`, for example, you name your reverse-lookup zone `10.in-addr.arpa`. If your network address is `172.16.0.0`, you name the reverse-lookup zone `16.172.in-addr.arpa`. If your network address is `192.168.10.0`, you name the reverse-lookup zone `10.168.192.in-addr.arpa`.

> **Reverse-Lookup Configuration Issue**
>
> It doesn't matter which subnet mask scheme you use for your network; the reverse-lookup zone should be based on the true class of the network address. You can use a less-specific reverse-lookup zone name, such as `168.192.in-addr.arpa` for a `192.168.x.0` network addresses. You cannot, however, use a more-specific reverse-lookup zone for a Class B or Class A address.

The configuration file can have any name. The common naming scheme for reverse-lookup files is `db.y.x.w.in-addr.arpa` for a Class C address.

In the configuration of DNS reverse-lookup zone files, it is common to configure at least two reverse-lookup zones. This includes reverse-lookup zone files for the following:

- The local network address of `127.0.0.0`
- The actual network address in use for the domain

Configuring the Local Network Reverse-Lookup Zone File

The following is an example of a typical local network address reverse-lookup configuration file:

```
0.0.127.in-addr.arpa.   IN   SOA   ns1.example.com.   admin.example.com (
                                    1998030501         ; serial
                                    10800              ;refresh
                                    3600               ;retry
                                    604800             ;expire
                                    86400              ;TTL
                                    )

                        IN   NS    ns1.example.com.
1                       IN   PTR   localhost.
```

An SOA record must exist within a reverse-lookup zone configuration file, just as in the forward-lookup zone file. The syntax of the SOA record is the same as in the forward-lookup zone file.

The NS server record also uses the same format as in the forward-lookup zone. The lack of hostname in the NS record indicates that the hostname should be the same as the previous resource record's hostname. In other words, this refers to 0.0.127.in-addr.arpa.

The pointer (PTR) resource record configures the IP address that is a pointer to a specific FQDN. Be sure you use periods correctly. If you want to append the address to the zone filename, enter the required address as previously shown with the entry for 1. This translates to the FQDN 1.0.0.127.in-addr.arpa.

Configuring the Reverse-Lookup Zone File for Your Network Address

The following is an example of the reverse-lookup zone for the southpark.com domain.

```
0.168.192.in-addr.arpa.  IN  SOA  ns1.example.com.  admin.example.com(
                                   1998030501        ; serial
                                   10800             ;refresh
                                   3600              ;retry
                                   604800            ;expire
                                   86400             ;TTL
                                   )

                         IN       NS      ns1.example.com.
3            IN    PTR    ns1.example.com.
4            IN    PTR    ns.example.com.
5            IN    PTR    zephyr.example.com.
6            IN    PTR    lynx.example.com.
```

As with the local network reverse-lookup zone, the reverse-lookup zone for your network address requires the following:

- A Start of Authority (SOA) record
- A name server (NS) record
- Pointer (PTR) records for any hosts named in address records in the forward-lookup zone configuration file

Although reverse-lookup zones are not required for your DNS implementation, it is recommended that you implement this feature within DNS. This enables users to identify which machine they are logging in from using the logical name rather than just the IP address. If you plan to run the NSLOOKUP utility for troubleshooting a DNS server, the reverse-lookup zone for your domain must be configured correctly.

7

Configuring a Windows DNS Server

Windows 2000 Server and Windows .NET server include a DNS service that can be optionally installed and implemented. The following section outlines the configuration of the *example* domain, including forward- and reverse-lookup zones using both Windows 2000 and Windows .NET Server.

Installing the DNS Service

The installation of the Windows 2000 DNS service is performed from the Add/Remove Programs applet in Windows 2000 and from the Add or Remove Programs applet in Windows .NET Server.

Note

A DNS server should have a static IP address assigned. If the computer on which you are installing the DNS service has a DHCP assigned address, you will be prompted to change the IP address to a static IP address.

The following procedure is used to install the DNS service:

1. Log on as a local Administrator at the computer that will act as a DNS server.
2. Open the Control Panel.
3. Double-click the Add/Remove Programs applet in Windows 2000, or the Add or Remove Programs applet in Windows .NET Server.
4. In the Add/Remove Programs dialog box, click the Add/Remove Windows Components button.
5. In the Windows Components dialog box (see Figure 7.6), select Networking Services, and then click Details.

FIGURE 7.6

Select Networking Services.

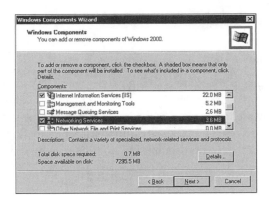

6. In the Networking Services dialog box (see Figure 7.7), click the check box next to Domain Name System (DNS), and then click OK.

FIGURE 7.7

Choosing the Domain Name System (DNS) for installation.

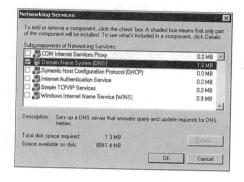

7. In the Windows Components dialog box, click Next.
8. The Configuring Components screen appears. If required, the Files Needed dialog box will appear, asking for the source media for service installation.
9. In the Completing the Windows Components Wizard dialog box, click Finish.
10. Close Add/Remove Programs.
11. Close the Control Panel.

After the DNS service is installed, you can configure it using the DNS Microsoft Management Console in the Administrative Tools.

Caution

When installing a service on Windows 2000, always ensure that you have the latest service pack and related hot fixes applied before you use the newly installed services. These service packs and hot fixes fix any bugs with the services, and more importantly, block any security holes identified since the software was released.

Configuring DNS Forwarders

If your DNS server must forward unresolved DNS requests to a specific DNS server on the Internet—typically your Internet service provider's DNS server—you must configure a forwarder resource record. This is done by configuring the forwarder option in the properties of the DNS server as shown in the following procedure.

1. From the Start menu, choose Programs, Administrative Tools, DNS.
2. In the console tree, expand *DNSServer* (where *DNSServer* is the name of your DNS server).

7

3. In the console tree, right-click *DNSServer*, and then click Properties.

4. In the *DNSServer* Properties dialog box, click the Forwarders tab. Figure 7.8 shows the Forwarders tab for Windows 2000 on the left and for Windows .NET Server on the right.

FIGURE 7.8

Configuring the Forwarders tabs.

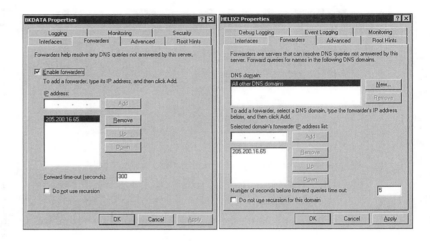

Tip

If the Forwarders tab is grayed out, then the DNS server is configured as a root DNS server. In the console tree, under Forward-Lookup Zones, delete the ".". Zone. The existence of this zone indicates that the DNS server is an Internet root server, meaning that it must know all DNS queries, and cannot forward the request elsewhere.

5. In the Forwarders tab, enter the IP address or addresses of the DNS servers that unresolved DNS queries are forwarded to and then click OK.

New Feature in Windows .NET Server

In Windows .NET Server, you can selectively forward unresolved DNS requests. By inputting a specific DNS domain name, you can configure which DNS server to forward the requests for that DNS domain.

Creating Reverse-Lookup Zones

The next step in configuring your Windows DNS server is to configure your reverse-lookup zone. As previously discussed, the reverse-lookup zone is named-based on the reverse order of the IP address for the network. The example.com domain assigns addresses in the 192.168.0 network.

Creating a Reverse-Lookup Zone in Windows 2000

The following procedure can be used to create a reverse-lookup zone in a Windows 2000 DNS server.

1. Open the DNS console as an Administrator of the server.
2. In the console tree, expand *DNSServer*, and then click Reverse Lookup Zones.
3. In the console tree, right-click Reverse Lookup Zones, and then click New Zone.
4. In the New Zone Wizard, click Next.
5. In the Zone Type page, click Standard Primary, and then click Next.

Active Directory Integrated Zones in Windows 2000 and Windows .NET Server

Windows 2000 and Windows .NET DNS servers can store their DNS zone data in traditional DNS text files or as objects in Active Directory. To create an Active Directory-integrated zone, the DNS service must be running on a Windows 2000 Server or Windows .NET Server configured as a domain controller.

Active Directory-integrated zones offer the following enhancements over traditional text file-based zones:

- More than one domain controller in a domain can accept DNS dynamic updates or manual DNS updates if they have the DNS service installed. This eliminates the single point of failure using traditional primary zone files where if the primary zone is unavailable, no new records may be added.

- Active Directory security can be applied to resource record objects so that only the owner of a resource record can modify the resource record. This feature prevents DNS dynamic updates from overwriting an existing resource record with incorrect information. You do this by enabling Secure dynamic updates.

An Active Directory-integrated zone can act as a master server to a secondary DNS zone, even if the secondary zone is hosted by a BIND DNS server. The necessary text file format is generated by the zone transfer mechanism for storage at the secondary DNS server.

---

6. In the Reverse Lookup Zone page (see Figure 7.9), enter the IP subnet address. In our example, we would enter 192.168.0. Note that Windows 2000 automatically generates the in-addr.arpa format of the filename, and then click Next.

7

FIGURE 7.9

Defining the reverse-lookup zone.

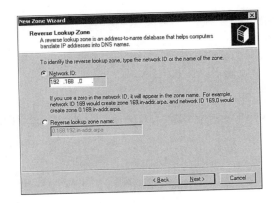

7. In the Zone File page, accept the proposed name, and then click Next.

8. In the Completing the New Zone Wizard page, click Finish.

When you investigate the zone in the DNS console, you will note that the New Zone Wizard automatically generated SOA and NS resource records for the zone. After the zone is created, you can modify these values by editing the properties of the SOA record.

From now on, you should not have to manually configure any more records for the reverse-lookup zone. If the DNS console allows automatic creation of PTR records in the zone when creating address (A) records. This reduces the chance that you will forget to create a pointer (PTR) record.

Additionally, you can configure the zone to accept dynamic updates. By right-clicking the DNS zone you just created, and then clicking Properties, you can define whether dynamic updates are allowed as shown in Figure 7.10.

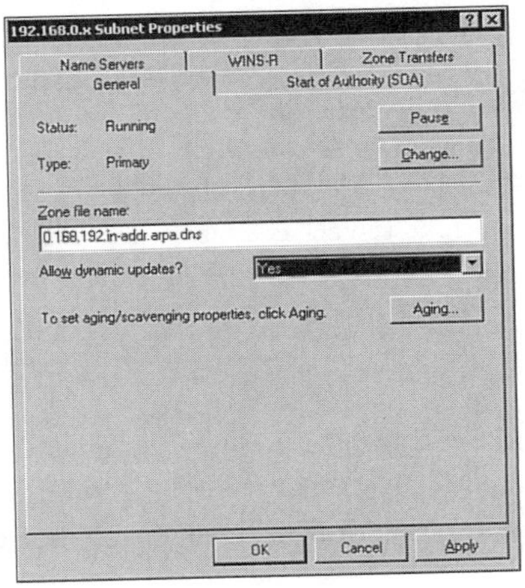

FIGURE 7.10

Enabling dynamic updates for the 192.168.0.x subnet.

Creating a Reverse-Lookup Zone in Windows .NET Server

The following procedure can be used to create a reverse-lookup zone in a Windows .NET Server running the DNS service.

1. Open the DNS console as an Administrator of the server.
2. In the console tree, expand *DNSServer*, and then click Reverse Lookup Zones.
3. In the console tree, right-click Reverse Lookup Zones, and then click New Zone.
4. In the New Zone Wizard, click Next.
5. In the Zone Type page, click Primary Zone, and then click Next.
6. In the Reverse Lookup Zone page, enter the IP subnet address (in our example, we would enter 192.168.0), and then click Next.
7. In the Zone File page, accept the proposed name, and then click Next.
8. In the Dynamic Update page, click Allow Any Dynamic Updates, and then click Next.
9. In the Completing the New Zone Wizard page, click Finish.

Creating a Forward-Lookup Zone File

Once the reverse-lookup zone is defined, you can create the actual domain zone file. For our example, we'll create the example.com domain that was created for a BIND DNS server.

Creating a Forward-Lookup Zone in Windows 2000 Server

The following steps are required to create a forward-lookup zone in Windows 2000 Server's DNS implementation:

1. Open the DNS console as an Administrator of the server.
2. In the console tree, expand *DNSServer*, and then click Forward Lookup Zones.
3. In the console tree, right-click Forward Lookup Zones, and then click New Zone.
4. In the New Zone Wizard, click Next.
5. In the Zone Type page, click Standard primary, and then click Next.
6. In the Name box in the Zone Name page, type **example.com**, and then click Next.
7. In the Zone File page, accept the proposed name, and then click Next.
8. In the Completing the New Zone Wizard page, click Finish.

As with the reverse-lookup zone creation, dynamic updates must be manually configured for the newly created zone. You can do this by right-clicking the newly created zone, and then selecting properties. In the General tab, set the Allow Dynamic Updates drop-down list to a value of Yes.

7

Securing Dynamic Updates

If the zone was configured as an Active Directory-integrated zone, the Allow Dynamic Updates drop-down list would allow you to set the value of Only secure updates. This option is only available for Active Directory-integrated zones.

The creation of the example.com zone automatically creates name server (NS), and start of authority (SOA) resource records. An address (A) record will also be created if the DNS server's DNS suffix matches the name of the DNS zone being created.

Creating a Forward-Lookup Zone in Windows .NET Server

The following procedure can be used to create a forward-lookup zone in a Windows .NET Server running the DNS service.

1. Open the DNS console as an Administrator of the server.
2. In the console tree, expand *DNSServer*, and then click Forward Lookup Zones.
3. In the console tree, right-click Forward Lookup Zones, and then click New Zone.
4. In the New Zone Wizard, click Next.
5. In the Zone Type page, click Primary Zone, and then click Next.

 Note

In the Zone Type page, the option to store the zone in Active Directory is enabled if the DNS server is a domain controller. This option is grayed out if the DNS server is not a domain controller.

6. In the Zone Name page, in the Zone name box, type **example.com** and then click Next.
7. In the Zone File page, accept the proposed name, and then click Next.
8. In the Dynamic Update page, click Allow Any Dynamic Updates, and then click Next.
9. In the Completing the New Zone Wizard page, click Finish.

Creating the Remaining Resource Records

Once the DNS forward lookup zone is created, the remaining static DNS resource records can be added using the DNS console. The steps do not really vary between Windows 2000 Server and Windows .NET Server so the process is described in one section.

As mentioned earlier, the SOA and NS resource records are automatically created during the creation of the zone by the New Zone Wizard. The resource records that must be manually created include the A, CNAME, and MX resource records.

Note

SRV resource records are registered by the Netlogon service of Windows 2000 and Windows .NET Server. The Netlogon service automatically registers all required SRV resource records with the domain controller's configured DNS server at startup or whenever the Netlogon service is restarted as long as the DNS zone is configured to allow dynamic updates.

A new Address (A) resource record is created by right-clicking the zone name in the console tree, and then clicking New Host. In the dialog box that appears (see Figure 7.11), enter the Name, IP address, and whether you want a Pointer (PTR) resource record to be created in the reverse-lookup zone.

FIGURE 7.11

Adding an Address (A) resource record.

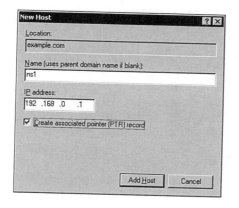

A CNAME resource record is created by right-clicking the zone name in the console tree, and then clicking New Alias. In the dialog box that appears (see Figure 7.12), enter the alias name and the fully qualified domain name (FQDN) of the host to which the alias refers.

A mail exchange (MX) resource record is created by right-clicking the zone name in the console tree, and then clicking New Mail Exchanger. In the dialog box that appears (see Figure 7.13), enter the Mail server name and the Mail server priority. Do not enter the Host or domain entry unless the mail server is for a child domain of the current domain.

7

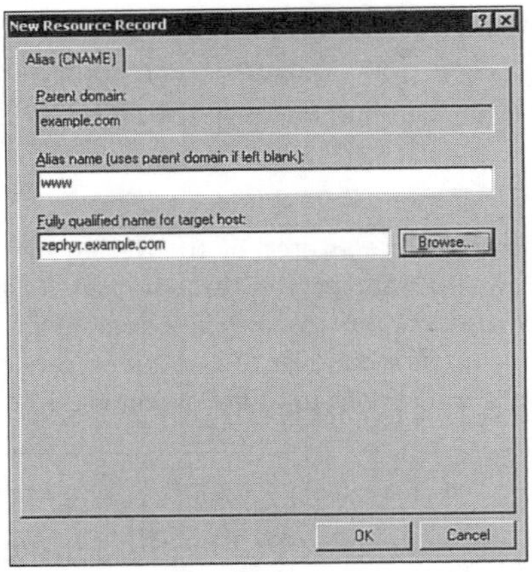

FIGURE 7.12

*Adding a canonical
name (*CNAME*) resource
record.*

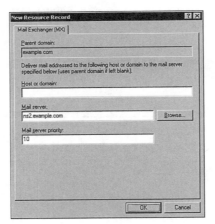

FIGURE 7.13

*Adding a Mail
Exchanger resource
record.*

Troubleshooting DNS with NSLOOKUP

The NSLOOKUP command can be used to troubleshoot hostname resolution problems.
It also is quite useful when determining whether your DNS server has been configured
correctly.

The NSLOOKUP command can be run in either interactive or batch mode. Batch mode
enables quick name resolution to take place. The following is the syntax for interactive
mode:

```
NSLOOKUP <hostname>     or NSLOOKUP <IP Address>
```

This returns the IP address for the queried hostname or the hostname for the queried IP address.

Interactive mode enables further inspection of the name space. Some common commands are shown in Table 7.3.

TABLE 7.3   NSLOOKUP Interactive Commands

Batch Command	Description
`<hostname>`	Prints info about the host/domain NAME using default server.
`<hostname> <DNS server>`	Same as `<hostname>`, but uses the indicated `<DNS Server>` as the name server.
`<help>` or `<?>`	Prints info about common commands.
`set all`	Shows all options currently in use.
`set [no]recurse`	Turns on or off recursive queries.
`Set d2`	Enables exhaustive debugging mode. This mode results in the display of all fields of every DNS packet.
`set querytype=X`	Sets query type, such as A, ANY, CNAME, MX, NS, PTR, or SOA.
`set type=X`	Synonym for `querytype`.
`set class=X`	Sets query class to IN, CHAOS, HESIOD, or ANY.
`set server <DNS Server>`	Sets default server to `<DNS Server>` using current default server.
`ls [opt] DOMAIN`	Lists addresses in DOMAIN: `-a` (Lists canonical names and aliases). `-d` (Lists all records—actually performs a zone transfer or dump of all resource records in the domain). `-t` TYPE (Lists records of the given type, such as A, CNAME, MX, NS, PTR, and so on).
`Exit`	Exit batch NSLOOKUP mode.

If you want to determine the SOA record for the example.com domain, you can enter the following information in batch mode:

```
[root@bklinux /root]# nslookup
Default Server:  ns1.example.com
Address:  192.168.0.1

> set type=soa
> example.com
Server:  ns1.example.com
Address:  192.168.0.1
```

7

```
example.com
        origin = ns1.example.com
        mail addr = administrator.example.com
        serial  = 3
        refresh = 3600 (1 hour)
        retry   = 600 (10 mins)
        expire  = 86400 (1 day)
        minimum TTL = 3600 (1 hour)

ns1.example.com    internet address = 192.168.1.2
```

 Note   In this example, the bold lines indicate the actual commands that you must type in a console. The non-bold lines are the data returned by the typed commands.

Applying What You Have Learned

Today's material reviewed the configuration of DNS servers in both BIND and Microsoft environments. Remember that the key is to configure DNS so hostname resolution is performed efficiently on your network. In the review questions, you will configure a DNS server using text files to be sure you understand the configuration of a DNS server.

Test Your Knowledge

Here are questions to check what you've learned today. The answers can be found in Appendix B, "Test Your Knowledge: Answers."

The network diagram shown in Figure 7.14 is used to create a DNS server's configuration files. Use this diagram for questions 1–3.

1. Create the `named.conf` file for the `Homer` computer.

2. Create the zone file for `simpsons.com` that would be stored on `HOMER`.

3. Configure the reverse-lookup zone for this network that would be stored on `HOMER`.

4. How do you acquire an updated version of `NAMED.CACHE`?

5. What `NSLOOKUP` command can be used to determine the mail exchange for the domain komarconsulting.com?

6. What `NSLOOKUP` command can be used to determine all the name servers for the komarconsulting.com domain?

7. What `NSLOOKUP` command can be used to dump all resources for the komarconsulting.com domain? How can this be prevented in a BIND DNS environment?

FIGURE 7.14

A sample network.

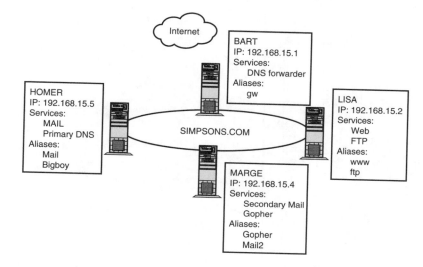

Preview of Day 8

Tomorrow, you will continue looking at name resolution configuration. The only difference is that you will look at NetBIOS Name Server configuration, rather than DNS server configuration.

For NetBIOS server configuration, we will look at the configuration of a Windows 2000 WINS server, and some of the configuration options that can be set to optimize NetBIOS name resolution.

7

DAY **8**

Configuring NetBIOS Name Servers

While NetBIOS is often considered a Microsoft-related protocol, NetBIOS services are also supported by IBM LAN Server and Unix Samba network systems. Today's material looks at how NetBIOS, an application-level protocol, is implemented in TCP/IP networks. As discussed in Day 6, "Resolution of IP Addresses and Logical Names," NetBIOS name servers can improve network performance by reducing NetBIOS' dependency on broadcast packets. Today we specifically look at

- NetBIOS message formats
- Implementing NetBIOS services over TCP/IP in a Windows 2000 network
- Troubleshooting NetBIOS with NBTSTAT

I conclude the day with a discussion of troubleshooting NetBIOS with the NBTSTAT command and look at the future of the NetBIOS protocol.

NetBIOS Message Format

 When data is transmitted across the network, the NetBIOS message format, shown in Figure 8.1, includes the following fields.:

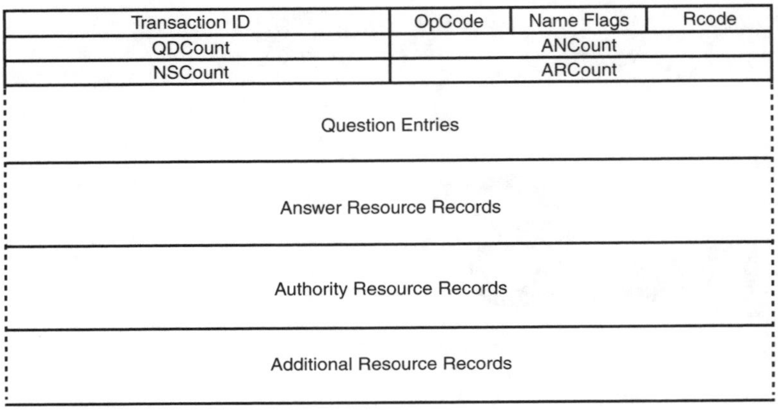

FIGURE 8.1

The NetBIOS message format.

Transaction ID		OpCode	Name Flags	Rcode
QDCount		ANCount		
NSCount		ARCount		
Question Entries				
Answer Resource Records				
Authority Resource Records				
Additional Resource Records				

- **Transaction ID.** A 16-bit field that contains a unique transaction ID. The requestor generates the unique value and the responder places this transaction ID into a response packet.

- **OpCode.** This 5-bit field defines the contents of the NetBIOS packet. The first bit represents whether the packet is a request packet ("0") or a response packet ("1"). The remaining four bits define the type of operation performed:

Bits	Operation
0000	NetBIOS name query
0101	NetBIOS name registration
0110	NetBIOS name release
0111	NetBIOS wait for acknowledgment (WACK)
1000	NetBIOS name refresh

- **Name Flags.** A 7-bit field that defines how operations will proceed. The Name Flags field is subdivided into seven fields (see Figure 8.2), two of which are reserved for future use.

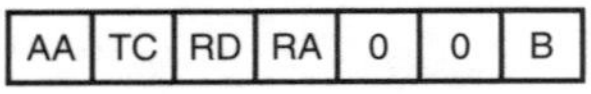

FIGURE 8.2

The NetBIOS Name Flags.

AA	TC	RD	RA	0	0	B

Field	Description
AA (Authoritative Answer)	A 1-bit field that indicates that the responding NetBIOS name server is authoritative (1) for the requested domain name, or nonauthoritative (0).
TC (Truncation Flag)	A 1-bit field indicates that the message was greater than 576 bytes and was truncated. This requires the client to use TCP for connections to the NetBIOS name server, instead of UDP.
RD (Recursion Desired)	A 1-bit field, only valid in requests sent to a NetBIOS name server, that if set to a value of 1, indicates that the NetBIOS client desires recursive queries, registrations, and releases.
RA (Recursion Available)	A 1-bit field, only valid in responses from a NetBIOS name server, that if set to a value of 1, indicates that the NetBIOS name server supports recursion. All other packets must be a value of 0.
B (Broadcast)	A 1-bit field that indicates if the packet is directed (0) or a broadcast/multicast (1).

- **RCode.** A 4-bit field that indicates the response of the request. The following values can exist.

Value	Meaning	Description
0	No Errors	The NetBIOS request was successful.
1	Format Error	The NetBIOS request was incorrectly formatted.
2	Server Error	The NetBIOS name server could not process the submitted name.
3	Name Error	The name requested was not found by the NetBIOS name server.
4	Unsupported Error	The request is not supported by the NetBIOS name server.
5	Refused Error	The name registration was refused by the NetBIOS name server.
6	Active Error	The name registration was refused because the name is owned by a different node.
7	Conflict Error	The name registration was refused because a UNIQUE name is owned by more than one node.

- **QDCount.** A 16-bit field indicating the number of questions included in the Question entries section. Set to a value of 0 for all response packets.

- **ANCount.** A 16-bit field indicating the number of responses included in the Answer entries section.
- **NSCount.** A 16-bit field indicating the number of resource records included in the Authority entries section.
- **ARCount.** A 16-bit field indicating the number of resource records included in the Additional Resource entries section.
- **Question Entries.** All NetBIOS requests in the NetBIOS packet. The number of entries is indicated by the QDCount field.
- **Answer Resource Records.** All NetBIOS responses in the NetBIOS packet. The number of entries is indicated by the ANCount field.
- **Authority Resource Records.** All NetBIOS authority resource records in the NetBIOS packet. The number of entries is indicated by the NSCount field.
- **Additional Resource Records.** All additional resource records in the NetBIOS packet. The number of entries is indicated by the ARCount field.

Implementing NetBIOS Services over TCP/IP

This section outlines the configuration of the most widely implemented NetBIOS name server—Microsoft's Windows Internet Name Service, or WINS, server.

Installing the Windows Internet Name Service (WINS)

The Windows Internet Name Service (WINS) provides a central repository with which configured NetBIOS clients can register their NetBIOS names. NetBIOS clients also use the WINS server to resolve NetBIOS names to IP addresses using unicasts rather than broadcasts, reducing the amount of broadcast traffic existing on the network related to NetBIOS name resolution.

Is WINS Required in Windows 2000?

NetBIOS is not technically required in a Windows 2000 network unless support for legacy clients, such as Windows 9*x* and Windows NT 4.0, or NetBIOS applications is required. Be sure to fully investigate your network when deciding whether to deploy WINS.

The WINS service is a component of Windows 2000 Server products. Because registrations are sent to a specifically configured WINS server by WINS clients, a static IP address is recommended for all WINS servers.

The WINS server can be installed in Windows 2000 using the following steps:

1. Log in to the Windows 2000 Server with an account that is a member of the local Administrators group on the server.
2. From the Start menu, click Settings, and then click Control Panel.
3. In the Control Panel, double-click the Add/Remove Programs applet.
4. In the Add/Remove Programs dialog box, click Add/Remove Windows Components.
5. In the Windows Components Wizard dialog box, in the Components list, select Networking Services, and then click Details.
6. In the Networking Services dialog box, in the Subcomponents of Networking Services list, click the Windows Internet Name Service (WINS) check box, and then click OK.
7. In the Windows Components Wizard dialog box, click Next.
8. The installation of the necessary files starts. If required, you may be prompted to input the installation location.
9. In the Completing the Windows Components Wizard page, click Finish.
10. Close the Add/Remove Programs dialog box.
11. Close the Control Panel.

 Note Windows 2000 allows installation of network services, such as WINS, without having to reboot the computer, as in Windows NT 4.0.

Configuring Clients to Reduce NetBIOS-Related Traffic

After the WINS server is configured, the next step is to configure clients to use the WINS server for NetBIOS-related traffic. This can be accomplished by manually configuring each client or by configuring clients using a DHCP server. Installation and configuration of a DHCP server will be discussed in detail on Day 10, "Auto-Configuration of Hosts Using RARP, BOOTP, and DHCP."

When manually configuring each client, you must enter the IP address of your WINS server in each client's TCP/IP properties dialog box (refer to Figure 8.3). This can be performed on all NetBIOS clients. After the WINS server's IP address is configured in the TCP/IP properties dialog box, the WINS client is configured as an h-node client by default. As discussed on Day 6, "Resolution of IP Addresses and Logical Names," this means the WINS client first queries the WINS server when resolving NetBIOS names to IP addresses. If they cannot resolve the name using the WINS server, they will then try a subnetwork broadcast to resolve the NetBIOS name.

FIGURE 8.3

Configuring WINS parameters at a Windows 2000 client.

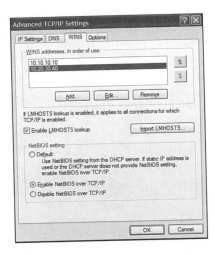

Changing the Default NetBIOS Node Type

You can change the default node type by editing the Registry value: `HKLM\System\CurrentControlSet\Services\NetBT\Parameters\NodeType` and setting the values to be 0x1 (Broadcast Node), 0x2 (Peer-to-Peer Node), 0x4 (Mixed Node), or 0x8 (Hybrid Node).

If clients are configured using a DHCP server, the following parameters must be configured within the DHCP scope to ensure that the clients correctly register their NetBIOS names with the WINS server and utilize the WINS server for NetBIOS name resolution:

- Configure option 44, WINS/NBNS Servers, to indicate the IP address of the WINS/NBNS for the DHCP clients
- Configure option 46, WINS/NBT Node Type, to indicate the NetBIOS name-resolution method used by the DHCP clients. The WINS/NBT Node Type is used to configure the NetBIOS resolution order that the NetBIOS client uses when resolving a NetBIOS name to an IP address. Valid Options include 0x1 (Broadcast Node), 0x2 (Peer-to-Peer Node), 0x4 (Mixed Node), or 0x8 (Hybrid Node).

Note

You may want to review the section "NetBIOS Name Resolution" in Day 6, "Resolution of IP Addresses and Logical Names."

8

Configuring the WINS Server Environment

Several configuration issues might arise when you implement WINS servers in your network. These issues can include the following:

- Adding static mappings for non-WINS clients
- Configuring WINS proxy agents
- Configuring WINS record timers
- Configuring replication between WINS servers
- Integrating WINS with DNS

Adding Static Mappings for Non-WINS Clients

Not all clients on a network can be configured to perform NetBIOS resolution using a WINS server, such as UNIX or Macintosh clients. The network administrator might want to add static mappings in the WINS database for these non-WINS clients. This enables WINS clients to resolve NetBIOS names to IP addresses for these hosts. A network with non-WINS clients is shown in Figure 8.4.

FIGURE 8.4

A networking consisting of WINS and non-WINS clients.

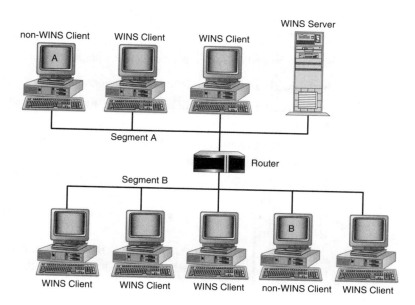

In this sample network, hosts A and B are not configured as WINS clients. This may be by choice or because a TCP/IP stack does not have a WINS configuration. What issues arise because these two hosts are not WINS clients? All the hosts on the same segment A can resolve NetBIOS names for host A to an IP address, because the resolution can be performed using a subnet broadcast. The hosts on segment B, however, cannot resolve any of the NetBIOS names for host A because the router cannot forward any NetBIOS resolution packets.

The problem can be corrected by adding static mappings to the WINS database. This can be accomplished using the WINS MMC console in the Windows 2000 Administrative Tools folder (see Figure 8.5).

FIGURE 8.5

The WINS MMC Console.

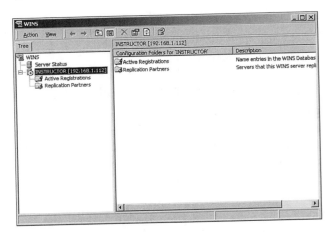

The following procedure can be used to define a static mapping:

1. In the console tree, expand the WINS server, and then select Active Registrations.

2. In the console tree, right-click Active Registrations, and then click New Static Mapping.

3. In the ensuing dialog box (see Figure 8.6), you can enter the host's NetBIOS name and the associated IP address.

   You can add static mappings for Unique, Group, Domain Name, Internet Group, or Multihomed NetBIOS names. (These were discussed in detail on Day 6, "Resolution of IP Addresses and Logical Names," in the section "NetBIOS Name Registrations.")

4. The mappings are now included in the WINS database, and WINS clients can resolve the non-WINS clients' NetBIOS names by querying the WINS database.

FIGURE 8.6

Configuring a static WINS mapping.

8

Viewing the Contents of the Database

Windows 2000 does not display all registered NetBIOS names by default. You can view all registered NetBIOS names by using the following procedure:

1. Open the WINS MMC console from Administrative Tools.

2. In the console tree, expand the WINS server, and then select Active Registrations.

3. In the console tree, right-click Active Registrations and then click Find by Name.

4. In the Find by Name dialog box, in the Find Names Beginning With box, type a matching pattern for the name you want to find. You can enter the "*" character as a wildcard to find all registrations, and then click OK.

5. The results of the find are displayed in the details pane.

Configuring a WINS Proxy Agent

Non-WINS clients only can resolve NetBIOS names using broadcast methods. They cannot resolve NetBIOS names stored in the WINS server database. This generally restricts NetBIOS name resolution to the local network segment.

A WINS client can be configured on each network segment as a *WINS proxy agent*. This computer acts as a proxy for non-WINS clients and forwards their NetBIOS name-resolution requests to the WINS server. The WINS proxy agent then broadcasts the result it receives from the WINS server on the local network segment.

In the sample network in Figure 8.3, you would have to configure one of the WINS clients on each network segment to function as a WINS proxy agent. This is accomplished by changing the setting for the value named EnableProxy to 1. The EnableProxy value is located in the following Registry location:

`HKLM\System\CurrentControlSet\Services\NetBT\Parameters`

After this value is set, the WINS proxy agent must be restarted before it can function.

Configuring WINS Record Timers

WINS clients, by default, register their NetBIOS names every time they restart. If a WINS client is not shut down regularly, timers can be configured to tune the name-registration process. These timers determine when a NetBIOS name entry can be removed from the WINS database.

The following timers can be configured for a WINS server:

- **Renewal timer.** This timer specifies how frequently a running client re-registers its NetBIOS name. The default interval on a WINS server is 6 days. The client actually renews its NetBIOS name at half this interval, or every 72 hours. When the timer expires, this entry is marked as released. This setting can be increased to reduce NetBIOS name-registration traffic.

 Note

Remember that a WINS client releases its NetBIOS names at shutdown, and renews its NetBIOS names at startup. The renewal timer only affects clients that are not shut down when not in use.

- **Extinction interval.** This timer specifies the interval between when an entry is marked as released and when it is marked as extinct. The default setting is 4 days. Marking an entry as extinct initializes the process of removing the entry from the WINS database.
- **Extinction timeout.** This timer specifies the interval between when an entry is marked extinct and when the entry is finally removed from the database. The default value for this setting is 6 days.
- **Verify interval.** This timer specifies the interval after which the WINS server must verify that old names it does not own are still active. The default depends on the extinction interval, which is the first step in removing an entry from the WINS database. The minimum value is 24 days. This is necessary when multiple WINS servers replicate their information between themselves.

To configure these timers, right-click the WINS server in the WINS MMC console, and then click Properties. In the WINS Server Properties dialog box, the timers are configured in the Intervals tab as shown in Figure 8. 7.

FIGURE 8.7

Defining timers for the WINS server

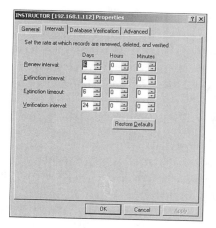

8

Configuring Replication Between WINS Servers

The final configuration commonly used in a network is replication between multiple WINS servers. These generally are larger-scale networks with thousands of NetBIOS clients (see Figure 8.8).

FIGURE 8.8

A network implementing WINS replication.

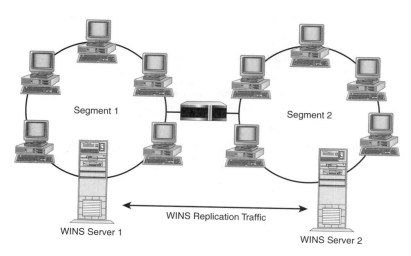

WINS replication must be configured when more than one WINS server is implemented in the network. The WINS replication process makes sure each WINS server contains a total copy of the NetBIOS names registered on the network. The records have an Owner designation that indicates which WINS server accepted the NetBIOS name registration.

WINS servers can perform two different roles during the replication process. They can be pull partners and push partners.

A *pull partner* is a WINS server that requests new database entries from its replication partner. This is configured to occur at regular time intervals. The WINS server requests only WINS records newer than the last record it received from its replication partner. Pull-partner replication often is used across slow WAN links because the replication can be configured to take place during lower network-utilization periods. Also, longer intervals for replication can eliminate the replication of entries that were released at a workstation's shutdown, but then re-registered when the workstation restarts. Slow WAN links are any links less than T1 speed (1.54Mbps).

A *push partner* is a WINS server that notifies its pull partners that a preconfigured number of changes have been registered to the WINS database. This message acts as a trigger for the pull partner to request the updated WINS records. Push partners generally are configured when fast network links exist. They tend to cause more frequent network traffic than pull replication alone, because the replicated data can include released entries, that will be re-registered in the near future.

A WINS replication partner can be configured using the following steps:

1. In the WINS console, in the console tree, expand the WINS server and select Replication Partners.

2. In the console tree, right-click Replication Partners, and then click New Replication Partner.

3. In the Replication Partner dialog box, enter the IP address of the WINS server with which you want to replicate, and then click OK.

4. The replication partner will appear in the details pane as a Push/Pull partner. You can modify the replication settings by double-clicking the replication partner object in the details pane.

5. In the Properties dialog box, in the Advanced tab (see Figure 8.9), you can define the following settings:

   - **Replication Partner Type.** The partner can be defined as a push partner, a pull partner, or both a push and pull partner. This setting defines what other properties are available in the dialog box.

   - **Pull Replication.** Defines all properties associated with pull replication, including using a persistent connection to the replication partner and replication interval settings.

   - **Push Replication.** Defines whether to use a persistent connection for push replication and how many changes must be made to the WINS database before a pull partner is informed that replication should take place.

6. Once the properties are defined, click OK.

FIGURE 8.9

Configuring replication partner settings.

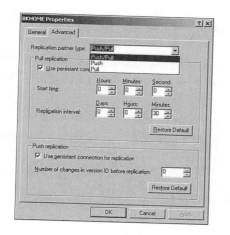

8

The other WINS server also must have its replication settings adjusted so it can send and receive WINS database changes. After the replication partner is defined in both directions, you can force replication in several ways. The options include

- *Triggering replication between all replication partners in both directions.* This is accomplished by right-clicking Replication Partners in the console tree, and then clicking Replicate Now.

- *Triggering a push replication with a specific replication partner.* This is accomplished by right-clicking the specific replication object in the details pane, and then clicking Start Push Replication. You can then select whether to start Push replication with this partner only, or with all configured partners.

- *Triggering a pull replication with a specific replication partner.* This is accomplished by right-clicking the specific replication object in the details pane, and then clicking Start Pull Replication.

After replication is performed, WINS clients can connect to any NetBIOS resources in the enterprise network. The WINS servers each contain the entire enterprise NetBIOS name database.

Integrating WINS with DNS

Windows 2000 allows you to integrate the names registered in the WINS database into DNS queries. This is done by configuring a DNS server to forward unresolved hostnames to a WINS server for a specific DNS zone.

When the DNS server receives a query for a hostname that is not in a zone file that the DNS server is authoritative for, the DNS server can be configured to forward the request to the WINS server for resolution. If the WINS server has a registration for the NetBIOS name, the IP address is returned to the DNS server. The DNS server then returns this IP address to the DNS client.

Integrating WINS is accomplished by configuring a DNS zone to forward unresolved hostname requests to a WINS server. This is done by performing the following procedure in Windows 2000.

1. Open the DNS console from Administrative Tools.
2. In the console tree, expand the DNS server, and then select the zone you want to integrate with WINS resolution.
3. In the console tree, right-click the zone, and then click Properties.
4. In the Zone Properties dialog box, select the WINS tab.
5. In the WINS tab (see Figure 8.10), you can configure the WINS server to which unresolved DNS queries are forwarded.

FIGURE 8.10

Configuring a WINS DNS resource record.

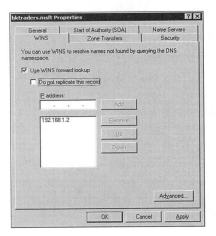

6. You can also choose to not replicate the resource record to secondary DNS servers. You *must* select this option if any of your secondary DNS servers are Unix BIND DNS servers. BIND DNS servers do not support the WINS resource record.
7. The Advanced button allows you to define the interval that a WINS-resolved hostname will be cached at the DNS server. The default value is 15 minutes.
8. After all WINS servers are configured, save the settings by clicking OK.

Using WINS for Reverse Lookups

You can also configure a reverse-lookup zone to forward unresolved PTR resource record queries to a WINS server. This is accomplished by defining a WINS-R resource record in the reverse-lookup zone.

Troubleshooting NetBIOS with NBTSTAT

Microsoft clients ship with a command-line tool that can be used to troubleshoot NetBIOS name problems in the network. The NBTSTAT command allows you to determine what NetBIOS names are in your NetBIOS cache, query other hosts for their NetBIOS names, and reload the NetBIOS cache with values configured in an LMHOSTS file.

The syntax of the NBTSTAT command is

NBTSTAT {[-a RemoteName]/[-A IPAddress] [-c] [-n] [-r] [-R] [-RR] [-s] [-S]}

where

- -a RemoteName lists all NetBIOS names of the host indicated by RemoteName.

- -A IPAddress lists all NetBIOS names of the host at the indicated IPAddress.

- -c displays the current contents of the NetBIOS name cache. This includes all cached entries and their current Time-To-Live (TTL).

- -n displays the NetBIOS names registered by the current host.

- -r displays statistics on how many requests are resolved by broadcast and Name Servers. It also displays names in the NetBIOS name cache and how they were resolved.

- -R empties the current contents of the NetBIOS name cache and reloads the name cache from entries in the LMHOSTS file.

- -RR causes the client to re-register all NetBIOS names using the configured NetBIOS settings of the client. For example, if using H-node, the client will first attempt registration by contacting the configured WINS server.

- -s lists all current NetBIOS sessions, and lists all remote computers by their NetBIOS names.

- -S lists all current NetBIOS sessions, and lists all remote computers by their IP addresses.

The NBTSTAT command is very useful for detecting what NetBIOS names are registered by a remote computer. The command NBTSTAT -A *ipaddress* is a common technique to determine what hostname a computer is using. It can also be used to determine what NetBIOS services are running on a computer. For example, if you see a *computer-name[20]* service running, you know that the computer is running a NetBIOS File and Print service. Likewise, if you see the entry *RonaldB[03]*, you know that RonaldB is currently logged on at the computer you are scanning.

The Movement Away from NetBIOS

Many of the operating systems that previously used NetBIOS have moved away from traditional NetBIOS solutions to solutions that are more dependent on DNS for name resolution services.

This does not mean that you can immediately remove the WINS server from your network. You should first audit your current applications to determine if any of the applications are WINS-dependent.

For example, in a Windows 2000 network, there are two services that still require NetBIOS name services:

- **Clustering.** The name applied to a Windows 2000 cluster is a NetBIOS name. You cannot connect to the cluster from a remote subnet unless you use a NetBIOS name resolution method such as a WINS server.
- **Computer restrictions.** If you want to restrict a user to only logging on at specific workstations, the workstations are determined using NetBIOS names. You must have a WINS server to determine if a remote computer is allowed as a workstation for a restricted user.

And just so you do not think that NetBIOS is only an issue with Microsoft software, another common application used by Engineering companies is AutoCAD. AutoCAD uses a NetBIOS licensing service in recent versions. When an AutoCAD client starts, it must contact the AutoCAD licensing service before the application starts. If the AutoCAD licensing service is running on a remote subnet, WINS is required to find the IP address of the AutoCAD licensing server.

Applying What You Have Learned

Today's material looked at how NetBIOS name servers are deployed on a network to provide NetBIOS name resolution. Although there is less need for NetBIOS name resolution in today's networks, be sure that you do not have NetBIOS-dependent applications before you remove the NetBIOS name server from your network.

8

Test Your Knowledge

Here are questions to check what you've learned today. The answers can be found in Appendix B, "Test Your Knowledge: Answers."

1. Describe the issues involved when multiple WINS servers are implemented in a network.

2. How do WINS proxy agents assist in the resolution of NetBIOS names for non-WINS clients?

3. When would you have to add static entries to a WINS database?

4. In a worst-case scenario, how much time will pass before a record is removed from the WINS database for a computer that has been permanently removed from the network?

5. What is the difference between a push partner and a pull partner in WINS replication?

6. What services in a Windows 2000 network still require NetBIOS name resolution?

7. In what circumstances would you consider integrating WINS with DNS for name resolution?

Preview of Day 9

Tomorrow's material examines the specifics of routing in a TCP/IP internetwork. You'll learn how to configure routing using both static routing tables and routing protocols to build your routing tables dynamically.

The material also covers the specific routing protocols in use today. It compares and contrasts the various routing protocols with one another.

Day 9

Gateway and Routing Protocols

Today's material examines various routing protocols that can be implemented in a network. The discussion starts with the basics of routing, including the following:

- Routing metrics
- Static routing
- Dynamic routing
- Common routing problems
- Methods for overcoming routing problems

Then more detailed information is provided about the following:

- Static routing concepts
- Exterior gateway protocols (including EGP and BGP)
- Interior gateway protocols (including RIP, IGRP, EIGRP, and OSPF)

Finally, we'll review some troubleshooting techniques using the `traceroute` command.

Routing Basics

Routing is the process of moving a packet of information from one physical network segment to another. Ultimately, the packet is delivered to a destination host.

People often compare the term *bridging* with routing. Bridging occurs at the data link layer of the OSI model; routing takes place at network layer three of the OSI model (see Figure 9.1).

FIGURE 9.1

Comparing bridging with routing.

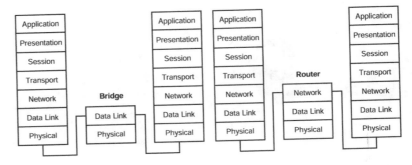

The Differences Between Bridges and Routers

A *bridge* examines the hardware destination address of a frame and, based on the tables it keeps of hardware addresses, either forwards or discards the frame. A new frame is generated to replace the original frame. Bridges are used only to connect locally managed networks.

A *router* is more intelligent than a bridge. It can make additional decisions, such as selecting the best route for a datagram to reach its destination. This enables routes to change and delivery still takes place to a destination host. Routers can connect both local and remotely managed networks.

Routers use various metrics to determine the best route for sending packets to a destination network. A *metric* is either a cost or a value assigned to a property of a network link. The following are some common metrics used by routing protocols:

- **Hop count.** This is the most common routing metric. It measures how many routers a packet crosses as it moves from the source network to the destination network.

- **Delay.** This metric measures the amount of time it takes to move a packet from the source to the destination network. Factors that can affect the delay include bandwidth of intermediate networks, size of queues waiting to be routed at each router, network congestion on intermediate networks, and total distance between two networks.

- **Throughput.** This metric measures the available traffic capacity of a network link. A 10Mbps ethernet link is preferred over a 56K frame-relay link.

- **Reliability.** This metric compares the reliability of network links. Some links are down more frequently than others, so the more reliable links are preferred. Other reliability ratings include determining how long it takes to get a failed link repaired and operational.

- **Communication costs.** Sometimes, delivering information to a destination network in the shortest amount of time is not the primary goal of the network designer. Reducing network transport costs often is the goal instead. It is less expensive to send data over public-switched networks than over privately-owned lines.

Different routing protocols use different routing metrics. Some routing protocols enable you to use different combinations of the preceding routing metrics and enable the network administrator to apply different weights to each metric when calculating the optimal route to a remote network.

Types of Routing Configuration

There are two primary ways to configure routing in a network. The first, *static routing*, involves manually configuring all preferred routing paths through the internetwork.

Static routing works best in smaller networks that do not change much in topology. If a change occurs in the network, manual reconfiguration must take place. If the manual reconfiguration changes are not performed, routing does not take place correctly. If static routing is implemented and a router goes down, the network must be manually configured to bypass the failed network segment.

The other way to configure routing in a network, *dynamic routing*, makes use of routing protocols to build routing tables that describe the network automatically. If a change in topology occurs, the dynamic routing protocol advertises the network changes to all routers. The routers then re-evaluate the best path to each network segment.

The two most common types of routing protocols in use today are distance vector protocols and link state protocols.

Distance vector protocols are broadcast-based protocols that commonly use hop count as their primary routing metric. Distance vector protocols are widely implemented because they are easy to configure. When you add a new router running the distance vector protocol, it advertises and builds its own routing table.

Distance vector protocols do have some disadvantages. They do not scale well to larger networks because each routing packet contains paths to the entire network. This can lead to a large amount of network traffic dedicated to routing. The routing information is sent only to the router's neighbors. *Neighbors* are routers connected to the same physical segment as the sending router.

Distance vector protocols also are characteristically slow to converge. *Convergence time* is the amount of time it takes the network to adjust to a topology change and to recalculate all routing tables for the network.

Link state protocols send routing information to all nodes in the network. This routing information only contains routes to directly attached networks. Even though these routing messages are sent to all routers on the network, their reduced size results in a more efficient exchange of routing information.

Each router stores the best route to a network ID. This results in a shorter convergence time when a router or network segment goes down. The shorter convergence time is a key reason link state protocols are used in larger network implementations. The only disadvantage of link state protocols is that they require more planning, configuration, and CPU power for the routing configuration.

Common Routing Problems

Common routing problems that occur in routed networks include routing loops and counting-to-infinity problems.

Routing loops usually occur when static routing is implemented incorrectly. Figure 9.2 shows a common routing loop.

In the figure, Router A believes that any packets destined for Network 4 must be routed to Router B. Router B is configured so that any packets destined for router 4 must be routed to Router C. Router C is configured so that packets destined for Network 4 must be routed to Router A. You are now back to where you started from, and you will never get to Network 4.

IP has some protection from routing loops in the Time-To-Live field. Every time the packet crosses a router, the TTL decreases by at least one. When the TTL reaches zero, the packet is discarded. This prevents a packet from continuing to circulate the network when there is no hope of it ever reaching its final destination.

A counting-to-infinity problem is more common in dynamic routing. The problem exists when a router fails, and the remaining routers continue to exchange routing information. The hop count to a network beyond the failed router continues to grow. Figure 9.3 shows a network about to suffer this type of problem.

FIGURE 9.2

A routing loop.

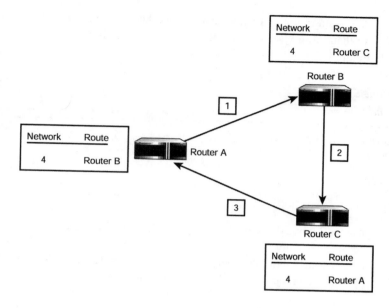

Network	Route
4	Router C

Router B

Network	Route
4	Router B

Router A

Network	Route
4	Router A

Router C

FIGURE 9.3

The network before a counting-to-infinity problem exists.

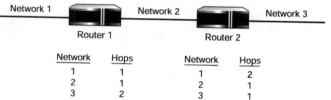

Network	Hops
1	1
2	1
3	2

Network	Hops
1	2
2	1
3	1

Assume that, because of an interface failure, the network interface attaching Router 2 to Network 3 fails. Router 2 immediately changes the hop count to infinity (∞) to indicate that Network 3 no longer is available (see Figure 9.4).

FIGURE 9.4

The router interface to Network 3 fails.

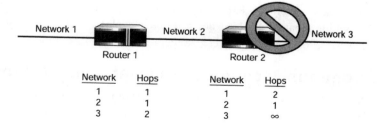

Network	Hops
1	1
2	1
3	2

Network	Hops
1	2
2	1
3	∞

A counting-to-infinity problem can occur as the result of a timing problem. If Router 1 sends its network advertisement before Router 2 sends its advertisement, Router 2 receives a routing advertisement stating that Network 3 is only 2 hops away. This is better than infinity, so the 2 is incremented to 3 and is entered as the new hop count (see Figure 9.5).

FIGURE 9.5

Router 2 receives incorrect routing information from Router 1.

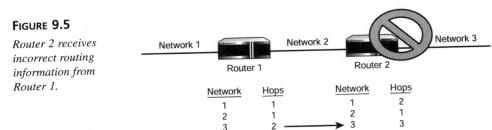

Router 2 now advertises its new routes. Router 1 receives a route update stating that Network 3 is now 3 hops away. Router 1 must update its routing table because it originally learned about the route to Network 3 from Router 2. The hop count is incremented by one and is recorded as 4 hops (see Figure 9.6).

FIGURE 9.6

Router 1 continues to update the incorrect information.

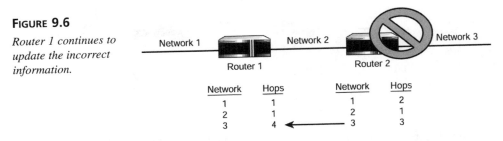

The routers continue to advertise new routes to Network 3. The hop count continues to grow by one with each advertisement until the hop count reaches infinity. The good news is that each routing protocol has a maximum hop count that it calls infinity. Routing Information Protocol (RIP), for example, has a maximum hop count of 15 hops. Anything greater than 15 is deemed unreachable. The counting-to-infinity problem has created a routing loop between Routers 1 and 2 for its duration.

Common Techniques to Overcome Routing Problems

Some common techniques are used to prevent routing loops and counting-to-infinity problems. These techniques include the following:

- Implementing hold-downs
- Implementing split horizons
- Implementing poison reverse

9

Hold-downs prevent regular update messages from erroneously updating a route that should be removed. Routers that are directly attached to the network detect when a route goes down. They send routing update messages to inform their neighbors of the new hop counts. In the counting to infinity example, a neighboring router sent an update message indicating that Network 3 was still reachable. A hold-down would have told Router 2 to maintain its configured change (that Network 3 is unreachable) for a specified period of time (called the *hold-down time*). This would prevent Router 2 from updating its routing table with the incorrect information from Router 1. The hold-down time should be a longer period of time than the update interval used to announce the routing table.

Split horizons are based on the principle that it is not wise to send routing information back in the direction from which it came. If you go back to the network example in Figure 9.4, split horizons would have prevented the counting-to-infinity problem. The counting-to-infinity problem was caused by Router 1 advertising that it could reach Network 3 in 2 hops. Router 1 should never pass this information to Router 2 because it learned about the route to Network 3 *from* Router 2. This would prevent the two-node routing loops associated with counting to infinity problems.

Poison reverse helps to speed up convergence in a network. When a router learns about a network from a particular interface, it sends RIP advertisements to that same interface advertising that the network is unreachable. This prevents a counting to infinity problem because the hop count immediately is set to an unreachable state. If the network is reachable, that hop count is maintained by receiving routers.

Figure 9.7 shows the implementation of poison reverse.

FIGURE 9.7

Poison reverse implementation.

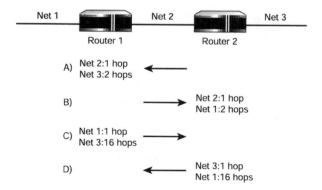

If Router1 and Router2 are configured to use poison reverse, the update of routing tables would proceed as follows:

A. Router1 sends a routing update packet to Router2 indicating that both Net1 and Net2 are 1 hop away.

B. On receipt, Router2 adds an entry to its routing table indicating that Net1 is two hops away (one more hop than what was received in the routing update from Router1). Because the route to Net1 is a newly learned network, Router2 sends a routing update packet to Router1 that includes a poison reverse update for Net1. The hop count for Net1 is set to 16 hops, or unreachable in this update packet. The update packet also contains routing updates for Net2 and Net3 indicating that the networks are 1 hop away.

C. Router1 inspects the received routing update packet. Because the route to Net1 exists in its routing table, the routing update indicating that Net1 is unreachable is discarded. Likewise, the routing table is not updated for Net2, as an existing route to Net2 exists in the routing table, and is shorter than the advertised route. Finally, the route to Net3 is new, and is added to the routing table with a hop count of 2 hops. Because the route to Net3 is newly discovered, a routing update packet is sent. The routing update includes an affirmation that the Net1 is 1 hop away and a poison reverse update indicating that Net3 is unreachable.

D. Router2 can now validate that the route to Net1 is valid. Likewise, after receiving the poison reverse update for Net3, a routing update packet is sent to Router1 indicating that the route to Net3 is valid, and that Net3 is 1 hop away.

Static Routing

In static routing, all routes are set by a network administrator. This most often is used in smaller networks because any topological changes to the network result in the need to modify the static routing tables.

Static routing requires that routes be set to each network address for each router on the network. If a route is not created for a network segment, packets cannot be sent to that network segment.

A default route can be set as a catchall route. Instead of explicitly naming each and every route to all segments of the network, several routes can be grouped by a default route entry in the routing table.

Figure 9.8 shows a small network requiring that static routes be configured for each router. These routing tables determine how a packet is transferred from a source network to a destination network.

Router 1 has interfaces on both the 192.168.1.0 and 192.168.2.0 networks. The router automatically configures routes for these two networks through the local interfaces when the router is started (see Table 9.1).

FIGURE 9.8

Configuring static routing.

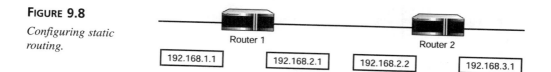

Router 1   Router 2

192.168.1.1   192.168.2.1   192.168.2.2   192.168.3.1

TABLE 9.1   Default Routes Autoconfigured for Router 1

Net Address	Netmask	Gateway Address	Interface	Metric
192.168.1.0	255.255.255.0	192.168.1.1	192.168.1.1	1
192.168.2.0	255.255.255.0	192.168.2.1	192.168.2.1	1

These routes indicate that the 192.168.1.0/24 network is reachable through interface 192.168.1.1. The 192.168.2.0/24 network is reachable through the interface 192.168.2.1.

A static route entry must be added for information to travel from Router 1 to the 192.168.3.0 network. The entry is shown in Table 9.2.

TABLE 9.2   Additional Static Route Required for Router 1

Net Address	Netmask	Gateway Address	Interface	Metric
192.168.3.0	255.255.255.0	192.168.2.2	192.168.2.1	2

This indicates that the 192.168.3.0/24 network is reachable through the gateway at 192.168.2.2. Information destined for this network should be sent from the local interface with IP address 192.168.2.1.

Another method that could be used is to add a default gateway entry. Adding the entry in Table 9.3 accomplishes this.

TABLE 9.3   A Default Gateway Static Route Entry

Net Address	Netmask	Gateway Address	Interface	Metric
0.0.0.0	0.0.0.0	192.168.2.2	192.168.2.1	1

This route indicates that, if a network address is not explicitly entered in the routing table, all packets destined for the network must be sent to the router interface at 192.168.2.2 through the local interface 192.168.2.1.

The major disadvantage of static routes is that they must be changed manually every time the topology changes. This includes changing the routes when a router interface fails. As you will see in upcoming sections, the use of routing protocols enables dynamic updates to the routing table.

Static Route Management in Windows

All static routing entries are made using the `route` command. The following is the syntax of the `route` command:

```
ROUTE [-f] [-p] [command] [destination] [MASK netmask] [gateway]
➥ [METRIC metric]]
```

- `[-f]`. Flushes the routing tables of all gateway entries. If this is used in conjunction with one of the commands, the tables are cleared prior to running the command.
- `[-p]`. When used with the ADD command, this option creates a persistent root that is re-created every time the router is restarted.
- `[command]`. Specifies one of four functions performed by the route command: `Print`, `Add`, `Delete`, or `Change`. `Print` shows the routing table onscreen, `Add` adds an additional route to the routing table, `Delete` removes a route from the routing table, and `Change` modifies an existing route in the routing table.
- `[destination]`. Specifies the destination IP address. This usually is a network address.
- `[MASK netmask]`. Indicates the subnet mask to be used with the destination address.
- `[gateway]`. Indicates the IP address to which packets destined for the indicated destination IP address/subnet mask should be sent.
- `[METRIC metric]`. Specifies the metric/cost for the destination network address. For example, if you wanted a metric of 3 hops for a route, you would include "METRIC 3" in the route command.

Static Route Management in Cisco

One of the most common routing solutions is to implement Cisco routers. All static routing entries are made using the `ip route` command. The following is the syntax of the `ip route` command:

```
[no] ip route [net id] [subnet mask] [gateway]
```

- `[no]`. Inclusion of the `[no]` parameter removes the indicated route from the Cisco router's routing table.
- `[net id]`. Specifies the destination network IP address.

> - [subnet mask]. Specifies the subnet mask to be used with the net id.
> - [gateway]. Indicates the IP address to which packets destined for the indicated [net id]/[subnet mask] should be sent.

Routing Protocols

9

Autonomous systems play a key part in defining whether a gateway protocol is an exterior gateway protocol (EGP) or an interior gateway protocol (IGP).

An autonomous system is a network managed by a single network management group. The phrase *autonomous system* usually represents your internal network. To identify the routers participating in your autonomous system, an autonomous system number can be acquired from InterNIC. Within an autonomous system, interior gateway protocols, such as RIP and OSPF, determine optimal routes between the locally managed networks.

Exterior gateway protocols transfer routing information between autonomous systems. If two companies want to establish an exchange of data between their networks, they use exterior gateway protocols, such as BGP, to exchange routing information between the two autonomous systems.

The following sections discuss various implementations of exterior gateway protocols and interior gateway protocols.

Exterior Gateway Protocols

Exterior gateway protocols exchange routing information between autonomous systems. When you need to exchange information with another organization's network, you can exchange entry-point information for each other's networks. This is much more efficient than exchanging entire routing tables.

The two most common exterior gateway protocols are Exterior Gateway Protocol (EGP) and Border Gateway Protocol (BGP).

Exterior Gateway Protocol (EGP)

RFC 904 The Exterior Gateway Protocol was developed as an interdomain reachability protocol in April 1984. EGP served as the first exterior gateway protocol to enable autonomous systems (AS) to exchange routing reachability information on the Internet. Some problems with this protocol, however, have led to its replacement by the Border Gateway Protocol (BGP) in most implementations.

Using EGP, information was passed from autonomous systems to the ARPAnet core routers by an EGP source router. This information was then exchanged throughout the core router network and was passed down to destination networks that belong to other autonomous systems (see Figure 9.9).

Figure 9.9

EGP usage on the ARPAnet backbone.

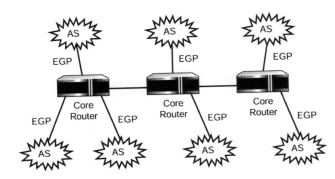

EGP is a dynamic routing protocol, but it does not calculate any routing metrics. As a result, it is unable to make intelligent routing decisions. The only time routing information from update messages can be used by EGP is when the routes being compared are from the same autonomous system. If the routes are from different autonomous systems, the results cannot be measured against each other. EGP only can inform another router of reachability to a remote network.

The following are the three primary functions of EGP:

- **Establishing neighbors.** Routers running EGP must define the routers with which they want to share their reachability information.
- **Polling neighbors.** Neighboring routers are polled to make sure they are still up.
- **Sending update messages.** EGP routers send update messages that contain information about the reachability of networks within their autonomous system.

The packet format for an EGP message (shown in Figure 9.10) includes the following:

- **EGP Version.** This field identifies the EGP version that sent the EGP message. The EGP versions must be compatible between sending and receiving EGP routers.
- **Type.** This field indicates one of five EGP message types. The message types are shown in Table 9.4.

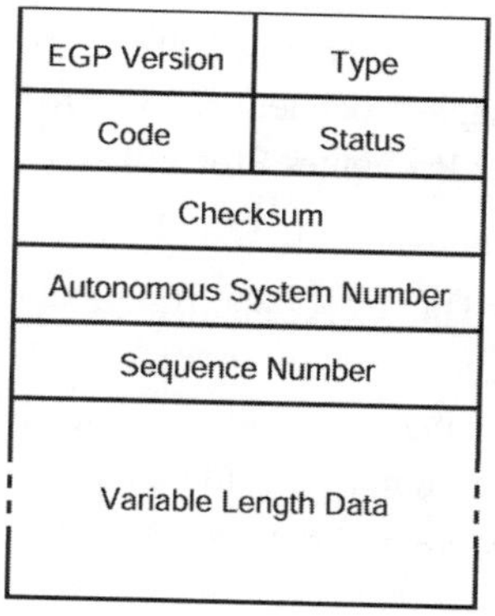

FIGURE 9.10

EGP message format.

EGP Version	Type
Code	Status
Checksum	
Autonomous System Number	
Sequence Number	
Variable Length Data	

9

TABLE 9.4 EGP Message Types

Message Type	Description
Neighbor acquisition	Establishes and de-establishes neighbors. This message includes the hello interval that establishes how frequently neighbor reachability messages should be sent and the poll interval that specifies how frequently routing update messages should be exchanged.
Neighbor reachability	Determines whether neighbors are alive. EGP uses an algorithm specifying that an EGP neighbor should be declared down only after a specified number of neighbor reachability messages have not been received.
Poll	Determines the reachability of the specified network. Using a poll message, an EGP router can determine the relative location of a host on a remote network. A poll message also provides reachability information about the remote network on which the host resides.
Routing update	Provides updated routing information. The routing update message contains additional fields in the Data section, such as the number of interior gateways, the number of exterior gateways, and the IP source network address included in the message. A series of gateway blocks provides the IP address for a gateway and the networks reachable through that gateway. The gateway blocks also include a Distance field. This distance only can be used to compare paths within an autonomous system because the paths are only relative to that autonomous system.
Error	Indicates that an error condition exists, such as a bad EGP header format or an excessive polling rate.

- **Code.** This field distinguishes between message subtypes.
- **Status.** This field contains message-dependent status information. Possible entries include Insufficient Resources or Parameter Problem.
- **Checksum.** This field identifies corruption of the EGP message in transit.
- **Autonomous System Number.** This field identifies the autonomous system to which the sending router belongs.
- **Sequence Number.** This field enables a sending and receiving router to match a request to a reply. This sequence number is initialized with a zero value and is incremented by one for each request or response.

Border Gateway Protocol (BGP)

RFC 1267   The primary function of the BGP protocol also is to exchange network reachability information with other autonomous systems. BGP improves on the functionality of EGP by including the full path of autonomous systems that traffic must transit to reach the destination network. Including the full path to each network provides enough information to construct a network layout graph that enables routing loops to be identified and removed from the routing tables.

BGP also includes some advertising rules that help prevent routing table corruption. An autonomous system can only advertise the routes it uses itself. If the autonomous system does not use a route, it cannot advertise that route because it is unsure whether that route is operational.

BGP uses the TCP protocol to transport routing messages between BGP routers. BGP uses port 179 to establish its connections. When two BGP systems communicate, they initially exchange the entire BGP routing table. After this occurs, only incremental updates are exchanged between the two BGP systems. BGP does not require a periodic refresh of the entire routing table.

To save time when a router goes down, each BGP router stores the most recent versions of its neighbors' routing tables. When the BGP router sends advertisements, it only sends the current optimal path in the routing messages. If a link goes down, it scans the neighbors' routing tables to determine a new optimal path.

In a BGP system, the routing metric assigns a degree of preference for a particular path to an autonomous system. Network administrators manually enter these metrics into router configuration files. The degree of preference can be based on the number of autonomous systems that must be crossed, the type of link, the reliability of the link, or other preferences.

The BGP message header is shown in Figure 9.11.

FIGURE 9.11

BGP message format.

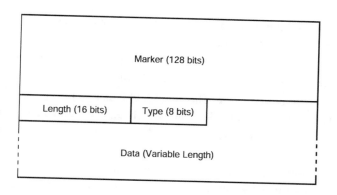

- **Marker.** This 128-bit field contains a value the recipient BGP system can predict. The computed value is based on the authentication mechanism. The Marker field also can identify when two BGP systems no longer are synchronized.

- **Length.** This 16-bit field indicates the total length of the BGP message in octets (including the header). This enables a stream of BGP messages to be sent one after the other. It also identifies where one message ends and the next one begins.

- **Type.** This 8-bit field indicates the type of BGP code transmitted by the BGP message and the format of the remaining fields in the BGP Data section. Possible types include OPEN, UPDATE, NOTIFICATION, and KEEPALIVE.

BGP Open Messages

After a TCP three-way handshake takes place between two BGP systems, the first message sent by each BGP system is an open message. If the open message is accepted by the receiving BGP system, a KEEPALIVE message is returned as confirmation.

Additional fields defined by a BGP open message, shown in Figure 9.12, are as follows:

FIGURE 9.12

BGP open message format.

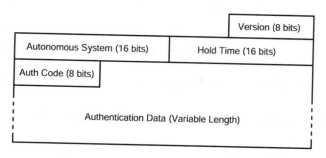

- **Version.** This 8-bit field indicates which BGP protocol version formed the BGP open message.

- **Autonomous System.** This 16-bit field contains the autonomous system number of the sending BGP system.
- **Hold Time.** This 16-bit field indicates the maximum interval between successive KEEPALIVE, UPDATE, or NOTIFICATION messages.
- **Authentication Code.** This 8-bit field indicates the authentication method used. The value in this field indicates which authentication code is implemented, the format of the authentication data, and the algorithm used to compute the values of the Marker field.
- **Authentication Data.** The contents of this variable-length field depend on the value set in the Authentication Code field. If the authentication code has a value of zero, the length of the Authentication Data field also must be zero.

BGP UPDATE Messages

BGP UPDATE messages transfer routing information between BGP neighbors. The information from each BGP Update message is used to build a graph that describes the relationships between the autonomous systems. By inspecting all the relationships, the BGP system can detect potential routing loops and can remove them from the routing table.

The additional fields in a BGP UPDATE message (shown in Figure 9.13) are as follows:

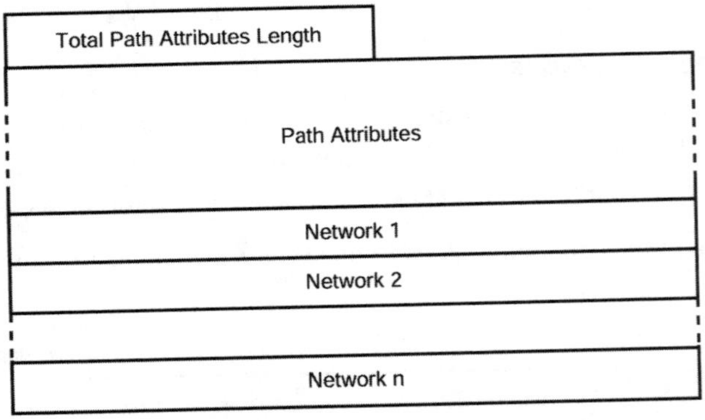

FIGURE 9.13

BGP UPDATE message format.

- **Total Path Attributes Length.** This 16-bit field indicates the total length of the Path Attributes field in octets.
- **Path Attributes.** This variable-length field contains three attributes: Type, Length, and Value.
- **Network #.** In this series of 32-bit fields, each field indicates a single network whose route is described by the Path Attributes field. This field does not report any information about subnet or host addresses.

Five different path attributes can be described in a BGP UPDATE message: Origin, AS path, Next hop, Unreachable, and Inter-AS metric.

The Origin defines whether the path was learned from an IGP (part of the same autonomous system), an EGP (another autonomous system), or some other means (incomplete). Paths learned from IGP are preferred over paths learned from EGP.

The AS path attribute lists autonomous systems that must be crossed to reach the destination network.

The Next hop attribute provides the IP address of the router to be used as the next hop en route to the network included in the update message.

The Unreachable attribute indicates that a formerly reachable network no longer is reachable.

The Inter-AS metric attribute provides a mechanism for a BGP router to advertise its cost to destinations within its own autonomous system. External BGP routers can choose the optimal route into the autonomous system to reach a destination network within the system.

BGP KEEPALIVE Messages

No explicit keep-alive mechanisms are defined within the BGP protocol. Instead, KEEPALIVE messages are exchanged between BGP neighbors at a more frequent rate than the configured hold time. This ensures that the hold timers do not expire. Keep-alive messages often are exchanged at a period equal to one-third the hold time.

A KEEPALIVE message does not contain any additional fields beyond the BGP header information.

BGP Notification Messages

BGP notification messages are sent whenever error conditions are detected. The notification message includes information about why the sending router is closing its connection to the destination router. Figure 9.14 shows the BGP notification message format, which includes the following fields:

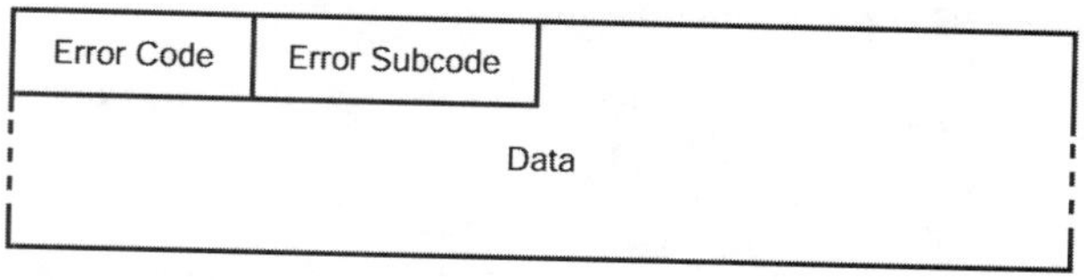

FIGURE 9.14

BGP notification message format.

Error Code	Error Subcode	
Data		

- **Error Code.** This 8-bit field contains an integer value that indicates the type of error notification included in the notification message. Table 9.5 shows a list of configured error codes.

TABLE 9.5   EGP Message Types

Error Code	Error Name	Description
1	Message Header Error	Indicates a problem with the format of the BGP message header.
2	Open Message Error	Indicates a problem with an open message format.
3	UPDATE Message Error	Indicates a problem with a BGP UPDATE message format.
4	Hold Timer Expired	Indicates that the hold timer has expired. The BGP node is declared dead at this point.
5	Finite State Machine Error	Indicates that the sending BGP system has received an unexpected message.
6	Cease	Indicates that the sending BGP system wants to close its BGP connection with the recipient BGP system.

- **Error Subcode.** This 8-bit field provides more detailed information about the reported error code. If an error code does not have an associated subcode, a zero value is set in the Error Subcode field.
- **Data.** This variable-length field can be used to diagnose the cause of a notification error. The size of this field depends on the contents of the Error Code and Error Subcode fields.

Interior Gateway Protocols

Interior gateway protocols exchange routing information between routers belonging to the same autonomous system. Because all the information gathered is from within an autonomous system, interior gateway protocols can depend more on routing metrics to make accurate decisions when building routing tables.

As previously mentioned, the two most common types of interior routing protocols are distance vector protocols and link state protocols. The following sections discuss two common interior routing protocols: Routing Information Protocol (RIP), a distance vector routing protocol, and Open Shortest Path First (OSPF), a link state routing protocol.

> **Note**
>
> The HELLO protocol sometimes is discussed in TCP/IP books as an example of an interior routing protocol. The HELLO protocol was used to synchronize clocks between hosts and to compute the path with the shortest delay between two hosts. RFC 891 contains more information about the HELLO protocol.

Routing Information Protocol Version 1 (RIPv1)

9

RFC 1058 The Routing Information Protocol version 1 (RIPv1) is a distance vector routing protocol originally developed for use in the Xerox Network Systems (XNS). RIP uses hop count as its routing metric. The *hop count* is the number of routers that must be navigated from the source network to the destination network.

RIP only maintains the best route to a destination network. RIP routers exchange routing information by sending RIP broadcast messages over UDP port 520. If a RIP router receives a broadcast suggesting a better route to a remote network, this better route replaces the existing route in the routing table.

Figure 9.15 shows a network structure and the resulting hop counts to each network segment.

FIGURE 9.15

A sample network and the resulting hop counts.

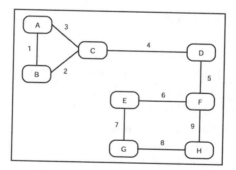

Router \ Network	1	2	3	4	5	6	7	8	9
A	1	2	1	2	3	4	5	5	4
B	1	1	2	2	3	4	5	5	4
C	2	1	1	1	2	3	4	4	3
D	3	2	2	1	1	2	3	3	2
E	5	4	4	3	2	1	1	2	2
F	4	3	3	2	1	1	2	2	1
G	6	5	5	4	3	2	1	1	2
H	5	4	4	3	2	2	2	1	1

Using a hop count metric might seem reasonable, but it does not show preference for routes that use fast network links over slower WAN links.

By default, RIP routers exchange routing information every 30 seconds. RIP broadcasts are sent out on all the routers' interfaces and contain a complete list of all network IDs to which they have been routed. The maximum number of networks that can be reported in a single RIP message is 25 networks. This can lead to scalability problems if a network grows to be quite large. It takes more than a single RIP packet to report the entire network layout. With broadcasts occurring every 30 seconds, a network easily can be overcome with RIP broadcast messages. The actual size at which this occurs is difficult to quantify. You need to consider the total number of RIP packets required to exchange the entire network routing table, the network utilization rates, and the total amount of network traffic.

To limit the number of paths reported by a single router, RIP assumes that a network located 16 or more hops away is considered unreachable.

Although RIPv1 is easy to implement, it has several key problems. The simplicity of the protocol does not lend itself to the routing problems faced by network administrators today. These problems include the following:

- **Subnet masks are not advertised.** RIP version 1 network advertisements do not include a Subnet Mask field. Without this field, it is assumed that networks use the default subnet mask based on the class of address. If a network interface on the router uses a variable-length subnet mask, it is assumed that any routes learned on that interface use the same subnet mask.
- **There is no authentication mechanism.** RIP version 1 does not implement any form of password. Nonauthorized RIP routers can be inserted into the network, potentially corrupting the routing tables.
- **The use of broadcast announcements.** The use of broadcast packets in RIP version 1 is an inefficient method of distributing routing information. Unicasts or multicasts are far more efficient.

RIP Version 2

RFC 2453   RIP version 2 was developed to overcome some of the shortcomings of RIP version 1. The following features have been added to RIP version 2:

- **Subnet Masks.** RIP version 2 router announcements include subnet masks with every network address. This enables network administrators to implement variable-length subnet masks and classless Internet domain routing in their networks.

- **Authentication.** RIP version 2 uses a password to be sure routes are accepted only from preferred routers on the network. If the password in a RIP packet does not match the necessary password, the RIP message is dropped.

- **Multicast announcements.** Instead of using inefficient broadcast announcements, RIP version 2 uses the multicast address 224.0.0.9 to send routing messages.

- **Route tags.** Route tags enable internal RIP routes to be distinguished from routes learned from other interior gateway protocols or from exterior gateway protocols. Route tags also can be configured to distinguish the source of external routes.

The RIP version 2 message format, shown in Figure 9.16, includes the following fields:

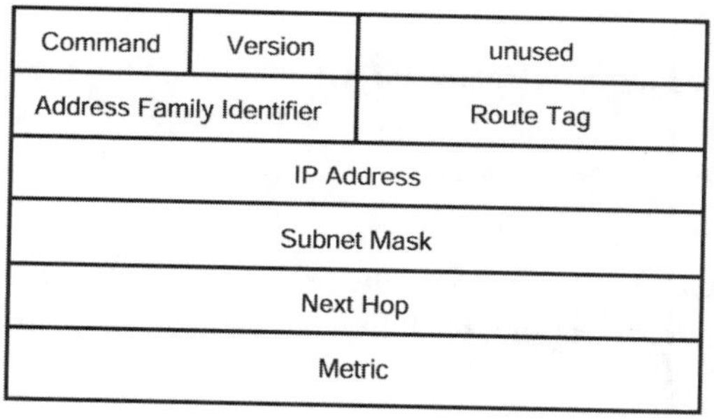

FIGURE 9.16

The RIPv2 message format.

Command	Version	unused
Address Family Identifier		Route Tag
IP Address		
Subnet Mask		
Next Hop		
Metric		

- **Command.** Indicates whether the RIP message is a request or a response. Response messages include all or part of the sending router's routing table.

- **Version.** Indicates which RIP version was used to form the RIP message. In a mixed system that contains both RIP version 1 and RIP version 2, this field indicates whether a router can interpret a RIP message.

- **Address Family Identifier.** Indicates the type of network addressing scheme in use. RIP can be implemented in non-TCP/IP environments such as IPX/SPX. For a TCP/IP environment, the address family identifier is set to a value of 2.

- **Route Tag.** Enables a method of distinguishing the origin of a route. Route tags should be configured as arbitrary values to represent the source of a route. Another common implementation is to use the autonomous system number of the network from which the route was learned. In a RIP version 1 message, this field is set to all zeros.

- **IP Address.** Contains the network IP address referred to in the RIP message.

- **Subnet Mask.** Contains the subnet mask applied to the IP Address field to determine the network portion of the IP address. In a RIP version 1 message, this field is set to all zeros.

- **Next Hop.** Indicates the next hop IP address to which packets destined for this network should be forwarded. This enables packets to be routed in a more efficient manner. This field is set to all zeros in a RIP version 1 message.
- **Metric.** Specifies the hop count to the indicated network.

Interior Gateway Routing Protocol

Interior Gateway Routing Protocol (IGRP) is a distance vector routing protocol developed by Cisco Systems, Inc., in the mid-1980s. IGRP is intended for routing within private networks. As with RIP, IGRP routing information is exchanged between adjacent IGRP routers.

Features of IGRP

IGRP was developed as an alternative to RIP due to limitations of the RIP protocol. Specifically, IGRP was designed to overcome RIP's weakness of only using hop count as a routing metric. To overcome these limitations, IGRP was designed with the capability to support multiple routing metrics:

- **Reliability and load.** A route in the routing table can be assigned a value between 1 and 255 to represent the reliability and the load endured by a specific network link.
- **Bandwidth.** A route can be assigned values representing the link speed from values of 1200bps up to 10Gbits per second.
- **Internetwork delay.** Assigning a value between 1 and 2^{24} can represent delays that may exist for specific network links.

These various metrics can be combined in a user-defined algorithm that reflects route selection for a specific organization.

In addition to multiple routing metrics, IGRP also permits *multipath routing*. Multipath routing enables multiple routes to be defined for a single network address. If the routes have equal metrics, IGRP can transmit a single stream of traffic between the two routes in a round-robin fashion. If the multiple paths have different metrics, data will be transmitted between the two paths using the same ratio. For example, if the metric for RouteA is 12 and the metric for RouteB is 3, four times more traffic will be transmitted using RouteB than the traffic sent using RouteA as shown in Figure 9.17.

In this example, RouteA is a frame relay link that is not too reliable, and has been assigned a metric of 12. In comparison, RouteB is comprised of two different hops that have a total metric of 3. If a file that is comprised of 5 TCP segments is transmitted from Host1 to Host2, multipath routing will send four of the segments using RouteB and one of the segments using RouteA.

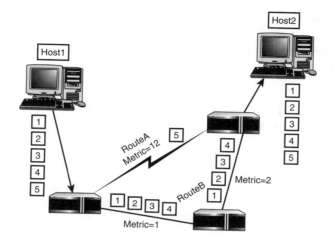

FIGURE 9.17

IGRP uses multipath routing.

IGRP Stability Features

Besides performance features, IGRP also supports hold downs, split horizons, and poison reverse updates to prevent common routing problems such as counting-to-infinity and routing loops from developing.

IGRP uses timers to exchange routing information. Some of the timers that can be defined in IGRP include:

- **Update timer.** Defines how frequently routing update messages should be sent to adjacent routers. The default value for this timer is every 90 seconds.

- **Invalid timer.** Defines how long a router should continue to maintain a specific route in its routing table once routing update messages are no longer received. By default, this timer is defined to be three times the updated period.

- **Hold-time period.** Indicates how long a router maintains configured changes. The default value is three times the update time plus an additional 10 seconds.

- **Flush timer.** Indicates how long a route can remain in the routing table before it is removed from the routing table. The default for IGRP is seven times the update timer.

Enhanced Interior Gateway Routing Protocol (EIGRP)

With Enhanced Interior Gateway Routing Protocol (EIGRP), Cisco improves on IGRP by making the exchange of routing information between adjacent routers more efficient.

EIGRP increases the efficiency by only transmitting changes in a router's routing table to adjacent routers, rather than the entire routing table. In addition, to ensure that an adjacent router does not erroneously designate a router as being offline, each router will send periodic "hello" packets. If a router does not receive a "hello" packet from an adjacent router after a specific period of time has passed, then the adjacent router is considered to be offline.

To determine the most efficient, least-costly route to a destination network, EIGRP uses the Diffusing-Update Algorithm (DUAL) developed at SRI International. The use of DUAL allows some of the features of link-state protocols to be integrated into the distance-vector–based EIGRP protocol.

In particular, the following features are found in EIGRP:

- **Fast convergence.** A router using EIGRP stores the routing tables of all adjacent routers, which allows faster fail-over to an alternate route in the event of router failure. If the EIGRP router cannot find an appropriate route from the cached routing information, the EIGRP router queries its neighboring routers until an alternate route is found. DUAL uses the collected routing information to determine the optimal route to a destination network.

- **Variable-length subnet mask support.** EIGRP can be configured to support different length subnet masks on any interface. No longer is the router required to use the same subnet mask on all interfaces.

- **Partial update support.** An EIGRP router will send a partial update of its routing table to adjacent routers when the metric for a route changes. This feature reduces the bandwidth required for route propagation in IGRP.

- **Multiple network-layer support.** An EIGRP router provides support for AppleTalk, IP, and NetWare routing environments. In addition, routes learned from other routing protocols can be redistributed by EIGRP. For example, when running IP routing, EIGRP can redistribute routes learned from OSPF, BGP, or EGP.

Open Shortest Path First (OSPF)

RFC 2328 The Open Shortest Path First (OSPF) protocol is a link state routing protocol developed to overcome the shortcomings of the RIP protocol. OSPF is more scalable than RIP and enables dynamic routing to be configured in large, diverse networks.

The OSPF algorithm for finding the best route to a destination network is based on the Dijkstra algorithm. This algorithm finds the shortest path from a single source node to all other nodes in the network. It is applied at every router in the network.

OSPF Segmentation of the Network

The network can be divided into autonomous systems to make it easier to manage. OSPF is a routing protocol that can be implemented in an autonomous system. OSPF enables an additional hierarchy to be implemented that cannot be performed in a RIP environment. OSPF can subdivide an autonomous system into groups of networks called *areas* (see Figure 9.18).

FIGURE 9.18

OSPF areas within an autonomous system.

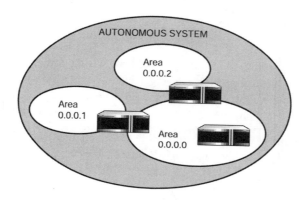

A network number identifies each area. Network area IDs use the same dotted decimal format as IP addresses, but they do not have to be the actual network IP addresses in use. In an OSPF network with multiple areas, one area is designated as the *backbone area*. This area is assigned the special area ID `0.0.0.0`. The backbone area acts as a routing hub for traffic between areas.

Dividing the autonomous system into areas reduces routing traffic for the entire autonomous system. If information needs to be routed entirely within an area, all routing information must be obtained from that area. No external area routing information is used.

Routing Table Construction Under OSPF

Each OSPF router in an autonomous system maintains a network map called the *link state database (LSDB)*. The link state database is updated whenever an area of the network topology changes. If a router has interfaces on multiple areas, an LSDB is maintained for each separate area. The LSDB is evaluated every 10 seconds. If no changes have occurred to the area's topology, no changes are made to the LSDB.

The LSDB contains entries for all the networks to which each router in an area is attached. It also assigns an associated outgoing cost metric to each network interface of a router. This metric measures the cost of sending traffic through an interface to the connected network. By assigning costs, router preferences can be set based on line cost or line speed.

The entries in the LSDB are based on information sent in link state advertisements (LSAs). An LSA contains the following information:

- Each OSPF interface on a router
- The attached networks for that router
- The cost to reach each of these networks

A network is in a *converged state* when the LSDB is the same for each router in the area. After the LSDB has reached this converged state, each OSPF router calculates the shortest path through the network for each network and each router. A Shortest Path First (SPF) tree stores this information. Every router maintains its own SPF tree.

After the SPF tree is built, the routing table can be calculated by determining the lowest-cost route to each destination network. Routing tables are calculated locally at each router.

A Sample OSPF Routing Table Calculation

This example walks you through the calculation of a routing table in an OSPF autonomous system. The routing table is calculated based on the network shown in Figure 9.19.

FIGURE 9.19

A sample OSPF network.

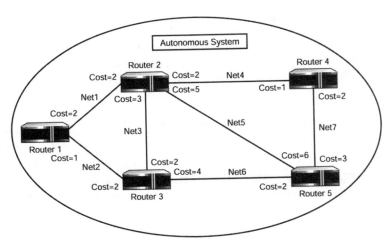

Based on the network in Figure 9.19, the link state database shown in Table 9.6 would be built based on the link state advertisements sent by each router.

TABLE 9.6   Determining the LSDB

Router	Attached Network	Network Usage Cost
Router 1	Net1	2
Router 1	Net2	1
Router 2	Net1	2
Router 2	Net3	3
Router 2	Net4	2
Router 2	Net5	5
Router 3	Net2	2
Router 3	Net3	2
Router 3	Net6	4
Router 4	Net4	1
Router 4	Net7	2
Router 5	Net5	6
Router 6	Net6	2
Router 7	Net7	3

Using this LSDB, a routing table now can be constructed by each router. To generate the routing table, determine the Shortest Path First (SPF) tree for each router. The SPF tree that can be built for Router 1 is shown in Figure 9.20.

FIGURE 9.20

The Shortest Path First tree for Router 1.

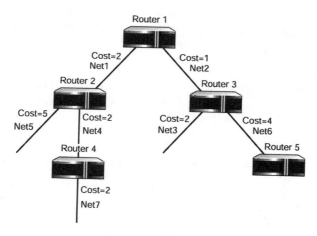

Based on the SPF tree for Router 1, the routing table shown in Table 9.7 could be built for Router 1.

TABLE 9.7   Router 1 Routing Table

Network	Gateway	Interface	Metric
Net1	-	1	2
Net2	-	2	1
Net3	Router 3	2	3
Net4	Router 2	1	4
Net5	Router 2	1	7
Net6	Router 3	2	5
Net7	Router 2	1	6

Communication Within an OSPF Network

In an OSPF environment, the key is to be sure the link state databases at each router are synchronized for all routers within an area. To simplify this process, OSPF only requires that adjacent routers remain synchronized. Instead of worrying about all routers within an area, each router only synchronizes with routers on adjacent networks.

Before synchronization can take place between two OSPF adjacent routers, the routers must decide which will function as the Master for the synchronization process. The Master usually is chosen based on the router ID. The router with the highest ID acts as the Master.

After the Master and Slave roles are defined, the Master OSPF router sends database description packets to the Slave. These packets contain descriptions of the Master router's LSDB and contain a list of link state advertisements (LSAs). The Slave router responds with its own database description packets.

Based on the information received in the database description packets, each router builds a set of link state request packets to complete its LSDB. The routers respond to these packets with link state update packets that contain the requested LSAs.

After the link state requests are exchanged, the two routers are said to be *fully adjacent*. When they are fully adjacent, they can exchange routing information. The routing tables now can be built after the Shortest Path First algorithm is run at each router.

Because there can be several routers within an area, one router acts as the *designated router*. This router becomes the central contact point for routing information exchange within the area. All routing changes are sent to the designated router first. These changes then are distributed to all other routers on the network. For the sake of fault tolerance, a backup designated router also is elected in case the designated router fails.

The designated router is selected based on a router priority. Each router is manually assigned a priority value, and the router with the highest priority value is selected as the designated router. If more than one router has the same router priority, the router ID becomes the value used for the election.

Within the OSPF network, OSPF routers use one of the following multicast IP addresses for communication (if the router supports multicasting):

- 224.0.0.5. This address sends information to all OSPF routers on a network.
- 224.0.0.6. This address sends information to the designated router and the backup designated router. This address sends link state updates and link state acknowledgments to the designated router.

Note

In Non-Broadcast Multiple Access (NBMA) networks, such as an X.25 network, there is no capability for multicasts. In this form of networks, all neighbors' IP addresses must be configured manually on the routers.

Router Types Within an OSPF Network

Several types of routers can exist within an OSPF autonomous system. These routers, shown in Figure 9.21, include the following:

FIGURE 9.21

Router roles in an OSPF autonomous system.

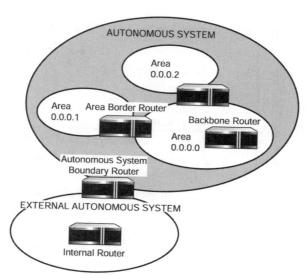

- An *internal router* is a router whose network interfaces are all connected to networks in the same area.

- An *area border router* is a router whose interfaces attach to networks belonging to multiple areas.

- A *backbone router* is any router with an interface to the backbone area. A backbone router can be either an area border router or an internal router that only connects to the backbone area.

- An *autonomous system boundary router* is a router that exchanges routing information with routers from an external autonomous system.

OSPF Message Header Format

Figure 9.22 shows the OSPF message header format. Its fields include the following:

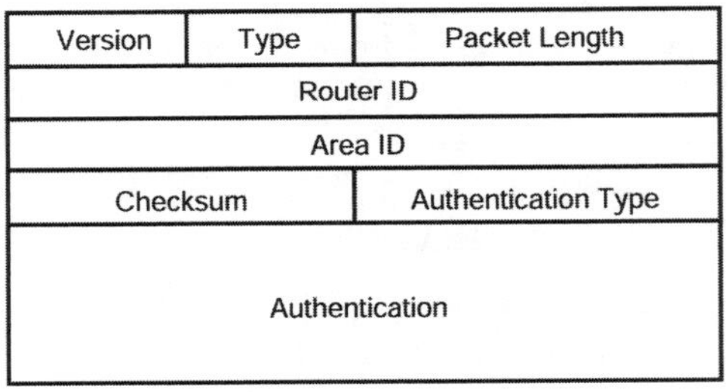

FIGURE 9.22

The OSPF message header.

Version	Type	Packet Length
Router ID		
Area ID		
Checksum		Authentication Type
Authentication		

- **Version.** This 8-bit field represents the version of OSPF in use.

- **Type.** This 8-bit field defines the type of OSPF information contained in the data. The various type values are outlined in Table 9.8.

TABLE 9.8 OSPF Message Types

Message Type	Description
Hello	Used to establish and maintain neighbor relationships.
Database description	Describes the LSDB and is exchanged during the establishment of full adjacency.
Link state request	A request for a portion of the destination router's LSDB, based on information exchanged in a database description message.
Link state update	The response message for a link state request.
Link state acknowledgment	Makes sure the link state update has been received successfully.
Router link advertisements	Describes the collected state of a router's links to a specific area. An RLA is sent for each area to which a router belongs. They do not go beyond the area.

TABLE 9.8 continued

Message Type	Description
Network link advertisements	Sent by the designated router, these messages describe all routers attached to a multiaccess network.
Summary link advertisements	These messages summarize routes to destinations outside the area but still within the autonomous network. Intra-area routes are advertised to the backbone area. Both intra-area and inter-area routes are advertised to all other areas.
AS external link advertisements	These messages describe routes to destination networks external to the autonomous system.

- **Packet Length.** This 16-bit field specifies the OSPF message length in bytes (including the OSPF header information).
- **Router ID.** This 32-bit field identifies the source router of the OSPF message.
- **Area ID.** This 32-bit field identifies the area to which the OSPF message belongs.
- **Checksum.** This 16-bit field makes sure the entire OSPF message has not been corrupted in transit. The checksum algorithm is performed against the entire OSPF message.
- **Authentication Type.** All OSPF messages are authenticated, and this 16-bit field designates the authentication method used. This can be configured uniquely for each area within an autonomous system.
- **Authentication.** This 64-bit field contains the authentication data based on the authentication type.

Troubleshooting Routing Problems

Most routing troubleshooting consists of inspecting the routing tables and tracing packets as they are routed through the network.

Troubleshooting Using Microsoft Windows

As previously mentioned in the "Static Routing" section, the ROUTE command can be used to inspect the routing table. You can type the following command to inspect the current routing table:

```
ROUTE PRINT
```

The default route (if defined) also should be inspected. Be sure the default route points to the correct gateway IP address.

Another common troubleshooting technique for routing problems, is to perform trace routes. A trace route indicates each router that is passed between the client that issues the trace route command and the target indicated in the parameter of the trace route command. Microsoft Windows uses the command TRACERT.EXE to perform trace routes. The following is the syntax of the TRACERT command:

```
tracert [-d] [-h maximum_hops] [-j host-list] [-w timeout] target_name
```

- [-d]. This option suppresses the resolution of IP addresses to hostnames for each intermediate host crossed to the target name.
- [-h maximum hops]. This option specifies the maximum number of hops that can be crossed en route to the target name.
- [-j host-list]. This option indicates specific hosts that must be crossed en route to the target name. This is useful if you expect a route to be used and want to test that route.
- [-w timeout]. This option indicates the timeout in milliseconds implemented for each reply from each router crossed.

> By inspecting the tracert output, a network administrator can determine where routing tables may be incorrect. The output of the tracert utility shows where the packet successfully crossed a router, and timeouts where the routing fails. To fully troubleshoot the problem, the tracert utility should be executed from both the source and destination hosts. If using Windows 2000 or higher, you can also use the pathping.exe command to further investigate routing. Pathping shows you the same output as a tracert command, but also computes statistics for lost and sent packets.

Troubleshooting Using Cisco IOS

The Cisco IOS also enables you to inspect the current routing table at a Cisco router by using the following command:

```
SHOW IP ROUTE
```

> To run this command, you must be in privileged mode. You enter privileged mode by typing the command **enable** at the Cisco IOS prompt and typing the enable password.

If the routing table is missing routes, the following steps must be taken at the Cisco router:

1. Ensure that you are in privileged mode, by typing the command **enable** at the Cisco IOS prompt and entering the enable password when prompted.

2. Once in privileged mode, you must enter configuration mode by typing **config terminal**.

3. In configuration mode, use the **ip route** command to add any missing static routes. For example, to add the route to the 172.16.7.0/24 network through the gateway located at 172.16.6.1, use the following command:

   `IP ROUTE 172.16.7.0  255.255.255.0  172.16.6.1`

4. Save the configuration changes by typing **CTRL Z**.

5. Save the running configuration to the startup configuration to ensure that the static routes persist in the event that the router is restarted by typing the following command:

   `COPY RUNNING STARTUP`

As with Microsoft Windows, the `traceroute` command can be used at a Cisco router to troubleshoot routing problems. In the Cisco IOS, you do not have to be in privileged mode to perform a traceroute. To perform a traceroute, use the following command at the Cisco IOS prompt:

`traceroute [IP address]`

where `[IP address]` is the IP address of the destination host.

Applying What You Have Learned

Today's material covered key issues related to gateway and routing protocols. Here are questions to check what you've learned today. The answers can be found in Appendix B, "Test Your Knowledge: Answers."

Test Your Knowledge

1. Explain the use of multicast addresses in RIP version 2 and OSPF.

2. Explain the difference between exterior gateway protocols and interior gateway protocols.

3. Which command can be used to determine the route taken by a packet to a remote host?

4. What are some of the primary differences between distance vector and link state protocols?

5. What are some of the common problems faced in a dynamic routing environment?

6. What features can be implemented to overcome these routing problems?

Based on the following routing table information, answer the following questions:

Network Address	Netmask	Gateway Address	Interface	Metric
0.0.0.0	0.0.0.0	203.196.205.1	203.196.205.254	2
127.0.0.0	255.0.0.0	127.0.0.1	127.0.0.1	1
172.16.2.0	255.255.255.0	172.16.2.8	172.16.2.8	1
172.16.2.8	255.255.255.255	127.0.0.1	127.0.0.1	1
172.16.255.255	255.255.255.255	172.16.2.8	172.16.2.8	1
172.16.3.0	255.255.255.0	172.16.2.1	172.16.2.8	2
172.16.4.0	255.255.255.0	172.16.2.1	172.16.2.8	2
172.16.5.0	255.255.255.0	172.16.2.1	172.16.2.8	3
203.196.205.254	255.255.255.255	127.0.0.1	127.0.0.1	1
203.196.205.255	255.255.255.0	203.196.205.254	203.196.205.254	1
224.0.0.0	224.0.0.0	172.16.2.8	172.16.2.8	1
255.255.255.255	255.255.255.255	172.16.2.8	172.16.2.8	1

7. What is the address of the default gateway for this router?

8. List all local IP addresses of this router.

9. Are requests to the IP address 172.16.2.8 placed on the network?

10. What is the significance of the multicast address 224.0.0.0 included in the routing table?

11. What metric is associated with reaching the network 172.16.4.0? Through which interface are packets destined for this network sent?

12. What metric is associated with reaching the network 172.16.5.0? Through which interface are packets destined for this network sent?

13. What Microsoft Windows command would be used to add a static route to network 172.16.6.0/24 through the gateway at IP address 172.16.2.1?

14. What Cisco IOS command would be used to add a static route to network 172.16.6.0/24 through the gateway at IP address 172.16.2.1?

Preview of Day 10

Tomorrow's material examines different methods of assigning IP addresses automatically to hosts on the network. This greatly reduces the amount of time spent individually configuring each host and helps limit the possibility of duplicate IP addresses on the network.

The following three protocols currently enable the automatic configuration of TCP/IP on hosts:

- Reverse Address Resolution Protocol (RARP)
- Bootstrap Protocol (BOOTP)
- Dynamic Host Configuration Protocol (DHCP)

9

Day 10

Auto-Configuration of Hosts Using RARP, BOOTP, and DHCP

One of the most common challenges facing network administrators is the distribution of valid IP addresses to their clients. Addressing must be consistent across a subnetwork, and no duplicates are allowed. Today we'll look at three techniques that can be used to auto-assign IP addresses to IP hosts. These methods reduce the initial configuration required for hosts and maintain an accurate pool of IP addresses without duplication.

The goals for today include

- Determining when to use an auto-configuration solution
- Understanding the RARP process
- Understanding the BOOTP process
- Understanding the DHCP process
- Configuring a DHCP server

The Need for Auto-Configuration

There are many scenarios in which the auto-configuration for IP addresses can be used successfully. These include:

- **The allocation of IP addresses.** Rather than maintaining a table of IP addresses for each host, you can create a pool of IP addresses that can be dynamically assigned to each host on the network. This reduces the configuration time for each host. Hosts can include desktop computers, workstations, servers, laptops, and wireless devices.

- **Diskless workstations.** Some clients do not have a hard disk on which to store their IP configuration. They cannot store this data on a network file server because they require an IP address to communicate with the file server.

- **Network hardware devices.** Some network hardware devices require an IP address to be assigned. These include devices such as HP Jet Direct cards. These clients require more information (such as a default gateway).

- **Pre-boot Execution Environment (PXE) clients.** PXE clients must retrieve an IP address to connect to the network and connect to a PXE Boot server for the installation of an operating system over the network.

By using an auto-assign method, network administrators ensure that clients have valid IP addresses with valid parameters.

Reverse Address Resolution Protocol (RARP)

RFC 903   The Reverse Address Resolution Protocol (RARP) builds on the Address Resolution Protocol (ARP). Rather than broadcasting an IP address for a target machine, the client broadcasts his MAC address on the network in a RARP message (see Figure 10.1).

A client host sends the RARP message to a RARP server. The RARP request specifies that the sending host is both the sender and target machine. The RARP request contains the sending host's MAC address in the target hardware address field. Only RARP servers respond to this message. These servers fill in the Target Protocol Address field and change the message type to a reply before sending the response packet. Due to the type of messaging being used, the RARP server must be on the same network segment as the calling host.

If the network is configured with only one RARP server, and it is unavailable, the client system could be locked up waiting for a response to the RARP request. You can remedy this by adding additional RARP servers. It is generally suggested to create a primary

RARP server. The RARP servers that are designated as secondary RARP servers respond to a RARP request only when they receive a second RARP request from a calling system. This prevents the network from being flooded with RARP responses.

FIGURE 10.1

The RARP process.

The final problem with RARP is that its IP address information is based on the client's MAC address. If a new client is added to the network, its IP address must be manually added to the RARP server before the client is assigned an IP address. There is no mechanism for assigning IP addresses to unknown MAC addresses. The following sections detail solutions that allow for the assignment of IP addresses in this manner.

Bootstrap Protocol (BOOTP)

RFC 951 **RFC 1542** The BOOTP protocol uses the User Datagram Protocol (UDP) as an alternative to RARP. BOOTP addresses are the primary fallback of RARP in that it can send configuration beyond just the IP address of a client.

The BOOTP process uses UDP messages to obtain an IP address and its necessary configuration for a BOOTP client. How does a BOOTP client use IP datagrams before it has received its own IP address? By using the limited broadcast address of 255.255.255.255. This address can be used before the host has obtained its own unique IP address.

The BOOTP response is also sent in a UDP broadcast message. The client knows the broadcast is meant for its system by investigating the packet's Client Hardware Address field.

Ensuring Reliability in the BOOTP Process

Because UDP is used, the delivery of BOOTP messages is said to be unreliable. It is the responsibility of the BOOTP client to ensure that all messages are sent and received correctly. This is accomplished using two UDP options:

- **BOOTP requires UDP checksums.** The checksum is used to verify the information has not changed in transit.
- **BOOTP requires that the Do Not Fragment bit be set.** Ensuring the information has not been fragmented prevents low memory clients from facing the scenario in which they do not have sufficient memory resources to reassemble the datagrams.

In addition, BOOTP uses the timeout and retransmission techniques to prevent data loss on the network. When the client transmits a BOOTP request, a timer starts. If the reply has not been received by when the timer expires, the request is retransmitted. The next time the data is retransmitted, the timer is set for double the previous duration.

The BOOTP Message Format

BOOTP messages use a simplified format. The same format is used for both BOOTP requests and BOOTP replies. Figure 10.2 shows the BOOTP message format.

FIGURE 10.2

The BOOTP message format.

Op	HTYPE	HLEN	HOPS	8 bits each
Transaction ID				32 bits
Seconds		Unused		16 bits each
Client IP Address				32 bits
Machine IP Address				32 bits
Server IP Address				32 bits
Gateway IP Address				32 bits
Client MAC Address				up to 128 bits
Server Host Name				up to 512 bits
Boot File Name				up to 1024 bits
Vendor-Specific Info				up to 512 bits

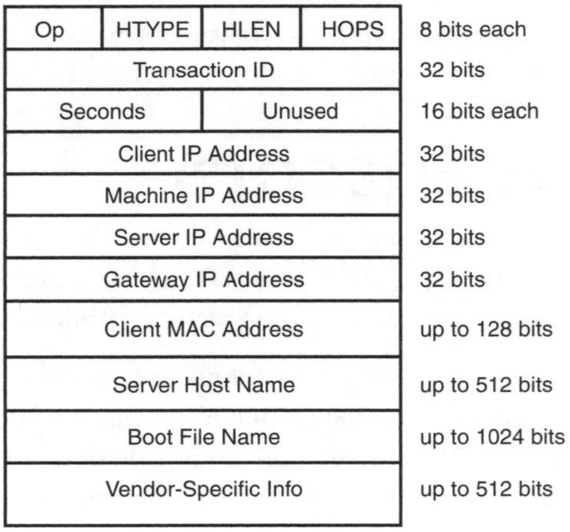

The fields used in a BOOTP message are as follows:

- **Op.** This 8-bit field indicates whether the message is a request (1) or a reply (2).
- **HTYPE.** This 8-bit field indicates what the client's network hardware type is. Ethernet uses a value of 1.
- **HLEN.** This 8-bit field indicates the client's hardware address length. Ethernet uses a hardware length of 6.

- **HOPS.** This 8-bit field indicates how many routers a BOOTP request has crossed on the way to a BOOTP server. The client initially sets this field to a value of 0. Each router that forwards this request increases this field by an increment of 1. This field generally indicates how many routers have been crossed by this BOOTP request.

- **Transaction ID.** This 32-bit field is used by diskless workstations to match the BOOTP reply to the proper BOOTP request. The client assigns this integer value.

- **Seconds.** This 16-bit field indicates the number of seconds since the client started its boot sequence.

- **Unused.** This 16-bit field is currently unused in the BOOTP message.

- **Client IP Address.** This 32-bit field is filled in if the client knows its IP address (or prefers an IP address). This information can be a partial network address (such as 172.16.0.0).

- **Machine IP Address.** The BOOTP server uses this 32-bit field when the client sends a client IP address of 0.0.0.0. The BOOTP server returns the assigned address for the client in the Machine IP Address field.

- **Server IP Address.** This 32-bit field contains either the IP address of a preferred BOOTP Server or 0.0.0.0 to allow any BOOTP server to respond to the BOOTP request.

- **Gateway IP Address.** This 32-bit field contains the IP address for the router or gateway that BOOTP requests are relayed on if a BOOTP server is not found on the local network.

- **Client MAC Address.** This field contains the MAC address of the BOOTP client. It can be up to 128 bits long as different hardware uses different length hardware addressing.

- **Server Host Name.** This field can be used in place of the Server IP Address field if the client is configured with the hostname of its BOOTP server. This field can be up to 512 bits in length.

- **Boot File Name.** This field (up to 1,024 bits in length) specifies a filename from which a memory image can be retrieved to boot the diskless workstation. A different protocol (such as TFTP) is used to download this image from the boot image server. This boot image server can be a different machine than the BOOTP server.

- **Vendor-Specific Information.** This field contains optional information that is passed from the server to the client. The information is specific to each vendor. This variable length field has a maximum size of 512 bytes. Table 10.1 shows the BOOTP vendor-specific types. The first four octets of information are known as the *magic cookie*. The magic cookie defines the format used for the option fields. The standard format described in the table uses a magic cookie value of 99.130.83.99.

TABLE 10.1   BOOTP Vendor-Specific Types

Item Type	Item Code	Length	Contents
Padding	0	X	Used to pad messages
Subnet Mask	1	4	Subnet mask for local network
Time of Day	2	4	Time of day
Gateways (routers)	3	# of entries	IP addresses of all gateways
Time Servers	4	# of entries	IP addresses of all Time Servers
IEN116 Server	5	# of entries	IP addresses of all IEN116 Servers
Domain Name Server	6	# of entries	IP addresses of all DNS Servers
Log Server	7	# of entries	IP addresses of all Log Servers
Quote Server	8	# of entries	IP addresses of all Quote Servers
Lpr Server	9	# of entries	IP addresses of all Lpr Servers
Impress	10	# of entries	IP addresses of all Impress Servers
RLP Server	11	# of entries	IP addresses of all RLP Servers
Hostname	12	# of entries	Client hostname
Boot Size	13	2	Integer size of the boot file
Reserved	128-254	X	Reserved for site-specific use
End	255	X	End of item list

Note   Although most network administrators deploy DHCP for automatic IP addressing, several applications and hardware devices require BOOTP support. For example, HP print devices use BOOTP for autoassignment of IP address information. Likewise, Remote Installation Services (RIS) in Windows 2000 and Windows .NET Server, utilizes BOOTP to initialize client workstations when they connect to the network to automatically load a preconfigured version of Windows 2000 Professional or Windows XP Professional.

Dynamic Host Configuration Protocol (DHCP)

RFC 2131   **RFC 2132**   The Dynamic Host Configuration Protocol (DHCP) is the next logical extension of the BOOTP protocol. DHCP allows for additional configuration items and provides support for dynamic IP address assignments. The use of DHCP on a TCP/IP network enables easier configuration of hosts and helps to prevent duplicate IP address assignment.

The DHCP Process

The DHCP process is made up of four distinct phases (see Figure 10.3).

FIGURE 10.3

The DHCP process.

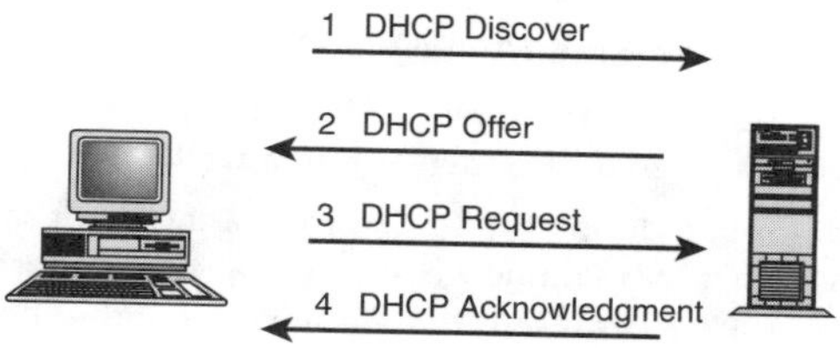

1. The *DHCP Discover* is issued by the DHCP client computer when it attempts to acquire an IP address. Because the client does not know the IP address of a DHCP server, nor does it know how many DHCP servers exist, all information for the DHCP process is issued as broadcasts. The destination IP address used is 255.255.255.255. The client includes its MAC address in the DHCP Discover request for registration in the DHCP database and populates the request with a unique value in the xid field to identify the client that issued the request.

2. The *DHCP Offer* is issued by any DHCP server that receives the DHCP Discover request. The DHCP server offers an IP address from a configured scope of IP addresses. The DHCP offer includes the requesting client's xid value in the xid field so that the client will know that the IP offer is meant for it. The DHCP client may receive more than one DHCP offer.

3. The *DHCP Request* is issued by the DHCP client. This DHCP packet is also issued as a broadcast. The reason for this is to indicate that a DHCP offer has been accepted and notifies other DHCP servers that their offer was rejected. When multiple DHCP offers are received, a Microsoft client uses the following decision process:

    a. The DHCP client always accepts the offer from the DHCP server from which it received its previous IP address.

    b. If the previous DHCP server does not offer an IP address to the DHCP request, the DHCP client accepts the first DHCP offer that it received.

   The DHCP request will also include a list of options that the DHCP client would like to receive from the DHCP server. Some of the more common DHCP options are detailed later today in Table 10.2, "DHCP Options."

4. The *DHCP Acknowledgment* is issued by the DHCP server to acknowledge that the IP lease has been assigned to the requesting client. The DHCP Acknowledgment includes all the optional parameters that were requested by the

client in the DHCP request. It also includes the total lease time and the renewal times for the IP address.

Automatic Private IP Addressing (APIPA)

Windows 2000, Windows XP, and Windows .NET server offer a feature to assign IP addresses to DHCP clients when a DHCP server is not available.

If a DHCP server is not found during the DHCP process, the client randomly selects an IP address from the 169.254.0.0/16 range. To ensure that the IP address is not in use on the network segment, an ARP packet is sent to determine if another host is using the selected IP address.

APIPA does allow limited network connectivity, but does not allow routing to take place. Only an IP address and subnet mask are assigned to the DHCP client. A default gateway IP address is not assigned.

The DHCP client will still attempt to contact a DHCP server. When contact is reached, the IP address will be changed to the IP address offered by the DHCP server.

DHCP Renewals

DHCP clients typically are assigned a limited lease on their IP addresses. The default lease duration is eight days in a Windows 2000 network. Three automatic triggers cause a DHCP client to renew the IP lease from a DHCP server:

- Every time a DHCP client restarts, it renews its IP lease by using a two-packet stream starting with a DHCP request. All DHCP packets are sent as broadcasts.

- At 50% of the lease duration, the DHCP client sends a directed packet to the DHCP server from which it received its IP lease. The packet is a DHCP request to renew its present configuration. If the DHCP server receives the packet, it sends a DHCP acknowledgment resetting the DHCP lease interval.

- At 87.5% of the lease duration, if the DHCP client was unable to renew its IP lease at the 50% renewal point, the DHCP client sends a broadcast DHCP request to renew its IP address. If the original DHCP server receives the DHCP request, it renews the IP address lease. If a different DHCP server receives the request, it either allows the DHCP request if the requested IP address is available in its scope, or sends a DHCP NACK so that the client will restart the IP renewal process with a DHCP discover request.

In some circumstances, the DHCP server can transmit an additional DHCP packet known as the DHCP NACK (Negative acknowledgment) packet. A DHCP NACK packet is sent when the DHCP client requests an IP address that is not applicable for the subnet in which it is presently located. This is most common with mobile users that obtain IP addresses on different segments of a network. When they request their previous IP address, the DHCP server sends a DHCP NACK that indicates the DHCP client should start the IP address renewal process as if it has never been assigned a previous IP address.

Configuring a DHCP Server

After you've decided to implement DHCP, you must configure the DHCP server to allow automatic IP address assignment for clients. Configuring a DHCP server is made up of three distinct phases:

- Installing the DHCP server software
- Configuring a scope of IP addresses
- Configuring options for the DHCP clients

The installation of the DHCP server software depends on your network operating system. The installation varies from vendor to vendor, but the actual configuration information remains the same, because the DHCP configuration options are defined in RFCs 2131, 2132, and 1542.

After the DHCP server has been installed, the first step is to create a scope (or pool) of IP addresses that can be leased to clients. Windows 2000 provides the New Scope Wizard for this process:

1. In the DHCP console, right-click the DHCP server and then click New Scope.
2. In the New Scope Wizard, click Next.
3. In the Scope Name page, enter a Name and Description for the scope, and then click Next.
4. In the IP Address Range page (see Figure 10.4), enter a Start IP address, End IP Address, and Subnet Mask for the scope, and then click Next.

FIGURE 10.4

Defining the Scope's IP addresses.

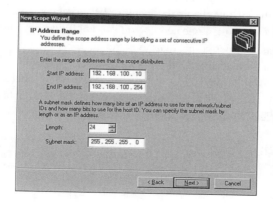

5. In the Add Exclusions page, enter the Start IP address and End IP address for each exclusion range. You can click Add to add new exclusion ranges, and click Remove to remove existing exclusion ranges. When all exclusions are defined, click Next to continue.

6. In the Lease Duration page, enter the duration by defining a combination of Days, Hours, and Minutes, and then click Next.

7. In the Configure DHCP Options page, select No, I Will Configure These Options Later, and then click Next.

8. Click Finish to complete the wizard.

The DHCP scope definition includes the beginning and ending addresses for the pool of IP addresses and any exclusion ranges. Exclusions are commonly used for IP addresses that have already been allocated as static IP addresses to hosts. The scope also defines the duration for any IP leases. You can set the duration to either a finite time period or an unlimited duration. The following strategies are commonly applied when setting the lease duration for a pool of DHCP IP addresses:

- If the number of clients is very close to the number of IP addresses available to lease, the lease duration should be kept to a short duration (such as one day), or the size of the scope should be increased.

- If the number of clients is very low compared to the number of IP addresses available, a longer lease duration can be set. I have seen lease durations up to three months in length in these circumstances.

- You can set lease durations on a scope-by-scope basis.

- Remember that DHCP clients renew their DHCP lease every time the computer is restarted, at 50% of the lease duration, and if there is no response at the 50% interval, at 87.5% of the lease duration.

After a scope has been created, options can be set for the scope. These options are applied to any of the DHCP clients that acquire IP addresses from this scope. If the DHCP server hosts more than one scope, you can configure options on either a global or scope-by-scope basis. Any options that do not change between scopes can be applied a single time using a global scope option. For example, the IP address of a DNS server may be the same for multiple scopes, allowing the use of a global scope option. Options that are specific to a scope of IP addresses (such as the default gateway) can be set in a scope option. Table 10.2 describes some of the more common options that are defined for DHCP clients.

TABLE 10.2 Basic DHCP Options

Option	Option Name	Description
1	Subnet mask	Specifies the subnet mask of the client subnet. This option is defined in the Create Scope or Scope Properties dialog box. It cannot be set directly in an Option dialog box.
3	Router	Specifies a list of IP addresses for routers on the client's subnet. Typically, this contains the IP address of the default gateway for the network segment. Multihomed computers can have only one list per computer, not one per adapter card.
6	DNS servers	Specifies a list of IP addresses for DNS name servers available to the client.
15	Domain name	Specifies the DNS domain name the client should use for DNS hostname resolution.
40	NIS domain name	Specifies the Network Information Service (NIS) domain name as an ASCII string.
41	NIS servers	Specifies a list of IP addresses for NIS servers available to the client.
42	NTP servers	Specifies a list of IP addresses for Network Time Protocol (NTP) servers available to the client.
44	WINS/NBNS servers	Specifies a list of IP addresses for NetBIOS Name Servers (NBNS).
46	WINS/NBT node type	Allows configurable NetBIOS over TCP/IP clients to be configured as described in RFC 1001/1002, where 1=b-node, 2=p-node, 4=m-node, and 8=h-node. On multihomed computers, the node type is assigned to the entire computer, not to individual adapter cards.
47	NetBIOS scope ID	Specifies a string that is the NetBIOS over TCP/IP scope ID for the client, as specified in RFC 1001/1002. On multihomed computers, the scope ID is assigned to the entire computer, not to individual adapter cards.
64	NIS+ Domain Name	Specifies the Network Information Service Plus (NIS+) domain name as an ASCII string.
65	NIS+ servers	Specifies a list of IP addresses for NIS+ servers available to the client.
66	Boot Server Host Name	TFTP Boot server hostname used by a BootP client to load the required Boot file.
67	Bootfile Name	The Boot file loaded by the TFTP protocol from the required Boot Server.

10

Advanced DHCP Deployment

Before wrapping up our discussion of DHCP, we need to address a few of the advanced configuration options that can be implemented with DHCP. These include the use of DHCP reservations and implementing DHCP in a multisegment network.

Using DHCP Client Reservations

Figure 10.5 shows the configuration screen for setting a client IP address reservation. The reservation ensures the desired client will lease a specific IP address. The most common use of this is to ensure that a server-class computer always leases the same IP address. The client lease is based on the MAC address of the client. Another case where reservations are used is to ensure that a Wireless Access Point receives the same IP address at all times.

FIGURE 10.5

Defining DHCP client reservations.

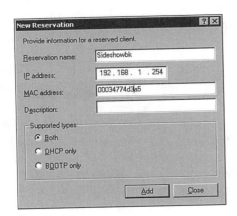

Reservations are also a good tactic when multiple DHCP servers exist on an intranet. You can set up DHCP servers with overlapping scopes as long as the overlapping addresses have been configured as IP lease reservations. This ensures the host is assigned the predetermined IP address no matter which DHCP server offers the successful lease.

Creating DHCP Superscopes

The latest RFCs on DHCP allow the creation of superscopes. A *superscope* is two or more DHCP scopes that are managed as a single unit. It is useful to define DHCP superscopes when the following circumstances arise:

- Your organization owns Internet-assigned IP address ranges that are noncontiguous. A superscope can combine the discontiguous scopes into a single scope for management.
- Your IP address requirements have grown for a subnet, where additional IP address must be added without changing any of the existing assigned addresses.

Deploying DHCP Servers in a Multisegmented Network

One of the most difficult questions when deploying DHCP servers is: How many DHCP servers do I need for my network? A common misconception is that you need a separate DHCP server for each segment of the network. This is not true.

In place of a DHCP server, you can install a DHCP Relay Agent on a network segment. A DHCP Relay Agent listens for DHCP broadcasts on its segment of the network. When it identifies a DHCP Discovery or DHCP Request broadcast packet on its segment of the network, the DHCP Relay Agent forwards the request as a directed packet to preconfigured DHCP servers. When the packet is forwarded, the IP address of the DHCP Relay Agent is added to the DHCP packet. This Relay Agent IP address is used to determine which scope of IP address should be used for the client's IP address assignment (see Figure 10.6).

10

FIGURE 10.6

Using a DHCP Relay Agent.

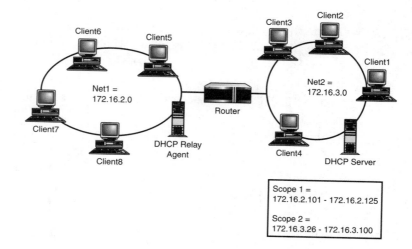

Clients on Net1 are assigned addresses from Scope 1. The DHCP server knows this scope should be used because the DHCP Relay Agent includes its address in all DHCP Discover and DHCP Request packets. Likewise, clients on Net2 are assigned addresses from Scope 2. The DHCP server knows to assign addresses from Scope 2 based on the fact that the DHCP Discover and DHCP Offer packets are broadcast on the local network.

By using DHCP Relay Agents, you can reduce the number of DHCP servers for an intranet. DHCP Relay Agents can also be located on segments that have a DHCP server. These provide backup capabilities in case the DHCP server on that segment fails. You can use the DHCP Relay Agent to forward the DHCP client requests to a remote DHCP server.

The final issue that needs to be dealt with is configuring multiple scopes on a single DHCP server. The most common implementation is to place the majority of the IP addresses for a network segment on a DHCP server located on that segment. It is also suggested to configure a smaller portion of the scope on a remote DHCP server. You should configure a DHCP Relay Agent that forwards DHCP requests to that remote DHCP server.

Preventing Rogue DHCP Servers

RFC 2131 introduces a new DHCP message type, a DHCPINFORM message, which allows DHCP servers to verify whether they are authorized to issue DHCP addresses.

Windows 2000 and Windows .NET Server use the process of authorizing DHCP servers in Active Directory to prevent rogue DHCP Servers from issuing incorrect IP addresses on a network. When a DHCP server initializes, the following process takes place:

1. The initializing DHCP server issues a DHCPINFORM message to the broadcast address 255.255.255.255. This process will be repeated every five minutes to verify that the DHCP server's status has not changed.

2. If other DHCP servers exist on the local subnet, the DHCP servers will respond with a DHCPACK message containing information about the name of the local Active Directory forest root domain.

3. The DHCP server will query its configured DNS server to find the closest domain controller. The domain controller can be in any domain in the forest, as the list of authorized DHCP servers is stored in the Configuration naming context.

4. The DHCP server will contact the domain controller and issue an LDAP query that returns a list of authorized DHCP servers.

5. If the DHCP server is authorized, the DHCP service will start. If not authorized, an error is logged at the DHCP server, and all DHCP client requests are ignored.

This Process Isn't Supported by All DHCP Servers

While this process appears to shut down all rogue DHCP servers on a network segment, the process works only if the DHCP servers support the DHCPINFORM message type and integrate with Microsoft's Active Directory. If a DHCP server does not support these parameters, the DHCP server can still issue erroneous address information.

Applying What You Have Learned

The use of automated IP address distribution is becoming more widespread in corporate networks. This chapter reviewed the three most common ways to assign IP addresses automatically to hosts.

The process of assigning IP addresses has evolved from RARP (which can assign an IP address only to a host), to BOOTP (which allows additional parameters such as a default gateway), to DHCP (which allows for automatic configuration and random IP address assignments).

Test Your Knowledge

Here are questions to check what you've learned today. The answers can be found in Appendix B, "Test Your Knowledge: Answers."

1. What problem is faced when adding new network hosts to a network if RARP is used for the assignment of IP addresses?

2. What advantage does BOOTP have over RARP for the assignment of IP addresses?

3. What IP address assignment protocol is used by Remote Installation Services in a Windows 2000 network?

4. If multiple IP address offers are received by a DHCP client, what selection algorithm does the DHCP client use to select an IP address?

5. When is a DCHP leased IP address renewed by a DHCP client?

6. What network configuration is required to allow a DHCP client to receive an IP address from a DHCP server located on a different network segment?

7. What security benefit does the DHCPINFORM message provide?

Preview of Day 11

The only way you can apply security in a network is to determine who is attempting to access your network's resources. The identification of individual users is handled by the authentication process.

Tomorrow's material looks at the common authentication methods that are used in TCP/IP networks to authenticate a user with a directory service. The authentication credentials are then used by the network to authorize access to the network's resources.

10

DAY 11

Authentication in a TCP/IP Network

One of the most important requirements for securing resources on a TCP/IP network is identifying who is attempting to access the resources. Identifying the users, computers, or services that access a resource is accomplished by *authenticating* the account.

Authentication can be performed in several ways. One of the easiest, but least-secure methods, is to pass the credentials to the application using clear text authentication.

To get around clear text authentication, other methods, such as Network Information System and Kerberos, use centralized databases to provide authentication. Rather than clear text, tokens and tickets are passed to identify and validate a user's credentials.

More and more digital methods are being used to authenticate users. A *public key infrastructure* provides the network framework to associate digital certificates with user accounts in your account database and authenticate users based on the possession of a private key associated with a presented certificate.

Finally, Web-based applications are being deployed increasingly, so we'll end today with methods available to authenticate Web-based applications and a discussion of the security merits of each method.

Clear Text Authentication

Many protocols that exist today use clear text authentication. Clear text authentication transmits a user's account name and password on the network in an unencrypted format that allows for the interception of network credentials.

Some of the more common protocols that use clear text authentication include:

- Post Office Protocol v3 (POP3)
- Internet Mail Access Protocol v4 (IMAP4)
- Telnet
- File Transfer Protocol (FTP)

The danger is that if these protocols use centralized account databases (such as Windows 2000 Active Directory), authentication with these protocols can result in the interception of credential information. Even though the password may be captured when a user checks his e-mail, the credentials could then be used to access other resources, such as using the credentials to dial in to a company's network.

There are four recommended strategies when using protocols that implement clear text authentication:

- Only use anonymous authentication. By removing the submission of credentials, you eliminate the possibility of credential interception. The only caveat is that you do not provide access to confidential information when using anonymous access. This access can be used for telnet and FTP sessions to prevent credential interception.
- Use application-level encryption to encrypt the credential exchange. Secure socket layers (SSL) or Transport Layer Security (TLS) can be used to encrypt the exchange of credentials. The only issue is that the application must be written to recognize and use application-level security. POP3 and IMAP4 are protocols that can use SSL encryption.
- Implement Internet Protocol Security (IPSec) to encrypt traffic between the client and the server. IPSec encrypts data at the IP layer so that the application does not even realize that the transmission is encrypted. While this does provide protection to the credentials, IPSec requires extensive configuration and that both client and server support IPSec.

Note   For more information on encrypting transmitted data at both the IP and Application layers, see Day 12, "Encrypting Transmitted Data."

- Do not use the protocols on the network. For example, alternative protocols can be used. For mail services, maybe consider using a Web-based e-mail client that is protected using SSL, or rather than using FTP, use WebDAV to protect network credentials.

Network Information System (NIS)

The network information system (NIS) provides a global and centralized database of information about a Unix network. NIS provides a service to keep user account information synchronized between hosts. This is important in the NFS environment, where the same account information must be used on both client and server hosts.

NIS comprises both NIS clients and NIS servers. An NIS client requests data from the NIS database on an NIS server. A system can function as both an NIS client and an NIS server. NIS (like NFS) uses Remote Procedure Calls and external data representation. This makes NIS portable between operating systems.

The following are key NIS features:

- Master and slave servers
- NIS maps
- NIS domains

Server Roles in NIS

NIS servers take on one of two roles: master or slave. Master servers maintain the original copy of the NIS databases. Any new information or updates are added to this copy of the database. A slave server maintains a duplicate copy of the master database. The information in the slave server database is kept up-to-date by the propagation process. If the NIS databases are kept in sync, it does not matter which NIS database an NIS client contacts when it is providing authentication information. This is known as a *steady state* situation.

The NIS Database

The NIS database includes several files known as *NIS maps*. These files initially are stored in ASCII text files. To provide better performance when querying the NIS

11

database, NIS tools convert the text files to DBM format. The maps contain keys and values. A *key* is a specific field in the map that the client specifies when it submits a query to the NIS server. A *value* is an attribute of the key returned in the response from the NIS server. In the map `hosts.byname`, for example, the keys are the individual names of the hosts, and the values returned are their assigned IP addresses.

NIS Domains

NIS domains include all hosts sharing the same NIS database. The actual name of an NIS domain often is not relevant to the users participating in the domain. The only part of NIS users see is that their user/password combination is accepted on all participating hosts. They do not have to set up separate accounts on each host on the network.

An application is configured to query a specific NIS domain. The application uses the `ypbind` daemon to detect a suitable NIS server in the NIS domain. The `ypbind` daemon broadcasts on the local network for an NIS server. The first server to respond is assumed to be the fastest NIS server and is used for all subsequent NIS queries.

Kerberos Authentication

RFC 1878   Kerberos authentication was developed at MIT to provide centralized authentication on a network. Typically, one of two versions of Kerberos is used in today's networks: Kerberos version 4 or Kerberos version 5.

Kerberos Components

There are several components that work together to allow Kerberos to provide secure authentication. These components include:

- **Key distribution center (KDC).** The KDC is a network service that issues ticket granting tickets (TGTs) and session tickets (STs) to an authenticating entity. The entity can be a computer, a user, or a service. The KDC manages the exchange of credentials between a client and a server. The KDC is made up of two separate services:

  - The Authentication Service (AS) performs the initial authentication of a user, computer, or service on the network and provides the user with a TGT for future service requests.

  - The Ticket Granting Service (TGS) receives the user's TGT in a request to authenticate with a network service and returns a session ticket (ST) to the user. The ST is used to authenticate with the indicated network service.

- **Ticket granting ticket (TGT).** A TGT is used to prove a user's or computer's identity on the network when it requests session tickets. Any time that a request is made to the ticket granting service, a TGT must be presented to indicate that initial authentication of the entity has taken place.

- **Session ticket (ST).** The ST provides authentication of an entity when it connects to a network service or to another computer.

- **Referral ticket.** A referral ticket is actually another form of a TGT. When a user attempts to connect to a resource in a different Kerberos realm, the TGS will issue a TGT that allows the user to acquire an ST from a KDC in a different Kerberos realm. Referral tickets allow authentication to take place between Kerberos realms.

The Kerberos Authentication Process

Kerberos uses three different message exchanges to provide network authentication. The message exchanges are

- **Authentication Service Exchange.** This exchange is performed between an end entity and the Authentication Service of the KDC. The end result of the authentication Service Exchange is that the end entity receives a TGT. The Authentication Service Exchange includes a Kerberos Authentication Service Request (KRB_AS_REQ) sent from the end entity to the AS and a Kerberos Authentication Service Reply (KRB_AS_REP) returned by the AS to the end entity containing the end entity's TGT.

11

Why Use the Term End Entity?

Kerberos authenticates more than just users. It also provides authentication services to computers and services. "End entity" covers all these (users, computers, and services).

- **Ticket Granting Service Exchange.** This exchange is used to distribute STs to end entities. A Ticket Granting Service Exchange includes a Kerberos Ticket Granting Service Request (KRB_TGS_REQ) sent from the end entity to the TGS and a Kerberos Ticket Granting Service Reply (KRB_TGS_REP) returned by the TGS to the end entity. The returned ST is encrypted using the master key shared by the TGS and the server hosting the requested service so that only the server can decrypt the ST.

- **Client/Server Authentication Exchange.** This exchange is used to authenticate an end entity with the target service. The message exchange includes a Kerberos

Application Request (KRB_AP_REQ) sent from the end entity to the server and a Kerberos Application Response (KRB_AP_REP) returned by the target server to the end entity.

Sometimes Authentication Fails

If the authentication attempt fails, a Kerberos error message (KRB_ERROR) is returned to the end entity indicating why it failed. The authentication attempt can fail because the incorrect password was provided, the account does not exist in the Kerberos database of accounts, or the client computer's clock is out of sync with the KDC.

The best example of how the messages work together is the scenario in which multiple Kerberos realms work together. Figure 11.1 shows two Kerberos realms integrated to provide authentication between the realms.

FIGURE 11.1

Kerberos authentication between two realms.

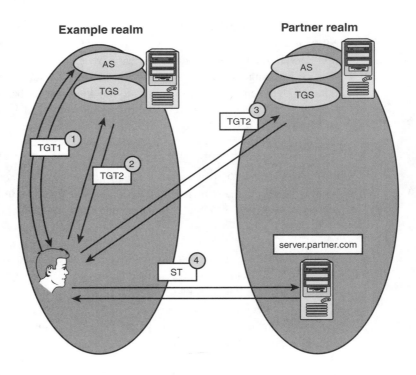

The Kerberos authentication of the user in the example.com domain that is attempting to access a service on the server.partner.com in the partner.com domain would proceed as follows:

1. The user sends a KRB_AS_REQ message to the AS service in the Example realm and the AS returns a KRB_AS_REP message containing TGT1. This TGT is used to acquire session tickets from the TGS service.

2. The user next submits a KRB_TGS_REQ message to the TGS in Example realm requesting access to the service on the server.partner.com server. Because the TGS cannot authenticate access to resources in the Partner realm, the KRG_TGS_REP is returned containing TGT2, a referral ticket to the TGS in the Partner realm.

3. The user submits another KRB_TGS_REQ message. The difference this time is that the KRB_TGS_REQ message is sent to the TGS in the Partner realm and now contains TGT2, the referral ticket to the TGS in the Partner realm. Because the TGS in Partner realm can authenticate requests to server.partner.com, the KRB_TGS_REP is returned containing an ST for server.partner.com.

4. The user then sends a KRB_AP_REQ to server.partner.com containing the ST returned by the TGS in the Partner realm. The server responds with a KRB_AP_REP message indicating that the user is authenticated.

User Still Can Be Denied Access to the Resource

Just because the user successfully authenticates with server.partner.com does not mean that he can access the requested resource. Kerberos provides authentication, the service that the user connects to must still *authorize* the user. Authorization is where the credentials are verified to ensure that the user has the necessary network permissions to access the requested resource.

11

Advantages of Kerberos

The major advantages of using Kerberos for your network authentication mechanism include the following:

- Kerberos version 5 is a standards-based protocol defined in RFC 1510.

- Kerberos version 5 interoperates between many network operating systems. For example, Kerberos realms in a Unix environment can interoperate with Windows 2000 domains using Kerberos authentication.

- Kerberos is time-sensitive. All Kerberos messages contain a time stamp. If the time included in a request message varies by more than five minutes with the time at the AS or TGS, the request is rejected and assumed to be a replay attack. This default time variance can be modified in most Kerberos implementations.

- By creating trusts between Kerberos realms, single sign-on is possible. Single sign-on exists when a user can use a single account to access all resources in an organization, rather than having to maintain separate accounts for separate systems.

- Kerberos reduces the network traffic associated with network authentication. When a client receives an ST from the TGS, the user can cache the ticket for future use. The next time that he connects to the same server, he only has to present the ST from his cache; he does not have to request another ST. The user only has to request a new ST when the current ST expires. The expiration time is based on the configuration of the TGS and AS services.

- Kerberos allows delegation. Delegation allows a service to impersonate a user account. This allows for the deployment of n-tiered client/server applications. The server can perform requests using the security context of the requesting user, and the responses from a database will include only records that the user is permitted to view.

Public Key Infrastructure

A method of authentication that is growing more popular is the use of *digital certificates* to prove one's identity on a network. The validation of digital certificates is provided by a public key infrastructure.

A public key infrastructure involves several components that work together to provide an infrastructure for authentication, encryption, and digital signatures:

- **Digital certificates.** Digital certificates are issued to users, computers, and services to prove their identities. Attributes in a certificate can limit the certificate to specific usages. The current version of certificates typically used are x.509 v3 certificates. X.509 is a standard format that allows for interoperability between certificate service solutions.

- **Certification authorities (CA).** A CA is the server that issues certificates to requesting users, computers, and services. All management of issued certificates takes place at the CA.

- **Certificate revocation list (CRL).** A CRL contains a listing of certificates that have been revoked by a CA. The CRL contains the serial number of all revoked certificates and a reason code describing why the certificate was revoked.

- **Public-key enabled applications.** To use a PKI, you must have applications that are certificate-enabled and can validate a presented certificate and map the certificate to an account in an account database.

- **CA hierarchies.** Typically, more than one CA exists in an organization. The CAs are usually chained in a hierarchy in which a single root CA exists (see Figure 11.2). To accept certificates from the CA hierarchy, the computer validating the presented certificate must *trust* the root CA of the hierarchy.

FIGURE 11.2

A CA hierarchy.

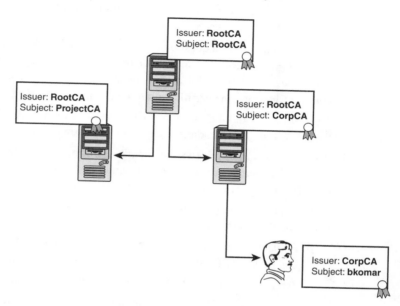

11

Acquiring a Digital Certificate

The first step in using digital certificates for authentication is actually acquiring a digital certificate. Where do you get one? In general, there are two choices: obtaining one from an internal CA (if your company has deployed a PKI), or obtaining one from an external CA.

Typically, the decision is made based on how the certificate is to be used. If the certificate is used for authenticating against internal systems, such as an intranet Web site or for remote access to the organization, then it is preferable to use a certificate from an internal CA. On the other hand, if you are using the certificate for secure e-mail between organizations, it might be better to acquire the certificate from an external CA, such as Verisign or Thawte—public CAs that are generally trusted by all organizations, allowing the certificates to be validated by all organizations.

The following steps take you through the actual process for acquiring a digital certificate:

1. A user launches a request for a certificate from a public-key enabled application, or by sending the request directly to a CA.

2. The client generates a public and private key pair to be associated with the certificate. The private key is stored locally at the client computer and the public key is transmitted with the certificate request so that the public key can be included as an attribute of the issued certificate.

3. The client completes a questionnaire used to populate the certificate with the required information. The questionnaire varies depending on the CA to which the request was sent. Typically, the request includes the user's name, company, and the purpose for which the certificate will be used.

4. The public key and the user information are sent to the CA. The CA usually holds the request until a CA administrator can validate the user's information.

5. A CA administrator reviews the submitted information, comparing it to the CA's *certificate practice statement*, a set of guidelines published by the CA that describes the rules for acquiring a certificate.

6. If the request is approved, the CA administrator issues the certificate. The certificate should contain the following attributes:

   - *Subject name.* The name of the user that requested the certificate. The name can be in any format, including e-mail address or LDAP distinguished name.
   - *Issuer name.* The LDAP distinguished name of the issuing CA.
   - *Public key.* The public key submitted by the user in the certificate request message.
   - *CRL Distribution Point (CDP).* The locations where the CA's CRL can be obtained to validate the revocation status of the certificate.
   - *Authority Information Access (AIA).* The location where the CA's certificate can be retrieved. The CA's certificate is required to validate the signature on the certificate issued by the CA.
   - *Constraints.* The certificate may be restricted in its usage. A constraint is typically an Object ID (OID) that limits what purposes the certificate may be used for. For example, the certificate may be limited to signing and encrypting e-mail messages.

7. The completed certificate is signed using the CA's private key and then sent to the user for installation. By using the private key, the user can retrieve the CA's public key from a directory service, and validate the signature on the certificate to ensure that the certificate is not modified.

Note that during the entire process, only public keys are transmitted on the network. In private/public key encryption, the private key is always secured at the workstation where the private/public key pair is generated. This ensures that the private key is never acquired during transmission.

Validating a Certificate

When a certificate is presented for authentication, the application that receives the certificate must validate the certificate to ensure that the certificate is valid or trusted. The presented certificate, and every CA certificate up to a trusted root, is validated to ensure that the presented certificate is valid.

For example, as shown in Figure 11.2, a certificate was issued to BKomar by the CorpCA. To validate this certificate, the following checks are performed by the application that receives this certificate:

1. The signature for BKomar's certificate is validated by creating a hash against the certificate and comparing it to the hash created when the CA signed the certificate. The hash created by the CA is retrieved by using the CA's public key to decrypt the hash stored in the attributes of the certificate.

2. The certificate's attributes are verified to ensure that the certificate is time-valid. All certificates have an expiration date. If the certificate is presented after the expiration date, it is considered invalid and not trusted by the application.

3. The CRL is downloaded from a location indicated in the CDP extension of the certificate. The CRL is downloaded only if a valid copy of the CRL is not cached locally at the computer where the application is running.

11

Revocation Status Checking

By default, a CRL is cached at a computer until it expires. This can lead to latency between the time a certificate is revoked and when all computers recognize that the certificate as revoked.

To reduce the latency in recognizing the revocation status for a newly revoked certificate, two different options exist today:

- **Delta CRLs.** In addition to base CRLs, a delta CRL, or a listing of all the revoked certificates since the last base CRL was published, can be implemented. Delta CRLs are published at much shorter intervals, reducing the amount of time before a certificate is recognized as a revoked certificate.

> - **Online Certificate Status Protocol (OCSP).** OCSP is a real-time service in which a public-key enabled application can request status information for a specific certificate. The OCSP responder immediately responds with the status of the certificate, allowing the application to receive up-to-date status of the certificate. Unfortunately, most OCSP responders use CRL checking to build their databases, so the information is still out-of-date.
>
> Both methods require that the application validating the certificate support either Delta CRLs or OCSP.

If the certificate's serial number is included in the CRL, the certificate is considered revoked.

4. The certificate for the issuing CA is retrieved. In this case, the certificate for the CorpCA is retrieved from a URL indicated in the AIA extensions of the BKomar certificate.

5. The CorpCA certificate signature is validated to ensure that it is not modified in any way.

6. The CorpCA certificate is validated to ensure that it is time-valid.

7. The CorpCA certificate is validated to ensure that it is not revoked by retrieving the CRL from the RootCA. The URL to the CRL is included in the CorpCA certificate.

8. The certificate for the RootCA is then retrieved. RootCA, in this example, issued the certificate for CorpCA. As with any certificate, the signature on the CorpCA certificate is validated.

9. The RootCA certificate is validated to ensure that it is time-valid.

10. The RootCA certificate is validated to ensure that it is not revoked.

11. Because the RootCA certificate is self-issued, this means that the RootCA is a root Certification Authority. The last test is to validate that the RootCA is considered a *trusted root CA*. A client can trust many root CAs, so the client will verify whether RootCA is included in the list of trusted root CAs.

If the CA is found to be trusted, the certificate is now considered validated. One of the key lessons learned by this process is that if a CA's certificate is revoked, all certificates issued by that CA, and any subordinate CAs below that CA, are considered revoked as well.

Mapping Certificates to User Accounts

To provide authentication to network services, digital certificates must be mapped to accounts in an account database. By performing a mapping, possession of the private key associated with a certificate equates to being the associated account in the account database.

There are two types of mappings that can be performed when doing certificate mapping. In a *one-to-one* certificate mapping, a certificate is mapped directly to a single user account. If the certificate is presented, it is related directly to a single user account. In a *many-to-one* mapping, the subject attribute of the certificate is ignored. In this case, if a certificate is issued by a specific CA, then the certificate is mapped to a single user account. In this type of mapping, many certificates map to the single user account.

Note

There are different ways that the actual certificate mapping is configured. Typically, the mapping is either performed in the application that supports certificate-based authentication, or in the directory service used on the network. An example of performing certificate mapping in Microsoft's Internet Information Server (IIS) is presented later in this chapter.

11

Combining a PKI and Kerberos: Smart Cards

Through Public Key Cryptography for Initial Authentication in Kerberos (PKINIT) extensions, it is possible to combine smart cards, a public key-based token, with Kerberos authentication. Rather than typing credentials for network authentication, smart cards are a form of *two-factor authentication*. It's called two-factor authentication because you must have one item—the physical smart card—in your possession, and you must know one item—the personal identification number (PIN) required to unlock the private key on the smart card.

Smart cards modify the Kerberos authentication process. In place of KRB_AS_REQ and KRB_AS_REP messages, PA_PK_AS_REQ and PA_PK_AS_REP messages are used. These messages are based on private/public key pairs associated with the inserted smart card.

The use of a smart card changes the initial Kerberos authentication process. The process, shown in Figure 11.3, is as follows:

FIGURE 11.3

Smart card logon process.

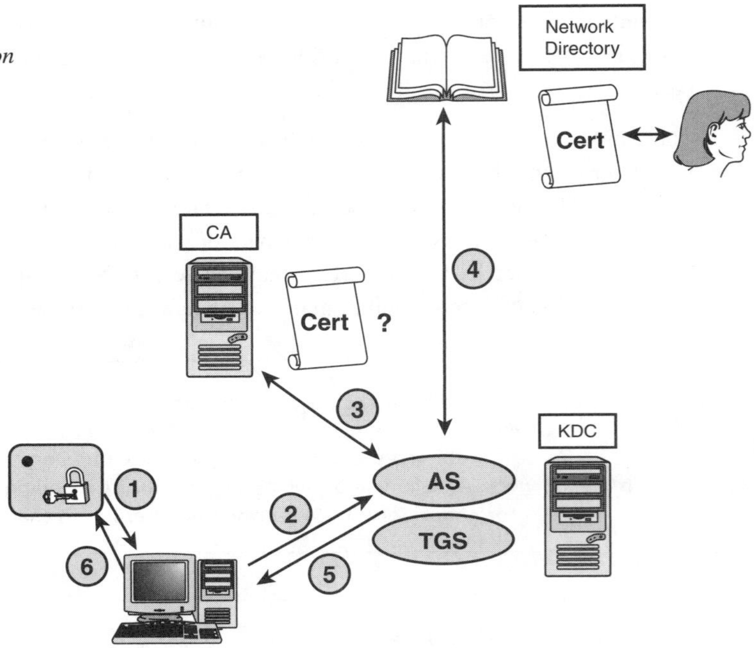

1. The smart card is inserted into a computer's smart card reader and the user types in the PIN for the smart card to retrieve the private key stored on the smart card.

2. A Kerberos Authentication Service Request (PA_PK_AS_REQ) message is sent to the Authentication Service on the KDC containing the user name, a time stamp, and a copy of the user's certificate from the smart card. The user name and time stamp are signed by the user's private key as preauthentication data.

3. The certificate submitted in the PA_PK_AS_REQ message is validated against a CA to ensure that the certificate is not revoked. This process may require the validation of multiple CA certificates as well.

4. The Authentication Service queries the network directory to determine what account in the directory is mapped to the certificate included in the PA_PK_AS_REQ. The account mapping is used to determine to what account the TGT is issued.

5. The Authentication Service sends the TGT back to the user in a modified Kerberos Authentication Service Response (PA_PK_AS_REP). Within the response, the session key is encrypted with the user's public key and the TGT is encrypted with the KDC's master key. This ensures that only the correct user can decrypt the session key.

6. The user retrieves the session key by decrypting the session key with the private key located on the smart card.

From this point on, authentication proceeds using the typical Ticket Granting Service and Client/Server Authentication message exchanges.

Web-Based Authentication

Web browser applications are becoming more prevalent. From applications that enable you to purchase airline tickets on the Internet to banking applications that allow you to pay bills, more and more browser-based applications are appearing. When you start working with browser-based applications, you still must provide credentials to identify the user performing the transactions.

Currently, there are five different methods for authenticating users when connecting to Web-based applications: anonymous, basic, digest, integrated, and certificate. The following sections outline each of these authentication methods.

Anonymous Authentication

Believe it or not, anonymous authentication is the most common authentication method used when connecting to Web-based resources. If you think about it, how often are you prompted for credential information when you connect to a Web site such as www.espn.com or www.cnn.com? When you connect to these Web sites, you do not send credentials to the Web server. Instead, the Web server uses a preconfigured account for the anonymous access.

When you are not prompted for credentials, you are probably using anonymous authentication. Instead, the Web server is using a preconfigured identity for all users that connect to the Web site.

For example, in Microsoft Internet Information Services (IIS), an account named IUSR_computername is created in the directory database of the Web server. This account is used for authentication anytime that anonymous authentication is used by a Web server.

By attaching an actual account to the anonymous account, access to the disk resources on the Web server can be restricted. You do this in Windows NT, Windows 2000, and higher, by assigning only the IUSR_computername account access to the desired Web sites. If an anonymous user attempts to access other areas on the Web server, the security system of Windows 2000 should prevent the access.

> These is an attack known as the Web Server Folder Directory Traversal attack. This assault takes advantage of a coding error that allows an attacker to gain access to any folder on the computer if security is not correctly defined. You can apply the latest IIS security patches to prevent this attack.

To allow only anonymous access to a Web site in IIS, use the following procedure:

1. From Administrative Tools, open Internet Services Manager.

2. In the console tree, expand the *WebServer* (where *WebServer* is the name of your Web server), and then click Default Web Site.

3. In the console tree, right-click Default Web Site, and then click Properties.

4. In the Default Web Site Properties dialog box, click the Directory Security tab.

5. In the Directory Security tab, in the Anonymous access and authentication control box, click Edit.

6. In the Authentication Methods dialog box (see Figure 11.4), select Anonymous access—clear all other check boxes—and then click OK.

FIGURE 11.4

Configuring anonymous authentication for IIS.

> If the Inheritance Overrides dialog box appears, you must decide whether to apply the authentication settings to all subsites of the Default Web Site.

7. In the Default Web Site Properties, click OK.

When combined with other authentication methods, anonymous authentication is always attempted first. Only if anonymous access fails will other authentication mechanisms be attempted.

Basic Authentication

RFC 1878 Basic authentication allows actual credentials to be passed to the Web browser to allow access to restricted Web sites. Because basic authentication is defined in RFC 1945, the HTTP 1.0 definition, all Web browsers support this form of authentication.

The problem with basic authentication is that the passwords are transmitted in an unencrypted format. Although not passed in clear text, credentials in basic authentication are only Base64 encoded before they are transmitted to the Web server. There are several utilities on the Internet that can intercept and decipher the Base64 encoding.

But do not disregard the use of basic authentication. Because the only risk involved with basic authentication is the risk of password interception, basic authentication can be combined with SSL encryption to secure the credential exchange.

Note
> For information on how to implement SSL with a Web server, please see Day 12.

11

To allow only basic authentication to a Web site in IIS, you use the same procedure as used for defining anonymous authentication, except that in the Authentication Methods dialog box (shown in Figure 11.4), you select only Basic Authentication.

Tip
> Windows 2000 uses domains as security boundaries. You can designate a default domain that will be appended to any credentials. If no domain is specified, or you must use an account from a domain other than the default domain, you provide the credentials as *domain\username*.

Digest Authentication

RFC 1878 Digest authentication is an improvement over basic authentication in that credentials are better secured as they are transmitted across the network.

In digest authentication, the Web browser applies a hash algorithm to a combination of a text string passed from the Web server to the user during session establishment, the user's name, the user's password, and other information required by the Web server. The additional information prevents anyone from capturing the password hash and reverse-engineering the password.

The Web server performs the same hash function against the same inputted values and compares the hash values. If the hash values are an exact match, the authentication is successful.

In addition, a time stamp is added to the hash to prevent replay attacks where the hash is captured and retransmitted on the network.

The only issues with digest authentication are that the user's password must be stored in an unencrypted or reversibly encryptable format in the directory service and that only HTTP 1.1–compliant Web-browsers support digest authentication. To prevent access to the password information, physical security must be maintained for the directory data-base server. To verify whether your Web browser is HTTP 1.1–compliant, review the release notes for your browser.

To allow only digest authentication to a Web site in IIS, you would use the same proce-dure that was used to define anonymous authentication, except that in the Authentication Methods dialog box (shown in Figure 11.4), you select only Digest Authentication for Windows Domain Servers.

In a Windows 2000 network, you also must configure any user accounts in the Active Directory store the user's password using reversible encryption. You can do this by using the following procedure:

1. From Administrative Tools, open Active Directory Users and Computers.
2. In the console tree, select the organizational unit where the user account exists.
3. In the details pane, double-click the user account that you want to configure for digest authentication.
4. In the User Properties dialog box, click the Account tab.
5. In the list of Account options (see Figure 11.5), enable the Store Password Using Reversible Encryption check box, and then click OK.
6. Ask the user to immediately change his password. The reversibly encrypted pass-word is only saved at the next password change. The current password cannot be reversibly encrypted.

FIGURE 11.5

FIGURE 11.5

Storing reversibly encrypted passwords.

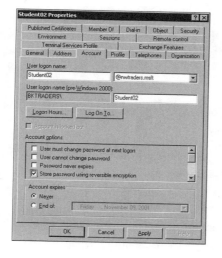

Integrated Authentication

Microsoft Windows supports a proprietary version of authentication that is supported only by Internet Explorer versions 2.0 and higher. This version, named Integrated Authentication or, in older versions, Windows NT Challenge/Response, uses either Kerberos or NTLM authentication to authenticate a Web client.

This provides a strong form of authentication that cannot be intercepted during transmission on the network wire, but is not compatible with other Web browsers such as Netscape.

Integrated authentication attempts to use the user's current credentials, and only prompts for credentials if the current credentials fail authentication, or cannot be determined. The user prompt varies from the basic authentication prompt in that the domain is also requested.

To allow only integrated authentication to a Web site in IIS, the same procedure as for anonymous authentication is used, except that in the Authentication Methods dialog box (shown in Figure 11.4), you select only Integrated Windows authentication.

Certificate Authentication

A Web site can also be configured to use certificate-based authentication. Certificate-based authentication provides the strongest form of authentication because only the holder of the private key can authenticate using a certificate.

The certificate that the user presents must be mapped to a user account in either IIS or in the Active Directory database (in a Windows 2000 network).

11

To implement client authentication using certificates, the Web server must first be configured to support SSL. (This information is covered in tomorrow's material.) The server must support SSL encryption because certificate-based authentication is a mutual authentication method, requiring that both the Web server and the Web client have certificates for authentication.

After the server is SSL-enabled, you can perform the certificate mapping using the following steps:

1. From Administrative Tools, open Internet Services Manager.

2. In the console tree, expand the *WebServer* (where *WebServer* is the name of your Web server), and then click Default Web Site, or the name of the site that you want to secure with basic authentication.

3. In the console tree, right-click Default Web Site, and then click Properties.

4. In the Default Web Site Properties dialog box, click the Directory Security tab.

5. In the Directory Security tab, in the Secure communications box, click Edit.

   If the Edit button is unavailable, you must enable the Web server for SSL by acquiring a server certificate.

6. In the Secure Communications dialog box, click the Enable client certificate mapping dialog box, and then click Edit.

7. In the Account Mappings dialog box, click Add to add a new account mapping.

8. In the Open dialog box, select the export certificate file received from the user, and then click OK. This certificate file must be in a Base-64 encoded format.

9. In the Map to Account dialog box, input a name for the mapping, the account that the certificate is mapped to, and a password, and click OK. The mapping is typically done for a user outside the organization. This account is created and the password set by an administrator expressly for the purpose of mapping a certificate to the account. The password is never actually used by the external user.

10. In the Confirm Password dialog box, retype the password and then click OK.

11. In the Account Mappings dialog box, click OK.

12. In the Secure Communications dialog box, click OK.

13. In the Directory Security tab, in the Anonymous access and authentication control box, click Edit.

14. In the Authentication Methods dialog box (see Figure 11.4), clear all other check boxes, and then click OK. This forces the Web server to only accept certificate-based authentication.

15. In the Default Web Site Properties, click OK.

Applying What You Have Learned

Today's material looked at several forms of authentication that are used in TCP/IP networks. The following questions will review your knowledge of the subject material. The answers can be found in Appendix B, "Test Your Knowledge: Answers."

Test Your Knowledge

1. What security issues exist when clear text authentication is used by an application?
2. What can be done to secure clear text authentication if the application only supports clear text authentication?
3. What are the server roles in an NIS authentication system?
4. What service is responsible for issuing a TGT to an authenticating user?
5. When a TGT is issued to another Kerberos realm, what is that TGT referred to?
6. Define the Kerberos message types in each of the six callouts in Figure 11.6.

FIGURE 11.6

Identify the Kerberos message types.

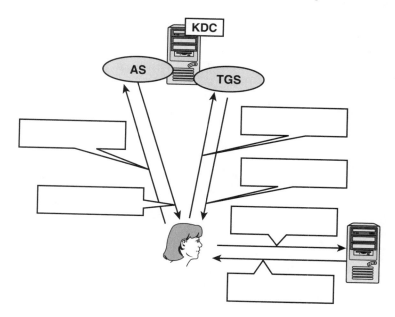

11

7. How does Kerberos authentication change when a smart card is used for authentication?
8. When using a PKI, how does CRL checking work?
9. What are some of the reasons that a certificate presented for authentication is rejected?

10. Of the available authentication schemes available for Web-based applications, which authentication scheme is proprietary?

11. What security issues exist when digest authentication is used?

Preview of Day 12

Tomorrow we'll look at how transmitted data can be encrypted on a TCP/IP network. With the more emphasis on security in today's network designs, you must consider how to protect transmitted data.

In general, two methods exist for encrypting transmitted data. You can encrypt data at the application layer using a protocol such as Secure Socket Layers (SSL), Transport Layer Security (TLS), or Secure Multipurpose Internet Mail Extensions (S/MIME). Alternatively, you can encrypt data at the IP layer of the TCP/IP layered model using Internet Protocol Security (IPSec).

DAY 12

Encrypting Transmitted Data

Today we delve into one of my favorite areas of TCP/IP networking: the encryption of transmitted data. Although time is spent securing data by encrypting the data while stored on disk drives, little has been done to encrypt the data as it is transmitted on the network, both wired and wireless.

When deciding to encrypt transmitted data, you must decide where to perform the encryption. Today's material looks at the two most common places: encrypting at the application layer of the TCP/IP model and encrypting at the IP layer of the TCP/IP model.

Application-layer encryption performs the encryption of data before it is passed to lower-level protocols for transmission. When the encrypted data is received at the destination client, the encrypted data is passed up the protocol stack until the application running at the server can decrypt the data and pass the decrypted data to the server-side application.

If an application does not know how to use encryption, the encryption can be configured to take place at the IP layer using Internet Protocol Security (IPSec). Applications do not have to know that IPSec is in use because the application

encryption and decryption take place before the data is passed to the transport layer.
Figure 12.1 illustrates the different layers of the TCP/IP layered model where application
and IP layer encryption takes place.

FIGURE 12.1

*Application and IP
layer encryption
locations.*

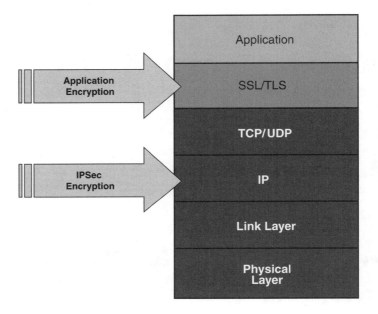

Encrypting Data at the Application Layer

Four protocols that can be used in TCP/IP networks for application-layer encryption of
transmitted data include:

- Secure Socket Layers (SSL)
- Transport Layer Security (TLS)
- Secure Multipurpose Internet Mail Extensions (S/MIME)
- Pretty Good Privacy (PGP)

The following sections detail how the protocols are used to provide encryption services
to transmitted data.

Secure Socket Layers (SSL) and Transport Layer Security (TLS)

Secure Socket Layers (SSL) is an application layer encryption method that was developed by Netscape Corporation to encrypt HyperText Transfer Protocol (HTTP) sessions

between a client and a server. With the increased use of the Internet, Netscape realized the need for encrypting transmissions between the client and the server if the Internet were to become a medium for secure transactions on the Internet.

Over time, other application protocols have added extensions to use SSL for encryption of transmitted data. The protocols that now support SSL encryption include NNTP, POP3, IMAP4, SMTP, HTTP, and LDAP. When SSL is used with these protocols, the application server will listen on an alternate port, rather than the default port used by the application. Table 12.1 shows the default ports used by applications with and without SSL encryption:

TABLE 12.1   SSL Port Usage

Protocol	Default Port	SSL Port
SMTP	TCP 25	TCP 465
POP3	TCP 110	TCP 995
NNTP	TCP 119	TCP 563
IMAP4	TCP 143	TCP 993
HTTP	TCP 80	TCP 443
LDAP	TCP 389	TCP 636

Transport Layer Security, discussed in RFC 2246, is a standards-track protocol that is based on SSL. The main difference between the two protocols is that SSL is managed by a specific corporation, Netscape, while TLS is defined by Internic.

Both protocols use the same method (see Figure 12.2) for encrypting data at the application layer:

1. The client makes an initial connection to the server. The SSL or TLS protocol is indicated by using HTTPS:// as the protocol in a Web browser, or by configuring the application, such as a mail client, to use SSL.

2. The server responds to the request by sending its digital certificate to the client. The client validates the certificate by performing revocation checking and ensuring that the certificate is time-valid and matches the name of the server.

3. After the identity of the server is validated, the client and the server will enter into a negotiation to determine what level of encryption is required for the symmetric key. The server may be configured to require strong encryption, say 128-bit encryption, or a mutually decided key length may be negotiated.

4. The Web client generates a symmetric session key that will be used for encrypting transmissions between the client and the server.

12

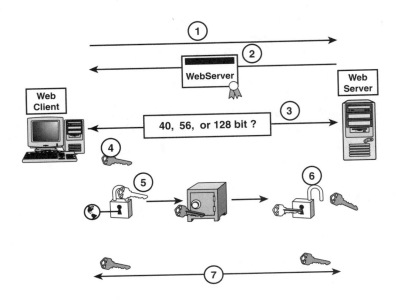

FIGURE **12.2**

SSL encryption.

5. From the server's certificate, the client extracts the public key associated with the certificate (it is stored as an attribute within the certificate), encrypts the session key using the public key, and sends the encrypted session key to the server.

6. The server receives the encrypted session key and decrypts the session key using the associated private key.

7. The session key is now used to encrypt traffic between the client and the server. When a new session is established between the client and the server, a new session key is generated.

SSL/TLS encryption is easy to configure in that the only configuration that is required is to acquire a certificate for the server and to configure the application running at the server to implement SSL. The problem with SSL/TLS is that the application must be coded to support SSL or TLS. For example, FTP does not support SSL or TLS. Because the protocol does not know how to implement SSL/TLS, you cannot implement SSL or TLS to provide application-level encryption.

Note

One area where TLS security is coming to the forefront is wireless security. Windows XP provides built-in support for 802.1x encryption using Extensible Authentication Protocol over TLS (EAP/TLS) to encrypt authentication and data transmission between wireless clients and the Wireless Access Point (WAP).

Secure Multipurpose Internet Mail Extensions (S/MIME) and Pretty Good Privacy (PGP)

Another common application that uses application-level security is an e-mail application. There are two common protocols used to provide mail security at the application layer: *Pretty Good Privacy (PGP)* and *Secure Multipurpose Internet Mail Extensions (S/MIME)*. Both protocols provide the ability to digitally sign or encrypt e-mail messages, but the two methods are not interoperable. For example, if you encrypt a message using an e-mail client that supports PGP encryption, you cannot decrypt the message using an e-mail client that only supports S/MIME.

PGP is an application-layer protocol that is managed by a private consortium, the OpenPGP Alliance. You can acquire PGP for free if you are a student or an individual, but must pay for the product if used for business.

S/MIME is an extension to MIME attachments. The main benefit in using S/MIME for mail encryption and signing is that S/MIME is an Internic standards track protocol.

Note

For details on how mail encryption and digital signatures work, see Day 16, "Electronic Mail over TCP/IP."

Protecting Data at the IP Layer

RFC 2401 *Internet Protocol Security (IPSec)* is a method of encrypting data at the IP layer so that the actual encryption and decryption process is transparent to the upper layer application protocols.

IPSec is performed by creating a *security association* between two computers that defines how transmitted data is secured between the two hosts. If a transmitted packet from one host matches the rules established in the security association, IPSec performs the actions defined in the security association before sending the packet on the network wire.

12

Note

Security associations can only be established between hosts on the network. You cannot define a security association between two users of the network. For example, if you wanted to ensure that Robert always used IPSec when connecting to the data server, you would configure IPSec so that Robert's computer used IPSec when communicating with the data server. If Robert uses more than one computer, all computers that Robert uses would have to be configured to use IPSec protection when communicating with the data server.

Besides providing encryption services, IPSec also provides integrity services to prevent modification of transmitted data.

This section starts by reviewing the two protocols used by IPSec to provide integrity protection (Authentication Header) and encryption protection (Encapsulating Security Payload).

Authentication Header (AH)

RFC 2402   An authentication header (AH) does not provide actual encryption to transmitted data, but is still considered an important part of transmitted data security. AH provides integrity protection by applying a digital signature to each transmitted packet, replay protection to prevent an attacker from capturing an authentication stream and replaying it to a server, and authentication of the two clients participating in the transmission of data.

AH works by calculating a hash against the non-mutable fields in a packet. Non-mutable means the fields do not change as a packet is routed through a network. For example, the Time To Live (TTL) field would not be included in the AH calculation because the field is decremented every time that a packet crosses a router enroute to the destination host.

The AH Packet

When AH is used to protect transmitted data, the protocol ID 51 is used to indicate that AH protection is applied to the packet. The actual AH header is composed of the following fields (see Figure 12.3):

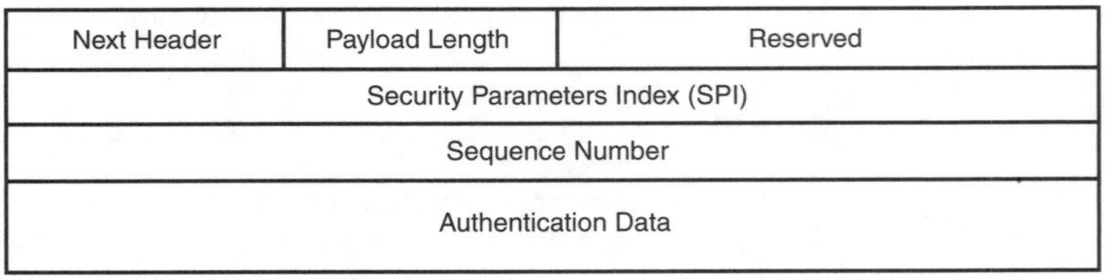

FIGURE 12.3

Authentication header (AH) packet.

Next Header	Payload Length	Reserved
Security Parameters Index (SPI)		
Sequence Number		
Authentication Data		

- **Next Header.** An 8-bit field that contains the protocol ID for the payload that immediately follows the Authentication Header. For example, if AH is used to protect a telnet transmission, the Next Header would contain a value of 6 to indicate that the next header was a TCP packet (telnet uses TCP port 23 at the server side).

- **Payload Length.** An 8-bit field that indicates the length of the Authentication Header in 32-bit words.

- **Reserved.** A 16-bit field reserved for future use. It must be set to a value of 0.

- **Security Parameters Index (SPI).** A 32-bit value that is used in combination with the destination IP address and security protocol (AH) to identify the specific security association that the AH packet is part of. Whenever a security association is established between two hosts, a unique SPI is assigned to identify that association.

- **Sequence Number.** A 32-bit field that contains a counter used to provide anti-replay protection. As each packet is transmitted in a security association, the counter is increased by one.

- **Authentication Data.** This variable-length field contains the *Integrity Check Value (ICV)* or signature calculated against the data packet. The field must be a multiple of 32 bits and may require padding to achieve this. If any nonmutable fields are modified during the transmission of the packet, the ICV will not match when calculated at the recipient host.

AH Integrity Protocols

Different algorithms are available to calculate the ICV for an AH packet. The two most common algorithms used to provide integrity protection are:

- **Message Digest 5 (MD5).** A digital signature algorithm that creates a 128-bit message digest from variable length data.

- **Secure Hash Algorithm 1 (SHA1).** A digital signature algorithm that creates a 160-bit message digest from variable length data.

The actual algorithm that is used for the security association is negotiated during the establishment of the security association.

Encapsulating Security Payload (ESP)

RFC 2406 Encapsulating Security Payload (ESP) provides both encryption and integrity to transmitted data. When most people discuss IPSec, they are actually describing the ESP protocol. ESP encrypts the contents of the original IP header and applies a digital signature to a portion of the original IP header. This differs from AH in that the digital signature for ESP is not applied to the entire packet, but only to nonmutable fields.

12

> **Note**
>
> You can use both AH and ESP protection within an IPSec security association. When both are used, ESP is performed first, encrypting the original IP packet, and then the AH digital signature is computed against the encrypted data. This combination is used when you want the signature to apply to the entire packet, not just the portions protected by the integrity checks provided by the ESP packet.

The ESP Packet

When ESP is used to protect transmitted data, the protocol ID 50 is used to identify that ESP protection is applied to the packet. The actual ESP header is composed of the following fields (see Figure 12.4):

FIGURE 12.4

Encapsulating Security Payload (ESP) packet.

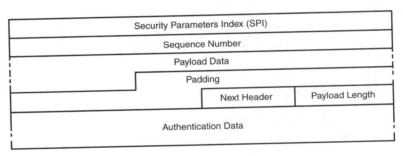

- **Security Parameters Index (SPI).** A 32-bit value that is used in combination with the destination IP address and security protocol (ESP) to identify the specific security association that the ESP packet is part of. Whenever a security association is established between two hosts, a unique SPI is assigned to identify that security association.

- **Sequence Number.** A 32-bit field that contains a counter used to provide anti-replay protection. As each packet is transmitted in a security association, the counter is increased by one.

- **Payload Data.** A variable-length field that contains the data described in the Next Header field. This is the encrypted form of the original IP packet.

The next three fields (Padding, Pad Length, and Next Header) are also referred to as the ESP trailer, because these fields follow the encrypted payload data.

- **Padding.** A variable length field between 0 and 255 bytes used to increase the size of the original data to a size boundary required by the encryption algorithm. Padding may also be used to ensure that the payload data terminates at a 4-byte boundary.

- **Pad Length.** An 8-bit field that indicates number of pad bytes appended to the Payload data.

- **Next Header.** An 8-bit field that contains the protocol ID for the data stored in the Payload Data field.

The Authentication Data field, if present, is also referred to as the ESP authentication trailer.

- **Authentication Data.** This optional, variable-length field contains the *Integrity Check Value (ICV)* or signature calculated against the data packet, if an integrity algorithm is enabled in the security association. The field must be a multiple of 32 bits and may require padding to achieve this. If any nonmutable fields are modified during the transmission of the packet, the ICV will not match when calculated at the recipient host.

ESP Integrity and Encryption Protocols

ESP can provide both integrity and encryption to an IP packet. As with AH, an ESP security association can use either MD5 or SHA1 to provide integrity protection to the ESP packet. Alternatively, you can choose not to use integrity protection to the ESP packet.

For encryption algorithms, three algorithms are available for encryption of the original IP header:

- **Null.** Null encryption means that there is no encryption applied to the original IP header. This algorithm is used only for testing purposes, and is not recommended for production networks.

- **Data Encryption Standard (DES).** An encryption algorithm originated by IBM that applies a 56-bit encryption key to each 64-bit block of data in the original IP packet.

- **Triple DES (3DES).** A modification to the DES algorithm that uses three 56-bit keys to encrypt the data. The first key is used to encrypt the data. The second key runs a decryption algorithm against the encrypted data produced by the first key. The final key runs another encryption process against the decrypted, encrypted data.

12

> **Processing Issues**
>
> The use of 3DES instead of DES encryption can result in performance issues due to the higher encryption processing. It is recommended to use offloading IPSec network cards when using 3DES to offload the 3DES processing to a processor on the network card, rather than having the computer's CPU performing the encryption calculations.

IPSec Modes

Whether you use AH or ESP to protect the transmitted data, IPSec offers two modes of protection: transport mode and tunnel mode (see Figure 12.5).

FIGURE 12.5

IPSec transport mode and tunnel mode.

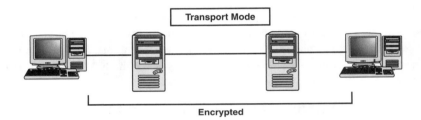

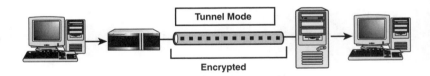

In transport mode, the data is protected from the originating host to the destination host. At no point is the data transmitted in an unprotected format.

In tunnel mode, the data is only encrypted over a partial path between the originating host and the destination host. In Figure 12.5, the client sends the data in an unprotected manner, When the data reaches the router at the boundary to the network, the router establishes a security association with the multihomed computer at the destination network. The tunnel mode security association establishes that the external NIC of the multihomed computer is the tunnel endpoint. Data is encrypted between the two boundary computers, and then is decrypted and sent to the target host.

> **Packets Must Get Back to Source**
>
> A separate security association is established for return traffic with the external interface of the router in Figure 12.5 designated as the tunnel endpoint.

Transport Mode Packet Construction

In transport mode, AH and ESP provide protection to the transmitted data from the originating host to the destination host.

For AH protected data, the AH header is placed between the original IP header and the transport protocol header as shown in Figure 12.6.

FIGURE 12.6

AH header placement for transport mode.

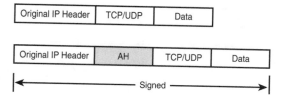

The AH header protects the entire packet (except mutable fields) against modification.

For ESP protected data, the ESP header is placed in between the original IP header and the transport protocol header, but the ESP trailer and ESP Authentication Trailer are placed after the original Data payload as shown in Figure 12.7.

FIGURE 12.7

ESP header placement for transport mode.

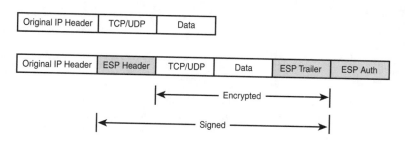

The encryption algorithm negotiated in the security association is applied to the TCP/UDP header, the data payload and the ESP Trailer fields, and the integrity algorithm (if included in the security association), is applied to the ESP header, the TCP/UDP header, the Data payload, and the ESP Trailer with the resulting digital signature stored in the ESP Authentication Trailer.

12

Tunnel Mode Packet Construction

The packet construction differs between transport and tunnel modes because the data is only protected as it is transmitted between the tunnel endpoints. The original packet must be decapsulated at the target tunnel endpoint and then transmitted unprotected to the target host.

For AH protected data, a tunnel mode packet appends a new IP header to the packet that contains the initiating host as the source IP address and the other tunnel endpoint as the destination IP address. The AH header is placed between the new IP header and the original IP header, as shown in Figure 12.8.

FIGURE 12.8

AH header placement for tunnel mode.

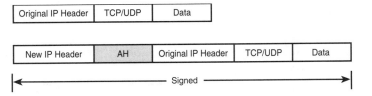

The AH protection is applied to the entire packet, excluding mutable fields, but including the new IP header and the Authentication Header.

For ESP protected data, a new IP header is also appended to the original IP packet as shown in Figure 12.9.

FIGURE 12.9

ESP header placement for tunnel mode.

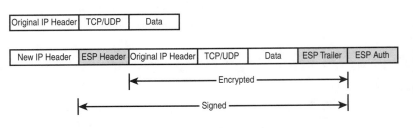

The original IP header, TCP/UDP header, Data, and ESP Trailer are encrypted. If integrity is negotiated for the security association, the integrity algorithm is applied to the ESP header, original IP header, TCP/UDP header, and Data and ESP Trailer, and the digital signature is stored in the ESP Authentication Trailer.

The IPSec Process

When two hosts are configured to implement IPSec, each host is configured with a security database that defines what IPSec protocols (ESP or AH) will be used to protect the transmitted data, how the data is to be protected, and the security algorithms (such as SHA1, or DES) used to protect the data. These settings are negotiated by using Internet Security Association and Key Management Protocol (ISAKMP), also referred to as Internet Key Exchange (IKE).

RFC 2408 ISAKMP is the protocol used to negotiate the security association between the two hosts implementing IPSec. During the ISAKMP process, the security association establishes two different modes: main mode and quick mode.

ISAKMP Main Mode

Main mode establishes what integrity and encryption algorithms are used to exchange negotiation packets when establishing Quick Mode settings.

In main mode, the following are negotiated:

- **Integrity Algorithm.** The algorithm (typically MD5 or SHA1) that is used to sign all transmitted packets during the security association establishment.
- **Encryption Algorithm.** The algorithm (typically DES or 3DES) that is used to encrypt all transmitted packets during security association establishment.
- **Diffie-Helman Group.** The Diffie-Helman Group settings determine the length of the initial key used when establishing a Security Association. The key length can be set to 768 bytes, 1024 bytes, or in some newer variants, 3072 bytes.
- **Rekey Interval.** The time interval when new integrity and encryption secret keys must be created.
- **Master Perfect Forward Secrecy.** Requires that when new secret keys are established, the keys cannot be based on previous key material. This adds security to the encryption by using unique keys each time a new key is generated.
- **Authentication Method.** A security association requires that the two hosts authenticate before the security association is established. Note that it is the actual network devices that authenticate, not the users at the network devices. The authentication methods supported for ISAKMP include
  - *Pre-shared key.* A text string is configured at each host participating in the security association and is exchanged during Quick Mode. If the key is the same at both hosts, authentication is successful. Pre-shared key is only recommended in cases where other authentication methods cannot be used, or during initial testing.
  - *Kerberos v5.* If the two hosts belong to the same Kerberos realm, or in realms that trust each other, the hosts can authenticate using Kerberos authentication.

12

- *Certificate-based authentication.* If the two hosts have certificates that chain to a common trusted root Certification Authority, the hosts are authenticated as long as the certificates are time-valid and are not revoked.

> **Note** Details on Kerberos and certificate-based authentication can be found in Day 11, "Authentication in a TCP/IP Network."

The following code snippet from an Oakley log shows the main mode (indicated by MM) negotiations between a Windows .NET Server router and a CheckPoint Firewall-1.

```
9-19: 13:54:57:68:214 Receive: (get) SA = 0x00000000 from 131.107.154.14.500
9-19: 13:54:57:68:214 ISAKMP Header: (V1.0), len = 164
9-19: 13:54:57:68:214   I-COOKIE fb1f246dc64bfa48
9-19: 13:54:57:68:214   R-COOKIE 0000000000000000
9-19: 13:54:57:68:214   exchange: Oakley Main Mode
9-19: 13:54:57:68:214   flags: 0
9-19: 13:54:57:68:214   next payload: SA
9-19: 13:54:57:68:214   message ID: 00000000
9-19: 13:54:57:68:214 Filter to match: Src 10.17.154.14 Dst 10.10.1.1
9-19: 13:54:57:68:214 MM PolicyName: 1
9-19: 13:54:57:68:214 MMPolicy dwFlags 2 SoftSAExpireTime 28800
9-19: 13:54:57:68:214 MMOffer[0] LifetimeSec 28800 QMLimit 0 DHGroup 1
9-19: 13:54:57:68:214 MMOffer[0] Encrypt: Triple DES CBC Hash: SHA
9-19: 13:54:57:68:214 Auth[0]:RSA Sig CN=IssuingCA
9-19: 13:54:57:68:214 Responding with new SA d68d0
9-19: 13:54:57:68:214 processing payload SA
9-19: 13:54:57:68:214 Received Phase 1 Transform 1
9-19: 13:54:57:68:214     Encryption Alg Triple DES CBC(5)
9-19: 13:54:57:68:214     Hash Alg SHA(2)
9-19: 13:54:57:68:214     Auth Method RSA Signature with Certificates(3)
9-19: 13:54:57:68:214     Oakley Group 2
9-19: 13:54:57:68:214     Life type in Seconds
9-19: 13:54:57:68:214     Life duration of 648000
9-19: 13:54:57:68:214 Received Phase 1 Transform 2
9-19: 13:54:57:68:214     Encryption Alg Triple DES CBC(5)
9-19: 13:54:57:68:214     Hash Alg SHA(2)
9-19: 13:54:57:68:214     Auth Method RSA Signature with Certificates(3)
9-19: 13:54:57:68:214     Oakley Group 1
9-19: 13:54:57:68:214     Life type in Seconds
9-19: 13:54:57:68:214     Life duration of 648000
9-19: 13:54:57:78:214 Phase 1 SA accepted: transform=2
9-19: 13:54:57:78:214 SA - Oakley proposal accepted
```

Note that the Oakley log shows that an ISAKMP header was received that contained two different main mode offers. The only difference between the two offers is the Diffie-Helman group settings. The first uses Oakley group 2 (1024 bits) and the second uses

Oakley group 1 (768 bits). The security association negotiation arrived at using Oakley Group 2 when transform 2 was selected.

ISAKMP Quick Mode

Quick mode is where the actual integrity and encryption algorithms for transmitted data are negotiated. The first process that takes place is the actual authentication of the hosts entering into a security association. The authentication method was negotiated during main mode, and if the authentication fails, the security association is not established, and ISAKMP negotiation terminates immediately.

If the authentication succeeds, the quick mode negotiation continues. The following settings can be negotiated:

- **IPSec protocols.** The security association can use AH, ESP, or a combination of AH and ESP.

- **Integrity/Encryption Algorithms.** Depending on the IPSec protocols selected, a mix of MD5, SHA1, NULL, DES, and 3DES can be designated.

> **Caution**
>
> More than one combination of IPSec protocols and integrity/encryption algorithms can be offered. The first match that is reached between the two hosts is ultimately selected, so you must be careful when ordering the selections at each host.

- **IPSec mode.** Determines whether IPSec tunnel mode or IPSec transport is required for the security association.

- **Rekey Interval (Seconds).** The lifetime of the security association in seconds. When the time elapses, a new Quick Mode session is established between the two hosts.

- **Rekey Interval (Kilobytes).** The lifetime of the security association in terms of data transferred. When the amount of data indicated is reached, a new Quick Mode session is established between the two hosts.

- **Perfect Forward Secrecy.** Requires that when new secret keys are established for Quick Mode, the keys cannot be based on previous key material. This adds security to the encryption by using unique keys each time a new key is generated.

The following Oakley log snippet shows the negotiation of quick mode between a CheckPoint Firewall-1 firewall and a Windows .NET Server router.

```
9-18: 16:03:59:186:214 processing payload SA
9-18: 16:03:59:186:214 Negotiated Proxy ID: Src 172.16.1.0.0 Dst 172.16.3.0
```

12

```
9-18: 16:03:59:186:214 Src id for subnet.  Mask 255.255.255.0
9-18: 16:03:59:186:214 Dst id for subnet.  Mask 255.255.255.0
9-18: 16:03:59:186:214 Checking Proposal 1: Proto= ESP(3), num trans=1 Next=0
9-18: 16:03:59:186:214 Checking Transform # 1: ID=Triple DES CBC(3)
9-18: 16:03:59:186:214     group description for PFS is 1
9-18: 16:03:59:186:214     SA life type in seconds
9-18: 16:03:59:186:214       SA life duration 00000e10
9-18: 16:03:59:186:214     HMAC algorithm is SHA(2)
9-18: 16:03:59:186:214     tunnel mode is Tunnel Mode(1)
9-18: 16:03:59:186:214 Finding Responder Policy for SRC=172.16.1.0.0000
➡ DST=172.16.3.0.0000, SRCMask=255.255.255.0, DSTMask=255.255.255.0,
➡ Prot=0 InTunnelEndpt 1016b83 OutTunnelEndpt e9a6b83
9-18: 16:03:59:186:214 QM PolicyName: ESP(SHA,3DES) dwFlags 1
9-18: 16:03:59:186:214 QMOffer[0] LifetimeKBytes 0 LifetimeSec 0
9-18: 16:03:59:186:214 QMOffer[0] dwFlags 0 dwPFSGroup -2147483648
9-18: 16:03:59:186:214  Algo[0] Operation: ESP Algo: Triple DES CBC HMAC: SHA
9-18: 16:03:59:186:214 Phase 2 SA accepted: proposal=1 transform=1
```

In this configuration, the initiating host matches an IPSec rule requiring IPSec tunnel mode between the 172.16.1.0/24 and 172.16.3.0/24 networks. Specifically, the following settings were negotiated:

- Tunnel Mode is used for the IPSec method.
- ESP using 3DES encryption and SHA1 integrity is used for all transmitted data.
- The Quick Mode security association will rekey every 3600 seconds. The value 00000e10 is 3600 in hexadecimal format.
- Perfect Forward Secrecy is enabled to ensure that when rekeying is implemented, the previous key material is not used to generate the new key.

Upcoming Changes in IPSec

One of the major issues with IPSec in its current implementation is that IPSec-protected packets cannot pass through firewalls or perimeter servers that implement Network Address Translation (NAT).

The Problem

NAT is used to translate private network addresses, as defined in RFC 1918, to public network addresses. This process is accomplished by replacing the source IP address and source port information in the IP header before the packet is transmitted over a public network (see Figure 12.10).

In the example shown in the figure, the packet originating from the host at the IP address 10.10.10.3 using TCP port 1098 is translated by a NAT device to have a source address of 126.17.2.3 and source port address of 7654. When the response packet is returned to the NAT device, the destination address information is translated back so that the response packet is returned to the host at IP address 10.10.10.3 and the port TCP 1098.

FIGURE 12.10

The NAT process.

Source IP	Source Port	Target IP	Target Port	Data
~~10.10.10.3~~ 126.17.2.3	~~TCP 1098~~ TCP 7654	41.10.54.3	TCP 23	Telnet

If you review the areas of the packet that are protected by IPSec in Figures 12.6 and 12.8, AH protects the original IP header and TCP/UDP header in transport mode and both the new IP header, the original IP header, and the TCP/UDP header in tunnel mode. If NAT translates the source IP address or source port address, this results in the digital signature stored in the Authentication Header being invalidated.

Likewise, Figure 12.7 shows that an ESP transport mode packet encrypts the TCP/UDP header, not allowing port translation, and an ESP tunnel mode packet encrypts both the original IP header and the TCP/UDP header. Because the TCP/UDP port information is encrypted, NAT cannot translate the packets.

Because of the demand to allow IPSec to pass through NAT devices, a series of drafts are now before the IETF that redesign IPSec to pass through NAT devices.

The Solution

The IETF has received recent drafts that propose encapsulating IPSec packets in UDP packets, allowing the IPSec packets to pass through the firewall. The solution, although simple, addresses the translation problems previously described.

UDP-Encapsulated ESP Header Format

The current draft only discusses ESP encapsulation, and will address AH encapsulation in its next release. The proposed UDP-encapsulated ESP header, shown in Figure 12.11, includes the following fields:

12

FIGURE 12.11

UDP-encapsulated ESP header format.

Source Port	Destination Port
Length	Checksum
Non-IKE Marker	
ESP Header	

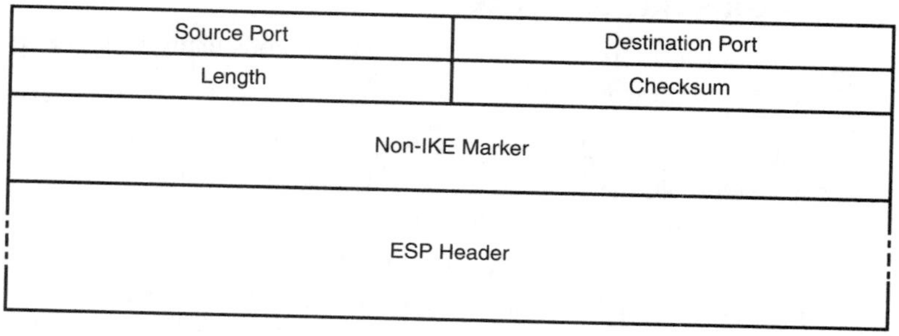

- **Source Port.** The 16-bit field containing the UDP port used by the source host. This source port is not protected by IPSec integrity or encryption. In the case of UDP-encapsulated ESP traffic, the source port would be UDP port 500, the port used for ISAKMP negotiation.
- **Destination Port.** The 16-bit field containing the UDP port used by the destination host. Like the source port, this field is not protected by IPSec integrity or encryption. In the case of UDP-encapsulated ESP traffic, the destination port would be UDP port 500, the port used for ISAKMP negotiation.
- **Length.** A 16-bit field containing the length in octets of the UDP header and its data payload.
- **Checksum.** A 16-bit field that is set to a zero value for UDP-encapsulated ESP traffic.
- **Non-IKE Marker.** A 64-bit field set to a value of zero so that the packet does not look like an ISAKMP packet.
- **ESP or AH Header.** The standard ESP header follows.

Besides a modified header to pass through NAT devices, another packet is required to ensure that the same NAT mappings are used for the duration of the connection between the two hosts. This is accomplished through a NAT-keepalive packet format, shown in Figure 12.12.

FIGURE 12.12

The NAT-keepalive packet format.

Source Port	Destination Port
Length	Checksum
Data (0×FF)	

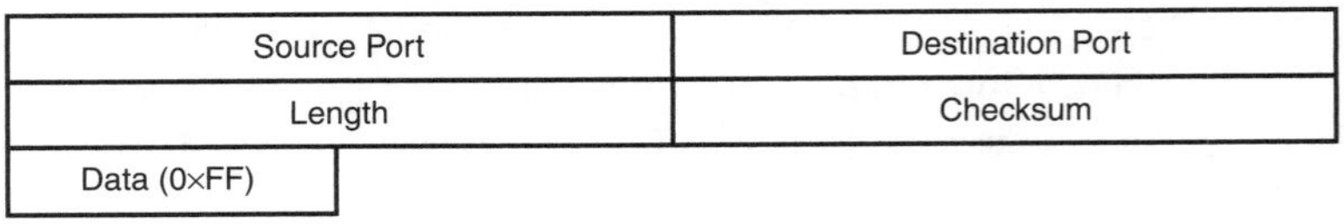

The only difference between the NAT-keepalive packet format and the UDP-encapsulated ESP header format is that after the zero value checksum, the payload is simply an 8-bit field containing the hexadecimal value 0xFF.

Encapsulation Process

For transport mode IPSec security associations using ESP, the transport mode packet is formed as shown in Figure 12.13.

As with today's ESP transport mode packets, the ESP header is inserted before the original TCP/UDP header and the ESP Trailer and ESP Authentication Trailer are added after the original data payload. The difference is that the new UDP header and non-IKE indicator header are placed between the original IP header and the added ESP header. The location of this header allows a NAT device to translate the source IP address from the original IP header and the source port UDP 500 from the newly inserted UDP header.

Note that neither of these fields is protected by UDP integrity or encryption algorithms, allowing the NAT device to translate the attributes.

FIGURE 12.13

Transport mode encapsulation.

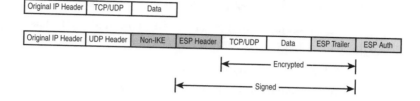

For tunnel mode IPSec security associations using ESP, the tunnel mode packet is formed from the original IP packet as shown in Figure 12.14.

FIGURE 12.14

Tunnel mode encapsulation.

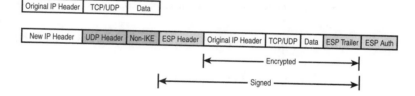

For tunnel mode encapsulation, the ESP header precedes the original IP header, the original TCP/UDP header, and the Data payload, and the ESP Trailer and ESP Authentication Trailer follow the original Data payload. The difference is that the new UDP header with source and destination ports set to UDP port 500 and the non-IKE header set to a value of 0 are inserted between the new IP header and the ESP header.

This format leaves the new IP header and the UDP header available for NAT translation as neither field is protected by ESP's integrity or encryption algorithms.

Note

> To follow the development of these drafts, search the Internet Drafts listing at http://search.ietf.org/search/brokers/internet-drafts/query.html for the keywords IPSec and NAT.

Applying What You Have Learned

Today you learned how data can be encrypted as it is transmitted over a network. Be careful not to fall into the trap of feeling that IPSec is the final word in network transmission security. Several protocols use application-level security methods such as SSL or S/MIME and should be investigated before deploying IPSec.

12

Remember that if a protocol can use application-layer security, there is no reason to also apply IPSec protection to the already encrypted data.

Test Your Knowledge

Here are questions to check what you've learned today. The answers can be found in Appendix B, "Test Your Knowledge: Answers."

1. What is required for an application to use application-layer security?

2. What is required for an application to use IP-layer security?

3. Can a Eudora e-mail client using PGP for mail encryption exchange encrypted mail with a Microsoft Outlook Express e-mail client using S/MIME for mail encryption? Why or why not?

4. Assume that your organization wants to use SSL to protect e-mail authentication. What protocols would you consider implementing to protect the mail authentication?

5. What configuration is required at the mail server to support the secured mail authentication?

6. What configuration is required at the e-mail clients to support the secured mail authentication?

7. What type of protection does an Authentication Header offer to transmitted data?

8. What type of protection does Encapsulating Security Payload offer to transmitted data?

9. Why would you consider using both AH and ESP for a security association, rather than just using the integrity protection offered by ESP packets?

10. What added security is provided by configuring Perfect Forward Secrecy for session key management?

11. What fields in an AH header identify a specific security association between two clients?

12. What methods can be used to authenticate IPSec security associations?

Preview of Day 13

Tomorrow we tackle network security—one of the most debatable network topics. We'll look at threats, some of the issues involved configuring the security of a network, various implementations of firewalls, and protecting local network resources.

DAY 13

Protecting Your Network

Today we'll tackle one of the most contentious topics discussed when referring to networks: network security. The discussion starts with some of the issues you face when configuring the security of a network.

After learning about common network threats, you'll examine various implementations of firewalls that can protect your network from external sources. The following types of firewalls are discussed:

- Packet-filter
- Circuit-level
- Proxy application
- Dynamic packet-filter
- Kernel proxy
- Stateful Inspection

We end the day with information about protecting local network resources. You'll see different Demilitarized Zone (DMZ) configurations and security options that can be implemented to securely expose resources to the Internet.

Threats to Network Security

As networks become more commonplace, several security issues are becoming more apparent. Some standard technologies currently used on the Internet are not secure. Awareness is key if you want to further secure your network from infiltration. The following are some examples of security holes in networks today:

- The use of clear-text passwords for authentication
- The ease of performing network monitoring
- The capability to spoof network addresses
- The poor quality of security implementations

Clear-Text Authentication

Many common, networked business applications in use today utilize clear-text passwords. These applications include the following:

- FTP
- Telnet
- POP3 mail clients

Anyone running a network monitor (also called a *network sniffer*) can capture network packets and reassemble them to determine account and password information.

Despite countless warnings, many passwords in use today are not secure. Passwords should not be names of family members or pets, birth dates, favorite colors, or phone numbers. Many users are guilty of sharing passwords with other users or even leaving passwords in readily accessible areas of the office. Some even stick Post-it notes on monitors or under keyboards with passwords written on them.

Even if more obscure passwords are used, it still is common practice to use words found in the dictionary. These passwords still are very insecure. Almost every operating system has password-cracking programs that use dictionary files to crack passwords. These password-cracking programs encrypt the contents of the dictionary file using the same encryption algorithm used by the network operating system to encrypt the password file. The contents are compared until a match is found.

How do you protect yourself from this network hacking routine? The key is to select alphanumeric, nondictionary words. Do not just tag a number to the end of a word. Many password-cracking programs tag the numbers 1 through 99 to the end of each word in their dictionaries. Also consider using the first letter of each word in a phrase and replacing some words with numbers. For example, you could use the phrase "I am going to the airport tomorrow" to generate the password "Iag2tAt!". Although your lips may move when typing the password, it is an easy method to build complex passwords that are easy to remember.

Proliferation of Network-Monitoring Software

Network-monitoring software packages (also called network *sniffers*) are readily available and can view packets as they traverse the network wire. If applications utilizing clear-text passwords are implemented, this security flaw enables anyone running network-monitoring software to capture passwords and account information for reuse later. The threat is not limited to the local network; it encompasses all network segments that the packets must cross from the user to the server. Any network-monitoring equipment between the two endpoints can capture the account and password information.

Network-monitoring software can be an expensive proposition, but several shareware and bundled versions of network-monitoring software are readily available.

Windows NT and Windows 2000 include the Network Monitor Tools and Agent as a service for users of all versions of the software. This utility sniffs out any traffic destined for the station running the network-monitoring software. This includes any traffic directed to the monitoring station and broadcast traffic destined for the host. System Management Server includes a full-service version of the network-monitoring software. This version has the capability to monitor all network traffic on the network, not just traffic destined for the station running the network-monitoring software. Figure 13.1 shows a network capture of a user's FTP account and password.

FIGURE 13.1

Capturing a password with Network Monitor.

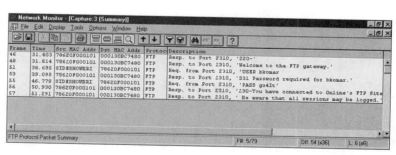

13

Network monitoring not only is related to external attempts to access the secure network; it also can be performed from within the interior network. Network administrators need to be aware of this. Verifying that no unauthorized network monitors are operating should be part of your regular monitoring activities.

In a Microsoft environment, the following NetBIOS name is registered whenever a client is running a network-monitoring software application:

```
SIDESHOWBRI    <BF>  UNIQUE      Registered
```

The <BF> entry also can be observed within the WINS database (if implemented) to determine which users have executed a network-monitoring software application.

 Note

> The latest version of the Network Monitor allows you to detect other monitoring stations from the Network Monitor itself. To determine other Network Monitor users, select Identify Network Monitor Users from the Tools menu.

Spoofing

Several methods are available for a host to masquerade as another host. This technique is commonly known as IP *spoofing*. The following steps show a common method of spoofing an IP address:

1. The attacking station creates a source route packet. This packet indicates the path an IP packet takes from the server on a return path. The trusted client being spoofed is the last hop in the indicated source route before reaching the server. This makes it appear that the packet originated at the masqueraded workstation.

2. The attacking station next sends a packet destined for the server using the source route packet.

3. Because the packet has been routed through the trusted client, the server accepts the packet.

4. The server returns its response to the trusted client.

5. Because of the source route implemented, the trusted client forwards the response to the attacking station.

This is one common method of spoofing an IP address. Another method consists of masquerading as the trusted host when the trusted host is turned off. As long as the correct account/password combination is used, the attacking station can masquerade as the trusted host.

Flawed Security Configuration

The most common form of network security breach relates back to improper configuration of security. This usually is the result of one of the following:

- Lack of experience on the part of the network administrator.
- Security patches, service packs, and hot fixes not being applied to the operating system.
- Installing operating systems using a default installation that results in nonrequired services, such as Web services, being installed on computers that are not acting as Web servers.
- Lack of security on a single host that compromises the entire network.

Lack of experience is a major cause of insecure networks. Many network administrators inherit their networks without knowing all the inherent risks involved in managing them. They learn their trade on the job, and the results can be disastrous. Sometimes default accounts and default passwords are not changed. Many networks are broken into using the default administrative account names and passwords.

As security holes are discovered in operating systems, patches or fixes are created to close these holes. A network administrator must keep up with the latest patches to be sure the system remains secure. If patches are not applied to the server, the network is left open to hackers who can exploit the unpatched security hole.

Obtaining Microsoft Security Updates

Microsoft now offers a subscription service for a security bulletin that informs you of any security updates that are released for Microsoft applications and operating systems. You can subscribe to the bulletin service at `http://www.microsoft.com/technet/security/notify.asp`. In addition, Windows 2000 and higher offers the Windows Update feature, which allows you to compare your current installation against a list of recommended updates. Any recommended updates can be applied immediately to your computer.

On most networks, if a single system is compromised, it can lead to the entire network being compromised. If a single host is compromised as a result of a bad or captured password, it can lead to other hosts being compromised. If the compromised system is included in an `.rhosts` file on another system, the hacker then can compromise that system as well. After that system has been compromised, the hacker can attack other systems that include a compromised system in the `.rhosts` file.

13

 Caution   Applying patches is important. The recent assaults against computers have attacked security holes in Microsoft Internet Information Services (IIS). Code

Red and Nimda actually went after the same security flaw in IIS. If administrators patched their servers after Code Red, they were not affected by
Nimda. Unfortunately, all it takes is one missed computer to result in an
infection to the corporate network.

Planning a Network Security Policy

RFC 1878 Before security can be implemented on a network, the organization must draft a
security policy. This document should detail the following information:

- What information should be accessible to all internal users of the network?
- What information should be accessible to remote users of the network?
- What external resources should be accessible to internal users of the network?
- What rules are in place for the removal of data from the office? These rules should
  include both physical and electronic forms of data.
- What rules of conduct should be implemented for electronic mail?
- What rules of conduct should be implemented for Web browsing?
- A password policy should be established. If text-based passwords are used, the pol-
  icy should include how frequently passwords are changed, the minimum length of
  a password, and the password requirements. Password requirements can force a
  password to be alphanumeric or to be a minimum length of characters.
  Alternatively, if biometric or certificate-based authentication is preferred, face-to-
  face meetings may be required to verify the identity of each user.

You cannot design network security without a security policy. The security policy outlines the organization's attitude about security. For example, should you deploy smart
cards, or use text-based authentication for the network. Without knowing what level of
security is required by an organization, this is an impossible question to answer. In fact,
the answer could be none of the above, with the actual answer ranging from no passwords are required to retinal scans are required.

 Note   Detailed information on what information should be included in a security
policy can be found in RFC 2196 "Site Security Handbook," available at
`www.ietf.org/rfc/`.

Firewalls

A *firewall* provides a boundary service to the local area network. In its simplest implementation, the firewall is located between the external world and the private network (see Figure 13.2).

FIGURE 13.2

Firewalls are typically placed between the external network and the private network.

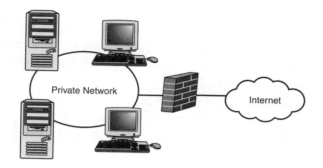

Being sure that all connections to and from the private network pass through the firewall inspection enforces security. A firewall can be configured to allow specific protocols to pass through it if predefined criteria are met. Criteria also can be set to reject a packet if it does not pass inspection.

The two most common implementations of firewalls are based on the following:

- Permitting all services to pass unless they are explicitly denied
- Denying all services unless they are explicitly allowed

The second implementation is the most common because it prevents newly developed protocols and applications from easily passing through the firewall. All unknown protocols are rejected by default.

Placing the firewall between the private and exterior networks masks the internal network characteristics from the exterior network. Common protocols that are blocked from revealing the interior network's characteristics include NIS, DNS, and FINGER. These protocols have the potential to reveal network configuration information that is invaluable to a hacker attempting to circumnavigate the firewall mechanism.

Besides enforcing security on the network, a good firewall also includes reporting and alert facilities. Usage reports can be generated to show commonly visited sites. They also can reveal security holes missed during the configuration of the network security policy. Alert services enable the firewall to notify a network or a security administrator when an intruder attempts to gain access using a prohibited service.

13

Additional Security Issues

After its initial configuration, a firewall must be maintained to provide continued protection against newer attack methods. As new services are released, a determination must be made whether each service will be allowed to navigate through the firewall. The following questions must be answered:

1. Is the service located on the internal network or the external network?

2. If the service is located on the external network, will all users on the internal network be allowed to connect to the service? Or will only a specific group of hosts be allowed to connect?

3. When connecting to the external service, will the clients connect directly or will they use a proxy service on the firewall?

4. If the service is located on the internal network, will external users be allowed to connect to the service?

5. If external users are allowed to connect, will a security mechanism be implemented to authenticate the users and to limit access?

6. What are the characteristics of the traffic related to the new service? Does it use UDP or TCP? What ports are used by the server service? What ports are used by the client service? Are any high-level protocols used that can be identified by a protocol ID number?

By answering these questions for a new service, you can be sure the service is implemented in a secure method that follows the security policy of the network.

The firewall should not be the last line of defense on your network. Be sure the actual network security for your network operating system is implemented correctly. If someone can crack your firewall, he or she should still have to break through your network security before data is compromised. Do not depend entirely on a firewall to provide all the security for your network.

You also need to be aware of backdoors to your network. It does not matter how well your firewall is configured if the network can be entered through a modem pool on the interior network that is not inspected by the firewall. Modem implementations must include authentication to be sure only known users are accessing the network.

Common Implementations

Firewall technology has six basic implementations. These implementations have evolved over the years to increasingly protect the internal network from external attacks.

The following are the six implementations:

- Packet-filter firewalls
- Circuit-level firewalls
- Application-level firewalls with proxies
- Dynamic packet-filter firewalls
- Kernel proxy firewalls
- Stateful Inspection firewalls

Packet-Filter Firewalls

Packet-filter firewalls (the earliest form of firewall) analyze network traffic at the transport layer of the OSI model. Each packet is compared to a set of rules configured for the interface. Rules can be set for both incoming and outgoing packets.

The rules are based on information in the transport protocol header and the IP header. Table 13.1 shows some of the packet-filter rules that can be established on a firewall.

TABLE 13.1   Packet-Filter Rules

Rule#	Interface	Protocol	Source IP	Source Port	Destination IP	Destination Port
1	Internal	TCP	172.16.2.0/24	Any	Any	80
2	Internal	TCP	172.16.2.0/24	Any	Any	23
3	Internal	TCP	172.16.2.0/24	Any	41.168.3.5	25
4	Internal	TCP	172.16.2.0/24	Any	41.168.3.5	110
5	Internal	UDP	172.16.2.0/24	Any	Any	69
6	External	TCP	Any	Any	172.16.2.100	80

This set of rules denies all packets except specified protocols and ports that are explicitly allowed through the firewall. The rules in Table 13.1 accomplish the following tasks:

1. Rule 1 allows any hosts in the 172.16.2.0/24 network to browse Internet resources with a Web browser on port 80.

2. Rule 2 allows any hosts in the 172.16.2.0/24 network to connect to telnet servers on the external network.

3. Rule 3 allows any host in the 172.16.2.0/24 network to send mail through SMTP to the SMTP server at IP address 41.168.3.5.

4. Rule 4 allows any host in the 172.16.2.0/24 network to receive POP3 mail from the POP3 server at IP address 41.168.3.5.

13

5. Rule 5 allows any host in the `172.16.2.0/24` network to use TFTP to connect to any TFTP servers on the external network.

6. Rule 6 allows all external hosts to connect to the internal Web server at IP address `172.16.2.100`.

Static Address Mapping or Service Publishing

For the sixth packet filter rule in Table 13.1 to work, an additional feature must be included on the firewall. This feature, called Static Address Mapping or Service Publishing in different firewall implementations, maps an external IP address and port to an internal IP address and port. When a packet is received addressed to the configured external IP address and listening port, the packet is redirected to an internal network host. The actual listening port can be translated at this time as well. In the list of packet filters, you always include the final destination and port of the redirected traffic, not the original IP address and port to which the external client would connect.

Packet filters often are implemented because they offer the following advantages:

- Client computers require no special configuration. The rules are based on traffic patterns that occur when a host attempts communication that traverses the firewall.

- Packet filters can be implemented with a strategy called *network address translation (NAT)*. The internal network can use a pool of IP addresses hidden from the external network. These addresses are overwritten with a common external address when a packet is sent through the firewall to the external network.

- Packet filters provide the best performance because of the small number of packet evaluations that have to be performed.

Despite these advantages, several disadvantages are related to packet-filtering firewalls. The following are some common disadvantages:

- Packet-filtering firewalls do not provide any additional capabilities such as Web page caching.

- Packet filters function based only on transport-layer information. They cannot determine application-level commands. This prevents more refined rules from being implemented, such as allowing FTP GET commands but disallowing FTP PUT commands. The only rules that can be implemented are to allow or disallow access to TCP ports 20 and 21.

- Packet filters often have little or no audit functionality. This can prevent you from determining whether an attack occurred if it was not initially noticed on the internal network.

Circuit-Level Firewalls

Circuit-level firewalls assume that each packet that passes through the firewall either is a connection request or is data being transported across a current connection that exists between a client and a server host.

A circuit-level firewall functions as a referee. When a TCP session is established, it makes sure a valid TCP three-way handshake occurs. If the handshake does not occur, the connection is terminated.

For each connection established through the firewall, a table of valid connections is maintained. This includes the current session state and the sequence information for both the client and host systems. By interpreting the sequence information, it can be determined whether another host is attempting to hijack a session and place its own packets into the TCP stream.

After a connection is terminated, its entry from the session state is removed.

The following advantages are associated with circuit-level firewalls:

- Circuit-level firewalls are quite efficient at moving traffic through the firewall.
- Connections can be prohibited from an entire network or from specific hosts in the rules table.
- Network address translation can be implemented to protect the internal network address scheme.

The following disadvantages are associated with circuit-level firewalls:

- Circuit-level firewalls cannot restrict access to protocols other than TCP. UDP protocol transactions are connectionless and no session is established.
- It is difficult to test the firewall rules unless they are implemented from the actual host to which restrictions are being applied.
- Packet-filtering firewalls do not provide any additional capabilities such as Web page caching.
- Circuit-level firewalls cannot perform higher-level protocol rule evaluations.

Application-Level Firewalls with Proxy Services

Application-level firewalls evaluate data at the application layer before allowing a connection to take place between two hosts. Information that can be evaluated includes connection state and sequencing information, user passwords, and service requests.

Application-level firewalls also generally include proxy services. A *proxy server* functions as a go-between for a client connecting to an external server. An internal client sends external network requests to a specific proxy server, which is configured in the client software. Figure 13.3 shows the Advanced configuration of proxy services in Microsoft Internet Explorer 6.0.

FIGURE 13.3

Configuring a Web browser to use proxy services.

When a client uses a proxy server, all requests for external network services are sent directly to the proxy server. The proxy server evaluates the request and compares it to rules configured for the proxy service. If the request is allowed, the proxy server issues the request on behalf of the calling client system. When the response is returned to the proxy server, it is forwarded on the internal network to the calling client. From the external service's point of view, the request originated at the proxy server and was returned to the source of the request.

Because proxy services understand the protocol used by the client, more precise rules can be developed based on the application data. This also provides the capability to log detailed session information by proxy clients.

Proxy servers can cache the Web resources they acquire for proxy clients. When subsequent requests are sent to the proxy server, it checks its cache to determine whether a cached copy of the page is stored locally. If it exists in cache, the client is served the resource from the cache. This results in faster delivery to the proxy client. It also reduces the amount of traffic sent over the network link from the internal network to the external network.

When a proxy service is implemented, packet-filtering services can be modified to allow only the proxy server to initiate communications from the internal network to the external network. Table 13.2 shows the modified packet-filtering rules based on the usage of a proxy server.

TABLE 13.2   Modified Packet-Filtering Rules Based on a Proxy Server at 172.16.2.7

Rule#	Interface	Protocol	Source IP	Source Port	Destination IP	Destination Port
1	Internal	TCP	172.16.2.7	Any	Any	80
2	Internal	TCP	172.16.2.7	Any	Any	23
3	Internal	TCP	172.16.2.7	Any	41.168.3.5	25
4	Internal	TCP	172.16.2.7	Any	41.168.3.5	110
5	Internal	UDP	172.16.2.7	Any	Any	69
6	External	TCP	Any	Any	172.16.2.100	80

The following are some common proxy services provided on firewalls:

- Telnet
- FTP
- HTTP
- NNTP
- Socks
- POP3
- SMTP
- IMAP4
- Real Audio

The following advantages are associated with application firewalls:

- The implementation of proxy services allows enforcement on application-level protocols such as HTTP and FTP.
- The proxy service hides the internal network addressing scheme from the external network.
- All allowed communications from the internal network must be performed by proxy services on the firewall. All other attempts to communicate with the external network can be denied.
- Client software can be configured so the use of proxy services is transparent to the clients using them.
- Proxy services can be configured to route external requests to specific internal servers without revealing their actual hostname or internal IP address. The service appears to be running on the proxy server, not the internal server where it truly resides.
- Proxy services keep detailed records of all the requests they handle.

13

The following disadvantages are associated with application servers:

- Proxy services run on the same ports as the applications they support. This prevents the implementation of the actual services on the firewall host, unless the services can be mapped to an available port, rather than using the default port.

- Performance delays can occur when using a proxy because all incoming data is processed twice—once by the proxy service and once by the actual client application.

- New protocols require that a specific proxy be created for them. In many cases, however, you can configure the protocol to work using a generic proxy or download updated protocol definitions to allow the proxy server to recognize the new protocol.

- In most cases, client software has to be configured manually to allow usage of the proxy server.

- Some proxy services require clients to first authenticate with the proxy server before they can use the proxy services. This can cause frustration with the user base.

Dynamic Packet-Filter Firewalls

Dynamic packet-filter firewalls combine the services of application-level firewalls and packet-filter firewalls. As an added benefit, this firewall technology allows firewall security rules to be created on-the-fly.

This technology also can support protocols that use UDP as their transport protocol. As previously mentioned, it is more difficult to monitor UDP communications because a session is not established between the client and the server. A dynamic packet-filter firewall remembers all UDP packets that cross it. When the other host sends a response message, the firewall makes sure it is destined for the original requestor. If this is the case, the UDP packet is allowed to cross the firewall boundary. If not, the packet is dropped. If the UDP response is not returned within a specific time frame, the association is deemed invalid and the response is dropped.

Kernel Proxy Firewalls

Kernel proxy firewalls are implemented at the kernel level of the underlying operating system. When information is discarded, it is done before the data is passed up the network stack.

When a new session request is received by the kernel proxy firewall, a new TCP/IP stack is generated on-the-fly. These stacks only contain the protocol proxies required for the requested session. This allows for additional customization to be implemented that will investigate the data transmission.

As data is transferred up through the levels of the network stack, the network packet can be examined and re-examined at each level. If any rules are broken at any level, the packet can be discarded immediately. There is no need to transfer data all the way up to the application level before the packet is discarded.

Stateful Inspection Firewalls

Checkpoint Systems patented a new technology for firewalls known as *stateful inspection*. Besides providing the firewall features provided by kernel proxy firewalls, stateful inspection firewalls are able to investigate each protocol stream that passes through the firewall to ensure that the rules of an application are followed.

For example, stateful inspection can identify when a client sends a request when instead it should have sent a response packet. The identification of such a transaction would result in the firewall blocking the client connection for not following protocol rules.

Stateful inspection is more secure than application proxies because the application rules are applied even before the packet reaches the application layer of the TCP/IP model. Stateful inspection also supports UDP-based protocols through the inspection of client and server ports used during a session. If a session is hijacked, the firewall would recognize that the source or destination socket was changed, and terminate the connection.

Other Network Protection Strategies

Besides firewalls, your network may also implement other services to protect the private network from attacks originating on the Internet. Two of the more common services implemented to further secure the network include Network Address Translation (NAT) and Intrusion Detection Systems (IDS).

Network Address Translation

Network address translation hides internal network addressing. All outbound packets are translated so that internal IP addressing is never exposed to the Internet. Rather than seeing the individual IP addresses used on the private network, it appears as if a single computer (with a single IP address) is really busy.

When a packet is sent outbound from the private network, the NAT intercepts the packet and translates both the source IP address and source port information (see Figure 13.4).

13

FIGURE 13.4

The NAT translation process.

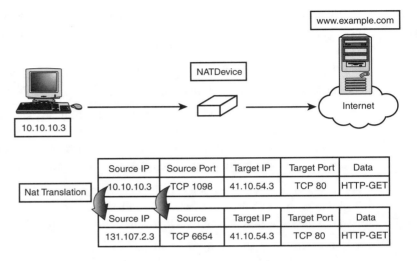

In this example, the host at IP address 10.10.10.3 attempts to connect to the Web server www.example.com, which is located at IP address 41.10.54.3. When the packet reaches the NAT device, which could be a firewall or a router, the source IP address and source port number are translated by the NAT service.

In this case, the source IP address is changed to 131.107.2.3 and the source port is changed to TCP port 6654. The mapping information is maintained in a NAT table, so that the response packet from the www.example.com Web server is returned to the correct internal client.

If network monitoring were to take place from the external network, the only IP addresses that would be exposed to the external network would be the external IP address of the NAT device, or 131.107.2.3.

InterNIC has set aside specific IP addresses for usage on private networks. These IP address ranges are guaranteed to not be in use on the Internet and are defined in RFC 1918. The RFC outlines three network address ranges reserved for internal networks:

- 10.0.0.0–10.255.255.255 (10.0.0.0/8)
- 172.16.0.0–172.31.255.255 (172.16.0.0/12)
- 192.168.0.0–192.168.255.255 (192.168.0.0/16)

These addresses are labeled as internal network addresses on firewall implementations that use network address translation. Other address pools can be used, but if you try to connect to any outside resource in the same network range, the connection fails because the range has been designated as part of the internal network.

If someone attempts to access the internal network from the external network using an address located in the internal network, the transaction is rejected because the internal network address is located on the wrong side of the firewall.

Intrusion Detection Systems (IDS)

Besides a firewall, your network may also require an *intrusion detection system (IDS)* to inspect the actual content of data that passes through the firewall to ensure that the data does not contain malicious content.

For example, a firewall may be configured to allow HyperText Transfer Protocol (HTTP) and secure HyperText Transfer Protocol (HTTPS) access to a Web server on the private network. Just allowing all Web-related traffic to pass to the Web server and blocking all other traffic does not necessarily protect the Web server from all attacks.

There are still attacks that work with malformed packets and other protocols disguised as an approved protocol that would still penetrate the firewall in this case.

An IDS such as Internet Security Systems' RealSecure and BlackICE allow protection of both the network and individual workstations against application attacks. The IDS monitors incoming traffic looking for both specific attacks and nontypical application transactions. When it recognizes an attack, the data transfer is immediately blocked and an administrator can be alerted about the attack.

Creating a Demilitarized Zone

Generally, an organization does not want to provide access to resources on the private network to Internet users. Rather than place the resources on the Internet directly, or on the private network, the resources are often placed on a separate network segment known as a *demilitarized zone* or DMZ.

In a demilitarized zone network implementation, all services made available to external network clients are located on a separate network segment. All access to the DMZ is monitored by a firewall. The firewall ensures that only protocols that you configure are allowed to enter the DMZ from the Internet. All other protocols are discarded at the firewall.

There are two common DMZ configurations:

- Three-pronged firewalls
- Mid-ground DMZs

13

Three-Pronged Firewalls

A three-pronged firewall uses a single firewall with three network cards to create three zones: the Internet, the private network, and the DMZ (see Figure 13.5).

FIGURE 13.5

A three-pronged fire-wall.

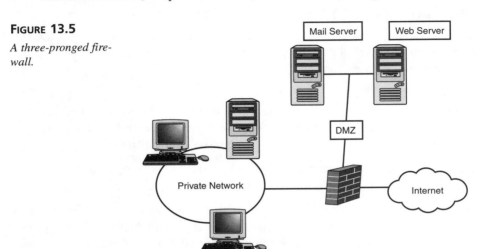

The firewall is configured to manage all traffic that is transferred between the three zones. Typically, the packet filters are most restrictive between the Internet and the private network, not allowing any traffic that originates on the Internet to enter the private network.

The firewall is configured to only allow the necessary protocols into the DMZ from the Internet. In this case, the firewall may be configured to allow HTTP and HTTPS to the Web server, and POP3 and SMTP to the Mail server.

Different rules may exist at the firewall for traffic that originates from the private network that enters the DMZ.

Mid-Ground DMZs

An alterative to using a three-pronged firewall for DMZ deployment is to implement the DMZ between two separate firewalls as shown in Figure 13.6. This implementation is often referred to as a mid-ground DMZ, or back-to-back firewalls.

In this configuration, the Web server and the Mail server are located in a separate network segment located between an exterior firewall and an interior firewall.

Additional security is gained in this configuration because two separate firewalls must be penetrated for an attacker to gain access to the private network.

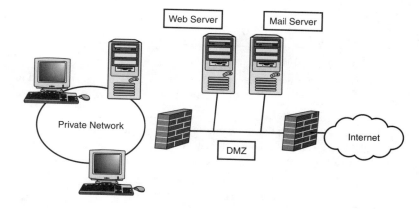

FIGURE 13.6

A mid-ground DMZ.

Comparing Three-Pronged Firewalls with Mid-Ground DMZs

Both the three-pronged firewall and the mid-ground DMZ provide an isolated network segment for Internet accessible resources. Table 13.3 shows the advantages and disadvantages to each configuration.

TABLE 13.3   Comparing DMZ Configurations

Advantages	Disadvantages
Three-Pronged Firewall	
The cost of deploying the DMZ is reduced because only a single firewall is required	The firewall is a single point of failure. If the firewall is compromised, both the DMZ and the private network are susceptible to attack.
Only a single packet filter list is defined, which reduces the packet filter management load.	The single packet filter listing can be quite complex. All the packet filters must be defined in a single listing, which can be very long and difficult to configure.
	Not all firewalls support more than two network interfaces.

13

TABLE 13.3   continued

Advantages	Disadvantages

Mid-Ground DMZ

Advantages	Disadvantages
If the exterior firewall is compromised, the interior firewall still protects the private network.	Extra cost is required for the purchase of the second firewall license.
Using two different firewall products adds additional security because different attacks must be launched against each firewall.	Two separate packet filters must be maintained to secure the private network.
It is easy to distinguish between exterior packet filter rules and internal packet filter rules.	

Choosing a Firewall

There is no easy answer to which firewall product you should buy. The best advice I can give you is to ensure that the firewall is International Computer Security Association (ICSA)-certified. You can retrieve a listing of ICSA-certified firewalls at `http://www.icsalabs.com/html/communities/firewalls`. The firewalls included in the listing have undergone an extensive security evaluation by an independent third party, TruSecure Corporation.

Applying What You Have Learned

Today's material looked at how firewalls and other security services can protect your network when connected to the Internet. Solutions ranged from a single firewall placed between the private network and the Internet to DMZ solutions using one or two firewalls.

Test Your Knowledge

Here are questions to check what you've learned today. The answers can be found in Appendix B, "Test Your Knowledge: Answers."

1. What are some of the common security threats faced on a network?

2. How does network address translation protect an interior network?

3. Why do you need a security policy for your organization before you can start protecting network resources?

4. Complete the following table of packet-forwarding rules based on the network configured in Figure 13.7.

FIGURE 13.7

A sample network.

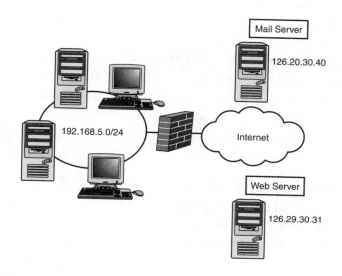

The following proxy rules should be established:

- All clients in the internal network (192.168.5.0/24) should be allowed to connect to the mail server using POP3, SMTP, or IMAP as protocols.

- All clients in the internal network should be allowed to connect to any Web server on the Internet.

- All clients in the internal network should be allowed to connect to any NNTP server on the Internet.

- All clients in the internal network should be allowed to connect to any telnet server on the Internet.

- Only the external client at IP address 126.29.30.31 should be allowed to telnet to the internal server at 192.168.5.10.

Rule#	Interface	Protocol	Source IP	Source Port	Destination IP	Destination Port
POP3						
IMAP						
SMTP						
HTTP						
NNTP						
Telnet Out						
Telnet In						

13

All source and destination port information can be found in the services file in your \etc directory.

5. Describe a process by which an intruder can spoof another host's address.

6. What benefits are derived by using an intrusion detection system with a firewall?

7. What are major decision factors that will lead you to deploy a DMZ with two firewalls, rather than with just a single firewall?

8. Why would you want to choose an ICSA-certified firewall over a firewall that is not ICSA-certified?

Preview of Day 14

Tomorrow we'll look at TCP/IP applications that allow a user or administrator to remotely execute commands on another computer. The applications range from the text-based telnet and Remote Unix command to graphical applications using X Window or Terminal Services.

I'll show you how each remote command works and what the security implications of each protocol selection are.

DAY 14

Remote Command Applications

Remote command applications enable users to perform tasks and run processes on a server while they are physically located at a remote host. The processes run as if the users are operating at the server console.

Telnet is a protocol commonly used for this type of functionality. It enables remote users to use a standardized interface to communicate with a remote server. Today I'll detail:

- Telnet communication flow
- Negotiation of additional Telnet options
- Telnet control functions
- The Telnet USASCII character set
- Telnet escape sequence commands

We'll also look at the Berkeley Unix "R-Utilities." These remote commands enable a user to execute processes on a remote system. The security involved with these remote commands will also be reviewed.

For those who prefer graphical administration of a network, both Microsoft and Citrix offer remote administration through thin clients connected to terminal servers. The implementation considerations of each solution will be reviewed and the two competing products will be compared.

Finally, some of the optional TCP/IP services will be reviewed. This section will include definitions of the optional TCP/IP utilities, installation of the utilities in a Windows 2000 environment, and using Telnet to inspect these optional services.

Telnet

RFC 854 The Telnet protocol provides a bidirectional communication session between two hosts. It allows the calling system to connect to a Telnet server service running on a TCP/IP host. When connected, the calling host can run commands and processes as if it were sitting at the console of the Telnet server.

Three key features are provided to the two hosts participating in a Telnet session:

- **Network Virtual Terminal (NVT).** An NVT provides a common endpoint at each end of a Telnet communication session that defines what functionality is provided (see Figure 14.1).

FIGURE 14.1

A Telnet communication session.

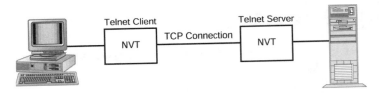

This eliminates the need for specific client and server software to be required. If you are running Telnet server software from one software vendor, you are not required to use that same vendor's client software to communicate with the Telnet server. The NVT creates an environment that can be extended if the client and server portion can agree to what options can be implemented beyond the scope of the NVT. It is also a minimum set of standards that must be provided. Therefore, a client that does not support all the options of a server will be able to operate using this minimum set of functions.

- **Negotiated options.** If a Telnet server or client can provide options above the base NVT, it can negotiate what options each will support to create a more option-inclusive Telnet session. Both the client and the server side of a Telnet session can request that options either be implemented or not implemented. In addition, the requesting system can ask for the option to be set on its NVT or on the server's NVT.

- **Symmetric view.** Because the negotiation syntax of options takes place in a symmetrical fashion, it can result in option loops. An option loop occurs when one NVT's acknowledgment of an option is mistakenly interpreted as a request to set an option on the other NVT. The Telnet protocol implements the following features to prevent option loops from occurring:

  - Option requests can be sent to another NVT only if they are requesting a change in option status. Option requests should not be sent simply to announce what an option is currently set to.

  - If an NVT receives a request to set an option and it already has that option set, it should not send an acknowledgment for this option. This helps to prevent option loops from starting.

  - Most options are set at the beginning of a Telnet session. If you need to change an option during a Telnet session, it can be implemented midstream. In other words, you can place the option in a data stream where it needs to take effect. All transmission of data beyond the point where the option is set follows the rules of that option being set.

What If the Option Is Rejected?

The NVT that requests the option change must keep a send buffer of all the data sent after the option change request has been sent. This way, if the option change is rejected, the NVT can resend the data with the option set to the original setting. If the option is accepted, the send buffer can be flushed.

The Telnet protocol uses the TCP protocol to ensure that reliable delivery of information takes place between the two hosts. The calling Telnet system uses a random TCP port above port 1024 and connects to the Telnet server's TCP port 23, a well-known port.

The Option Negotiation Process

The negotiation of options between two NVTs generally occurs during the initial creation of a Telnet session. The actual setting of options makes use of four negotiation options (see Table 14.1).

14

TABLE 14.1 NVT Negotiation Request Types

Negotiation Option	Meaning as Offer/Request	Meaning as Acknowledgment
DO	Requests that the receiving NVT implements the requested option.	Indicates that the receiving NVT agrees to the requesting NVT implementing the indicated option.
DON'T	Requests that the receiving NVT ceases to implement the requested option.	Indicates that the receiving NVT does not agree to the requesting NVT implementing the indicated option.
WILL	Offers to implement the indicated option.	Indicates that the receiving NVT has implemented the requested option.
WON'T	Offers to cease supporting the indicated option.	Indicates that the receiving NVT did not implement the requested option.

The option negotiation asks either that the remote NVT implements an option or that the remote NVT accepts the local NVT setting an option. Figure 14.2 shows the sending of a WILL and DO option request and the expected acknowledgments that follow.

FIGURE 14.2

The Telnet option negotiation process.

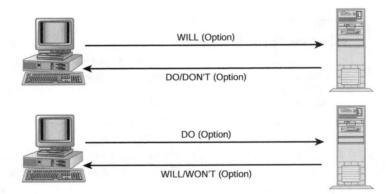

As you can see, the acknowledgment of an option uses the same negotiation options as a request. This is what can lead to option loops.

The options that can be set through negotiation include:

- **Echo.** If enabled, the configured side of the Telnet session echoes the data it receives.

- **Transmit Binary.** This option changes the transmission from 7-bit U.S. ASCII to 8-bit binary.

- **Terminal Type.** This option allows information to be exchanged about the type and model of a terminal being used. This allows output to be optimized for that terminal type.

- **End of Record.** This option indicates whether data will be terminated with an end-of-record code.

- **Suppress Go Ahead (GA).** This option suppresses the sending of a Go Ahead signal after data has been transmitted.

- **Status.** This option requests the status of other Telnet options from a remote host.

- **Timing-Mark.** This option inserts a timing mark in a return data stream to allow the two ends of the connection to synchronize their clocks.

- **Linemode.** This option allows a Telnet client to perform local editing on input lines. This sends complete lines rather than individual characters to the Telnet server.

- **Com Port Control.** This option provides the client with the ability to send COM port configuration information to the access server that is connected to the outbound modem if connecting to the Telnet server via a serial line.

- **Character Set.** This option allows a negotiation to take place to determine what character set to use for transmission between the client and server.

- **Environment.** This option allows the exchange of environment variable information between two hosts. This includes both global and user environment variables.

- **Authentication.** This option provides a framework to be created for the passing of authentication information through a Telnet session. This removes the security risk of sending clear-text authentication—the default with Telnet.

Improvement in Authentication

There have been great improvements in authentication in recent years. Some Telnet servers now support Kerberos authentication, rather than the default clear-text authentication.

The Telnet client in Microsoft Services for Unix, Windows 2000, and Windows .NET Server support NT Lan Manager (NTLM) authentication, to use a challenge/response mechanism, rather than clear-text authentication.

Both provide a great improvement, and should be implemented to increase the security of Telnet. Be sure to select clients that support the authentication protocol you implement.

14

- **Remote Flow Control.** This option provides a method of remotely toggling flow control between a user Telnet process and the attached terminal. This flow control pertains only to data being transmitted over the Telnet session.

Standard Control Functions

Because you can implement Telnet servers and clients on heterogeneous systems, some standard control functions had to be implemented in the Telnet protocol. The standardization of these functions recognizes that different systems might implement these functions differently, but the functions must be defined the same. One Telnet client, for example, might use the key combination Ctrl+C to represent an Interrupt Process (IP) function whereas another client might use the Esc key. The caveat is that if the local system does not implement one of the seven control functions locally, it does not have to provide support for that function to remote users.

The seven common control functions are:

- Interrupt Process: IP
- Abort Output: AO
- Are You There: AYT
- Erase Character: EC
- Erase Line: EL
- Synchronize: SYNCH
- Break: BRK

The Interrupt Process (IP) control function enables you to suspend or interrupt a process running on the Telnet server. A common use for this function is to terminate a looping process that the user feels has not completed in a timely fashion. IP is also used by protocols other than Telnet; if other protocols are used, the Interrupt Process control function must be implemented.

The Abort Output (AO) function allows the running process to continue running until it's completed, but it stops the sending of output to the remote user's terminal screen. This function often also clears output that has been produced but not yet sent to the remote terminal. Typically, the remote terminal is placed back at a prompt screen and asked for its next command to be issued.

The Are You There (AYT) function enables remote users to determine whether their connection to the Telnet server is still functioning. The Telnet server may appear to be "down" due to heavy usage or a large computation.

The Break (BRK) function is used by many systems to indicate that the Break or Attention key has been invoked. This function emulates these keys in a Telnet session.

The Erase Character (EC) function deletes the last character input by the remote user. This is most commonly used when a remote user wants to edit his input before submitting it to the Telnet server.

The Erase Line (EL) function is used to delete the contents of the current "line" of input. This is the case in which the entire line needs to be erased and replaced with an alternate command.

The Synchronize (SYNCH) function provides a method for remote users to ensure that they can regain control of the Telnet session in the case of a runaway process. The IP and AO functions provide this function commonly, but in the case of a remote host, these commands might not reach the Telnet server and will have no effect. The SYNCH function consists of a TCP segment with the URGENT flag set and the Telnet Data Mark (DM) command. The TCP URGENT flag ensures the receiving host reads the accompanying data stream immediately. The DM command discards all the characters between the remote host that sent the SYNCH function and the Telnet server.

Definitions of ASCII Control Characters

Within the NVT, the U.S. ASCII character set is used to represent all input and output characters on the screen. This includes all printable characters, such as lowercase letters, uppercase letters, and punctuation. Table 14.2 shows the standard definitions of the recognized U.S. ASCII control codes between characters 0 and 31.

TABLE 14.2 U.S. ASCII Cursor Control Codes

U.S. ASCII	Decimal Value	U.S. ASCII Control Code Meaning
0	Null [NUL]	No operation.
7	Bell [BEL]	Produces a sound at the terminal. This character does not move the cursor.
8	Back Space [BS]	Moves the cursor one character position toward the left margin.
9	Horizontal Tab [HT]	Moves the cursor to the next horizontal tab stop. The location of the tab stop is configured in the Telnet client software.
10	Line Feed [LF]	Moves the cursor to the next print line, keeping the cursor in the horizontal location on screen.

14

TABLE 14.2   continued

U.S. ASCII	Decimal Value	U.S. ASCII Control Code Meaning
11	Vertical Tab [VT]	Moves the cursor to the next vertical tab stop. The location of the tab stop is configured in the Telnet client software.
12	Form Feed [FF]	Moves the cursor to the top of the next page, keeping the cursor in the same horizontal location on screen.
13	Carriage Return [CR]	Moves the cursor to the left margin of the current line.

The most common combination of these control codes is the combination of [CR][LF]. You should treat this combination as a single "new-line" character. It moves the cursor to the leftmost column of the next line when sent to the Telnet server.

Telnet Escape Sequence Commands

Each command issued in a Telnet session is actually made up of a two-command sequence. The first command is always the Interpret as Command (IAC)-Escape character sequence. The second command is the actual code for the command being issued. When the command codes are not preceded by the Interpret as Command code, they do not have the same meaning.

Requiring the IAC character to precede each command sequence leaves no doubt whether a data stream is intended to be a command or simply some data sent to the other host. Table 14.3 shows the defined Telnet commands.

TABLE 14.3   Telnet Command Codes

U.S. ASCII Decimal Value	Control Code	Meaning
240	SE	End of sub-negotiation parameters.
241	NOP	No operation.
242	Data Mark	The data stream portion of a SYNCH operation. This should always be accompanied by a TCP Urgent notification.
243	Break	The Break (BRK) function.
244	Interrupt Process	The Interrupt Process (IP) function.
245	Abort Output	The Abort Output (AO) function.
246	AYT	The Are You There (AYT) function.
247	EC	The Erase Character (EC) function.

TABLE 14.3 continued

U.S. ASCII Decimal Value	Control Code	Meaning
248	EL	The Erase Line (EL) function.
249	GA	The Go Ahead signal.
250	SB	Indicates the following data stream is a sub-negotiation of the indicated option.
251	WILL [Option code]	If sent initially, indicates the desire to begin performing the indicated option. If sent as an acknowledgment, indicates a confirmation that the receiving host is currently performing the indicated option.
252	WON'T [Option code]	If sent initially, indicates the desire to not perform the indicated option. If sent as an acknowledgment, indicates a confirmation that the receiving host has ceased to perform the indicated option.
253	DO [Option code]	If sent initially, indicates the desire for the receiving host to perform the indicated option. Can also represent an acknowledgment that the receiving host will perform the indicated option.
254	DON'T [Option code]	If sent initially, indicates the desire for the receiving host to cease performing the indicated option. Can also represent a response that the receiving host should not implement the indicated option.
255	IAC	The Interpret as Command (IAC) function that precedes all the command functions.

Connecting to a Telnet Server

To connect to a Telnet server, you need to use Telnet client software. Most operating systems now come with Telnet software, including all Windows platforms since

14

Windows 95 and all Unix operating systems. On most systems, the executable for the
Telnet client is `TELNET.EXE`.

The next process depends on whether the Telnet client you are using is a graphical user
interface (GUI) or text-based client.

In Windows 95, Windows 98, and Windows NT 4.0, the Telnet client is a GUI-based
client. After running `TELNET.EXE`, you need to indicate the host you want to connect to
for a Telnet session. Select Remote System from the Connect menu. The connection dialog box shown in Figure 14.3 appears.

FIGURE 14.3

*Connecting to a Telnet
server using a GUI
client.*

Text-based clients require that you actually input the commands to connect to the Telnet
server. After you run `Telnet.exe`, you must enter the following commands once you
reach the `telnet>` prompt:

```
telnet> open ds.internic.net
```

If successful, you will see output much like the following, showing that you are attempting connection and ultimately achieving connection to the Telnet server.

```
Trying 198.49.45.10...
Connected to ds.internic.net.
Escape character is '^]'.
```

Tip

> You can reduce the keystrokes to achieve a Telnet session by simply typing
> **telnet term.example.com**. This command automatically launches Telnet and
> issues the open `term.example.com` command.

After you connect to the Telnet server, you need to authenticate with the Telnet server.
This includes providing your user account and password combination when prompted
(see Figure 14.4). The account and password are commonly transported using clear text.

FIGURE 14.4

Authenticating with a Telnet server.

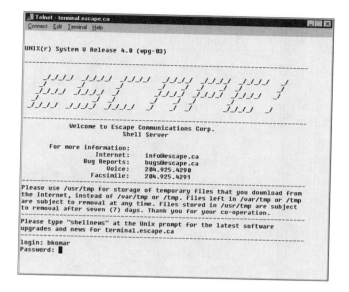

NTLM Authentication Difference

When NTLM authentication is implemented in Microsoft Services for Unix, Windows 2000, or Windows .NET Server, the user's current credentials are passed to the Telnet server. If the user is not granted Telnet access, the authentication will fail. No credentials are typed when NTLM authentication is implemented.

After you connect to the Telnet server, the level of commands you can execute depends on your privilege level on the system hosting the Telnet server and the actual Telnet server application that you are connecting to. Table 14.4 shows some of the common Telnet commands.

TABLE 14.4 Telnet Commands

Telnet Command	Description
? [specific command]	Shows a list of available commands. If [specific command] is included, this command will provide help information about [specific command].
Close	Closes the connection to the Telnet server and returns you to the Telnet command prompt.

14

TABLE 14.4   continued

Telnet Command	Description
Display [*argument*]	Displays all the set and toggle values if no arguments are specified. The arguments limit the listing to only those values that match the argument.
Open [*host*] [*port*]	Opens a connection to the indicated host. The host can be represented as either an IP address or a hostname. The use of a hostname requires a functioning hostname resolution process. If no port is indicated, Telnet defaults to TCP port 23.
Quit	Closes a connection and terminates the Telnet program.
Control-D	Has the same effect as the Quit command when in command mode.
Status	Shows the status of the Telnet session, including the current mode and connected remote host.
z	Opens a shell on the local host as specified in the SHELL environment variable.

Anonymous Access in Telnet

When you attempt to connect to a Telnet server with an anonymous account, the most common account you use is the GUEST account with no password. If the server does not support anonymous clients, your authentication request will be rejected.

Remote Unix Commands

A set of remote commands, known as the *Berkeley R-Utilities*, was developed at the University of California at Berkeley. The "R" stands for "remote." These utilities enable remote users to run processes and applications as if they were local users on the systems running the remote daemons. These utilities are found most often in Unix systems, but several of the R-Utilities have been ported to other operating systems.

Other Remote Commands

This section covers only the rlogin, rsh, and rexec commands. Day 15, "File Transfer Protocols," discusses the rcp (remote copy) command. Other R-Utilities include rwho (remote who) and ruptime (remote uptime). The rwho command displays a list of users on the network. The ruptime command displays a list of all machines on the network. It includes statistics on their status, the time they have been up, the number of active users, and their current load.

Configuring Security

Determining who can run these remote commands is a key issue when configuring the security level of your network. Two files can be configured to grant remote users access to a system to run the R-Utilities: HOSTS.EQUIV and .RHOSTS. The combination of entries in these two files and entries in the /etc/passwd file control which users can access the local system using the R-Utilities and without having to provide a password.

The HOSTS.EQUIV File

The HOSTS.EQUIV file is located in the /etc directory on a Unix system. The file can contain entries for trusted hosts or for specific users on a host. The danger in trusting all users on a remote system is that if a single account were compromised on the remote system, the system with the remote system in its HOSTS.EQUIV file is also compromised.

The following is an example of a HOSTS.EQUIV file:

```
#Sample HOSTS.EQUIV file
ironman bphillips
calgary mgrasdal
winnipeg dneilan
development
```

Any user that has a valid account on development can connect to the system with this HOSTS.EQUIV file. The other three systems name specific users that can connect from the remote system to the local system.

The .RHOSTS File

The .RHOSTS file allows specific accounts to be named for a remote host for granting access to the local host. The .RHOSTS file contains entries for hosts and users that can gain access to the local system. Each entry consists of a hostname and a login name. The following is a sample .RHOSTS file:

```
#Sample .RHOSTS file
ironman bphillips
ironman dchaze
ironman bkomar
calgary mgrasdal
calgary bkomar
winnipeg dneilan
winnipeg jsmith
winnipeg bkomar
```

The .RHOSTS file commonly resides in the user's home directory. This means that the network administrator can lose control of the security environment. It is very possible that a user could place an undesirable user in the .RHOSTS file.

14

rlogin (Remote Login)

The rlogin command enables a user to remotely log in to another system on the network. The host that accepts the remote login runs the rlogind daemon to allow this connection.

The rlogin command connects using TCP port 513. Once connected, the client sends the following four null-terminated strings:

- <NULL>. An empty string to begin the session.
- *CLIENT-USER-NAME*<NULL>. The username the client uses at the client host.
- *SERVER-USER-NAME*<NULL>. The username the client uses on the remote server. Generally, this is the same as *CLIENT-USER-NAME*, but it can be different.
- *TERMINAL-TYPE/SPEED*<NULL>. The final string contains the name and transmission speed of the remote user's terminal.

An example of this initialization sequence could occur as follows:

```
<NULL>
bkomar<NULL>
briank<NULL>
VT100/14400<NULL>
```

The server returns a zero byte to indicate that it received these four strings and is ready for data transfer.

The syntax of the rlogin command is as follows:

```
rlogin rhost [-ec] [-8] [-L] [-l username]
```

- **rhost.** The name of the remote host to which you are connecting.
- **[-ec].** Enables you to define an alternate escape character. The default is the tilde (~) character.
- **[-8].** Sets the data input path to be 8 bits all the time.
- **[-L].** Runs the session in litout mode. This provides backward compatibility with version 4 of Berkeley Software Development (BSD) Unix. Litout mode enables 7-bit with parity data transmission. All lowercase characters are translated to uppercase.
- **[-l *username*].** Indicates the username you want to use on the remote system. If not indicated, uses your current login name.

The following is a sample rlogin command for logging in to the ironman remote server using the dchaze login name:

```
rlogin ironman -l dchaze
```

After your `rlogin` session has completed, you must type the following on a separate line to exit the session:

~.

rsh (Remote Shell)

The `rsh` (remote shell) utility enables you to execute a single command on a remote host without logging in to the remote host. If you need to run multiple commands, you should use either `rlogin` or Telnet.

The `rsh` command is not suited for processes that return data to the screen, because the connection is completed before the data would be returned. Likewise, no return codes are ever returned to the calling system when using the `rsh` command.

The `rsh` command also uses the HOSTS.EQUIV and .RHOSTS files to determine whether the calling user is authorized to execute remote commands on the local host.

A host must run the `rshd` daemon to allow remote users to run the `rsh` command against it.

The syntax of the `rsh` command is as follows:

```
rsh [-l username] rhost command
```

- **[-l username].** Indicates the username you want to use on the remote system. If not indicated, `rsh` uses your current login name.
- **rhost.** The name of the remote host to which you are connecting.
- **command.** The command you want to execute on the remote host.

For example, if you want to concatenate the file `remote_file_1` on the remote host `Earl` to the local file `myfile`, use the following command:

```
rsh Earl cat remote_file_1 >>myfile
```

rexec (Remote Execute)

The `rexec` (remote execute) command allows remote execution of programs to take place. Unlike `rlogin` and `rsh`, `rexec` does not use the HOSTS.EQUIV or .RHOSTS files to determine trusted hosts. Instead, the client must specify the username, password, and command that it wants to execute. Depending on the version of the `rexec` and `rexecd` being run, the password may be sent in encrypted format across the network.

14

The syntax of the `rexec` command is as follows:

```
rexec [-l username] [-p password] rhost command
```

- **[-l *username*].** Indicates the login name that should be used on the remote host.
- **[-p *password*].** Provides the password for the login name on the remote host.
- **rhost.** The name of the remote host being communicated with.
- **command.** The command to be executed on the remote host.

Administration Using Terminal Services

Terminal Services allows processing responsibility to be shifted to large, back-end servers (similar to the days of the mainframe computer). Instead of having high-powered clients that execute programs locally utilizing their own processors, clients run sessions hosted on a centralized server (see Figure 14.5). These sessions appear to be local Windows sessions. The clients in this configuration are typically referred to as *thin clients*.

FIGURE 14.5

A thin client connecting to a terminal server.

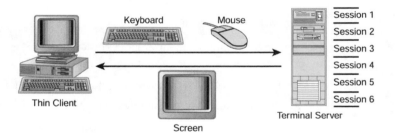

The thin client sends only keyboard and mouse input to the terminal server. After processing is complete, the terminal server sends updated screen information to the remote client. To provide security, the data transmitted between the client and the server can be encrypted. No other data is transmitted between the client and the server. All processing takes place in memory space and on the processor of the terminal server.

This ability to remotely connect to a terminal server also provides remote administration capability. A network administrator can connect to a remote server using either a thin client, or terminal services software, and manage the configuration of the terminal server.

The following are goals of implementing Terminal Services:

- Reducing the total cost of ownership (TCO) by deploying low-cost and low-maintenance systems to the desktop.

- Reducing hardware costs by redeploying older client systems with sufficient resources to function as thin clients, but not enough to function as PC clients.

- Reducing support costs by removing configuration requirements from the client systems and moving toward a centrally administered system.

- Reducing LAN/WAN bandwidth requirements by performing all processing on the back-end server.

- Improving performance over slow WAN links by sending only screen images and mouse/keyboard inputs across the WAN link.

- Increasing security by running server-side processes only at the security level of the connecting client.

Note | In Unix Systems, X Window has enabled graphical screen information from remote servers to be displayed locally. Using either the KDE or GNOME X Window shells, the same functionality described using Citrix or Windows can be used in a Unix environment.

Models in Use

Currently, two different client architecture models provide Terminal Service functionality:

- Citrix Metaframe
- Microsoft Terminal Services

The clients that connect to the terminal servers can include

- Native clients developed by Citrix and Microsoft for use with their Terminal Servers
- Web-based Netscape plug-ins
- ActiveX controls downloaded to an Internet Explorer Web browser

Terminal Server Technology

Terminal server models use a central server that hosts all user sessions. To the client, it appears as if she is sitting at the server console working directly at the server. In truth, she is operating in a session established on the terminal server for the workspace.

Each user session has the following characteristics:

- All keyboard and mouse input from the client is received and processed by the terminal session.

- Each user has an independent session that is not affected by other sessions.

14

> **Caution** If a client connected to a remote terminal server launches a virtual private network (VPN) connection to a remote network, all terminal server sessions will have access to the network. This is because the network interfaces of the terminal server, including the VPN connection, are shared among all terminal server sessions.

- All display output is redirected to the client's video display.
- All passwords and data are transported over an encrypted connection.

Two different protocols exist that are used to provide terminal services: Microsoft's Remote Desktop Protocol (RDP) and Citrix's Independent Computing Architecture (ICA) protocol.

RDP is a physical line protocol that allows a remote client to connect to a Windows 2000 server running Terminal Services. The client connects to TCP port 3389 on the terminal server. RDP requires the use of the TCP/IP protocol suite for communications.

ICA is the physical line protocol used for communication between the client system and the Citrix server. ICA is a higher-layer protocol that can run on top of any transport protocol. Most frequently, this protocol is TCP, but ICA can run over SPX, IPX, NetBEUI, and Direct Asynch in addition to TCP. When using TCP/IP, an ICA client resolves server and application names using ICA Browser data sent to UDP port 1604. Actual connections to the MetaFrame server are sent to TCP port 1494.

Table 14.5 provides a more detailed comparison of RDP and ICA.

TABLE 14.5   Comparing RDP and ICA

Feature	RDP	ICA
Windows clients	X	X
DOS clients		X
Unix, Macintosh, Java clients		X
Browser-based client	X	X
TCP/IP communications	X	X
IPX/SPX, NetBEUI, Direct Asynch		X
Connect over WAN and LAN	X	X
Connect directly to server using but no dial-up service		
Supports audio	X[1]	X

TABLE 14.5 continued

Feature	RDP	ICA
Print to local printer attached to client	X	X
Connect to client local disk	X[1]	X
Cut and paste between client and server	X	X
Connect to an application rather than desktop	X	X
Advertise server-based applications to client		X
Shadowing of client sessions	X	X
Multilevel security for client communications	X	X

[1] *Requires the Windows XP client and Windows .NET Terminal Services*

Microsoft Terminal Services

Windows NT Terminal Server edition was the first to provide Terminal Services capabilities using the RDP protocol. In Windows 2000, the services were improved by modifying Terminal Services to be an add-on service, rather than a separate version of the operating system.

In Windows 2000, Terminal Services can be installed in one of two configurations:

- **Remote Administration Mode.** This mode only allows a maximum of two concurrent remote sessions to the terminal server. In addition, only members of the local Administrators group are allowed to connect to the terminal server.

Things Are Changing Again

In Windows 2000, you still had to install Terminal Services to install Remote Administration mode. In Windows XP and Windows .NET Server, remote administration mode is automatically enabled when you install the operating system. In Windows XP, you can remotely access a computer using Remote Desktop. You can also request help from a network administrator by using the Remote Assistance application that sends a request to the administrator to initiate a Remote Desktop connection. In Windows .NET Server, all servers support Remote Desktop for administrative connections.

- **Application Server mode.** This mode allows any user to connect to the Terminal Server to provide a Windows shell for applications. There are no special group requirements other than the user must have the permission to connect using Terminal Services and no limits on the number of connections.

14

The Optional TCP/IP Services

A TCP/IP network has several optional services that users and applications can use. These services include:

- Active Users
- Character Generator
- Daytime
- Discard
- Echo
- Quote of the Day
- Time

The Active Users service returns a message to the calling system informing it of all the users currently active on the system running the Active Users service. The Active Users service monitors both TCP and UDP ports 11 to establish a session.

The Character Generator service returns a list of all 95 printable ASCII characters. Both TCP and UDP port 19 are monitored for connections, but they behave differently. A connection on TCP port 19 returns the list of printable characters until the connection is broken. A connection on UDP port 19 responds with a datagram that contains a random set of the printable ASCII characters (with a maximum of 512 characters being returned). This service is useful for testing whether a printer is capable of printing all ASCII characters correctly.

The Daytime service returns a message that contains the current date and time to the connection system. The format of the response is Day of Week, Month, Day, Year, HH:MM:SS, with each field separated by a single space. The Daytime service monitors both TCP and UDP port 13 for connections.

The Discard service discards all information sent to it on either TCP or UDP port 9. Although this might seem rather pointless, it can be quite useful for testing routing.

The Echo service returns any information passed to it. In the case of a TCP connection on port 7, the Echo service returns whatever data is sent until the connection is broken. For a UDP connection on port 7, the exact datagram that is received is retransmitted back to the originating host. This can be used to measure response times on the network. The ping utility uses this service to test whether another host is reachable.

The Quote of the Day service returns a quotation from a central file of quotations. This central file must exist for the service to function. The Quote of the Day service listens for requests on both TCP and UDP port 17.

The Time service returns the number of seconds that have elapsed since midnight, January 1, 1900. This number is sent as a 32-bit binary number that must be translated by the requesting host. All requests to the Time service are sent to TCP or UDP port 37. This service is useful for synchronizing clocks on the network.

> **Note**
>
> All time values are sent using coordinated universal time (UTC), formerly known as Greenwich mean time (GMT). All time zone offsets are determined by the time zone settings at the computer connecting to the time service.

Installing the Optional TCP/IP Services in Windows 2000

In a Windows 2000 and Windows .NET Server environment, these optional TCP/IP services are referred to as the Simple TCP/IP Services. They are installed through the Add or Remove Programs applet in the Control Panel.

> **Note**
>
> Only the Character Generator, Daytime, Discard, Echo, and Quote of the Day services are installed in a Windows 2000 and Windows .NET Server environment.

To install the Simple TCP/IP Services, follow these steps:

1. From the Start Menu, select Settings, Control Panel.
2. In the Control Panel, double-click the Add or Remove Programs applet.
3. In the Add or Remove Programs dialog box, click Add/Remove Windows Components.
4. In the Windows Components dialog box, select the Networking Services item, and then click Details.

> **Caution**
>
> Do not enable the check box next to Networking Services, because this will install *all* networking services. You only want to select the words *Networking Services*, so that you can select the individual services you require.

14

5. In the Networking Services dialog box, click the check box next to Simple TCP/IP Services, and then click OK.

6. In the Windows Components dialog box, click Next.

7. If the Files Needed dialog box appears, insert your Windows CD-ROM in the CD-ROM drive, and then ensure that the Copy Files From box refers to the *CD*:\i386 folder, and then click OK.

8. After the installation is complete, click Finish.

9. In the Add or Remove Programs dialog box, click Close.

10. Close the Control Panel.

Testing the Optional TCP/IP Services

If you want to connect to the optional TCP/IP services, you can use a Telnet client. The catch is that you must change to the port of the optional TCP/IP service to which you are connecting.

To connect to the Quote of the Day service on the host named simple, for example, execute the following commands:

```
-% telnet simple 17
Trying 207.161.165.73...
Connected to 207.161.165.73.
Escape character is '^]'.
"Oh the nerves, the nerves; the mysteries of this machine called man!
 Oh the little that unhinges it, poor creatures that we are!"
 Charles Dickens (1812-70)
Connection closed by foreign host.
```

Likewise, to check out the current date and time using the Daytime service on simple, use the following sequence of commands:

```
/home/orgs/online/users/b/bkomar 14% telnet 207.161.165.73 13
Trying 207.161.165.73...
Connected to 207.161.165.73.
Escape character is '^]'.
Saturday, March 14, 1998 21:01:00
Connection closed by foreign host.
```

You can also generate these commands from within the Telnet client software that ships with Microsoft operating systems. Figure 14.6 shows the dialog box that is configured to connect to the Echo service on simple from the Windows NT Telnet client software.

FIGURE 14.6

Connecting to the
Echo service.

Sometimes Things Become More Difficult

Starting with Windows 2000, the Telnet client changed from a GUI-based client to a text-based client. With the text-based client you must type in the actual port information when connecting to the client. For example, to connect to the echo service, you would have to type `telnet simple 7`.

As you can see in Figure 14.6, you can choose from Telnet, Daytime, Echo, Qotd (Quote of the Day), and Chargen (Character Generator). As with the Windows 2000 Telnet client, you can also type the specific port to which you want to connect, rather than selecting one of the provided port names.

Applying What You Have Learned

Today's material investigated the Telnet process, the R-Utilities, and the optional TCP/IP services. The following section tests your knowledge of these topics and indicates areas you might want to review further.

Test Your Knowledge

Here are questions to check what you've learned today. The answers can be found in Appendix B, "Test Your Knowledge: Answers."

1. Match each TCP/IP service in Table 14.6 to its correct TCP port number.

TABLE 14.6   Associating Port Numbers with the Correct TCP/IP Service

Service	Port
1. Telnet	A. 19
2. rlogin	B. 9
3. Quote of the Day	C. 7
4. Daytime	D. 23
5. Echo	E. 17
6. Discard	F. 13

14

TABLE 14.6   continued

Service	Port
7. Character Generator	G. 37
8. Time	H. 513

9. Compare the security implications of a Telnet session with an rlogin session.

10. What is the syntax of an rlogin command to connect to a host named BART using the username LISA?

11. Describe the interaction between the DO/DON'T and WILL/WON'T functions during a Telnet option negotiation.

12. What is the significance of the Interpret as Command (IAC) sequence?

13. Describe the concept of the Network Virtual Terminal.

14. What are some uses of the Telnet client software besides connecting to a Telnet server?

15. What optional TCP/IP services are supported under Windows 2000 Server?

16. Under what circumstances would you choose to deploy Citrix Metaframe rather than Windows 2000 Terminal services for your organization?

17. What ports must be opened at a firewall to provide external access to a Citrix Metaframe server?

18. What ports must be opened at a firewall to provide external access to a Windows 2000 server running Terminal Services?

Preview of Day 15

Tomorrow's material investigates the next class of application software that runs on a TCP/IP network: file transfer applications. Specifically, we'll look at:

- FTP (File Transfer Protocol)
- TFTP (Trivial File Transfer Protocol)
- RCP (remote copy)
- HTTP (HyperText Transfer Protocol)
- NFS (Network File System)
- WebDAV (Web Distributed Authoring and Versioning)

We'll also review several of the popular Web servers available today.

DAY **15**

File Transfer Protocols

Today we'll look at an overview on the major protocols used for transferring files on a TCP/IP network. These include the following:

- File Transfer Protocol (FTP)
- Trivial File Transfer Protocol (TFTP)
- Remote Copy (RCP)
- Hypertext Transmission Protocol (HTTP)
- Network File System (NFS)
- Web Distributed Authoring and Versioning (WebDAV)

In addition to discussing common connection sequences, security, and characteristics of these protocols, the chapter also includes a brief mention of Web servers most commonly used on today's Internet.

File Transfer Protocol (FTP)

File Transfer Protocol (FTP) is one of the most commonly used protocols for transferring data files from one host to another in a TCP/IP network. The advantage of FTP is that it uses the TCP protocol to provide a session-oriented, reliable method to transfer data between two hosts.

The FTP protocol uses two separate processes during the transfer of data:

- The Data Transfer Process (DTP) is used for the actual transmission of data between an FTP client and an FTP server. The DTP on the client listens for a connection from the server's DTP process.

- The Protocol Interpreter (PI) is used to transmit the commands between the FTP client and the FTP server. The PI initiates the FTP process and is used to govern the FTP client-side DTP service.

The actual FTP session is really two separate sessions between the client and the FTP server (see Figure 15.1).

FIGURE 15.1

An FTP session.

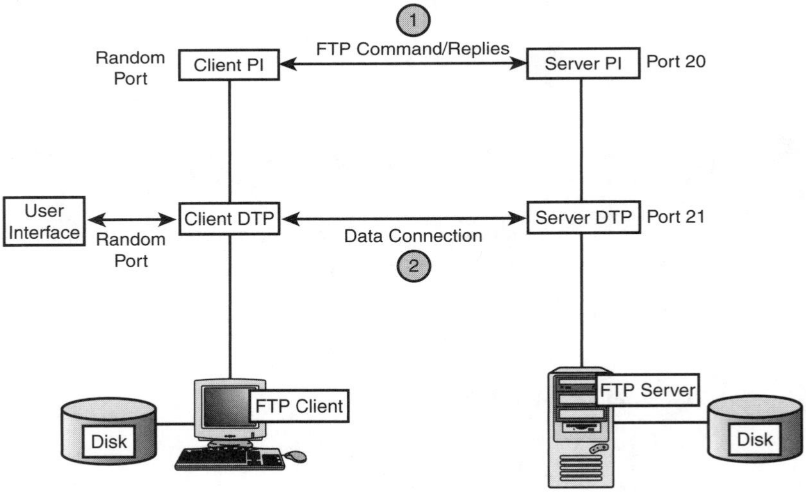

The following transactions take place when an FTP session is established between an FTP client and an FTP server:

1. The first session takes place between the server and client PI services. The client-side protocol interpreter initiates the control connection between the client and server sides. For each command sent to the FTP server, a response is returned over the control connection to the FTP client. The client side of this connection uses a randomly assigned port number and connects to TCP port 21 on the FTP server.

2. When a data transfer is requested, the server's DTP initiates a connection with the client's DTP service. Only data is transmitted over the data connection. The connection is initiated from the FTP server's TCP port 20, to a random port on the client computer negotiated by the DTP service.

During the actual transmission of data, the control connection must remain established so that commands and responses can be exchanged between the server and client processes. Both the control connection and the data connection will allow data to flow in both directions between the client and server.

Using Passive FTP

There is an additional way that FTP transfers can be established. As already discussed, normal FTP connections are initiated by the client for the FTP control connection. Then, the FTP server initiates the data transfer to the client connection.

An alternative method exists for FTP transfers, known as an *FTP passive transfer*. As with a normal FTP transfer, the FTP client initiates the connection to TCP port 21 at the FTP server. The differences start when the client issues the PASV command.

When the PASV command is received, the FTP server responds with the port (above and including TCP port 1024) to be used for FTP data connections and then listens for connections to that port.

The second difference is that the FTP client establishes the data connection to the server, rather than the server initiating the connection as with a normal FTP transfer. The connection binds to the data port received in the PASV response from the FTP server.

Many organizations do not allow passive FTP transfers because of the requirement for the FTP server to listen on random ports above and including TCP port 1024. Opening these ports at an external firewall is considered too much of a security risk.

Common Commands and Reply Codes Used in FTP

The following sections outline many of the common commands used during an FTP session. They are broken out into the following categories:

- Access control commands
- Transfer parameter commands
- File transfer commands
- Directory and file management commands
- Help and status commands
- FTP reply codes

Access Control Commands

FTP access control commands are used during the establishment and termination of an FTP session between client and server. These commands are often issued in a specific sequence. The PASS command, for example, is always expected to follow the USER command to provide the accompanying password for a user account. Table 15.1 shows the FTP access control commands.

TABLE 15.1 FTP Access Control Commands

Command	Description
OPEN [*hostname*]	The OPEN command is used to establish an FTP session with the FTP service running on [*hostname*].
USER [*username*]	The USER command is used to identify the user who is performing the FTP commands. This command is the first command sent after the control connection is established.
PASS [*password*]	The PASS command immediately follows the USER command. It is used to pass the user's password via the telnet protocol to the FTP server. An FTP client generally does not display the user's password onscreen. Unfortunately, the default FTP specification does transmit the password over the network using clear text.
ACCT [*account*]	This optional parameter is required by some FTP servers to identify the user's account on the FTP server. The account does not have to be related to the USER command.
SMNT	The SMNT (Structure Mount) command allows a different file system data structure to be mounted without having to relog on to the FTP server.
REIN	The REIN (Reinitialize) command terminates the session for the current user account. All input/output information is terminated (except for a current transfer). This places the user in the same state as when he initially connected to the FTP server.
QUIT	The QUIT (Logoff) command terminates the session between the FTP client and server. Some implementations also use the command BYE with the same meaning.

Protecting Password Information with IPSec

Internet Protocol Security (IPSec), discussed in Day 12, "Encrypting Transmitted Data," can be used to provide encryption of all data transmitted between the client and the server by defining rules that require Encrypting Security Payloads (ESP) to be used for all connections to the FTP server on TCP ports 20 and 21.

> **Note**
>
> **Anonymous FTP Sessions**
>
> The FTP protocol allows anonymous connections to take place between an FTP client and server. The account is commonly presented by the user to indicate an anonymous connection is anonymous or ftp. In addition to typing the anonymous or ftp account name, the user provides his e-mail address as the password.

Transfer Parameter Commands

The FTP transfer parameter commands allow the default parameters for an FTP session to be changed. The FTP server generally has defaults preserved. They need to be modified only if your implementation requires new methods to be used. Table 15.2 shows the FTP transfer parameter commands.

TABLE 15.2   FTP Transfer Parameter Commands

Command	Description
PORT ##	This command allows for the FTP client-side socket to be defined. The ## parameter includes the 32-bit IP address of the host that the DTP connection should be established with and the 16-bit port address on that host.
PASV	The PASV (Passive) command changes the behavior of the server during a data session establishment. Rather than initiating the establishment of the data connection, the server listens on a data port and waits for the client to initiate the data connection.
TYPE	The TYPE (Representation Type) command indicates whether the data representation on the server is ASCII, EBCDIC, or Image.
STRU	The STRU (File Structure) command is a single code that indicates whether the default file structure is files, records, or pages.
MODE	The MODE (Transfer Mode) command specifies the transfer mode that will be used during the transmission of data. Options include Stream, Block, and Compressed.

File Transfer Commands

After you have established your session with the FTP server and have set any defaults that you want for the data transfer session, you are ready to start the transfer of data files. Table 15.3 explains some of the more common file transfer commands used within FTP client software.

TABLE 15.3 FTP File Transfer Commands

Command	Description
ASCII	This file transfer type is used to transfer text files. This is the default transfer type. You can also use the shortened version, ASC, for this command.
BINARY	The BINARY file transfer type should be used to transfer all nontext files. This includes graphics, archives, and executables. You can also use the shortened version, BIN, for this command.
TYPE	The TYPE command indicates whether the data transfer method has been set for BINARY or ASCII.
RECV [remfile] [locfile]	This command copies the file [remfile] from the remote FTP server to the local file [locfile]. If [locfile] is not specified, the file is copied using the same filename as on the remote FTP server.
SEND [locfile] [remfile]	This command copies the local file [locfile] to the FTP server using the filename [remfile]. If [remfile] is not indicated, the remote file will use the filename [locfile].
GET [remfile] [locfile]	The GET command works the same as the RECV command.
PUT [locfile] [remfile]	The PUT command works the same as the SEND command.
MGET [remfile]	The MGET (Multiple Get) command allows multiple files to be transferred from the FTP server to the local host. This command allows the use of wildcards when designating the remote file to copy.
MPUT [locfile]	The MPUT (Multiple Put) command allows multiple files to be transferred to the FTP server. This command also allows the use of wildcard characters.
PROMPT	This command enables/disables the use of prompts when using an MPUT or MGET command. If enabled, you are prompted whether to transfer the files on a one-by-one basis. If disabled, no prompts display.

Directory and File Management Commands

After you have connected to the FTP server, you may have to do some file or directory management in addition to transferring files to and from the FTP server. Table 15.4 shows many of the directory and file management commands used by an FTP client.

TABLE 15.4   FTP Directory and File Management Commands

Command	Description
DELETE [remfile]	The DELETE command deletes the indicated [remfile] on the FTP server.
MDELETE [remfile]	The MDELETE command deletes all files that match the wildcard indicated in [remfile].
LCD	The LCD (Local Change Directory) command changes the default directory on the local host. This is commonly used to choose a new location to transfer files to the local host.
CD	The CD (Change Directory) command is used to change the current directory on the FTP server.
CDUP	The CDUP (Change Directory Up) command changes the directory to the parent directory of the current working directory. This command was created to handle the various representations of the parent directory that are implemented by different systems.
MKDIR	The MKDIR (Make Directory) command is used to create a new directory on the FTP server.
RMDIR	The RMDIR (Remove Directory) command is used to remove a directory on the FTP server.
DIR	The DIR command shows a detailed listing of the contents of the FTP server's current directory.
LS	The LS (List) command can be used to view the contents of the FTP server's current directory. Common flags used with the LS command include -F and -all. The -F flag shows subdirectory names with a following slash (/) character. The -all flag produces the same screen output as the DIR command.
PWD	The PWD command displays the name of the current directory on the FTP server.
RENAME [fromfile] [tofile]	The RENAME command renames the [fromfile] filename to the new name [tofile] on the FTP server.

Help and Status Commands

The FTP help and status commands help you to investigate the syntax of an FTP command if you are unsure of its parameters. You can also use them to determine what options are currently set for your FTP sessions. Table 15.5 shows some of the more common help and status commands for FTP.

TABLE 15.5   FTP Help and Status Commands

Command	Description
!	The ! command shells out of FTP to a local shell or command interpreter. Most often you return to your FTP session by typing in the command EXIT.
?	The ? command displays all the available commands in the FTP client software.
HELP	The HELP command works the same as the ? command.
STATUS	The STATUS command displays the current status information for your FTP session. This includes the transfer mode, connection status, prompt status, and timeout value.
VERBOSE	The VERBOSE command toggles between VERBOSE and non-VERBOSE screen output. VERBOSE output includes all FTP server responses and transmission rates on file transfers.

FTP Server Reply Codes

When an FTP client issues a command to the FTP server, the FTP server returns a reply code to indicate whether the command was carried out successfully. If not, an error code is returned so that the FTP client is informed on how to proceed from this point.

All FTP server reply codes are three-digit alphanumeric codes. The first digit of the three-digit code indicates the general status of the preceding command. In general, the first digit indicates the next appropriate action the FTP client should take. Table 15.6 shows the five values that can be returned in the first digit of the FTP reply code.

TABLE 15.6   First-Digit Values of FTP Server Reply Codes

Value	Definition	Description
1yz	Positive Preliminary Reply	A value of 1 in the first digit of the FTP reply code is a Positive Preliminary Reply. It indicates that the request action has been started and another reply will be sent before the next command should be issued. Only a single 1yz reply can be sent in a row.
2yz	Positive Completion Reply	A value of 2 in the first digit of an FTP server response indicates that the requested action has been performed successfully and the FTP server is ready for the next client command.

TABLE 15.6   continued

Value	Definition	Description
3yz	Positive Intermediate Reply	A value of 3 in the first digit of an FTP server reply code indicates that the command has been accepted from the FTP client, but more information is required. This is the common response when a sequence of commands is expected, such as a USER command followed by a PASS command.
4yz	Transient Negative Completion Reply	A value of 4 in the first digit of an FTP server reply code indicates that the submitted command did not execute correctly. But, the failure was due to a temporary error connection and the command should be tried again.
5yz	Permanent Negative Completion Reply	A value of 5 in the first digit of an FTP server reply code indicates that the requested action could not be performed. This could result from a mistyped command or a security privilege not being assigned to the current user.

The second digit of the reply code provides further detailed information about an FTP server reply. Table 15.7 describes the possible values for the second digit of the FTP server reply codes.

TABLE 15.7   Second-Digit Values of FTP Server Reply Codes

Value	Definition	Description
x0z	Syntax	A 0 indicates that an error is returned because of a syntax error. It is also used for a syntactically correct command issued at the incorrect time.
x1z	Information	A 1 is used in response to FTP status commands such as STATUS or HELP.
x2z	Connections	A 2 is used for replies that refer to maintenance of data connections.
x3z	Authentication and Accounting	A 3 is used during the user authentication process.

TABLE 15.7   continued

Value	Definition	Description
x4z	Unspecified	This reply code is not implemented as of yet.
x5z	File System	A 5 indicates the status of the FTP server file system or the local client file system.

The final digit gives even more granular information about the reply code that is dependent on the specific first and second digits of the reply code. RFC 959 provides details on specific third-level reply codes. You can download RFC 959 from www.ietf.org/rfc.

FTP Security Issues

RFC 1878   RFC 2228 outlines the need for standardized security mechanisms for the FTP protocol. Although there is awareness of FTP's security issues, passwords continue to be passed in FTP using clear text. This can lead to passwords being captured by network sniffers.

These security mechanisms also ensure that servers are authenticated to prevent masquerading, and the encryption of information transferred on the data channel.

RFC 2228 introduced commands that can be optionally implemented in an FTP system. Table 15.8 outlines these commands.

TABLE 15.8   FTP Security Extension Commands

Command	Description
AUTH	The AUTH (Authentication/Security Mechanism) command is used by the client to state what mechanism it wants to use for a secure transfer of information. This command may be sent several times as the authentication method is negotiated between client and server.
ADAT	The ADAT (Authentication/Security Data) command sends additional information to implement any optional features for the chosen security mechanism.
PROT	The PROT (Data Channel Protection Level) command indicates what level of protection the client and server will implement on the data channel. If set to Clear, only raw data is transmitted. If set to Safe, data integrity is verified. If set to Confidential, the data is transmitted in an encrypted state. Finally, if set to Private, the data is both encrypted and verified for data integrity.
PBSZ	The PBSZ (Protection Buffer Size) command indicates the maximum in size of the encoded data blocks that will be transmitted during a file exchange. This size is indicated in bytes.

TABLE 15.8 continued

Command	Description
CCC	The CCC (Clear Command Channel) command is used to quit using the security implementation. This is commonly used when TCP security is implemented on a network. After the authentication has taken place, the CCC command can be used to terminate all authentication and data integrity checks.
MIC	The MIC (Integrity Protected Command) is used for the transmission of data when the data protection level is set to Safe.
CONF	The CONF (Confidentiality Protected Command) is used for the transmission of data when the data protection level is set to Confidential.
ENC	The ENC (Privacy Protected Command) is used for the transmission of data when the data protection level is set to Private.

An actual security exchange begins with an FTP client telling the security mechanism that it wants to enable a secure FTP session by using the AUTH command. The FTP server accepts the mechanism requested in the AUTH command, rejects the mechanism, or rejects the command entirely (when the server does not implement FTP security).

If the FTP server requires any additional security information, it requests that the client using an ADAT command send this information. This exchange continues until a security association has been established.

After the secure connection has been established, the data protection can be set using the PROT command. Depending on the level set, MIC, CONF, or ENC commands are used to transport the data in a secure manner over the data connection. The size of these packets of data is determined using the PBZ command.

> **Not All RFCs Are Implemented**
>
> Although an RFC exists for implementing security for FTP authentication, not many FTP clients have implemented these changes at this time. I recommend that you use IPSec to encrypt the FTP session information between the FTP client and the FTP server, or implement anonymous authentication to prevent network credentials from being transmitted in clear text.

Caution If you use anonymous authentication, never store important documents on your FTP server, or allow write access to your FTP server. Only provide public-level security documents for download in this scenario.

A Typical FTP Session

The following set of commands shows a typical FTP session. All commands are preceded by either CLIENT> or SERVER> to indicate the source of the information. (The actual commands that you type are in bold.)

```
CLIENT> D:\>ftp
CLIENT> ftp> open bkdata
SERVER>  Connected to bkdata.
SERVER>  220 bkdata Microsoft FTP Service (Version 5.0).
CLIENT> User (bkdata.example.com:(none)): ftp
SERVER>  331 Anonymous access allowed, send identity (e-mail name) as _password.
CLIENT> Password:bkomar@komarconsulting.com
SERVER>  230-Welcome to the BKDATAb FTP Server
SERVER>  =====================================
SERVER>   Anonymous access allowed!

SERVER>  230 Anonymous user logged in.
CLIENT> ftp> ls -F
SERVER>  200 PORT command successful.
S 150 Opening ASCII mode data connection for /bin/ls.
SERVER>  lanma256.bmp
SERVER>  Telnet Utilities/
SERVER>  226 Transfer complete.
SERVER>  33 bytes received in 0.01 seconds (3.30 Kbytes/sec)
CLIENT> ftp> cd "Telnet utilities"
SERVER>  250 CWD command successful.
CLIENT> ftp> ls
SERVER>  200 PORT command successful.
SERVER>  150 Opening ASCII mode data connection for file list.
SERVER>  teld4_x86_beta.exe
SERVER>  telftp32.exe
SERVER>  226 Transfer complete.
SERVER>  34 bytes received in 0.01 seconds (3.40 Kbytes/sec)
CLIENT> ftp> binary
SERVER>  200 Type set to I.
CLIENT> ftp> get telftp32.exe
SERVER>  200 PORT command successful.
SERVER>  150 Opening BINARY mode data connection for telftp32.exe(743758
_bytes).
SERVER>  226 Transfer complete.
SERVER>  743758 bytes received in 3.11 seconds (238.84 Kbytes/sec)
CLIENT> ftp> bye
SERVER>  221 Thanks for visiting!
```

As you can see, the actual commands used are generally limited to the commands you require for acquiring a file. In this example, we connected to the FTP server `bkdata.example.com`. The FTP session used anonymous authentication by supplying the username FTP. After the session was established, the command `ls -F` was used to determine the contents of the FTP server's current directory. The `-F` option enabled us to distinguish between directories and files on the FTP server. After we changed directory to the directory `Telnet Utilities`, the file `telftp32.exe` was transferred using a binary transmission.

Trivial File Transfer Protocol (TFTP)

Trivial File Transfer Protocol (TFTP) allows the transfer of files between two hosts using the UDP protocol. It does not provide as many features as FTP, but does allow for the reading and writing of data files between two TCP/IP hosts. Because of TFTP's use of UDP, rather than TCP, TFTP is not intended for reliable data transmissions. TFTP is commonly implemented to download initializing code to printers, hubs, and routers. DHCP or BOOTP clients that are diskless workstations use another implementation of TFTP. A reference is supplied to a TFTP server from which the client can download an image of its initialization code. A recent example of technology that implements TFTP in this manner is Microsoft's Remote Installation Service (RIS). RIS uses TFTP to download the files used to boot a client computer and install Windows 2000 over the network using a network bootable network card.

All data transferred using TFTP uses fixed-length packets of 512 bytes. A packet of less than 512 bytes is considered the last packet of the data transfer. After a data packet is sent to the destination host, the data is held in a buffer space until an acknowledgment is received to indicate that the data has been received successfully. If the sending host does not receive the acknowledgment before the retransmit timer expires, the data packet will be re-sent. This does add a level of protection to the data stream above and beyond the UDP checksum. Only the last packet must be maintained to ensure reliable delivery, as there is only a single outstanding data packet at any one time.

TFTP Message Formats

The following five types of messages can be sent during a TFTP session:

- Read Request (RRQ)
- Write Request (WRQ)
- Data (DATA)
- Acknowledgment (ACK)
- Error (ERR)

Both the Read Request (RRQ) and Write Request (WRQ) use the same message format, which is shown in Figure 15.2. The format fields include the following:

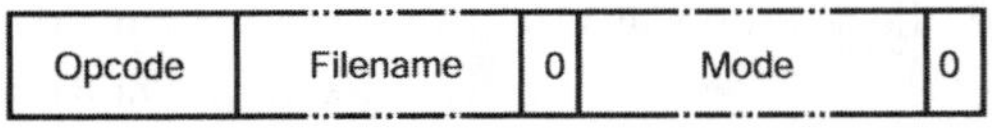

FIGURE 15.2

A Read Request/Write Request TFTP packet format.

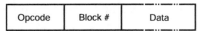

| Opcode | Filename | 0 | Mode | 0 |

- **Opcode.** This field contains 1 for a Read Request or 2 for a Write Request.
- **Filename.** This field indicates the name of the file that is either being uploaded or downloaded from the TFTP server. The filename is transmitted as NETASCII characters using a variable-length field.
- **0.** A 0 is used to indicate the end of the Filename field.
- **Mode.** This field indicates the type of transfer that is to take place. Allowable values include NETASCII and OCTET. The NETASCII mode is used to transfer text documents. NETASCII is 8-bit ASCII as used in the telnet protocol. OCTET is used for the transfer of binary data using raw 8-bit bytes.
- **0.** A 0 is used to indicate the end of the Mode field.

Actual data is transferred in TFTP using the DATA message format (see Figure 15.3). The DATA message contains the actual file contents as the file is transferred from one host to another. Its fields include the following:

FIGURE 15.3

A TFTP DATA packet.

| Opcode | Block # | Data |

- **Opcode.** This field is set to a value of 3 to indicate that data is being transmitted the TFTP message.
- **Block #.** This field is set to a value of 1 for the initial DATA packet. Each additional packet's Block # is incremented by 1 until the entire file has been transmitted.
- **Data.** The Data field can be up to 512 bytes in length. A Data field containing less than 512 bytes indicates that it is the final block of data from the file. If the field is 512 bytes long, additional blocks of data are expected to be transmitted to complete the file transfer.

Figure 15.4 shows a TFTP Acknowledgment (ACK) packet. Each DATA packet and WRQ packet are responded to with either an ACK packet (if received successfully) or an ERROR packet if the data was corrupted or incorrect.

FIGURE 15.4

A TFTP Acknowledgment packet.

15

An ACK packet has two fields:

- **Opcode**. The Opcode field in an ACK packet has a value of 4.
- **Block #.** The Block # field contains the Block # of the DATA packet that is being acknowledged. If the acknowledgment is in response to a Write Request (WRQ) packet, the Block # is set to 0 to indicate that data transfer can commence.

Figure 15.5 shows the TFTP Error (ERR) message format, which contains the following fields:

FIGURE 15.5

The TFTP Error packet.

- **Opcode.** This field is set to a value of 5.
- **Error Code.** This field is set to one of the values shown in Table 15.9.

TABLE 15.9   TFTP Error Codes

Error Code	Description
0	Undefined error. The error message provides any additional information as to the cause of the error.
1	File not found. An incorrect filename has been provided.
2	Access violation. Insufficient security rights have caused an error during the transmission of the data.
3	Disk full or allocation exceeded.
4	Illegal TFTP operation.

TABLE **15.9** continued

Error Code	Description
5	Unknown transfer ID.
6	File already exists.
7	No such user.

- **Error Message.** The data in this field is stored in NETASCII format and adds a text description to assist in debugging TFTP error messages.
- **0.** Because the Error Message field is of variable length, the error message is always terminated with a 0.

Connecting to a TFTP Server

Two common transactions take place when a client connects to a TFTP server. The client either uploads data to the TFTP server using a Write Request or downloads data from the TFTP server using a Read Request.

Figure 15.6 shows the communication sequence that takes place when a Write Request is sent to the TFTP server.

FIGURE 15.6

A TFTP Write Request sequence.

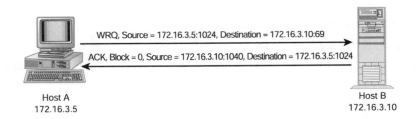

WRQ, Source = 172.16.3.5:1024, Destination = 172.16.3.10:69

ACK, Block = 0, Source = 172.16.3.10:1040, Destination = 172.16.3.5:1024

Host A
172.16.3.5

Host B
172.16.3.10

The sending host (Host A) sends a TFTP message with the Opcode set to 2 for a Write Request. Within the TFTP message, the source port is set to a random port number over port 1024. The destination port for the Write Request is always UDP port 69 by default. The TFTP server (Host B) responds with a TFTP acknowledge message. This message sets the Block # to be a value of 0, indicating that the TFTP server is ready to begin receiving data from the sending host. Within the TFTP message, the TFTP server sets the UDP port that it will listen on for future data transmissions for this data transfer. This change in listening port number makes it difficult for firewalls to match the response to the earlier TFTP request. Data is then transferred in 512-byte packets until all the data has been sent. The final packet contains less than 512 bytes.

Figure 15.7 shows the communication sequence that takes place when the TFTP client wants to download a file from the TFTP server.

FIGURE 15.7

A TFTP Read Request sequence.

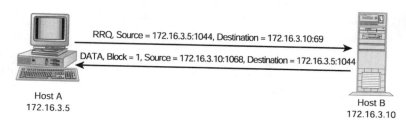

RRQ, Source = 172.16.3.5:1044, Destination = 172.16.3.10:69

DATA, Block = 1, Source = 172.16.3.10:1068, Destination = 172.16.3.5:1044

Host A
172.16.3.5

Host B
172.16.3.10

Host A sends a TFTP Read Request message to Host B. The Opcode is set to a value of 1 to indicate that the request is a Read Request. Within the Read Request message, Host A sets its Transport ID to be the random UDP port that it has selected for the data transmission. In this case, port 1044 was selected. The Read Request is always sent to UDP port 69 on the TFTP server by default. The TFTP server responds with a TFTP DATA packet. The initial DATA packet has Block # of 1 and includes the first 512 bytes of data. Within the first DATA packet, the TFTP server sets its Transport ID. Each successive DATA packet contains 512 bytes of data and increments the Block # by 1 for each DATA packet. The final packet has a size less than 512 bytes.

TFTP Client Software

The TFTP command in most Unix shells and Windows operating systems is a text-based command that enables you to transmit data either to or from a TFTP server. The syntax of the TFTP command is as follows:

TFTP [-i] *host* [GET | PUT] *source* [*destination*]

- [-i]. Including the optional -i parameter sets the data transfer to use OCTET mode for the transmission of a binary file. If not used, the default transfer mode is NETASCII, which is used for text files.
- *host*. Indicates the hostname of the TFTP server.
- [GET]. This transaction copies a file from the TFTP server to the host running the client software.
- [PUT]. This transaction copies a file from the host running the TFTP client software to the TFTP server.
- *source*. The name of the file to be downloaded from or uploaded to the TFTP server.
- [*destination*]. The name that is to be used for the file after it has been transferred. This is often referred to as the *target filename*.

Common Uses of TFTP

The TFTP protocol is not used that often for actual transmission of data. It is most commonly used for downloading configuration information to hosts. The two most common implementations include the configuration of routers and the configuration of BOOTP hosts.

Routers can store the configuration parameters on a TFTP server. This provides a method of fault tolerance for routers. If a router crashes, the correct configuration can be downloaded from the TFTP server to either the repaired router or to a replacement router.

 Caution

Be sure that the router being used as a replacement router has the same router operating system, and if possible, the same version of the router operating system. In the case of Cisco routers, the router operating system has added many new configuration parameters with each new version of the Cisco IOS.

The BOOTP protocol contains a reference to a TFTP server that can contain the configuration files for the BOOTP client. After an initial IP configuration has been retrieved from the BOOTP server, the TFTP server is contacted for downloading the operating system. This is an extremely efficient method for transferring the data to the BOOTP client. This can also be performed in some implementations of the DHCP protocol. The best example of using TFTP with DHCP is Microsoft's RIS deployment method for installing Windows 2000 Professional and Windows XP Professional client software.

Remote Copy Protocol (RCP)

The Remote Copy Protocol (RCP) is part of the Berkeley R-Utilities suite. It enables you to copy directories and their contents to and from a remote host.

As with the RSH and RLOGIN utilities discussed in yesterday's material, the RCP command makes use of the hosts.equiv and .rhosts files to determine which hosts and users can run the RCP command.

The syntax of the RCP command is as follows:

```
RCP [-r] host1:file1 host2:file2
```

- [-r]. This option allows a recursive copy to take place, which includes the contents of the indicated directory and all its subdirectory contents.
- host1:file1. This is the file to be copied from. If host1 is the local computer, the directory and filename are all that must be provided.

- `host2:file2`. This is the destination file and directory for the copy process.

If you wanted to copy the file `budget.txt` from the local directory `/usr/bkomar/reports` to the remote host `DNEILAN` in the directory `/usr/dneilan`, for example, you would use the following syntax:

```
RCP /usr/bkomar/reports/budget.txt dneilan:/usr/dneilan
```

Likewise, if you wanted to copy the entire contents of the `/data/accounting` directory to the `/data/budget` directory on the remote host named `IRONMAN`, you would use the following command:

```
RCP -r /data/accounting ironman:/data/budget
```

Finally, if you wanted to copy the directory structure `/data/marketing` on the host named `DNEILAN` to the directory structure `/data/marketing/2001` on the host named `IRONMAN`, you would use the following command:

```
rcp -r dneilan:/data/marketing ironman:/data/marketing/2001
```

Hypertext Transfer Protocol (HTTP)

RFC 1878 Hypertext Transfer Protocol (HTTP) is the protocol used when exploring the World Wide Web (WWW). HTTP is implemented as a request/response protocol. A client requests that a page be transferred to him from the Web server. The Web server responds with the contents of that page.

The HTTP protocol works at the application level. A client sends a request to the HTTP server (normally on TCP port 80); the HTTP server interprets the request and sends an appropriate response to the client. The actual communication is connectionless and stateless. After the HTTP server has responded to the client's request, the connection is dropped until the next request is posted. The exception to this scenario is when the client implements HTTP keep-alives that are supported under HTTP 1.1. In this case, the client would maintain the connection rather than establish a new session.

Several methods are used in HTTP requests, including the following:

- GET
- HEAD
- POST
- PUT
- DELETE
- TRACE
- CONNECT

The GET method is used to retrieve the indicated information in an HTTP request. GET allows additional flexibility through the use of IF statements. This can lead to what is known as a conditional GET. When the condition in the IF statement is met, the data is transferred. This enables HTTP clients to utilize cached copies of Web pages if they have not been recently updated, which leads to a better utilization of network bandwidth.

The HEAD method works much the same as the GET method except that the message body is not returned to the client. This method is often used to determine whether a link is still valid or has been recently modified. The modification is tested by comparing the information sent in the REQUEST header with the response received in the RESPONSE header.

The POST method is used to request that the HTTP server accept the attached data as a new posting to the HTTP server. This can be used to post messages to a newsgroup, the submission of an HTML form to the HTTP server, or the addition of a record of data to a database hosted on an HTTP server.

The PUT method is used to request that the data sent in the request be stored on the resource indicated in the REQUEST message. This differs from the POST method in that the target can be specified for the data. If the data already exists, the data should be considered to be a modification of the existing data.

The DELETE method is used to request that the HTTP server delete the resource indicated in the REQUEST message. This method may be overridden by human intervention or by security set on the HTTP server. A success response should be sent only if the HTTP server intends to delete the resource.

The TRACE method is used to ensure that the data received at the HTTP server is correct. The TRACE response is the actual HTTP request that was received by the HTTP server. This allows for testing and debugging of the HTTP request to take place.

The CONNECT method is reserved for use by TLS (Transport Layer Security) connections.

HTTP 1.1 is the current standard for the HTTP protocol. Some of the features that were introduced in this version of the HTTP protocol include the following:

- **Persistent connections.** HTTP 1.1 now allows for multiple requests to be serviced in the same connection. Previous implementations of the protocol required that a separate connection be established for each graphic embedded on a Web page.
- **Pipelining.** This feature allows additional requests to be sent to a Web server before the response to their initial request has been received. This results in a greater performance boost.
- **Caching directives.** The implementation of caching directives allows default caching algorithms on both the client and server to be overridden and optimized.

- **Host headers.** This HTTP 1.1 option allows multiple fully qualified domain names to be associated with a single IP address. This eliminates the need for multiple IP addresses to be assigned to a Web server that is hosting many virtual servers. The host header is used to determine to which virtual server the request should be directed.

- **PUT and DELETE options.** These commands enable a remote administrator to post and remove content from a Web server by using a standard Web browser.

- **HTTP redirects.** This feature enables an administrator to redirect a user to an alternative page or Web site if the original page is unavailable or has been removed.

> **Note**
>
> Three common HTTP servers are being implemented today. The most popular being the shareware APACHE Web server that runs on most Unix and Linux systems. Other popular Web servers include Netscape's SuiteSpot and Microsoft's Internet Information Server. The Netscape SuiteSpot runs on the most platforms including Windows NT, Linux, and SCO Unix. Internet Information Server (IIS) runs only on the Windows NT Server, Windows 2000 Server, and Windows .NET Server platforms.

Security in HTTP

RFC 1878 Several methods can be implemented for securing information transmitted via an HTTP connection. The two most common methods—Secure Sockets Layers (SSL) or Transport Layer Security (TLS)—involve *encryption* of the actual data transmission and *authentication* of both the client and server components.

Both SSL and TLS function between the TCP/IP transport layer and the application layer. All transmissions between the client and server are encrypted and decrypted by SSL and TLS. The major difference between SSL and TLS is that SSL, although a widely used security protocol, is not defined in RFCs. TLS, on the other hand, was introduced in RFC 2246 and TLS's interaction with the HTTP 1.1 protocol is defined in RFC 2817 and RFC 2818.

The encryption process performed by SSL and TLS is accomplished through the use of SSL digital certificates. The following is a typical SSL communication sequence (shown in Figure 15.8).

FIGURE 15.8

The SSL handshake process.

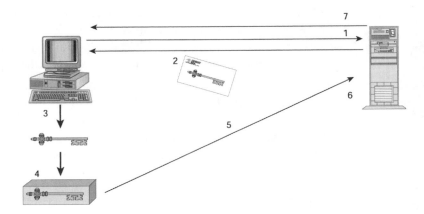

1. The client makes a security request to the server.
2. The server sends its certificate to the client. One of the attributes of the certificate is the server's public key. Also included in the response are the server's cipher preferences.

> **Caution**
>
> At this point, the client may generate an error condition when it receives the server's certificate. This commonly is due to one of two reasons:
>
> The first is that the subject name of the certificate does not match the fully qualified domain name (FQDN) of the Web server. This is typically the case when an organization moves a Web site to a different server and moves the SSL certificate to the new server without renaming the new server.
>
> The second is that the certificate was not issued by a Certification Authority (CA) that is trusted by the client computer. For a certificate to be deemed trusted, the certificate must be traced back to a root certification authority that both the client and the server trust.

3. The client generates a master key.
4. The client encrypts the master key using the server's public key that it received in step 2. The master key of the client can now only be decrypted by the server's private key located at the server.
5. The client transmits the encrypted master key to the server.
6. The server decrypts the client's master key using the server's private key.
7. The server authenticates with the client by returning a message to the client that is encrypted using the client's master key. This authenticates both sides of the session.

All following data is encrypted and decrypted using the master key that was sent to the server.

Public and Private Keys

Many encryption mechanisms use what are known as public/private key pairs. If a public key is used to encrypt a package, only its matching private key can be used to decrypt the package. Likewise, if the private key is used to digitally sign a package, only its matching public key can be used to verify the signature.

How to Know When SSL Is Being Used

All Web pages that institute SSL have HTTPS:// (the HTTP is followed with an S) in the Universal Resource Locator (URL) for the Web page. If you do not see HTTPS:// for what is supposed to be a secure Web site, do not input any valuable information such as a credit-card number. Look for additional indicators that a secure connection has been established in both Netscape and Internet Explorer. In Netscape, a key appears at the bottom of the window. In Internet Explorer, a lock appears at the bottom of the window.

Network File System (NFS)

RFC 1878 The network file system (NFS) was created by Sun Microsystems to enable transparent access to remote file services for network clients. Transparent means the client does not realize it is accessing files from a remote server. The files appear to be stored locally. The network client performs an action called mounting to create a file handle that connects them to the remote file source. This file handle makes the network file source appear to be a local file resource. Assigning a drive letter to the remote file source accomplishes this. This functionality is provided by using Remote Procedure Calls (RPCs) at the session level and external data representation at the presentation level of the OSI model (see Figure 15.9).

FIGURE 15.9

NFS software implementation.

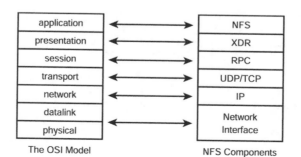

The OSI Model   NFS Components

NFS usually runs on the UDP protocol, but it has been able to run on TCP since NFS 3.0 (its latest revision is 4.0). The client connects to TCP or UDP port 2049 on the NFS server when accessing remote file sources.

NFS is implemented as a stateless protocol. The server does not keep track of any ongoing disk transactions. It is the responsibility of the client to manage and track all operations. This model of operation is known as *idempotent*. The client must fully describe the operation it is going to perform. It cannot depend on the server to remember anything about previous transactions.

If a write transaction is taking place, for example, the client has to specify the following information:

- The file to be written to (using the file handle)
- The number of bytes to be written
- The starting point for the write operation

Because NFS operations historically ran on UDP, the NFS client must wait for an acknowledgment before proceeding with its next transaction. If an acknowledgment is not received, the client retries the transaction when its retransmit timer reaches zero. This is repeated until the client's retry threshold fails, at which time the transaction fails.

Although this seems to be an inefficient method of operation, it removes complexity from the NFS server. The NFS server can fail, restart, and still maintain client connections. The clients retry their operations until the server once again is available.

 Note

> NFS 3.0 introduced the capability for an NFS client and an NFS server to communicate using TCP as the transport protocol. TCP is also supported in the current version, NFS 4.0. The primary advantage of using TCP is the capability to use sliding windows when transmitting transactions. Instead of having to wait for an acknowledgment of every request, multiple requests can be transmitted in a more efficient manner. This provides roughly a 200-percent performance gain over using UDP.

Remote Procedure Calls (RPCs)

Remote Procedure Calls (RPCs) play a major role in the implementation of NFS. Using RPCs, a client can utilize the file resources of a remote server. RPCs make the remote file-sharing process on the NFS server appear to be a local file resource.

The manner in which RPCs are implemented is similar to a function call in programming. When the RPC is executed on the remote host, the RPC is run at the security level of the calling user. This ensures that security is maintained, even though the procedure actually is running on a remote host.

The communications involved when an RPC is executed on a remote host (shown in Figure 15.10) are as follows:

FIGURE 15.10

RPC communications.

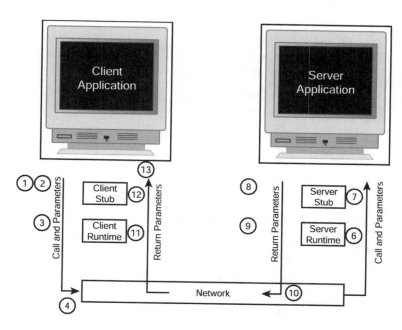

1. The client application issues a normal function call to the client stub.

2. The client stub converts the input arguments from the local data representation to a common data representation that can be used between hosts that utilize different internal data representations. In this example, data representation refers to the scheme the local host uses to store all characters and data internally. An example of data representations differing is when an ASCII-based machine requires communication with an EBCDIC-based machine.

3. The client stub calls the client runtime. The client runtime usually is a library of routines that provides functionality to the client stub.

4. The client runtime transmits a message containing the encapsulated XDR representation of the function call across the network to the server runtime. The server runtime also is a library of routines that provides the necessary functionality to the server stub.

5. The server runtime issues a call to the server stub.

6. The server stub converts the encapsulated arguments from the common data representation to its native data representation.

7. The server stub calls the server application and passes the original client inputs for processing.

8. After the processing has completed, the server application returns the result set to the server stub.

9. The server stub converts the result set and any associated arguments to the common data representation for transmission. This is encapsulated within a message passed to the server runtime.

10. The server runtime transmits this message over the network to the client runtime.

11. The client runtime passes the message to the client stub.

12. The client stub extracts the result set from the message and converts the message to the local data representation.

13. The client stub returns the result set and any accompanying arguments to the calling function.

External Data Representation (XDR)

External data representation (XDR) provides the common data representation used by RPCs when transmitting data between the client and server systems. The XDR format was created to solve the following problems when binary data is exchanged between heterogeneous systems:

- Different byte orders
- Different data type representation (EBCDIC versus ASCII)
- Structure alignment

Whenever data is transmitted between client and server systems, XDR is used as the data's format during transmission. This ensures that the data is presented in a format with which the receiving system can work.

Portmapper

NFS is not the only application that makes use of Remote Procedure Calls. Because different applications can use RPCs simultaneously, a portmapper program operates on all servers that provide client/server connectivity using RPCs. When a client connects to the server to communicate with a server application using RPCs, the portmapper first determines whether the application is running on the server. If it is, the correct port number is

15

returned to the client system. The client continues to use this port number until the application terminates.

The portmapper uses UDP and TCP port 111. When an RPC-based service is launched on the server, it reports its port usage to the portmapper.

NFS RPC Procedure Calls

The following Remote Procedure Calls have been defined for use with NFS. These RPCs provide functionality to NFS clients.

- **NULL.** The do-nothing procedure tests whether the NFS server is responding. It does not perform an actual task.
- **GETATTR.** The Get File Attributes procedure gets the attributes of a file found on the server. These attributes include protection, owner, size, and access times.
- **SETATTR.** The Set File Attributes procedure changes the attributes of a file.
- **ROOT.** This procedure now is obsolete. It originally was used to mount file systems. (The mount protocol, discussed later today, now accomplishes this.)
- **LOOKUP.** The Lookup Filename procedure performs a directory lookup for the client. This procedure returns both a file handle for the client to use to access the file and the attributes of the file.
- **ACCESS.** The Access procedure checks the access permissions for the user.
- **READLINK.** The Read From Symbolic Link procedure reads the value stored within a symbolic link.
- **READ.** The Read From File procedure is used by the client to read data from a file.
- **WRITE.** The Write to File procedure is used by the client to write data to a file.
- **CREATE.** The Create File procedure creates a file in a directory.
- **MKDIR.** The Create Directory procedure creates a directory.
- **SYMLINK.** The Create Symbolic Link procedure creates a symbolic link to an existing file.
- **MKNOD.** The Create Special Device procedure creates device files or named pipes.
- **REMOVE.** The Remove File procedure deletes a file.
- **RMDIR.** The Remove Directory procedure removes an empty directory.
- **RENAME.** The Rename procedure renames a file or a directory.
- **LINK.** The Link Procedure creates a hard link to an existing file.

- **READDIR.** The Read From Directory procedure views the contents of a directory. It requires the client and server to maintain the state of the connection so a long directory listing can be returned fully to the client. This is accomplished with a magic cookie. The magic cookie contains the state information to be maintained between client and server. The READDIR function returns the filename and the file ID.

- **READDIRPLUS.** The Extended Read From Directory procedure also returns the contents of a directory using the same methodology as the READDIR function. Besides the filename and file ID, attributes and file handles also are returned. This function greatly increases the performance of directory browsing.

- **FSSTAT.** The Dynamic File System Information procedure returns volatile file system state information. If the NFS server does not support all attributes, it makes a best effort and returns all the attributes it can. This command previously was implemented as STATFS in earlier versions of NFS.

- **FSINFO.** The Get Static File System Information procedure retrieves nonvolatile file system state information and general information about the NFS server implementation.

- **PATHCONF.** The Path Configuration procedure returns POSIX-specific information including the maximum number of hard links, the maximum object name length, how to handle name truncation, and case-sensitivity issues.

- **COMMIT.** The Commit procedure forces or flushes cached data to permanent disk storage that was previously written with a WRITE procedure call. This prevents data from being lost because it was not committed from cache.

Authentication Methods

Remote Procedure Calls enable authentication of the calling client. In addition, NFS 4.0 supports callback RPC, which ensures that the client performing the Remote Procedure Call has sufficient permissions to perform the desired task. The following authentication mechanisms are supported under NFS 4.0:

- AUTH_NONE

- AUTH_UNIX

- AUTH_SHORT

- AUTH_DES

- AUTH_SYS

- AUTH_DH

- AUTH_KRB4

- RPCSEC_GSS

AUTH_NONE

The AUTH_NONE authentication method means no authentication is required. This often is used for read-only data stores that are not confidential. User authentication is not required to access this type of data store.

AUTH_UNIX

The AUTH_UNIX authentication method is based on traditional Unix authentication. When using this mechanism, the NFS client provides a user ID (UID), a group ID (GID), and group information to the NFS server.

When implementing AUTH_UNIX as the authentication mechanism, it generally is best to use the network information service (NIS). This provides a common and consistent account database for all participating hosts.

The major issue with the AUTH_UNIX mechanism is that all authentication information is transmitted in clear text. It is possible a network sniffer might intercept the data transmission and then spoof the calling client to connect to the server.

AUTH_SHORT

In the AUTH_SHORT authentication method, the client generates an authentication sequence. The server returns the authentication mechanism. This generally is used when an RPC connection previously has been established. This previous RPC connection is referenced to shorten the authentication process.

AUTH_DES

The AUTH_DES method uses data encryption standard (DES) authentication when transferring RPC packets. Session keys are exchanged using a public/private key model.

The following are advantages of using DES rather than Unix authentication:

- The authentication method is not tied to a specific operating system.
- The authentication mechanism utilizes encrypted transfer of authentication information.
- For outsiders to perform impersonation, they must acquire the private key or the client's network password.

AUTH_SYS

The AUTH_SYS authentication method uses the credentials used by the client to authenticate with the operating system. These are the credentials used by the client when it sets up the delegation to the NFS server.

AUTH_DH

In the AUTH_DH authentication method, the client generates an authentication sequence. The server returns the authentication mechanism. This generally is used when an RPC connection previously has been established. This previous RPC connection is referenced to shorten the authentication process.

AUTH_KRB4

The AUTH_KRB4 authentication mechanism utilizes the Kerberos v4 authentication mechanism.

In a Kerberos authentication scheme, the client presents a session ticket (ST) issued by a Kerberos Distribution Center (KDC). The advantage of Kerberos security is that the client also can authenticate the service. In other words, the client can make sure that the service to which it is connecting is the correct service, not an imposter.

RPCSEC_GSS

The use of RPCSEC_GSS allows an extensible authentication mechanism for NFS. By using the GSS API, protocols such as Kerberos v5 and public key authentication, using the LIPKEY API, can be used as authentication protocols.

RPCSEC_GSS is not an authentication mechanism itself, but an API that allows other commonly authentication mechanisms to interface with NFS and provide mutual authentication services.

Mounting a File System

NFS 4.0 now provides the ability to provide an initial mapping between the network pathname and the file handle established at the NFS client. NFS 4.0 provides this ability natively, rather than using the mount protocol, used by previous versions of NFS.

Previous Versions of NFS

In previous versions of NFS, the mount protocol was a separate protocol used in an NFS implementation. The following tasks were assigned to the mount protocol:

- Determining server pathnames
- Validating users
- Verifying access permissions
- Providing clients with access to the root of a remote file system (by providing a file handle to the access point)

This information is kept separate from the NFS protocol so that methods of access and validation can be changed without having to change the NFS protocol. The mount protocol currently uses AUTH_NONE, AUTH_UNIX, AUTH_SHORT, AUTH_DES, and AUTH_KERB for authentication mechanisms.

The following procedures are used by the NFS protocol to establish and terminate mounts:

- **OPEN.** TheOPEN procedure performs all file lookup, creation, and share operations. Rather than using separate functions, all active operations are performed using the single procedure.

- **CLOSE.** The CLOSE procedure terminates the state established by an OPEN procedure.

When an NFS client initially connects to the NFS server, the client must establish a file handle to initiate the connection. When using NFS 4.0, one of two file handles are used as the starting point for the NFS client:

- **Root file handle.** This file handle is considered to be the root of the file system name space by the NFS client. A client will connect to the root file handle by using the PUTROOTFH operation. When connected to the root file handle, an NFS client can search and use files within the entirety of the servers' file tree using the LOOKUP procedure.

- **Public file handle.** This file handle can be bound to any file system object on the NFS server, rather than the root of the NFS namespace.

Note

It is possible for both the public and root file handles to reference the same file system object. It is up to the NFS administrator to define the security for the file handles, and ensure that they do not map to the same file system object.

File Locking Under NFS

In NFS versions prior to NFS 4.0, NFS was implemented as a stateless protocol. This resulted in an additional protocol being required to implement file locking. File locking ensures that multiple clients cannot access a data file simultaneously (unless this is required by the application). The network lock manager (NLM) provides this functionality for NFS versions prior to version 4.0.

In version 4.0, the model is changed. Rather than use NLM, file-lock state is maintained using a lease-based model. When an NFS client connects to an NFS resource, the NFS server defines a lease period for all states held by the NFS client. If the lease is not renewed by the NFS client within the period defined by the NFS server, the lease is released, allowing other clients to access the resource. Typically, the lease is renewed by using either the RENEW operation, or by simply reading the resource.

This process is less complicated than using NLM protocol in previous versions. The NLM protocol indicated which client held a lock on a file. A lock could be either an *exclusive* lock (access to the file is not allowed until the lock is removed) or a *shared* lock (multiple clients can connect to the file in question).

To prevent a permanent lock in the case of a failed client connection, timers were implemented in NLM. When the timer expired, the file lock was released.

Using NFS with Microsoft Windows

Microsoft Windows operating systems do not ship with an NFS client or an NFS server. You can add this software to interoperate with Unix NFS servers and NFS clients by adding either third-party software, or by installing Services for Unix 2.0.

The most common third-party software used to connect to NFS servers is NetMANAGE's ViewNOW InterDrive client software. The ViewNow InterDrive client software operates under Windows 9x, Windows NT 4.0, and Windows 2000 operating systems and allows the client to mount NFS volumes using the Windows interface (see Figure 15.11).

FIGURE 15.11

Browsing for NFS resources on the network.

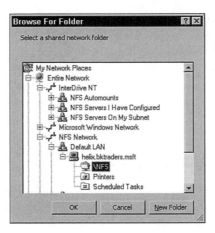

By right-clicking Network Neighborhood (or My Network Places in later versions of Windows operating systems), and selecting Map Network Drive, you can browse for NFS resources, just as you would for Windows or Novell NetWare resources.

> Alternatively, the same functionality can be obtained by installing either the NFS Server or NFS client software included in Services for Unix 2.0.
>
> Whatever solution you choose, this allows you to interoperate with Unix NFS servers and NFS clients.

15

Web Distributed Authoring and Versioning (WebDAV)

RFC 1878 Web Distributed Authoring and Versioning (WebDAV) offers a method for file sharing over the Internet using HTTP as the underlying protocol. The main purpose of WebDAV is to allow secure file sharing between clients using a common protocol allowed to traverse firewalls.

WebDAV is a fully interoperable solution supported by Apache, Adobe, Macromedia, Netscape, Oracle, and Microsoft.

Note

In Windows 2000, Windows XP, and Windows .NET Server, WebDAV folders are defined as *Web Folders* in the user interface. The two are equivalent, and just an example of alternate names that are used for WebDAV.

When connected to a WebDAV share, the use of HTTP is transparent to the WebDAV clients as the publish and manage resources at the WebDAV server.

WebDAV Security

One of the primary reasons for developing WebDAV was to overcome the security issues with using FTP for data transfers. WebDAV offers the following improvements in security over FTP:

- **Password Security.** By implementing a combination of basic authentication and SSL encryption, all passwords entered to access the WebDAV share are encrypted by SSL. Alternatively, certificate-based user authentication can be deployed to prevent interception of credentials.

- **Data Transmission Encryption.** If SSL is enabled at the Web server hosting the WebDAV share, all data transmitted to the Web server is encrypted.

- **Data Storage Encryption.** Windows .NET Server introduces the ability to use Encrypting File System (EFS) with WebDAV. This allows the encryption of a file to take place at the remote client, and then the encrypted file is transferred to the WebDAV share.

Using EFS and WebDAV Together

EFS is an encryption technology supported by both Windows 2000 Professional and Windows XP Professional. In Windows .NET Server, the ability to combine EFS and WebDAV is introduced. In Windows .NET Server, a file encrypted at the local client can be stored securely at the WebDAV server and is never transmitted in an unencrypted format, preventing interception of unencrypted data on the network wire.

Figure 15.12 shows how EFS can be used to protect data as it is transmitted to the Web server and as it is stored at the Web server. These are the steps:

FIGURE 15.12

Using EFS with WebDAV.

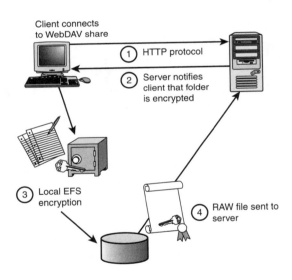

1. The client connects to the WebDAV share by connecting to either `http://webserver/WebDAVshare` or `\\webserver\WebDAVshare` (where `webserver` is the name of the server hosting the WebDAV share, and `WebDAVshare` is the name that the WebDAV folder is shared as).

   If security is implemented at the WebDAV server, the user now has to authenticate. The authentication mechanism used depends on how the Web server is configured to authenticate Web clients.

2. If the WebDAV folder is configured to require EFS encryption, the Web server notifies the client that the folder is encrypted, and that all files saved to the WebDAV folder must be encrypted.

15

3. A symmetric key is generated and the file is encrypted. This File Encryption Key (FEK) is then encrypted using the user's private key and the encrypted FEK is stored in the Data Decryption Field (DDF) of the file.

4. The encrypted file is sent to the Wininet process and then the RAW data file is uploaded to the Web server.

The RAW data file appears as a binary blob file when viewed on the local file system of the Web server. Only when the file is viewed using the WebDAV share do the attributes of the encrypted file appear.

Applying What You Have Learned

Today's material reviewed many of the file transfer protocols available in a TCP/IP network. Most of the file transfers that you will be performing on a TCP/IP network will probably involve the FTP protocol, but due to an increase in awareness about security, alternative methods, such as WebDAV are becoming more prevalent. Remember that several freeware and shareware utilities can be used for file transfers, and that these are much more intuitive than the text-based methods discussed in this book.

Test Your Knowledge

Here are questions to check what you've learned today. The answers can be found in Appendix B, "Test Your Knowledge: Answers."

1. What are some of the key differences between the FTP and TFTP protocols?

2. What is meant by the term *anonymous FTP*?

3. Compare the security of Remote Copy Protocol (RCP) and the File Transfer Protocol (FTP).

4. What are the two communication channels used during an FTP session? What ports are used on the server side during this session?

5. Describe the steps involved in the establishment of a Secure Socket Layer session.

6. What functionality does NFS provide in a networked environment?

7. What functionality is provided to an NFS server by the mount protocol?

8. Explain the concept of file locking. Why is it important in a network environment?

9. How does WebDAV provide increased security over FTP file transmissions?

10. Describe how Windows XP and Windows .NET Server use encryption with WebDAV.

11. Of the various authentication mechanisms supported by NFS, which offer(s) extensibility to provide authentication using future protocols?

Preview of Day 16

Tomorrow we focus on the use of electronic mail in a TCP/IP network. Topics include the protocols used for e-mail transport. These include Simple Mail Transfer Protocol (SMTP), Post Office Protocol 3 (POP3), and Internet Mail Access Protocol (IMAP).

We'll also look into the issues involved with attaching documents to e-mail messages and securing confidential e-mail attachments.

DAY **16**

Electronic Mail over TCP/IP

Today we investigate the various protocols required to implement an e-mail system in a TCP/IP network. The protocols used to send and retrieve e-mail include the following:

- Simple Mail Transfer Protocol (SMTP)
- Post Office Protocol 3 (POP3)
- Internet Message Access Protocol version 4(IMAP4)

Besides the protocols used to send and receive e-mail, you also need to find a recipient's e-mail address and related information. The Lightweight Directory Access Protocol (LDAP) provides the capability to view directory information and find specific attributes of a recipient, such as his digital certificate for transmitting encrypted e-mail.

We'll finish up the day with a look at two areas of concern for e-mail users. The first is e-mail attachments. Many people receive attachments from other users, but find that they are unable to open the attachments. We'll look at the various methods that exist today for sending binary attachments within an e-mail message. The second area of concern is the encryption of sensitive e-mail messages and protecting messages from being modified in transit. Protocols such as Pretty Good Privacy (PGP) and Secure Multipurpose Internet e-mail Extensions (S/MIME) provide a private/public key method of encrypting and digitally signing e-mail messages.

Internet E-Mail at a Glance

Internet e-mail is probably the most used of all applications running on a TCP/IP network. With the explosive growth of the Internet, the use of e-mail in the business place is becoming more and more a required tool.

Some of the reasons that offices are moving toward using e-mail as a standard of communication include the following:

- It is a cheaper alternative than faxing or sending a floppy disk through the post office or by courier.
- E-mail offers quick delivery of a message to the recipient. Time is generally measured in terms of seconds and minutes rather than days and weeks.
- E-mail can reach a recipient even if she is not at her normal location (such as on a business trip). The recipient can connect to her e-mail server from anywhere in the world and access her e-mail account.
- Through the use of protocols such as Pretty Good Privacy (PGP) and Secure Multipurpose Internet e-mail Extensions (S/Mime), data can be secured to prevent both modification and interception as it is transmitted across the Internet.

Although there are many positives, e-mail has some negative points also, including the following:

- Malicious attachments. Several viruses and worms use e-mail as a method to transmit the virus or worm to other computers on the Internet.
- SPAM. Sometimes e-mail is abused. Today, you receive large volumes of unsolicited e-mail in the form of chain letters and SPAM. While Internet e-mail filters can block some of the unwanted messages, many still get through to your inbox.

Internet e-mail uses a unique method of addressing for recipients. The address contains both the mailbox of the recipient whom you want to contact and the domain that hosts the recipient's mailbox.

The format of an Internet e-mail address is `mailbox@domain.tld`, in which `mailbox` is generally the recipient's account name and `domain.tld` is the name of the company or Internet service provider's domain name on the Internet.

My e-mail address is `bkomar@komarconsulting.com`, for example. This indicates that my mailbox name is `bkomar` and it is hosted by the Internet domain `komarconsulting.com`. Besides addresses for mailboxes, there are also addresses known as aliases. *Aliases* are commonly used for e-mail addresses that serve some functionality in the organization. At my company, Komar Consulting Inc, you can send an e-mail message to `admin@komarconsulting.com`. This is an alias that allows e-mail intended for the administrator of my network to also be received by my personal mailbox. Whether you send e-mail to `admin@komarconsulting.com` or `bkomar@komarconsulting.com`, the message ultimately arrives at the same mailbox.

Another common type of e-mail address is known as a distribution list. The addresses do not have to be members of the same Internet domain. They are just referred to by a single name. For example, for a Microsoft course that I worked on, I created a distribution list that included all the reviewers of the material. When I sent a message to `reviewers`, the client-side distribution list was parsed and e-mail was sent to all the individual reviewers of the course material. Likewise, distribution lists can be created for your own organization, so that e-mail messages sent to a distribution list are sent to all members of the distribution list.

Tip

> If your organization implements a centralized help desk, it may be a wise decision to create a distribution list named `helpdesk@company.com` that includes all members of the help desk. This is an example of a server-side distribution list, where the server maintains a distribution list and ensures messages sent to the list are received by all members of the list.

Simple Mail Transfer Protocol (SMTP)

RFC 821 **RFC 2821** Simple Mail Transfer Protocol (SMTP) provides message transfer between two hosts. SMTP uses the TCP protocol for transport. An SMTP server listens on TCP port 25 for connections by default.

SMTP defines both the message format and the methods that will be used for transferring e-mail between two SMTP hosts. The sending host uses SMTP commands to transfer the e-mail to the receiving host. After the transport has completed, the connection is closed between the two hosts.

The SMTP Process

A typical SMTP connection involves six steps (see Figure 16.1).

FIGURE 16.1

The SMTP process.

CLIENT

SERVER

① Connection Initiated ⟶
← 220 <Ready>

② HELO <FQDN> ⟶
← 250 <OK>

③ MAIL FROM: <Address> ⟶
← 250 <OK>

④ RCPT TO: <Address> ⟶
← 250 <OK>

⑤ DATA ⟶
← 250 <OK>
Message Body ⟶

⑥ Quit ⟶
← 221 <Closing>

1. The SMTP client initiates a connection to the SMTP server. The client uses a random port above 1024 and connects to the server's TCP port 25. On accepting the connection, the SMTP server responds with a 220 <Ready> message.

2. The SMTP client requests that the SMTP session be established by sending a HELO (Hello) or EHLO (Extended Hello) command. This command should include the fully qualified domain name (FQDN) of the SMTP client. The SMTP server should respond with a 250 <OK> message.

Note

> Both HELO and EHLO are used by an SMTP client to identify themselves to an SMTP server. EHLO not only allows the SMTP client and SMTP server to identify each other, but it also allows the SMTP server to identify what SMTP extensions it supports.

3. The SMTP client informs the SMTP server who is sending the message with the e-mail FROM: <Address> command, in which the <Address> parameter is the Internet e-mail address of the sending user. This is generally configured as the reply address in the e-mail client software. The SMTP server should respond with a 250 <OK> message.

4. The SMTP client now identifies all the recipients for whom the message is intended using the RCPT TO: <Address> command. If multiple recipients are hosted on the SMTP server, a RCPT TO: command is issued for each of the recipients. The SMTP server responds to each recipient with a 250 <OK> message.

5. The SMTP client indicates that it is prepared to transmit the actual e-mail message by issuing the DATA command. The server responds with a 250 <OK> message. It also indicates the string that it expects to end the body text of the message. Most often this is the string [CR][LF].[CR][LF]. The actual message is now transmitted to the SMTP server. The message is transmitted using 7-bit ASCII characters. If any attachments exist in the message, the attachments must be encoded into a 7-bit stream using BinHex, uuencode, or MIME.

6. After the message has been successfully transmitted, the SMTP client sends a QUIT command to terminate the SMTP session. The SMTP server responds with a 221 <Closing> message to indicate that the session termination has taken place. If the SMTP client had another message to transmit, it could issue the FROM: command again.

The following code sample shows a typical SMTP connection. Client commands are shown in bold in the transcript.

```
/users/bsmith% telnet mail.escape.ca 25
220 wpg-01.escape.ca ESMTP Sendmail 8.8.7/8.7.5 ready at Sun, 22 Nov 2001
➥19:35:25 -0600 (CST)
helo escape.ca
250 wpg-01.escape.ca Hello bsmith@wpg-03.escape.ca [198.163.232.252],
➥pleased to meet you
mail from:bsmith@escape.ca
250 bsmith@escape.ca... Sender ok
rcpt to:bkomar@komarconsulting.com
250 bkomar@komarconsulting.com... Recipient ok
data
354 Enter e-mail, end with "." on a line by itself
subject:This is a test

This was sent by connecting to an SMTP server
.
250 TAA16829 Message accepted for delivery
QUIT
```

This session connected to the SMTP server mail.escape.ca. Once connected, issuing the command HELO started an SMTP session. After the SMTP session was established, a message was sent from bsmith@escape.ca to bkomar@komarconsulting.com. This message sent had the subject This is a test. To complete the message, a single period was entered on a line as the SMTP server indicated.

Other SMTP Requirements

For e-mail to be successfully delivered to an SMTP server, the SMTP client must be able to resolve the domain portion of the Internet e-mail address to an IP address. This is normally done through DNS. For more information on the DNS, review Day 7, "Configuring Domain Name Servers."

DNS has special records that indicate the mail exchanger for a domain. The mail exchangers are represented using an MX (mail exchanger) record. When a client is sending e-mail to bkomar@komarconsulting.com, for example, the SMTP client performs a resolution for the MX record for the domain komarconsulting.com. The MX record indicates the hostname of the mail exchanger for komarconsulting.com. An additional DNS lookup may have to take place to determine the IP address of the mail exchanger so that the SMTP process can be established to the SMTP server.

Within the DNS configuration files, MX records appear as follows:

```
komarconsulting.com          IN    MX    10    mail.komarconsulting.com.
komarconsulting.com          IN    MX    20    mail2.komarconsulting.com.
```

There can be more than one MX record for a domain to provide alternative delivery points for Internet e-mail. The preference number in the MX record is used to rank the preference of mail servers for a domain. The SMTP servers are contacted in an order based on the preference numbers. A lower preference number indicates a higher priority for the mail exchanger. In the example shown, e-mail is sent to mail.komarconsulting.com for the komarconsulting.com domain. If mail.komarconsulting.com is not available, the e-mail is sent to mail2.komarconsulting.com. If neither mail server is available, the sending SMTP server holds the message in an outbound queue and retries transmission at scheduled intervals. Once a preconfigured time passes, the message is returned to the sender with a nondelivery report (NDR).

Securing SMTP Sessions

SMTP is a protocol that is continually used by hackers to send SPAM e-mail to unsuspecting e-mail recipients. This is due to the trusting nature of the SMTP protocol.

SMTP works using a method known as SMTP relaying. An SMTP client will connect to an SMTP server, and then relay SMTP messages to a recipient by "bouncing" the message off the SMTP server. This process is known as *SMTP relaying*.

Typically, an SMTP server allows any clients to relay messages. But, with the increase in SPAM e-mail messages, many organizations are locking down their SMTP servers to restrict the use of SMTP relaying. Some common solutions include:

- **Restricting SMTP relaying to specific IP subnets.** An SMTP server can be configured to only allow hosts within a specific IP subnet to relay messages using the SMTP server. While this works for clients on a local area network, it does not work for organizations that have users that travel. Because the users may connect using different Internet service providers (ISPs) in each city that they travel to, it is almost impossible to define what IP address ranges they will use.

- **Enabling SMTP authentication.** The SMTP protocol allows for authentication to be required by SMTP clients. Before a client can send a message, she must authenticate with the SMTP server. While this sounds like the best solution, it does create a security risk, in that the authentication is performed in clear text.

- **Preventing SMTP relaying.** In the case of mail servers, such as Microsoft Exchange Server 2000, that use proprietary methods to connect to the mail server, SMTP relaying can be disabled, so that only services within the mail server can forward e-mail messages to the Internet. If any Post Office Protocol v3 (POP3) or Internet Message Access Protocol v4 (IMAP4) clients exist on the network, this option is not possible.

Besides restricting SMTP relaying, SMTP can be protected using public key technology-based SSL protection. SSL uses the secure exchange of a session key that is used to encrypt all transmissions between the SMTP client and the SMTP server.

When the SMTP client connects to the SMTP service running on the Mail server, the SMTP client is sent the SMTP's server public key (see Figure 16.2). The process proceeds as follows:

FIGURE 16.2

Securing SMTP authentication with SSL.

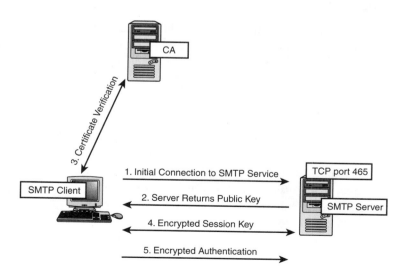

16

1. The SMTP client connects to the SMTP server. Rather than connecting to the default SMTP port (TCP port 25), the SMTP server connects to TCP port 465.

Note

> Some SMTP servers continue to use TCP port 25 for secure SMTP connections.

2. The SMTP server returns its certificate to the SMTP client. One of the attributes of the digital certificate returned to the SMTP client is the certificate's public key.

3. The SMTP client verifies the certificate of the SMTP server by ensuring that the certificate chains to a trusted root Certification Authority (CA), the certificate is time-valid, the name in the certificate matches the fully qualified domain name of the SMTP server, and that the certificate is not revoked.

4. If the certificate is verified, the SMTP client generates a random session key. The session key is encrypted using the SMTP server's public key and transmitted in an encrypted state to the SMTP server. The SMTP server decrypts the session key using its associated private key and sends an acknowledgement that proves the SMTP Server's identity to the SMTP client.

5. The user's account and password are sent to the SMTP server. The credentials are encrypted using the previously created session key.

Post Office Protocol 3 (POP3)

RFC 1939 The Post Office Protocol 3 (POP3) protocol is the most common client protocol that is used for the retrieval of e-mail messages. Initially, SMTP was used for both sending and receiving e-mail. This worked well in an environment when all hosts were on the same network and were available at all hours of the day. As time has progressed, most people are now connecting to the mail servers from varying computers or from different locations. This intermittent checking for messages has resulted in the development of protocols such as POP3.

A POP3 server is best compared to a mail-drop system. The POP3 server holds the e-mail until the user connects and moves the e-mail from the server to the POP3 client. Some POP3 clients do allow you to leave the e-mail on the POP3 server, but this is a client configuration. It is not part of the POP3 protocol itself. POP3 servers sometimes don't support this feature or impose limits on the amount of e-mail that can be left on a POP3 server.

The POP3 Process

As with an SMTP session, POP3 sessions are established using a specific set of steps. Figure 16.3 shows the steps involved in a POP3 session.

FIGURE 16.3

A POP3 client session.

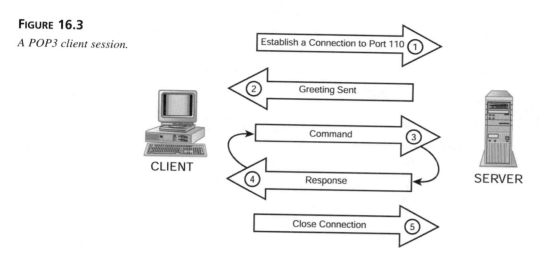

CLIENT   SERVER

1. The POP3 client connects to the POP3 server. The POP3 server will be listening on port 110 for client connections.
2. The POP3 server sends the client a greeting. The greeting generally contains the name and version of the POP3 server that is running.
3. All the following steps consist of commands and responses from the POP3 server. The initial command involves authentication with the POP3 server. The client must provide his identity with USER <username> and PASS <password> commands. After the user has been authenticated, several commands can be executed. Table 16.1 lists the specific POP3 commands that can be sent from the client to the server.

TABLE 16.1 POP3-Supported Commands

Command	Description
AUTH	Specifies the type of authentication that is to be used for the session.
USER <username>	Identifies the mailbox to which the user is connecting.
PASS <password>	Sends the password for the mailbox to the POP3 server. This password is sent by clear text by default. Secure Socket Layers can be implemented in some cases to better protect the user's password.
QUIT	Terminates the POP3 session.

TABLE 16.1   continued

Command	Description
STAT	Indicates the number of messages that are stored on the server and the total amount of disk space that they occupy.
LIST *<msg #>*	Indicates the approximate size of the listed message.
RETR *<msg #>*	Retrieves the indicated message number.
NOOP	Indicates that no operation should take place.
TOP *<msg #> n*	Displays the first *n* lines of the indicated message number.

4. For each command, the server sends an appropriate response. The responses are prefaced with either +OK for successful responses or -ERR for commands that were not successfully interpreted.

5. On completion of the POP3 session, the client terminates the session using the QUIT command.

The following code sample shows a POP3 session transcript. The client commands are shown in bold.

```
/user/bsmith% telnet mail.escape.ca 110
+OK QPOP (version 2.4b2) at wpg-01.escape.ca starting.
user bsmith
+OK Password required for bsmith.
pass Passw0rd
+OK smith has 2 messages (2767 octets).
stat
+OK 2 2767
retr 2
+OK 1057 octets
Return-Path: bkomar@komarconsulting.com
Received: by wpg-01.escape.ca (8.8.7/8.7.5) with SMTP id TAA16267 for
➥<bsmith@escape.ca>;
 Sun, 25 Nov 2001 19:33:08 -0600 (CST)
Message-ID: <000301bd55fc$20eb8f30$080810ac@bkhome.komarconsulting.com>
From: "Brian Komar" <bkomar@komarconsulting.com>
To: <bsmith@escape.ca>
Subject: Another Test Message
Date: Sun, 25 Nov 2001 19:36:38 -0600
MIME-Version: 1.0
        charset="iso-8859-1"
Content-Transfer-Encoding: 7bit
Content-Type: text/plain;

Did you receive this okay!!!
```

```
Brian
QUIT
+OK Pop server at wpg-01.escape.ca signing off.
Connection closed by foreign host.
```

As you can see, the client bsmith connected to the POP3 server using the password Passw0rd. The STAT command showed that there were two messages on the POP3 server using a total disk space of 2767 bytes. The second message was retrieved. This was a message from bkomar@komarconsulting.com with the subject Another Test Message.

Securing POP3 Authentication

The major problem with the POP3 protocol is that the authentication is sent to the POP3 server using clear text authentication. This means that a network packet sniffer can be used to intercept the authentication packets and determine the credentials used by the POP3 client.

To prevent inspection of the authentication, the POP3 server can be configured to require SSL encryption. When a POP3 server requires SSL encryption, the POP3 server's listening port is changed from TCP port 110 to TCP port 995. A POP3 encrypted authentication using SSL takes places as shown in Figure 16.4.

FIGURE 16.4

Securing POP3 authentication with SSL.

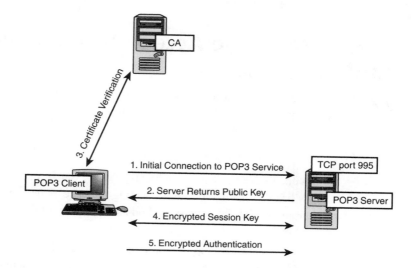

1. The POP3 client connects to the POP3 server. Rather than connecting to the default POP3 port (TCP port 110), the POP3 client connects to TCP port 993.

Caution A POP3 server must be configured to use SSL by installing a digital certificate. If the POP3 server is not configured to support SSL, then the connection to TCP port 993 will fail.

2. The POP3 server returns its certificate to the POP3 client. One of the attributes of the digital certificate returned to the POP3 client is the certificate's public key.

3. The POP3 client verifies the certificate of the POP3 server by ensuring that the certificate chains to a trusted root Certification Authority (CA), the certificate is time-valid, the name in the certificate matches the fully qualified domain name of the POP3 server, and the certificate is not revoked.

4. If the certificate is verified, the POP3 client will generate a random session key. The session key is encrypted using the POP3 server's public key and transmitted in an encrypted state to the POP3 server. The POP3 server decrypts the session key using its associated private key and sends an acknowledgement that proves the POP3 Server's identity to the POP3 client.

5. The user's account and password are sent to the POP3 server. The credentials are encrypted using the previously created session key.

Internet Message Access Protocol Version 4 (IMAP4)

RFC 2060 Internet Message Access Protocol version 4 (IMAP4) is a newer form of e-mail transport protocol. It has been built with more features than the older POP3 protocol, but is not used as much.

IMAP4 offers the following advantages over the POP3 protocol:

- IMAP4 clients are not sent the contents of every e-mail message. The IMAP4 server sends header information for all waiting messages; this results in quicker transmission times. The actual message bodies can be downloaded on a message-by-message basis.

- IMAP4 allows messages to be stored in a hierarchical structure on the IMAP4 server. Rather than storing the messages locally (as is the default for POP3), the messages are stored on the server. This allows support for common folders such as Inbox, Sent Items, and Drafts on the IMAP4 server.

- Because the messages are stored on the IMAP4 server, the messages can be accessed from multiple IMAP4 clients and users can still see the same status information for all messages. This includes Read and Reply status.

- IMAP4 servers understand MIME file extensions. This enables an IMAP4 client to select which portions of a message he wants to retrieve. If an important message also includes a 5MB AVI attachment, for example, the user could choose to retrieve only the text message.

- IMAP4 supports online, offline, and disconnected access modes. POP3 supports only online mode.

IMAP4 Message Attributes

One key feature of IMAP4 e-mail is that messages are stored on a central IMAP4 server. This allows multiple clients to connect to the same mailbox. This requires the implementation of flags to indicate the current status of a message. Each message can be assigned one or more separate flags to indicate the status of a message.

Currently defined system flags include the following:

\Seen	Indicates that the message has been previously read.
\Answered	Indicates that a Reply has been sent in response to this message.
\Flagged	Indicates that an Urgent or Special Attention flag has been set for this message.
\Deleted	Indicates that this message has been marked for deletion by an EXPUNGE command.
\Draft	Set on a message that has been saved for later delivery on the IMAP4 client. This is commonly referred to as a draft message.
\Recent	Assigned to messages that have just arrived in the mailbox. This flag exists only during the first session in which the message arrives. Thereafter, this flag is not set.

IMAP4 States and Their Associated Commands

The following four states can exist for an IMAP4 session between an IMAP4 client and an IMAP4 server:

- Non-authenticated

- Authenticated

- Selected

- Logout

Within each of these states, the client can execute associated IMAP4 commands. Each command is issued with an alphanumeric prefix used to tie a response back to the original command. If you were to request the language capabilities of the IMAP4 server, for example, you would proceed through the following command sequence:

```
Client: 0001 Capability
Server: * CAPABILITY IMAP4 4 IMAP4 4rev1 AUTH=Kerberos_v4 AUTH=NTLM
Server: 0001 OK Capability Completed
```

where `0001` is the alphanumeric prefix that indicates that the response was in regard to the `CAPABILITY` command issued in the first line.

Some IMAP4 client commands can be issued in any of the four states. Table 16.2 shows these commands.

TABLE 16.2 IMAP4 Commands Valid in Any State

Command	Description
CAPABILITY	a listing of all capabilities that the server will support. If a capability is prefixed by AUTH=, this represents an authentication method that can be used to authenticate with the server.
NOOP	Polls for new messages and prevents the session from disconnecting because of the auto-logout timer expiring. This command always succeeds.
LOGOUT	Informs the server that the client is ready to terminate the connection. The server sends a BYE response before responding OK to the LOGOUT request.
QUIT	Terminates the IMAP4 session.

Non-Authenticated State Commands

The non-authenticated state is limited in the commands that can be issued. The goal of this state is to authenticate users so that they can start to manage their server-based mail store. This state is entered after the connection has been started between the IMAP4 client and the IMAP4 server.

Table 16.3 shows the two commands that are available in the non-authenticated state.

TABLE 16.3 IMAP4 Commands Valid in the Non-Authenticated State

Command	Description
AUTHENTICATE method	Indicates the authentication method that will be used for this session. If the server supports the authentication mechanism, it performs the selected authentication routine. The actual exchange depends on the authentication mechanism indicated. After the mechanism is negotiated, it is applied to all subsequent data transmitted in the session.
LOGIN user password	Identifies the user to the server and sends the associated password. This password may or may not be sent as clear text across the network, depending on the authentication method selected.

Caution   IMAP4, like POP3, uses clear-text authentication by default, and this can lead to a user's account and password being compromised. To prevent password interception, consider using authentication protocols such as Kerberos, or configuring the IMAP4 server to use SSL to protect the authentication session as described later in this section.

16

Authenticated State Commands

The authenticated state is entered after the IMAP4 client has successfully authenticated with the IMAP4 server. In this state, the client's primary task is to indicate the mailbox to which he will be connecting. This is the mailbox to which the client will be issuing e-mail management commands. Other tasks that can be performed in this state include creating and deleting mailboxes, adjusting subscriptions, and checking the status of mailboxes. Table 16.4 shows the commands available in the authenticated state.

TABLE 16.4   IMAP4 Commands Valid in the Authenticated State

Command	Description
Select *mailbox*	Selects the *mailbox* to be inspected in the selected state. If another mailbox is currently selected, the select command automatically deselects the preceding mailbox.
Examine *mailbox*	This command is much like the Select command. The difference is that the Examine command gives read access only to a mailbox; the Select command can provide read/write access.
Create *mailbox*	Allows a new mailbox to be created with the mailbox name. If the mailbox that is named includes parent folders in its name, these parent folders are also created if they do not already exist.
Delete *mailbox*	Permanently removes the indicated mailbox. The indicated mailbox cannot be removed if subfolders exist below it.
Rename *mailbox newmailbox*	Renames the existing mailbox to *newmailbox*. There is one special case for this command. If the mailbox being renamed is the Inbox, all the messages in the original Inbox are moved to the new mailbox. However, the original Inbox remains with no messages in it.
Subscribe *mailbox*	Adds the specified mailbox to the list of "Active" mailboxes displayed in the IMAP4 client software.
Unsubscribe *mailbox*	Removes the specified mailbox from the list of "Active" mailboxes displayed in the IMAP4 client software.

TABLE 16.4   continued

Command	Description
List *reference mailbox*	Returns a subset of names from the complete set of all names available to the client. The *reference* parameter allows the hierarchy in which the *mailbox* exists to be indicated.
LSUB *reference mailbox*	Returns only a subset of names from the mailboxes that the user has subscribed to by marking "Active." This is common when a user subscribes to various IMAP4 folders.
Status *mailbox status item*	Indicates the status of the *mailbox*. This allows a different mailbox to be inspected without terminating the connection to the current mailbox. Status items that can be inspected include messages, \Recent flagged files, the UID value that will be assigned to the next new message, the number of unread messages, and the unique identifier validity value for the mailbox.
Append *mailbox message*	Appends a new e-mail message to the specified *mailbox*.

Selected State Commands

The selected state is entered after the IMAP4 client has selected a mailbox to work with. At this point, commands can be entered to investigate the contents and manage the contents of the selected mailbox. Besides the selected state commands listed in Table 16.5, all authenticated state commands can also be issued in this state.

TABLE 16.5   IMAP4 Commands Valid in the Selected State

Command	Description
Check	Launches any native housekeeping functionality implemented by the IMAP4 server. If the IMAP4 server does not have any housekeeping functionality, this command is the equivalent of the NOOP command.
Close	Returns to the authenticated state from the selected state. It also permanently removes all messages that have the \Delete flag set.
Expunge	Permanently removes all messages with the \Delete flag set, but it continues in the selected state.
Search [*Charset*] *parameters*	Searches the mailbox for all messages that meet the indicated search *parameters*. Optionally, the character set can be specified by using the *Charset* option.

TABLE 16.5 continued

Command	Description
Fetch message_set Message data_items	Retrieves data associated with a message in the mailbox. When used, the specific contents of a message can be retrieved. Message data_items include ALL, BODY, ENVELOPE, FLAGS, FULL, and UID.
Store message_set message_data_item value	Alters the data associated with a message in the mailbox. This is generally used to change the flags associated with a message.
Copy message_set mailbox	Copies the specified message(s) to the mailbox indicated. The copy operation maintains the flags and date stamps.
Uid command arguments	Allows commands to be executed against Unique ID numbers rather than message sequence numbers. The UID command can be used with the COPY, FETCH, STORE, and SEARCH commands.

16

Logout State Commands

In the logout state, the connection is being prepared for termination. After the server is prepared, it closes the connection between client and server. This state is entered after a client performs a CLOSE request or the auto-logout timer expires.

Securing IMAP Authentication

As with SMTP and POP3 authentication, the IMAP4 server can be configured with a digital certificate that allows encryption of IMAP4 authentication. As with POP3 and SMTP, the following modifications must be made to the IMAP4 clients and IMAP4 server:

- The IMAP4 server must have acquired a digital Web server certificate to allow for encryption of sessions between the IMAP4 server and the IMAP4 clients.

- The certificate for the IMAP4 server must chain to a root certification authority trusted by the IMAP4 client.

- The IMAP4 clients must be configured to connect to the SSL port for IMAP4, TCP port 995, to provide SSL-protected authentication.

Lightweight Directory Access Protocol (LDAP)

One of the major issues with e-mail is that you do not always know the e-mail address of another person. Lightweight Directory Access Protocol (LDAP) provides a directory service that an e-mail client can connect to when trying to determine a recipient's e-mail address.

LDAP has been developed by the IETF to standardize access to X.500 and non-X.500 directory systems. Several e-mail systems have been deployed on the Internet. Each of these systems has its own proprietary directory service. LDAP provides a methodology that uses a common framework for finding names in the diverse directory services.

LDAP's Evolution from X.500

LDAP has evolved from the X.500 directory service. The X.500 standard defines different object classes that can be used to identify objects within the directory services tree. These objects include the following:

- Aliases
- Country codes
- Localities
- Organizations
- Organizational units
- People

Within these object classes, several common objects have a defined set of attributes. Some of the more common objects that are used within X.500 include the following:

- Common name (cn)
- Organization name (o)
- Organizational unit name (ou)
- Country (c)
- State or province (s)

Figure 16.5 shows a typical X.500 tree structure.

Within this tree, you can define distinguished names. The distinguished name for a person is built from the end object, also known as the leaf object, back to the root of the X.500 structure. For example, the distinguished name (dn) for Krista would be:

```
cn=Krista, ou=sales, o=Acme, c=US
```

FIGURE 16.5

An X.500 tree structure.

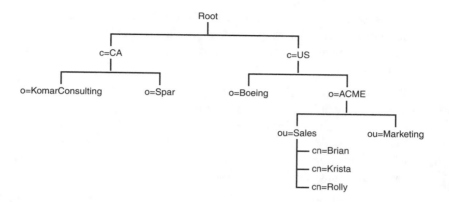

16

The LDAP protocol provides a method of access to the directory. Within the protocol, the operations of searching, addition, deletion, and modification are all defined. When you perform a search of the directory using LDAP, the following parameters are provided:

- A base distinguished name, where the search is to be started. You could limit the search to start in "c=US, o=Acme", for example.
- A filter that can be applied to set the criteria for the search. The criteria can include attribute types and wildcard characters.
- A scope that can be set to indicate which part of the directory to search. The scope can include only the base distinguished name, the level just below the distinguished name, or the entire subtree starting at the distinguished name.

LDAP Operations

All LDAP queries are directed to the LDAP server on TCP port 389 by default. When the client initially contacts the LDAP server, this is known as the *bind operation*.

The LDAP client initiates the LDAP protocol session between the client and the server and performs client authentication. The `BindRequest` uses the following format:

```
BindRequest ::=
    [APPLICATION 0] SEQUENCE{
                    version            INTEGER (1..127)
                    name         LDAPDN,
                    authentication CHOICE {
                        simple     [0] OCTET STRING,
                        krbv42LDAP    [1] OCTET STRING,
                        krbv42DSA        [2] OCTET STRING
                    }
    }
```

In this format, version indicates the LDAP protocol version being used; name is the name that the client is using to bind to the directory object (this is used for authenticating the client); and the authentication parameter is used to authenticate the name indicated in the BindRequest.

The simple authentication method passes the password as clear text. This should be used only in anonymous situations because of the possibility of passwords being compromised. Other authentication methods supported include Kerberos authentication to the LDAP server and to the Directory Service Agent. The OCTET STRING passed with these would be the Kerberos session ticket. Finally, you can simply disable authentication altogether and allow anonymous access.

After the bind operation has been processed, the LDAP server must send a BindResponse in the following format:

```
BindResponse ::= [Application 1] LDAPResult
```

The LDAPResult is the notification of a successful or unsuccessful authentication with the LDAP server.

The most common operation that is performed next by the LDAP client is a search operation. This is performed by using a SearchRequest. The SearchRequest uses the following format:

```
SearchRequest ::=
    [Application 3] SEQUENCE {
            baseObject      LDAPDN,
            scope           ENUMERATED {
                                    baseObject      (0),
                                    singleLevel     (1),
                                    wholeSubtree    (2)
                            },
            drefAliases     ENUMERATED {
                                    neverDerefAliases       (0),
                                    derefInSearching        (1),
                                    derefFindingBaseObj     (2),
                                    derefAlways             (3)
                            },
            sizeLimit       INTEGER (0 .. maxInt),
            timeLimit       INTEGER (0 .. maxInt),
        attrsOnly       BOOLEAN,
        filter          Filter,
        attributes      SEQUENCE of AttributeType
    }

Filter ::=
    CHOICE {
            and                       [0] SET OF Filter,
```

```
            or                    [1] SET OF Filter,
            not                   [2] Filter,
            equalityMatch         [3] AttributeValueAssertion,
            substrings            [4] SubstringFilter,
            greaterOrEqual        [5] AttributeValueAssertion,
            lessOrEqual           [6] AttributeValueAssertion,
            present               [7] AttributeType,
            approxMatch           [8] AttributeValueAssertion,
    }

SubstringFIlter
    SEQUENCE {
            Type                  AttributeType,
            SEQUENCE OF CHOICE    {

            Initial               [0] LDAPString,
                    Any           [1] LDAPString,
                    Final         [2] LDAPString
            }
    }
```

16

Within the search request, the following parameters are used:

BaseObject   The directory entry used as the starting point for the search.

Scope   This indicator represents the scope of the search. This can be set to be only the base object, the layer below the base object, or the entire subtree starting at the base object.

derefAliases   An indicator as to how alias objects should be handled when performing the search. You can set this to never use aliases in searching, only use aliases when searching for a directory entry (not the base object), only use aliases for locating the base object of the search, or freely use aliases at any time during a search.

sizeLimit   This parameter restricts the number of entries that are returned by a search request. Setting this parameter to 0 indicates that all entries should be returned that match the criteria of the search.

timeLimit   This parameter sets a maximum amount of time (in seconds) for the search. If set to 0, there are no time limit constraints on the search.

attrsOnly   This indicator sets the search results to contain attribute types and values, or just attribute types.

Filter   This parameter defines the criteria for the search to be performed.

Attributes   A listing of the attributes the search wants returned for each matching directory object. If this parameter is null, all attributes are returned.

The server responds with a `Search Response`, using the following format:

```
Search Response ::=
    CHOICE {
        Entry         [APPLICATION 4] SEQUENCE {
                          ObjectName    LDAPDN,
                          Attributes    SEQUENCE OF SEQUENCE {
                                            AttributeType,
                                            SET OF AttributeValue
                                            }
                      },
        ResultCode    [APPLICATION 5] LDAPResult
    }
```

The `Search Response` contains zero or more matching objects based on the filter set in the `SearchRequest`. Each entry contains all the attributes specified in the Search Request and their associated values. In addition, a `resultCode` is returned that indicates whether the search was a success or failure.

After the LDAP process is complete, the LDAP client sends an unbind operation to terminate the protocol session. The unbind operation uses the following syntax:

```
UnbindRequest ::= [Application 2] NULL
```

There is no associated response to the unbind operation. Upon receipt of the unbind request, the protocol server assumes the client has disconnected. If there are any outstanding requests, they are discarded at this point.

Securing Your LDAP Directory

LDAP directories are a potential vulnerability when they are exposed to the Internet. There is a potential that an attacker will use your LDAP directory to populate a distribution list with the intent to send SPAM e-mail.

You can secure your LDAP directory by using the following strategies:

- Rather than making your entire LDAP directory available to the Internet, consider hosting a mirror of your directory that only contains those accounts that you want to make available to the Internet.

- Configure a directory synchronization service that will configure the account information between the internal directory and the external directory at regular intervals.

- Ensure that security for the LDAP directory is configured so that external clients can only read information in the directory, and not modify any of the attributes in the externally-accessible directory.

- Consider using certificate-based authentication for users connecting to the LDAP server. The certificates will map, or be associated with, a specific user account. By authenticating the users, you can restrict which accounts are exposed in the LDAP directory. This is done by configuring browser permissions to only specific containers in the LDAP directory structure.

- If using typed credentials, consider acquiring a server certificate for the LDAP server to enable SSL-encryption of LDAP sessions. The LDAP server will listen for LDAP requests on TCP port 636, rather than TCP port 389. You must combine this approach with the other security strategies to prevent harvesting of the LDAP information by an attacker.

16

E-Mail Attachment Issues

With the continued use of e-mail, the need for sending and translating attachments is becoming a familiar support issue for e-mail administrators. The following three common methods are used for attaching nontext attachments to e-mail messages:

- BinHex
- uuencode/uudecode
- Multipurpose Internet Mail Extensions (MIME)

The purpose of each of these file-encoding schemes is to convert binary data into text data for transmission by SMTP clients. The biggest problem encountered is having the correct decoding software installed on the client. The following sections detail specifics about each of the file-encoding schemes.

BinHex

BinHex is a storage protocol that was developed initially for use by Macintosh systems. BinHex translates a binary data file into an encrypted text version using hexadecimal. This enables e-mail clients to send the "BinHexed" version of a binary file.

A BinHex attachment is generally stored with the extension .hqx. If you receive an attachment with the .hqx extension, you need a BinHex utility such as the latest version of Stuffit or WinZip to open the data stored in the attachments.

BinHex is the preferred method of file encoding on Macintosh systems because BinHex can handle data fork and resource fork information. BinHex preserves this information when file encoding so that this information is correctly transferred between systems.

BinHex is also available as an attachment method in Eudora and Pegasys e-mail clients.

uuencode/uudecode

uuencode (Unix-to-Unix encoding) is an alternative method for converting raw binary data into a text representation. This is mainly performed for the purpose of sending binary attachments via a text-based Internet e-mail system.

uuencode converts the binary file into a series of 7-bit ASCII characters. The encoded files do not have a standard naming convention, but you often see the .uu extension on Unix systems and .UUE extension on DOS- and Windows-based systems.

A uuencoded file can also be identified by the first line of the file. It always appears in this format:

```
Begin ### afile.avi
```

The ### represents a permissions flag for the file. This is used in Unix systems. The afile.avi represents the name of the file that the uudecode uses for the re-expanded file. Each additional line begins with the letter M and terminates with a [CR][LF] character combination. If this is not the case, either the file is not a uuencode file or the file is damaged.

The utility uudecode is used for translating the uuencoded file back into its native format. Most versions of uuencoding software available today have both the uuencode and uudecode programs built in to one software interface. For example, the latest versions of WinZip fully support working with uuencoded files.

Lotus Corporation's defunct mail package cc:Mail used uuencoding for binary attachments. Lotus has replaced cc:Mail with Lotus Notes as its e-mail solution.

MIME

The Multipurpose Internet Mail Extensions (MIME) standard was developed by the IETF to provide a mechanism for formatting non-ASCII messages so that they can be transmitted over the Internet. Most current e-mail clients now support the MIME standard. The added benefit of MIME is that it supports character sets other than ASCII.

The existence of MIME data in an e-mail message is determined by examining an e-mail's message header. A text-only e-mail message header might look something like this:

```
From: bkomar@komarconsulting.com
To: ronald@beekelaar.com
Subject: How have you been doing
... Message Text ...
```

If an e-mail message has MIME data included, five additional fields can be included within the message header. These additional fields are

- MIME-Version
- Content-Type
- Content-Transfer Encoding
- Content-ID
- Content-Description

The MIME-Version Field

The MIME-Version field is used to indicate the MIME version that was used to create the e-mail message. Currently, this would be version 1.0. This field must be located at the top level of a message. If the message is a multipart message, the MIME-Version needs to be declared only once at the top of the message.

The Content-Type Field

The Content-Type field is used to indicate the type of data contained in the message body. The recipient's e-mail client software can select the correct application to present the data based on the Content-Type field. The Content-Type is based on a top-level media type and a subtype value. The top-level media type declares the general type of data. There are five discrete top-level media types:

- **text.** Used for encoding text-based information. Three subtypes are predefined for the Text media-type: plain, enriched, and html. plain and enriched encoding are used when the text can be displayed as is. Recently, more and more e-mail products are using the html subtype so that Hypertext Markup Language can be used to generate graphic e-mail solutions.

- **image.** Used for graphics attachments, and requires that a display device be present. Two subtypes were initially defined for the media type: JPEG and GIF.

- **audio.** Used for sound producing attachments and requires headphones or speakers for output. Several subtypes are defined, such as BASIC and WAV.

- **video.** Used for video attachments. Defined subtypes include MPEG, QT (QuickTime), and AVI.

- **application.** Used for data that must be processed by a native application. post-script is one of the most common subtypes.

There are also two composite top-level media types.

- **multipart.** Used when data from multiple entities is included within a single e-mail message. Four basic subtypes exist:
  - **mixed.** Subtype specifies that there are multiple attachments using different media types in the message.
  - **alternative.** Subtype indicates that the data is attached in multiple formats to facilitate different clients reading the information.
  - **parallel.** Subtype indicates that the MIME attachments should be viewed simultaneously at the receiving host.
  - **digest.** Subtype represents that the message has many entities and all the entities have a default type of message/rfc822.
- **message.** Indicates that an encapsulated message is included in the message body. The message can be an entire message or part of a message.
  - **rfc822.** Subtype indicates that the message is plain text and shorter than 1,000 characters as per RFC 822.
  - **partial.** Subtype used when an RFC822 message has been broken apart because of size restrictions.
  - **external-body.** Subtype references an external data source for the message instead of including the actual message.

If the Content-Type is not indicated, it is assumed that the Content-Type is text/plain, using the US-ASCII character set.

The Content-Transfer-Encoding Field

Because the natural format of many attachments is not compatible for transport across the SMTP protocol, the attachments must be encoded into a 7-bit ASCII format. MIME uses several methods for encoding the data into a 7-bit short-line format. The Content-Transfer-Encoding field is used to indicate the method of encoding that was used and provides the decoding method for the receiving client to use when reading the attachment.

Accepted encoding mechanisms include the following:

- **7-bit.** This is used when the data is exclusively using ASCII characters that are no greater than value 127 and do not contain null characters. Each line has fewer than 998 octets and ends with the [CR][LF] sequence. No actual encoding is performed for this mechanism.

- **8-bit.** This is used when data includes octets with values greater than 127 from the ASCII character set. As with 7-bit encoding, each line has fewer than 998 octets and each line is terminated with a [CR][LF] combination. No actual encoding is performed for this mechanism.

- **binary data.** This mechanism is not currently valid in today's Internet e-mail. It has been provided for the time when a binary attachment can be transmitted over the Internet without being encoded. This mechanism would transmit the data without any encoding.

- **quoted-printable.** This mechanism transforms the original attachment into material that is 7-bit in nature. This mechanism is used when the data is largely made up of data from the 7-bit US-ASCII character set. The following rules are used for encoding under quoted-printable:

  - Any 8-bit characters will be represented with = followed by the two-digit hexadecimal representation of the characters ASCII number. The hexadecimal digit must be represented in uppercase letters.

  - Lines will be truncated to no more than 76 characters per line. A "soft line break" will be implemented. Simply put, an = symbol is used as the last character on an encoded line.

- **base64.** This mechanism converts binary data into a text format. Unfortunately, an encoded document will be roughly 33% larger after this encoding has been performed.

The base64 encoding process breaks the binary data into 24-bit streams of data by concatenating three 8-bit input groups. These 24 bits are treated as four 6-bit groups. These 6-bit groupings are translated into a single digit of the Base64 alphabet s (see Table 16.6).

TABLE 16.6   The Base64 Alphabet

Value	Encoding	Value	Encoding	Value	Encoding	Value	Encoding
0	A	16	Q	32	g	48	w
1	B	17	R	33	h	49	x
2	C	18	S	34	i	50	y
3	D	19	T	35	j	51	z
4	E	20	U	36	k	52	0
5	F	21	V	37	l	53	1
6	G	22	W	38	m	54	2

16

TABLE 16.6   continued

Value	Encoding	Value	Encoding	Value	Encoding	Value	Encoding
7	H	23	X	39	n	55	3
8	I	24	Y	40	o	56	4
9	J	25	Z	41	p	57	5
10	K	26	a	42	q	58	6
11	L	27	b	43	r	59	7
12	M	28	c	44	s	60	8
13	N	29	d	45	t	61	9
14	O	30	e	46	u	62	+
15	P	31	f	47	v	63	/

If fewer than 24 bits are available at the very end of the data being encoded, the data will be padded with the = character to provide 24 bits for conversion. These bits are considered as zero bits when calculations are performed.

The Content-ID Field

This field is an optional field used when referencing one body to another body. These Content-ID fields must be globally unique so that duplicate IDs are not created. This field is required in the case where the MIME media type is set to `message/external-body`.

The Content-Description Field

The Content-Description field is provided to associate a descriptive text phrase to an attachment. This is generally displayed as the attached document's icon title when working in a graphical interface. This field is an optional MIME header field.

A Sample MIME Header

The following message was transmitted using Outlook Express. This product allows messages to be sent using HTML formatting.

```
From: scrim@scrimtech.ca
To:bkomar@komarconsulting.com
Subject: How is it going.
Date: Sun, 25 Nov 2001 12:32:58 -0600
MIME-Version: 1.0
Content-Type: text/html;
        charset="iso-8859-1"
Content-Transfer-Encoding: quoted-printable
```

```
<!DOCTYPE HTML PUBLIC "-//W3C//DTD W3 HTML//EN">
<HTML>
<HEAD>

<META content=3Dtext/html;charset=3Diso-8859-1 =
http-equiv=3DContent-Type>
<META content=3D'"MSHTML 4.72.2106.6"' name=3DGENERATOR>
</HEAD>
<BODY bgColor=3D#ffffff>
<DIV><FONT color=3D#000000 size=3D2>Talk to you =
next week!</FONT></DIV></BODY></HTML>
```

Note that the MIME-Version is set to `1.0`. Also note that the Content-Type is set to `text/html`. The Content-Type also used the optional parameter to indicate the character set that was used for the message.

This message was encoded using `quoted-printable`. Notice that the longer HTML lines were split into multiple lines by using = as the last character of the line.

Securing E-Mail Messages

One of the major issues faced when sending e-mail messages is that the SMTP, POP3, and IMAP4 protocols send all data in clear text. This means that if someone were using a network packet sniffer, they would be able to read the contents of the messages as the messages are transmitted on the wire.

To provide encryption of e-mail messages, e-mail software makes use of a Public Key Infrastructure (PKI) to allow protection of the transmitted e-mail messages.

In this section, we'll look at the following topics:

- Mail content security protocols
- Mail encryption
- Digital signatures

Mail Content Security Protocols

Two protocols exist today for the encryption and signing of Internet e-mail messages: Pretty Good Privacy (PGP) and Secure Multipurpose Internet Mail Extensions (S/MIME). Both protocols accomplish the same task, but are not interoperable.

PGP uses public and private keys to provide encryption and digital signature abilities to e-mail applications. PGP is free for personal users and can be downloaded from `http://www.pgp.com/products/freeware/default.asp`. The only concern with PGP is that it is not controlled by a centralized standards organization, such as the IETF.

16

RFC 2632 **RFC 2633** **RFC 2634** S/MIME is similar in functionality to PGP. As with PGP, S/MIME uses private and public keys to provide encryption and digital signing services to e-mail applications. The major difference in S/MIME is that the protocol is governed by the IETF and is documented in RFC 2632, 2633, and2634.

Where Is the Encryption Performed?

Both PGP and S/MIME perform the actual encryption and decryption processes at the client computers, and not at the mail servers. This removes any requirement for the mail servers to support PGP or S/MIME, but does prevent antivirus software at the mail server from scanning for viruses in the e-mail content or attachments.

Digital Signatures

Digital signatures are used to ensure that the contents of an e-mail message are not modified in transit. In addition, a digital signature provides nonrepudiation, because the digital signature is created using the user's private key, to which only the user has access.

Digital signing uses the combination of a well-known hash algorithm and private/public key pairs to protect the contents of an e-mail message from modification as shown in Figure 16.6.

FIGURE 16.6

The digital signing process.

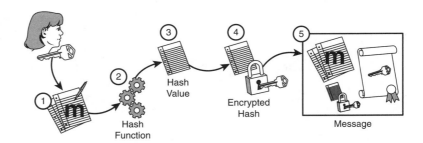

1. The sender creates an e-mail message that contains content that must not be modified in transit and indicates in her e-mail application that the messages must be digitally signed.

2. The e-mail application passes the message content through a hash algorithm, typically SHA1 or MD5. The result of the hash algorithm is stored in a hash value. This hash value will be no longer than 160 bits.

Can Two Messages Arrive at the Same Digital Hash Value?

Although it is technically possible that two different messages can arrive at the same hash value, it is improbable that the two messages would make sense. You cannot change a single word, sentence, or paragraph in an e-mail message and arrive at the same digital hash value.

3. The hash value is now encrypted using the sender's private key. The usage of the sender's private key ensures that the content was created by the sender of the e-mail message.

4. The original e-mail message, the encrypted hash, and the sender's digital certificate are sent by the e-mail application to the recipient. The digital certificate is included so that the recipient has access to the sender's public key.

The recipient can now verify the digital signature when he receives the e-mail message as shown in Figure 16.7 and in the following steps:

FIGURE 16.7

Verifying a digital signature.

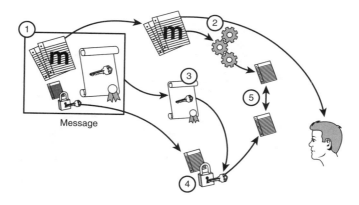

Message

1. The e-mail recipient retrieves the message from his mail server.

2. The recipient passes the message content through the same hash algorithm used by the sender. The result of the hash algorithm is stored in a separate hash value for later use.

3. The sender's public key is retrieved from the digital certificate included in the signed e-mail message.

4. The sender's public key is used to decrypt the original message hash.

5. The two hash values are compared. If the hash values match, the original content has not been modified. Any difference in the two hash values indicates that the message was modified in transit.

Mail Encryption

Mail encryption uses a symmetric key, generated uniquely for each e-mail message, which is protected using public/private key encryption as it is transmitted across the network.

In the case of e-mail encryption, the recipient's public key is used to encrypt the symmetric key, so that only the recipient of the message can decrypt the symmetric key, and then decrypt the contents of the message.

The process of e-mail encryption is shown in Figure 16.8 and in the following steps:

FIGURE 16.8

The e-mail encryption process.

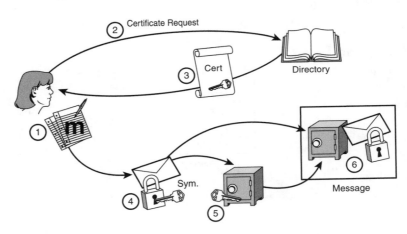

1. The sender creates an e-mail message and addresses it to a recipient. In the e-mail application, the sender indicates that he wants to encrypt the e-mail message.

2. The sending user must acquire the recipient's public key. In most e-mail systems, this is performed using an LDAP query to a directory service. The LDAP query asks to retrieve the recipient's digital certificate. One of the attributes of the digital certificate is the recipient's public key.

16

What If No Directory Service Exists?

Many e-mail users have acquired e-mail certificates for sending and receiving secure e-mail, but do not belong to a common directory. In this case, digitally signed e-mail messages can be exchanged between the two users. After the e-mail message is received, the recipient can add the sender as a personal contact. The contact object contains the sender's digital certificate and associated public key. This method only works if the e-mail client uses the same public/private key pair for both digital signatures and e-mail encryption.

---

3. The directory service returns the recipient's digital certificate to the e-mail client. The e-mail program uses the public key attribute of the digital certificate for encrypting the symmetric key.

What About Sending to Distribution Lists?

When you send encrypted e-mail messages to a distribution list, you must have access to the public key of all recipients. If you are missing just one public key, the message will not be sent, or will only be sent in an encrypted format to the recipients whose public keys you have access to.

---

4. The e-mail application generates a one-time symmetric key that is used to encrypt the contents of the original e-mail message.

5. The symmetric key is encrypted using the recipient's public key so that only the recipient can decrypt the symmetric key.

6. The encrypted symmetric key and the encrypted contents of the e-mail message are sent to the recipient using SMTP.

After the e-mail message reaches the recipient's mail server and the recipient attempts to open the message, the decryption process begins, as shown in Figure 16.9 and in the following steps:

1. The encrypted e-mail message arrives at the recipient's mailbox. Remember that the e-mail message includes the encrypted e-mail message and the encrypted symmetric key.

2. The recipient uses his private key to decrypt the symmetric key. Depending on the e-mail package, the user may have to provide a password to access the private key.

3. The decrypted symmetric key is used to decrypt the e-mail message.

4. The recipient can read the decrypted e-mail message in his e-mail package.

FIGURE 16.9

Decrypting an e-mail message.

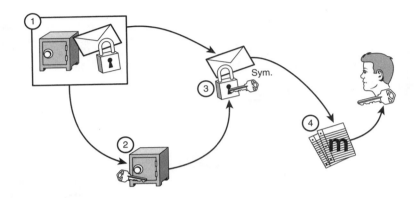

Dual Key Pairs

Several e-mail applications increase security by using separate key pairs for digital signing and for e-mail encryption. This ensures that a digital signing certificate can only be used for digital signatures, and that an e-mail encryption certificate can only be used for e-mail encryption.

Applying What You Have Learned

Today's material reviewed the common methods of implementing e-mail applications in a TCP/IP environment. Although SMTP is still the most common method for sending e-mail, there seems to be more and more of a movement toward using IMAP4 for retrieving messages because of the performance gains over POP3 clients.

We also reviewed the issue of attachments. The key thing to remember when dealing with attachments is that you may require additional software to read attachments that have been encoded using a method that your e-mail software does not support.

Test Your Knowledge

Here are questions to check what you've learned today. The answers can be found in Appendix B, "Test Your Knowledge: Answers."

1. What are the steps involved in an SMTP session between an SMTP client and an SMTP server?

2. With an Internet e-mail client, what function does the SMTP protocol provide? What function does POP3 or IMAP4 provide?

3. What type of record is queried in DNS by an SMTP client?

4. What advantages do IMAP4 e-mail clients offer over POP3 e-mail clients?

5. Why is the LDAP protocol being developed?

6. Describe the meaning of the following X.500-style name:

   `cn=Beekelaar, Ronald; ou=Utrecht; o=Beekelaar Consulting, c=nl`

7. If you were working primarily with Macintosh systems, which method of file encoding would you use for e-mail attachments?

8. What are the field headers used when a MIME attachment exists in an e-mail message?

9. What protocols are used to protect e-mail message authentication?

10. What protocols are used to protect e-mail message content?

11. What is the difference between PGP and S/MIME? Can they interoperate?

12. How does the use of public and private keys vary when comparing digital signing to e-mail encryption?

13. What additional feature can be used to further secure e-mail applications that perform both digital signing and e-mail encryption?

16

Preview of Day 17

Tomorrow's material looks at managing a TCP/IP network using the Simple Network Management Protocol (SNMP). It looks at how SNMP tackles the task of managing a network and overviews some of the common products used for managing an SNMP network.

DAY 17

Managing a Network with SNMP

Today's material looks at the use of the Simple Network Management Protocol (SNMP) to manage the infrastructure of a network. The material includes an overview of the following:

- Roles in a network management system
- SNMP communities
- The structure of the Management Information Base (MIB)
- SNMP transactions
- Security considerations

An Overview of Network Management

Two different thoughts come to mind when the term *network management* is brought up. The first thought deals with the management of resources of the network. These include user accounts, file resources, and print resources. This management is more specific to the network operating system implemented.

Network management can also encompass the management of the physical devices that make up the network, such as routers, bridges, and hubs. The management of these devices is many times a reactive style of management. When failures occur, users notify the network administrator that they cannot perform normal day-to-day activities. Although this eventually leads to the solution of the problem, early notification would assist greatly in solving the problem.

Simple Network Management Protocol (SNMP) enables the network administrator to detect a problem before the user base even notices the problem. SNMP management systems can determine immediately when a network interface on a router has failed and can help to build a solution to the problem. SNMP provides a standard for the monitoring and controlling of a network. SNMP most commonly runs on TCP/IP networks, but it can also run on AppleTalk, IPX, and OSI networks.

SNMP Management Systems and SNMP Agents

There are two key components in an SNMP system: the SNMP management system and the SNMP agents. SNMP management systems are used to issue queries to the systems running SNMP agents. The SNMP agents respond with values filled in for the queried information. SNMP management systems are able to query and manage network devices remotely. A key feature of some network devices is the fact that they are SNMP-enabled. This means they have been configured to respond to SNMP requests from an SNMP management system. SNMP agents are implemented via either software loaded on the host or firmware loaded on the actual device.

You can also configure SNMP agents to initiate conversations with an SNMP management system, by using SNMP traps. Traps are messages issued by the SNMP agent because a specified threshold or situation has been exceeded for an SNMP-monitored resource. A router, for example, might send an SNMP trap when one of its configured interfaces fails.

In some cases, the SNMP agent cannot be implemented on the device that needs to be managed. Instead, the agent is loaded onto a different system that functions on behalf of the network device. This system is known as an *SNMP proxy agent*. When the proxied network device needs to be managed, the SNMP management system sends the management request to the proxy agent. The proxy agent then contacts the proxied device. The device either uses a different protocol to query the device or monitors the device using other methods to determine the results to any queries.

> **SNMP Agent Implementations**
>
> You are likely to see SNMP agents implemented as firmware on actual networking hardware devices, such as routers, switches, bridges, and hubs. Generally, host computers implement SNMP agents as actual software packages or services.

SNMP Communities

Each SNMP transaction contains a tag known as the community name. The community name is used as a low-level method of security. When the request is made, the SNMP agent determines whether the request has come from a management system within the same community. If the community name does not match, the request is not processed.

Community names are case sensitive and can be a maximum of 32 characters. It is imperative that all systems within the same management domain share the same community name.

Three types of communities exist in an SNMP implementation. They include

- **Monitor community.** The management system in the Monitor community is able to perform read-only queries of all SNMP agents that belong to the same community name. For each query that is posed, the SNMP management system includes the Monitor community name in the request. This is compared to the monitor agent's community name as a low-level security check. If they match, the request is responded to.

- **Control community.** The management system in the Control community is able to perform read/write functions to the SNMP agents. Write operations are allowed only for properties that can be modified by a management system. This community is normally disabled to protect against accidental modification of properties of the SNMP agents.

- **Trap community.** The Trap community name is set on the SNMP agent system. When a trap event occurs, the SNMP agent sends a message to its configured SNMP management system. The Trap community name configured in the SNMP trap message must match the community name of the SNMP network management system.

17

> **Caution**
>
> An SNMP management system is able to query an SNMP agent for many details that could compromise network security. Ensure that you do not use default community names, such as `public`, in your SNMP deployment. Use

of `public` eases the task for an attacker to use SNMP to find out details about your internal network infrastructure.

The Components of an SNMP System

The following are requirements for implementing SNMP:

- The traffic involved with network management should not adversely affect the network traffic within the system as a whole.
- The network monitor agent should not cause additional processor usage.

Several components make up the SNMP system, including

- The Structure of Management Information (SMI)
- The SNMP protocol
- Management Information Bases (MIB)

Structure of Management Information (SMI)

RFC 1155 The Structure of Management Information (SMI) provides a standardized framework for defining the information that an SNMP manager can manage. It does not describe the actual objects that can be managed. Instead, it provides the basic format for all managed objects.

In addition, the SMI defines the hierarchy used to store MIB database information. By defining the hierarchy, it is guaranteed that there will be no ambiguity when an SNMP request is made.

Each object within the SNMP hierarchy is assigned a unique object identifier. Object identifiers are allocated in a hierarchical tree method (see Figure 17.1).

When an object is referred to within the object identifier tree, either the object identifiers or the object descriptions are used. When discussing the management object in the object identifier hierarchy, for example, you can refer to it by its object identifiers, or as follows:

`iso.org.dod.internet.management`

This can also be identified using the following object identifier values:

`1.3.6.1.2`

FIGURE 17.1

The object identifier hierarchy.

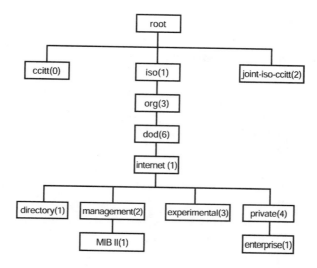

Each object is defined using Abstract Syntax Notation One (ASN.1), which provides a common mechanism for defining objects so that there is no ambiguity with the function and properties of the object. Each object contains the following properties:

- name
- syntax
- encoding

The name property is used to identify each managed object. The name is based on the actual object identifier for the managed object. Each managed object must have a unique object identifier based on the SMI. The object identifier is created by traversing the object hierarchical tree starting at the root and ending at the managed object.

The syntax property is used to define the structure of the object type. This is defined using the ASN.1 notation. The use of ASN.1 removes any ambiguity as to the contents and properties of each managed object. Within the syntax, the following defined types are used for the properties of an object:

- Integer   This data type is a whole number between 1 and the largest integer value allowed on the host system.
- Octet_string   This data type is used for data stored in strings of 8-bit bytes (the term "octet" is used rather than "byte" because it can't be assumed that all computers will have 8 bits in a byte).

- `Object_identifier` This data type is used to store the object identifiers used to name unique objects within the MIB.
- `NetworkAddress` This data type is used to define the protocol family for an address.
- `IpAddress` This data type contains an IPv4 32-bit address.
- `Counter` This data type is a non-negative integer incremented by values of 1 until the maximum value of $2^{32}-1$ is reached. At this point, the count reverts to 0 and restarts from that point.
- `Gauge` This data type is used to contain non-negative integers that can increase or decrease based on performance variables. A maximum value of $2^{32}-1$ is allowed for this data type.
- `TimeTicks` This data type is used to indicate the time in hundredths of a second since a specific event occurred.
- `Opaque` This data type is used to pass arbitrary ASN.1 syntax. A value is first encoded using ASN.1 rules into a string of octets. This is then encoded again as an `octet_string`. This second encoding is performed so that a recognized ASN.1 format is used for the transport of the data. The receiving system needs only to know how to interpret the `octet_string` data, not the encoded internal data.

The `encoding` property is used to transmit the value of an object to a management station based on the syntax describing the object type.

Finding Who Owns an Object Identifier

It is possible to find out what object identifier is owned by an organization by viewing the comprehensive list of SMI network management private enterprise codes maintained at the following URL:

> http://www.isi.edu/in-notes/iana/assignments/enterprise-numbers.txt

This listing can be used to find the specific enterprise numbers registered by organizations with the IANA. This listing can be used as the starting point when deciphering SNMP commands captures using a network packet sniffer.

The SNMP Protocol

RFC 1441 SNMP is a simple protocol that uses the following User Datagram Protocol (UDP) destination ports during transmission:

- **UDP Port 161.** This is the destination port for all SNMP request and response messages. Remember that the SNMP management station initiates SNMP requests.

- **UDP Port 162.** This is the destination port for all SNMP trap messages. Remember that the SNMP agent initiates SNMP trap messages when a preconfigured event takes place.

Why Not Use TCP?

The UDP protocol is used as the transport protocol, rather than TCP, because of the requirement for timely delivery of SNMP messages. The need to get the information to the SNMP management system as quickly as possible outweighs the need for reliable transmission. Using UDP bypasses the additional transmission packets involved in establishing a TCP session.

Within the SNMP protocol, six basic operations have been defined. Each operation is encoded using ASN.1 and is defined in separate Protocol Data Units (PDUs). These PDUs define the format of the SNMP message.

RFC 1448 The defined operations include:

- `GetRequest` The SNMP management station uses the `GetRequest` PDU to query an MIB on an SNMP agent (see Figure 17.2).

FIGURE 17.2

The traffic flow for an SNMP `GetRequest` *PDU.*

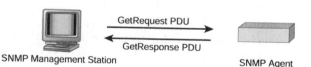

SNMP Management Station

GetRequest PDU

GetResponse PDU

SNMP Agent

- `GetNextRequest` An SNMP management station uses the `GetNextRequest` PDU to read sequentially through an MIB. It allows a value in a table to be retrieved without knowing its exact object ID. This is extremely valuable when the SNMP management station is unaware of the number of instances of an object that exist.
- `GetBulk` The `GetBulk` PDU has been added in SNMP v2. It was created to provide a more efficient retrieval mechanism for values in a table. Rather than having to send a `GetNextRequest` for each entry in a table, `GetBulk` allows the table to be retrieved in a single request.
- `SetRequest` The SNMP management station uses the `SetRequest` PDU to change the value of an MIB object. This object must allow Read/Write access.
- `GetResponse` The SNMP agent to the SNMP management station sends the `GetResponse` PDU. Its format is identical to `GetRequest` except that the `Type` and `Value` portions of the variables are completed with the current values.

17

- Trap The Trap PDU (see Figure 17.3) is the only PDU initiated by the SNMP agent. It provides a mechanism for the agent to signal out the occurrence of an event that may require special attention.

FIGURE 17.3

The SNMP Trap *message flow.*

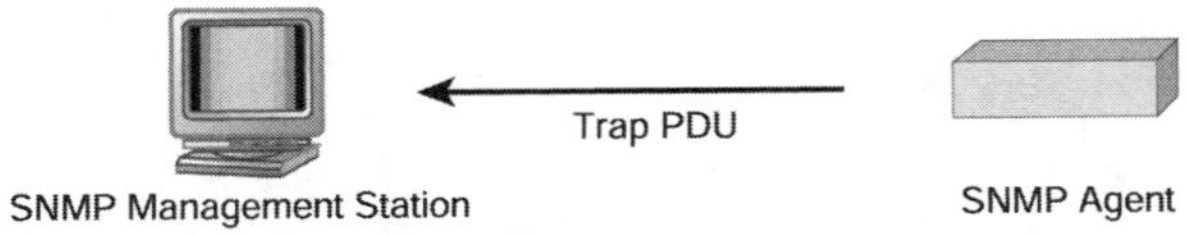

Trap PDU

SNMP Management Station

SNMP Agent

The following seven traps have been predefined for use by MIBs that implement the Trap PDU:

- coldStart This trap is sent when the SNMP agent is in the state of reinitializing itself and has significant changes to its configuration. Rebooting the system causes this trap to be sent.
- warmStart This trap is sent when the SNMP agent reinitializes itself with no changes in its configuration.
- linkDown This trap is sent to indicate that one of the communication links of the sending SNMP agent has failed.
- linkUp This trap is sent by the SNMP agent to indicate that a downed communication link has been restored to normal operation.
- authenticationFailure This trap implies that an SNMP management station has made an SNMP request to the SNMP agent and has failed the authentication procedure. This can be due to a nonmatching community name or noninclusion in the list of accepted SNMP management stations.
- egpNeighborLoss This trap is sent by an SNMP agent when an EGP peer relationship has been lost.
- enterpriseSpecific This trap is an enterprise-specific defined trap event.

Management Information Base (MIB)

RFC 1213 The Management Information Base (MIB) is used to specify the details that a managed device will report to an SNMP management system. There are actually several MIB files that can be implemented. Each vendor can produce a unique MIB for its hardware device that will have specific management objects exposed for queries. Objects within the MIB are defined based on the structures and object types defined in the SMI. These objects are stored together within a subtree of the object identifier hierarchy. Several different MIBs exist for each distinct part of the object hierarchy.

The current version of the MIB is MIB-II. The MIB is divided into logically related groups of objects. These groups are defined using the following criteria:

- The object must be essential for either fault or configuration management to be included in the MIB.
- Objects included in the MIB should allow only limited damage when an SNMP manager tampers with them.
- The object must be in current use.
- Each object must be independent. If an object can be derived from others in the MIB, it should not be included in the MIB.
- Implementation-specific objects, such as a specific attribute of an HP LaserJet printer, are not included in the MIB.

Internet MIB-II is divided into the following categories:

- **System.** Used to contain general information about the network device.
- **Interfaces.** Defines information about a network interface. This includes both physical network interfaces such as ethernet or token ring and point-to-point links.
- **Address Translation.** Used to contain address translation information. The information is contained in a single table used to convert a network address (such as an IP address) into subnet-specific addresses (such as a physical address). This category exists solely for compatibility with MIB-I nodes.
- **IP.** Used for querying and setting information specific to the IP protocol.
- **ICMP.** Used for querying and setting information specific to the ICMP protocol.
- **TCP.** Used for querying and setting information specific to the TCP protocol. In the TCP group, objects that represent specific TCP connections exist only for the duration of the TCP session.
- **UDP.** Used for querying and setting information specific to the UDP protocol.
- **EGP.** Used for querying and setting information specific to the UDP protocol. Exterior routers use the EGP protocol to allow autonomous systems to exchange routing reachability information on the Internet.
- **Transmission.** Based on the actual transmission media used by each interface. Currently, as the definitions for transmission media progress through the standardization process, they reside in the experimental portion of the MIB.
- **SNMP.** Used for querying and setting information specific to the SNMP protocol.

All SNMP-capable devices must implement these groups. The only caveat is that an SNMP-capable device must implement only groups that are relevant to that device. If a device, such as a wireless bridge, does not use EGP, it is not required to implement the EGP group.

Internet MIB-II Updates

Internet MIB-II has been updated in RFC 2011, RFC 2012, and RFC 2013.

Specific Internet MIB-II Objects

Appendix C, "Internet MIB—II OIDs," contains definitions of all default objects included in the Internet MIB-II. You do not have to know every object within this MIB. This information is provided so that you can use these tables to troubleshoot specific SNMP events or to perform specific SNMP requests.

Deploying an SNMP Management System

The deployment of SNMP management software requires two separate configuration tasks. First, SNMP agent software must be acquired for all devices you want to manage on the network. You must configure each device to load the SNMP agent software. Second, an SNMP management software package must be acquired, from which all SNMP management operations are performed.

Installing the SNMP Agent

In a Windows XP environment, the SNMP agent software is distributed freely with the Windows XP Professional software. Complete the following steps to configure the SNMP agent on a Windows XP workstation:

1. From the Start Menu, click Control Panel.
2. In the Control Panel, double-click Add or Remove Programs.
3. In the Add or Remove Programs dialog box, click Add/Remove Windows Components.
4. In the Windows Components Wizard dialog box, select Management and Monitoring Tools from the list of components, and then click Details.
5. In the Management and Monitoring Tools dialog box, enable the check box for Simple Network Management Protocol (see Figure 17.4), and then click OK.
6. In the Windows Components Wizard dialog box, click Next.

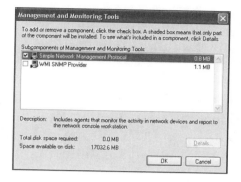

7. In the Files Needed dialog box, provide the path to the installation files (typically the CD:\i386 folder), and then click OK.

8. In the Completing the Windows Components Wizard, click Finish.

9. Close the Control Panel.

Configuring the SNMP Agent

After the SNMP Agent is installed, you need to configure the SNMP agent for your environment. Use the following steps to configure the SNMP Agent:

1. From the Start menu, click Administrative Tools, and then click Services.

2. In the Services console, double-click the SNMP Service in the list of installed services.

3. In the Agent tab (see Figure 17.5), you can configure information such as contact name and location. You also determine which levels of the network will be monitored by SNMP.

4. Click the Traps tab. For each community name that exists on your network, configure the destination IP address to which SNMP trap messages are sent. See Figure 17.6.

> **Caution**
>
> Do not use the default community name of public when configuring your SNMP agent. Doing so is considered a security weakness.

5. Click the Security tab (see Figure 17.7). Configure the accepted community names for SNMP requests and define what Rights are allowed for each community name. The Security tab is also used to configure which IP addresses will be allowed to perform SNMP requests to this SNMP agent.

17

FIGURE **17.5**

*Configuring the SNMP
Agent properties.*

FIGURE **17.6**

*Configuring the
SNMP Traps proper-
ties.*

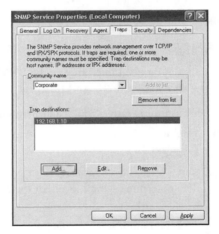

Caution

For added security, configure the SNMP agent to only accept SNMP packets
from specific hosts. If an SNMP packet is received from an SNMP management station that does not match the community name or list of approved
management stations, an SNMP trap will be sent to the defined trap destination from the Traps page.

6. Click OK to close the SNMP Service Properties (Local Computer) dialog box.

7. Close the Services console.

FIGURE 17.7

Configuring the SNMP Security properties.

Using an SNMP Management Station

Windows XP and Windows 2000/.NET Server do not ship with a prepackaged SNMP management station. Several SNMP management packages are available to provide SNMP management capability to Windows 2000/.NET Server, including:

- HP OpenView
- Tivoli Enterprise Console
- Intel LanDesk
- CA-Unicenter

The Windows .NET Server Resource Kit provides a limited Graphical User Interface (GUI) utility called SNMPUTILG, which can do basic queries against SNMP agents (see Figure 17.8).

This utility enables you to perform Get, GetNext, or Walk operations. The Walk operation shows the text equivalents of the object IDs. You must also provide the agent name to which you want to send the GetRequest PDU and the community name you want to use.

Although SNMPUTILG provides the ability to perform SNMP queries, it does not provide a mechanism to perform SNMP SetRequest operations. Third-party versions of SNMP management software provide many benefits, including:

- More intuitive features
- Network mapping capabilities
- Increased functionality

FIGURE 17.8

Using the SNMPUTILG *utility.*

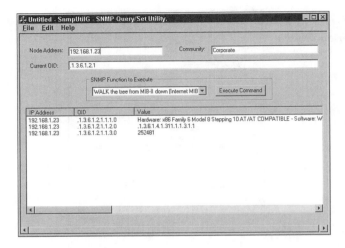

Figure 17.9 shows an example of how CA-Unicenter shows a network mapping of the 131.107.3.0 network segment.

FIGURE 17.9

The 131.107.3.0 *network segment.*

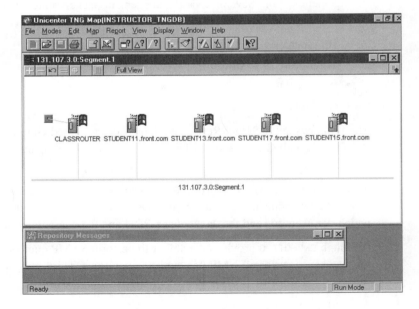

Note how each device on the network segment is identified. The identification includes the hostname for each device and an icon to indicate that these are all Windows 2000 Server hosts.

A request for determining system uptime is much easier when using a graphical SNMP manager. Rather than having to manually determine that the object ID for sysUpTime is .1.3.6.1.2.1.1.3, CA-Unicenter allows you to navigate the MIB tree using logical names. Figure 17.10 shows an SNMP request for sysUpTime being performed to the device named classrouter in the 131.107.3.0 network.

FIGURE 17.10

A query on sysUpTime *using CA-Unicenter.*

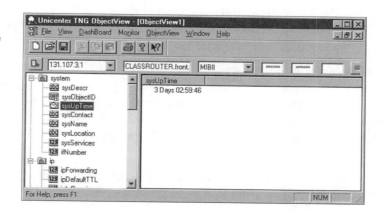

17

Practical Application of SNMP

At this time, your eyes are probably blurring at the thought of using SNMP on a network, especially if you have looked at the SNMP object ID tables in Appendix C. Let's discuss a true application of SNMP in a network.

One of my clients was having a problem with network broadcast traffic. First thing in the morning, their SNMP management station noticed that there were high volumes of network broadcast traffic saturating the network. After about an hour had passed, the broadcasts disappeared, other than the occasional broadcast storm.

I was brought in to determine what was causing the broadcast storms. I used a network packet sniffer to find out what was causing the broadcasts. Through the packet sniffer, I determined that several hosts were sending out SNMP requests to all IP addresses in the local subnet. Normally this would not be a problem, except that the client was using a Class B IP address with a Class B subnet mask. In other words, each host was sending out 65,534 packets.

On further inspection, the following SNMP request was being sent:

```
SNMP Get .1.3.6.1.4.1.11.2.3.9.4.2.1.1.3.1
```

To troubleshoot the problem, I had to identify what the OID referred to. The following steps were used to determine the meaning of the OID.

1. Using the listing of SMI Network Management Private Enterprise Codes at `http://www.isi.edu/in-notes/iana/assignments/enterprise-numbers.txt` I established that Hewlett Packard owned the `1.3.6.1.4.1.11` object ID.

2. I next retrieved the HP MIBs to determine what the specific OID was referencing. I did not have any luck finding the MIBs at `www.hp.com`, but I was able to find the MIBs I needed at `http://www.snmplink.org/`.

3. At the `www.snmplink.org` Web site, I discovered that the OID I was researching was related to HP LaserJet 5Si Mopiers.

In the actual MIB file, I was able to determine that the `.1.3.6.1.4.1.11.2.3.9.4.2.1.1.3.1` OID referred to the model-number identifier for the printers. The cause of the problem was that the computers originally had a proprietary HP5 printer management software package installed. This software package allowed remote management of HP5 Si Mopier printers.

When the computer started, it would send out ARP requests to all addresses in its local subnet. Because the network used a Class B address, this resulted in 65,534 broadcast ARP requests being sent out. This was the source of the broadcast traffic.

After the responses were received, all responding workstations were sent an SNMP request performing a SNMP GET on `.1.3.6.1.4.1.11.2.3.9.4.2.1.1.3.1`.

To put it in English, the computer asked each network host if it was an HP 5Si Mopier, because if it was, the computer could manage it remotely.

To solve the problem, the software was correctly uninstalled, so that the SNMP GET requests were stopped. Secondly, HP was informed of the problem with the uninstall process, so that all software was correctly uninstalled. Finally, a recommendation was sent to the client to consider *not* using a Class B subnet mask for the network. If subnet masking had been performed more efficiently, the number of broadcasts sent by the computers would have been limited.

Applying What You Have Learned

The material discussed today walked you through the various aspects of network management using the SNMP protocol. SNMP is used widely in enterprise networks because of its capability to attack problems at an early stage.

Here are questions to check what you've learned today. The answers can be found in Appendix B, "Test Your Knowledge: Answers."

Test Your Knowledge

1. What are the two major categories of network management?
2. What protocols (in addition to IP) can an SNMP system be implemented on?
3. What role does the SNMP management system play in the SNMP process?
4. What role does the SNMP agent play in the SNMP process?
5. What additional network management functionality does the SNMP Trap PDU provide?
6. What measures can you apply in an SNMP environment to provide additional security?
7. What are the three types of community names used in an SNMP implementation?
8. How are object identifiers assigned to objects in the MIB?
9. What are the major categories in the MIB-II database?
10. What advantage does the GetBulk PDU provide in SNMP v2?

Preview of Day 18

Tomorrow's material looks into the issues involved with providing remote access to your network. The topics include

- The methods used to provide dial-in capabilities to the network
- The SLIP and PPP protocols
- An overview on the use of tunneling protocols, including two of the more common tunneling protocols available today: PPTP and L2TP
- Using remote access over broadband networks
- Centralizing remote access security configuration and authentication using the RADIUS protocol

17

DAY 18

Dial-Up Networking Using TCP/IP

Today we look at the technology used to access networks remotely. There are more options available than using a modem to connect to a network.

We'll discuss dial-up solutions for connecting to remote networks. Two methods exist for dial-up connectivity using public phone networks: Serial Line Internet Protocol (SLIP) and Point-to-Point Protocol (PPP).

We'll also examine "tunneling" solutions, where connections to a remote network can be securely created over public networks. Currently, three solutions exist for connecting remote clients to remote access servers over public and broadband networks: Point-to-Point Tunneling Protocol (PPTP), Layer Two Tunneling Protocol (L2TP), and Point-to Point-Protocol over Ethernet (PPPoE).

No matter which method you use to connect to your remote network, you must authenticate with that network to access resources on the network. Besides standard remote access authentication protocols, you can centralize authentication using Remote Authentication Dial In User Service (RADIUS). RADIUS allows you to decentralize authentication services, yet centralize management of authentication and accounting services for remote access users.

Connecting to Networks Remotely over Phone Lines

This book so far has discussed connecting systems over traditional network media including ethernet, token ring, and wide-area networking technologies. Now we'll discuss implementation over analog phone lines. The following are two commonly implemented protocols:

- Serial Line Internet Protocol (SLIP)
- Point-to-Point Protocol (PPP)

These protocols are similar to frame types implemented on local area networks. They define how data is formatted as it transmits over analog phone lines.

Serial Line Internet Protocol (SLIP)

RFC 1055   *Serial Line Internet Protocol (SLIP)* is the original method developed for TCP/IP communication over serial phone lines. SLIP forms a point-to-point connection that runs the TCP/IP protocol.

The SLIP protocol is implemented as a packet-framing protocol. SLIP defines a specific sequence of characters that frame each IP packet as it is transported over the serial line. SLIP does not have a standardized maximum packet size. The two most common sizes are 1,006 bytes and 1,500 bytes.

Two special characters are defined—the END character (decimal 192) and the ESC character (decimal 219). This ESC character should not be confused with the ASCII escape character.

The END character indicates the end of the packet being transmitted. If the data packet contains the decimal 192 character, the END character is represented with a two-byte sequence comprising the ESC character and the decimal 219 character.

The ESC character is used when the END character has to be represented as a two-byte sequence because the decimal 192 character exists in the data stream.

Although the SLIP protocol is a simple protocol to implement, the following deficiencies exist:

- Both computers need to know each other's IP address for routing purposes. A script often is required to allow the server to assign an IP address to the client at dial-in. No mechanism is provided to automatically assign the IP address to the client.

- SLIP is designed for use with the IP protocol. Without a Type field, it is impossible to use an alternative protocol, such as IPX, over the connection.

- No error detection or error correction is provided. SLIP leaves these tasks to the transport protocols instead of implementing its own checksums. This leads to inefficiencies because it is up to a higher-level protocol to determine whether a packet has been corrupted in transit.

- The user's account and password are transmitted as clear text across the phone network.

- No compression is provided. Many of the packets transmitted over a SLIP connection are fragmented. A compression algorithm can be implemented on the common fields of the fragmented packets, including the IP header and the TCP header. If these fields are included in compression algorithms, only the changed fields between fragmented fields can be transmitted.

Point-to-Point Protocol (PPP)

RFC 1661 *Point-to-Point Protocol (PPP)* is a standardized protocol developed to solve the problem of encapsulating the IP protocol over point-to-point links. PPP has the following features:

- Automatic assignment and management of IP addresses for remote clients.

- The capability to transmit multiple protocols over a single point-to-point link.

- Negotiation of options between the client and server, including network addresses and data-compression options.

- Automatic error detection.

The following are the main components of the PPP protocol:

- A method to encapsulate multiple-protocol datagrams.

- A Link Control Protocol (LCP) used to establish, configure, and test the data link connection. This actually is an extension of the PPP protocol.

- A family of Network Control Protocols (NCPs) used to establish and configure different network-layer protocols.

The PPP Packet

The PPP protocol can transmit multiple protocols during a single communication session. To accomplish this, the PPP packet, shown in Figure 18.1, uses framing to indicate the beginning and end of the encapsulated data.

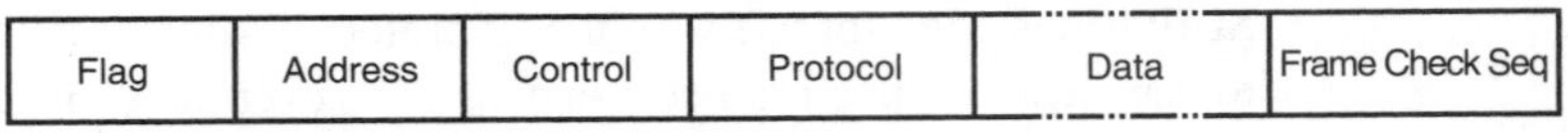

FIGURE 18.1

PPP packet format.

Flag	Address	Control	Protocol	Data	Frame Check Seq

The packet contains the following fields:

- **Flag.** This 8-bit field indicates the beginning or end of a frame of data. It is a static value set to the binary sequence 01111110.

- **Address.** This 8-bit field is set to the standard broadcast address 11111111. PPP does not assign addresses to each station in the point-to-point link.

- **Control.** This 8-bit field contains the binary sequence 00000011, which calls for the transmission of user data in unsequenced frames.

- **Protocol.** This 16-bit field identifies the protocol encapsulated in the data payload. This protocol ID is based on the values stored within the current STD002, the Assigned Numbers standard document. The following protocol IDs have been reserved by the PPP specification:

    - *c021.* Link Control Protocol (LCP)

    - *c023.* Password Authentication Protocol (PAP)

    - *c025.* Link Quality Report

    - *c223.* Challenge Handshake Authentication Protocol (CHAP)

- **Data.** This variable-length field contains the actual protocol data encapsulated within the PPP packet. The maximum length of this field, called the *Maximum Receive Unit (MRU)*, is set to the default of 1,500 bytes. Two hosts can negotiate for this to be set to a different value. The end of the data field is indicated by the 01111110 flag sequence.

- **Frame Check Sequence (FCS).** This 16-bit checksum makes sure the PPP packet has not been corrupted in transit. Some implementations can use a 32-bit check sum for improved error detection.

Link Control Protocol Phases

The Link Control Protocol provides the PPP protocol with a methodology for establishing, configuring, maintaining, and terminating a point-to-point connection. The following four phases are involved in the Link Control Protocol:

- Link establishment

- Authentication

- Network-layer protocol

- Link termination

The Link Establishment Phase

The link establishment phase uses the Link Control Protocol to establish a point-to-point connection by exchanging configuration packets.

At the beginning of the negotiation, it is assumed that all configurations are set to their default values. Negotiation only needs to occur for values being changed from their defaults.

Options configured during this phase are network-layer protocol independent. Network protocol-specific configuration is handled by the separate network-control protocol during the network-layer configuration phase.

The following options can be configured during this phase:

- **Maximum Receive Unit (MRU).** This option informs its peers that they can receive larger packets than the default size of 1,500 bytes. It also can request smaller packets for transmission.

- **Authentication Protocol.** This option selects a protocol for authentication. Valid options include the Password Authentication Protocol and the Challenge Authentication Protocol.

- **Quality of Link Protocol.** This option determines whether link monitoring is enabled. Link monitoring can determine how often the link drops data.

- **Magic Number.** This option detects a looped-back link. When a magic-number request is sent, the receiving host compares the magic number received to the magic number in the last configuration request sent to the peer. If the magic numbers do not match, the link is not looped back. If they match, the link might be looped back. To determine whether it gets looped back, a new magic number is selected by the protocol, and a new configure request is sent using this new magic number. If the magic numbers match again when the next configure request is received, the link is in a looped-back state.

- **Protocol field compression.** This option enables the compression of the PPP protocol field. Protocol field values are chosen so they can be compressed into a single octet (rather than the default 16 bits). If both peers agree to this option, the smaller, 8-bit version of the protocol field can be transmitted.

- **Address and Control field compression.** This option provides a method to negotiate the compression of the address and control fields. In a PPP link, the address and control fields have static addresses that easily can be compressed during transmission.

18

The Authentication Phase

This optional phase enables a peer to authenticate before network-layer protocols are exchanged. If authentication takes place, it should occur as soon as possible after the link is established.

 Note   The common authentication protocols used to authenticate remote access clients are described later today in the "Authenticating PPP Clients" section.

Network-Layer Protocol Phase

After the link establishment and authentication phases are complete, each network-layer protocol to be implemented during the session must be configured using the appropriate Network Control Protocol (NCP). Remember that PPP can be used to transport multiple protocols during the same session. After the network-layer protocol negotiation is complete, the link can transmit those protocols.

An example of network-layer protocol negotiation is the negotiation of an IP address for a remote client.

Link Termination Phase

PPP can terminate a link at any time. Any of the following can cause the termination of a link:

- Loss of carrier
- Authentication failure
- Link-quality failure
- Expiration of the idle-time timer
- Administrative closing of the link

The termination of the link is processed through an exchange of terminate packets.

Tunneling Solutions

Many organizations are examining other methods of enabling remote users to access the internal network. One method being implemented more frequently is tunneling. *Tunneling* enables a routable protocol (such as IP) to transfer the frames of another protocol to a destination network. The data can traverse public networks, private networks, and even wireless networks.

With the spread of broadband solutions for Internet access, you are now more likely to hear that a friend is connecting to the Internet using a cable modem or an Asynchronous Digital Subscriber Line (ADSL). These broadband solutions provide higher bandwidth connectivity to the Internet, but cost far less than traditional high bandwidth solutions.

At the sending end of the connection, software encapsulates the network packets so it can be transferred to the remote network. At the destination network, the receiving router decapsulates the original frame and sends it to the destination host.

Three solutions exist for the transfer of data over public networks through a tunnel:

- Point-to-Point Tunneling Protocol (PPTP)
- Layer Two Tunneling Protocol (L2TP)
- Point-to-Point Protocol over Ethernet (PPPoE)

The following sections look at each tunneling solution in detail, and discuss the network infrastructure required to support each tunneling protocol.

Components of a Virtual Private Network

Figure 18.2 shows the components in a Virtual Private Network (VPN).

FIGURE 18.2

Components of a Virtual Private Network.

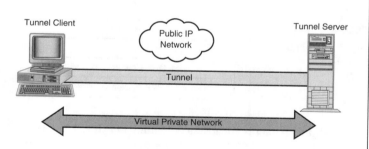

- **Tunnel server.** The tunnel server is configured with a protocol (such as PPTP) that can support a Virtual Private Network. The tunnel server can be configured to host multiple virtual network interfaces to enable connections from remote clients.
- **Tunnel client.** The tunnel client is configured with the same tunneling protocol as the tunnel server. The virtual network interface on the tunnel client must be configured to provide dial-out access.
- **Tunnel.** The tunnel is a logical connection established between the tunnel client and the tunnel server. Although the tunnel might cross several routers between the client and the server, it logically appears to be a single network hop. All data transmitted over the tunnel can be encrypted for secure communications.

18

> The tunnel client will either be connected to an IP network that provides connectivity to the tunnel server, or the tunnel client will use a dial-up connection to establish a PPP connection to the Internet, before launching a tunnel connecting the tunnel client to the tunnel server.

Point-to-Point Tunneling Protocol

RFC 2637 Point-to-Point Tunneling Protocol is a tunneling solution developed by a vendor consortium that was led by Microsoft Corporation and first made available in Windows NT 4.0 operating system and Windows 95 (with the installation of additional software). PPTP is now included as a default in all of its latest operating systems.

PPTP Packet Definitions

PPTP allows PPP packets to be transmitted over networks by encapsulating the packets in a Generic Routing Encapsulation (GRE) header. The only difference between the PPP packets used by PPTP and traditional PPP packets, is that the PPP packets used by PPTP do not have any media-specific framing information.

Figure 18.3 shows the general structure of PPTP packets as they are sent between a PPTP client and a PPTP server.

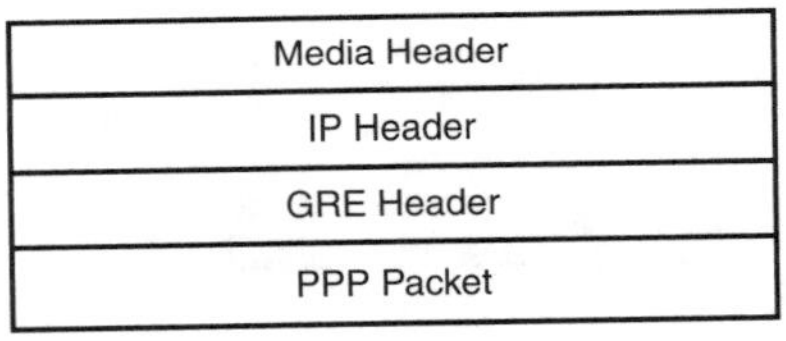

FIGURE 18.3

The PPTP packet structure.

Media Header
IP Header
GRE Header
PPP Packet

All PPTP data is encapsulated within a GRE header. The GRE header (defined in RFC 1701 and RFC 1702) is modified slightly for use with PPTP. The main modification is the inclusion of the Acknowledgement Number field. Rather than determining if GRE packets have successfully arrived at the other participant, the Acknowledgement Number field is used to determine the rate at which packets are transmitted through the tunnel. Figure 18.4 shows the GRE header format.

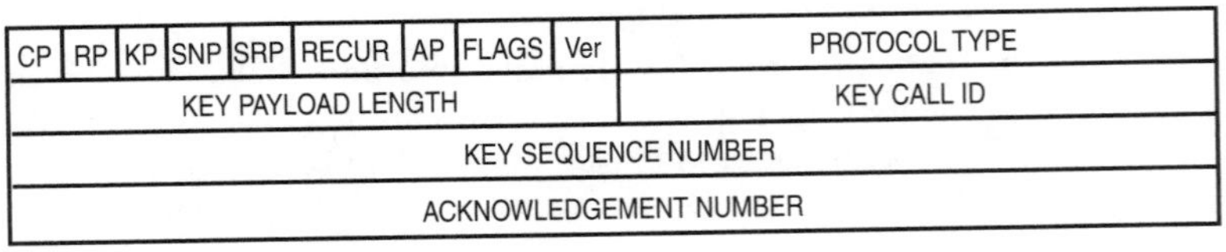

FIGURE 18.4

The GRE header format.

CP	RP	KP	SNP	SRP	RECUR	AP	FLAGS	Ver	PROTOCOL TYPE
KEY PAYLOAD LENGTH									KEY CALL ID
KEY SEQUENCE NUMBER									
ACKNOWLEDGEMENT NUMBER									

The GRE header includes the following fields:

- **Checksum Present (CP).** A 1-bit field that is set to 0. A separate checksum is not maintained for the GRE header.

- **Routing Present (RP).** A 1-bit field that is set to 0. All routing is handled by the IP header.

- **Key Present (KP).** A 1-bit field that is set to 1, indicating that an encryption key is included in the GRE header.

- **Sequence Number Present (SNP).** If the GRE packet contains data, the SNP is set to a value of 1; otherwise, the SNP is set to a value of 0 when the GRE packet is an acknowledgement only.

- **Strict Source Route Present (SRP).** A 1-bit field that is set to 0. Source routing options are set in the IP header.

- **Recursion Control (RECUR).** A 3-bit field set to a value of 0. All recursion control is defined by the IP header.

- **Acknowledgement Sequence Number Present (AP).** A 1-bit field that is set to a value of 1 if the packet contains an acknowledgement number for a previously transmitted GRE packet, or 0 if no acknowledgement number is present.

- **Flags.** A 4-bit field that is set to a value of 0.

- **Version (VER).** A 3-bit field that is set to a value of 1 to indicate an enhanced GRE packet format.

- **Protocol Type.** A 16-bit field that is set to a hexadecimal value of 880B.

- **Key Payload Length.** A 16-bit field that contains the size of the key payload, not including the GRE header.

- **Key Call ID.** A 16-bit field that contains the call ID used by the peer connection.

- **Key Sequence Number.** A 32-bit field that will contain the sequence number of the payload. This field value is only defined if the SNP field is set to a value of 1.

- **Acknowledgement Number.** A 32-bit field sent in acknowledgement packets indicating the highest numbered GRE packet received from the sending peer for the session. This field is only present if the AP field is set to a value of 1.

The actual payload of the GRE packet is contained in the PPP data packet.

PPTP Encryption

PPTP uses Microsoft Point-to-Point Encryption (MPPE) protocol to encrypt the payload information within the PPTP packet. The encryption key used by MPPE is based on a hash of the user's password when he authenticates with the PPTP server. While there

18

were some initial security issues with this method of generating the encryption key, enhancements in authentication security have reduced the fear of encryption failure.

PPTP Security Concerns

When PPTP first was released as a tunneling protocol, there were security issues found with the generation of key material used to encrypt the GRE payload. The problem was that the user's password provided to authenticate the PPTP connection was also used to derive the key material for the session.

When PPTP was first released, the authentication protocols used for the connection were not as strong as improved authentication protocols available today. In response to the security issues, Microsoft released modifications to PPTP that enabled stronger authentication schemes, such as MS-CHAPv2 and EAP/TLS that better secure the credential information provided for the PPTP connection.

For more information on the available authentication protocols for remote access connections, please see "Authenticating PPP Clients," the final section of today's material.

PPTP Server Deployment

PPTP servers can be deployed to allow connectivity to private network resources over a public network, such as the Internet. The benefit of using PPTP, when compared to L2TP/IPSec, is that GRE packets can pass through firewalls performing Network Address Translation (NAT).

Because the actual PPTP data is encapsulated in GRE packets, the actual connection to the PPTP server is a combination of a PPTP and GRE connection. The connection to the PPTP server is made to TCP port 1723 (the PPTP listening port) and all packets will be defined as containing protocol ID 47 (the protocol ID for GRE packets).

If you are configuring a firewall to allow connections to a PPTP server, you must configure the packet filters shown in Table 18.1.

TABLE 18.1 PPTP Packet Filters

Protocol	Source IP	Source Port	Destination IP	Destination Port	Action
TCP	Any	Any	PPTP Server IP	1723	Allow
ID 47	Any		PPTP Server IP		Allow

The first packet filter allows any client on the Internet to connect to the IP address of the PPTP server, if the connection is to TCP port 1723. The second packet filter allows GRE packets (protocol ID 47) to be sent from any client on the Internet to the IP address of the PPTP Server.

Layer Two Tunneling Protocol (L2TP)

RFC 2661 Layer Two Tunneling Protocol (L2TP) is an Internet standards-track protocol that also allows tunneling of sessions over TCP/IP networks. L2TP evolved from both Microsoft's PPTP protocol and Cisco's Layer Two Forwarding (L2F) protocol.

As with PPTP, an L2TP tunnel can be established between a client and a server or between two servers providing secure network connectivity over a public network such as the Internet.

The major difference between L2TP and PPTP is that L2TP does not have an encryption protocol built in to the protocol. Instead, encryption of L2TP packets is achieved by using Internet Protocol Security (IPSec) with Encrypting Security Payloads (ESP).

Note

> The use of IPSec for encryption prevents L2TP tunnels from passing through firewalls that perform Network Address Translation (NAT). While this is true at the time of writing this book, there are currently drafts before the Internet board on modifying IPSec to pass through NAT services.

18

The use of IPSec not only provides encryption services, but it also provides machine authentication of the tunnel endpoints. For the IPSec association to be established, both tunnel endpoints must authenticate using Kerberos, certificate-based authentication, or a shared secret. Besides the machine authentication, user authentication is also required for the successful establishment of an L2TP tunnel.

The establishment of an L2TP tunnel consists of two separate steps: the establishment of a control connection for the tunnel and the establishment of a session based on the call request.

Establishing the Control Connection

The first connection that is established between an L2TP client and a L2TP server is the control connection. In the control connection, the identity of the hosts at the tunnel endpoints, framing information, and L2TP versions is determined. This is done with an exchange of three messages.

1. Start-Control-Connection-Request (SCCRQ). A control message used to initialize a tunnel between an L2TP client and an L2TP server. The request is sent from a random UDP port at the client computer to UDP port 1701 at the L2TP server.

2. Start-Control-Connection-Reply (SCCRP). A control message that acknowledges that the SCCRQ was accepted and that tunnel establishment should continue.

3. Start-Control-Connection-Connected (SCCCN). A control message sent as a response to an SCCRP message. The SCCCN completes the tunnel establishment.

> **Control Message Contents**
>
> Each control message contains mandatory and optional attribute value pairs (AVPs). An AVP is the combination of a unique attribute and the value assigned to that attribute. For example, an SCCRQ must contain AVPs for Message Type, Protocol Version, Host Name, Framing Capabilities, and Assigned Tunnel ID.

L2TP allows authentication of the endpoints of the L2TP session. This is above the authentication of the host computers performed during the IPSec session establishment. The authentication can use any of the authentication protocols discussed at the end of today's material, and is performed by including the Challenge AVP in the SCCRQ or SCCRP messages. If the Challenge AVP is included in an SCCRQ or SCCRP message, the following SCCRP or SCCCN message must include the Challenge Response AVP to complete the authentication. Failure to do so, or if the response does not match the expected response, the tunnel establishment fails.

Establishing Sessions in the L2TP Tunnel

Once the L2TP control connection is established, individual sessions can be created. For each unique session, two sessions exist. One from the L2TP client to the L2TP server, and a second from the L2TP server to the L2TP client.

The initial session that is established occurs when the L2TP client requests that the L2TP server establish an incoming call session. This is done using a three-message exchange initiated by the L2TP client.

1. Incoming-Call-Request (ICRQ). An ICRQ message is sent from the L2TP client to the L2TP server when traffic destined to the network beyond the L2TP server is received by the L2TP client. The ICRQ message contains the parameter information required by the L2TP server to establish a session within the L2TP tunnel.

Note This traffic may originate from the client in a client-to-server connection, or from a client on the L2TP client's network in a server-to-server connection.

2. Incoming-Call-Reply (ICRP). An ICRP message is sent by the L2TP server to indicate that the ICRQ was successful and provides the L2TP client with any necessary parameters required by the L2TP server.

Note

In the case where the L2TP client is actually an L2TP server providing tunneling services between two networks, the L2TP client may actually wait before establishing a session with the initiating computer until the L2TP client receives an ICRP message from the L2TP server.

3. Incoming-Call-Connected (ICCN). An ICCN message is used to indicate that the ICRP was accepted, the call from the initiating computer has been answered, and that the session can now be designated as established. If any additional parameters must be defined for the session, they can be provided here.

Besides the incoming call being established, an outgoing call must also be established between the L2TP server and the L2TP client. This is also established using an exchange of three messages:

1. Outgoing-Call-Request (OCRQ). An OCRQ message is sent from the L2TP Server to the L2TP client to indicate that an outbound call from the L2TP client is to be established. The OCRQ message contains parameter information required by the L2TP server to establish a session within the L2TP tunnel.

2. Outgoing-Call-Reply (OCRP). An OCRP message is sent by the L2TP client to indicate that the OCRQ was successful and that the L2TP client can attempt the outbound call. The OCRP message contains parameter information about the call.

3. Outgoing-Call-Connected (OCCN). An OCCN message is sent from the L2TP client to the L2TP server to indicate that the result of a requested outgoing call was successful. If any additional parameters are required by the L2TP client, they are sent to the L2TP server at this time.

After the two sessions are established, PPP frames received at the L2TP client are stripped of Cyclic Redundancy Checking (CRC), link framing, and transparency bytes and then encapsulated into L2TP packets. The L2TP packets are assigned the negotiated session and tunnel IDs defined by the receiving host and then transmitted to the receiving host where the L2TP packet is decapsulated and treated as an incoming PPP packet.

18

L2TP Packet Definitions

L2TP uses the header format shown in Figure 18.5 to encapsulate data transferred between two hosts.

FIGURE 18.5

The L2TP header format.

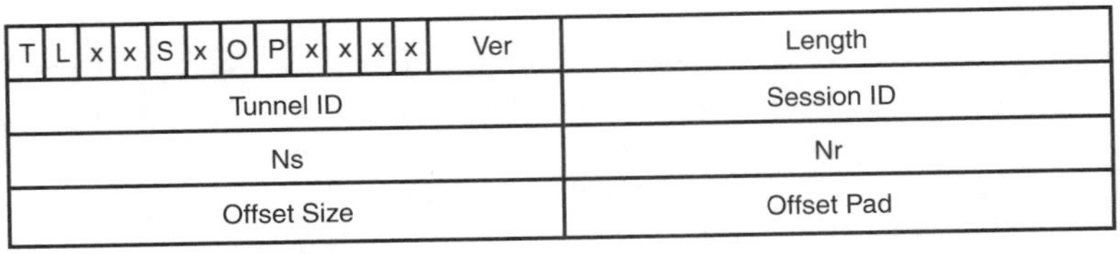

T	L	x	x	S	x	O	P	x	x	x	x	Ver	Length
Tunnel ID													Session ID
Ns													Nr
Offset Size													Offset Pad

The x bits in the header are reserved for future extensions and must be set to a value of 0 for outgoing messages and ignored for incoming messages. The other fields are as follows:

- **Type (T).** A 1-bit field that indicates whether the message is a data message (0) or a control message (1).
- **Length (L).** A 1-bit indicator field that indicates whether the Length field is present in the L2TP header.
- **Sequence (S).** A 1-bit field that indicates whether the Ns and Nr fields are present.
- **Offset (O).** A 1-bit field that indicates if the Offset Size field is present.
- **Priority (P).** A 1-bit field used to indicate that preferential treatment is required for the L2TP header for queuing and transmission. Priority is enabled by setting the Priority field to a value of 1.
- **Versions (Ver).** A 4-bit field that indicates the version of the L2TP message header. This is set to a value of 2 for L2TP packets. A value of 1 is reserved to detect L2F packets.
- **Length.** A 16-bit field that indicates the total length of the message in octets. This field is optional and must only be defined if the Length (L) field has a value of 1.
- **Tunnel ID.** A 16-bit field that indicates the identifier for the control connection. An L2TP tunnel has two unique identifiers, one for each end of the tunnel. When an L2TP packet is sent, the tunnel ID is set to the value of the recipient host, not the sending host. The tunnel ID is created during tunnel establishment.
- **Session ID.** A 16-bit field that uniquely identifies a session within the L2TP tunnel. As with tunnel IDs, two session IDs exist for a single session: one session ID in each direction.
- **Ns.** A 16-bit field that indicates the sequence number for the outbound data or control message. The initial value is always set to 0, and then incremented by one for each message sent.

- **Nr.** A 16-bit field that indicates the sequence number expected in the next control message to be received. The Nr field's value is set to the Ns value of the last message received incremented by one.
- **Offset Size.** An optional 16-bit field that indicates how many octets past the L2TP header exist before the payload data starts.
- **Offset Pad.** If an offset size is defined, and additional data is needed to end the data on a 16-bit boundary, offset padding is defined.

L2TP Server Deployment

As with PPTP servers, L2TP servers can be deployed to allow connectivity to private network resources over a public network such as the Internet. The major consideration you must face when deploying the L2TP server is that the L2TP server cannot be located behind a NAT service. In other words, if the L2TP server has an IP address in the RFC 1918 range (10.0.0.0/24, 172.16.0.0/20, or 192.168.0.0/16 are the network ranges defined by RFC 1918), then you will not be able to connect to the L2TP server. This is because of L2TP's dependence on IPSec using ESP for encryption services. At the time of this book's writing, IPSec cannot pass through NAT services. Currently, Internet drafts exist that propose a solution, but they have not become widely accepted.

So, if you want to deploy L2TP servers for remote access, then you must choose one of two deployment scenarios:

- Deploy the L2TP server on a network segment that is not protected by NAT.
- Deploy the L2TP server as a perimeter server that performs the NAT function itself, or has two interfaces, one on the Internet segment and one on the NAT'd segmented.

Caution

> If you are using two L2TP servers to tunnel information between two network segments, rather than having clients connect to an L2TP server, the firewall rules in the following section must be modified: You have to change the source IP address information from Any to the specific IP address of the other L2TP server.

Deploying an L2TP Server Behind a Firewall that Performs NAT

If an L2TP server is deployed behind a firewall that is not performing NAT, then the firewall must be configured to allow both Internet Key Exchange (IKE) and ESP packets to pass to the L2TP server.

18

> **Note** For more information on IKE and ESP packets, please review the material for Day 12, "Encrypting Transmitted Data."

If the L2TP server will allow connections to the L2TP server by numerous remote clients, the firewall packet filters must be configured to allow *any* client to connect to the L2TP server. This requires the packet filters in Table 18.2 to be configured at the firewall.

TABLE 18.2   L2TP Packet Filters for Multiple Clients

Protocol	Source IP	Source Port	Destination IP	Destination Port	Action
UDP	Any	500	L2TP Server IP	500	Allow
ID 50	Any		L2TP Server IP		Allow
ID 51	Any		L2TP Server IP		Allow*

* This packet filter is only required if the L2TP connection uses AH protection.

The first packet filters allow any client to negotiate an IPSec security association with the L2TP server using IKE. Of course, this also requires that the L2TP client authenticate the IPSec main mode connection using Kerberos, certificates, or shared secrets for the machine authentication.

Microsoft: No Kerberos Support

While IPSec supportsKerberos, certificates, and shared secrets for machine authentication, an L2TP client running Windows 2000 or Windows XP can only use certificates or shared secrets for machine authentication with the L2TP server. Kerberos authentication is not supported.

The second packet filter allows ESP packets to be transmitted from any L2TP client to the L2TP server.

> **Note** Even though L2TP packets are sent to UDP port 1701 at the L2TP server, you do not have to configure a packet filter for this port at the firewall. The data is encrypted as it passes through the firewall, and the firewall cannot see the port information with the ESP packets, only the protocol ID 50 indicating that the data is encrypted using ESP.

Deploying an L2TP Server as a Perimeter Server

If an L2TP server is deployed either as a perimeter server (with interfaces on both the Internet and the private network or DMZ), or as a service running on a firewall (as with Microsoft's Internet Security and Acceleration [ISA] Server), then different packet filters must be established at the L2TP server as shown in Table 18.3.

TABLE 18.3   L2TP Packet Filters on a Perimeter Server

Protocol	Source IP	Source Port	Destination IP	Destination Port	Action
UDP	Any	500	L2TP Server IP	500	Allow
ID 50	Any		L2TP Server IP		Allow
UDP	Any	Any	L2TP Server IP	1701	Allow

The first packet filters allow any client to negotiate an IPSec security association with the L2TP server using IKE. Of course, this also requires that the L2TP client authenticate the IPSec main mode connection using Kerberos, certificates, or shared secrets for the machine authentication. The second packet filter allows ESP packets to be transmitted from any L2TP client to the L2TP server.

The new packet filter that must be implemented is one that allows UDP 1701 packets to be sent to the L2TP server's IP address. This is because the firewall component of the L2TP server must inspect the transmitted data after the ESP packets are decapsulated. Now, the firewall does see that the L2TP packets are destined to UDP port 1701 on the L2TP server.

Point-to-Point Protocol over Ethernet (PPPoE)

RFC 2516   Point-to-Point Protocol over Ethernet (PPPoE) allows features of PPP to be deployed in ethernet networks so that individual connections can be authenticated, and makes use of LCP to negotiate options between a client and a server. PPPoE is targeted at broadband solutions, such as Internet Service Providers (ISPs) providing Asynchronous Digital Subscriber Line (ADSL) Internet access, to authenticate individual connections. Another scenario where ISPs use PPPoE is for cable modem deployments. The individual cable modems authenticate with the ISP to identify the individual cable modems, and prevent unauthorized cable modems from accessing Internet Services through the ISP.

PPPoE is used because it offers the ISP the ability to configure access control, service restrictions, or billing on a user-by-user basis.

18

PPPoE Session Establishment

A PPPoE connection consists of two separate stages: a discovery stage and a PPP session stage.

The discovery stage allows the client and the server to learn each host's Ethernet Media Access Control (MAC) address for communications and establish a session ID for the PPPoE session. Because there could be multiple servers available to which a client can connect, the discovery stage allows the host to discover all available servers.

There are different PPPoE packets that are involved in the PPPoE discovery stage:

- **PPPoE Active Discovery Initiation (PADI) packet.** A PADI packet has the destination address set to the ethernet broadcast address and the session identifier set to a value of 0x0000. This packet is sent to discover all available servers supporting PPPoE.

- **PPPoE Active Discovery Offer (PADO) packet.** A PADO packet is sent by a PPPoE server (also referred to as an Access Concentrator) in response to a PADI packet that it can process. The destination address is set to the ethernet MAC address of the requesting host. The PADO packet contains information (in TAG fields) that indicates the Access Concentrator's name and services offered by the Access Concentrator.

- **PPPoE Active Discovery Request (PADR) packet.** A PADR indicates which Access Concentrator the host has chosen (in the event that multiple PADO packets are received). The destination address of the PADR packet is set to the ethernet MAC address of the selected Access Concentrator.

- **PPPoE Active Discovery Session-confirmation (PADS) packet.** A PADS packet is sent by the Access Concentrator to the requesting host to generate the unique session identifier for the session. If the PADR packet requests a service type that is not supported by the Access Concentrator, a service name error is returned to the requesting host.

- **PPPoE Active Discovery Terminate (PADT) packet.** A PADT packet is used to terminate a PPPoE session and can be sent by either the host or the Access Concentrator.

After a server is selected and the ethernet MAC address information is determined for the client and the server, the two hosts can enter into a PPP session. When the PPP session stage is entered, the session moves from being a stateless to a stateful session.

The PPP session stage progresses like a PPP connection over public phone lines. For all data transmitted, the session identifier established in the discovery stage is used for all packets.

PPPoE Packet Definitions

PPPoE ethernet frames use the header format defined in Figure 18.6 to encapsulate data transferred from a client to a server over an ethernet network.

FIGURE 18.6

The PPPoE header format.

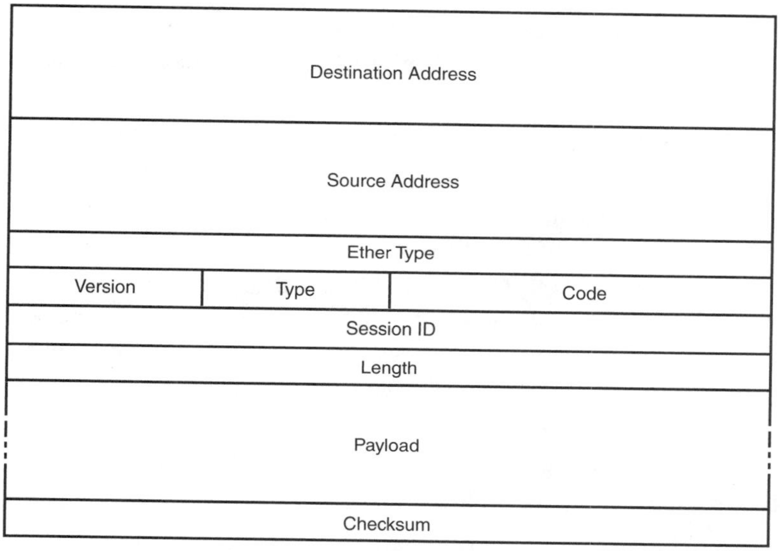

The header includes the following fields:

- **Destination Address.** A 48-bit field that contains either the ethernet Media Access Control (MAC) Address of the destination, or the ethernet broadcast address (0xffffffff).
- **Source Address.** A 48-bit field containing the ethernet MAC address of the originating host.
- **Ether Type.** A 16-bit field that contains the value 0x8863 during the discovery phase or 0x8864 during the PPP session stage.
- **Version.** A 4-bit field that is set to a value of 0001 for PPPoE packets.
- **Type.** A 4-bit field that is set to a value of 0001 for PPPoE packets.
- **Code.** An 8-bit field that is set to different values, depending on the PPP Discovery or PPP Session Stage:
  - 0x00. Used to identify that a PPP session is established.
  - 0x07. Used to identify a PPPoE Active Discovery Offer (PADO) packet.
  - 0x09. Used to identify a PPPoE Discovery Initiation (PADI) packet.

18

- 0x19. Used to identify a PPPoE Active Discovery Request (PADR) packet.
- 0x65. Used to identify a PPPoE Active Discovery Session-confirmation (PADS) packet.
- 0xa7. Used to identify a PPPoE Active8 Discovery Terminate (PADT) packet.

- **Session ID.** A 16-bit field that is set for a given PPP session and is used in combination with the Destination Address and Source Address to identify a specific PPP session.
- **Length.** A 16-bit field that defines the length of the PPPoE payload, excluding the ethernet or PPPoE headers.
- **Payload.** The payload of the PPPoE packet consists of zero or more tags. The tags consist of three fields:
    - *TAG_TYPE.* A 16-bit field that indicates what type of information is contained within the payload. For example, tag types exist for Denial of Service protection, Service Names, or error status information.
    - *TAG_LENGTH.* A 16-bit field that indicates the length of the TAG_VALUE field.
    - *TAG_VALUE.* A variable length field that contains the data based on the TAG_TYPE.
- **Checksum.** A 16-bit field that contains a checksum protecting the PPPoE packet against corruption or modification.

Authenticating PPP Clients

There are several protocols that are used by PPP clients to authenticate with a remote access server. The protocols are the same if the client is connecting using a dial-up connection, or a tunneling solution.

Analyzing Available Authentication Protocols

The protocols most commonly used for authentication of a remote access client include the following:

- **Password Authentication Protocol (PAP).** When PAP authentication is used, the user name and password of the remote access client are sent to the remote access server unencrypted. Because of the risk of password interception, PAP is not recommended unless you are troubleshooting a connection problem, or are connecting to an older remote access service that does not support more advanced authentication protocols.

- **Shiva Password Authentication Protocol (SPAP).** SPAP improves on PAP by having the remote access client send a Base64 encoded password to the Shiva remote access server. By using Base64, a two-way encoding algorithm, the Shiva remote access server can decode the password and compare the decrypted password to the clear-text version stored at the Shiva remote access server.

- **Challenge Handshake Authentication Protocol (CHAP).** CHAP improves security over PAP, by eliminating the unencrypted transmission of the user's account and password information. Instead, the remote access server sends a random challenge string to the remote access client. The remote access client then takes the challenge string and the user's inputted password and computes a Message Digest-5 (MD5) hash. The calculated hash is sent to the remote access server, where the same hash function is performed using the password stored in the local directory store. If the hashes match, the user is successfully authenticated.

Caution

> CHAP requires that either clear text versions of the password be stored in the directory, or at the minimum, a reversibly encryptable format. This too is considered a security risk, reducing the urge to deploy CHAP authentication.

18

- **Microsoft CHAP and Microsoft CHAP v2 (MS-CHAP and MS-CHAPv2).** Microsoft has implemented a custom version of CHAP that improves the security involved with the challenge response mechanism. MS-CHAP uses a Message Digest 4 (MD4) hashing algorithm and the Data Encryption Standard (DES) encryption algorithm to generate the challenge and response data. The authentication protocol was further enhanced in version 2 to support mutual authentication of both client and server, rather than just authenticating the client. In addition, different encryption keys are used for sent and received data.

- **Extensible Authentication Protocol (EAP).** EAP is an extension to PPP that allows new authentication methods to be used for remote access connections. EAP allows for stronger authentication methods such as smart cards, secure ID tokens, or biometric authentication to be implemented.

Note

> Windows 2000 introduced EAP-MD5 and EAP-TLS as authentication protocols. EAP-TLS allows smart card authentication for remote access authentication.

Deciding Whether to Centralize or Decentralize Authentication

One of the biggest decisions faced when deploying a remote access solution is whether to centralize authentication against a single account database.

In earlier deployments, authentication was always performed by the remote access server that receives the connection from the remote access client.

Remote Authentication Dial-In User Service (RADIUS) allows the authentication to be centralized at a single account repository. Rather than having each remote access server individually authenticate remote access connections, the authentication attempts are forwarded to a RADIUS server. This allows multiple remote access servers to forward their authentication requests to the same RADIUS server. The RADIUS server then authenticates the remote access clients using PAP, SPAP, CHAP, or EAP.

> **RADIUS Accounting Services**
>
> Besides centralizing remote access authentication, RADIUS also provides a centralized remote access accounting service, which includes information such as who connected using a remote connection and how long they remained connected. This assists in analyzing connection habits for an organization and billing to specific departments or individuals.

Examining RADIUS Roles

In a RADIUS deployment, there are several roles that are fulfilled by the components of the RADIUS system:

- **RADIUS Client.** A RADIUS client is a remote access server that is configured to forward authentication and/or accounting requests to a configured RADIUS server.
- **RADIUS Server.** A RADIUS server receives an authentication request on UDP port 1812 and validates the authentication request using a central database such as a Unix Network Information Services (NIS) or Windows Active Directory database. If configured to perform centralized accounting requests, the RADIUS server will look for these requests on UDP port 1813.
- **RADIUS Proxy.** In some instances, an organization such as an ISP, will accept remote access connections from users in multiple organizations. A RADIUS proxy can inspect prefixes and suffixes provided by the remote access user and determine which RADIUS server to forward the request to.

> ### Remote Access Clients
>
> The only time that configuration must be performed at a remote access client is when a RADIUS proxy exists in your RADIUS solution. If a RADIUS proxy exists, the remote access client must be configured to add a prefix, suffix, or both a prefix and suffix, to the user-name so that the RADIUS proxy can forward the authentication request to the correct RADIUS server.

RADIUS Packet Format

RFC 2138   A UDP packet is used to transmit a single RADIUS packet in the UDP packet's data field. The RADIUS packet is sent to UDP port 1812 for authentication requests and UDP port 1813 for accounting requests.

> ### Port Changes for RADIUS
>
> An earlier version of the RADIUS RFC recommended using UDP port 1645 for authentication and UDP port 1646 for accounting, but these ports conflicted with the datametrics service and were changed.

18

The format of a RADIUS packet is shown in Figure 18.7.

FIGURE 18.7

The RADIUS packet format.

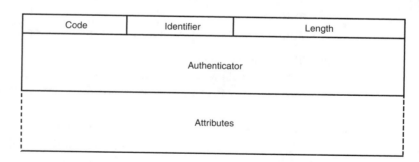

The format includes the following fields:

- **Code.** An 8-bit field that contains one of the following RADIUS codes:
    - *Access-Request (1).* A code value of 1 indicates that the RADIUS client has forwarded authentication information for a user attempting to authenticate against the RADIUS server. The access-request contains information specific to the authentication attempt. This can include the user-name attribute, NAS-identifier, and user-password or CHAP-password.

- *Access-Accept (2)*. A code value of 2 indicates that the access-request submitted by a RADIUS client is acceptable to the RADIUS server and remote access is granted.

- *Access-Reject (3)*. A code value of 3 indicates that the access-request submitted by a RADIUS client contains one or more attributes that are not acceptable to the RADIUS server. The message may contain a text message that is displayed to the authenticating user.

- *Accounting-Request (4)*. A code value of 4 indicates that an accounting request is being sent from a RADIUS client or a RADIUS proxy to a RADIUS server. The RADIUS packet is re-sent until an acknowledgement is received from the RADIUS server.

- *Accounting-Response (5)*. A code value of 5 indicates that an account-response is being sent from the RADIUS server to a RADIUS proxy or RADIUS client indicating that the accounting information was recorded at the RADIUS server.

- *Access-Challenge (11)*. A code value of 11 indicates that the RADIUS server wants to challenge the user. The access-challenge is matched to a previous access-request by the identifier field.

- *Status-Server (12)*. A code value of 12 is reserved for experimental purposes as of today.

- *Status-Client (13)*. A code value of 13 is reserved for experimental purposes as of today.

- *Reserved (255)*. A code value of 255 is reserved for future use.

- **Identifier.** An 8-bit field that is used to match RADIUS requests with RADIUS replies. This field allows a RADIUS server to identify duplicate requests by comparing the Identifier field with the source IP and source port fields from the UDP and IP headers.

- **Length.** A 16-bit field that identifies the length of the packet. The length includes the Code, Identifier, Length, Authenticator, and Attribute fields. The length must be a value between 20 and 4096, or the RADIUS packet is discarded.

- **Authenticator.** A 128-bit field that has varying content depending on whether the RADIUS packet is a request or a response.

  - A request authenticator contains an unpredictable, unique value that only exists for a single access attempt. The shared secret between the RADIUS client and the RADIUS server is put through a one-way MD5 hash, resulting in a 128-bit value. The hash value is then compared to the password entered by the user using an Exclusive Or function, and the Exclusive Or function result is placed in the User-password attribute of an Access-Request packet.

- A response authenticator contains a one-way MD5 hash calculated against the following fields in an Access-Accept, Access-Reject, or Access-Challenge message: Code, Identifier, Request Authenticator field, Attributes, and the shared secret.

- **Attributes.** This variable length field contains specific authentication, authorization, and configuration details for an authentication request and reply. The actual amount of attributes is defined by the Length field for the RADIUS packet.

Applying What You Have Learned

Today we looked at technologies that enable remote users to connect to an organization's private network remotely. As more users take part in mobile computing, the need to provide remote access to the internal network increases. Expect to see more advances in securing remote access, and propagation of tunneling solutions. With Internet drafts on passing IPSec through NAT, the solutions that we see may change greatly, once the IPSec through NAT standard is defined.

18

Test Your Knowledge

Here are questions to check what you've learned today. The answers can be found in Appendix B, "Test Your Knowledge: Answers."

1. What are some of the deficiencies of the SLIP protocol?
2. What forms of authentication can the PPP protocol use?
3. How does SLIP frame the data it transmits over a serial line?
4. Can PPP be used to transmit multiple protocols over a single dial-up session?
5. What role does the Link Control Protocol (LCP) play in a PPP connection?
6. What are the three main components of a Virtual Private Network (VPN)?
7. What packet filters are required at a firewall to pass through PPTP traffic?
8. What packet filters are required at a firewall to pass through L2TP traffic?
9. Under what scenarios is PPPoE used to provide tunneling services?
10. What function does a RADIUS proxy play in remote access authentication?
11. What RADIUS component allows an ISP to support multiple client RADIUS implementations at the same time?

Preview of Day 19

Tomorrow you'll see some of the future applications of the TCP/IP protocol. Specifically, the following "bleeding edge" uses of TCP/IP are overviewed:

- Using IP in an ATM network
- Using IP in a Wireless Network
- Transmitting Voice data over IP networks

DAY 19

ATM, Wireless, and Voice over IP

TCP/IP is being used in alternative network architectures. Although these architectures are not implemented in every network, it is important to be familiar with them. In the first part of the day you examine the issues involved with implementing TCP/IP on an ATM network. These issues exist because ATM devices do not have a physical hardware address. The following details of implementing TCP/IP over ATM are discussed:

- Using TCP/IP in an ATM environment
- The ATMARP packet structure
- Implementing an ATMARP server
- ATMARP transactions

Then we discuss using IP in a wireless network environment. The 802.11 frame type allows IP packets to be used in a wireless environment. We look at how IP works in a wireless network and two methods of securing the wireless transmissions.

We end the day with a look at voice communication over an IP network.

Using TCP/IP in an ATM Network

RFC 2225 Asynchronous Transfer Mode (ATM) is used to transmit data, voice, and video over a network at speeds exceeding 145Mbps. The enhanced speed enables simultaneous transmission of all three data types. With the increasing demand for multimedia presentations over TCP/IP networks, the use of technologies such as ATM will continue to grow.

A major issue with running IP over an ATM network is that ATM devices do not have a hardware address. Instead, they have an ATM address that can be extended to represent the hardware address for an ATM device. For TCP/IP to function correctly in an ATM network, a modified version of the address-resolution protocol ATMARP must be used to resolve an IP address to an ATM address. A modified version of reverse ARP, InATMARP, resolves an ATM address to an IP address.

Another issue when TCP/IP is implemented in an ATM network is that ATM does not support the use of broadcasts. As a result, there is no way to map an IP broadcast address to an ATM broadcast address.

The ATMARP Packet

An IP address is assigned directly to each ATM device, independent of its ATM address. For IP addressing to function in an ATM environment, each host must have the following configuration information:

- The ATM host must know its ATM address.
- The ATM host must know its IP address and subnet mask configuration.
- The ATM host must respond to any address-resolution requests to resolve an IP address to its ATM address, or vice versa.
- The ATM host must use ATMARP and InATMARP to resolve IP addresses to ATM addresses when necessary.
- Each ATM host must have an ATMARP request address configured. This is the ATM address of an ATMARP server located on the network where the ATM host is located. In a switched virtual-connection environment, all ATMARP requests are sent to this address for resolution of IP addresses to ATM addresses.

ATMARP and InATMARP packets are similar in format to an ARP packet. Figure 19.1 shows the detailed ATMARP packet format.

FIGURE 19.1

The ATMARP packet.

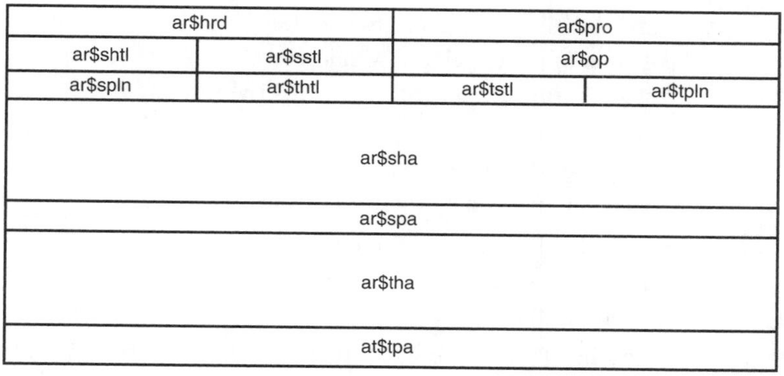

ar$hrd		ar$pro	
ar$shtl	ar$sstl	ar$op	
ar$spln	ar$thtl	ar$tstl	ar$tpln
ar$sha			
ar$spa			
ar$tha			
at$tpa			

Fields in the packet include the following:

- **ar$hrd.** The Hardware Type field is a 16-bit field that contains the hexadecimal value 0x0013 to indicate that the hardware in use is an ATM device.

- **ar$pro.** The Protocol Type field is a 16-bit field that contains the hexadecimal value 0x0800 to indicate that the protocol in use is IP.

- **ar$shtl.** The Sender's Hardware Length field is an 8-bit field that contains the length of the sender's ATM address. If the ATM address implemented is a 20-octet address (as recommended by the ATM forum), this field is set to a value of 20.

- **ar$sstl.** The Sender's Sub-address Length field in an 8-bit field that contains the length of the sender's ATM sub-address. If the ATM address scheme is implemented as recommended by the ATM forum, this field is set to a value of 0.

- **ar$op.** The Operation Type field is an 8-bit field that contains the operation in the ATMARP packet. Table 19.1 shows the allowed values for the operation type.

TABLE 19.1 The ATM Operation Types

Operation Code	Description
1	An ATMARP request
2	An ATMARP reply
8	An Inverse ATMARP request
9	An Inverse ATMARP reply
10	An ATMARP negative acknowledgment

- **ar$spln.** The Sender's Protocol Address Length field is an 8-bit field that contains the length of the source protocol address in octets. For an IP address, this field is set to a value of 4.

19

- **ar$thtl.** The Target's Hardware Length field is an 8-bit field that contains the length of the target's ATM address. If the ATM address implemented is a 20-octet address (as recommended by the ATM forum), this field is set to a value of 20.

- **ar$tstl.** The Target's Sub-address Length field in an 8-bit field that contains the length of the target's ATM sub-address. If the ATM address scheme is implemented as recommended by the ATM forum, this field is set to a value of 0.

- **ar$tpln.** The Target's Protocol Address Length field is an 8-bit field that contains the length of the source protocol address in octets. For an IP address, this field is set to a value of 4.

- **ar$sha.** The Source ATM Address field is a 160-bit field that contains the source's ATM address. The length of this field is based on the ATM forum recommended addressing scheme.

- **ar$ssa.** The Source ATM Sub-address field is not shown in Figure 19.1 because the figure shows the ATMARP packet structure when the ATM forum recommended addressing scheme is utilized.

- **ar$spa.** The Source Protocol Address field's length is based on the information stored in the ar$spln field. For an IP address, the length of this field is 32 bits, and it contains the source host's IP address.

- **ar$tha.** The Target ATM Address field is a 160-bit field that contains the target's ATM address. The length of this field is based on the ATM forum recommended addressing scheme.

- **ar$tsa.** The Target ATM Sub-address field is not shown in Figure 19.1 because the figure shows the ATMARP packet structure when the ATM forum recommended addressing scheme is utilized.

- **ar$tpa.** The Target Protocol Address field's length is based on the information stored in the ar$tpln field. For an IP address, the length of this field is 32 bits, and it contains the target host's IP address.

Dividing the Network into Logical IP Subnets

Logical IP subnets (LISs) are used in an ATM environment to group ATM hosts into a closed IP subnetwork. Every ATM host in an LIS has the same network and subnetwork IP addressing scheme. If two hosts in the same LIS want to communicate with each other, they do so using a direct connection. To communicate with an ATM host that is not a member of the same LIS, IP transmission must take place through an IP router. In this case, the IP router is an ATM device configured as a member of one or more LISs. The router can also have an alternate interface that is not an ATM device.

The following conditions must be met for all ATM hosts participating in an LIS:

- All members must be part of the same IP network and subnetwork.
- All members in an LIS must be directly connected to the same ATM network.
- All members outside the LIS must be accessed using an IP router.
- All members of the LIS must implement a mechanism to resolve IP addresses to ATM addresses (ATMARP).
- All members of the LIS must implement a mechanism to resolve ATM addresses to IP addresses (InATMARP).
- The ATM network must be fully meshed. The term fully meshed means that all members of an LIS must be able to communicate with all other members of their LIS.

Multiple LISs on the Same Physical Network

Multiple LISs can exist on the same ATM network. A different IP network address must be implemented for each LIS. Even though multiple LISs can exist on the same physical network, communication between hosts in different LISs must occur using an IP router that is a member of both LISs (see Figure 19.2).

FIGURE 19.2

The ATM network with two logical IP subnets.

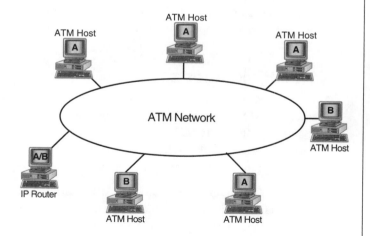

In Figure 19.2, the ATM hosts are broken into two LISs, A and B. Any communication between hosts in different LISs must be transmitted using the ATM host labeled as the IP router. This ATM host has been configured to belong to both LISs.

19

The ATMARP Server

A single ATMARP server must be configured within each LIS. This server resolves all ATMARP requests by IP ATM hosts within the LIS.

The ATMARP server is a passive server. It depends on its clients to initiate the ATMARP registration process. Remember, all ATM hosts that utilize TCP/IP must have a configured ATM request address.

Registering an IP Address with the ATM Server

When the ATM host starts, it connects to the ATMARP server using a point-to-point virtual connection. After the server has been established, the ATMARP server sends an inverse ATMARP (InATMARP) request to determine the configured IP address of the ATM host. The ATM server uses information in the InATMARP reply to build its ATMARP table cache. This cache is used to generate replies to ATMARP requests.

When the ATM server receives the InATMARP reply, the ATM server examines the ATM address and the IP address. If the entry is not found in the ATMARP table cache, the entry is added. If a matching entry is found on both the IP address and the ATM address, the ATM server updates the time stamp on the entry with the new date and time. If the InATMARP reply matches on the IP address but not the ATM address, the packet is discarded because this represents a duplicate IP address on the network. This occurs only when there is also an open virtual circuit with the entry in the current ATMARP table cache.

ATMARP Requests

When an ATM host sends an ATMARP request to the ATM server, the ATM server generates an ATMARP reply based on information in the ATMARP table cache. If no entry is found, a negative ATMARP reply is returned. Sending a negative ATMARP reply indicates to the client that the ATM server received the request but did not have an ATM address mapping for the requested IP address.

When the ATM server receives an ATMARP request, it updates the timeout for the source's entry in the ATMARP table cache. This indicates that the client is still alive. If the source IP address is in the ATMARP request, the ATM server checks to see whether the IP address is registered in the ATMARP table cache. If it is not, the server adds the ATM address, IP address, and time stamp into the ATMARP table. It associates the entry with the virtual circuit used to send the ATMARP request.

When the client receives the ATMARP reply, it adds the ATM and IP address information to its own ATMARP table cache.

Aging of ATMARP Table Entries

On a client system, an ATM host sets a lifetime of 15 minutes on each ATMARP table entry. On the ATMARP server, each table entry is valid for a minimum of 20 minutes. When the timer expires on an ATMARP entry, the table entries are handled differently than in the case of normal ARP aging.

On the ATM server, an InATMARP request is sent on the virtual circuit associated with the entry. If an InATMARP reply is received, the table entry is updated rather than deleted. If the associated virtual circuit is not open, the ATMARP table entry is deleted.

An ATMARP client, however, must prove that the table entry no longer is valid before it can remove the ATMARP table entry. As with the ATMARP server, the table entry is deleted if a virtual circuit is not open. If a virtual circuit is open, the ATMARP client must revalidate the entry before regular traffic can resume. With a permanent virtual circuit, an InATMARP request is sent directly over the virtual circuit. With a switched virtual circuit, an ATMARP request is sent to the ATMARP server. The ATMARP reply is used to update the client's ATMARP table cache.

TCP/IP in a Wireless Network

One of fastest growing areas in network connectivity is the use of wireless networks. Wireless networks allow connectivity between computers using radio transmissions in the unlicensed 2.4GHz band.

Wireless LANS have become more popular or used more because of the increased use of mobile computing. When attending a meeting, the use of wireless networking allows network connectivity for laptops without having to install a hub or switch in the meeting room with a connection for each participant in the meeting.

In a more personal application, rather than do the "geek" thing and put ethernet drops in each room of my house, I found it more cost effective and flexible to install a 3Com Wireless network. This allows me to connect to the Internet and to the office from anywhere in the vicinity of my home, including the neighbor's backyard.

Wireless Network Configurations

The most common wireless network in use today is a network that makes use of the IEEE's 802.11 standard. The 802.11 standard proposes two different methods of configuring a network: ad-hoc networking and infrastructure networking.

In an ad-hoc network (see Figure 19.3), every node in the wireless network establishes links with the other nodes in the wireless network.

19

FIGURE 19.3

A wireless ad-hoc network.

An ad-hoc network is a good choice for cases such as the meeting example mentioned earlier. The attendees at the meeting could communicate with each other in an ad-hoc mode. While the ad-hoc network is great for quick-and-dirty networks, it does not scale well for larger networks.

The infrastructure network provides the capability to scale to larger networks as shown in Figure 19.4.

In an infrastructure network, Access Points (AP) are deployed and the wireless clients (or stations) associate with an AP. As shown in Figure 19.4, the APs can be connected to the physical ethernet network and act as a bridge between the wireless stations and the corporate network. In an infrastructure network, multiple APs can exist and a wireless station can associate with the nearest AP. Each AP will have a configured Service Set Identifier (SSID) that is used by the wireless stations to identify the Access Point that the wireless station is associated with.

FIGURE 19.4

A wireless infrastruc-
ture network.

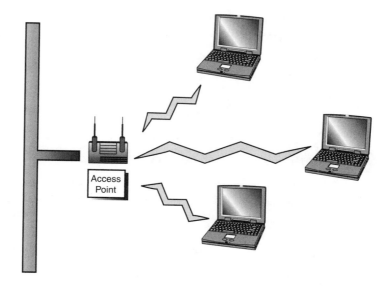

MAC Addressing

When a wireless station is started, the wireless station uses the following algorithm to
connect to a wireless network.

1. If the wireless station is not associated with an AP, the wireless station will attempt
   to associate with any wireless network that is beaconing its network name. For
   example, Windows XP provides you with the capability to view the available
   wireless networks as shown in Figure 19.5.

19

FIGURE 19.5

Browsing available
wireless networks.

2. If the initial association fails, the wireless station will attempt to associate with any
   other available wireless networks.

3. The process is repeated until no more wireless networks are available. At this point, the wireless station switches to ad-hoc network mode.

4. The wireless station periodically attempts to connect to any new wireless networks that become available.

When the wireless station associates with an AP, the wireless station opens the communication path, allowing TCP/IP communications to proceed as if the wireless station were physically connected to the network.

Security in Wireless Networks

One of the major concerns with wireless networks is the need for security. By their very nature, wireless networks have more potential for security risks than a wired network. A wireless network transmits data to an area that may extend beyond the physical boundaries of the organization. For example, without security, my neighbors could connect to the Internet and my home network using wireless adapters.

This could lead to an attacker intercepting network data transmissions and viewing the contents of the transmitted data.

To provide security in a wireless network, the initial proposal involved the Wired Equivalent Privacy (WEP) algorithm. While this algorithm provides encryption of transmitted data, it was found that the encryption was not strong enough, and could lead to data being compromised.

To further secure wireless transmission, the 802.1x standard is coming to the forefront to provide stronger and more flexible security for wireless networks by using EAP/TLS.

Wireless Network Component Authentication

When a wireless station connects to an AP, the following process is used to authenticate the wireless station with the AP:

1. The wireless station sends an Authentication frame to the AP.

2. The AP replies with an authentication frame containing a 128-bit random challenge text string.

3. The wireless station encrypts the challenge text string using a shared key and then sends the encrypted data to the AP.

 Note

802.11 is not specific in how the shared key is distributed to each wireless station. Whatever method is used to distribute the key, the actual key value is stored at both the wireless station and the AP.

4. The AP decrypts the encrypted data and compares the decrypted data with the challenge string sent to the wireless station. If the strings match, the authentication is successful.

Wireless Equivalent Privacy (WEP)

The WEP algorithm was introduced in the 802.11b standard to provide a method for encryption and protecting against modification of data transmitted in a wireless network. WEP uses a symmetric encryption algorithm, meaning that the same key is used for both encryption and decryption of data. Figure 19.6 describes the WEP encryption process:

FIGURE 19.6

WEP encryption and integrity protection.

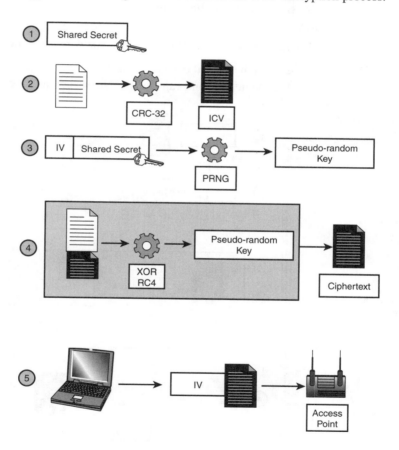

1. A shared secret used by the wireless station when connecting to the AP is retrieved from the station's Management Information Base (MIB). One of the security concerns with WEP is that many implementations generate the secret key based on the

user's password. If a poor password is selected, this can lead to a weakness in the secret key.

2. The Integrity Check Value (ICV) is calculated by passing the plaintext message through the CRC-32 integrity algorithm. This produces a 32-bit ICV.

3. A random Initialization Vector (IV) is concatenated with the shared secret. This combined package is inputted into the Pseudo-Random Number Generator (PRNG). The PRNG uses the RC4 algorithm to produce a pseudo-random key.

4. Ciphertext is created by putting the ICV/plaintext pair through an RC4 Exclusive/Or (XOR) function with the pseudo-random key between the plaintext and ICV.

5. The IV and ciphertext are sent to the AP by the wireless station.

When the AP receives the IV and ciphertext, the following process (shown in Figure 19.7) is used to decrypt and validate the data sent from the wireless station.

FIGURE 19.7

WEP decryption and integrity verification.

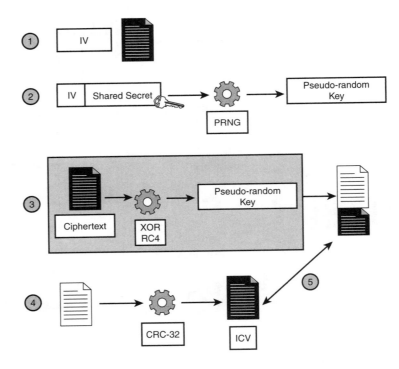

1. The IV is stripped from the packet received from the wireless station.

2. The IV is concatenated with the shared secret, and the combined data is passed through the PRNG RC4 algorithm to calculate the pseudo-random key.

3. The ciphertext is put through an RC4 XOR function with the pseudo-random key to arrive at the ICV/plaintext pair.

4. The extracted plaintext has the CRC-32 algorithm applied to arrive at an ICV value.

5. The calculated ICV value is compared with the ICV value decrypted in step 3. If the two ICV values are equivalent, the message has not been modified. If they differ, then an error is sent back to the wireless station.

The WEP algorithm depends on the IV. Remember that the shared secret remains constant for the wireless station and the AP. It is the IV that extends the lifetime of the shared secret by making the total key material random. Unfortunately, with the total length of the key material being 64 bits (a 40-bit shared secret and a 24-bit IV), over time, the same key material is re-used. This can ultimately result in a decryption of the protected data.

Note

Although 40-bit is the length defined in the 802.11b standard, most vendors implement 128-bit encryption using a 104-bit shared secret and a 24-bit IV.

802.1x Wireless Authentication

The use of symmetric key encryption using a nonchanging key is leading to the downfall of the WEP algorithm. Many papers released recently have exposed that the WEP algorithm did not use a strong enough key and that it allows for the determination of the secret key. By determining the secret key, decryption of confidential data is possible.

To provide better security to wireless networks, the IEEE 802.1x draft standard uses RADIUS authentication to protect the exchange of the WEP key. The RADIUS authentication requires that certificate-based authentication is used to authenticate the wireless station with the AP using Extensible Authentication Protocol with Transport Layer Security (EAP/TLS). This authentication requires that the client will have previously obtained a certificate. Typically, the certificate is obtained using a wired, rather than a wireless, network.

19

Note

EAP provides a defined set of services that the network can provide in an 802.1x frame that standard upper-layer security protocols like Kerberos and TLS can be used to provide encryption, authentication, and key exchange.

In addition, 802.1x enhances security in the following ways:

- A wireless station can't connect to the network until the user at the wireless station is successfully authenticated.
- The WEP encryption keys are no longer a shared secret. The keys are rotated on a per-session basis and can be renewed based on time or amount of data transmitted.
- Industry standard authentication schemes, including RADIUS and EAP/TLS, are used to mutually authenticate the authentication server and the user at the wireless station.

When 802.1x is implemented, the AP acts as a RADIUS proxy to a RADIUS server. All authentication requests sent to the AP are forwarded by the AP to the configured RADIUS server.

The AP provides what is known as port-based access control. A single 802.11 port becomes many IEEE 802.1x ports. When wireless stations are associated with the AP, each association ID is mapped to one of the virtual ports.

At the AP, the first logical access point is an uncontrolled port. This uncontrolled port allows the exchange of data between the AP and wireless stations no matter what the authentication state of the wireless stations is. The second logical port is a controlled port. Only data exchanges between authorized wireless stations and the AP are allowed through this port.

The 802.1x authentication is shown in Figure 19.8.

FIGURE 19.8

The initial stages of 802.1x authentication.

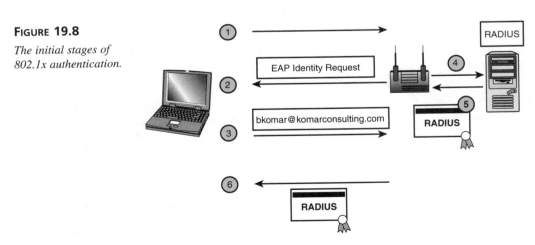

It proceeds as follows:

1. The Wireless station forms an 802.11 association with an AP.

2. The AP sends the wireless station an EAP identity request.

3. The wireless station responds by sending its EAP identity to the access point. The identity consists of the user's username and domain. For example, bkomar@komar-consulting.com.

4. The AP forwards this request to the RADIUS server over its uncontrolled port.

5. After receiving the wireless station's EAP identity, the RADIUS server requests a user certificate that is associated with the identity it just received and sends the RADIUS server's certificate to the AP.

6. The AP forwards the certificate request to the wireless station.

7. The wireless station validates the server certificate it receives and sends its own user certificate back to the AP (see Figure 19.9).

FIGURE 19.9

The final stages of 802.1x authentication.

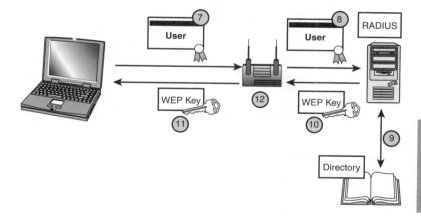

8. The AP forwards the certificate to the RADIUS Server.

9. The RADIUS Server checks with its configured directory service to ensure that the user information in the identity packet is indeed associated with the user certificate received from the client. If not, the RADIUS server sends an authentication failure message to the access point.

10. Upon successful authentication, the RADIUS server sends a success message to the AP along with a usable WEP key for the session.

11. The AP forwards the WEP Key to the wireless station. This WEP key is used for the entire session in which the wireless station is associated with the Access Point.

12. The AP opens the controlled port to give the wireless station access to network resources.

When the AP opens its controlled port to the wireless station, the wireless station can now use the provided WEP key to encrypt all transmissions to the AP. After encryption is established, the wireless station either initializes its preconfigured IP address information, or contacts a DHCP server to acquire a network IP address. From this point on, communications proceed as they did in a pure 802.11b network, with the difference that both the WEP key and the IV are randomized.

Voice over IP

More and more people are discussing the concept of using the Internet as a backbone for voice conversations. *Voice over IP (VoIP)* technology uses the Internet, a packet-switched network, to transport digitized voice data to a destination host. This technology is being researched because of the cost savings for the participants, who can use local phone calls to access the Internet for any-distance voice conversation instead of having to use long-distance phone service. If a participant has a broadband connection to the Internet, then a local phone call is not recognized.

The Conversion of the Voice Input

The actual voice input is transported as digitized data. The digitization of voice data falls into one of these categories: voice coders or waveform coders.

Voice coders use speech input to create a signal that resembles the original voice input. The voice coder is configured to use a specific speech model. The created signal is analyzed against the speech model, and a set of parameters is generated. It is this set of parameters that is transmitted to the destination station. The destination station uses these parameters to reconstruct the speech input.

Waveform coders directly encode the waveform generated by analog speech. It does so by sampling the voice input and converting the amplitude of each sample to the nearest value from a finite set of discrete values. An example of this technology is Pulse Code Modulation (PCM).

Issues Affecting the Implementation of VoIP

The following issues need to be resolved before Voice over IP becomes a day-to-day reality:

- Voice over IP requires timely delivery. If a packet of a voice message is delayed, there are long pauses in the transmission while the destination hosts await delivery of the missing packet.

- Many users connect to the Internet using modems over *Public Switched Telephone Networks (PSTN)*. When users connect to the Internet, they generally are assigned random IP addresses. Without a centralized directory service, it is difficult to ascertain the IP address of your destination host.

- Originally, VoIP required the two connecting hosts to have similar equipment. Each end of the connection required a modem, the same Voice over IP software (such as the Internet Telephone), and a voice input device such as a microphone (see Figure 19.10).

FIGURE 19.10

Performing Voice over IP using modems.

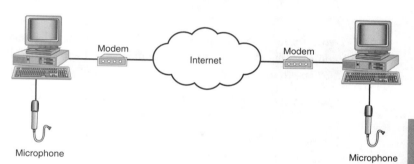

- Voice over IP requires a large amount of bandwidth for timely transport of digitized voice data. The *Resource Reservation Protocol (RSVP)* is a solution to this problem. Routers can request a specific size of bandwidth pipe through the network using the RSVP protocol. This protocol can be used by Voice over IP software to set minimum performance requirements that must be met for transmission to be attempted.

The Future Direction of VoIP

The next generation of Voice over IP will enable users to connect to remote users using a regular phone. This functionality is facilitated by the use of phone gateways (see Figure 19.11).

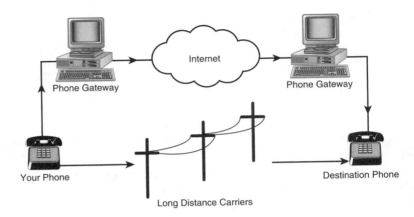

FIGURE 19.11

*Voice over IP utilizing
phone gateways.*

By using phone gateways, this methodology hides the fact that participants are using the
packet-switched technology of the Internet rather than the circuit-switched technology of
the PSTN. To users, the phone call appears to be taking place over normal long-distance
carriers.

The VoIP forum has been operating as a group in the International Multimedia
Teleconferencing Consortium. This forum is working to further the progress of Voice
over IP. The following are the main tasks of the VoIP forum:

- Defining and establishing a set of open, consistent guidelines for the implementation of devices that perform voice communications over IP protocol data networks.

- Ensuring seamless product interoperability and high quality of service.

- Developing a standard for addressing so routers will know how to locate and
  address remote users.

You can use Voice over IP using clients such as Microsoft's Windows Messenger or
Net2Phone. Both applications allow free PC to PC communications, but you can also
perform PC to phone communications for additional charges.

Applying What You Have Learned

Many networks now are looking to implement ATM as a transport mechanism for network traffic. TCP/IP requires a revised version of the Address Resolution Protocol,
known as ATMARP, to work within the nuances of an ATM network. This protocol
enables address resolution to take place, even though ATM devices do not have a physical address.

Test Your Knowledge

Here are questions to check what you've learned today. The answers can be found in Appendix B, "Test Your Knowledge: Answers."

1. What are some of the reasons that a modified version of the Address Resolution Protocol must be implemented in an ATM network?

2. How are ATM hosts grouped for a TCP/IP network?

3. What process is followed to remove an entry whose timer has expired in the ATMARP cache for a client?

4. What two network configurations are supported by 802.11 wireless networks?

5. What security risks in the initial deployment of WEP led to the development of 802.1x authentication?

6. What authentication protocols are used in 802.1x authentication to mutually authenticate the user at the wireless station with the RADIUS server?

7. What two methods convert voice input into a digital format for transport over the Internet?

8. What issues need to be resolved before Voice over IP is widely implemented?

Preview of Day 20

Tomorrow we'll look at the manual process of configuring TCP/IP on the common operating systems used in today's networks. The operating systems discussed range from Windows 95 to Windows 2000 in the Microsoft family of operating systems; NetWare 6.1; Linux; and Unix servers.

19

DAY **20**

Configuring Network Client and Server Software to Use TCP/IP

Today we'll look at configuring the TCP/IP protocol for the following client and server operating systems:

- Windows 9*x* (includes Windows 95, Windows 98, and Windows ME)
- Windows 2000 Professional and Server
- NetWare 6.1 Server
- Red Hat Linux
- Unix Servers

Installing TCP/IP on a Windows 9*x* Client

The Windows 95, Windows 98, and Windows ME operating systems are widely used today because most computers that you buy come preloaded with one of these operating systems. The following sections detail the steps to install

TCP/IP on these operating systems. The following steps are based on a Windows 98 client, but it should be easy to apply the steps to the other versions of Microsoft's client operating system.

Adding a Network Adapter

When configuring your Windows 9*x* system to take part in a TCP/IP network, the first step is to install the network adapter in your computer. Windows 9*x* is a Plug and Play operating system. This means that if the peripheral you are adding supports the Plug and Play architecture, the operating system should be able to autodetect and autoinstall the correct drivers for your system.

If the network adapter is not autodetected, you must launch the Add New Hardware Wizard to install the necessary drivers. Use the following steps to install a network adapter's drivers:

1. From the Start menu, select Settings, and then click Control Panel.
2. In the Control Panel, double-click the Add New Hardware applet.
3. In the Add New Hardware Wizard, click Next.
4. To start a search for any Plug and Play devices, click Next.
5. If no Plug and Play devices are found, the Add New Hardware Wizard can perform an invasive search for the added hardware. It is recommended that you let Windows search for new hardware. To start the invasive search, click Next.
6. After the detection process completes, you can click the Details button in the Add New Hardware Wizard to see the detected hardware (see Figure 20.1).

FIGURE 20.1

Viewing the detected hardware.

7. Click the Finish button to install the necessary drivers. You need the original Windows 9*x* media to install the drivers.
8. You must restart the computer for the drivers to be activated.

Adding the TCP/IP Protocol Stack

After your client system restarts, the next step is to add and configure the TCP/IP protocol stack that ships with your operating system. This is where the versions differ in the implementation of TCP/IP. Windows 95 does not automatically install the TCP/IP protocol, whereas TCP/IP is the only protocol installed under Windows 98 and Windows ME. The following steps are required to add the TCP/IP protocol under Windows 95.

1. From the Start menu, select Settings, and then click Control Panel.

2. In the Control Panel, double-click the Network applet.

3. Click the Add button to add a new protocol.

4. In the Select Network Component Type dialog box, select Protocol, and click the Add button.

5. In the Select Network Protocol dialog box (see Figure 20.2), select Microsoft from the list of manufacturers, select TCP/IP from the list of protocols, and then click OK.

FIGURE 20.2

The Select Network Protocol dialog box.

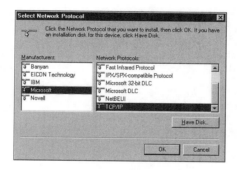

6. You might be prompted to insert your Windows 9*x* media for the installation of the drivers. After these drivers and support files are installed, you must restart your computer.

Configuring the TCP/IP Protocol

After you install the TCP/IP protocol, you probably need to make some changes to your TCP/IP configuration. The configuration tasks can include the following:

- Assigning a static IP address or selecting to use a DCHP-assigned address
- Assigning a default gateway
- Configuring DNS parameters
- Configuring whether NetBIOS is used on the network

20

- Configuring WINS parameters (if running on a network that requires NetBIOS)
- Configuring whether TCP/IP is the default protocol (if multiple protocols exist)
- Selecting which of your installed adapters use TCP/IP

All these options are configured in the TCP/IP properties dialog box. This can be opened using the following steps:

1. Open the Control Panel.
2. In the Control Panel, double-click the Network applet.
3. In the Network dialog box, select TCP/IP from the list of installed network components, and then click Properties.

Assigning an IP Address

The first step is to configure the IP address for your computer. You can either use automatic IP addressing (using a DHCP server) or manually configure an IP address. The setting is configured in the IP Address tab (see Figure 20.3).

FIGURE 20.3

*Configuring IP
address settings.*

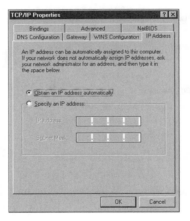

If you configure the IP address manually, you must enter both the IP address and the subnet mask for your network.

Configuring the Default Gateway

The second step in configuring TCP/IP on a Windows 9*x* client is to set the default gateway entry (see Figure 20.4).

You do not have to configure the default gateway if the computer's IP address is configured using DHCP or your network is a single segment network without a router.

FIGURE 20.4

Configuring the default gateway.

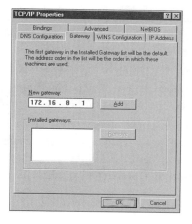

After you manually enter the IP address of the default gateway, click the Add button. This adds the IP address to the list of installed gateways.

Configuring DNS Properties

The DNS Configuration tab of the TCP/IP properties dialog box enables you to configure DNS settings (see Figure 20.5).

FIGURE 20.5

Setting DNS properties.

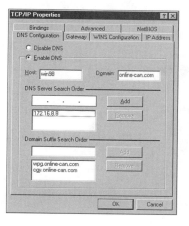

If you enable DNS resolution, then you must also configure the following options:

- **Host.** The Host field provides the hostname for the Windows 9*x* client. This usually is set to the computer name assigned during installation. It can, however, be set to a different value if desired.

20

- **Domain.** The Domain field provides the host's Internet domain. The Fully Qualified Domain Name (FQDN) for the client is a combination of the Host and Domain fields.

- **DNS Server Search Order.** The listing of DNS servers (by IP address) specifies the order in which a client attempts to connect to multiple DNS servers. If a connection is established to a DNS server, no further connection attempts result.

- **Domain Suffix Search Order.** This parameter enables the host to try different Internet domain names as suffixes when you ping a hostname. If you configure the Domain Suffix Search order as shown in Figure 20.5, and then type **ping smallguy** at the command prompt, you actually are performing the following DNS queries:

  - `smallguy`
  - `smallguy.online-can.com`
  - `smallguy.wpg.online-can.com`
  - `smallguy.cgy.online-can.com`

Enabling NetBIOS over TCP/IP

If you use a WINS server for NetBIOS name resolution, you must enable NetBIOS over TCP/IP on the Windows 9x client. In the WINS Configuration tab (see Figure 20.6), you can disable WINS resolution, enable WINS resolution and enter the IP addresses of available WINS servers, or use DHCP assigned settings.

FIGURE 20.6

Configuring WINS settings.

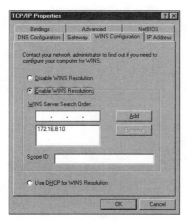

You can optionally configure a Scope ID that restricts communications to computers using the same NetBIOS scope ID.

Setting TCP/IP as the Default Protocol

If you are running multiple protocols, the Windows 9*x* operating system enables you to designate one protocol as the default protocol. In the Advanced tab, you can enable the Set This Protocol To Be The Default Protocol check box.

Installing TCP/IP on a Windows 2000 Computer

Windows 2000 Professional and Server ship with a TCP/IP protocol stack and additional TCP/IP services. The following sections guide you through implementing TCP/IP in a Windows 2000 environment.

Windows 2000 should detect a network adapter during the installation process. If you add an additional network adapter, the plug and play service should autodetect and install the drivers for the network adapter.

Configuring TCP/IP

On a Windows 2000 computer, only the TCP/IP protocol is installed. You can configure the TCP/IP configuration using the following steps:

1. On the desktop, right-click My Network Places, and then click Properties.
2. In the Network and Dial-Up Connections windows, right-click the LAN connection you want to configure and then select Properties. The default name for your LAN connection is Local Area Connection.
3. In the Local Area Connection Properties dialog box, select Internet Protocol (TCP/IP) from the list of components, and then click Properties.
4. In the Internet Protocol (TCP/IP) Properties dialog box (see Figure 20.7), you can configure the following options:

   - Choose whether to use DHCP or a static IP address.
   - If a static IP address is selected, you must enter the IP address, subnet mask, and default gateway information.
   - Choose whether to use the DNS information assigned by DHCP, or manually enter preferred and alternate DNS server IP information.

20

FIGURE 20.7

*Configuring the IP
Address information.*

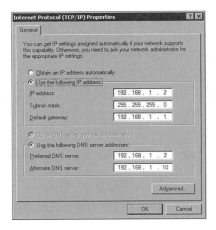

Configuring Additional TCP/IP Properties

In the Internet Protocol (TCP/IP) Properties dialog box, you can configure additional properties by clicking the Advanced button to reveal the Advanced TCP/IP Settings dialog box as shown in Figure 20.8.

FIGURE 20.8

*Configuring Advanced
TCP/IP Settings.*

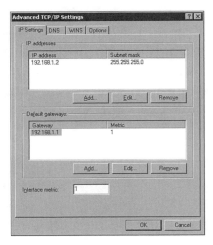

The following parameters can be configured in the Advanced TCP/IP Settings dialog box:

- **IP Settings.** Allows you to assign additional IP addresses and default gateways to the adapter.

- **DNS.** Allows you to configure additional DNS servers for hostname resolution, define additional DNS suffixes, and enable dynamic updates for DNS by registering the connection's addresses in DNS (see Figure 20.9).

FIGURE 20.9

Configuring DNS settings.

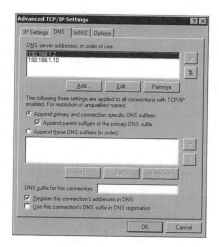

- **WINS.** Allows you to define any WINS servers on the network and enables you to choose whether to enable or disable NetBIOS over TCP/IP.

- **Options.** Allows you to enable Internet Protocol Security (IPSec) or TCP/IP Filtering for the adapter.

Windows XP and Windows .NET Server

At the time of writing this book, Windows XP has just shipped and Windows .NET Server development is in the homestretch. You will find that configuring IP in this environment has not changed all that much. The two major changes that you should be aware of are Alternate IP address configuration and the Internet Connection Firewall (ICF).

The Alternate Configuration tab (see Figure 20.10) allows you to choose whether to use Automatic Private IP Addressing (APIPA) or to use a preconfigured IP address configuration if a DHCP server is unavailable.

This allows you to configure more specific IP address information, rather than being assigned an IP address in the APIPA (169.254.0.0/16) address range.

The Internet Connection Firewall (see Figure 20.11) allows you to enable a connection firewall when connected to the Internet. This blocks most incoming ports but still allows you to browse the Internet.

20

FIGURE 20.10

Configuring alternate IP address.

FIGURE 20.11

Enabling the Internet Connection Firewall.

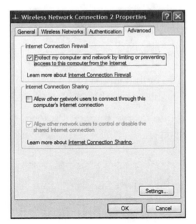

Configuring TCP/IP on a Linux Computer

An operating system that more corporations are looking at as both a client and as a server is Linux. Linux, a Unix variant, is easily downloaded from the Internet, or purchased at your local computer store. The following section looks at configuring TCP/IP on a Red Hat Linux host.

Configuring TCP/IP During Installation

During the Red Hat installation process, you are prompted to enter the Network Configuration if a network adapter is detected in your computer (see Figure 20.12).

FIGURE 20.12

Configuring TCP/IP during Linux installation.

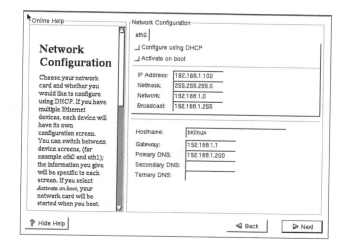

The Network Configuration utility allows you to configure the following information for each network adapter. There is a separate tab for each installed (and detected) network adapter:

- **Configure Using DHCP.** Do not enter any configuration information manually; retrieve all configuration from the local DHCP server.
- **Activate on Boot.** You can choose to disable a network interface by not enabling this option.
- **IP Address.** The manually configured IP address for the adapter.
- **NetMask.** The subnet mask configured for the assigned IP address.
- **Network and Broadcast addresses.** After the IP address and subnet mask are configured, these fields are automatically generated.
- **Hostname.** The logical name to be used by the Linux computer.
- **Gateway.** The IP address of the default gateway.
- **DNS Servers.** You can enter up to three DNS IP addresses for hostname resolution.

The adapter settings for the network adapter are written into the Linux kernel and are applied when the Linux computer restarts after installation.

Modifying TCP/IP Configuration

If you want to modify the TCP/IP configuration after installation, the following procedure can be used:

1. Log on as root with the root account password.
2. Type **cd /sbin**.

20

3. Type `./linuxconf` to run the Linux configuration utility.

4. In the Linuxconf utility main menu (see Figure 20.13), select Basic Host Information, and then press Enter.

FIGURE 20.13

The Linuxconf main menu.

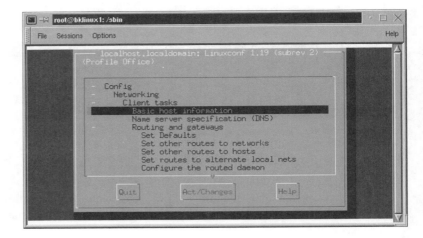

5. In the host basic configuration (see Figure 20.14), you can enter the fully qualified domain name, choose between static, DHCP, or BOOTP addressing, and assign an IP address and subnet mask for each installed adapter. Configure the configuration, and then select the Accept button and press Enter.

FIGURE 20.14

Using Linuxconf to change the host's IP address.

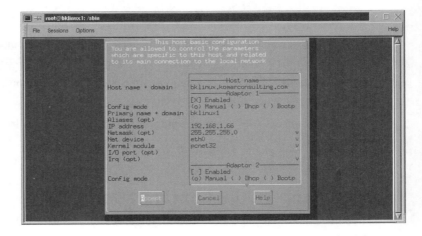

6. In the Linuxconf main menu, select Name Server Specification (DNS) to configure DNS settings, and then press Enter.

7. In the Resolver Configuration screen (see Figure 20.15), you can configure
    whether DNS is used, the default domain, DNS server IP address, and DNS suffix-
    es for the adapter. Configure the required settings, click the Accept button, and
    press Enter.

FIGURE 20.15

Using Linuxconf to set DNS resolver configuration.

8. In the Linuxconf main menu, under Routing and Gateways, select Set Defaults,
    and then press Enter.

9. In the Defaults screen (see Figure 20.16), you can configure the IP address of the
    default gateway. If the Linux host has more than one network adapter installed, you
    can also enable routing in this menu. After your routing information is configured,
    click the Accept button and press Enter.

FIGURE 20.16

Using Linuxconf to define the default gateway.

20

10. In the Linuxconf main menu, press Tab until the Act/Changes button is selected, and then press Enter.

11. In the Status of the System menu, select Activate the Changes, and then press Enter.

12. In the Linuxconf main menu, press Tab until the Quit button is selected, and then press Enter.

This activates the IP configuration for the LINUX host. You can verify the IP configuration by typing ./ifconfig at a console (see Figure 20.17).

FIGURE 20.17

Reviewing the IP con-figuration using IFCONFIG.

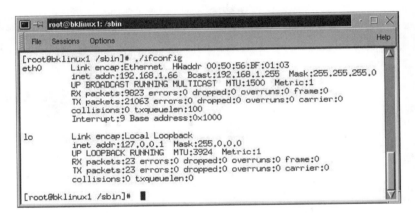

Configuring TCP/IP on a Unix Server

As described in Day 1's history lesson of the TCP/IP protocol, Unix and TCP/IP have evolved together. As a result, the TCP/IP protocol is a standard configuration option in all Unix systems. This section details the steps to configure TCP/IP on a Berkeley Software Distribution (BSD) version of Unix.

The configuration of TCP/IP includes the following:

- Creating a kernel that contains your network adapter.
- Configuring the network adapter.
- Reviewing the TCP/IP configuration files.
- Configuring the Internet daemon.
- Configuring routing.
- Testing the TCP/IP configuration.

Adding the Network Adapter to Your Unix Host

To use TCP/IP on a Unix host, the Unix kernel must understand each piece of hardware on the system and how to use it. This can be compared to NetWare's use of LAN drivers and Windows' use of device drivers.

To add a new network adapter to the Unix station, you need to re-create the Unix kernel. The new device generally contains all the necessary steps for installing the new device.

The actual creation of the new kernel is a series of compilations of C-language programs. The compilation is based on the script stored in the configuration file in the /usr/sys/conf directory. This configuration file typically uses the same name as the hostname for the Unix workstation.

The following is an example of a typical kernel configuration file:

```
Options              INET

pseudo-device        loop
pseudo-device        ether
pseudo-device        pty

device ix0 at isa? port 0x300 net irq 10 iomem 0xd0000 iosiz 32768 vector
➥ixintr
```

- The INET option is mandatory. It indicates that the kernel supports TCP/IP networking.

- Pseudo devices are device drivers that do not have corresponding hardware. In this configuration file, pseudo devices are created for the loopback device, ethernet is a low-level networking scheme for ethernet connectivity, and pty enables users to connect to the network as if they were connected by a terminal directly attached to the Unix workstation.

- The device statements indicate actual hardware devices installed on the system. This device line is the configuration line for an Intel EtherExpress 10.

After the configuration file has been edited, the kernel must be recompiled using the updated configuration file. In the following, note that the user executes only the first two steps:

1. cd /etc

2. config [config file]

3. The system creates a new directory in /usr/sys based on the configuration file's name. If the configuration file is named beard, for example, the directory is /usr/sys/beard.

20

4. The system copies all C-language files necessary for the compilation into the newly created directory.

5. The system calls the program /bin/make. This file reads its own configuration file and begins compiling the code. The output of this compilation is a new kernel named vmunix.

After the compilation is complete, the newly created kernel must be transferred to the root directory. The following steps make sure the previous kernel is not overwritten (just to be safe). These steps assume the hostname is beard.

1. mv /vmunix /vmunix.old

2. cp /usr/sys/beard/vmunix /vmunix

Other Versions of Unix

Other versions of Unix provide easier methods of creating the kernel. The System V kernels launch a program that prompts you to enter information about the options you want to include on your system. This program also can be used any time you want to reconfigure your system. When you finish running the program, a new kernel is created. In SCO Unix, this program is called netconfig. The name varies between flavors of Unix, but the operation generally is the same.

Configuring the Network Adapter

When the Unix host is prepared to run TCP/IP, the next step is to configure the TCP/IP information for the network adapter. This is accomplished using the ifconfig utility. The ifconfig utility enables you to assign IP addresses to an interface, to define the subnet mask, to define the broadcast address, and to enable or disable the network interface.

The following is the syntax of the ifconfig command:

```
ifconfig [interface] [address] netmask [subnet mask]
➡ broadcast [broadcast address]
```

- [interface]. This is the name of the network adapter as named in the kernel. If multiple devices exist on the host, you need to run ifconfig once for each adapter.

- [address]. This is the IP address to be assigned to the network adapter. This can be either a dotted-decimal notation of the address or a hostname to be resolved from the /etc/hosts configuration file.

- netmask [subnet mask]. This is the subnet mask to be used with the configured IP address. Be sure to enter the correct subnet mask or communication might not work as expected between other hosts.

- broadcast [broadcast address]. The address to which local subnet broadcasts are sent.

For example, if you want to configure the interface ix0 to have the IP address 192.168.20.15 with subnet mask 255.255.255.0 that uses the broadcast address 192.168.20.255, use the following command:

```
ifconfig ix0 192.168.20.15 netmask 255.255.255.0 broadcast 192.168.20.255
```

As previously mentioned, the ifconfig command also can enable or disable an interface. The following is the syntax for this:

```
ifconfig interface down|up
```

If you want to enable the interface, execute this command with the UP option. To disable the device, use the DOWN option.

If you want to view the configuration for an IP address, execute the following command:

```
ifconfig interface
```

In this case, you would receive the following screen output:

```
# ifconfig ix0

epro0: flags=63<UP, BROADCAST, NOTRAILERS, RUNNING>
        inet 192.168.20.15 netmask ffffff00 broadcast 192.168.20.255
        ether 08:00:20:19:e3:bc
```

Reviewing the TCP/IP Configuration Files

After you verify that your network adapter is configured correctly, be sure all the TCP/IP configuration files are configured correctly. The following configuration files in the /etc directory should be verified:

- hosts. Contains mappings of IP addresses to hostnames. Programs such as ping and ifconfig consult this file for name resolution.

- ethers. Contains mappings of MAC addresses to hostnames. The ARP utility uses this file to load the ARP cache with static entries.

- networks. (Optional) Assigns logical names to network addresses. This can be used by the route command when creating the routing table.

20

- protocols. This configuration file is used when a packet arrives on the host. The protocol ID is extracted from the IP header to determine which upper-level protocol this packet should be sent to for further processing.
- services. Determines which service is responding to requests on a specific port number. This configuration file assumes that the server and the client are using the same version of the file.
- hosts.equiv. Contains the list of trusted hosts that can connect to the Unix server over the network.
- resolv.conf. Configures the DNS properties for the DNS server. This file includes the domain name for the host and the primary and secondary DNS servers for the host.

All these files can be edited using an ASCII text editor such as VI.

Configuring the Internet Daemon

After you configure the TCP/IP settings for your Unix host, you need to configure which services should run on your system. These programs generally are launched as *daemons* that run at all times. Some programs, however, need to be configured to launch on demand.

The *Internet daemon (inetd)* provides the functionality to listen on specific ports for incoming service requests. If a request is received, the Internet daemon launches the appropriate daemon to handle the request. After the request is completed, the Internet daemon shuts down the configured daemon.

This information is based on the entries in the configuration file /etc/inetd.conf. The following is the format of each entry in the inetd.conf file:

```
service-name socket-type protocol wait-status user server-pathname arguments
```

- service-name. This parameter must match an entry in the /etc/services file.
- socket-type. This parameter describes the type of socket used by the service. Possible entries include stream, datagram (dgram), raw, and reliably delivered message (rdm).
- protocol. This is the protocol used by the service. This protocol must match a protocol in the /etc/protocols file.
- wait-status. This field determines how inetd moderates the service. If set to wait, inetd must wait until the server releases the socket before allowing another process to access the service. If set to no-wait, inetd can allow additional server requests to access the service.

- user. This field contains the user account used by the service to determine the security level of the process. The process executes with the permissions assigned to this user account.

- server-pathname. This is the actual name of the program inetd launches when a request is received. This entry should include the full path to the program. If the word internal appears instead of a program name, inetd services the request itself instead of calling a separate process.

- arguments. This field contains any additional arguments required by the process to launch correctly. As a minimum, this field contains the actual program name.

The only time you should edit the inetd.conf file is when you add a service. Most software includes the necessary entries to be added to the inetd.conf file. When modifications are made to the inetd.conf file, the inetd process must be restarted for the changes to take place. The following commands accomplish this:

```
#ps -acx | grep inetd
131 ? IW 0:04 inetd

kill -HUP 131
```

The following is an example of the inetd.conf file from a SUN Unix box:

```
##ident   "@(#)inetd.conf 1.22    95/07/14 SMI"   /* SVr4.0 1.5
➥ */### Configuration file for inetd(1M).  See inetd.conf(4).
➥## Syntax for socket-based Internet services:
# <service_name> <socket_type> <proto> <flags> <user> <server_pathname> <args>
#
# Ftp and telnet are standard Internet services.
#
ftp     stream  tcp     nowait  root    /usr/sbin/tcpd in.ftpd -d
telnet  stream  tcp     nowait  root    /usr/sbin/tcpd  in.telnetd
#
# identd is to support RFC 1413 authentication / identity lookups
#
ident   stream  tcp     nowait  root    /usr/sbin/in.identd     in.identd
#
# Shell, login, exec, comsat and talk are BSD protocols.
#
shell stream  tcp     nowait  root    /usr/sbin/tcpd  in.rshd
login stream  tcp     nowait  root    /usr/sbin/tcpd  in.rlogind
exec  stream  tcp     nowait  root    /usr/sbin/tcpd  in.rexecd
comsat dgram  udp     wait    root    /usr/sbin/in.comsat     in.comsat
talk    dgram   udp     wait    root    /usr/sbin/tcpd  in.talkd
ntalk   dgram   udp     wait    root    /usr/sbin/in.ntalkd in.ntalkd

# Tftp service is provided primarily for booting.  Most sites run this
# only on machines acting as "boot servers."
#
```

20

```
tftp dgram   udp     wait    root    /usr/sbin/tcpd  in.tftpd -s /tftpboot
#
# Finger, systat and netstat give out user information which may be
# valuable to potential "system crackers."  Many sites choose to disable
# some or all of these services to improve security.
#
finger          stream  tcp     nowait  nobody  /usr/sbin/tcpd  in.fingerd
#systat stream  tcp     nowait  root    /usr/bin/ps       ps -ef
netstat stream  tcp     nowait  root    /usr/bin/netstat   netstat -f inet
#
# Time service is used for clock synchronization.
#
time   stream  tcp     nowait  root    internal
time   dgram   udp     wait    root    internal
#
# Echo, discard, daytime, and chargen are used primarily for testing.
#
echo   stream  tcp     nowait  root    internal
echo   dgram   udp     wait    root    internal
discard         stream  tcp     nowait  root    internal
discard         dgram   udp     wait    root    internal
daytime         stream  tcp     nowait  root    internal
daytime         dgram   udp     wait    root    internal
chargen         stream  tcp     nowait  root    internal
chargen         dgram   udp     wait    root    internal
#
```

Services in the inetd.conf file with duplicate entries can respond to requests on both the TCP and UDP protocols.

Configuring Routing

If your network consists of multiple TCP/IP segments, you need to configure routing for the Unix host. This can be accomplished using the program command /usr/etc/route to define the routing table.

The syntax of the route command was discussed on Day 9, "Gateway and Routing Protocols," in the section, "Static Routing." The syntax of the Windows NT route command is not that different from the FreeBSD version.

When configuring routes, you should include the following:

- A route to the local host address. This prevents communication with services on the local computer from being transmitted on the network interface.

- The local network broadcast address.

- A default gateway address. This address is used when a specific route to a destination network is not defined.
- Any specific network routes. If a specific route to a destination network must be defined, it should be configured for the Unix host.

After the routing table is configured, the `ping` command and the `traceroute` command can be used to make sure routing has been configured correctly. The `ping` command also can be used to make sure that the correct address has been bound to the network interface and that remote hosts can be reached using the routing table's information.

The `traceroute` command can be used to determine whether specific routes are used to reach a remote network. The `traceroute` command indicates each router crossed enroute to the destination host.

You can view the configured routing table using the `traceroute  -r` command.

Configuring TCP/IP on a NetWare 6 Server

This configuration information assumes NetWare 6 is currently installed and configured correctly running the IPX/SPX protocol. This section details the steps involved in performing the following tasks:

- Installing the TCP/IP protocol
- Verifying the TCP/IP configuration
- Configuring NetWare/IP
- Configuring the NetWare DNS Server
- Configuring the NetWare DHCP server

All these products are included on the NetWare 6.0 installation CD-ROM.

Installing the TCP/IP Protocol

The TCP/IP protocol can be installed as part of the default installation of NetWare 6. The following installation instructions assume the TCP/IP protocol was not installed during the initial installation of the network operating system:

1. To configure the TCP/IP protocol on the NetWare 6 server, you must run the Internetworking Configuration utility by entering the following command at the system console of the NetWare server:

```
load inetcfg
```

20

Or, you may access the Internetworking Configuration utility remotely by accessing the NetWare Remote Manager and choosing the system console interface and issuing the `load inetcfg` command. Either method starts the Internetwork Configuration Netware Loadable Module or NLM (see Figure 20.18).

FIGURE 20.18

The Internetworking Configuration NLM.

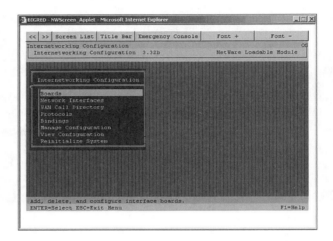

Note

Utilities that are executed on the NetWare system console are called *NetWare Loadable Modules* (NLMs). They are loaded using the LOAD command and are unloaded using the UNLOAD command. You can determine which NLMs are loaded by issuing the MODULES command.

2. From the Internetworking Configuration menu, select Protocols. In the ensuing menu, select TCP/IP. The TCP/IP Protocol Configuration dialog box opens.

This dialog box enables you to configure the following features:

- **TCP/IP Status.** Enables or disables the TCP/IP protocol.
- **IP Packet Forwarding.** Enables NetWare 6 to act as a router.
- **RIP.** Enables or disables the RIP routing protocol.
- **OSPF.** Enables or disables the OSPF routing protocol.
- **OSPF Configuration.** Configures the OSPF routing protocol.
- **LAN Static Routing.** Configures static routing information.
- **LAN Static Routing Table.** Build your list of static routes here.
- **Dead Gateway Detection.** Enables or disables the detection of dead routers.

- **Dead Gateway Detection Configuration.** Configures the dead gateway detection (DGD) parameters.
- **SNMP Manager Table.** Configures the SNMP management system.
- **DNS Resolver Configuration.** Configures your DNS domain name and up to three DNS servers.
- **Load Balancing.** Enables or disables the load balancing features of NetWare 6.
- **Load Balancing Configuration.** Configures the load balancing features.
- **Fault Tolerance.** Enables or disables the fault tolerance support in NetWare.
- **Fault Tolerance Configuration.** Configures the fault tolerance parameters.
- **Filter Support.** Enables or disables packet filtering.
- **NAT Implicit Filtering.** Configures Network Address Translation for this interface.
- **Expert Configuration Settings.** Includes Directed Broadcast Forwarding; Forward Source Route Packets; BootP Forwarding Configuration; EGP and EGP configuration.

3. After your TCP/IP protocol configuration is set, press Esc and select Yes to update the TCP/IP configuration.

4. Press Esc again to return to the Internetworking Configuration menu. From this menu, select Bindings to configure which network cards use the TCP/IP protocol.

5. Press Insert and select the TCP/IP protocol from the list of configured protocols. Press Enter.

6. Select the desired board name and press Enter to bind TCP/IP to that network card. This opens the TCP/IP configuration dialog box shown in Figure 20.19.

   This dialog box enables you to configure the IP address and subnet mask assigned to the network card. It also provides specific configuration options for the RIP and OSPF protocols. The Expert Options section enables you to configure the frame type and broadcast address.

7. Press Esc to exit the dialog box. Select Yes to update the TCP/IP configuration. A dialog box opens that shows the configured IP address for the interface (see Figure 20.20).

8. Press Esc until you are asked whether you want to exit configuration. Select Yes to complete the TCP/IP configuration.

9. Reinitialize the NetWare 6 server by pressing the Escape key, until you return to the Inetcfg main screen and choose the Reinitialize System command from the Internetworking Configuration menu.

20

FIGURE 20.19

Binding TCP/IP to a LAN interface screen.

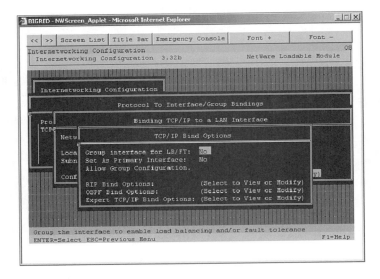

FIGURE 20.20

Viewing the TCP/IP bindings.

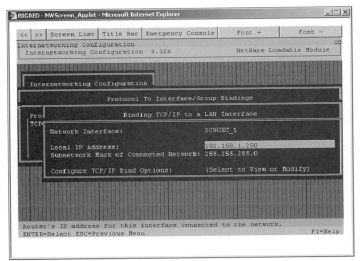

Verifying the TCP/IP Configuration

To verify the assigned IP address, you can use the PING NLM included with NetWare 6.

1. Load the PING NLM by issuing the following command at the system console:

```
load ping
```

2. Enter the IP address (or hostname) you configured for the NetWare 6 server (see Figure 20.21), the seconds between each ping packet, and the size of each ping packet. To begin the ping process, press Escape.

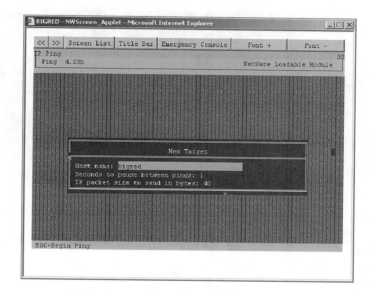

3. You should see something similar to the screen shown in Figure 20.22 indicating that 100% of the packets were received.

4. Press Escape to exit the PING session.

You also can ping other hosts on your segment. At this point, however, you only can use IP addresses because you have not configured a DNS server.

Configuring NetWare/IP

The next step in the TCP/IP installation process is to configure Novell/IP. This defines the DNS and DSS servers used by the NetWare 6 server.

1. From the IntranetWare server console, enter the following command to load the NWCONFIG NLM:

```
load nwconfig
```

2. The NetWare 6 Server NWCONFIG NLM provides a menu of options (see Figure 20.23). From the Configuration Options menu, select Product Options.

20

FIGURE 20.22

Reviewing the ping results.

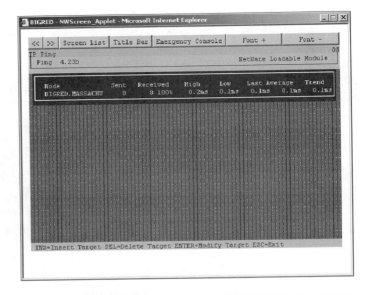

FIGURE 20.23

The NetWare Server Configuration Options screen.

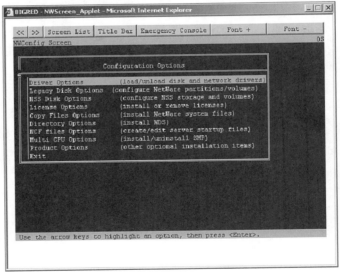

3. From the Other Installation Items/Products menu, select Install NetWare/IP. This starts the transfer of necessary configuration files to the NetWare 6 server. The installation program asks whether you want to read the online documentation first. This generally is a good idea; it prepares you for the installation requirements.

4. After reading the documentation of Novell/IP, you can proceed with the installation.

   Switch to the system console using the Alt+Esc key combination.

5. The installation program prompts you for the hostname you want to assign to the NetWare 6 server.

   In this example, the hostname BIGRED was assigned. After the hostname is entered, the initial configuration files are defined.

6. A warning states that you must have NDS installed to access network resources.

7. Select Yes to exit the NetWare/IP Configuration Console.

8. You must reinitialize the system for the configured changes to take effect.

9. At the NetWare console, type **DOWN**.

10. At the NetWare console, type **EXIT** to return to DOS.

11. Restart the NetWare server, by typing **SERVER**.

Configuring the NetWare DNS Server

The installation of DNS and DHCP in a NetWare 6 environment requires that the client has access to the \\NWSERVER\SYS\Public\DNSDHCP volume on the NetWare 6 server.

You can map the NetWare drive by using My Network Places on the Windows 2000 Desktop by browsing the NetWare network. After the drive is mapped, install DNS by using the following procedure:

1. From the drive mapped to \\server\sys\public\DNSDHCP, run SETUP.EXE. This program installs a shortcut on the desktop for the DNS configuration tool.

2. The installation of DNS requires that the NDS schema be extended to include the DNSDHCP locator object. If this is not performed before running SETUP.EXE, you will see the error message shown in Figure 20.24.

FIGURE 20.24

Error indicating the NDS schema must be extended.

3. From the NetWare server console, load the DNIPINST NLM, by typing **load dnipinst.nlm**.

4. At the NDS Context Query Form, press Enter to create the necessary objects.

5. A message appears (see Figure 20.25) indicating that the schema extensions were successfully installed allowing use of the Java-based DNS/DHCP console.

FIGURE 20.25

Successful extension of the NDS schema.

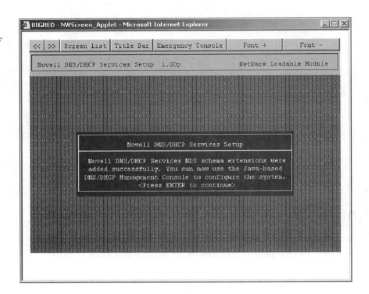

After the schema is extended and the Java console interface is installed at a client computer, you can now configure DNS/DHCP services.

1. On the client workstation, double-click the DNSDHCP shortcut on the desktop.

2. When prompted, selected the NDS tree in your organization to launch the console.

3. The DNS/DHCP Management Console (see Figure 20.26) appears. Notice that there are two separate tabs for configuration of the interface: one for DNS and the other for DHCP.

   The DNS/DHCP Management console is composed of three separate windows. The left window displays all available DNS resources. The right window displays the details of the object selected on the left. The lower window shows all available NetWare DNS servers.

   You may either import DNS configuration from an existing DNS BIND format file or you may manually configure a new zone.

4. To create a new forward lookup zone, click the Create icon on the toolbar and choose the object to create. Your choices are DNS Server, Zone, or Resource Record. Choose Zone, and then click OK.

FIGURE 20.26

*DNS/DHCP
Management Console.*

FIGURE 20.26

*DNS/DHCP
Management Console.*

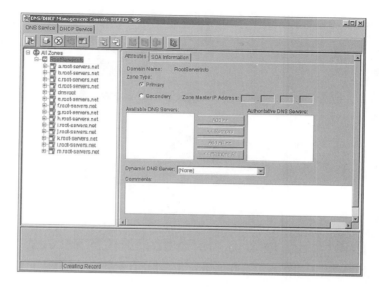

5. In the Create Zone dialog box (see Figure 20.27), choose Create New Zone, and set the other options as shown to create the REDDOM.COM zone.

FIGURE 20.27

Create the REDDOM.COM
forward lookup zone.

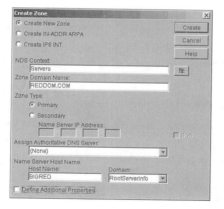

20

6. To create a new reverse lookup zone, click the Create icon on the toolbar, choose Zone, and then click OK.

7. In the Create Zone dialog box (see Figure 20.28), choose Create IN-ADDR.ARPA, and set the other options as shown to create the 1.168.192.in-addr.arpa zone.

FIGURE 20.28

Create the REDDOM.COM
reverse lookup zone.

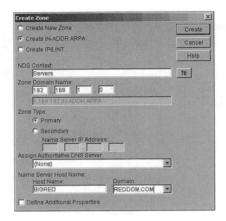

Configuring the NetWare DHCP Server

NetWare 6 ships with a fully functional DHCP server. It is managed using the same Java console used to manage DNS.

1. In the DNS/DHCP Management Console, click the DHCP Service tab.

2. To create a new DHCP server, in the DHCP Service tab, click the Create icon in the toolbar.

3. In the ensuing dialog box, choose DHCP Server, select which NetWare server will host the DHCP service, and then click Create.

4. To create a new DHCP scope, in the DHCP Service tab, click the Create icon in the toolbar.

5. In the ensuing dialog box, select Create Subnet.

6. In the Create Subnet dialog box (see Figure 20.29), enter the information defining the subnet of IP addresses in the DHCP scope. Ensure that you select the Define Additional Properties check box to define scope-specific options.

FIGURE 20.29

*Configuring the
DHCP scope pool.*

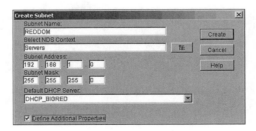

7. In the next screen, define the DHCP Lease duration and the address of a BootP server and file to execute for BootP clients.

8. In the Modify DHCP Options dialog box (see Figure 20.30), you can configure any specific options for the DHCP scope and then click OK to confirm the settings.

FIGURE 20.30

Configuring DHCP scope options.

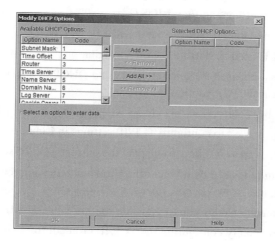

9. Start the DHCP service by clicking the Start/Stop icon on the toolbar.

Applying What You Have Learned

Today you learned the steps for configuring TCP/IP in both client and server environments. Step-by-step instructions showed you how to implement and configure TCP/IP in your Windows 9x, Windows 2000, Linux, BSD Unix, or NetWare 6 environment.

Whatever environment you deploy, always plan ahead and ensure that you know what configuration settings you must use before you proceed with the configuration. Items to know beforehand include:

- The IP addressing scheme used on the network
- The logical names you intend to use for the new host
- All other default TCP/IP settings, such as DNS servers, default gateways, and subnet masks

20

Test Your Knowledge

Here are questions to check what you've learned today. The answers can be found in Appendix B, "Test Your Knowledge: Answers."

1. How can a network adapter be added to a Windows 9x installation if it was not detected by the Plug and Play BIOS?

2. What does the Domain Suffix Search order provide?

3. What NLM is used to start the TCP/IP installation process on a NetWare 6 server?

4. How do the tools used to configure DNS and DHCP in a NetWare environment differ from basic TCP/IP configuration?

5. What must be rebuilt on a Unix server when a new network adapter is installed?

6. What utility is used to configure TCP/IP settings in Linux post installation?

7. What utility is used in Linux to display the current TCP/IP settings?

8. Which daemon is used by a Unix server to launch the correct daemon to handle an Internet request from a remote client?

9. What command enables you to view the routing table on a Unix server?

10. If you are manually configuring the TCP/IP protocol for a client running on a single-segment LAN, what is the minimum configuration required?

11. If your client's TCP/IP configuration is provided by a DHCP server, which takes precedence: a DHCP configuration setting or a manually entered configuration setting?

Preview of Day 21

Tomorrow we'll examine future trends in the world of TCP/IP. We'll look at the new version of the IP protocol, called IPv6, and discuss the major changes in IPv6 from IPv4. We'll examine the packet format and security extensions for IPv6, as well as methods for migrating from IPv4 to IPv6.

DAY 21

IPv6, the Future of TCP/IP?

With the growth of the Internet, there will come a time when the current IPv4 addressing scheme will run out of available addresses. Recognizing that even the use of private network addressing and Network Address Translation (NAT) cannot prevent this from occurring, the IETF has been commissioned to create the next generation of the IP address.

Several published RFCs lay out the needs for the new protocol. The new release of the IP protocol, called IPv6, should eventually replace the current IPv4 in the next decade, unless other stop-gap measures delay IPv6 deployment.

Today's material gives you some insight into the design of IPv6. It also discusses the effect this new addressing scheme will have on networks that need to integrate both IPv4 and IPv6.

What Are the Major Changes in IPv6?

IPv6 is being designed as the successor to the current 32-bit addressing scheme, IPv4. Major changes in the IPv6 include the following:

- **Expanded addressing capabilities.** The address size for IPv6 will be 128 bits. This will provide a larger pool of IP addresses for the Internet. Each user will have access to a pool of IP addresses greater than the total number of IP addresses currently available on the Internet. A 128-bit address allows for potentially 2^{128} or 3.4028236692093846346337460743177 x 10^{38} possible addresses (less a few for reserved pools).

- **Simplification of the IP header.** Much of the IPv4 header information has been made optional in IPv6 or dropped entirely. This will result in faster processing of IP header information by receiving hosts.

- **Improved extensibility of the IP header.** The IP header has been formatted to provide more efficient forwarding, more flexibility on the length of option fields, and easier inclusion of new options in the future. This will enable the IP header to change as the protocol evolves over the years, without having to redesign the entire header format.

- **Improved flow control.** IP datagrams will be able to request a better quality of service. This will include time-specific delivery of information and the capability to request a minimum bandwidth availability or real-time service. Today this is possible, but not built in to the existing IP packet.

- **Increased security.** The IP header will include extensions to support authentication of source and destination hosts and better assurance that data will not be corrupted. This also will provide the option of encrypting data as it is transported over the network. While IPSec exists today to provide encryption of transmitted data, IPSec is built in to the IP header information in IPv6.

Address Formats Under IPv6

 Hosts using IPv6 will be assigned 128-bit addresses. These addresses will fall into the following address classes:

- Unicast
- Anycast
- Multicast

A *unicast* address is a unique identifier assigned to a single interface.

An *anycast* address is an identifier assigned to multiple interfaces, generally on distinct routers. When a packet is sent to an anycast address, the packet is delivered to only one of the interfaces associated with the address. This usually is the nearest address based on routing table distance.

Anycast addresses use the same syntax as unicast addresses. They become any-cast addresses when assigned to more than one network interface. Routers that are assigned anycast addresses must be explicitly configured to know that the address is an anycast address.

A *multicast* address also is an identifier assigned to multiple interfaces on distinct hosts. A packet delivered to a multicast address is delivered to all the interfaces assigned this multicast address.

Multicast addresses use the format shown in Figure 21.1.

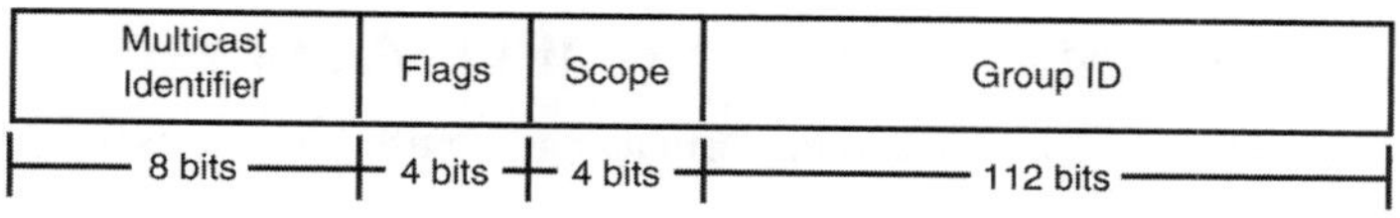

FIGURE 21.1

Multicast IPv6 address format.

- **Multicast Identifier.** The first eight bits are set to 1. This identifies the IPv6 address as a multicast address.

- **Flags.** This 4-bit field indicates whether the address is a permanently assigned multicast address (as set by the global Internet numbering authority) or a specially created multicast address. The first three bits are set to 0 and are reserved. The fourth bit is set either to 0 for a permanent multicast address or to 1 for a transient, or not permanently assigned, multicast address.

- **Scope.** This 4-bit field sets the address space in which the multicast address is effective. Allowable values are shown in Table 21.1.

TABLE 21.1 Allowable Multicast Scope Field Values

Value	Meaning
0	Reserved
1	Node-local scope
2	Link-local scope
5	Site-local scope
8	Organization-local scope

21

TABLE 21.1 continued

Value	Meaning
E	Global scope
F	Reserved
3,4,6,7,9,A,B,C,D	Unassigned

- **Group ID.** This 112-bit field identifies the group address. This address is effective only within the defined scope.

You might notice that there are no broadcast addresses under IPv6. This is because all functionality handled by broadcast addresses in IPv4 has been replaced by more efficient multicast addresses in IPv6. In other cases, the anycast functionality also removes the need to use broadcast messages.

Representations of the IPv6 Address

The following three accepted formats can be used to represent IPv6 addresses:

- The preferred format represents the address in eight fields of 16 bits. The 16 bits are represented as a string of four hex digits. The following is an example of an IPv6 preferred format:

  `1079:0005:AB45:5f4C:0010:BA97:0043:34AB`

  In the preferred format, you can suppress leading zeros in any of the eight fields. There must, however, be at least one digit in each of the eight fields. The preceding address also can be represented as the following:

  `1079:5:AB45:5f4C:10:BA97:43:34AB`

- Many assigned IPv6 addresses contain long strings of zeros. A special syntax has been created that represents multiple 16-bit fields of zeros with ::. This can only be used to represent entire 16-bit fields of all zeros and can only be used once within an IPv6 address. Table 21.2 shows how various IPv6 addresses can be shortened using this syntax.

TABLE 21.2 IPv6 Address Representations

Address Type	Original Address	Shorter Address Syntax
Unicast	`1090:0:0:0:0:876:AABC:1234`	`1090::876:AABC:1234`
Multicast	`FF01:0:0:0:0:0:0:67AB`	`FF01::67AB`
Loopback	`0:0:0:0:0:0:0:1`	`::1`
Unspecified	`0:0:0:0:0:0:0:0`	`::`

- In mixed environments of IPv4 and IPv6, it might be easier to work with an address format of H:H:H:H:H:H:d.d.d.d. The Hs are hexadecimal notation for the six high-order fields of the IPv6 address. The ds are the IPv4 format of the address in dotted-decimal format representing the last two fields of the IPv6 address (32-bits). The following are examples of this address format:

```
0:0:0:0:0:0:10.16.234.15 where the IPv4 address was 10.16.234.15
FFFF::1234:172.16.4.34 where the IPv4 address was 172.16.4.34
```

Special IPv6 Addresses

You should be familiar with the following special unicast IPv6 addresses when you start working with IPv6:

- **0:0:0:0:0:0:0:0.** This unspecified address indicates the absence of an assigned IPv6 address. An example of this is a DHCP client that has initialized but has not received an IP address from the DHCP server. This address can only be used in the source address field. It cannot be used as the destination address.

- **0:0:0:0:0:0:0:1.** An IPv6 host uses this loopback address to send IPv6 packets to itself. It can only be used in the destination field of an IPv6 packet. An easy mnemonic (if you worked with IPv4) is that the IPv6 address is 127 zeros 1. The IPv4 loopback address is 127.0.0.1.

- **IPv4-compatible IPv6 addresses.** IPv6 hosts that also will communicate with IPv4 hosts need a special IPv6 unicast address that contains a valid IPv4 address in its lower 32 bits. The first 96 bits are all zeros.

- **IPv4-mapped IPv6 addresses.** This IPv6 address represents nodes that will support only IPv4 and are incapable of working with IPv6 addressing.

  The actual IPv6 address is front loaded with 80-0 bits. The next 16 bits are set to a value of 1. The IPv4 address makes up the last 32 bits of the address. Figure 21.2 shows this format.

FIGURE 21.2

IPv4-mapped IPv6 address format.

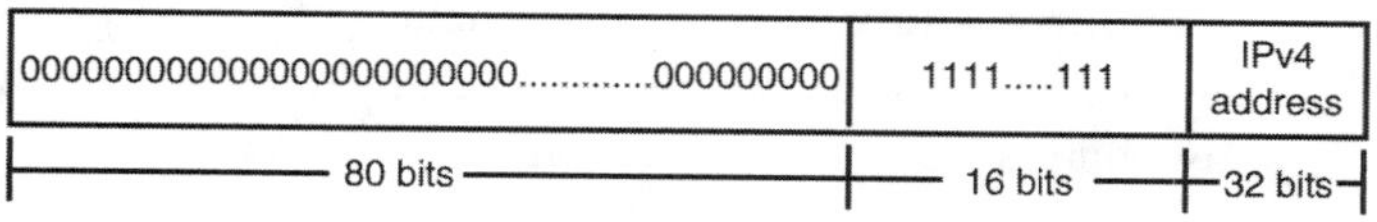

The IPv6 Header Format

The IPv6 header, shown in Figure 21.3, has the following properties:

21

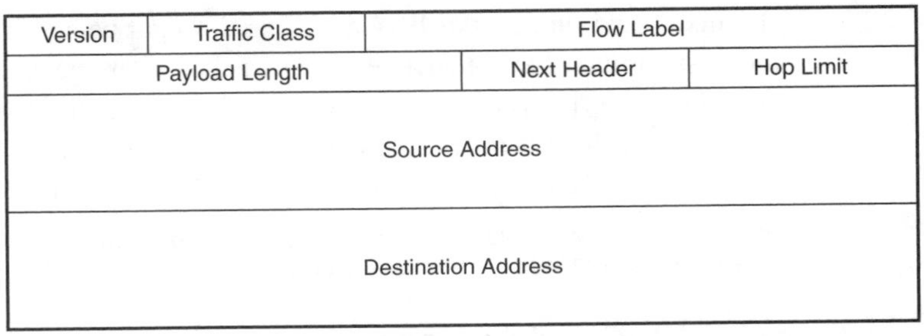

FIGURE 21.3

The IPv6 header format.

- **Version.** This 4-bit field contains the IP version number. It is set to 6.

- **Traffic Class.** This 8-bit field enables a source host or forwarding router to prioritize its packets. At this time, Quality of Service is being investigated in IPv4, and the findings of this research will be used as the basis of traffic classes in IPv6.

- **Flow Label.** This 20-bit field labels packets from a source host that require special handling by IPv6 routers. Flow options could include real-time service or nonstandard quality of service requirements. This portion of the IPv6 header is under review and may change in the future.

- **Payload Length.** This 16-bit field indicates the length of the remainder of the IP packet. This is the total length of the packet minus the IP header. If this value is set to 0, it indicates a payload longer than 65,536 bytes. This is known as a *jumbo payload Hop-by-Hop Option*.

- **Next Header.** This 8-bit field indicates the option header that immediately follows the IP header. The values in this field are the same as the IPv4 protocol field options.

- **Hop Limit.** This 8-bit field is the IPv6 equivalent of the Time-To-Live (TTL) field in IPv4. Every time a packet is forwarded between network segments, this value is decremented by one. When the Hop Limit reaches a value of 0, it is discarded.

- **Source Address.** This 128-bit field contains the source host's IPv6 address.

- **Destination Address.** This 128-bit field contains the destination host's IPv6 address. In IPv6, this destination field might not contain the ultimate destination host address if the Routing header option is included.

IPv6 Extension Headers

RFC 2460 In IPv6, optional Internet-level information from the TCP/IP layered model is included in separate option headers. These headers are located between the IP header and the upper-layer header of the packet. An IPv6 packet can contain zero, one, or many extension headers (see Figure 21.4).

FIGURE 21.4

IP option header examples.

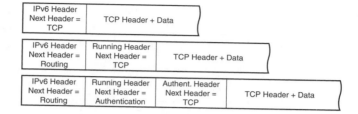

> **There's Always an Exception to the Rule**
>
> The Hop-by-Hop option header, discussed in more detail in the following section, is the only exception. Because intermediary hosts can examine the Hop-by-Hop option header, it must immediately follow the IP header in the packet. This option header's presence is indicated by a value of 0 in the Next Header option field of the IP header.

Extension headers are not examined or processed by routers along a packet's delivery path. Only the designated destination address investigates the option headers. Option headers are processed in the order they appear in the IPv6 packet. A receiving host cannot scan the option headers looking for a specific extension header. All preceding extension headers must be processed first.

A full implementation of IPv6 contains support for the following extension headers:

- Hop-by-Hop Options
- Destination Options
- Routing
- Fragment
- Authentication Header
- Encapsulating Security Payload
- No Next Header

Figure 21.5 shows the order in which these extension headers must appear if they are used in the same packet.

Each extension header should appear no more than once in an IPv6 packet. The only exception is the Destination Options header. A Destination Options header can be located before the routing header. Options in this header are processed by every destination address in the routing header. A destination header also can exist before the Upper-Layer Protocol header. The Upper-Layer Protocol header is a header related to an application-layer protocol. The ultimate destination host of the packet can only process this header.

21

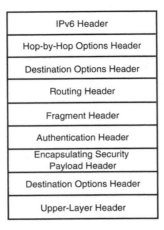

| IPv6 Header |
| Hop-by-Hop Options Header |
| Destination Options Header |
| Routing Header |
| Fragment Header |
| Authentication Header |
| Encapsulating Security Payload Header |
| Destination Options Header |
| Upper-Layer Header |

Hop-by-Hop Options Header

The Hop-by-Hop Options header carries information that must be examined by every node a packet crosses along the path to a destination host. A Next Header value of 0 in the IPv6 header indicates the existence of a Hop-by-Hop Options header.

Hop-by-Hop Options also can indicate a jumbo payload. Jumbo payloads are IPv6 packets with payloads longer than 65,536 octets, which must be known by routers for fragmentation purposes.

The format of the Hop-by-Hop Options header is shown in Figure 21.6.

FIGURE 21.6

The Hop-by-Hop extension header.

| Next Header | Header Ext. Len | |
| Options | | |

The Hop-by-Hop Options header contains the following fields:

- **Next Header.** This 8-bit field identifies what type of header immediately follows the Hop-by-Hop header.
- **Header Extension Length.** This 8-bit field indicates the length of the Hop-by-Hop options field in 8-octet units (not including the first 8 octets).
- **Options.** This variable-length field depends on the number and type of options. These options generally are of type-length-value (TLV) style (see Figure 21.7).

Figure 21.7

TLV option field format.

Any options in the Hop-by-Hop header must be processed in sequential order. The Option Type field is encoded so that the leftmost two bits indicate what action should be taken if an IPv6 node does not recognize the included option type. The following bit values can be used:

- 00. Indicates that this option should be skipped and the next header should be processed.

- 01. Indicates that the packet should be discarded.

- 10. Indicates that the packet should be discarded and the source address should be informed using ICMP that the packet was dropped as a result of an unknown option. This is done if the destination is a unicast or multicast address.

- 11. Indicates that the packet should be discarded and sends the source host an ICMP packet that indicates an unrecognized option was received. This is sent only if the destination address was not a multicast address.

Destination Options Header

The Destination Options header contains information that can be investigated only by the destination host or by intermediate hosts. This depends on the location of the destination header in comparison to other headers.

The Destination Options header uses the same format as the Hop-by-Hop header (refer to Figure 21.6). It also uses the same TLV option format.

Routing Header

An IPv6 source host uses the Routing header to list which nodes must be crossed during the transmission of a packet to a destination host. A Routing header is identified in the previous header's Next Header field with a value of 43.

The format of a Type 0 Routing header, shown in Figure 21.8, includes the following fields:

- **Next Header.** This 8-bit field identifies what type of header immediately follows the Routing header. This field uses the same values as the IPv4 protocol field.

- **Header Extension Length.** This 8-bit field indicates the length of the Routing header in 8-octet units (not including the first 8 octets). For a Type 0 Routing header, this value equals two times the number of addresses in the header.

21

- **Routing Type.** This 8-bit field identifies the format of the Routing header. This is an example of a Type 0 Routing header and would be set to a value of 0.
- **Segments Left.** This 8-bit field indicates how many explicitly listed nodes still need to be visited before reaching the destination host.
- **Reserved.** This 32-bit field is initialized with a value of 0 by the source host and is ignored by the destination host.
- **Address[1..n].** This is a list of 128-bit IPv6 addresses that must be navigated from source host to destination host.

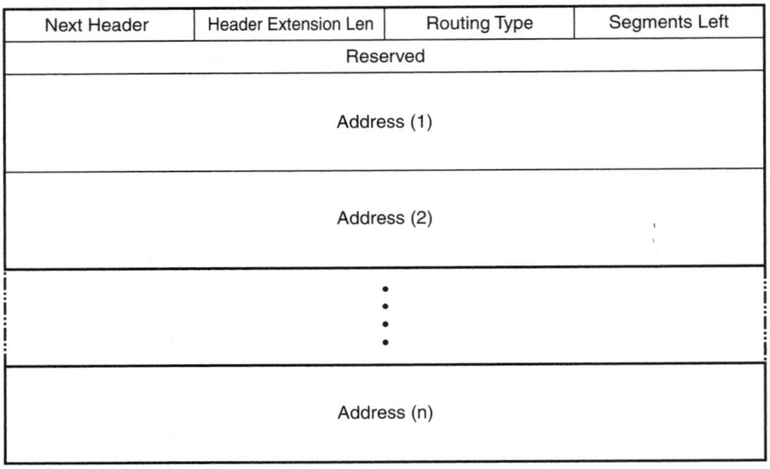

FIGURE 21.8

Type 0 Routing option header format.

Next Header	Header Extension Len	Routing Type	Segments Left
Reserved			
Address (1)			
Address (2)			
⋮			
Address (n)			

Fragment Header

In IPv6, a key feature is the recognition of the Maximum Transmission Unit (MTU) for the entire path between source and destination hosts. The MTU is the smallest packet size (in octets) required on any of the networks traversed between source and destination.

Because the path MTU is determined before transmission, the source nodes handle all fragmentation. Routers along the delivery path, as is currently done in IPv4, never fragment the packet. The Fragment header is indicated by a value of 44 in the Next Header field of the preceding extension option header.

The format of a Fragment header, shown in Figure 21.9, includes the following:

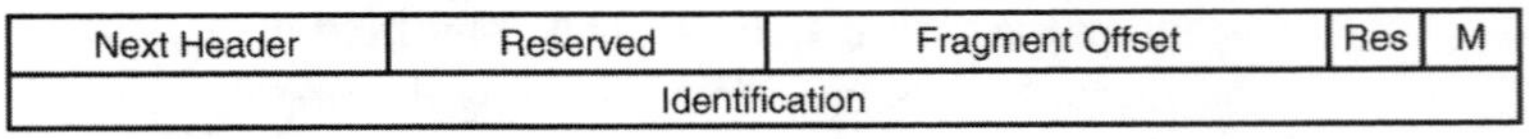

FIGURE 21.9

IPv6 Fragment header format.

Next Header	Reserved	Fragment Offset	Res	M
Identification				

The following is the format of a Fragment header:

- **Next Header.** This 8-bit field identifies what type of header immediately follows the Fragment header. This field uses the same values as the IPv4 protocol field.
- **Reserved.** This 8-bit field is initialized to 0 transmission but is ignored on reception.
- **Fragment Offset.** This 13-bit field is the offset location of the data following this header in 8-octet units. The offset is based on the start of the fragmentable part of the original packet.
- **Res.** This 2-bit field is initialized to 0 transmission but is ignored on reception.
- **M.** The more fragments flag is set to 1 if more fragments from the original packet are to follow. It is set to 0 if this is the last fragment of the original packet.
- **Identification.** This unique identifier created by the source host identifies that the fragments together represent an original, unfragmented packet.

The original, unfragmented packet comprises two component parts: the unfragmentable and fragmentable parts. The unfragmentable part consists of the IPv6 header and any extension headers that precede the routing header (including the routing header). This is known as the unfragmentable part of the packet because this information is required in every fragment created. The fragmentable part contains the remaining data within the packet.

Each fragment packet includes the unfragmentable part of the original packet, a fragment header, and a portion of the fragmentable data from the original packet (see Figure 21.10).

FIGURE 21.10

IPv6 fragmented packet contents.

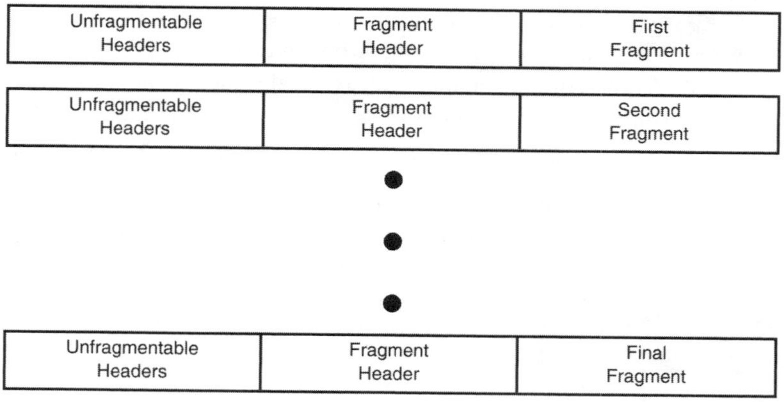

Unfragmentable Headers	Fragment Header	First Fragment

Unfragmentable Headers	Fragment Header	Second Fragment

Unfragmentable Headers	Fragment Header	Final Fragment

21

When the fragment packets are received at the destination host, the reassembly process begins with the identification and offset fields. The payload length of the original fragment is calculated using the following formula:

$$Payload_{original} = Payload_{first} - Frag\ Len_{first} - 8 + (8 * Frag\ Offset_{Last}) + Frag\ Len_{Last}$$

where

- $Payload_{original}$ is the length of the original packet.
- $Payload_{first}$ is the payload length of the first fragment packet.
- $Frag\ Len_{first}$ is the length of the fragment following the fragment header in the first fragment packet.
- $Frag\ Offset_{Last}$ is the Fragment offset field of the last fragment header. Multiply this value by 8 to convert the octet value into bytes.
- $Frag\ Len_{Last}$ is the length of the fragment following the fragment header of the last fragment packet.

This process is similar to the fragmentation process in IPv4. IPv4 uses the Identification field, the More Fragment flag, and the Fragment Offset field to determine how a fragmented packet is reassembled.

In IPv6, collecting all the packets with the same Identification field value reassembles the packet. Together, they make up the original packet. They are reassembled based on the offset field values. The offset field indicates the fragment's position in the original packet.

Authentication Options Header

RFC 2402 The Authentication Header is used by Internet Protocol Security (IPSec) to provide a mechanism for strong authentication for IP datagrams and is built in to the IPv6 protocol. This authentication is calculated using all nonmutable fields (fields that do not change in transit) in the IP datagram. This does not include fields such as Hop Count. These fields are assigned a value of 0 when the authentication information is calculated.

The authentication data is carried in the data of the authentication header so it will work properly without changing the underlying infrastructure of the Internet.

An Authentication header is indicated by a value of 51 in the Next Header field of the preceding extension option. Figure 21.11 shows the format of an Authentication Packet header.

FIGURE 21.11

*IPv6 Authentication
Header format.*

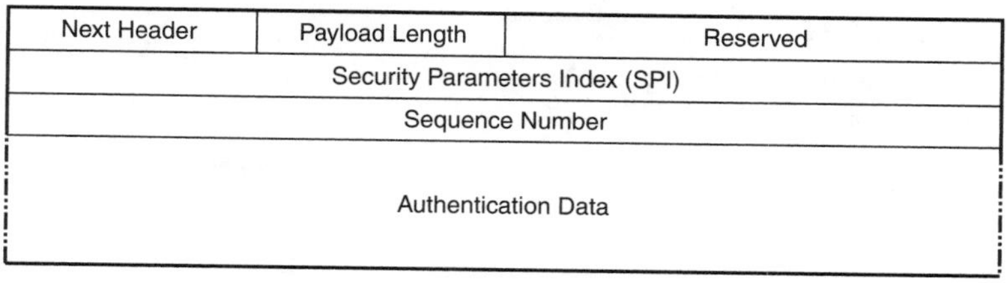

Next Header	Payload Length	Reserved
Security Parameters Index (SPI)		
Sequence Number		
Authentication Data		

The following is the format of the Authentication header:

- **Next Header.** This 8-bit field identifies the header that follows the Authentication header. This field uses the same values as the IPv4 protocol field.

- **Payload Length.** The length of the Authentication Data field in 32-bit words less 2 32-bit words.

- **Reserved.** This 16-bit field is reserved for future use. It is set to a value of 0 by the source host but is ignored by the destination host.

- **Security Parameters Index.** This 32-bit pseudorandom value identifies the security association for a packet. If the value is set to 0, no security association exists. The security association is unidirectional in nature. The recipient of the packet assigns the SPI value to the security association of that specific sender.

- **Sequence Number.** This 32-bit field contains a monotonically increasing sequence number that is initially set to zero when a security association is established between two hosts. The recipient host uses the sequence number to prevent replay attacks.

- **Authentication Data.** This variable-length field contains the authentication information for the Security Parameters Index. The destination host uses the destination address and SPI value in the IP authentication header to determine the correct security association for the client. The information in the Authentication Data field and the data packet received are compared to be sure they are consistent.

Encapsulating Security Payload Header

RFC 2406 The Encapsulating Security Payload (ESP) header provides integrity and confidentiality to IP datagrams using IPSec. This is provided by encrypting the data portion of the encapsulating security payload. Depending on the selected level of security, this can include encrypting the entire IP datagram or just the upper-layer data.

The Next Header field of the previous extension option header must point to option 50 for an ESP header. The ESP header is inserted into an IP packet just before a transport-layer protocol header such as Transmission Control Protocol (TCP) or User Datagram Protocol (UDP). Figure 21.12 shows the format of an ESP header.

21

FIGURE 21.12

IPv6 Encapsulating Security Payload header format.

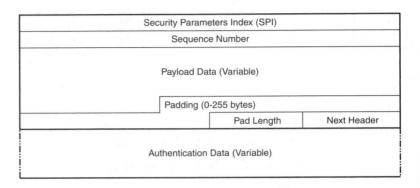

- **Security Parameters Index.** This field, in combination with the destination IP address and the ESP security protocol, uniquely identifies the security association for the datagram.

- **Sequence Number.** This 32-bit field contains a monotonically increasing sequence number that is initially set to 0 when a security association is established between two hosts. The recipient host uses the sequence number to prevent replay attacks.

- **Payload Data.** This variable-length field contains the encrypted data referenced by the Next Header field in the ESP header.

- **Padding.** Some encryption algorithms require that the data to be encrypted be of a specific block size, and this field enables expansion of the data to the required block size. Additionally, padding may be used to ensure that the encrypted cyphertext ends at a 4-byte boundary.

- **Pad Length.** This field indicates the number of pad bytes immediately preceding this field. The field can be defined for values from 0 to 255 bytes where a value of 0 represents no padding is present.

- **Next Header.** This 8-bit field identifies the type of information stored in the Payload Data field, based on IP protocol numbers defined in Standard 2 (STD2) "Assigned Numbers."

- **Authentication Data.** This variable-length field contains the authentication information for the Security Parameters Index. The destination host uses the destination address and SPI value in the IP authentication header to determine the correct security association for the client. The information in the Authentication Data field and the data packet received are compared to make sure they are consistent. This field is only used if a security association requires the use of authentication for ESP packets.

ESP can be implemented in two modes. In *tunnel-mode ESP*, the original IP datagram is placed in the encrypted portion of the ESP payload. The entire ESP frame is then placed within an unencrypted IP datagram used to route the datagram from the source host to the destination host. In *transport-mode ESP*, the ESP header is inserted in the IP datagram immediately prior to the Transport-Layer Protocol header. This provides more bandwidth because there are no encrypted headers or options to be decrypted at the destination host.

 Note | For more information on ESP headers and the use of ESP to encrypt transmitted data, review the material in Day 12, "Encrypting Transmitted Data."

No Next Header

If the Next Header field in an IPv6 header or extension header contains a value of 59, nothing follows that header. If the Payload field indicates that information exists beyond the end of the header, even though the Next Header value is set to 59, this information is ignored. If the packet is forwarded, the information is passed on unchanged to the next node. It is not truncated.

The Transition from IPv4 to IPv6

RFC 2893 In the near future, the transition from IPv4 to IPv6 will begin to take place. This section discusses the mechanisms being put in place to make this transition easier.

The Internet will soon enter a transition state, just as it did when ARPAnet switched from NCP to TCP/IP as the standard protocol for transport. The goal of this transition is for IPv6 to be compatible with the large installed base of IPv4. An immediate switch is not possible for migration to IPv6.

All mechanisms to help with this transition must be placed in IPv6. This is because the IPv4 packet does not use IPv6 addressing and packet formats.

The following mechanisms are proposed:

- Installing a dual IP layer that supports both IPv4 and IPv6 for all hosts and routers.
- Including IPv6 over IPv4 tunneling. This method encapsulates an IPv6 packet within an IPv4 header, enabling transit over an IPv4 network using IPv4 routing mechanisms.

21

- Using Transport Relay Translators (TRT). This method uses a TRT system that acts as a middle device that translates TCP and UDP transmissions between IPv6 and IPv4 and between IPv4 and IPv6.

At this time, all three mechanisms are possibilities. I believe as the arrival of IPv6 draws nearer, the ultimate solution between IPv4 and IPv6 will be the use of dual stacks.

The use of tunneling and TRTs will probably not fall in the domain of companies, but of ISPs and routing companies that must route information between IPv4 and IPv6 networks. Companies that are researching IPv6 are more likely to load a dual stack on test computers during the research period.

Using IPv6 Today!

If you want to investigate using IPv6 addressing in your network, you can use the following links and instructions to load an IPv6 implementation for your operating system.

For Windows 2000, Microsoft Research makes available a version of IPv6 that can be loaded on a Windows 2000 computer for research, education, and testing purposes. You can download the protocol stack at

`http://research.microsoft.com/msripv6/msripv6.htm`.

Windows XP includes an IPv6 implementation in the operating system. This prerelease version of IPv6 is also intended for testing, and can be loaded from a command prompt, by typing `ipv6 install`. There is also an excellent help file on IPv6, `ipv6.chm`, that provides information on using the IPv6 protocol in Windows XP.

The Linux IPv6 Development Project, also known as the USAGI (UniverSAl playGround for Ipv6) project, provides a test version of the IPv6 protocol that can be loaded on various Linux versions at `www.linux-ipv6.org/`.

Finaly, the KAME project (`www.kame.net`), provides an IPv6 stack for BSD variants, including FreeBSd, OpenBSD, NetBSD, and BSD/OS.

Using a Dual IP Layer

This is the easier implementation for coexistence of IPv4 and IPv6. Each IPv6 host also would include a complete IPv4 implementation. These nodes would be known as IPv6/IPv4 nodes. They would have the capability to send and receive both IPv6 and IPv4 packets. This would enable them to communicate directly with IPv4-only and IPv6-only hosts.

IPv6/IPv4 hosts would require assignment of both IPv4 and IPv6 addresses. These addresses usually would be related to each other, but they also can be totally independent. When IPv4 and IPv6 addresses are related to each other, the IPv6 address would be represented as the IPv4 address prefixed with 96 bits set to 0. The IPv4 address would be the last 32 bits of the IPv6 address (see Figure 21.13).

FIGURE 21.13

An IPv4-compatible IPv6 address.

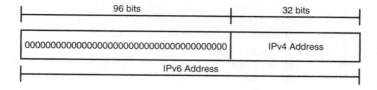

Other issues that must be addressed for IPv6/IPv4 hosts include the following:

- IPv6/IPv4 hosts should be able to acquire their IPv4 addresses from IPv4 configuration methods such as a BOOTP or DHCP server so that these IPv4 configuration methods are leveraged.

- IPv6/IPv4 hosts must treat both the IPv6 address ::1 and the IPv4 compatible address ::127.0.0.1 as loopback addresses. Any packets addressed to either of these addresses should not be put on the network; they should stay local to the node.

- DNS should support A records for IPv4 addresses and A6 and AAAA records for IPv6 addresses. IPv6/IPv4 hosts should have DNS resolver libraries that can handle both A,A6, and AAAA records.

IPv6 and DNS

A new resource record type named "A6" has been defined for DNS to support IPv6 addresses. Depending on the IPv6 implementation, your DNS server may also have to support the previous IPv6 resource records known as "AAAA" resource records.

- If the DNS resolver finds both an A record and an A6/AAAA record for a host, it does not have to return both addresses. It can return the IPv4 address only, the IPv6 address only, or both addresses. The major issue is that the returned address determines whether IPv4 or IPv6 methods are used to communicate with the destination host.

- A6/AAAA resource records should only be added to DNS if the following three conditions are met:
  - The host has an IPv6 address assigned to one of its interfaces.
  - The interface is properly configured with IPv6 address information.
  - The interface with the IPv6 address is connected to an IPv6 infrastructure.

21

Caution If a host with an IPv6 assigned address is not connected to an IPv6 infrastructure, there can be communication problems when connections to other IPv6
hosts take place. If DNS returns an A6 or AAAA resource record for a target
host, the IPv6 host will attempt to connect using IPv6, even if the host does
not register its own IPv6 address in DNS. This act will result in the communication attempt failing, and a communication delay waiting for the TCP connection to timeout, before an attempt is made using IPv4.

IPv6 over IPv4 Tunneling Options

Tunneling IPv6 over IPv4 networks enables IPv6 to be deployed using existing routing
infrastructure. The IPv6 packet is encapsulated within IPv4 packets for transmission
across the IPv4 network. Tunneling can be implemented in one of the following four
configurations:

- **Router-to-router.** IPv6/IPv4 routers connected by an IPv4 infrastructure can create
  a tunnel that spans the IPv4 network.

- **Host-to-router.** An IPv6/IPv4 host can tunnel IPv6 packets to an intermediary
  IPv6/IPv4 router that can only be reached over an IPv4 network.

- **Host-to-host.** Two IPv6/IPv4 hosts can create a tunnel that spans an entire IPv4
  network between the two hosts. This provides an end-to-end tunnel between the
  two hosts.

- **Router-to-host.** An IPv6/IPv4 router can form a tunnel to an IPv6/IPv4 host over
  an IPv4 network.

In the case of router-to-router or host-to-router implementation, the router being connected to complete the tunnel is not the ultimate destination host. This creates a need for configured tunneling. The IPv6 packet being transmitted does not have the tunnel endpoint's
IPv4 address in its destination address. Based on the ultimate destination address, the
source host must have a preconfigured tunnel endpoint to which it sends the encapsulated
data. This usually is determined from the source host's routing table.

Another possibility is to configure all tunnels to connect to a common router on an IPv6
backbone. This backbone could include several IPv6/IPv4 routers that have been
assigned an IPv4-compatible anycast address (see Figure 21.14).

In this figure, the three border routers all have been assigned the anycast address of
::172.16.2.1. When the IPv6/IPv4 host at ::172.16.4.5 sends an encapsulated IPv6
packet to the anycast address, it is delivered to the nearest border router with the anycast
address based on routing distance. Setting the default tunnel to an anycast address

provides a high degree of fault tolerance because traffic automatically switches to one of the other border routers if one fails.

FIGURE 21.14

Default configured tunnel using an anycast address.

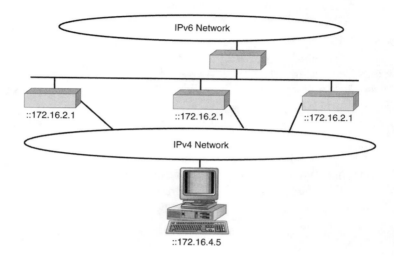

In the case of host-to-host or router-to-host tunneling, the ultimate destination host is the endpoint of the tunnel. The IPv4 address of the host can be determined from the IPv4-compatible address in the IPv6 Destination Host field. This requires that an IPv4-compatible address be used. If it is not used, a configured tunneling solution needs to be implemented.

Implementing a Transport Relay Translator (TRT)

RFC 3142 In June 2001, an informational RFC was released that proposed using a translation device between IPv6 and IPv4 hosts that translates TCP and UDP traffic exchanged between the hosts.

The TRT uses TCP relaying, a technology used in today's firewalls. When a packet is received from an IPv6 host using a specific prefix, the TRT examines the packet for IPv4 address information. The TRT then relays the packet to the destination IPv4 host. In this scenario, there are two separate TCP connections that are established:

- A TCP connection between the initiating host and the TRT.
- A TCP connection between the TRT and the destination host.

The way that the TRT knows that the destination packet must be translated is through the use of a predefined IPv6 prefix of c6::/64. To allow translation to take place, routing tables must be adjusted so that packets sent to c6::/64 are routed to the TRT system.

21

For example, if `c6::/64` is equal to `fec0:0:0:1::/64` and the destination IPv4 address is `10.10.1.4`, the destination address that should be used by the originating IPv6 host is `fec0:0:0:1::10.10.1.4` (see Figure 21.15).

FIGURE 21.15

Using a TRT to translate traffic from an IPv6 host to an IPv4 host.

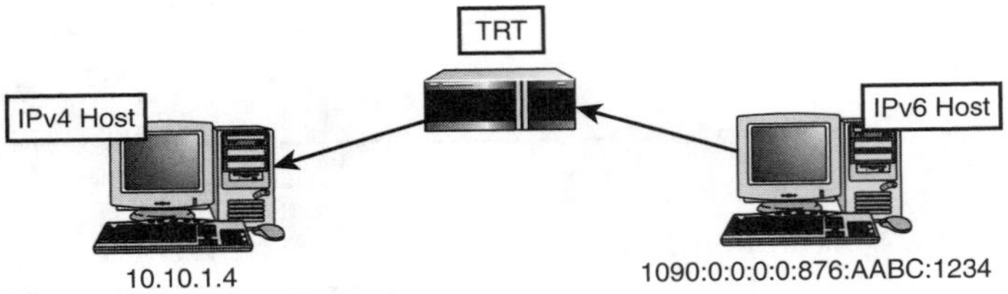

TRT

IPv4 Host

IPv6 Host

10.10.1.4

1090:0:0:0:0:876:AABC:1234

The TRT in this case accepts an initial TCP connection from the IPv6 host (1090::867:AABC:1234) to the TRT host (FEC0:0:0:1::10.1.1.4). The TRT host then strips the IPv4 address from the address and establishes a second TCP connection to the IPv4 host at `10.10.1.4` from its IPv4 interface using IPv4 address `10.10.1.1`. From this point on, the TRT translates data transmission sent between the IPv4 and IPv6 hosts.

> **Caution**
>
> The proposal for TRT is only informational at this time and may not be accepted for the standards track. Due to the load that may exist at the TRT device, this may not become a standard, unless load-balancing solutions are defined, and support for additional protocols other than TCP and UDP are defined.

Applying What You Have Learned

The IP protocol continues to evolve to meet our ever-changing needs. The migration to IPv6 will lead to an addressing scheme that should provide sufficient address space into the next century. It also will provide more efficient use of the network because it eliminates communication methods such as broadcasts.

Here are questions to check what you've learned today. The answers can be found in Appendix B, "Test Your Knowledge: Answers."

Test Your Knowledge

1. What fault tolerance is provided by using an anycast address?
2. What is the difference between sending data to an anycast address and sending data to a multicast address?
3. Identify the IPv6 reserved addresses in Table 21.3:

TABLE 21.3   Identify the IPv6 Address Type

Address	Address Type
0:0:0:0:0:0:0:1	
0:0:0:0:0:FFFF:AC10:0210	
0:0:0:0:0:0:0:0	
0:0:0:0:0:0:C0A8:0344	
FF0E:2322::AD56:0230	

4. How is fragmentation handled differently in IPv6 than it was in IPv4?
5. What methods have been proposed to help the conversion of networks from IPv4 to IPv6?
6. What IPv6 resources are available to you if you wish to start testing IPv6 on your network?

21

APPENDIX A

RFC Reference

The following tables of RFCs are based on the maturity level of each RFC. The following levels are included in this appendix:

- Standard protocols
- Network-specific standard protocols
- Draft standard protocols
- Proposed standard protocols
- Experimental protocols
- Informational protocols
- Historic protocols
- Internet Drafts

Note

> By the time you read this book, new RFCs will be introduced into the pool of RFCs. You can always review the updated list of RFCs at www.ietf.org/rfc.htm or, for a more user-friendly version, at www.networksorcery.com.

Standard Protocols

The Internet Engineering Steering Group (IESG) has established the protocols in Table A.1 as official standard protocols for the Internet. These standard protocols each have been assigned a standard number, and they apply to the entire Internet. Table A.1 shows the current listing of standard protocols.

TABLE A.1   Standard Protocol RFCs

STD	Protocol	Name	RFC
1		Internet Official Protocol Standards	2900
2		Assigned Numbers	1700
3		Host Requirements—Communications	1122
3		Host Requirements—Applications	1123
5	IP	Internet Protocol	791
5	IP	IP Subnet Extension	950
5	IP	IP Broadcast Datagrams	919
5	IP	IP Broadcast Datagrams with Subnets	922
5	ICMP	Internet Control Message Protocol	792
5	IGMP	Internet Group Multicast Protocol	1112
6	UDP	User Datagram Protocol	768
7	TCP	Transmission Control Protocol	793
8	TELNET	Telnet Protocol	854
8	TELNET	Telnet Option Specification	855
9	FTP	File Transfer Protocol	959
10	SMTP	Simple Mail Transfer Protocol	2821
11	MAIL	Format of Electronic Mail Messages	822

TABLE A.1 continued

STD	Protocol	Name	RFC
11	CONTENT	Content Type Header Field	1049
12	NTP	Network Time Protocol (Version 3)	1305
13	DOMAIN	Domain Name System	1034,1035
14	DNS-MX	Mail Routing and the Domain System	974
15	SNMP	Simple Network Management Protocol	1157
16	SMI	Structure of Management Information	1155
17	MIB-II	Management Information Base-II	1213
18	EGP	Exterior Gateway Protocol	904
19	NETBIOS	NetBIOS Service Protocols	1001,1002
20	ECHO	Echo Protocol	862
21	DISCARD	Discard Protocol	863
22	CHARGEN	Character Generator Protocol	864
23	QUOTE	Quote of the Day Protocol	865
24	USERS	Active Users Protocol	866
25	DAYTIME	Daytime Protocol	867
26	TIME	Time Server Protocol	868
27	TELNET	Binary Transmission Telnet Option	856
28	TELNET	Echo Telnet Option	857
29	TELNET	Suppress Go Ahead Telnet Option	858
30	TELNET	Status Telnet Option	859
31	TELNET	Timing Mark Telnet Option	860
32	TELNET	Extended Options List Telnet Option	861
33	TFTP	Trivial File Transfer Protocol	1350
34	RIPv1	Routing Information Protocol (RIP)	1058[*]
35	TP-TCP	ISO Transport Service on top of the TCP	1006
36		Transmission of IP and ARP over FDDI Networks	1390
37	ARP	Ethernet Address Resolution Protocol	826
38	RARP	Reverse Address Resolution Protocol	903
39		IMP/Host Interface	n/a[**]
40	HAP	Host Access Protocol specification	907
41		Transmission of IP datagrams over Ethernet networks	894
42		Transmission of IP datagrams over Experimental Ethernet networks	895

A

TABLE A.1   continued

STD	Protocol	Name	RFC
43	IP-IEEE 802	Transmission of IP datagrams over IEEE 802 networks	1042
44		DCN Local-Network Protocols	891
45	IP-HYPER	Internet Protocol on Network System's HYPERchannel	1044
46	IP-ARCNET	Transmitting IP traffic over ARCNET networks	1201
47		Transmission of IP datagrams over serial lines	1055
48	IP-NETBIOS	Transmission of IP datagrams over NetBIOS networks	1088
49		Transmission of 802.2 packets over IPX networks	1132
50	ETHER-MIB	Ethernet MIB	1643
51	PPP	Point-to-Point Protocol (PPP)	1661
51	PPP-HDLC	PPP in HDLC Framing	1662
52	IP-SMDS	IP Datagrams over the SMDS Service	1209
53	POP3	Post Office Protocol, Version 3	1939
54	OSPF v2	Open Shortest Path First version 2	2328
55		Multiprotocol Interconnect over Frame Relay	2427
56	RIPv2	RIP Version 2	2453
57	RIPv2	RIP Version 2 Protocol Applicability Statement	1722
58	SMIv2	Structure of Management Information Version 2	2578, 2579
59		Remote Network Monitoring Management Information Base	2819
60	SMTP	SMTP Service Extension for Command Pipelining	2920
61		One-Time Password System	2289

* Standard 34—Replaced by Standard 56 when RIP was updated to version 2.

** Standard 39—Now obsolete. The content can be found in Bolt, Beranek, and Newman Report 1822

Network-Specific Standard Protocols

The Internet Engineering Steering Group (IESG) has established the protocols in Table A.2 as official standard protocols for the Internet. Some network-specific standard protocols have been assigned a standard number but are implemented only on a network-specific basis. Not every TCP/IP installation must implement these protocols. Table A.2 shows the current network-specific standard protocols.

TABLE A.2 Network-Specific Standard Protocol RFCs

Protocol	Name	RFC
ARP	Address Resolution Protocol	826
IP-DC	Internet Protocol on DC Networks	891
IP-E	Internet Protocol on Ethernet Networks	894
IP-EE	Internet Protocol on Exp. Ethernet Nets	895
RARP	A Reverse Address Resolution Protocol	903
IP-WB	Internet Protocol on Wideband Network	907
IP-IEEE	Internet Protocol on IEEE 802	1042
IP-HC	Internet Protocol on Hyperchannel	1044
IP-SLIP	Transmission of IP over Serial Lines	1055
IP-NETBIOS	Transmission of IP over NETBIOS	1088
IP-IPX	Transmission of 802.2 over IPX Networks	1132
IP-FDDI	Internet Protocol on FDDI Networks	1188
IP-ARC	Transmitting IP Traffic over ARCNET Nets	1201
IP-SMDS	IP Datagrams over the SMDS Service	1209
IP-X.25	X.25 and ISDN in the Packet Mode	1356
IP-HIPPI	IP and ARP on HIPPI	1374
IP-FDDI	Transmission of IP and ARP over FDDI Net	1390
IP-TR-MC	IP Multicast over Token-Ring LANs	1469
ATM-ENCAP	Multiprotocol Encapsulation over ATM	1483
IP-FR	Multiprotocol over Frame Relay	1490
IP-ATM	Classical IP and ARP over ATM	1577

Draft Standard Protocols

Draft standard protocols are being considered by the IESG to become standard protocols. Widespread testing is performed on draft standard protocols. Table A.3 shows the current draft standard protocols.

TABLE A.3 Draft Standard Protocol RFCs

Protocol	Name	RFC
BOOTP	Bootstrap Protocol	951, 1497
NICNAME	WhoIs Protocol	954

TABLE A.3 continued

Protocol	Name	RFC
IP-MTU	Path MTU Discovery	1191
BGP3	Border Gateway Protocol 3 (BGP-3)	1267, 1268
FINGER	Finger Protocol	1288
NTPV3	Network Time Protocol (Version 3)	1305
BRIDGE-MIB	BRIDGE-MIB	1493
802.3-MIB	IEEE 802.3 Repeater MIB	1516
MIME	Multipurpose Internet Mail Extensions	1521
-------	Message Header Ext. of Non-ASCII Text	1522
DECNET-MIB	DECNET MIB	1559
ISO-TS-ECHO	Echo for ISO-8473	1575
OSPF2	Open Shortest Path First Routing V2	1583
OSI-NSAP	Guidelines for OSI NSAP Allocation	1629
SMTP-EXT	SMTP Service Extensions	1651
SMTP-8BIT	SMTP Service Ext or 8bit-MIMEtransport	1652
SMTP-SIZE	SMTP Service Ext for Message Size	1653
BGP-4-MIB	BGP-4 MIB	1657
-------	Def Man Objs Character Stream	1658
-------	Def Man Objs RS-232-like	1659
-------	Def Man Objs Parallel-printer-like	1660
SIP-MIB	SIP Interface Type MIB	1694
RIP2-APP	RIP Version 2 Protocol App. Statement	1722
RIP2	RIP Version 2-Carrying Additional Info	1723
RIP2-MIB	RIP Version 2 MIB Extension	1724
POP3	Post Office Protocol, Version 3	1725
802.5-MIB	IEEE 802.5 Token Ring MIB	1748
RMON-MIB	Remote Network Monitoring MIB	1757
PPP-DNCP	PPP DECnet Phase IV Control Protocol	1762
BGP-4	Border Gateway Protocol 4	1771
BGP-4-APP	Application of BGP-4	1772
X.500lite	X.500 Lightweight	1777
X.500syn	X.500 String Representation	1778
STR-REP	String Representation	1779

Proposed Standard Protocols

Proposed standard protocols are in the first stages of consideration to become standard protocols. Several groups are involved with the implementation and testing of these protocols. Table A.4 shows the current proposed standard protocols.

A

TABLE A.4   Proposed Standard Protocol RFCs

Protocol	Name	RFC
NNTP	Network News Transfer Protocol	977
IPSO	DoD Security Options for IP	1108
IP-CMPRS	Compressing TCP/IP Headers	1144
IS-IS	OSI IS-IS for TCP/IP Dual Environments	1195
GINT-MIB	Extensions to the Generic-Interface MIB	1229
IPX-IP	Tunneling IPX Traffic through IP Nets	1234
STD-MIBs	Reassignment of Exp MIBs to Std MIBs	1239
OSI-UDP	OSI TS on UDP	1240
OSPF-MIB	OSPF Version 2 MIB	1253
ICMP-ROUT	ICMP Router Discovery Messages	1256
BGP-MIB	Border Gateway Protocol MIB (Version 3)	1269
-------	COSINE and Internet X.500 Schema	1274
-------	Replication and Distributed Operations	1276
-------	Encoding Network Addresses	1277
FDDI-MIB	FDDI-MIB	1285
IARP	Inverse Address Resolution Protocol	1293
NETFAX	File Format for the Exchange of Images	1314
FRAME-MIB	Management Information Base for Frame	1315
TCP-EXT	TCP Extensions for High Performance	1323
-------	Mapping between X.400 (1988)	1327
-------	X.400 1988 to 1984 downgrading	1328
PPP-IPCP	PPP Control Protocol	1332
PPP-LINK	PPP Link Quality Monitoring	1333
PPP-AUTH	PPP Authentication	1334
TOS	Type of Service in the Internet	1349
SNMP-ADMIN	SNMP Administrative Model	1351
SNMP-SEC	SNMP Security Protocols	1352

TABLE A.4 continued

Protocol	Name	RFC
SNMP-PARTY-	MIB Administration of SNMP	1353
TABLE-MIB	IP Forwarding Table MIB	1354
PPP-OSINLCP	PPP OSI Network Layer Control Protocol	1377
PPP-ATCP	PPP AppleTalk Control Protocol	1378
SNMP-LAPB	SNMP MIB Extension for X.25 LAPB	1381
SNMP-X.25	SNMP MIB Extension for X.25 Packet Layer	1382
--------	Route Advertisement in BGP2 and BGP3	1397
BGP-OSPF	BGP OSPF Interaction	1403
DS1/E1-MIB	DS1/E1 Interface Type	1406
DS3/E3-MIB	DS3/E3 Interface Type	1407
IDENT	Identification Protocol	1413
IDENT-MIB	Identification MIB	1414
FTP-FTAM	FTP-FTAM Gateway Specification	1415
SNMP-OSI	SNMP over OSI	1418
SNMP-AT	SNMP over AppleTalk	1419
SNMP-IPX	SNMP over IPX	1420
PEM-ENC	PEM - Message Encryption and Auth	1421
PEM-CKM	PEM - Certificate-Based Key Management	1422
PEM-ALG	PEM - Algorithms, Modes, and Identifiers	1423
PEM-KEY	PEM - Key Certification	1424
SNMPv2	Introduction to SNMPv2	1441
SNMPv2	SMI for SNMPv2	1442
SNMPv2	Textual Conventions for SNMPv2	1443
SNMPv2	Conformance Statements for SNMPv2	1444
SNMPv2	Administrative Model for SNMPv2	1445
SNMPv2	Security Protocols for SNMPv2	1446
SNMPv2	Party MIB for SNMPv2	1447
SNMPv2	Protocol Operations for SNMPv2	1448
SNMPv2	Transport Mappings for SNMPv2	1449
SNMPv2	Management Information Base for SNMPv2	1450
SNMPv2	Manager-to-Manager MIB	1451
SNMPv2	Coexistence between SNMPv1 and SNMPv2	1452

TABLE A.4 continued

Protocol	Name	RFC
X25-MIB	Multiprotocol Interconnect on X.25 MIB	1461
PPP/LCP MIB	Link Control Protocol of PPP MIB	1471
PPP/SEC MIB	Security Protocols of PPP MIB	1472
PPP/IP MIB	IP Network Control Protocol of PPP MIB	1473
PPP/Bridge	MIB Bridge PPP MIB	1474
IDPR-ARCH	Architecture for IDPR	1478
IDPR	Inter-Domain Policy Routing Protocol	1479
Equiv	X.400/MIME Body Equivalences	1494
Mapping	MHS/RFC-822 Message Body Mapping	1495
HARPOON	Rules for Downgrading Messages...	1496
--------	X.400 Use of Extended Character Sets	1502
DASS	Distributed Authentication Security	1507
GSSAPI	Generic Security Service Application	1508
GSSAPI	Generic Security Service API: C-bindings	1509
KERBEROS	Kerberos Network Authentication Ser (V5)	1510
FDDI-MIB	FDDI Management Information Base	1512
--------	Token Ring Extensions to RMON MIB	1513
HOST-MIB	Host Resources MIB	1514
--------	802.3 MAU MIB	1515
CIDR-APP	CIDR Applicability Statement	1517
CIDR-ARCH	CIDR Architecture	1518
CIDR-STRA	CIDR Address Assignment	1519
SRB-MIB	Source Routing Bridge MIB	1525
DHCP	Dynamic Host Configuration Protocol	1531
BOOTP	Clarifications and Extensions BOOTP	1532
DHCP-BOOTP	DHCP Options and BOOTP Vendor Extensions	1533
DHCP-BOOTP	Interoperation Between DHCP and BOOTP	1534
CON-MD5	Content-MD5 Header Field	1544
IPXCP	PPP Internetworking Packet Exchange Control	1552
CIPX	Compressing IPX Headers over WAM Media	1553
NSM-MIB	Network Services Monitoring MIB	1565
MAIL-MIB	Mail Monitoring MIB	1566

A

TABLE A.4   continued

Protocol	Name	RFC
X500-MIB	X.500 Directory Monitoring MIB	1567
PPP-LCP	PPP LCP Extensions	1570
--------	Evolution of the Interfaces Group of MIB-	1573
RIP-DC	Extensions to RIP to Support Demand Cir.	1582
OSPF-Multi	Multicast Extensions to OSPF	1584
OSPF-NSSA	The OSPF NSSA Option	1587
SONET-MIB	MIB SONET/SDH Interface Type	1595
PPP-X25	PPP in X.25	1598
FR-MIB	Frame Relay Service MIB	1604
DNS-S-MIB	DNS Server MIB Extensions	1611
DNS-R-MIB	DNS Resolver MIB Extensions	1612
PPP-ISDN	PPP over ISDN	1618
PPP-SONET	PPP over SONET/SDH	1619
AAL5-MTU	Default IP MTU for use over ATM AAL5	1626
UPS-MIB	UPS Management Information Base	1628
PPP-BCP	PPP Bridging Control Protocol	1638
TN3270-En	TN3270 Enhancements	1647
--------	Postmaster Convention X.400 Operations	1648
BGP-4-IMP	BGP-4 Roadmap and Implementation	1656
PPP-TRANS	PPP Reliable Transmission	1663
SNANAU-MIB	SNA NAUs MIB using SMIv2	1665
ATM-MIB	ATM Management Version 8.0 Using SMIv2	1695
MODEM-MIB	Modem MIB - Using SMIv2	1696
RDBMS-MIB	RDMS MIB - Using SMIv2	1697
PPP-MP	PPP Multilink Protocol	1717
IMAP4	Internet Message Access Protocol V4	1730
IMAP4-AUTH	IMAP4 Authentication Mechanisms	1731
POP3-AUTH	POP3 Authentication Command	1734
URL	Uniform Resource Locators	1738
MacMIME	MIME Encapsulation of Macintosh Files	1740
AT-MIB	Appletalk MIB	1742
BGP4/IDRP	BGP4/IDRP for IP/OSPF Interaction	1745

TABLE A.4 continued

Protocol	Name	RFC
SDLCSMIv2	SNADLC SDLC MIB Using SMIv2	1747
802.5-SSR	802.5 SSR MIB Using SMIv2	1749
IPNG	Recommendation for IP Next Generation	1752
ATM-SIG	ATM Signaling Support for IP over ATM	1755
Print-MIB	Printer MIB	1759
BVCP	PPP Banyan Vines Control Protocol	1763
XNSCP	PPP XNS IDP Control Protocol	1764
Lang-Tag	Tags for Identification of Languages	1766
MIME-EDI	MIME Encapsulation of EDI Objects	1767
OSI-Dir	OSI User Friendly Naming	1781
TFTP-Ext	TFTP Option Extension	1782
TFTP-Blk	TFTP Blocksize Option	1783
TFTP-Opt	TFTP Options	1784

Experimental Protocols

Experimental protocols are in the earliest stage of development and are not intended for general use yet. Although they might enter the standards track later, they currently are not intended for operational use unless you are participating in the experiment. Table A.5 lists the current experimental protocols.

TABLE A.5 Experimental Protocol RFCs

Protocol	Name	RFC
RLP	Resource Location Protocol	887
RDP	Reliable Data Protocol	908,1151
LDP	Loader Debugger Protocol	909
IRTP	Internet Reliable Transaction Protocol	938
NETBLT	Bulk Data Transfer Protocol	998
COOKIE-JAR	Authentication Scheme	1004
VMTP	Versatile Message Transaction Protocol	1045
IP-DVMRP	IP Distance Vector Multicast Routing	1075
--------	Mapping Full 822 to Restricted 822	1137

TABLE A.5   continued

Protocol	Name	RFC
TCP-ACO	TCP Alternate Checksum Option	1146
DMF-MAIL	Digest Message Format for Mail	1153
NTP-OSI	NTP over OSI Remote Operations	1165
IMAP2	Interactive Mail Access Protocol	1176
DNS-RR	New DNS RR Definitions	1183
SNMP-BULK	Bulk Table Retrieval with the SNMP	1187
ST-II	Stream Protocol	1190
MPP	Message Posting Protocol	1204
ALERTS	Managing Asynchronously Generated Alerts	1224
IP-AX.25	IP Encapsulation of AX.25 Frames	1226
SNMP-DPI	SNMP Distributed Program Interface	1228
CFDP	Coherent File Distribution Protocol	1235
CLNS-MIB	CLNS-MIB	1238
IN-ENCAP	Internet Encapsulation Protocol	1241
--------	X.500 and Domains	1279
DSLCP	Dynamically Switched Link Control	1307
MSP2	Message Send Protocol 2	1312
TCP-HIPER	TCP Extensions for High Performance	1323
RMCP	Remote Mail Checking Protocol	1339
DNS-IP	Experiment in DNS-Based IP Routing	1383
TRACE-IP	Traceroute Using an IP Option	1393
MAP-MAIL	X.400 Mapping and Mail-11	1405
TEL-KER	Telnet Authentication: Kerberos V4	1411
TEL-SPX	Telnet Authentication: SPX	1412
DIR-ARP	Directed ARP	1433
SIFT/UFT	Sender-Initiated/Unsolicited File Transfer	1440
TOS-LS	Link Security TOS	1455
IRCP	Internet Relay Chat Protocol	1459
DNS	Storing Arbitrary Attributes in DNS	1464
X400	Routing Coordination for X.400 Services	1465
TP/IX	TP/IX: The Next Internet	1475
RAP	Internet Route Access Protocol	1476

TABLE A.5 continued

Protocol	Name	RFC
REM-PRT	An Experiment in Remote Printing	1486
EHF-MAIL	Encoding Header Field for Internet Messages	1505
REM-PRINT	TPC.INT Subdomain Remote Printing - Technical	1528
CLNP-TUBA	Use of ISO CLNP in TUBA Environments	1561
SNMP-DPI	SNMP Distributed Protocol Interface	1592
X500-DIR	Representing IP Information in the X.500 Directory	1608
X500-CHART	Charting Networks in the X.500 Directory	1609
FOOBAR	FTP Operation over Big Address Records	1639
MIME-UNI	Using Unicode with MIME	1641
UTF-7	A Mail-Safe Transformation Format of Unicode	1642
T/TCP	TCP Extensions for Transactions	1644
-------	DNS to Distribute RFC1327 Mail Address Mapping Tables	1664
TCP-POS	An Extension to TCP: Partial Order Service	1693
DNS-ENCODE	DNS Encoding of Geographical Location	1712
DNS-DEBUG	Tools for DNS debugging	1713
NARP	NBMA Address Resolution Protocol	1735
RWP	Remote Write Protocol - Version 1.0	1756
OSPF-OVFL	OSPF Database Overflow	1765
CLNP-MULT	Host Group Extensions for CLNP Multicasting	1768

Informational Protocols

Informational protocols are developed outside the influence of the IESG. Some are published as RFCs so the Internet community can have easier access to the demos. Some informational protocols are developed by outside organizations or vendors. Table A.6 lists the current informational protocols.

TABLE A.6 Informational Protocol RFCs

Protocol	Name	RFC
PCMAIL	Pcmail Transport Protocol	1056
SUN-RPC	Remote Procedure Call Protocol Version 2	1057
SUN-NFS	Network File System Protocol	1094
LPDP	Line Printer Daemon Protocol	1179

TABLE A.6 continued

Protocol	Name	RFC
MD4	MD4 Message Digest Algorithm	1186
DAS	Directory Assistance Service	1202
SNMP-TRAPS	Defining Traps for Use with SNMP	1215
SUBNETASGN	On the Assignment of Subnet Numbers	1219
HAP2	Host Access Protocol	1221
OSI-HYPER	OSI and LLC1 on HYPERchannel	1223
IP-X.121	IP to X.121 Address Mapping for DDN	1236
DIXIE	DIXIE Protocol Specification	1249
-------	Replication Requirements	1275
BSD Login	BSD Login	1282
MTP	Multicast Transport Protocol	1301
LISTSERV	Listserv Distribute Protocol	1429
-------	Data Link Switching: Switch-to-Switch Protocol	1434
GOPHER	The Internet Gopher Protocol	1436
TACACS	Terminal Access Control Protocol	1492
AUBR	Appletalk Update-Based Routing Protocol...	1504
ADSNA-IP	Advanced SNA/IP: A Simple SNA Transport Protocol	1538
IPXWAN	Novell IPX over Various WAN Media	1634
SNPP	Simple Network Paging Protocol - Version 2	1645
TMUX	Transport Multiplexing Protocol	1692
GRE	Generic Routing Encapsulation	1701
GRE-IPv4	Generic Routing Encapsulation over IPv4	1702
RADIO-PAGE	TPC.INT Subdomain: Radio Paging—Technical Procedures	1703
DNS-NSAP	DNS NSAP Resource Records	1706
RWHOIS	Referral Whois Protocol	1714
BINHEX	MIME Content Type for BinHex Encoded Files	1741
SNOOP	Snoop Version 2 Packet Capture File Format	1761
SNTP	Simple Network Time Protocol	1769
SDMD	IPv4 Option for Sender Directed MD Delivery	1770

Historic Protocols

Historic protocols have been superseded by later revisions during the development process. Table A.7 lists the current historic protocols. It also includes the status each attained as it developed.

TABLE A.7 Historic Protocol RFCs

Protocol	Name	RFC
RJE	Remote Job Entry	407
NETED	Network Standard Text Editor	569
SUPDUP	SUPDUP Protocol	734
NETRJS	Remote Job Service	740
MPM	Internet Message Protocol	759
CLOCK	DCNET Time Server Protocol	778
RTELNET	Remote Telnet Service	818
GGP	Gateway Gateway Protocol	823
HMP	Host Monitoring Protocol	869
EGP	Exterior Gateway Protocol	904
SFTP	Simple File Transfer Protocol	913
THINWIRE	Thinwire Protocol	914
RATP	Reliable Asynchronous Transfer Protocol	916
HFEP	Host - Front End Protocol	929
POP2	Post Office Protocol, Version 2	937
HOSTNAME	HOSTNAME Protocol	953
STATSRV	Statistics Server	996
--------	Gateway Requirements	1009
HEMS	High Level Entity Management Protocol	1021
SGMP	Simple Gateway Monitoring Protocol	1028
NFILE	A File Access Protocol	1037
SUN-RPC	Remote Procedure Call Protocol Version 1	1050
--------	Mail Privacy: Procedures	1113
--------	Mail Privacy: Key Management	1114
--------	Mail Privacy: Algorithms	1115
MIB-I	MIB-I	1156
BGP	Border Gateway Protocol	1163, 1164

A

TABLE A.7 continued

Protocol	Name	RFC
CMOT	Common Management Information Services	1189
IMAP3	Interactive Mail Access Protocol Version 3	1203
OIM-MIB-II	OSI Internet Management: MIB-II	1214
SNMP-MUX	SNMP MUX Protocol and MIB	1227
802.4-MIP	IEEE 802.4 Token Bus MIB	1230

Internet Drafts

The RFC process never stands still. Regularly, new proposals are researched by the IETF working group. In addition, drafts are sometimes submitted from outside the IETF working group. The drafts may propose modifications to existing RFCs or even introduce new protocols. Rather than listing the ever-changing drafts, you can view the current listing of drafts at http://www.ietf.org/1id-abstracts.html.

Note

The IETF Web site includes a search engine for locating Internet Drafts on a specific topic. You can find the Internet Draft search engine at http://search.ietf.org/search/brokers/internet-drafts/query.html.

APPENDIX **B**

Test Your Knowledge: Answers

Answers for Day 1

1. The Internet is based on a packet-switching network. Paul Baran developed the concept of a network that breaks data into datagrams (or packets) that are labeled to include a source and destination address. These packets are forwarded from computer to computer until they reach the intended destination computer.

2. RFCs 854 and 855 and the Internet Standard RFCs that describe the telnet protocol. In addition, there are several RFCs that describe telnet options. A listing of specific telnet Option RFCs can be found in the document STD001.

3. The Internet Engineering Task Force (IETF) is in charge of short- to medium-term research projects within the Internet Society. Each separate project under research is assigned a manager to head the research effort. These managers and the chairman of the IETF make up the Internet Engineering Steering Group (IESG).

4. No. Each RFC is maintained and kept for historical reference (even when it has been designated as obsolete). This allows for comparisons to the updated RFCs to see what has been changed.

5. No. An RFC remains "as is" for its lifetime. If changes need to be applied to an RFC, a new RFC is released and the original's status is changed to obsolete.

6. RFCs can be retrieved from the World Wide Web by connecting to the URL `http://www.ietf.org/rfc/rfc####.txt` (where #### is the number of the RFC you want to retrieve). Alternatively, in Internet Explorer, you can type **find RFC ####** in the address bar, and Internet Explorer will automatically load the indicated RFC.

7. There exist RFC numbers that were assigned for proposed RFCs that never made it to the standards track. These "missing" RFC numbers are never reassigned.

8. Modifications can be made to a developing RFC during the Draft stage. All Internet drafts are made available for comment during the Internet draft stage, and this can result in modifications taking place.

Answers for Day 2

1. X.25 networks were developed to run over public switched telephone networks. Due to the unreliability of the lines, extensive error-checking was built in to the protocol. Frame relay was developed to run in digital and fiber-optic environments. Due to the reliability of the lines, less error-checking needs to be performed in a frame relay environment. Only a simple cyclic redundant check (CRC) is performed.

2. An ATM network allows Quality of Service (QoS) parameters to be included in any network request. QoS parameters set minimum thresholds that must be met for transmission. These include values for peak bandwidth, average sustained bandwidth, and burst size. If the actual traffic flow does not meet this QoS specification, the cell can be marked as discard eligible. Frame relay does not include any QoS parameters.

3. An FDDI network is comprised of a primary and a secondary ring. This provides fault tolerance if the primary ring were to stop functioning. In addition, a computer on an FDDI network can transmit as many frames as it can produce in a preset time interval before letting the token go. Several frames can be circulating the ring at once, which gives an FDDI network an overall edge in speed compared with a token-ring network.

4. Peer-to-peer networks are comprised of hosts that function as both a client and a server. The clients determine which resources they are willing to "share" with the other users of the network. In a server-based network, at least one host is dedicated to the purpose of sharing resources with the other host on the network. The peer-to-peer model is generally implemented in smaller, decentralized networks. Server-based networks are more common in larger, centralized networks.

5. Quality of Service (QoS) allows a calling host to request that specific performance levels be met for a connection to be established. Parameters include peak bandwidth, average sustained bandwidth, and burst size. If the actual traffic flow does not meet this QoS specification, an ATM switch can discard the cell.

6. B. The Application layer allows programs to access network resources.

7. E. The Presentation layer is responsible for translation of all data.

8. G. The Session layer coordinates service requests and responses between two hosts.

9. D. The Transport layer provides an end-to-end connection between a source and destination host.

10. A. The Network layer determines the best route from a source to a destination host.

11. F. The Data Link layer is divided into the Logical Link Control and the Media Access Control layers.

12. C. The Physical layer performs the actual binary transmission of data between networked hosts.

13. The four layers of the TCP/IP layered model are the Network Interface layer, the Internet layer, the Transport layer, and the Application layer.

14. When a new product is developed, it will fit into one of the layers of a layered model. The new product needs to communicate only with the layers above and below it. This simplifies the development of new products. For example, a new transport protocol would need to communicate only with the Application layer and the Internet layer in the TCP/IP layered model. It would depend on the Internet layer to communicate with the Network Interface layer.

15. The following comparisons between the layers of the OSI model and the TCP/IP model can be made. The Physical and Data Link layers of the OSI model are comparable to the Network Interface layer of the TCP/IP layered model. The Network layer of the OSI model matches the Internet layer of the TCP/IP model. The Transport layer is the same for both the OSI and TCP/IP models. Finally, the Presentation, Session, and Application layers of the OSI model map to the Application layer of the TCP/IP layered model.

B

16. The Transport layer provides end-to-end communication between hosts. Two protocols exist in the Transport layer. TCP provides guaranteed, connection-oriented communication. UDP provides connectionless, nonguaranteed communication.

Answers for Day 3

1. Convert the decimal numbers in Table 3.3 to binary representation.

Decimal	Binary
127	01111111
0	00000000
76	01001100
248	11111000
224	11100000
57	00111001
135.56.204.253	10000111 00111000 11001100 11111101

2. Convert the following binary numbers to decimal format:

Binary	Decimal
11100110	230
00011100	28
01010101	85
11001100	204
11001010 00001100 10100011 11110010	202.12.163.242
00011011 10001001 01111111 10000101	27.137.127.133

3. Identify the address class of the following IP addresses:

IP Address	IP Address Class
131.107.2.8	Class B
127.0.0.1	No Class—reserved for loopback functions
225.34.56.7	Class D
129.33.55.6	Class B
10.2.4.5	Class A
223.223.223.223	Class C

4. The broadcast address for a host with IP address 172.30.45.67 is 172.30.255.255. The address is a Class B address, which means that the first two octets represent the network component of the IP address. The broadcast address is always the network component of the IP address with the remaining bits set to a value of 1.

5. The IP address 201.200.200.15 is a Class C IP address. This means that the first three octets represent the network component of the IP address. The network address would be 201.200.200.0 for this host.

B

6. An ISP in Malaysia would contact its own ISP, or the regional authority, Asia Pacific Network Information Centre (APNIC) (http://www.apnic.net/) to obtain additional pools of IP addresses.

7. The host SUSAN would not be able to communicate with the host KELLY, because based on the subnet mask implemented, SUSAN would believe that KELLY is on the same network segment, when it is actually on a remote network segment.

8. A subnet mask that would allow SUSAN to communicate with KELLY, would be 255.255.255.0. If the ANDing process is then performed on the two IP addresses, they would result in different results, indicating that the two hosts are on different network segments. Other subnet masks that would also work in this case include 255.255.240.0, 255.255.248.0, 255.255.252.0, and 255.255.254.0.

9. RFC 1918 reserves three pools of addresses for local area networks: 10.0.0.0/8, 172.16.0.0/12, and 192.168.0.0/16.

10. NAT reduces the demand for public network addresses by allowing hosts using private network addressing as defined in RFC 1918 to share an ISP-assigned outbound address. As packets are transmitted through the NAT service, the original source IP address and port address information is translated to the IP address and port used by the external interface of the NAT device.

11. IPv6 offers the following benefits over IPv4:

   - Expanded addressing capabilities
   - Simplified IP header
   - Improved extensibility of the IP header
   - Improved flow control
   - Increased security

Answers for Day 4

1. ARP returns the actual MAC address of the destination host when the destination host exists on the same network segment as the source host.

2. ARP returns the MAC address of the router on the local segment, typically the default gateway configured at the client computer, that is used to route traffic destined for the remote destination host.

3. ICMP provides error reporting and control messaging to the TCP/IP protocol suite. Some of the specific functions include:

   - Redirecting traffic when a more efficient route to a destination network is found
   - Informing a source host when a datagram's TTL has expired
   - Determining the address of all available routers on a network segment
   - Informing a host to slow down communications when they are saturating a router or network segment
   - Discovering what subnet mask is in use on a network segment

4. IP provides connectionless service. It is left up to the higher layer protocols to implement guaranteed service (if desired).

5. Multicasting is preferred over broadcasting because it limits the number of hosts on a segment that will have to examine the data being transmitted. A broadcast is directed to every host on the network segment. This increases network traffic and bandwidth usage. All the messages sent to a multicast group are sent to an Internet Class D address. Members of the multicast group will know if that address is intended for their group.

6. TCP provides guaranteed, connection-oriented delivery of data. UDP, on the other hand, provides nonguaranteed, connectionless delivery of data. The use of UDP does not mean that the application does not require that all data be delivered; it simply means that the guarantee of delivery is left to a higher level.

7. TCP provides reliable transport by using acknowledgments. When the destination host receives a series of TCP segments, it acknowledges it has received the segments by requesting the next segment it expects to receive.

8. A delayed acknowledgment timer causes an acknowledgment to be sent to the sending host when the timer reaches a value of zero. This allows for acknowledgments to be sent even if two contiguous segments have not been received at the destination host.

9. The TCP three-way handshake establishes a TCP session between two hosts. It is comprised of three steps.

   In the first step, the source host sends a TCP packet containing its current sequence number with the SYN (synchronize) flag enabled. This indicates that it wants to synchronize sequence numbers with the destination host.

   In the second step, the destination host sends an acknowledgment packet. This acknowledgment has the following properties: It contains the next sequence number expected by the source host, the SYN flag is enabled, and the current sequence number of the destination host is sent to the source host.

   In the final step, the original source host sends an acknowledgment packet containing the next sequence number the destination host expects to use. The completion of this step establishes a full duplex connection between the two hosts.

10. Yes. If the sliding window is configured to be too large, it can result in too many segments being lost during transmission. This results in retransmission timers expiring, which causes the lost segments to be re-sent. The overall effect is excess network traffic due to the resending of data, and delays due to the expiration of retransmission timers.

11. The receiving host adjusts its receive window size to be equal to the sending host's transmit window size.

12. The UDP header contains a 16-bit checksum field that ensures the UDP packet has not been corrupted in transit. The checksum is based on the UDP pseudo header, which contains fields from both the IP header and the UDP header. The Source IP address, Destination IP address, and protocol fields are taken from the IP header, and the Length field is taken from the UDP header.

13. The TCP header's checksum field is based on the fields contained in the TCP pseudo header. The pseudo header is comprised of the Source IP address, Destination IP address, and protocol fields from the IP header and the TCP Length field from the TCP header.

14. The following output shows the port usage when connected to the site `http://www.microsoft.com` using the Internet Explorer Web browser:

```
netstat -a
  TCP    bkhome:1169           www.microsoft.com:80   ESTABLISHED
  TCP    bkhome:1171           www.microsoft.com:80   ESTABLISHED
  TCP    bkhome:1173           www.microsoft.com:80   ESTABLISHED
  TCP    bkhome:1174           www.microsoft.com:80   ESTABLISHED
```

   As you can see, all the connections on the server side are `www.microsoft.com:80` (or port 80, the HTTP port). My host computer is using random assigned ports.

For this connection, it used TCP ports 1169, 1171, 1173, and 1174. All the traffic is using the TCP protocol for this transaction.

Answers for Day 5

1. You would require an additional 7 bits from the host portion of the IP address to provide 115 subnets. This would provide you with 126 subnets.

2. The extended network prefix in this subnetwork example would be `255.254.0.0`.

3. Using the subnet shortcut table, we see that using a 254 subnet mask, the increment value would be 2. Assuming that zero subnetting is not implemented, the third pool of IP addresses would begin with 6 (2×3). The addresses requested would map as follows:

Network address	`10.6.0.0`
Broadcast address	`10.7.255.255`
Beginning address	`10.6.0.1`
Ending address	`10.7.255.254`

4. Using the subnet shortcut table, you would require 4 additional bits to create 14 subnets from this Class B address of `172.30.0.0`.

5. The extended network prefix for this example would be `255.255.240.0`.

6. Using the subnet shortcut table, we see that using a 240 subnet mask, the increment value would be 16. Assuming that zero subnetting is not implemented, the third pool of IP addresses would begin with 48 (16×3). The addresses requested would map as follows:

Network address	`172.30.48.0`
Broadcast address	`172.30.63.255`
Beginning address	`172.30.48.1`
Ending address	`172.30.63.254`

7. Using the subnet shortcut table, you would require 4 bits from the host portion of the address to provide 10 subnets. In this case, you would actually have 14 subnets available for use.

8. This addressing scheme leaves 4 bits to represent the host portion of the address. This provides $2^4-2 = 14$ hosts per subnet. The two addresses not included are the network address and the broadcast address.

9. Complete the following table of addresses:

Network Address	Beginning Address	Ending Address	Broadcast Address
192.168.23.16	192.168.23.17	192.168.23.30	192.168.23.31
192.168.23.32	192.168.23.33	192.168.23.46	192.168.23.47
192.168.23.48	192.168.23.49	192.168.23.62	192.168.23.63
192.168.23.64	192.168.23.65	192.168.23.78	192.168.23.79
192.168.23.80	192.168.23.81	192.168.23.94	192.168.23.95
192.168.23.96	192.168.23.97	192.168.23.110	192.168.23.111
192.168.23.112	192.168.23.113	192.168.23.126	192.168.23.127
192.168.23.128	192.168.23.129	192.168.23.142	192.168.23.143
192.168.23.144	192.168.23.145	192.168.23.158	192.168.23.159
192.168.23.160	192.168.23.161	192.168.23.174	192.168.23.175
192.168.23.176	192.168.23.177	192.168.23.190	192.168.23.191
192.168.23.192	192.168.23.193	192.168.23.206	192.168.23.207
192.168.23.208	192.168.23.209	192.168.23.222	192.168.23.223
192.168.23.224	192.168.23.225	192.168.23.238	192.168.23.239

B

10. The following network address and broadcast address would be used for the following host and subnet masks:

172.16.67.16 with subnet mask 255.255.240.0

network = 172.16.64.0 and broadcast = 172.16.79.255

192.168.54.76 with subnet mask 255.255.255.224

network = 192.168.54.64 and broadcast = 192.16.54.95

157.76.2.198 with subnet mask 255.255.255.128

network = 157.76.2.128 and broadcast = 157.76.2.255

11. Assuming that the networks will be assigned their IP addresses based on the lowest addresses being assigned to the leftmost networks, the network address 192.168.30.0/25 could be used for subnetwork #1.

12. Keeping this assumption, the following network addresses could be used for subnetwork #3, subnetwork #4, and subnetwork #6.

Subnetwork #3 = 192.168.30.128/27

Subnetwork #4 = 192.168.30.160/27

Subnetwork #6 = 192.168.30.224/27

I have skipped the pool 192.168.30.192/27 and have left it to be divided up between subnetworks 7, 8, 9, and 10.

13. What could be the broadcast addresses for subnetworks 7, 8, 9, and 10?

Subnetwork #7 = 192.168.30.199

Subnetwork #8 = 192.168.30.207

Subnetwork #9 = 192.168.30.215

Subnetwork #10= 192.168.30.223

14. The first network address in this pool is 198.163.32.0/24 and the final address is 198.163.39.0/24. The difference between these is that the third octet is 7. Because 7 is greater than 4, but less than 8, you must reference the 8 column in the subnet shortcut table. The number of bits required for an increment value of 8 is 5 bits. Therefore, the network address that can be used to aggregate this pool of IP addresses would be 192.163.32.0/21.

15. The missing information for each of the CIDR networks is as follows:

Beginning address: 200.200.64.1

Ending address: **200.200.67.254**

Subnet mask: 255.255.252.0

Beginning address: **172.32.0.1**

Ending address: 172.39.255.254

Subnet mask: 255.248.0.0

Beginning Address: 198.16.0.1

Ending Address: 198.31.255.254

Subnet Mask: **255.240.0.0**

Answers for Day 6

1. Hostname resolution is used to resolve hostname or fully qualified domain names to an IP address. NetBIOS name resolution resolves both a NetBIOS computer name and a NetBIOS service to an IP address. NetBIOS support is not required within a TCP/IP stack unless the network uses NetBIOS services.

2. The top-level domain names that exist on the Internet today include the following: COM, EDU, ORG, NET, GOV, MIL, NUM, and ARPA. In addition, country code

top-level domains exist using a two-letter abbreviation for countries. For example, Canada is represented with CA and New Zealand is represented with NZ. Recently, several generic top-level domains have been added as the names available in the COM domain have dwindled. The new generic top-level domains include BIZ, INFO, AERO, PRO, COOP, NAME, and MUSEUM. These names were added to provide additional expansion room for registering domain names on the Internet.

3. No. This computer will not be able to initiate communication with the target host using the hostname. This is because the HOSTS file is referred to before DNS in a hostname resolution process. The incorrect address would be communicated instead of the correct address that would be obtained from DNS. It may be possible for the target host to initiate communications if the target host does not have an incorrect entry for the computer in its hosts file.

4. Yes. As mentioned in the answer to question 3, the HOSTS file is checked before DNS when resolving a hostname to an IP address. If the IP address were correct in the HOSTS file, the target hostname would be successfully resolved to an IP address.

5. A recursive DNS query requires the responding name server to respond with either the resulting IP address or an error that the hostname could not be resolved. An iterative DNS query, on the other hand, allows the responding name server to provide its best answer when resolving the hostname to an IP address. The best answer may be a reference to another name server that may be able to resolve the hostname to an IP address.

6. You can increase performance on a DNS server by using caching. By increasing the cache parameter for zones, you allow the hostname to IP address resolutions to be cached for longer intervals. This provides a speedier resolution process.

7. The four NetBIOS node types are B-Node (broadcast), P-Node (peer), M-Node (mixed), and H-Node (hybrid). The node types that help to reduce network traffic most are the P-Node and the H-Node. The P-Node will submit NetBIOS name resolution requests only to a NetBIOS name server. No broadcasts are used to resolve NetBIOS names. Likewise, the H-Node will first query a NetBIOS name server to resolve a NetBIOS name to an IP address. The difference is that it will use a broadcast if the NetBIOS name server cannot resolve the NetBIOS name to an IP address. This allows resolution of NetBIOS names for hosts that are not configured to register the NetBIOS names with a NetBIOS name server.

8. The three basic NetBIOS name transactions that occur on a NetBIOS network are name registrations, name discoveries, and name releases.

9. Dynamic DNS allows a host that changes its IP address to register its new hostname/IP address combination with a DNS server that supports dynamic updates.

10. The following lines would be required to refer to the shared LMHOSTS file referred to in this question:

```
172.18.56.35    PRIMARY    #PRE

#INCLUDE \\PRIMARY\NETLOGON\LMHOSTS
```

The first line is required so that the IP address for PRIMARY is loaded into the NetBIOS name cache. The second line indicates the location of the shared LMHOSTS file that should be included in the resolution of NetBIOS names to IP addresses.

11. BIND 8.x and higher and Microsoft Windows 2000 and higher versions of DNS support dynamic DNS updates.

12. The main security risk that exists when dynamic updates are implemented in DNS is that an unauthorized computer can "hijack" a resource record that currently exists in the DNS zone file, unless some method of security is used to protect the resource records from unauthorized updates.

Answers for Day 7

1. The NAMED.CONF file for the Homer computer would be as follows:

```
#
# conf file for the HOMER DNS Server
#
options {
    directory "/usr/named";
    forwarders {192.168.15.1;};
};
zone "simpsons.com" in {
    type master;
    file "db.simpsons";
    allow-update {192.168.15/24;};
    allow-transfer {none;};
};

zone "15.168.192.in-addr.arpa" in {
    type master;
    file "db.192.168.15.0";
    allow-update {192.168.15/24;};
    allow-transfer {none;};

zone "0.0.127.in-addr.arpa" in {
    type master;
    file "db.127.0.0";
    allow-update {192.168.15/24;};
    allow-transfer {none;};
};
```

2. The zone file for `simpsons.com` that would be stored on HOMER is as follows:

```
@           IN     SOA     homer.simpsons.com      matt.simpsons.com. {
                1998030501     ; serial
                10800          ;refresh
                3600         ;retry
                604800         ;expire
                86400        ;TTL
            )
                       IN     NS      homer.simpsons.com.

homer.simpsons.com.     IN     A      192.168.15.5
bart.simpsons.com.      IN     A      192.168.15.1
lisa.simpsons.com.      IN     A      192.168.15.2
marge.simpsons.com.     IN     A      192.168.15.4

mail            IN     CNAME       homer.simpsons.com.
bigboy          IN     CNAME       homer.simpsons.com.
gw              IN     CNAME       bart.simpsons.com.
www             IN     CNAME       lisa.simpsons.com.
ftp             IN     CNAME       lisa.simpsons.com.
gopher          IN     CNAME       marge.simpsons.com.
mail2           IN     CNAME       marge.simpsons.com.

simpsons.com        IN     MX     10      homer.simpsons.com.
simpsons.com        IN     MX     20      marge.simpsons.com.
```

3. The reverse lookup zone for this network that would be stored on HOMER is as follows:

```
15.168.192.in-addr.arpa. IN SOA homer.simpsons.com. matt.simpsons.com. (
                                1998050301      ; serial
                                10800           ;refresh
                                3600            ;retry
                                604800          ;expire
                                86400           ;TTL
            )
            NS                  homer.simpsons.com.
    1       IN     PTR          bart.simpsons.com.
    2       IN     PTR          lisa.simpsons.com.
    4       IN     PTR          marge.simpsons.com.
    5       IN     PTR          homer.simpsons.com.
```

4. The latest version of the `named.cache` file can be obtained using anonymous FTP from the following site:

`ftp://rs.internic.net/domain/named.cache`

5. The `NSLOOKUP` command that can be used to determine the mail exchange record for the domain `komarconsulting.com` is:

`ls -t MX komarconsulting.com`

6. The `NSLOOKUP` command that can be used to determine the name server for the komarconsulting.com domain is:

   `ls -t NS komarconsulting.com`

7. The `NSLOOKUP` command that is used to dump all resource records for the komarconsulting.com domain is:

   `ls -d komarconsulting.com`

   You can prevent this command from succeeding by configuring your DNS server to either not allow zone transfers, or restricting zone transfers only to configured secondary name servers.

Answers for Day 8

1. If multiple WINS servers exist in a single network, replication must be configured between the WINS servers to ensure that the entire WINS database is available to all WINS clients for NetBIOS name resolution.

2. A WINS proxy agent forwards NetBIOS name resolution packets to a WINS server on behalf of a non-WINS client. When the WINS server responds to the packet, the WINS proxy agent broadcasts the response on the network segment so that the non-WINS client can retrieve the data.

3. Static entries must be added to a WINS server for non-WINS NetBIOS clients so that a WINS client can resolve the NetBIOS name for the non-WINS clients to an IP address. This helps to reduce broadcast traffic and enables non-WINS clients on a remote network to be accessed without implementing `LMHOSTS`.

4. In the worst-case scenario, a record will exist in the WINS database for 16 days before being removed entirely from the WINS database after a WINS client has been removed from the network. The first six days encompass the Renewal timer. After six days have elapsed, the WINS record is marked as released. The next four days are the days associated with the Extinction interval. At the completion of these four days, the WINS record is marked as extinct. After the final six days pass, the Extinction timeout elapses and the WINS record is removed from the database.

5. A push partner informs its pull partner that it should pull the changed WINS records when a configured number of changes has been recorded to the WINS database. A pull partner requests all changed records from the WINS database at regularly configured intervals.

6. Windows 2000 Advanced Server's clustering services registers a NetBIOS name for the shared quorum drie, or logical name, used by the clustered disk device.

In addition, Active Directory uses NetBIOS names to enforce computer restrictions configured for individual user accounts.

7. You would consider integrating WINS with DNS in environments where a DNS server that does not support dynamic updates is implemented. Another case where you could use WINS integration with DNS would be where a DHCP server did not support dynamic update of pre-Windows 2000 client resource records.

Answers for Day 9

1. Multicast addresses enable RIP version 2 and OSPF to propagate routing information in a more efficient manner. Rather than using a broadcast address that non-routers would have to inspect, these protocols use a predetermined multicast address that is registered only by the RIP and OSPF routers themselves. RIP version 2 uses the multicast address `224.0.0.9`, and OSPF uses the address `224.0.0.5` for all OSPF routers and `224.0.0.6` for the designated router and the backup designated router.

2. Exterior gateway protocols are used to exchange routing information between other organizations or autonomous systems. Interior gateway protocols are used to exchange routing information between routers that belong to the same autonomous system.

3. The `traceroute` command can be used to determine the route a packet takes to a remote host. The Microsoft implementation of this command is `tracert.exe`.

4. Distance vector protocols are broadcast-based protocols that are commonly used in smaller networks due to their usage of broadcasts to propagate routing information. A distance vector protocol propagates the entire routing table between neighboring routers. A link state protocol floods routing information to all nodes in the network. This routing information will contain only routes to directly attached networks. Even though these routing messages are sent to all routers on the network, their reduced size results in a more efficient exchange of routing information.

5. Common problems faced in a dynamic routing environment include routing loops and the counting to infinity problem. A routing loop exists when a series of routers creates a circular route to a destination network that simply goes around in circles. A counting to infinity problem occurs when an interface fails on a router. Before the router can announce this to the rest of the network, it receives a routing announcement from a neighboring router that it can reach the network on the other side of the dead interface. Rather than removing the route, it increments the hop count from the neighboring router. This leads to the hop count increasing until infinity is reached.

6. Some of the techniques that can be used to prevent routing loops and counting to infinity problems are

   - The use of hold-downs
   - Implementing split horizons
   - Implementing poison reverse

7. The default gateway address is 203.196.205.1. This was found in the following routing entry:

   ```
   0.0.0.0      0.0.0.0      203.196.205.1      203.196.205.254      2
   ```

8. The local IP addresses for this router are 172.16.2.8 and 203.196.205.254. You can find the local IP addresses for a router by determining which addresses have a subnet mask of 255.255.255.255 and are routed to the loopback address of 127.0.0.1.

9. No. The routing table shows that this is a local IP address. Any requests to this address are redirected to the loopback address 127.0.0.1.

10. The multicast address 224.0.0.0 shows that all packets destined to a multicast address are sent to the local network segment through the interface with IP address 172.16.2.8.

11. The metric associated with reaching the network 172.16.4.0 is 2. This means that another router must be crossed after the packet is sent through the router at IP address 172.16.2.1.

12. The metric associated with reaching the network 172.16.5.0 is 3. This means that two more routers must be crossed after the packet is sent through the router at IP address 172.16.2.1.

13. The following Microsoft Windows command is used to add a static route to network 172.16.6.0/24 through the gateway at IP address 172.16.2.1:

   ```
   route  -p  add  172.16.6.0  mask  255.255.255.0  172.16.2.1
   ```

14. The following Cisco IOS commands are used to add a static route to network 172.16.6.0/24 through the gateway at IP address 172.16.2.1:

   ```
   enable
   config terminal
   IP ROUTE 172.16.6.0  255.255.255.0  172.16.2.1
   {Control-Z}
   Copy Running Startup
   ```

Answers for Day 10

1. A new host must have its MAC address to IP address mapping entered in the RARP servers listing of IP addresses.

2. Rather than just IP address information, BOOTP can send additional information such as the default gateway and send a boot file to diskless workstations allowing the workstation to boot and connect to a network server.

3. Remote Installation Services use BOOTP for IP address assignment. BOOTP is used because a boot file is loaded to the RIS client using TFTP.

4. A DHCP client has an affinity to the DHCP server from which it previously obtained its IP address. If a DHCPOFFER is not received from the previous DHCP server, then the DHCP client will use the first DHCP offer that it received from alternate DHCP servers.

5. A DHCP-leased IP address is renewed every time a DHCP client restarts. At 50% of the lease duration, the DHCP client will renew its IP address by directly contacting the DHCP server it received its IP address from. If the 50% renewal request is not answered, the DHCP client broadcasts a DHCP request for renewal at 87.5% of the lease duration.

6. A DHCP relay agent, or an RFC 1542-compliant router, must exist on the network segment where the DHCP client is located so that the DHCP requests and responses are forwarded to the DHCP server on the other network segment.

7. The DHCPINFORM message is used by DHCP servers to determine if their name and IP address are registered in Active Directory. If the name and IP address are not found, the unauthorized DHCP servers will not issue IP addresses (as long as the DHCP server supports the DHCPINFORM message type).

Answers for Day 11

1. It is possible to capture the account and password submitted to an application that uses clear text authentication. The account and password information can be captured using a network sniffer. Once the password is captured, an attacker can authenticate with the network using the captured credentials.

2. If an application supports only clear-text authentication, encryption protocols such as Internet Protocol Security (IPSec) can be used to encrypt the clear-text authentication. Alternatively, if the data used by the application is not critical, anonymous authentication, where no credentials are presented, can be used.

3. In an NIS authentication system, an NIS server can be either a master or a slave server. Master servers maintain the original, writable, copy of the NIS database and slave servers maintain a duplicate, read-only, copy of the NIS database.

4. The Authentication Service (AS), running on a Kerberos Key Distribution Center (KDC), is responsible for issuing TGTs to an authenticating user.

5. A TGT issued to another Kerberos realm is sometimes called a Referral ticket.

6. Figure B.1 shows the Kerberos message types.

FIGURE B.1

The Kerberos message types.

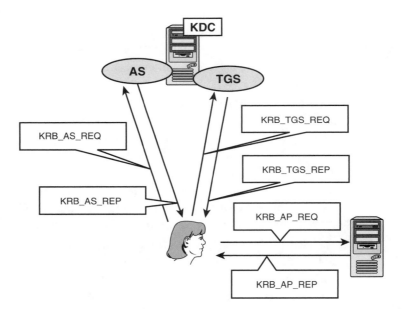

7. Smart cards use PKINIT extensions to allow public keys to be used with Kerberos authentication. The KRB_AS_REQ message is replaced with a PA_PK_AS_REQ message and the KRB_AS_REP message is replaced with a PA_PK_AS_REP message.

8. When a certificate is presented, the computer validating the certificate checks its cache to see if it has a cached version of the issuing CA's CRL. If it doesn't, it retrieves the latest version of the CRL from the presented certificate's CDP extension. The CRL is then checked to see if the certificate's serial number is included in the CRL.

The process is then repeated for the issuing CA's certificate all the way up to the trusted root CA's certificate. If any certificate in the chain is revoked, the presented certificate is considered revoked.

B

9. A certificate presented for authentication can be rejected by a server if the certificate is revoked, if the certificate is time invalid, if the certificate is not intended for authentication purposes, or if the certificate does not chain to a RootCA trusted by the server.

10. Windows Integrated Authentication is a proprietary authentication scheme only supported by Internet Explorer Web browsers.

11. Digest authentication requires that the user's password be stored in an unencrypted, or reversibly encryptable format in the directory service. The storage format requires that physical security be deployed for the directory service server.

Answers for Day 12

1. The application must be coded to support the desired application layer security protocol. If the application does not support the application layer security protocol, then the security protocol cannot be implemented.

2. There are no requirements for an application to use IP layer security. All encryption and decryption takes place at lower levels of the IP stack—and the application only sends and receives unencrypted data.

3. No. S/MIME and PGP are not interoperable. The two users must decide on a mail encryption protocol that is supported by both mail clients.

4. To secure e-mail authentication, you must implement SSL protection for POP3 and IMAP4 protocols. Additionally, you can consider implementing SSL for HTTP connections if a Web-based mail client is implemented.

5. The mail server must have a digital certificate installed that supports machine authentication and encryption.

6. The e-mail clients must be configured to use SSL for POP3 or IMAP4, depending on the mail retrieval protocol used by the e-mail client.

7. The Authentication Header ensures that unauthorized clients cannot connect to a network and protects transmitted data from being modified or replayed on the network.

8. An Encapsulating Security Payload protects transmitted data by encrypting the original data payload. As an option, ESP can also apply integrity protection to a portion of the transmitted data.

9. You would consider using both AH and ESP for a security association to both encrypt the transmitted data and apply integrity protection to the entire IPSec protected packet, and not just to the encrypted portion of the packet.

10. Perfect Forward Secrecy ensures that the previous session key material is not used to generate the new session key material.

11. In an AH header, the Security Parameters Index (SPI), destination IP address, and security protocol identify the specific security association.

12. IPSec can use Kerberos, shared secrets, or certificate-based authentication to authenticate the two hosts participating in a security association.

Answers for Day 13

1. Some of the common security threats faced on a network include:

   - The capture of clear text passwords for authentication by the attacker
   - The ease of performing network monitoring
   - The ability to "spoof" network addresses
   - Poor security implementations

2. Network address translation protects an interior network by never exposing the interior-addressing scheme to the exterior network. A proxy server replaces any internal addressing information with its external address when data is transmitted outside of the internal network.

3. The security policy outlines the organization's attitude about security and allows the organization to design network security to protect network resources that meets the objectives outlines in the organization's security policy.

4. The following proxy rules must be established:

Rule	Interface	ProtocolSource IP	Source Port	Destination IP	Destination Port
POP3	Internal	TCP192.168.5.0/24	Any	126.10.30.40	110
IMAP	Internal	TCP192.168.5.0/24	Any	126.10.30.40	143
SMTP	Internal	TCP192.168.5.0/24	Any	126.10.30.40	25
HTTP	Internal	TCP 192.168.5.0/24	Any	Any	80
NNTP	Internal	TCP192.168.5.0/24	Any	Any	119
Telnet Out	Internal	TCP 192.168.5.0/24	Any	Any	23
Telnet In	External	TCP 126.29.30.31	Any	192.168.5.10	23

5. An intruder can spoof another host's IP address using the following method.

   1. The attacking station next creates a source route packet. This packet indicates the path an IP packet takes from the server on a return path. The trusted client

being spoofed is the last hop in the indicated source route before reaching the server. This makes it appear that the packet originated at the masqueraded workstation.

2. The attacking station next sends a packet destined for the server using the source route packet.

3. Because the packet has been routed through the trusted client, the server accepts the packet.

4. The server returns its response to the trusted client.

5. Because of the source route implemented, the trusted client forwards the response to the attacking station.

6. An intrusion detection system (IDS) allows inspection of data at the application layer, not just at the transport and IP layers as is commonly performed at firewalls. An IDS protects against attacks such as malformed packets that contain malicious commands in allowed protocols, such as HTTP.

7. The main decision factor that would make you choose to deploy a DMZ with two firewalls, rather than with just a single firewall, would be depth in defense. With a single firewall DMZ, there is only a single point of failure between the private network and the public network. With a mid-ground DMZ, there are two firewalls that must be breached before the private network is compromised.

8. An ICSA-certified firewall has undergone an extensive security evaluation by an independent third party, TruSecure Corporation. This certification is considered an industry standard certification that firewalls are measured under for effectiveness and security levels.

Answers for Day 14

1. D. Telnet uses TCP port 23.

2. H. Rlogin uses TCP port 513.

3. E. Quote of the Day uses TCP or UDP port 17.

4. F. Daytime uses TCP or UDP port 13.

5. C. Echo uses TCP or UDP port 7.

6. B. Discard uses TCP or UDP port 9.

7. A. Character Generator uses TCP or UDP port 19.

8. G. Time uses TCP or UDP port 37.

9. Telnet sends clear text authentication information across the network, which is subject to being intercepted by a network sniffer. rlogin uses entries within the

hosts.equiv and .rhosts files to determine which users or hosts can perform rlogin sessions. No actual account and password information is transferred over the network.

10. The syntax of the rlogin command to connect to a host named BART using the username LISA is:

```
rlogin bart -l lisa
```

11. A telnet option negotiation is based on a series of exchanges using the DO, DON'T, WILL, and WON'T functions. When the sending host sends a DO or DON'T request, the receiving host responds with WILL or WON'T to indicate whether it will implement the requested option. Likewise, when the sending host sends a WILL or WON'T function suggesting an option that it could implement, the receiving host replies with a DO or DON'T function indicating whether it agrees to the option.

12. The Interpret as Command (IAC) character precedes each command sequence to leave no doubt as to whether a data stream is intended to be a command or simply some data sent to the other host.

13. A network virtual terminal provides a common endpoint at each end of a telnet communication session that defines what functionality is provided. This provides a minimum environment that must be provided on all telnet clients and servers. These environments can be enhanced via option negotiation.

14. Telnet client software can be used to connect to various optional TCP/IP services by changing the port that the client software connects to on the server. Telnet can also be used to troubleshoot connectivity problems to SMTP and POP3 mail servers.

15. The following optional TCP/IP services are supported under Windows NT Server: Character Generator, Daytime, Discard, Echo, and Quote of the Day.

16. Citrix would be selected over using Microsoft Terminal Services in the following cases:

    - You require support for DOS clients.
    - You require support for Unix, Macintosh, or Java clients.
    - You require connectivity using IPX/SPX, NetBEUI, or Direct Asynchronous connections.

17. The firewall must be configured to allow connections to UDP port 1604 (ICA browser) and to TCP port 1494 (the ICA protocol) on the Citrix MetaFrame server.

18. The firewall must be configured to allow connections to TCP port 3389 (the RDP protocol) on the Windows 2000 Terminal Server.

Answers for Day 15

1. The FTP protocol uses TCP as its transport protocol, whereas TFTP uses UDP as its transport protocol. When a file is transferred using FTP, two sessions are actually established between the client and the server. The first session is a protocol interpreter session that is used to transmit FTP commands. The second session is the data transfer process over which data is transported. TFTP does not use sessions, because of the use of UDP as the transport protocol.

2. Anonymous FTP is a common method of granting access to an FTP server to unknown or nonregistered users. Users log in to the FTP server using the account anonymous or ftp and provide their Internet e-mail address as their password.

3. The Remote Copy Protocol (RCP) depends on the .rhosts or hosts.equiv file to contain the user account and hostname for allowed connections. No passwords are transmitted across the network unless the user's name does not exist in either file. FTP, on the other hand, sends the account/password information in clear text across the network.

4. The two communication channels used during an FTP session are the Data Transfer Process (DTP) and the Protocol Interpreter (PI). The DTP is used for the actual transmission of data between the client and the server. The PI is used to transmit commands between the client and the server. The FTP server uses TCP port 21 for the PI and TCP port 20 for the DTP. The client uses a random port number above port 1024 for each of the two sessions.

5. The steps involved in the establishment of a Secure Socket Layer (SSL) session are as follows:

    1. The client makes a security request to the server.

    2. The server sends its certificate to the client. This certificate contains the server's public key and the server's cipher preferences.

    3. The client generates a master key.

    4. The client encrypts the master key using the server's public key that it received in step 2. The master key of the client can now be decrypted only by the server's private key that is located only on the server.

    5. The client transmits the encrypted master key to the server.

    6. The server decrypts the client's master key using the server's private key.

    7. The server authenticates with the client by returning a message to the client that is encrypted by using the client's master key. This authenticates both sides of the session.

B

6. NFS allows files to be made available to remote clients. Clients have transparent access to the remote file services. The files appear to be stored locally.

7. The mount protocol provides NFS with the necessary tools to mount an NFS file system on the underlying operating system.

8. File locking ensures that multiple clients are not able to access a data file simultaneously, unless required by the application. This prevents a file from being corrupted by multiple users attempting to modify the same file simultaneously. The Network Lock Manager (NLM) provides this functionality for NFS.

9. WebDAV offers the following security improvements when compared to FTP:

   - **Password security.** Using a combination of Basic authentication and SSL encryption can protect passwords.

   - **Data Transmission encryption.** The actual data transmitted between the client and the WebDAV server is encrypted by SSL.

   - **Data Storage Encryption.** If WebDAV is implemented in a Windows XP or Windows .NET Server environment, the files can be encrypted at the client using EFS, and then the encrypted file is transmitted to the WebDAV server.

10. Windows XP and Windows .NET Server allow EFS files that are locally encrypted to be stored remotely on a WebDAV server. The encrypted files are transmitted to the WebDAV server in their encrypted format.

11. The `RPCSEC_GSS` authentication mechanism is an API that allows other common authentication mechanisms to interface with NFS and provide mutual authentication services. Through this API, future authentication protocols can be implemented in an NFS environment.

Answers for Day 16

1. The steps involved in an SMTP session between an SMTP client and an SMTP server are

   1. The SMTP client initiates a connection TCP port 25 on the SMTP server. The SMTP server responds with a `220 <Ready>` message.

   2. The SMTP client requests that the SMTP session be established by sending a `HELO` (Hello) command including the Fully Qualified Domain Name (FQDN) of the SMTP client. The SMTP server should respond with a `250 <OK>` message.

   3. The SMTP client informs the SMTP server that is sending the message with the `MAIL FROM:` command. The SMTP server should respond with a `250 <OK>` message.

4. The SMTP client identifies all the recipients the message is intended for by using the RCPT TO: command. A separate RCPT TO: command is issued for each recipient of the message. The SMTP server responds to each of the recipients with a 250 <OK> message.

5. The SMTP client indicates that it is prepared to transmit the actual e-mail message by issuing the DATA command. The actual message is now transmitted to the SMTP server by using 7-bit ASCII characters. If any attachments exist in the message, the attachments must be encoded into a 7-bit stream using BinHex, uuencode, or MIME.

6. After the message has transmitted successfully, the SMTP client sends a QUIT command to terminate the SMTP session. The SMTP server responds with a 221 <Closing> message to indicate that the session has terminated.

2. The SMTP protocol allows an Internet e-mail client to send Internet e-mail. POP3 or IMAP allows an Internet e-mail client to receive Internet e-mail.

3. A Mail Exchange (MX) record is queried in DNS by an SMTP client to determine the mail exchanger for the domain name it is sending mail to.

4. IMAP mail clients have the following advantages over POP3 mail clients:

  • Initially, IMAP clients are not sent the contents of every mail file, just the header information.

  • IMAP allows messages to be stored in a hierarchical structure on the IMAP server.

  • Messages are stored on the IMAP server, which allows the messages to be accessed from multiple IMAP clients and still see the same status information for all messages.

  • IMAP servers understand MIME file extensions.

  • IMAP supports online, offline, and disconnected access modes. POP3 supports only the online model.

5. The LDAP protocol has been developed by the IETF to standardize access to X.500 and non-X.500 directory systems. This allows for easier integration of foreign e-mail systems.

6. In the X.500 name cn=Beekelaar, Ronald; ou=Utrecht; o=Beekelaar Consulting, c=nl, cn=Beekelaar, Ronald represents the common name "Ronald Beekelaar." Mr. Beekelaar is located within the organizational unit (ou) "Utrecht" within the organization (o) "Beekelaar Consulting." The organization is located within the country (c) of The Netherlands (NL).

B

7. Macintosh systems primarily use BinHex for encoding e-mail attachments.

8. The following field headers are used when a MIME attachment exists in an e-mail message:

   - MIME-Version
   - Content-Type
   - Content-Transfer Encoding
   - Content-ID
   - Content-Description

9. POP3/S, IMAP/S, and SMTP/S are used to protect e-mail message authentication. In these cases, the mail servers will use SSL to encrypt the authentication traffic.

10. Both PGP and S/MIME can be used to protect e-mail message content when e-mail messages are sent between recipients.

11. Both PGP and S/MIME are public-key methods of encrypting and signing e-mail data. The difference is that PGP is free for personal use, while S/MIME must be purchased with your mail system, or supported by your e-mail software. The other major difference is that PGP is not controlled by a central standards organization, while S/MIME is defined in RFCs and managed by the IETF.

12. When you sign an e-mail message, the sender's private key is used to sign a hash of the message. The encrypted hash is decrypted by the recipient using the sender's public key. The recipient then calculates a hash of the mail message using the same algorithm as the sender and compares the two hashes. If they match, the message is intact, and has not been modified. When an encrypted message is sent, the message is encrypted with a one-time symmetric key. The symmetric key is then encrypted using the public key of the recipient. When the recipient retrieves the message, the symmetric key is decrypted by using the recipient's private key, and then the message content is decrypted using the symmetric key.

13. E-mail security can be increased by using dual key pairs. This means that separate private/public key pairs are used for the digital signing and mail encryption services.

Answers for Day 17

1. The first category of network management encompasses the management of network resources, including user accounts and security issues. The second category of network management includes the management of the physical devices that form the network.

2. SNMP can also be implemented on AppleTalk, IPX, and OSI networks.

3. The SNMP management system is used to send SNMP requests to SNMP agents. It is also the destination of SNMP trap messages.

4. An SNMP agent responds to SNMP requests and fills in the requested information before sending an SNMP response to the SNMP management system. In addition, an SNMP agent can send an SNMP trap when a preconfigured event takes place, such as a cold boot of a host.

5. The SNMP trap PDU provides the capability for an SNMP agent to alert the SNMP management system when a threshold has been exceeded or a significant event has taken place. This allows for a quicker response to a network device failure.

6. Additional security can be provided by one of two methods. The first method involves changing the community name from the default of public (it is easily guessed). The second method involves configuring which SNMP management systems that an SNMP agent will accept SNMP requests from. This limits which SNMP management systems can perform requests on an SNMP agent. It is also a good idea to configure the SNMP agent to send an SNMP trap if a nonconfigured SNMP management system attempts an SNMP request.

7. The three types of community names that can be implemented in an SNMP network are the monitor community, the control community, and the trap community. The monitor community indicates which community name SNMP requests will be responded to. The control community is used to configure which SNMP management systems can perform write functions to an SNMP agent. Finally, the trap community is used to indicate the community's SNMP management system to which all SNMP trap messages are sent.

8. Object identifiers are assigned to objects in the Management Information Base (MIB) in a hierarchical fashion. This hierarchy defines whether the object is a common object or a private enterprise object based on its location in the hierarchy.

9. The major categories within the MIB-II database are System, Interfaces, Address Translation, IP, ICMP, TCP, UDP, EGP, Transmission, and SNMP.

10. The `GetBulk` PDU provides a more efficient retrieval mechanism for values in a table. Rather than having to send a `GetNextRequest` for each entry in a table, the `GetBulk` allows the table to be retrieved in a single request.

Answers for Day 18

1. Deficiencies of the SLIP protocol include the inability to automatically assign IP addresses to clients, the inability to use protocols other than IP, the lack of error detection or correction, and the fact that account information is sent as clear text and there is no compressions built in to the protocol.

2. PPP can use Password Authentication Protocol (PAP), Shiva Password Authentication Protocol (SPAP), Challenge Handshake Authentication Protocol (CHAP), Microsoft CHAP, Microsoft CHAP v2, or Extensible Authentication Protocol (EAP) for authentication. PPP can also choose to not enable authentication at all.

3. SLIP frames data using the END character (decimal 192). The END character is placed at the end of each packet transmitted.

4. Yes. PPP provides the ability to multiplex multiple protocols over a single dial-up session. This functionality is provided by the inclusion of a protocol field in the PPP header.

5. The Link Control Protocol is used to establish, configure, and test the data link connection between the dial-in client and the dial-in server. Four phases are involved in the Link Control Protocol: link establishment, authentication phase, network-layer protocol, and link termination.

6. The three main components of a virtual private network are a tunnel server, a tunnel client, and the tunnel. The tunnel is the logical connection established between the tunnel server and the tunnel client over a public data network. All data transmitted over the tunnel can be encrypted to provide for a secure communications mechanism.

7. A firewall must implement the following packet filters to allow PPTP to connect to a VPN server protected by the firewall:

Protocol	Source IP	Source Port	Destination IP	Destination Port	Action
TCP	Any	Any	PPTP Server IP	1723	Allow
ID 47	Any		PPTP Server IP		Allow

8. A firewall that does not implement NAT must implement the following packet filters to allow L2TP/IPSec to connect to a VPN server protected by the firewall:

Protocol	Source IP	Source Port	Destination IP	Destination Port	Action
UDP	Any	500	L2TP Server IP	500	Allow
ID 50	Any		L2TP Server IP		Allow
ID 51	Any		L2TP Server IP		Allow*

This packet filter is only required if the L2TP connection uses AH protection.

9. PPPoE is used to provide tunneling for broadband solutions, such as Internet Service Providers (ISPs) providing Asynchronous Digital Subscriber Line (ADSL) and cable modems for Internet access. PPPoE allows authentication of the

individual connections to prevent unauthorized modems from accessing Internet Services through the ISP.

10. A Radius proxy provides intelligent routing of authentication traffic to the correct Radius server, based on a prefix, suffix, or combination of prefix and suffix provided by the remote access client.

11. A Radius proxy allows an ISP to support multiple Radius implementations at the same time. Prefixes and suffixes are used to identify which Radius server the authentication must be forwarded to.

B

Answers for Day 19

1. A modified version of ARP must be implemented in an ATM environment, because ATM devices do not have a physical network address. ATMARP resolves an IP address to an ATM address instead.

2. ATM hosts are grouped into Logical IP Subnets (LIS) to form a logical IP subnetwork. Each host in an IP subnetwork belongs to the same LIS.

3. A client must attempt to prove that the ARP cache table entry is no longer valid before it can remove the ATMARP table entry. If there is no open virtual circuit to the destination, the table entry is deleted. If there is an open virtual circuit, the ATMARP client must revalidate the entry before regular traffic can be resumed. In a permanent virtual circuit, an InATMARP request is sent directly over the virtual circuit. In a switched virtual circuit, an ATMARP request is sent to the ATMARP server. The ATMARP reply is used to update the client's ATMARP table cache.

4. The 802.11 standard proposes two different methods of configuring a network: ad-hoc networking and infrastructure networking. In an ad-hoc network, every node in the wireless network establishes links with the other nodes in the wireless network. In an infrastructure network, the wireless clients (or stations) associate with an Access Point (AP).

5. WEP was found to use an encryption scheme that was not strong enough. The weak encryption scheme could lead to the transmitted data being compromised. The encryption key used by WEP is comprised of a 40-bit shared secret and a 24-bit IV. The shared secret remains constant for the lifetime of the session, and only the IV changes. Because of the short length of the IV, it is possible for the same key material to be reused.

6. EAP/TLS provides authentication with a RADIUS server to users at wireless stations.

7. You can use voice coders or waveform coders to convert voice input into a digital format for transport over the Internet. Voice coders use the speech input to create a

signal that resembles the original voice input. Waveform coders directly encode the waveform generated by analog speech by sampling the voice input and converting the amplitude of each sample to the nearest value from a finite set of discrete values.

8. The issues that need to be resolved before Voice over IP becomes widely implemented include the following:

   - Voice over IP requires timely delivery.
   - Because most users are assigned random IP addresses when they connect to the Internet, a centralized directory service is required to allow hosts to be found for communication sessions.
   - The need for similar equipment at each end of the connection must be removed.
   - Voice over IP requires a large amount of bandwidth for the timely transport of digitized voice data.

Answers for Day 20

1. You can add a network adapter to a Windows 9*x* installation by launching the Add New Hardware Wizard to install the necessary drivers. The Add New Hardware Wizard can be launched from the Add New Hardware applet in the Control Panel.

2. The Domain Suffix Search order provides additional Internet domain names that will be appended to a hostname when a hostname is resolved using DNS.

3. The `inetcfg` NLM is used to start the TCP/IP installation process on a NetWare 6 server. This NLM also enables you to configure TCP/IP on the NetWare 6 server.

4. The DNSDHCP configuration utility is Java console, rather than an NLM-based management tool in NetWare 6. The Java console allows management of the DNS and DHCP environments using a GUI tool.

5. The Unix kernel must be rebuilt on a Unix server when a new network adapter is installed. Depending on the version of Unix, this could involve a compilation of C language programs. The compilation is based on the script stored in the configuration file stored in the `/usr/sys/conf` directory.

6. The Linuxconf utility, in the `/sbin` directory, is used to configure TCP/IP settings in Linux after installation is completed.

7. To display the current TCP/IP settings in Linux, you can use the `IFCONFIG` utility. Alternatively, if you want to view and modify the TCP/IP settings, you can use the `LINUXCONF` utility. Both utilities are found in the `/SBIN` directory.

8. A Unix server uses the `inetd` daemon to determine which daemon is launched to satisfy an Internet request from a remote client. The `inetd` daemon also determines how the daemon will act when the session is closed.

9. You can use the command `netstat -r` to view the routing table on a Unix server.

10. If a TCP/IP client is installed on a single segment LAN, it requires an IP address and a subnet mask for a minimum TCP/IP configuration.

11. A manually entered configuration setting takes precedence over a DHCP setting if a manual configuration is set. To prevent this from taking place, you must implement system policies that restrict a user's access to the Network Control Panel applet.

B

Answers for Day 21

1. You can assign an Anycast address to multiple interfaces that are generally on distinct routers. When a packet is sent to an Anycast address, the packet is delivered to only one of the interfaces associated with the Anycast address. This is generally the "nearest" address based on routing table distance. If one of the routers goes down, the packet can be sent to another host with the same Anycast address.

2. When data is sent to an Anycast address, it is sent to only one of the interfaces that has the same Anycast address. Data sent to a multicast address is sent to all interfaces that have registered the multicast address.

3. The following IPv6 addresses are

Address	Address Type
0:0:0:0:0:0:0:1	The loopback address
0:0:0:0:0:FFFF:AC10:0210	An IPv4-mapped IPv6 address
0:0:0:0:0:0:0:0	The unspecified address
0:0:0:0:0:0:C0A8:0344	An IPv4-compatible IPv6 address
FF0E:2322::AD56:0230	A Global Scope Multicast Address

4. Under IPv6, the Maximum Transmission Unit (MTU) for the entire path between source and destination hosts is determined. This allows all fragmentation to be performed by the source node. The packet does not have to be fragmented again as it crosses routers along the delivery path as in IPv4, resulting in a more efficient fragmentation process.

5. The following methods have been proposed to help convert from IPv4 to IPv6: Installing a dual IP layer that supports both IPv4 and IPv6 for all hosts and routers,

IPv6 over IPv4 tunneling, where an IPv6 packet is encapsulated within an IPv4 header, and Transport Relay Translator (TRT), where an intermediate host translates IPv6 addresses to an IPv4 address, and relays the packets between the two networks.

6. IPv6 resources are available from many locations. For Microsoft products, a Windows 2000 IPv6 stack can be downloaded from Microsoft Research at `http://research.microsoft.com/msripv6/msripv6.htm` and Windows XP includes an IPv6 protocol stack that can be loaded from the command line. A Linux IPv6 stack is available at `http://www.linux-ipv6.org/` and the KAME project (`www.kame.net`) provides IPv6 stacks for BSD Unix variants.

APPENDIX C

Internet MIB-II Category Definitions

Internet MIB-II is divided into the following categories:

- System
- Interfaces
- Address Translation
- IP
- ICMP
- TCP
- UDP
- EGP
- Transmission
- SNMP

This appendix describes the commonly used SNMP object identifiers within each category. If you want to search for other MIBS that exist for SNMP, you can find most MIB definitions at www.snmplink.org/mibs.html.

The System Group

The System group contains general information about the network device. Table C.1 shows some of the more commonly used objects within the System group.

TABLE C.1   The MIB-II System Group Objects

Object	Object ID	Description
SysDescr	.1.3.6.1.2.1.1.1	A textual description of the device. It should include the full name of the device.
SysObjectID	.1.3.6.1.2.1.1.2	The vendor's authoritative identification of the network management subsystem. This is the hierarchy object ID for the vendor's enterprise MIB.
SysUpTime	.1.3.6.1.2.1.1.3	The time, in seconds, since the device was last initialized.
SysContact	.1.3.6.1.2.1.1.4	The contact person for the network device. This should include information on how to contact this person.
SysName	.1.3.6.1.2.1.1.5	The fully qualified domain name of the device.
SysLocation	.1.3.6.1.2.1.1.6	The physical location of the device.
SysServices	.1.3.6.1.2.1.1.7	A value that indicates the set of services the device offers as its primary function.

The Interfaces Group

The Interfaces group defines information about a network interface. This includes both physical network interfaces, such as ethernet or token ring and point-to-point links. Table C.2 shows the objects in the Interfaces group.

TABLE C.2   The MIB-II Interfaces Group Objects

Object	Object ID	Description
IfNumber	.1.3.6.1.2.1.2.1	The number of network interfaces present on a device.
IfTable	.1.3.6.1.2.1.2.2	A list of interface entries. The total number of entries in the table is the value of IfNumber.
IfEntry	.1.3.6.1.2.1.2.2.1	An interface entry that contains objects at the subnetwork layer and below for a particular interface.

TABLE C.2 continued

Object	Object ID	Description
IfIndex	.1.3.6.1.2.1.2.2.1.1	A unique value for each interface. The value ranges between 1 and the value of IfNumber.
IfDescr	.1.3.6.1.2.1.2.2.1.2	A textual description of the interface, which commonly contains the manufacturer, the product name, and the version of the interface.
IfType	.1.3.6.1.2.1.2.2.1.3	The type of interface. This defines whether the device is an ethernet card, a token ring card, an ISDN interface, or other.
IfMTU	.1.3.6.1.2.1.2.2.1.4	The size of the largest datagram that can be sent or received on the interface.
IfSpeed	.1.3.6.1.2.1.2.2.1.5	An estimate of the interface's current bandwidth in bits per second.
IfPhysAddress	.1.3.6.1.2.1.2.2.1.6	The physical address of the network interface. If the device (such as a serial line) does not have a physical address, the object should contain an octet string of length zero.
IfAdminStatus	.1.3.6.1.2.1.2.2.1.7	This describes the desired state of the interface. It can be listed as up, down, or in testing mode.
IfOperStatus	.1.3.6.1.2.1.2.2.1.8	This describes the current state of the interface in terms of up, down, or testing.
ifLastChange	.1.3.6.1.2.1.2.2.1.9	The value of sysUptime at the time the interface entered its current operational state.
ifInOctets	.1.3.6.1.2.1.2.2.1.10	The total number of octets received on the interface.
ifinUcastPkts	.1.3.6.1.2.1.2.2.1.11	The number of subnetwork unicast packets delivered to a higher-level protocol.
ifInNUcastPkts	.1.3.6.1.2.1.2.2.1.12	The number of non-unicast packets delivered to a higher-layer protocol. This is the total number of broadcasts and multicasts received.
ifInDiscards	.1.3.6.1.2.1.2.2.1.13	The number of inbound packets that were discarded without an error condition existing.
InInErrors	.1.3.6.1.2.1.2.2.1.14	The number of inbound packets that contained errors and were not delivered to a higher-level protocol.

C

TABLE C.2 continued

Object	Object ID	Description
ifInUnknownProtos	.1.3.6.1.2.1.2.2.1.15	The number of inbound packets that contained unknown or unsupported protocols and were discarded.
IfOutOctets	.1.3.6.1.2.1.2.2.1.16	The total number of octets transmitted out the interface.
IfOutUcastPkts	.1.3.6.1.2.1.2.2.1.17	The total number of unicast packets transmitted out the interface.
IfOutNUcastPkts	.1.3.6.1.2.1.2.2.1.18	The total number of non-unicast packets transmitted out the interface. This includes both broadcasts and multicasts.
IfOutDiscards	.1.3.6.1.2.1.2.2.1.19	The total number of outbound packets discarded even though no error condition existed.
IfOutErrors	.1.3.6.1.2.1.2.2.1.20	The number of outbound packets that were not transmitted due to errors.
IfOutQlen	.1.3.6.1.2.1.2.2.1.21	The length, in packets, of the output packet queue.
IfSpecific	.1.3.6.1.2.1.2.2.1.22	A reference to MIB definitions specific to the media being used by the interface.

The Address Translation Group

The Address Translation group exists solely for compatibility with MIB-I nodes. It contains address translation information. The information is contained in a single table used to convert a network address (such as an IP address) into subnet-specific addresses (such as a physical address). Table C.3 shows the objects contained in the Address Translation group.

TABLE C.3 The MIB-II Address Translation Group Objects

Object	Object ID	Description
AtTable	.1.3.6.1.2.1.3.1	This table contains the network address to physical address entries.
AtEntry	.1.3.6.1.2.1.3.1.1	Each entry contains a single network address to physical address mapping.
AtIfIndex	.1.3.6.1.2.1.3.1.1.1	The interface on which the network address to physical address mapping is based.

TABLE C.3   continued

Object	Object ID	Description
AtPhysAddress	.1.3.6.1.2.1.3.1.1.2	The media-dependent physical address of the interface.
AtNetAddress	.1.3.6.1.2.1.3.1.1.3	The network address that corresponds to the physical address (such as an IP address).

The IP Group

The IP group contains information specific to the IP protocol. Table C.4 shows the primary objects contained in the IP group.

TABLE C.4   The MIB-II IP Group Objects

Object	Object ID	Description
IpForwarding	.1.3.6.1.2.1.4.1	This indicates whether the device is functioning as an IP router or as a nonrouting IP host.
IpDefaultTTL	.1.3.6.1.2.1.4.2	The default value inserted into the TTL field of an IP header for datagrams that originate at this device. This is used only if an upper layer protocol does not supply a TTL value.
IpInReceives	.1.3.6.1.2.1.4.3	The total number of IP datagrams received from interfaces (including errors).
IpInHdrErrors	.1.3.6.1.2.1.4.4	The number of input errors discarded due to errors in the IP header.
IpInAddrErrors	.1.3.6.1.2.1.4.5	The number of input datagrams discarded at the device because the IP address in their IP header's destination field was not a valid address to be received at this device. This can be due to a destination address of 0.0.0.0 or a nonsupported class of IP address (such as a Class E address).

C

TABLE C.4   continued

Object	Object ID	Description
IpForwDatagrams	.1.3.6.1.2.1.4.6	The number of input datagrams that were received that this device was not the final destination and they were forwarded. This includes source route packets that were routed via this device successfully.
IpInUnknownProtos	.1.3.6.1.2.1.4.7	The number of locally addressed datagrams received successfully but that were dropped due to an unknown or unsupported protocol.
IpInDiscards	.1.3.6.1.2.1.4.8	The number of IP datagrams that were discarded even though an error condition was not detected. This includes IP fragment packets that were discarded while awaiting reassembly.
IpInDelivers	.1.3.6.1.2.1.4.9	The total number of input datagrams successfully delivered to IP user protocols (including ICMP).
IpOutRequests	.1.3.6.1.2.1.4.10	The total number of IP datagrams that local IP user protocols (including ICMP) supplied to IP in requests for transmission.
IPOutDiscards	.1.3.6.1.2.1.4.11	The number of output datagrams that were discarded even though no error conditions were detected.
IpOutNoRoutes	.1.3.6.1.2.1.4.12	The number of IP datagrams discarded because no route could be determined for the next hop.
IPReasmTimeout	.1.3.6.1.2.1.4.13	The maximum number of seconds an incoming fragment is held for the reassembly process.
IPReasmReqds	.1.3.6.1.2.1.4.14	The number of IP fragments received that need to be reassembled at this device.
IpReasmOKs	.1.3.6.1.2.1.4.15	The number of IP datagrams successfully reassembled at this device.

TABLE C.4   continued

Object	Object ID	Description
IpReasmFails	.1.3.6.1.2.1.4.16	The number of failures detected by the IP reassembly process.
IpFragOKs	.1.3.6.1.2.1.4.17	The number of IP datagrams that have been successfully fragmented by this device.
IpFragFails	.1.3.6.1.2.1.4.18	The number of IP datagrams that have been discarded because they needed to be fragmented but could not be. This can be caused by a datagram having the Don't Fragment flag set.
IPFragCreates	.1.3.6.1.2.1.4.19	The number of IP fragments that have been generated by the fragmentation process by this device.
IpAddrTable	.1.3.6.1.2.1.4.20	The table of addressing information for this device's IP addresses.
IpAddrEntry	.1.3.6.1.2.1.4.20.1	The addressing information for one of this device's IP addresses.
IpAddEntAddr	.1.3.6.1.2.1.4.20.1.1	The IP address to which this entry's addressing information pertains.
IpAdEntIfIndex	.1.3.6.1.2.1.4.20.1.2	The index value that uniquely identifies the interface to which this entry is applicable.
IpAdEntNetMask	.1.3.6.1.2.1.4.20.1.3	The subnet mask associated with the IP address of this entry.
IpAdEntBcastAddr	.1.3.6.1.2.1.4.20.1.4	The value of the least significant bit in the IP broadcast address used for sending datagrams on the (logical) interface associated with the IP address of this entry.
IpAdEntReasmMaxSize	.1.3.6.1.2.1.4.20.1.5	The size of the largest IP datagram this entry can reassemble from incoming IP fragmented datagrams received on this interface.
IpRouteTable	.1.3.6.1.2.1.4.21	The IP routing table for a device.
IpRouteEntry	.1.3.6.1.2.1.4.21.1	A route to a specific destination.

C

TABLE C.4 continued

Object	Object ID	Description
IpRouteDest	.1.3.6.1.2.1.4.21.1.1	The destination IP address of this route. An entry with the value 0.0.0.0 is considered to be the default route.
IpRouteIfIndex	.1.3.6.1.2.1.4.21.1.2	The index value that uniquely identifies the local interface through which the next hop of this route should be reached.
IpRouteMetric1	.1.3.6.1.2.1.4.21.1.3	The primary routing metric for this route. The specifics of the metric are based on the IPRouteProto.
IpRouteMetric2	.1.3.6.1.2.1.4.21.1.4	An alternate routing metric for this route. If this route is not used, the value is set to −1.
IpRouteMetric3	.1.3.6.1.2.1.4.21.1.5	An alternate routing metric for this route. If this route is not used, the value is set to −1.
IpRouteMetric4	.1.3.6.1.2.1.4.21.1.6	An alternate routing metric for this route. If this route is not used, the value is set to −1.
IpRouteNextHop	.1.3.6.1.2.1.4.21.1.7	The IP address for the next hop in this route.
IpRouteType	.1.3.6.1.2.1.4.21.1.8	The type of route. Generally, this value is set to either direct or indirect.
IpRouteProto	.1.3.6.1.2.1.4.21.1.9	The routing mechanism by which the route was learned. This can include protocols such as RIP, OSPF, and BGP.
IpRouteAge	.1.3.6.1.2.1.4.21.1.10	The number of seconds since this route was last updated or otherwise determined to be correct.
IpRouteMask	.1.3.6.1.2.1.4.21.1.11	The subnet mask to be used for the ANDing process with the destination IP address value in the ipRouteDest field.
IpRouteMetric5	.1.3.6.1.2.1.4.21.1.12	An alternate routing metric for this route. If this route is not used, the value is set to −1.

TABLE C.4 continued

Object	Object ID	Description
IpRouteInfo	.1.3.6.1.2.1.4.21.1.13	A reference to MIB definitions specific to the particular routing protocol responsible for this route, as determined by the value specified in the route's ipRouteProto value.
IpNetToMediaTable	.1.3.6.1.2.1.4.22	The IP Address Translation table used for mapping from IP addresses to physical addresses.
IpNetToMediaEntry	.1.3.6.1.2.1.4.22.1	Each entry contains one IP address to physical address mapping.
IpNetToMediaIfIndex	.1.3.6.1.2.1.4.22.1.1	The interface on which this IP address to physical address mapping is based.
IpNetToMediaPhysAddress	.1.3.6.1.2.1.4.22.1.2	The media-dependent physical address.
IpNetToMediaNetAddress	.1.3.6.1.2.1.4.22.1.3	The IP address corresponding to the physical address.
IpNetToMediaType	.1.3.6.1.2.1.4.22.1.4	The type of mapping. Valid entries include Invalid, Static, Dynamic, or Other.
IpRoutingDiscards	.1.3.6.1.2.1.4.23	The number of IP routing entries that were chosen to be discarded even though they were valid.

The ICMP Group

The ICMP group contains information specific to the ICMP protocol. Table C.5 shows the primary objects contained in the ICMP group.

TABLE C.5 The MIB-II ICMP Group Objects

Object	Object ID	Description
IcmpInMsgs	.1.3.6.1.2.1.5.1	The total number of ICMP messages the device has received.
icmpInErrors	.1.3.6.1.2.1.5.2	The number of ICMP messages the device received but that were determined to have ICMP-specific errors.

TABLE C.5   continued

Object	Object ID	Description
icmpInDestUnreachs	.1.3.6.1.2.1.5.3	The number of ICMP destination unreachable messages received.
icmpInTimeExcds	.1.3.6.1.2.1.5.4	The number of ICMP time exceeded messages received.
icmpInParmProbs	.1.3.6.1.2.1.5.5	The number of ICMP parameter problem messages received.
icmpInSrcQuenchs	.1.3.6.1.2.1.5.6	The number of ICMP source quench messages received.
icmpInRedirects	.1.3.6.1.2.1.5.7	The number of ICMP redirect messages received.
icmpInEchos	.1.3.6.1.2.1.5.8	The number of ICMP echo request messages received.
icmpInEchoReps	.1.3.6.1.2.1.5.9	The number of ICMP echo reply messages received.
icmpInTimestamps	.1.3.6.1.2.1.5.10	The number of ICMP timestamp request messages received.
icmpInTimestampReps	.1.3.6.1.2.1.5.11	The number of ICMP timestamp reply messages received.
icmpInAddrMasks	.1.3.6.1.2.1.5.12	The number of ICMP address mask request messages received.
icmpInAddrMaskReps	.1.3.6.1.2.1.5.13	The number of ICMP address mask reply messages received.
IcmpOutMsgs	.1.3.6.1.2.1.5.14	The total number of ICMP messages this entity attempted to send, including all IcmpOutErrors.
IcmpOutErrors	.1.3.6.1.2.1.5.15	The number of ICMP messages the device did not send due to problems discovered within ICMP. This does not include errors discovered outside the ICMP layer.
IcmpOutDestUnreachs	.1.3.6.1.2.1.5.16	The number of ICMP destination unreachable messages sent.
IcmpOutTimeExcds	.1.3.6.1.2.1.5.17	The number of ICMP time exceeded messages sent.
IcmpOutParmProbs	.1.3.6.1.2.1.5.18	The number of ICMP parameter problem messages sent.

TABLE C.5 continued

Object	Object ID	Description
IcmpOutSrcQuenchs	.1.3.6.1.2.1.5.19	The number of ICMP source quench messages sent.
IcmpOutRedirects	.1.3.6.1.2.1.5.20	The number of ICMP redirect messages sent.
IcmpOutEchos	.1.3.6.1.2.1.5.21	The number of ICMP echo request messages sent.
IcmpOutEchoReps	.1.3.6.1.2.1.5.22	The number of ICMP echo reply messages sent.
IcmpOutTimestamps	.1.3.6.1.2.1.5.23	The number of ICMP timestamp request messages sent.
IcmpOutTimestampReps	.1.3.6.1.2.1.5.24	The number of ICMP timestamp reply messages.
IcmpOutAddrMasks	.1.3.6.1.2.1.5.25	The number of ICMP address mask request messages sent.
IcmpOutAddrMaskReps	.1.3.6.1.2.1.5.26	The number of ICMP address mask reply messages sent.

C

The TCP Group

The TCP group contains information specific to the TCP protocol. In the TCP group, objects that represent specific TCP connections exist only for the duration of the TCP session. Table C.6 shows the primary objects contained in the TCP group.

TABLE C.6 The MIB-II TCP Group Objects

Object	Object ID	Description
TcpRtoAlgorithm	.1.3.6.1.2.1.6.1	The algorithm used to determine the timeout value for the retransmission timer.
TcpRtoMin	.1.3.6.1.2.1.6.2	The minimum value, in milliseconds, permitted by a TCP implementation for the retransmission timeout.
TcpRtoMax	.1.3.6.1.2.1.6.3	The maximum value, in milliseconds, permitted by a TCP implementation for the retransmission timeout.

TABLE C.6   continued

Object	Object ID	Description
TcpMaxConn	.1.3.6.1.2.1.6.4	The limit on the total number of TCP connections a device can support.
TcpActiveOpens	.1.3.6.1.2.1.6.5	The number of times TCP connections have made a direct transition to the SYN-SENT state from the CLOSED state.
TcpPassiveOpens	.1.3.6.1.2.1.6.6	The number of times TCP connections have made a direct transition to the SYN-RCVD state from the LISTEN state.
TcpAttemptFails	.1.3.6.1.2.1.6.7	The number of times TCP connections have made a direct transition to the CLOSED state from either the SYN-SENT state or the SYN-RCVD state. This also includes the number of times a connection made a direct transition to the LISTEN state from the SYN-RCVD state.
TcpEstabResets	.1.3.6.1.2.1.6.8	The number of times TCP connections made a direct transition to the CLOSED state from either the ESTABLISHED state or the CLOSE-WAIT state.
TcpCurrEstab	.1.3.6.1.2.1.6.9	The number of TCP connections for which the current state is ESTABLISHED or CLOSE-WAIT.
TcpInSegs	.1.3.6.1.2.1.6.10	The total number of TCP segments received, including TCP segments that were received with errors.
TcpOutSegs	.1.3.6.1.2.1.6.11	The total number of TCP segments sent. This does not include segments that contained only retransmitted octets.
TcpRetransSegs	.1.3.6.1.2.1.6.12	The total number of segments that were contained in one or more of the previously transmitted octets.
TcpConnTable	.1.3.6.1.2.1.6.13	A table that contains TCP connection-specific information.
TcpConnEntry	.1.3.6.1.2.1.6.13.1	Information about a specific, currently existing TCP connection. The connection is removed when the connection state enters the CLOSED state.

TABLE C.6   continued

Object	Object ID	Description
TcpConnState	.1.3.6.1.2.1.6.13.1.1	The state of this TCP connection. Allowable values include CLOSED, LISTEN, and ESTABLISHED.
TcpConnLocalAddress	.1.3.6.1.2.1.6.13.1.2	The local IP address for this TCP connection. If the connection is in a LISTEN state that is willing to accept connection on any available IP interface on the device, the IP address 0.0.0.0 is used.
TcpConnLocalPort	.1.3.6.1.2.1.6.13.1.3	The local port number for this TCP connection.
TcpConnRemAddress	.1.3.6.1.2.1.6.13.1.4	The remote IP address for this TCP connection.
TcpConnRemPort	.1.3.6.1.2.1.6.13.1.5	The remote port number for this TCP connection.
TcpInErrs	.1.3.6.1.2.1.6.14	The total number of segments received with errors (such as bad TCP checksums).
TcpOutRsts	.1.3.6.1.2.1.6.15	The number of TCP segments sent with the RST flag set.

The UDP Group

The UDP group contains information specific to the UDP protocol. Table C.7 shows the primary objects contained in the UDP group.

TABLE C.7   The MIB-II UDP Group Objects

Object	Object ID	Description
UdpInDatagrams	.1.3.6.1.2.1.7.1	The total number of UDP datagrams delivered to UDP users.
UdpNoPorts	.1.3.6.1.2.1.7.2	The total number of received UDP datagrams for which there was no application at the destination port.

TABLE C.7   continued

Object	Object ID	Description
UdpInErrors	.1.3.6.1.2.1.7.3	The number of received UDP datagrams that could not be delivered for reasons other than the absence of an application at the indicated UDP destination port.
UdpOutDatagrams	.1.3.6.1.2.1.7.4	The total number of UDP datagrams sent from this device.
UdpTable	.1.3.6.1.2.1.7.5	A table containing information about all UDP listeners.
UdpEntry	.1.3.6.1.2.1.7.5.1	Information about a specific, currently operating UDP listener.
UdpLocalAddress	.1.3.6.1.2.1.7.5.1.1	The local IP address for this UDP listener. If the device is able to accept datagrams on any of its IP interfaces, the value 0.0.0.0 is used.
UdpLocalPort	.1.3.6.1.2.1.7.5.1.2	The local port number for this UDP listener.

The EGP Group

The EGP group contains information specific to the EGP protocol. The EGP protocol is used by exterior routers to allow autonomous systems to exchange routing reachability information on the Internet. Table C.8 shows the primary objects contained in the EGP group.

TABLE C.8   The MIB-II EGP Group Objects

Object	Object ID	Description
EgpInMsgs	.1.3.6.1.2.1.8.1	The number of EGP messages received that have no errors.
EgpInErrors	.1.3.6.1.2.1.8.2	The number of EGP messages received that have errors.
EgpOutMsgs	.1.3.6.1.2.1.8.3	The total number of locally generated EGP messages.
EgpOutErrors	.1.3.6.1.2.1.8.4	The number of locally generated EGP messages not sent due to resource limitations within an EGP device.

TABLE C.8 continued

Object	Object ID	Description
EgpNeighTable	.1.3.6.1.2.1.8.5	The EGP neighbor table.
EgpNeighEntry	.1.3.6.1.2.1.8.5.1	Information about this device's relationship with a specific EGP neighbor.
EgpNeighState	.1.3.6.1.2.1.8.5.1.1	The EGP state of the local system with respect to this entry's EGP neighbor.
EgpNeighAddr	.1.3.6.1.2.1.8.5.1.2	The IP address of this entry's EGP neighbor.
EgpNeighAs	.1.3.6.1.2.1.8.5.1.3	The autonomous system of this EGP peer. This is set to zero if the AS number is not known at this time.
EgpNeighInMsgs	.1.3.6.1.2.1.8.5.1.4	The number of EGP messages received from this EGP peer that did not have errors.
EgpNeighInErrs	.1.3.6.1.2.1.8.5.1.5	The number of EGP messages received from this EGP peer that were found to have errors.
EgpNeighOutMsgs	.1.3.6.1.2.1.8.5.1.6	The number of locally generated EGP messages to this EGP peer.
EgpNeighOutErrs	.1.3.6.1.2.1.8.5.1.7	The number of locally generated EGP messages not sent to this EGP peer due to a resource limitation on this EGP device.
EgpNeighInErrMsgs	.1.3.6.1.2.1.8.5.1.8	The number of EGP-defined error messages received from this EGP peer.
EgpNeighOutErrMsgs	.1.3.6.1.2.1.8.5.1.9	The number of EGP-defined error messages sent to this EGP peer.
EgpNeighStateUps	.1.3.6.1.2.1.8.5.1.10	The number of EGP state transitions to the UP state with this EGP peer.
EgpNeighStateDowns	.1.3.6.1.2.1.8.5.1.11	The number of EGP state transitions from the UP state to any other state with this EGP peer.
EgpNeighIntervalHello	.1.3.6.1.2.1.8.5.1.12	The interval, in hundredths of a second, between EGP Hello command retransmissions.
EgpNeighIntervalPoll	.1.3.6.1.2.1.8.5.1.13	The interval, in hundreths of a second, between EGP poll command transmissions.

C

TABLE C.8 continued

Object	Object ID	Description
EgpNeighMode	.1.3.6.1.2.1.8.5.1.14	The polling mode of the EGP device. This is set to either passive or active.
EgpNeighEventTrigger	.1.3.6.1.2.1.8.5.1.15	A control variable used to trigger an operator-initiated Start or Stop event. This returns the most recent value set for this object.
EgpAs	.1.3.6.1.2.1.8.6	The autonomous system number of this EGP device.

The Transmission Group

The objects in the Transmission group are based on the actual transmission media used by each interface. Currently, as the definitions for transmission media progress through the standardization process, they reside in the experimental portion of the MIB.

The SNMP Group

The SNMP group contains information specific to the SNMP protocol. Table C.9 shows the primary objects contained in the SNMP group.

TABLE C.9 The MIB-II SNMP Group Objects

Object	Object ID	Description
SnmpInPkts	.1.3.6.1.2.1.11.1	The total number of messages delivered to the SNMP device from the transport service.
SnmpOutPkts	.1.3.6.1.2.1.11.2	The total number of SNMP messages passed from the SNMP protocol device to the transport services.
SnmpInBadVersions	.1.3.6.1.2.1.11.3	The total number of SNMP messages delivered to the SNMP protocol device from an unsupported SNMP version.
SnmpInBadCommunityNames	.1.3.6.1.2.1.11.4	The total number of SNMP messages that contained an unrecognized community name.

TABLE C.9   continued

Object	Object ID	Description
SnmpInBadCommunityUses	.1.3.6.1.2.1.11.5	The total number of SNMP messages delivered to the SNMP protocol device that requested an SNMP operation not allowed by the referenced SNMP community name.
SnmpInASNParseErrs	.1.3.6.1.2.1.11.6	The total number of ASN.1 errors encountered by the SNMP protocol device when decoding an SNMP message.
SnmpInTooBigs	.1.3.6.1.2.1.11.8	The total number of SNMP PDUs delivered to the SNMP protocol device that had the error status value set to tooBig.
SnmpInNoSuchNames	.1.3.6.1.2.1.11.9	The total number of SNMP PDUs delivered to the SNMP protocol device that had the error status value set to noSuchName.
SnmpInBadValues	.1.3.6.1.2.1.11.10	The total number of SNMP PDUs delivered to the SNMP protocol device that had the error status value set to badValue.
SnmpInReadOnlys	.1.3.6.1.2.1.11.11	The total number of SNMP PDUs delivered to the SNMP protocol device that had the error status value set to readOnly.
SnmpInGenErrs	.1.3.6.1.2.1.11.12	The total number of SNMP PDUs delivered to the SNMP protocol device that had the error status value set to genErr.
SnmpInTotalReqVars	.1.3.6.1.2.1.11.13	The total number of MIB objects retrieved successfully by the SNMP protocol device as the result of receiving valid SNMP Get-Request and Get-Next PDUs.
SnmpInTotalSetVars	.1.3.6.1.2.1.11.14	The total number of MIB objects retrieved successfully by the SNMP protocol entity as the result of receiving valid SNMP Set-Request PDUs.

C

TABLE C.9 continued

Object	Object ID	Description
SnmpInGetRequests	.1.3.6.1.2.1.11.15	The total number of SNMP Get-Request PDUs accepted and processed by the SNMP protocol device.
SnmpInGetNexts	.1.3.6.1.2.1.11.16	The total number of SNMP Get-Next Request PDUs accepted and processed by the SNMP protocol device.
SnmpInSetRequests	.1.3.6.1.2.1.11.17	The total number of SNMP Set-Request PDUs accepted and processed by the SNMP protocol device.
SnmpInGetResponses	.1.3.6.1.2.1.11.18	The total number of SNMP Get-Response PDUs accepted and processed by the SNMP protocol device.
SnmpInTraps	.1.3.6.1.2.1.11.19	The total number of SNMP Trap PDUs accepted and processed by the SNMP protocol device.
SnmpOutTooBigs	.1.3.6.1.2.1.11.20	The total number of SNMP PDUs generated by the SNMP protocol device that had an error status value set to tooBig.
SnmpOutNoSuchNames	.1.3.6.1.2.1.11.21	The total number of SNMP PDUs generated by the SNMP protocol device that had an error status value set to noSuchName.
SnmpOutBadValues	.1.3.6.1.2.1.11.22	The total number of SNMP PDUs generated by the SNMP protocol device that had an error status value set to badValue.
SnmpOutGenErrs	.1.3.6.1.2.1.11.24	The total number of SNMP PDUs generated by the SNMP protocol device that had an error status value set to genErr.
SnmpOutGetRequests	.1.3.6.1.2.1.11.25	The total number of SNMP Get-Request PDUs generated by the SNMP protocol device.
SnmpOutGetNexts	.1.3.6.1.2.1.11.26	The total number of SNMP Get-Next Request PDUs generated by the SNMP protocol device.

TABLE C.9   continued

Object	Object ID	Description
SnmpOutSetRequests	.1.3.6.1.2.1.11.27	The total number of SNMP Set-Request PDUs generated by the SNMP protocol device.
SnmpOutGetResponses	.1.3.6.1.2.1.11.28	The total number of SNMP Get-Response PDUs generated by the SNMP protocol device.
SnmpOutTraps	.1.3.6.1.2.1.11.29	The total number of SNMP Trap PDUs generated by the SNMP protocol device.
SnmpEnableAuthenTraps	.1.3.6.1.2.1.11.30	Indicates whether the SNMP agent process is permitted to generate authentication-failure traps.

The SNMP object IDs .1.3.6.1.2.1.11.7 *and* .1.3.6.1.2.1.11.23 *are not implemented.*

C

APPENDIX D

Glossary of Terms

802.1x   The standard proposed for secure wireless communications using digital certificates to authenticate and authorize a wireless client with a wireless access point and secure communications using PKI-based encryption. If the authentication and authorization process fails, the client is prevented from accessing the wireless network.

802.11b   The standard proposed for connectivity between wireless access points and wireless network cards. The 802.11b standard supports communications up to 11Mbps.

10BASE-2   Also known as thin ethernet, this wiring standard allows for network segments of up to 185 meters on coaxial cable.

10BASE-5   Also known as thick ethernet, this wiring standard allows for network segments up to 500 meters on coaxial cable.

10BASE-T   This wiring standard is commonly used with both star and ring networks. The 10-BASE-T wiring standard allows for cable length segments of 100 meters from the central wiring hub.

Abort Output (AO)   This allows the running process to continue running until completed. It stops the sending of output to the remote user's terminal screen, however, during a Telnet session.

Abstract Syntax Notation One (ASN.1)   The notation used to define each object within the Management Information Base (MIB). ASN.1 describes the name of the object and the syntax used to access the object.

Active Directory-integrated zones   A Microsoft DNS zone format that stores DNS zone data in Active Directory. This format allows Active Directory replication of resource records and application of Active Directory security to all resource records.

Active Users   This service returns a message to the calling system informing it of all the users currently active on the system running the Active Users service. The Active Users service can be called on both TCP and UDP ports 11.

Address (A)   An address resource record is used to map a hostname to an IP address.

Address Resolution Protocol (ARP)   This Internet layer protocol provides address resolution between IP addresses and physical MAC addresses on network interfaces.

aliases   E-mail addresses that actually reference a different e-mail mailbox. Aliases are commonly set up to reference a function within an organization (for example, personnel@org.com), rather than a person.

ANDing process   The process of determining whether a source host is located on a local network or on a remote network in the TCP/IP protocol. The process involves comparing the source and destination IP addresses to the source's subnet mask.

anycast address   An IPv6 address that can be assigned to multiple interfaces that are generally on different hosts. Data sent to an anycast address is delivered to the "nearest" interface that is assigned the anycast address.

Application-level firewalls   These firewalls perform an evaluation of data at the application layer before a connection between two hosts is established. Connection states, sequencing information, user passwords, and specific service requests are all monitored.

Are You There (AYT)   This function enables remote users to determine whether their connection to the Telnet server is still functioning.

area border router   An OSPF router with interfaces that attach to networks belonging to different areas.

ARPA   In 1957, ARPA, the Advanced Research Projects Agency, was commissioned to take the United States' lead in science and technology.

ARPAnet   ARPAnet, the Advanced Research Projects Agency Network, was the originator of the network that today is known as the Internet.

ASCII   ASCII, the American Standard Code for Information Interchange, is an 8-bit character set used to define all alphanumeric characters. It is the most common implementation of text transmissions on computers.

ATM   Asynchronous Transfer Mode (ATM) is an advanced method of packet switching that makes use of fixed-length cells of data. Transmission rates on an ATM network reach 155Mbps but could theoretically reach 1.2Gbps. An Asynchronous Transmission Mode backbone was introduced on the Internet in 1996 when NSFNET officially contracted out the Internet backbone to privatized companies.

ATMARP   A revised version of ARP used in an ATM network that resolves an IP address to an ATM address rather than a physical MAC address.

authentication   The validation of a user/password combination to a server's account information database. Different mechanisms can be implemented to validate the user with the server.

Authentication header (AH)   An IPSec protocol that provides protection against modification of data as it is transmitted across a network.

authentication server   The server at which users and network services register their private/public key pairs.

authenticator   A Kerberos message that contains the current time and other identifying information about the user establishing the session that is locked using the assigned session key. Authenticators are used to prevent impersonation.

Authority Information Access (AIA)   A digital certificate extension that indicates URLs where the digital certificate of the issuing CA may be retrieved.

autonomous system   A network that is managed by a single network administrator. This is commonly used to represent your internal network.

autonomous system boundary router   An OSPF router that exchanges routing information with routers from an external autonomous system.

B-Node   A NetBIOS name resolution method that uses broadcast methods to resolve a NetBIOS name to an IP address after the NetBIOS name cache is checked. If this fails, the host attempts to resolve the NetBIOS name to an IP address using the LMHOSTS file, the HOSTS file, and DNS.

backbone area   A special area in an OSPF network that has been assigned the area ID of 0.0.0.0. The backbone area acts as a routing hub for traffic between areas.

backbone router   An OSPF router that has an interface attached to the backbone area.

backup designated router   A backup router used to exchange routing information within an OSPF area elected in case the designated router fails.

BBN   Bolt, Beranak, and Newman (BBN) were contracted by ARPA to build the ARPAnet.

Berkeley Internet Name Daemon (BIND)   A common method of configuring DNS name servers that utilizes a `named.boot` file to configure the DNS name server.

Berkeley R-Utilities   A set of remote commands that enable remote users to run processes and applications as though they were local users on the systems hosting the remote daemons.

binary   The binary notation system is the underlying method used to represent IP addresses assigned to hosts.

BinHex   A file encoding system initially implemented for Macintosh systems. BinHex converts a binary file into an encrypted text version using hexadecimal characters. BinHex attachments are generally saved with the extension .hqx.

BNC   British Naval Connectors (BNC) are used to connect coaxial cable in a bus topology network.

BOOTP protocol   This protocol is used to automatically configure a host with an IP address. Besides an IP address, additional options can also be assigned to the client.

Border Gateway Protocol (BGP)   This protocol allows autonomous systems to exchange network reachability information. BGP improves on the EGP protocol by including all autonomous systems that must be crossed in transit to the destination network. This helps to develop a network layout graph and identify routing loops for removal from the routing tables.

boundary layers   A protocol located in one layer of a layered model needs to interact only with protocols located in the layers immediately above or below its layer. This helps the development of new protocols because they have to interface only with their defined boundary layers.

Break (BRK)   This Telnet function is used by many systems to indicate that the Break or Attention key has been invoked.

bridging   The process of transferring data between two segments of a network that share the same logical network address. This occurs at the data link layer of the OSI model.

broadcasting   This transmission method is used to send a message to every host on a network segment. Broadcasting is not an efficient communication mechanism in that all hosts on a network segment must inspect the datagram to determine whether it is intended for them.

bus network   A network topology in which every computer is connected by a single cable segment.

caching-only name server   A DNS name server that does not store any zone data locally. All information is obtained via DNS requests to other DNS name servers. The results are cached and DNS responses are formulated from the cache (if found in the cache).

Callback RPC   NFS 4.0 uses callback RPCs to allow mutual authentication of the NFS client and the NFS server for NFS file transactions.

CAN   A campus area network (CAN) uses wide area network (WAN) technologies to join local area networks (LANs) on a university campus.

Canonical Name (CNAME)   This resource record is used to provide alias names to a hostname. It is configured in forward-lookup zones.

Certificate Revocation List (CRL)   A listing published by a CA that contains the serial numbers of all revoked certificates and the revocation reason for each revoked certificate.

Certification Authority (CA)   A server that issues digital certificates to users, computers, and services for the purposes of authentication, digital signing, and encryption purposes.

Challenged Handshake Authentication Protocol (CHAP)   An authentication mechanism that uses a three-step process. In the first step, the server sends a challenge string and its hostname to the client. In the second step, the client uses the hostname to determine the shared secret between the client and server. This shared secret is used to encrypt the challenge string. In the final step, the encrypted challenge string is returned to the server. The server performs the same encryption and compares the results. If they match, the client is authenticated.

Character Generator   This service returns a list of all 95 printable ASCII characters. It can be called on both TCP and UDP ports 19.

Circuit-level firewalls   These firewalls act as a referee for connections. Each connection request is monitored to ensure that a correct TCP three-way handshake takes place. If it does not, the connection is dropped. In addition, a session table is established that

D

contains all the current sessions. If any communication sequences do not follow their normal course, the connection is terminated.

Citrix Winframe   This thin client methodology allows clients to use sessions on a central terminal server. This server is capable of running DOS, WIN16, and WIN32 applications.

Class A addresses   This class of IP address allocates the first 8 bits to the network portion of the IP address and the remaining 24 bits to the host portion of the address.

Class B addresses   This class of IP address allocates the first 16 bits to the network portion of an IP address and the remaining 16 bits to the host portion of the address.

Class C addresses   This class of IP address allocates the first 24 bits to the network portion of an IP address and the remaining 8 bits to the host portion of the address.

Class D addresses   This class of address is used for addressing multicast groups. The first 4 bits are set to 1110, and the remaining 24 bits represent the actual multicast group address.

Classless Inter-Domain Routing (CIDR)   An addressing scheme that removes the concept of classes of IP addresses. Each address is simply a combination of network and host portions that do not have a specific number of bits assigned to each part.

community name   A low-level method of security implemented in SNMP. The community name must match the SNMP management system and the SNMP agent for SNMP requests to take place.

Compressed Serial Line Internet Protocol (CSLIP)   A version of the SLIP protocol that allows compression of data over the point-to-point connection.

configured tunneling   A preconfigured tunnel endpoint that an IPv6 packet uses to transmit data to an IPv6 destination address over an IPv4 network. The encapsulated data is delivered to this endpoint where it is unencapsulated and delivered to the IPv6 destination host.

convergence time   The amount of time it takes a network to adjust to a topology change and recalculate all the routing tables for the network.

count-to-infinity problem   A routing scenario in which each router informs its neighbor that it knows the route to a no longer accessible network. Each exchange causes the metric to increase by one until the maximum hop count is reached, at which time the route is discarded.

CRL Distribution Point (CDP)   A digital certificate extension that indicates URLs where the latest CRL of the issuing CA may be retrieved.

CSMA/CD Generally, carrier-sense multiple access with collision detection is used with bus topologies. A station listens to the physical network to determine whether another host is currently transmitting data on the network. If a collision occurs, the sending stations must wait a random period of time before attempting to retransmit.

CSU/DSU A channel service unit/data service unit converts network data into digital bipolar signals that are able to traverse a synchronous communications environment.

DARPA ARPA was renamed the Defense Advanced Research Projects Agency in 1972.

Data Transfer Process (DTP) The FTP protocol uses the Data Transfer Process for the actual transfer of data between the FTP client and FTP server.

database description packets Packets sent from the master OSPF router to slave OSPF routers that contain descriptions of the master router's Link State Database (LSDB).

Daytime This service returns a message that contains the current date and time to the connection system. A connection is established using TCP or UDP port 13.

DCE A Data Communications Equipment device takes input from a DTE (Data Terminal Equipment) device and transforms the input signal before sending it across a wide area network. A modem is an example of a DCE device.

default route A catchall route used if an explicit route is not defined in the routing table for a destination network.

demilitarized zone A network configuration in which all services available to the outside world are located on their own private network segment rather than in the internal network.

designated router The router used as a central contact point for routing information exchange within an OSPF area.

DHCP Ack The final phase in a DHCP exchange. The DHCP server acknowledges that the DHCP lease has been assigned to the client. Any options requested by the DHCP client are sent at this time.

DHCP Discover The first phase in a DHCP exchange. This message is sent by a DHCP client to indicate that it requires an IP address from a DHCP server.

DHCP Nack This DHCP message is sent from the DHCP server to a DHCP client when the DHCP client has requested an IP address that cannot be used on that segment of the network.

D

DHCP Offer   The second phase in a DHCP exchange. This message, sent by a DHCP server, indicates an IP address that it is willing to assign to the DHCP client.

DHCP relay agent   An agent that forwards DHCP broadcast requests to DHCP servers located on remote subnets.

DHCP Request   The third phase in a DHCP exchange. This message is sent by the DHCP client to indicate the DHCP offer that it has accepted.

Digital Signature   A hashing method used to protect data, such as an e-mail message, from modification. The sender computes a hash of the original message, and then sends the encrypted hash to the recipient. The recipient performs the same hash function and compares the two hashes to ensure they are identical.

Dijkstra algorithm   A routing algorithm used to find the shortest path from a single source node to every other node in the network.

Discard   This service discards all information that is sent to it on either TCP or UDP port 9. It is often used to test routing.

distance vector protocols   Broadcast-based protocols that primarily use hop counts as the routing metric. These protocols propagate the entire routing table between neighboring routers.

Distinguished Name   The full X.500 name for an object within the X.500 directory services tree. This includes all containers back to the ROOT of the X.500 tree.

distribution list   A single e-mail address that refers to a group of e-mail addresses.

DLCI   Data link connection identifiers are used to identify a circuit ID in a frame relay network. DLCIs provide addressing between network segments in a frame relay network.

DNS cache file   A text-based configuration file for a DNS name server that contains the ROOT DNS name servers and their IP addresses.

DNS Manager   The Windows NT utility that provides the capability to configure a DNS name server in Windows NT.

DNS resolvers   The client that performs the query to resolve a hostname to an IP address.

Domain Name Space (DNS)   The hierarchical name database containing the entire name space for the Internet. DNS provides name resolution to every host on the Internet.

Domain SAP/RIP Server (DSS)   A distributed Btrieve database that replicates all the services and routes within a NetWare/IP domain. DSS is used to reduce the number of broadcasts associated with SAP and RIP by storing the same information in a Btrieve database.

DTE   Data Terminal Equipment is any device that has the capability to transmit information in a digital format over a communications line. A data terminal is an example of a DTE device.

Dual-ring network   A network topology, consisting of a primary and secondary ring, in which data flows in opposite directions. The secondary ring is used only when a break in the primary ring occurs.

Dynamic DNS   A modified DNS methodology that allows for the dynamic registration and release of DNS names.

Dynamic DNS NOTIFY   A DNS message that allows a Master name server to inform its configured Slave name servers that a DDNS update should take place.

Dynamic DNS UPDATE   A DNS message that includes updated information for a hostname participating in the DDNS system.

Dynamic Host Configuration Protocol (DHCP)   This protocol allows a pool of IP addresses (scope) to be created that can be dynamically assigned to configured clients. Each scope can have options configured that will be assigned to DHCP clients.

dynamic packet filter firewalls   These firewalls combine the services of application-level firewalls and packet filter firewalls. The added advantage of this firewall is that security rules can be implemented as the service is running. This allows filters to be created for UDP connections.

dynamic routing   The automatic configuration of all routing paths through the network. This is accomplished by implementing routing protocols that advertise changes to the network topology.

EBCDIC   The Extended Binary Coded Decimal Interchange Code is a text representation method used extensively on IBM mainframe and mini computers.

Echo   This service returns as a response any information that is passed to it. Connections are established on either TCP or UDP port 7.

Encrypting Security Payloads (ESP)   An IPSec protocol used to encrypt and sign data as it is transmitted across a network. ESP protects against data being viewed as it is transmitted across the network.

encryption   The protection of transmitted data by scrambling the data with a method that can be deciphered only by the intended recipient.

D

Enhanced B-Node   A Microsoft-specific resolution method that first uses a broadcast to resolve a NetBIOS name to an IP address once the NetBIOS name cache has been checked. If that fails, the LMHOSTS file will be consulted to attempt to resolve the NetBIOS name to an IP address. If the Enable DNS for Windows option is selected, the client will also check the HOSTS file and DNS for name resolution.

Erase Character (EC)   This Telnet function deletes the last character input by the remote user.

Erase Line (EL)   This Telnet function is used to delete the contents of the current line of input.

ethernet   This network is based on Carrier-Sense Multiple Access with Collision Detection (CSMA/CD). The development of ethernet allowed for the proliferation of local area networks.

extended network prefix   The combination of the network and subnetwork portions of a subnet mask.

Exterior Gateway Protocol (EGP)   An interdomain reachability protocol that allows autonomous systems to exchange routing reachability information on the Internet.

exterior gateway protocols   Protocols used to exchange routing information between other organizations or autonomous systems.

eXternal Data Representation (XDR)   XDR is used by applications such as NFS and NIS to provide a universal format for text transmission between two hosts. It is used to facilitate text transmissions between two hosts using different internal text representations (such as EBCDIC and ASCII).

FDDI   Fiber Distributed Data Interface networks allow for high-speed, fiber-optic, local area networks running at speeds of 100Mbps. FDDI uses a dual-ring topology.

file encoding   A method of converting binary data into text data so that SMTP clients can transmit binary attachments.

File Transfer Protocol (FTP)   This protocol is used to transfer data from one host to another computer using TCP as the transport protocol.

Firewall   A host that provides a boundary service between the local area network and the external world. Rules can be implemented at the firewall to determine which specific traffic is allowed to cross this boundary service.

forward-lookup zone   A DNS configuration file containing resource records that generally provide hostname to IP address name resolution.

fragmentation   This process occurs when a packet is too large for the underlying network. The packet is broken into smaller fragments that can be transported on the underlying network.

frame relay   An advanced packet switched network that transmits variable length data using Permanent Virtual Circuits over digital networks. Due to the conditioned lines of a digital network, less error correction is built in to frame relay than X.25, which results in faster transmission rates.

full adjacent routers   The term used to indicate two routers that have exchanged link state requests.

fully qualified domain name (FQDN)   The combination of the hostname and the Internet domain of which it is a member. For example, the hostname www in the domain xyz.org would have a FQDN of www.xyz.org.

Generic Routing Encapsulation (GRE)   This protocol is used by the PPTP protocol to transport all data over a virtual private network.

H-Node   A specialized NetBIOS name resolution method that first queries a NetBIOS name server to resolve a NetBIOS name to an IP address. If this does not work, a local broadcast is sent to attempt to resolve the NetBIOS name to an IP address. If this fails, the host attempts to resolve the NetBIOS name to an IP address using the LMHOSTS file, the HOSTS file, and DNS.

hold-downs   The ignoring of routing messages that indicate a dead link is still reachable for a configured period of time (known as the hold-down time).

Host header   Host headers, introduced in HTTP version 1.1, allow a Web server to host multiple Web sites but use only a single IP address for each site. The site being accessed by a client is referenced in the host header.

hostname   A logical name that is assigned to an IP address. It does not relate directly to any service.

HOSTS file   This locally stored TCP/IP configuration file is used to resolve hostnames to IP addresses.

hosts.equiv   This file contains entries for hosts, or specific users on a host, that are trusted to connect remotely to a Unix host. This file is stored in the /etc directory.

hypertext transfer protocol (HTTP)   A request/response protocol that enables a user to view resources stored on the Web. A client requests a page from a Web server, and the Web server responds with the contents of that Web page.

D

IAB   The Internet Architecture Board (IAB) is in charge of strategic planning for the Internet.

IANA   The Internet Assigned Number Authority (IANA) is in charge of setting the policies of how IP addresses are assigned and is in charge of these assignments.

idempotent   A disk operation model that leaves the management and tracking of all operations to the client rather than to the server.

IESG   The Internet Engineering Steering Group (comprised of the area managers and the chairman of the IETF) determines which RFCs can enter the standards track.

IETF   The Internet Engineering Task Force is concerned primarily with short- to medium-length projects that resolve technical problems and needs that arise as the Internet develops.

InATMARP   A modified version of Reverse ARP (RARP) used in an ATM network. InATMARP resolves an ATM address to an IP address.

increment value   The value used to determine the starting address for each pool of addresses in a subnetted network.

Independent Computing Architecture (ICA)   The line protocol used to communicate between the client system and the Citrix server in a Citrix Winframe environment. This line protocol can run over any transport protocol.

interior gateway protocols   Protocols that are used to exchange routing information within an autonomous system.

internal router   An OSPF router whose network interfaces are all connected to networks belonging to the same area.

Internet Control Message Protocol (ICMP)   This Internet layer protocol provides an error reporting mechanism and control messages to the TCP/IP protocol suite.

Internet Daemon (inetd)   This service is used to launch the appropriate daemon when an Internet protocol request is received by a Unix host. The inetd daemon reviews the `inet.conf` file to determine which daemon is associated with the requested service.

Internet Group Management Protocol (IGMP)   This protocol is used to define groups of computers that share a common multicast address.

Internet Mail Access Protocol (IMAP)   A protocol that allows clients to retrieve e-mail messages from a server. It also allows messages to be stored in a hierarchical structure on the IMAP server.

Internet Protocol (IP)   This Internet layer protocol provides the logical addressing used for hosts in a TCP/IP network. This protocol is also used in determining whether a packet must be routed to a remote network or sent on the local network.

Internet Protocol Security (IPSec)   A method of protecting data as it is transmitted across a network. Data can be protected against modification by using Authentication Headers and against inspection by using Encrypting Security Payloads.

Interrupt Process (IP)   This provides the ability to suspend or interrupt a process running on the Telnet server.

Intrusion Detection System (IDS)   A software application that works with a firewall to detect common attacks that take place at the application layer against a computer on the Internet.

inverse query   A DNS resolution method that resolves a queried IP address to a fully qualified domain name.

IPv6   The next implementation of the Internet Protocol (IP) that expands the address space from a 32-bit address scheme to a 128-bit address scheme. IPv6 also uses a simplified header that allows for easier extensibility of the protocol.

IRSG   The Internet Research Steering Group sets the priorities and coordinates all research projects for the IRTF.

IRTF   The Internet Research Task Force is in charge of all research activities related to TCP/IP protocols (including any proposed changes to the Internet architecture).

ISDN   Integrated Services Digital Network is a digital service that is available in two formats: Basic Rate ISDN and Primary Rate ISDN. In North America, Basic Rate ISDN provides two B channels of 64Kbps and one D channel that can provide transmission rates of 16Kbps. Primary Rate ISDN can provide up to 1.544Mbps over 23 B channels and uses a D channel of 64Kbps for signal and link management.

ISO   The International Standards Organization works to establish global standards for communications and information exchange.

iterative query   A DNS name resolution method that returns an answer from the DNS name server to the DNS resolver. This answer can be a referral to a different DNS name server that may be able to resolve the logical name to an IP address, the IP address of the host, or a response that the hostname could not be resolved.

Java Virtual Machine   This thin client architecture allows small JavaScript applets to be launched from a central server and executed on a local client device.

D

Jumbo Payload hop-by-hop option   An IPv6 packet that has a payload greater than 65,636 bytes. This is indicated by a payload length field that is set to a value of 0.

Kerberos authentication   A method of authentication and data encryption that enables users to authenticate with services and to validate themselves to users based on secret key technology.

kernel proxy firewalls   These firewalls are implemented at the kernel level of the underlying operating system. Kernel proxy firewalls increase security because data is not passed up the levels of the network stack if a rule is broken.

LAN   Local area network computers operate together in a contained area connected with high bandwidth media.

Layer 2 Tunneling Protocol (L2TP)   This tunneling protocol is in the draft stage for becoming an RFC. It combines the technology of Microsoft's PPTP protocol and Cisco's Layer Two Forwarding (L2F) protocol. L2TP requires the use of IPSec to encrypt the tunneled data.

Lightweight Directory Access Protocol (LDAP)   A protocol that allows names to be found in a diverse directory services implementation. LDAP offers a standardized method for storing and retrieving names from directory services.

Line Printer Daemon (LPD)   This service allows a server to accept print jobs from remote TCP/IP hosts and print them to a local printer.

Line Printer Router (LPR)   This service is used to send a print job to a server running the Line Printer Daemon (LPD) or to a TCP/IP printer.

Link Control Protocol (LCP)   A PPP extension used to establish, configure, and test a data link connection.

Link State Advertisement (LSA)   The network advertisements used to build the OSPF link state database. These advertisements include each OSPF interface on a router, the attached networks for the router, and the cost to reach each of the attached networks.

Link State Database (LSDB)   Existing on each router interface in the network, this database contains entries for each network and the outgoing cost assigned to each network interface of a router.

link state protocols   These protocols flood routing information to all nodes in the network. This routing information contains routes to directly attached networks only. Even though these routing messages are sent to every router on the network, their reduced size results in a more efficient exchange of routing information.

link state requests   Requests for link state advertisements based on the database description packets received from a Master or Slave router. The link state request contains the entries required to complete its own link state database.

LMHOSTS (LAN Manager Hosts) file   This Microsoft-specific TCP/IP configuration file is used to auto-load NetBIOS names into the NetBIOS name cache, resolve NetBIOS names to IP addresses, and configure important NetBIOS servers on the network.

logical IP subnets (LIS)   Logical IP subnets are used in an ATM environment to group ATM hosts into a closed IP subnetwork. Multiple LISs can exist on the same physical network segment. For traffic to be routed between the LISs, one ATM device must be configured as a member of each LIS.

longest match route   The route in a routing table that most specifically defines the route to the destination network. This is used when variable length subnet masking is implemented.

Loopback adapter   A virtual network card that can be installed on a Windows NT-class computer to allow TCP/IP to be installed on the computer and bound to the loopback adapter.

M-Node   A specialized NetBIOS name resolution method that first uses broadcasts to resolve a NetBIOS name to an IP address after checking the NetBIOS name cache. If this fails, a query is sent to the configured NetBIOS name server. If this fails, the host attempts to resolve the NetBIOS name to an IP address using the LMHOSTS file, the HOSTS file, and DNS.

MAC address   The Media Access Control address is the physical address of a network interface card.

Mail Exchange (MX) records   Mail Exchange records are used to indicate the host that accepts e-mail messages for an Internet domain. Priorities can be configured so that multiple mail exchangers can be configured for a single Internet domain using the preference field.

MAN   A metropolitan area network is a distributed computer network joined by telecommunication links that reside in a close geographic area.

Management Information Base (MIB)   A database used to specify the details that a managed device will report to an SNMP management system.

master name server   A DNS name server that transfers its zone information to a secondary name server. Both a primary name server and a secondary name server can function as a Master name server.

D

Master servers   NIS servers that maintain the original copy of the NIS database.

MAU   A Multistation Access Unit is the connecting mechanism in a ring topology network.

maximum receive unit (MRU)   The maximum length of the data field in a PPP packet. It is the largest size of data stream that can be received by a PPP client/server. The default value is 1,500 bytes.

maximum transmission unit (MTU)   The largest packet size that can be used on a network segment. Routers use the MTU to determine whether a packet must be fragmented during transmission over a network segment.

mesh network   A mesh network connects remote sites over telecommunication links. The defining characteristic of a mesh network is that routers are able to search multiple paths to determine the best route to take at that moment.

metrics   Costs or values assigned to a property of a network link. Metrics are used to determine the lowest cost route to a destination network. Common metrics include hop count, delay, throughput, reliability, and communication costs.

Microsoft Point-to-Point Encryption (MPPE)   The encryption protocol used by Microsoft dial-up connections and PPTP tunnel connections.

MILNET   The Military Network evolved in 1983 when the ARPAnet was split into military and public access networks.

mount protocol   A protocol that provides the NFS protocol with the necessary tools to share a network drive based on the underlying operating system.

mounting   The process that creates a file handle to connect a client to a remote file source so that it appears to be a local resource.

multicast address   An IP address that is assigned to multiple interfaces on different hosts. Data sent to a multicast address is delivered to every interface assigned the multicast address.

multicasting   This transmission method is used to send a single message to a predefined group of computers. All multicast messages are sent using UDP as the transport protocol.

multiplexing ports   A method that allows multiple sessions to be connected to a single port on a host. This is possible because the other end of the connection always has a unique combination of IP address, port, and protocol.

multipurpose Internet mail extensions (MIME) A file encoding system that provides a mechanism for translating non-ASCII messages into an ASCII format for transmission over the Internet. Different MIME types are defined that allow each file category to be encoded in a defined manner.

name discovery The process of resolving a NetBIOS name to an IP address.

name registration The process of registering a NetBIOS name on a network.

name release The process of releasing a NetBIOS name from the network.

name server (NS) The Name Server resource record is used to indicate which hosts contain copies of a domain's zone file.

named daemon On a Unix-based DNS name server, this is the daemon (service) that provides the DNS name server services.

Named.conf A configuration file in BIND-compatible DNS name servers that provides startup information for the named daemon.

NBTSTAT A Microsoft text-based utility used to troubleshoot NetBIOS name issues on a network.

NCP The Network Control Protocol (NCP) was the initial protocol used to communicate between hosts on the ARPAnet. The TCP/IP protocol suite replaced this protocol on January 1, 1983.

NETASCII A TFTP mode used for the transfer of 8-bit ASCII data between a TFTP client and a TFTP server.

NetBIOS Name Server (NBNS) A centralized server configured to accept NetBIOS registrations and releases from clients. NBNS also resolves queried NetBIOS names to an IP address.

NetBIOS names Logical names assigned to computers, domains, and users in a network, such as Windows NT, that use NetBIOS as an upper-layer protocol.

NetBIOS Node Type A NetBIOS configuration parameter that determines the resolution methods used to resolve a NetBIOS name to an IP address. The NetBIOS Node Type can be configured to be either B-Node, P-Node, M-Node, or H-Node.

Netconfig This program is used by SCO Unix to update the Unix kernel when configuration changes are performed to the Unix host.

NETSTAT This TCP/IP command enables the network administrator to investigate current port usage and port connections.

D

NetWare Loadable Modules (NLMs)   The utilities that are executed on a NetWare system console using the `load name.nlm` command.

network address translation (NAT)   An addressing scheme in which the internal network's IP addresses are hidden from the external network. Every internal address is replaced with a common external address when packets are passed through a firewall to the external world.

Network Control Protocol (NCP)   Used by a PPP connection to establish and configure different network-layer protocols.

network file system (NFS)   A protocol that allows transparent access to remote file services for networked clients.

Network Information System (NIS)   A global and centralized information database that allows user account information to be synchronized between hosts in a Unix environment.

Network Lock Manager (NLM)   This service provides file-locking capabilities to the NFS protocol.

network management   In the case of SNMP, network management is the management of the physical devices that make up the network infrastructure. This includes routers, bridges, and hubs. This can also refer to the logical management of the network, such as the management of users, groups, disk and printer resources, and network security.

Network News Transfer Protocol (NNTP)   This protocol is used to facilitate the reading and posting of documents stored on Internet News servers.

network segment   A physical section of the network that is separated from all other areas of the network by a routing device.

network sniffers   These devices (or software applications) capture network traffic and analyze what is being transmitted.

Network Virtual Terminal (NVT)   This provides a common endpoint at each end of a Telnet communication session that defines what functionality is provided. An NVT defines the minimum feature set for a Telnet session.

NETWORKS file   This locally stored TCP/IP configuration file is used to assign logical names to network IP addresses.

NIS domain   A collection of hosts that share the same NIS database for user authentication.

NIS maps   The configuration files that contain the NIS database consisting of keys and values.

Non-Broadcast Multiple Access (NBMA) networks   Networks that do not have the capability of transporting multicasts or broadcasts. An example of this network is an X.25 network.

NSFnet   In 1985, the National Science Foundation created a T1 backbone network that replaced the ARPAnet as the primary network backbone.

NSLOOKUP   A tool commonly used to troubleshoot and verify the configuration of a DNS name server. This tool can be run in either batch mode or interactive mode. Interactive mode allows for multiple DNS queries to be performed at once.

object identifier   The unique hierarchical identifier that defines each object within the Management Information Base (MIB).

octet   A collection of eight bits of information. An IPv4 address consists of four octets of data.

octet mode   A TFTP transfer mode used for transferring binary data between a TFTP client and a TFTP server using raw 8-bit bytes.

one's complement   A mathematical method used to calculate a checksum on both TCP and UDP headers to ensure that the data has not been corrupted in transit from the source host to destination host.

Open Shortest Path First (OSPF)   A link state routing protocol that builds a link state database at each router interface. From this database, the shortest path to each network address is determined.

OSI   The Open Systems Interconnect reference model is a seven-layer networking model that describes the flow of data from the physical network connection to an end-user network application.

P-Node   A NetBIOS name resolution method that queries a NetBIOS name server to resolve NetBIOS names to IP addresses only after the NetBIOS name cache is checked. If this fails, the host attempts to resolve the NetBIOS name to an IP address by using the LMHOSTS file, the HOSTS file, and DNS.

packet filter firewalls   A firewall implementation that analyzes traffic at the transport layer of the OSI model. Each incoming/outgoing packet is scrutinized and compared to a set of rules that will either accept or reject the packet.

Packet Internet Groper (PING)   The PING utility is commonly used to inspect the TCP/IP configuration of a TCP/IP host or to test the reachability of a network host. This utility uses the ICMP protocol to determine reachability.

packet switched network   A network that delivers data by breaking it into smaller packets. These packets are routed from the source to the destination host on an individual basis. Each packet may take a different route through the network but is reassembled at the destination host.

PAD   A Packet Assembler/Disassembler breaks large blocks of data into packets for transmission over an X.25 network. At the destination network, the PAD reassembles the packets.

passwd file   This file is used for determining valid login accounts on a Unix system.

Password Authentication Protocol (PAP)   An authentication mechanism that uses a two-step process. In the first step, clients transmit their account/password combination. In the second step, the server compares the account/password combination to its secret database and either accepts or rejects the connection attempt.

peer-to-peer network   A LAN configuration where all the participants function as both clients and servers.

phone gateways   A next-generation voice-over IP solution that enables a person to dial directly into a phone gateway using a normal phone, and use the Internet as a backbone network to connect to another phone in a remote location.

Point-to-Point Protocol (PPP)   A standardized protocol that has been developed to solve the problems of encapsulating the IP protocol over point-to-point links. PPP allows the automatic assignment of IP addresses to remote clients, the capability to transport multiple protocols over the same link, the capability to negotiate options between the client and server, and automatic error detection.

Point-to-Point Tunneling Protocol (PPTP)   A Microsoft-specific protocol that allows IP, NetBEUI, or IPX to be encapsulated within an IP header for transmission across an intermediary network. The data is encapsulated using GRE packets.

Pointer (PTR)   This resource record is found in reverse-lookup files. These records relate an IP address to a specific hostname.

poison reverse   When a router learns about a network on a specific interface, it will send out advertisements on that interface that the network is unreachable. If the network is up, the receiving routers will maintain their current routing information. If the network is down, the routes will be dropped, because the infinity value has already been reached.

portmapper   A service that determines whether a requested application is running on a specific server. This service returns the correct port number on which the application is accepting connections to the calling client.

ports   A host can provide access to multiple applications. When a client connects to the host for a specific application, a port is used to provide access to that specific application. Well-known ports are assigned port addresses between 0 and 1023.

Post Office Protocol 3 (POP3)   A protocol used by e-mail clients to retrieve e-mail messages from a server using TCP as the transport protocol.

primary name server   The DNS name server in which the actual zone configuration files are stored. All updates to the zone data files should be performed on this name server.

protocol   A method of packaging information as it is transferred between two networked hosts.

Protocol Data Unit (PDU)   The actual definitions of the SNMP message formats. The following PDUs are supported in SNMPv2: `GetRequest`, `GetNextRequest`, `GetBulk`, `SetRequest`, `GetResponse`, and `Trap`.

PROTOCOL file   This locally stored TCP/IP configuration file contains the protocol ID numbers that have been configured for the standard TCP/IP protocols.

Protocol Interpreter (PI)   The FTP protocol uses the Protocol Interpreter to transfer FTP commands between the FTP client and FTP server.

proxy services   Services that act on behalf of a client performing requests to the external world. The client issues the request to the proxy service and the proxy service performs the request. When a response is received, the proxy service returns the result set to the calling client.

pseudo header   A pseudo header is a header that is comprised of fields from more than a single header in a data stream. In TCP and UDP, the pseudo header is comprised of fields from the TCP/UDP header and fields from the IP header.

PSTN   Public Switched Telephone Networks are circuit-switched networks that can be used for data traffic as a wide area networking solution as well as for voice data.

Public Key Infrastructure (PKI)   An infrastructure of certification authorities that provides certificate issuances, revocation, and renewal services to a network. The certificates are used for authentication, encryption, and integrity services.

Quote of the Day   This service returns a quotation from a central file of quotations by connecting to it on TCP or UDP port 17.

D

reassembly   The reassembly process occurs when the fragmented packets reach the destination network. The fragmented packets are reassembled into their original packet based on the fragment IDs.

recursive query   A DNS name resolution method that returns either the answer to the DNS query or an error stating that the name could not be resolved.

Remote Access Service (RAS)   The Windows NT service that is used to configure the Windows NT PPP server and SLIP/PPP client software.

Remote Copy Protocol (RCP)   This utility enables you to copy directories and their contents to and from a remote host. The RCP utility is part of the Berkeley R-Utilities suite.

Remote Desktop Protocol (RDP)   A protocol based on the ITU T.120 protocol. It allows Microsoft terminal servers to send optimized transmissions to remote clients, which includes the transmission of the screen, mouse, and keyboard data between the terminal server and the thin client.

Remote Procedure Call (RPC)   A procedure executed on a remote system at the security level of the calling user.

RESOLV.CONF file   This TCP/IP configuration file is used to store the DNS configuration information for a Unix host. This file is located on a DNS resolver.

resource records   The records that are stored in a DNS name server configuration file. Resource records can include Address (A), Pointer (PTR), Mail Exchange (MX), and Canonical Name (CNAME) records.

Resource Reservation Protocol (RSVP)   A protocol that is able to request a specific amount of bandwidth from the source host to the destination host. This provides the minimum bandwidth pipe required for the transmission of Voice-over IP.

retransmission timers   These timers are used during a TCP connection to determine a resend time if an acknowledgment is not received in a timely manner from the destination host.

Reverse Address Resolution Protocol (RARP)   This protocol is used by a terminal to receive an IP address from an RARP server. The client will broadcast its MAC address, and the RARP server will send a preconfigured IP address to the client.

reverse lookup file   This DNS name server configuration file provides IP address to hostname resolution.

rexec   The rexec (Remote Execute) command allows for remote execution of programs to take place. Unlike rlogin and rsh, the rexec command does not use the HOSTS.EQUIV or .RHOSTS files for determining trusted hosts.

RFCs   Request for Comments are the documents that define the TCP/IP protocol suite.

.rhosts   This file allows specific accounts to be named for a remote host. It contains entries for hosts and users that can gain access to the local system.

ring network   A network topology where all computers are connected in a circle. Data travels around the circle in a single direction using a method known as token passing.

rlogin   This command enables a user to remotely log in to another system on the network.

root domain   The starting point of the name space for the Internet.

route aggregation   The use of a single route into an enterprise network that can be used to contain the address space of several networks. This is used to reduce the size of Internet backbone routing tables.

router discovery   An extension of the Internet Control Message Protocol (ICMP) that enables hosts attached to multicast or broadcast networks to discover the IP addresses of their neighboring routers.

routing   The process of moving a packet of information from one physical network segment to another physical network segment. This takes place at the Network layer of the OSI model.

Routing and Remote Access Service (RRAS)   The Windows 2000 service that is used to configure routing protocols, remote access settings, and virtual private network settings.

Routing Information Protocol (RIP)   A distance vector routing protocol that uses hop count as its routing metric. The hop count is measured as the number of routers that must be navigated from source to destination network. All routing information is exchanged using broadcasts directed to UDP port 520.

Routing Information Protocol (RIP) version 2   An enhancement to the original RIP protocol that includes subnet masks in router announcements, authentication included in routing packets, the use of multicasts instead of broadcasts, and route tags to distinguish internal routes from external routes.

routing loops   The situation that occurs when a series of routers create a circular route to a destination network that simply goes around in circles without ever arriving at the destination network.

D

routing protocols   Protocols that exchange routing information to build routing tables for a network. After all the known routes are gathered, the routing protocol determines the best route to each destination network.

rsh   The remote shell utility enables you to execute a single command on a remote host without logging in to the remote host.

ruptime   This command displays a list of all machines on the network. It includes statistics on each machine's status, the time it has been "up," the number of active users, and its current load.

rwho   This command displays a list of users on the network.

scope   A pool of IP addresses that can be leased from a DHCP server.

second-level domains   These domains are located below the top-level domains. These names are registered with InterNIC.

secondary name server   A DNS name server that obtains its zone configuration files from another DNS name server known as its master name server. A secondary name server is used to provide redundancy in a DNS environment.

Secure Socket Layer (SSL)   A layer implemented between the TCP/IP transport layer and the application layer that encrypts all transmissions between a client and a server.

Serial Line Internet Protocol (SLIP)   A packet framing protocol, SLIP is used for transporting data over a point-to-point connection using a serial line. SLIP defines a specific sequence of characters that frame each IP packet.

Server-based network   A LAN configuration in which all data is stored on centralized server locations.

Service Locator (SRV) resource record   A DNS resource record used to find services on a TCP/IP network. The resource record defines the service, the protocol and port the service is listening on, a priority and weight for the server, and the server providing the service.

SERVICES file   This locally stored TCP/IP configuration file is used to assign text names to well-known TCP/IP port addresses. This is used for both TCP and UDP ports.

session key   A separate key that is generated by the authentication server for a specific connection session between a client and a server. This key expires at the completion of the session.

shortest path first (SPF) tree   This tree contains the shortest path through the network for each network and each router. Each router in the network maintains its own unique shortest path first tree.

Simple Mail Transfer Protocol (SMTP)   This protocol provides mail transfer between two hosts using TCP as the transport protocol.

Simple Network Management Protocol (SNMP)   An application-level protocol that allows for management of network devices including routers, hubs, and switches.

Slave name servers   An alternate name for secondary name servers. This highlights that the secondary name server receives its zone information from a configured DNS Master name server.

Slave servers   NIS servers that maintain a duplicated copy of the master database. A slave server is maintained using the propagation process.

SNMP agent   This component of SNMP exists on managed devices. The SNMP agent responds to queries by filling in the request values and sends SNMP traps to the SNMP management system.

SNMP-enabled   A network device with an SNMP agent built in that responds to SNMP requests.

SNMP Management System   This component of SNMP is used to issue queries against SNMP agents to determine the status of an SNMP agent.

SNMP proxy agent   An SNMP agent that functions on behalf of another network device. All SNMP requests are sent to the SNMP proxy agent. The proxy agent then queries the network device by using alternative methods to fulfill the SNMP response.

SNMP trap   A communication in an SNMP system sent from the SNMP agent to the SNMP manager. This occurs when a preconfigured event takes place that the SNMP management system wants to be notified about.

SNMPUTIL   A Windows NT Resource Kit utility that allows queries to be performed against an SNMP agent.

socket   A socket provides an endpoint for a communication session. It is comprised of an IP address, a transport protocol, and a port address.

split horizons   The prevention of sending routing information back in the direction from which it is received. Under split horizons, routes that originated from a specific neighboring router are never sent back to that neighboring router.

star network   A network topology in which each computer is connected to a central hub by a cable segment.

Start of Authority (SOA)   The prime configuration resource record for a domain, the SOA provides configuration parameters that describe how primary and secondary name servers interact. It also contains configuration information about how long a DNS name server will cache resolved hostnames to IP address resolutions.

static routing   The manual configuration of all routing paths through an internetwork. Generally, this is implemented only in smaller networks.

static WINS mappings   These mappings are added to a WINS server for non-WINS clients that are not able to register their NetBIOS names with the WINS server.

Structure of Management Information (SMI)   A standardized framework for defining the information that can be managed by an SNMP manager. SMI provides a basic format for all managed objects.

sub-domains   These domains exist below the second-level domains. These names are registered with the second-level domain below which they exist.

subnet mask   A subnet mask determines the dividing point between the network and host portions of an IP address.

supernetting   Another term used to represent Classless Inter-Domain Routing (CIDR).

Synchronize (SYNCH)   This Telnet function provides a method for remote users to ensure they are able to regain control of the Telnet session in the case of a runaway process.

T1 service   A digital line service that provides transmission rates of up to 1.544Mbps. It can carry both voice and data transmissions.

T3 service   A digital line service that provides transmissions of up to 45Mbps. It can carry both voice and data transmissions.

TCP (Transmission Control Protocol)   This transport layer protocol provides connection-oriented, reliable delivery of data on a network. The use of TCP requires that a session be established between the source and destination hosts.

TCP sliding windows   A method of providing improved transmissions in a TCP session. Multiple TCP segments can be sent that require only a single acknowledgment from the receiving host.

TCP/IP (Transmission Control Protocol/Internet Protocol)   A suite of protocols that allows connectivity between heterogeneous environments.

Telnet   A protocol that provides a bidirectional communication session between two hosts. Telnet uses the TCP protocol to ensure the reliable delivery of information between the two hosts.

Terminal Server   The central server in the Citrix Winframe/Microsoft Terminal Server implementation of thin clients. The terminal server hosts all remote users' client sessions.

thin client   A technology that allows a client to connect to a central server and perform all its processing on the remote server. The only information transmitted to the client is the screen output from the central server. The client transmits only keyboard and mouse input to the central server.

Thinwire   The data protocol used by Citrix Winframe to send the actual screen image from the Terminal server to the client station.

ticket   A Kerberos message that contains a copy of the session key and an identifier for the user that wants to communicate with a service. This message is locked by using shared secret key between the user and the Kerberos Distribution Center.

Ticket-Granting Server (TGS)   A server in a Kerberos environment that grants tickets that can increase security. All future tickets are requested from the TGS using the Ticket-Granting Ticket. Each reply is encrypted using the session key for the TGS and client. The session key for the requested server is encrypted by the TGS session key.

Ticket-Granting Ticket (TGT)   A ticket granted that establishes a session between the client and the ticket-granting server.

Time   This service returns the number of seconds that have elapsed since midnight, January 1, 1900, on a connection to TCP or UDP port 37.

Time-To-Live (TTL)   This option is used to set a maximum lifetime on a datagram. Each time a datagram crosses a router, the datagram's TTL is decremented by at least one. When the TTL reaches a value of zero, the datagram is dropped from the network.

top-level domains   The first level of domain names below the root domain in the domain name space. Top-level domains are broken into types of business and country codes.

total cost of ownership (TCO)   This term refers to the total cost involved with purchasing, operating, and maintaining your organization's computers and computing resources.

traceroute   A command used to determine the route to an external network. This command shows each router that is crossed en route to the destination network. In Microsoft networking, the `tracert.exe` command offers the same functionality.

D

Transmission Control Protocol (TCP)   This transport layer protocol provides connection-oriented, reliable delivery of data on a network. The use of TCP requires that a session be established between the source and destination hosts.

Transmission Control Protocol/Internet Protocol (TCP/IP)   A suite of protocols that allows connectivity between heterogeneous environments.

Transport Layer Security (TLS)   An RFC-based proposal for encrypting data at the application level. TLS is based on the SSL protocol developed by Netscape.

Transport Mode   An IPSec configuration where data is encrypted or signed end-to-end between the client and the server.

Trivial File Transfer Protocol (TFTP)   This protocol allows the transfer of files between two hosts using the UDP protocol. The client will connect to UDP port 69 on the TFTP server.

Tunnel Mode   An IPSec configuration where data is only encrypted between boundary servers. The data is transmitted unprotected until the initial boundary server is reached. The data is then signed or encrypted as it is transmitted to the destination boundary server. The data is then decrypted and delivered to the ultimate destination.

tunneling   A network transfer method that allows a routable protocol to transfer the frames of another protocol to a destination network by encapsulating those frames. The frames are decapsulated at the receiving end.

unicast address   A unique IP address that is assigned to a single interface.

uniform resource locator (URL)   The combination of the protocol, fully qualified domain name, and content that you want to view in a Web browser. For example, `http://www.komarconulting.com/default.asp` is comprised of the protocol `http`, the fully qualified domain name `www.komarconulting.com`, and the content to be viewed `default.asp`.

User Datagram Protocol (UDP)   This transport layer protocol provides connectionless, nonguaranteed delivery of data on a network. Applications that use UDP as their transport protocol must provide their own acknowledgment mechanism for reliable delivery.

UTP   Unshielded twisted pair wiring is a cable where the interior wires are twisted around each other a minimum number of twists per foot. This cabling standard does not have any insulation or shielding.

UUEncode   Unix-to-Unix Encoding is a file encoding system that converts binary data into a series of 7-bit ASCII characters for the transmission of binary data using SMTP. uuencoded files are usually stored with the extension .uu or .uue.

variable length subnet masking (VLSM) This method of allocating subnet masks allows for different subnet masks to be implemented in the same network. This requires that the routing protocols transmit the subnet mask in their routing information.

virtual circuit A method that allows communication between two defined endpoints to take place through any number of intermediate nodes on a mesh network.

virtual private network (VPN) The completed link between a tunneling client and a tunneling server. Logically, a VPN appears to be a single hop between the client and the server, even though multiple routers may be crossed in transit.

virtual Web server This term refers to a Web server that hosts multiple Web sites that appear to be unique Web servers. Each Web site within the Web server is known as a virtual Web server. To the external user, virtual Web servers appear to be independent Web servers.

voice codecs A method of digitizing voice data that converts speech input into a signal that resembles the original voice input. The created signal is analyzed against a speech model and a set of parameters is generated. These parameters are what are transferred to the destination station.

Voice over IP The use of the Internet as a transport medium for digitized voice data.

Voice over IP (VoIP) Forum A working group in the International Multimedia Teleconferencing Consortium to further the progress of the Voice over IP development.

WAN A wide area network is a computer network that uses telecommunication links to join computers over a vast geographic area.

waveform codecs A method of digitizing voice data by sampling the voice input and converting the amplitude of each sample to the nearest value from a finite set of discrete values.

WINS (Windows Internet Name Service) The Microsoft NetBIOS name server that ships with Windows NT Server. This product functions as a central repository from which NetBIOS clients can register, resolve, and release NetBIOS names.

WINS Lookup A Windows NT-specific DNS resource record that provides the ability to look up IP addresses of hosts that register their NetBIOS names with a WINS server.

WINS proxy agent A NetBIOS host that forwards NetBIOS requests from a non-WINS client to a WINS server for resolution. After the request is resolved, the WINS proxy agent broadcasts the resolution to the local network segment.

WINS pull partner A WINS server that requests new database entries from its replication partner at regularly scheduled intervals.

D

WINS push partner   A WINS server that is configured to send notification to its replication partner when a preconfigured number of changes have been applied to its WINS database. This notification acts as a trigger for the replication partner to pull the changes across to its database.

WINS Reverse Lookup (WINS-R)   A Windows NT–specific DNS resource record that provides a method for a DNS name server to look up IP addresses dynamically from a configured WINS server and provide hostname resolution.

Wireless Access Point (WAP)   The central access point for a wireless network that is comparable to a hub in an Ethernet network.

World Wide Web (WWW)   The collection of HTML Web servers that are located on the Internet.

X Window   This thin client system allows graphical screen information from a remote server to be displayed locally. It is commonly used in Unix environments.

X.25   X.25 defines the electrical connection between a terminal and the network, the transmission protocol, and the implementation of virtual circuits between network users. Together, these definitions create a synchronous, full-duplex terminal to network connection. The X.25 protocol has error correcting built in due to its initial implementation on public data networks.

X.500 directory service   A directory standard that defines the different objects and object classes that can be implemented in a directory services tree.

zero subnetting   This is an option available on routers that support the transmission of both the network address and the subnet mask when routing tables are created. The use of zero subnetting allows for a subnet mask of all zeros to be implemented.

zone transfer   The process of transferring DNS zone information from a Master name server to a Slave name server.

INDEX

A

M

P